HISTORICAL DICTIONARY

The historical dictionaries present essential information on a broad range of subjects, including American and world history, art, business, cities, countries, cultures, customs, film, global conflicts, international relations, literature, music, philosophy, religion, sports, and theater. Written by experts, all contain highly informative introductory essays of the topic and detailed chronologies that, in some cases, cover vast historical time periods but still manage to heavily feature more recent events.

Brief A–Z entries describe the main people, events, politics, social issues, institutions, and policies that make the topic unique, and entries are cross-referenced for ease of browsing. Extensive bibliographies are divided into several general subject areas, providing excellent access points for students, researchers, and anyone wanting to know more. Additionally, maps, photographs, and appendixes of supplemental information aid high school and college students doing term papers or introductory research projects. In short, the historical dictionaries are the perfect starting point for anyone looking to research in these fields.

HISTORICAL DICTIONARIES OF SPORTS

Jon Woronoff, Series Editor

Competitive Swimming, by John Lohn, 2010.
Basketball, by John Grasso, 2011.
Golf, by Bill Mallon and Randon Jerris, 2011.
Figure Skating, by James R. Hines, 2011.
The Olympic Movement, Fourth Edition, by Bill Mallon and Jeroen Heijmans, 2011.
Tennis, by John Grasso, 2011.
Soccer, by Tom Dunmore, 2011.
Cycling, by Jeroen Heijmans and Bill Mallon, 2011.
Skiing, by E. John B. Allen, 2012.
Track and Field, by Peter Matthews, 2012.
Baseball, by Lyle Spatz, 2013.
Ice Hockey, by Laurel Zeisler, 2013.
Football, by John Grasso, 2013.
Boxing, by John Grasso, 2014.

Historical Dictionary of Boxing

John Grasso

The Scarecrow Press, Inc.
Lanham • Toronto • Plymouth, UK
2014

Published by Scarecrow Press, Inc.
A wholly owned subsidiary of The Rowman & Littlefield Publishing Group, Inc.
4501 Forbes Boulevard, Suite 200, Lanham, Maryland 20706
http://www.scarecrowpress.com

10 Thornbury Road, Plymouth PL6 7PP, United Kingdom

British Library Cataloguing in Publication Information Available

Library of Congress Cataloging-in-Publication Data

Grasso, John.
Historical dictionary of boxing / John Grasso.
pages cm. -- (Historical dictionaries of sports)
Includes bibliographical references.
ISBN 978-0-8108-6800-7 (cloth : alk. paper) -- ISBN 978-0-8108-7867-9 (ebook) 1. Boxing--History--Dictionaries. I. Title.
GV1118.G73 2013
796.8303--dc23
2013018838

Printed in the United States of America

Contents

Editor's Foreword

Boxing, like wrestling, doubtlessly goes back as far as there were men who engaged in one form of fighting or another, certainly back to the Ancient Greeks. But it was a rough-and-tumble activity, occasionally even a cruel and vicious one, throughout most of its history, until during the modern period it was increasingly refined, given rules that had to be obeyed, a referee who could intervene to enforce them, and sports organizations to regulate the field. Gradually, it has become accepted as an ordinary sport . . . almost. This transition was largely engineered by boxers and boxing enthusiasts who, for the sake of the sport, developed and refined the rules of modern boxing, most notable among them being Jack Broughton and the Marquess of Queensberry. Moreover, it was further consecrated by being accepted into the modern Olympic Games. Whether professional or amateur, boxing was mainly of interest to men, who turned out massively to witness major bouts, although it has become a sport for women as well. But fashions change, and any "refinement" was not enough for some, who thought it was still too brutal and should be done away with. That was obviously not the view of the fans, who still watch it in person or over television, in major and lesser bouts, and learn more about it through often popular, if fictionalized, films.

This *Historical Dictionary of Boxing* will certainly be of interest to the remaining fans since, for starters, it does delve into a long and intriguing history from earliest times to the present, partly in the chronology, which traces the major events to as early as 688 BC. This is further elaborated on in the introduction, which provides more of an overview, tracing the various trends and in so doing mentioning some of the top boxers of their time, including Jack Dempsey, Joe Louis, and Muhammad Ali (Cassius Clay). The dictionary section, however, is the largest and most interesting part. It presents dozens and dozens of boxers, mostly men but also women, from a growing circle of countries in Europe, Latin America, Asia, and especially, the United States. As noted above, rules are very important, and they are explained here, too, as is some of the technical terminology and jargon. And there are also entries on the international and national organizations that govern the sport as best they can. Last, but most certainly not least in this context, there are precious appendixes giving among other things lists of champion boxers, their nicknames and ring names, winners of the fighter of the year awards, weight classes, and rules. This book will certainly provide much of the essential information, more than any other book presently, but more can certainly be gleaned from the other books included in an extensive bibliography.

This volume was written by John Grasso, who has written extensively on boxing, including (with Bert Randolph Sugar) *The 100 Greatest Boxers of All Time* and *505 Boxing Questions Your Friends Can't Answer*, as well as contributing to the *1984 Ring Record Book and Boxing Encyclopedia*. He has also provided material for biographical works and done several columns for *Ring* magazine and *Boxing Illustrated*. While he closely follows boxing, this is not the only sport of interest to him, as can be gathered from his authorship of three other books in the Scarecrow sports series, the *Historical Dictionary of Tennis*, the *Historical Dictionary of Basketball*, and the *Historical Dictionary of Football*. Moreover, he is currently working on a companion volume to this one on boxing, the *Historical Dictionary of Wrestling*. This all makes him an excellent guide to a very exciting sport that has been around for a long time and will continue to impassion aficionados whether or not others join in.

Jon Woronoff
Series Editor

Preface

It is impossible in a book of this size to cover all aspects of an activity that has been participated in for more than 200 years. I have tried to include a fair representation of boxers and others involved with the sport such as trainers, managers, and promoters from all eras. As can be seen by the list of people inducted into the International Boxing Hall of Fame (Appendix A), many contributors to the sport have had to be omitted from this volume. Space limitations have restricted entries to brief sketches, but readers interested in more details are advised to make use of the extensive bibliography. It is hoped that the information contained within this book will provide the neophyte with a general introduction, and that some of the anecdotal details will be of interest to the reader with a broader background.

I'd like to thank Dorothy A. Grasso, for condoning my reclusive hobbies for nearly 50 years; Steve Grasso, manufacturing engineer and Corvette and motocross racer, and Dr. Laurel Zeisler, speech therapist and ice hockey expert, for their encouragement and support; also new home owner and former Charlotte Valley soccer star James Hernandez, international clarinetist Trinity Grasso, percussionist and Egyptologist Lindsey Zeisler, and artist and trumpeter Dorothy Rose Zeisler, for putting up with a silly grandpa; Dr. Bill Mallon, orthopedic surgeon and Olympic Games expert, for getting me involved with this project; Dr. Tomasz Małolepszy, for help with Polish boxing; Mort O'Shea, for help with boxing in Ireland; the late Bert Randolph Sugar, for opening the door for my entry into the world of boxing; and Jon Woronoff, editor, for helping to bring this book to fruition.

This book is dedicated to my late father, John Charles Grasso. My first experience with boxing occurred in 1950 when my father allowed me to stay up past my bedtime to watch the great Joe Louis fight Ezzard Charles. During the 1950s, we would watch the Friday Night Fights together, and in 1959 he took me to Sunnyside Garden to see New York Golden Gloves bouts in person (mainly because his helper, Joe Duran, was fighting that night). Duran won, and we returned the following week to Sunnyside only to see him lose a decision and exit the tournament. Golden Gloves (usually at Sunnyside) became an annual tradition. I became hooked on that tournament and had aspirations to enter myself. My father wisely talked me out of it, saying that the one thing I had going for me was my brain and I shouldn't get it pounded senseless.

During the 1960s, my girlfriend, Dorothy Cwihun (now my wife for the past 49 years), lived only five blocks from Sunnyside Garden and her father, Bill Cwihun, often joined me and my father for the fights. Since many of the top Golden Glovers later became professional boxers, and quite a few of them champions, I wondered if there were any champion boxers who had entered the Golden Gloves only to be defeated in that tournament. In 1969, I wrote to the *New York Daily News*, the tournament's sponsor since its inception in 1927, and was told by tournament director Jack Smith that that information was unavailable. That started me on a 10-year project researching every one of the more than 30,000 bouts since the tournament began. I put together a 300-page book with my findings and attempted to get the *New York Daily News* to publish it. Although they lauded my accomplishment, they were unable to help me.

My quest for a publisher landed me at the offices of *Ring* magazine. Fortunately, Bert Sugar had just become owner. While he too thought the work was outstanding, he also was unable to help me. He did recognize my research abilities and asked me to research the complete results of boxing at the Olympic Games, which to that time had not been published anywhere. The results of that project appeared in the *1980 Ring Record Book*. He also put me in touch with other boxing researchers and encouraged me to form the International Boxing Research Organization (IBRO) along with the *Ring*'s managing editor, Herbert G. Goldman. In 1984, I self-published the *Olympic Games Boxing Record Book* under the auspices of IBRO. Dr. Bill Mallon, the world's foremost expert on the Olympic Games, discovered the book and in 1992 invited me to join the International Society of Olympic Historians, and since that time various doors have been opened to me resulting in my being selected to write this historical dictionary.

Reader's Note

In order to facilitate the rapid and efficient location of information and to make this book as useful a reference tool as possible, extensive cross-references have been provided in the dictionary section. Within individual entries, terms that have their own entries are in **boldface** the first time they appear. Related terms that do not appear in the text of an entry are indicated in the *See also*. *See* refers to other entries that deal with the same topic.

Professional boxing records used in this book have been taken from the files of Boxrec, one of the better boxing record-keeping organizations. They are, for the most part, quite accurate although in the case of many boxers in the first half of the 20th century, not all of their fights were recorded. On the other hand, amateur records included in the book should be taken with a grain of salt since there is no one comprehensive record-keeping institution for amateur boxing, and published amateur totals have often been the product of a manager's promotional abilities.

Bouts that ended short of the distance due to one boxer's inability to continue are often referred to as knockouts even though the losing boxer was still on his feet and are more properly recorded as technical knockouts. Heights and weights have been listed as whole numbers, disregarding fractions of inches and pounds.

Although attempts have been made to obtain each entrant's complete given name, there are several instances in which that was not possible (Ray Arcel, Tony Canzoneri, etc.), and the individual is simply listed by his common name.

A final note—throughout the dictionary, reference is frequently made to "*Ring* magazine." The correct title of the publication is "*The Ring*" although it is seldom referred to in that way.

Acronyms and Abbreviations

ORGANIZATIONS

AAU	Amateur Athletic Union
ABC	American Broadcasting Company
AIBA	Association Internationale de Boxe Amateur
BBBC	British Boxing Board of Control
CYO	Catholic Youth Organization
EBU	European Boxing Union
ESPN	Entertainment and Sports Programming Network
GBA	Global Boxing Association
GBC	Global Boxing Council
GBF	Global Boxing Federation
GBO	Global Boxing Organization
GBU	Global Boxing Union
HBO	Home Box Office
IBA	Independent Boxing Association
IBA	International Boxing Association
IBB	International Boxing Board
IBC	International Boxing Commission
IBC	International Boxing Council
IBC	International Boxing Club
IBF	International Boxing Federation
IBL	International Boxing League
IBO	International Boxing Organization
IBRO	International Boxing Research Organization
IBU	International Boxing Union
IOC	International Olympic Committee
IRS	Internal Revenue Service
JBC	Japan Boxing Commission

NABA	North American Boxing Association
NABF	North American Boxing Federation
NABO	North American Boxing Organization
NBA	National Boxing Association
NCAA	National Collegiate Athletic Association
NCBA	National Collegiate Boxing Association
NHL	National Hockey League
NYSAC	New York State Athletic Commission
NYU	New York University
PABA	Pan Asian Boxing Association
PAL	Police Athletic League
TWBA	Transcontinental World Boxing Association
UBA	Universal Boxing Association
UBC	Universal Boxing Council
UBF	Universal Boxing Federation
UBO	Universal Boxing Organization
USBA	United States Boxing Association
USBC	United States Boxing Council
WAA	World Athletic Association
WBA	World Boxing Association
WBB	World Boxing Board
WBC	World Boxing Council
WBCC	World Boxing Championship Committee
WBE	World Boxing Empire
WBF	World Boxing Federation
WBF	World Boxing Foundation
WBI	World Boxing Institute
WBL	World Boxing League
WBN	World Boxing Network
WBO	World Boxing Organization
WBU	World Boxing Union
WCOB	World Cup of Boxing
WJBF	World Junior Boxing Federation
WTBF	World Tournament Boxing Federation
WUBA	World United Boxing Association

COUNTRIES

ALG	Algeria
ARG	Argentina
AUS	Australia
BEL	Belgium
BUL	Bulgaria
CAN	Canada
CHN	China
CUB	Cuba
DEN	Denmark
DOM	Dominican Republic
ENG	England
ESP	Spain
FIN	Finland
FRA	France
FRG	West Germany
GBR	Great Britain
GDR	East Germany
GER	Germany
HUN	Hungary
IRL	Ireland
ITA	Italy
JPN	Japan
KAZ	Kazakhstan
KEN	Kenya
KOR	Korea
MEX	Mexico
MGL	Mongolia
NED	The Netherlands
NOR	Norway
NZL	New Zealand
POL	Poland
PRK	North Korea
ROU	Romania
RSA	South Africa

TCH	Czechoslovakia
THA	Thailand
UKR	Ukraine
URS	Soviet Union
USSR	Soviet Union
USA	United States
UZB	Uzbekistan
VEN	Venezuela
YUG	Yugoslavia

RESULTS

D	Draw
Dec	Decision
DQ	Disqualification
Exh	Exhibition
KO	Knockout
KO by	Knocked Out by Opponent
L	Lost
LF	Lost on Foul
Maj. Dec.	Majority Decision
NC	No Contest
ND	No Decision
RSC	Referee Stops Contest
Spl. Dec.	Split Decision
TD	Technical Draw
TKO	Technical Knockout
TL	Technical Loss
TW	Technical Win
Unan. Dec.	Unanimous Decision
W	Won
WF	Won on Foul

WEIGHT CLASSES

STR	Strawweight
LFL	Light Flyweight
FLY	Flyweight
SFL	Super Flyweight
BAN	Bantamweight
SBA	Super Bantamweight
FEA	Featherweight
SFE	Super Featherweight
LIT	Lightweight
LWE	Light Welterweight
WEL	Welterweight
LMD	Light Middleweight
MID	Middleweight
SMD	Super Middleweight
LHV	Light Heavyweight
CRU	Cruiserweight
HVY	Heavyweight
SHV	Super Heavyweight

OTHER

MMA	Mixed Martial Arts
MSG	Madison Square Garden
NSC	National Sporting Club

Chronology

688 BC Olympia, Greece: Boxing is first contested at the Olympic Games during the 23rd Olympiad. Onomastus of Smyrna becomes the first Olympic champion boxer.

385 AD Olympia, Greece: Varazdates of Armenia is the last winner of the boxing competition in the original Olympic Games, which are discontinued shortly thereafter.

1719 Thame, Oxfordshire, England. Englishman Jim Figg opens a boxing academy and is considered to be the first bareknuckle boxing champion.

1743 London, England, 16 August: After severely beating George Stevenson in a fight, causing Stevenson's death a few days afterward, Jack Broughton draws up a set of boxing rules for the members of his boxing academy. The rules, known as Broughton's rules, govern boxing until 1838.

1751 Harlston, England, 29 July: Englishman Jack Slack defends his championship claim by defeating the "giant" Frenchman Jean Petit in 25 minutes in the first international championship bout.

1810 Shenington Hollow, Oxfordshire, England, 18 December: After winning several bouts for his owner in Virginia, Tom Molineaux is granted his freedom from slavery and travels to England to earn a living as a professional boxer. He wins his first bout in July but is defeated by champion Tom Cribb in the 35th round of their championship bout.

1816 New York, New York, October: Jacob Hyer, a butcher, meets Tom Beasley, an English sailor, in a bout open to the public, held under English prize ring rules, in what is considered to be the first professional boxing match in America. Reports vary as to the winner.

1838 London, England: A revision to Broughton's rules is published as the London Prize Ring Rules. They are again revised in 1853 and govern boxing until 1867, when the Marquess of Queensberry rules are written.

1860 Farnborough, England, 17 April: American champion John Camel Heenan meets English champion Tom Sayers in the first bout between champions of the two countries. The bout is ruled a draw after unruly spectators break into the ring after 42 rounds of boxing.

1867 London, England: A set of 12 rules governing boxing and requiring gloves to be worn is written by John Graham Chambers and published in London with the endorsement of John Sholto Douglas, the ninth Marquess of Queensberry.

1870 Kennerville, Louisiana, 10 May: English champion Jem Mace comes to America to fight the American champion, Tom Allen. Mace claims both the English and American titles after defeating Allen in 10 rounds.

1882 Mississippi City, Mississippi, 7 February: John L. Sullivan wins the world's heavyweight championship by defeating Paddy Ryan in nine rounds.

1889 Richburg, Mississippi, 8 July: John L. Sullivan knocks out Jake Kilrain in the 75th round and retains his title in the last bareknuckle heavyweight championship bout.

1892 New Orleans, Louisiana, 5–7 September: Three championship bouts billed as the "Carnival of Champions" are held in three days. On the first day, Jack McAuliffe knocks out Billy Myer in the 15th to retain his world's lightweight championship. On the second day, George Dixon defeats Jack Skelly for the world featherweight title on an eighth-round knockout. Jim Corbett knocks out John L. Sullivan in the 21st round to become the new world's heavyweight champion on the third day.

1893 New Orleans, Louisiana, 6 April: Lightweights Andy Bowen and Jack Burke box for 110 three-minute rounds. The referee, Professor John Duffy, rules the bout a draw after more than seven hours as both fighters are too exhausted to continue. The following year, Bowen is fatally injured in a bout with George "Kid" Lavigne.

1894 West Orange, New Jersey, 7 September: Heavyweight champion Jim Corbett and Peter Courtney box a six-round exhibition that is filmed using the newly invented Edison Kinetoscope.

1897 Carson City, Nevada, 17 March: Bob Fitzsimmons, who weighs only 167 pounds, knocks out Jim Corbett in the 14th round and becomes the new world's heavyweight champion.

1899 Coney Island, New York, 9 June: Jim Jeffries becomes the new heavyweight champion after he knocks out Bob Fitzsimmons in the 11th round.

1902 Hot Springs, Arkansas, 26 December: Battling Nelson knocks out Christy Williams in the 17th round of their lightweight bout. Nelson was knocked down nine times while Williams was reportedly knocked down a record 42 times.

1903 Detroit, Michigan, 22 April: After knocking down his opponent seven times, Jack Root wins a 10-round decision over Charles "Kid" McCoy in the first world's light heavyweight championship bout.

1904 San Francisco, California, 26 August: Jim Jeffries knocks out Jack Munroe in two rounds in a successful defense of his heavyweight title. Shortly afterward, Jeffries retires from the ring, citing a lack of qualified opponents. **St. Louis, Missouri, 21–22 September:** The modern Olympic Games includes a boxing tournament for the first time. Eighteen boxers, all from the United States, participate in seven weight classes. Oliver Kirk enters both the 115-pound and the 125-pound classes and wins both titles.

1905 Reno, Nevada, 3 July: Jeffries selects Marvin Hart and Jack Root to compete for his vacated heavyweight championship. With Jeffries as referee, Hart stops Root in the 12th round to claim the title.

1906 Los Angeles, California, 23 February: Tommy Burns wins a 20-round decision over Marvin Hart and is declared the new heavyweight champion.

1908 London, England, 27 October: The Olympic Games includes boxing in five weight classifications with all bouts being held on only one day. Forty-two boxers from four nations enter, and Australian Reginald "Snowy" Baker and Englishman Fred Spiller each compete in four bouts in one day, although both lose their final bout. **Sydney, Australia, 26 December:** Jack Johnson stops Tommy Burns in the 14th round in a bout that is stopped by police. Johnson becomes the first black heavyweight champion.

1910 Reno, Nevada, 4 July: In an effort to restore the heavyweight championship to the white race, Jim Jeffries comes out of retirement to face Jack Johnson. Jeffries is no match for Johnson, who knocks him out in the 15th round of their scheduled 45-round match.

1911 Bronx, New York, 29 August: The first boxing card under the new Frawley Law governing boxing in New York state, limiting matches to 10 rounds and prohibiting decisions, takes place at the Fairmont Athletic Club. Five bouts are contested, with the main event being between heavyweights Dan "Porky" Flynn and Joe Jeannette. **London, England, 25 September:** The British Boxing Board of Control sanctions a bout between Sid Smith and Stoker Bill Hoskyne as a British flyweight championship bout. The bout, won by Smith by decision, is the first for a "flyweight" title although some historians do not accept the claim as it was contested over 20 two-minute rounds rather than the customary three-minute rounds.

1912 Stockholm, Sweden, 5 May–27 July: The Olympic Games does not include boxing, as the sport is illegal in Sweden at this time.

1915 Havana, Cuba, 5 April: Jack Johnson is knocked out in the 26th round of a scheduled 45-round bout by Jess Willard, who becomes the world's heavyweight champion.

1919 Toledo, Ohio, 4 July: Jack Dempsey knocks out Jess Willard in three rounds and wins the heavyweight championship. Willard is knocked down seven times in the first round but stays on his feet until the fight is stopped by referee Ollie Pecord.

1920 Albany, New York, May: New York State Governor Al Smith signs a bill known as the Walker Law, which legalizes boxing in New York State and permits decisions to be rendered at the conclusion of the bout. It also provides for a commission to oversee boxing in the state. The law repeals the Frawley Law. **Antwerp, Belgium, 21–24 August:** The Olympic Games has a full program of eight weight classes, with 116 boxers from 12 countries entering the tournament. American Frank Genaro wins the flyweight class and later becomes the professional world's champion. Although Belgium has 13 entrants, they fail to win a medal.

1921 Jersey City, New Jersey, 2 July: Jack Dempsey knocks out Frenchman Georges Carpentier in four rounds to retain his heavyweight title. The paid attendance of $1,789,238 is the first time that proceeds from a boxing match exceed one million dollars.

1922 New York, New York. Nat Fleischer begins publication of a monthly boxing and wrestling magazine called the *Ring*. The magazine eventually becomes known as "The Bible of Boxing" and is the sport's most prestigious publication.

1923 Shelby, Montana, 4 July: Jack Dempsey wins a 15-round decision over Tommy Gibbons in the small mining town of Shelby. Dempsey receives a guarantee of $300,000 for the bout, and as this sum far exceeds the gate proceeds, it causes the Shelby banks to close. **New York, New York, 14 September:** Jack Dempsey knocks out Luis Ángel Firpo in the second round of their heavyweight championship bout. Firpo had knocked Dempsey down twice in the first round. There are a total of nine knockdowns in the bout.

1924 Paris, France, 15–20 July: The Olympic Games again has a full program of eight weight classes, with 181 boxers from 27 nations entering the tournament. Americans Fidel LaBarba and Jackie Fields both win gold medals and later become professional world's champions. Sixteen French boxers enter, but only bantamweight Jean Ces wins a medal. The tournament is marred by poor officiating.

1926 Philadelphia, Pennsylvania, 23 September: Gene Tunney wins a 10-round unanimous decision over Jack Dempsey in a bout that draws 120,557 people to Sesquicentennial Stadium. Tunney becomes the new world's heavyweight champion.

1927 New York, New York, 11 March: The first bouts in the New York Golden Gloves amateur boxing tournament are held at the Columbus Council Knights of Columbus Hall in Brooklyn and at the Knights of St. Antony Hall in Manhattan. The first bout held in Brooklyn is in the 135-pound sub-novice class. John Williams of the Wolverine AC stops Jim Garrie of the Athos AC in 2:04 of the second round in the first bout there. In Manhattan, the program begins with William Anderson of the Swedish-American AC stopping Plino Imbelli, unattached, in 1:30 of the first round. **Chicago, Illinois, 22 September:** Gene Tunney defends his heavyweight title with a 10-round unanimous decision over Jack Dempsey before 104,943 spectators at Soldier Field. Dempsey knocks Tunney down in the seventh round, but referee Dave Barry does not begin counting until Dempsey goes to a neutral corner. Tunney gets up at the count of nine although he is on the canvas for 14 seconds.

1928 Chicago, Illinois, 28 March: The first Intercity Golden Gloves Championships are held at the Chicago Coliseum. Winners of the New York Golden Gloves tournament meet winners of the Chicago Golden Gloves tournament. Two boxers from each weight class for each team compete, and the result is a tie, with each team winning eight bouts. **New York, New York, 23 July:** Tunney knocks out Tom Heeney in the 11th round in a successful title defense and one week later announces his retirement from boxing. **Amsterdam, The Netherlands, 7–11 August:** The Olympic Games has a full program of eight weight classes, with 144 boxers from 29 nations in the tournament. For the first time, entries are limited to one boxer in each class per country. Dutchman Lambertus "Bep" Van Klaveren wins the featherweight championship.

1930 New York, New York, 11 June: In his bout with Jack Sharkey, Max Schmeling is declared the winner by referee Jim Crowley on a foul in the fourth round and becomes the new world's heavyweight champion. **San Francisco, California, 25 August:** Future world's heavyweight champion Max Baer hits Frankie Campbell with a barrage of punches as Campbell leans on the ropes in the fifth round. After the referee finally steps in to halt the bout, Campbell collapses. The following day, Campbell dies.

1932 Lake Placid, New York, 8–15 February: Eddie Eagan is a member of the United States gold medal–winning Olympic four-man bobsleigh team. In 1920, he won a gold medal in the light heavyweight boxing class at the Olympic Games in Antwerp and as of 2013 is still the only person to win gold medals in both summer and winter Olympic Games. **Long Island City,**

New York, 21 June: Jack Sharkey wins a 15-round decision over Max Schmeling and wins the heavyweight championship of the world. **Los Angeles, California, 9–13 August:** The Olympic Games has a full program of eight weight classes, but only 85 boxers from 18 countries enter the tournament. The host nation, the United States, wins two gold and two bronze medals.

1933 Long Island City, New York, 29 June: Six-foot, six-inch, 245-pound Italian-born Primo Carnera knocks out Jack Sharkey in the sixth round and becomes the world's heavyweight champion.

1934 Long Island City, New York, 14 June: Max Baer knocks out Primo Carnera in the 11th round and wins the heavyweight championship. Carnera is knocked down 11 times in the bout.

1935 Long Island City, New York, 13 June: In one of boxing's major upsets, James J. Braddock is awarded a 15-round decision over Max Baer and is the new world's heavyweight champion.

1936 Berlin, Germany, 10–15 August: The Olympic Games has a full program of eight weight classes, with 179 boxers from 31 countries in the tournament. Two rings are used for the first time, with simultaneous action. Germany wins five medals—two gold, two silver, and one bronze.

1937 Chicago, Illinois, 22 June: Joe Louis knocks out Jim Braddock in the eighth round and becomes the new world's heavyweight champion. Louis, a soft-spoken, gentle black man, is considered by boxing fans as "a credit to his race," in contrast to the previous black heavyweight champion, Jack Johnson, whose flamboyant, abrasive personality resulted in dislike by many. **New York, New York, 23 September:** Promoter Mike Jacobs puts on a series of four world championship bouts at the Polo Grounds and bills the event "the Carnival of Champions." Bantamweight, lightweight, welterweight, and middleweight title bouts are contested before a disappointing crowd of just 30,969 fans in the 60,000-seat outdoor arena.

1938 New York, New York, 22 June: Joe Louis meets the German Max Schmeling, who had knocked out Louis in 12 rounds in 1936, the only loss in Louis's career to that date. Schmeling is portrayed by the press as Hitler's emissary, and there is much joy throughout the United States as Louis knocks him out in the first round. **New York, New York, 17 August:** Despite being penalized four rounds, Henry Armstrong wins a split 15-round decision over Lou Ambers and wins the world's lightweight championship. Armstrong, who also holds the world's featherweight and welterweight championships, becomes the first boxer to hold three world titles simultaneously.

1940 Los Angeles, California, 1 March: Henry Armstrong boxes a 10-round draw with middleweight champion Ceferino Garcia in a bout recognized by the California Boxing Commission for the world's middleweight championship. The three-time champion Armstrong nearly wins his fourth title of the eight divisions then recognized.

1941 New York, New York, 18 June: Joe Louis defends his title against light heavyweight champion Billy Conn. Conn is ahead on points when Louis knocks him out in the 13th round. **Milwaukee, Wisconsin, 16 August:** The largest crowd ever to see a boxing match attend the Tony Zale–Billy Pryor match at Juneau Park. The six-bout card featuring free admission and sponsored by the Pabst Brewing Company is held during the national convention of the Fraternal Order of Eagles and draws 135,132 fans. The nontitle featured bout is won by middleweight champion Zale via a ninth-round knockout with former heavyweight champion Jack Dempsey as referee.

1942 New York, New York, 9 January: Joe Louis knocks out Buddy Baer in one round and donates his entire purse from the bout to the Naval Relief Fund. **New York, New York, 12 January:** After successfully defending his heavyweight title 20 times since winning it in 1937, Joe Louis enlists in the U.S. Army, and the heavyweight championship is declared frozen "for the duration." **New York, New York, 27 March:** Louis knocks out Abe Simon in six rounds and donates his entire purse to the Army Relief Fund.

1946 New York, New York, 19 June: In an eagerly awaited rematch of the 1941 bout, Joe Louis easily handles Billy Conn and knocks him out in the eighth round. **Lewiston, Maine, 23 September:** Welterweight Al Couture is credited with a 10-and-a-half-second knockout over Ralph Walton. Couture rushed across the ring and hit Walton as Walton was adjusting his mouthpiece. The 10-second count is included in the total elapsed time. **New York, New York, 27 September:** In a bout selected as the "Fight of the Year" by *Ring* magazine, Tony Zale successfully defends his world's middleweight title with a sixth-round knockout of Rocky Graziano at Yankee Stadium.

1947 New York, New York, 18 April: Former lightweight champion Benny Leonard, now a prominent referee, is stricken with a heart attack and dies in the ring during the first round of a bout at St. Nicholas Arena after refereeing the six previous bouts. **Chicago, Illinois, 16 August:** The second bout between Tony Zale and Rocky Graziano is another classic and again wins *Ring* magazine's award for "Fight of the Year." This time, Graziano rallies from a third-round knockdown, closed eye, and near defeat to stop Zale in the sixth round to win the world's middleweight championship at Chicago Stadium. **New York, New York, 5 December:** Joe Louis is awarded a split 15-round decision over Jersey Joe Walcott in a bout that most spectators, and Louis himself, thought Walcott had won.

1948 Ridgewood, New York, 1 March: Rocco "Socko" Marchegiano of Lowell, Massachusetts, loses his only bout in the New York Golden Gloves Eastern Regionals tournament to Coley Wallace on a close decision. Marchegiano, later known as Rocky Marciano, becomes world's heavyweight champion in 1952 and retires in 1956 undefeated as a professional. **London, England, 7–13 August:** The Olympic Games has a full program of eight weight classes. Weight limits are changed to use metric weights, and 205 boxers from 39 countries enter the tournament. Pascual Pérez of Argentina wins the flyweight class and later becomes the world's champion. British boxers win only two medals.

1949 Redondo Mountain, Sao Miguel Island, Azores, 28 October: A Lockheed Constellation flight from Paris to New York crashes while landing for refueling, killing all 48 passengers and crew. Former middleweight champion Marcel Cerdan, en route to New York for a rematch with Jake LaMotta, is one of the passengers.

1950 New York, New York, 27 September: Ezzard Charles wins a unanimous 15-round decision over Joe Louis and wins universal recognition as heavyweight champion.

1951 Pittsburgh, Pennsylvania, 18 July: Ezzard Charles is stopped in the seventh round by 37-year-old Jersey Joe Walcott and loses his heavyweight title. Walcott had been unsuccessful in four previous attempts at the heavyweight crown. **New York, New York, 26 September:** Featherweights Willie Pep and Sandy Saddler meet at the Polo Grounds for their fourth bout. The bout features many unsportsmanlike tactics by both boxers. Saddler successfully defends his world championship as Pep retires after the ninth round due to a cut eye. **New York, New York, 26 October:** Joe Louis's attempted comeback is ended when Rocky Marciano knocks him out in the eighth round of a scheduled 10-round bout.

1952 New York, New York, 25 June: Joey Maxim defends his light heavyweight championship against middleweight champion Sugar Ray Robinson at Yankee Stadium. The bout takes place in the midst of a heat wave, and referee Ruby Goldstein collapses from the heat after the 10th round and is replaced by Ray Miller. Robinson, although ahead on points, collapses after the 13th round and cannot answer the bell for the 14th round. **Helsinki, Finland, 28 July–2 August:** The Olympic Games boxing program adds two weight classes—light welterweight and light middleweight; 249 boxers from 43 countries take part in the tournament. The United States wins four gold medals, with future heavyweight champion Floyd Patterson winning the middleweight class. Heavyweight Ingemar Johansson of Sweden, another future heavyweight champion, is disqualified for "not trying" in the heavyweight final and is not awarded the second place medal. **Philadelphia, Pennsylvania, 23 September:** Undefeated Rocky Marciano knocks out Jersey Joe Walcott in the 13th round to become the new heavyweight champion.

1954 Bangkok, Thailand, 2 May: Undefeated world's bantamweight champion Jimmy Carruthers travels from his native Australia to face Thai challenger Chamrern Songkitrat in an outdoor bout. After a week's worth of monsoon rains, the fight takes place in a ring filled with water. The boxers, to have better footing, agree to fight barefoot. Twice during the bout, strong winds cause the riggings supporting the lights to break and drop broken glass on the ring, with the barefoot fighters cutting their feet. Carruthers is declared the winner by sole arbiter referee Bill Henneberry at the end of the scheduled 12 rounds, and Songkitrat, to forestall a potential riot, takes the microphone to calm the fans.

1956 Brockton, Massachusetts, 27 April: After successfully defending his heavyweight title six times, Rocky Marciano announces his retirement. Unlike many other fighters, he does not attempt a comeback and retires undefeated with 43 knockouts in 49 bouts. **Melbourne, Australia, 23 November–1 December:** The Olympic Games attracts fewer nations than in the last two games due to the extra travel required. Hungarian László Papp becomes the first man to win three gold medals in boxing, as 161 boxers from 34 countries compete in 10 weight classes. He was the 1948 middleweight and 1952 light middleweight champion and repeats in the light middleweight class by defeating American José Torres in the final. Torres later has a fine professional career and becomes world's light heavyweight champion. **Chicago, Illinois, 30 November:** Former Olympic champion 21-year-old Floyd Patterson knocks out 39-year-old Archie Moore in the fifth round to win the vacant heavyweight title and becomes the youngest heavyweight champion.

1957 Seattle, Washington, 22 August: In his second heavyweight title defense, Floyd Patterson survives a second-round knockdown to defeat 1956 Olympic heavyweight champion Pete Rademacher by knockout in the sixth round. Rademacher is making his professional debut. **New York, New York, 23 September:** World's welterweight champion Carmen Basilio wins the world's middleweight championship on a 15-round split decision over Sugar Ray Robinson at Yankee Stadium in a bout named the "Fight of the Year" by *Ring* magazine.

1959 New York, New York, 26 June: Undefeated Swedish heavyweight Ingemar Johansson defeats Floyd Patterson and becomes the world's heavyweight champion. Patterson is down seven times in the third round before referee Ruby Goldstein stops the fight at 2:03 of that round in the bout held at Yankee Stadium.

1960 Madison, Wisconsin, 9 April: Charlie Mohr, cocaptain of the University of Wisconsin's boxing team, is knocked out in the second round of the 165-pound class finals at the National Collegiate Athletic Association (NCAA) national tournament and dies eight days later. One month later, the university discontinues its boxing program. **New York, New York, 20 June:** Floyd Patterson becomes the first man to regain the world's heavyweight championship when he knocks out Ingemar Johansson at 1:51 of the fifth round in their rematch at the Polo Grounds. **Rome, Italy, 25 August–5 September:** The Olympic Games boxing tournament has 281 contestants from 54 nations—the most to date. American light heavyweight Cassius Marcellus Clay defeats Zbigniew Pietrzykowski of Poland in the final. As a professional heavyweight, Clay dominates the sport for the next two decades.

1961 Pittsburgh, Pennsylvania, 11 January: At its annual meetings, the NCAA votes to discontinue its national boxing championship tournament, claiming that not enough colleges had boxing teams.

1962 New York, New York, 24 March: Emile Griffith regains the world's welterweight championship by stopping Benny "Kid" Paret at 2:09 of the 12th round at Madison Square Garden. Griffith, upset over a homosexual slur that Paret made about him during the weigh-in, pounds Paret on the ropes for nearly 30 seconds before referee Ruby Goldstein stops the bout. Paret never regains consciousness and dies the following day. **Chicago, Illinois, 25 September:** Ex-convict Charles "Sonny" Liston knocks out Floyd Patterson at 2:05 of the first round to win the world's heavyweight championship.

1963 Mexico City, Mexico, 14 February: Representatives from 11 countries meet and form the World Boxing Council (WBC), whose aim is to regulate professional boxing worldwide. **Los Angeles, California, 21 March:** Ultiminio "Sugar" Ramos stops Davey Moore at the end of the 10th round of their world's featherweight championship bout. Moore dies two days later as a result of whiplash to his brain stem after his neck hits the bottom rope during the bout. **Las Vegas, Nevada, 22 July:** Charles "Sonny" Liston duplicates his performance of a year earlier by again knocking out Floyd Patterson in the first round of their world's heavyweight championship fight. This is the first heavyweight championship bout fought in Las Vegas, but there would be many more in the future.

1964 Miami Beach, Florida, 25 February: Loquacious Olympic champion Cassius Clay, a 7–1 underdog, stops Sonny Liston and wins the world's heavyweight championship. Liston, claiming a shoulder injury, refuses to come out for the seventh round. **Tokyo, Japan, 11–23 October:** In the first Olympic Games held in Asia, 269 boxers from 56 countries compete. American Joe Frazier wins the heavyweight gold medal and later would have an exceptional professional career.

1965 Lewiston, Maine, 25 May: In a bout held in a converted hockey arena before only 2,434 fans, Muhammad Ali (formerly known as Cassius Clay) stops former heavyweight champion Sonny Liston in the first round. After a brief exchange of punches, Liston goes down and does not get up before the count of 10. The fight ends in chaos as referee Jersey Joe Walcott has the fighters continue, but writer Nat Fleischer climbs into the ring to tell Walcott that Liston failed to rise in time and the bout is stopped. The "official" time of the ending of the bout is given as one minute of the first round, although in actuality 2:12 elapses before the end.

1967 Houston, Texas, 28 April: Muhammad Ali refuses induction into the U.S. Armed Forces, claiming that as a Muslim, the Vietnam War is against the teachings of the Qur'an. He is quoted as saying, "I ain't got no quarrel with them Viet Cong." **Houston, Texas, 20 June:** In a jury trial, Muhammad Ali is convicted of draft evasion and is sentenced to five years in prison, given a $10,000 fine, and is stripped of his passport and prohibited from boxing in the United States.

1968 New York, New York, 4 March: Joe Frazier stops Buster Mathis in the 11th round and wins the world's heavyweight championship as sanctioned by the New York State Athletic Commission in the first main event held at the new Madison Square Garden. **Mexico City, Mexico, 13–26 October:** For the third time in consecutive Olympic Games boxing tournaments, one of the gold medalists will later become the world's professional heavyweight champion. American George Foreman stops Lithuanian Jonas Čepulis (competing for the Soviet Union) in the second round of the heavyweight final; 307 entrants from 65 countries take part in the tournament.

1969 Newton, Iowa, 31 August: Rocky Marciano, a passenger in a Cessna 172 plane flying from Chicago to Des Moines, Iowa, is killed when the pilot, flying at night in bad weather, crashes into a tree attempting to land at a small airport, killing himself and his two passengers.

1970 20 January: A filmed simulated fight between Muhammad Ali and Rocky Marciano, based on a computer simulation with Marciano knocking out Ali in the 13th round, is shown at 1,500 theaters in the United States and Canada. **Atlanta, Georgia, 26 October:** Muhammad Ali, out on bail pending an appeal, is given a license by the City of Atlanta Boxing Commission and meets Jerry Quarry in Ali's first competitive bout since his conviction. Ali stops Quarry on cuts at the end of the third round, and the bout draws a large number of celebrities dressed to the nines in attendance.

1971 New York, New York, 8 March: Undefeated heavyweight champions Muhammad Ali and Joe Frazier meet in Madison Square Garden in a bout to determine the undisputed champion. Each boxer is paid $2.5 million dollars.

Frazier wins a hard-fought 15-round unanimous decision. **Washington, D.C., 28 June:** The Supreme Court of the United States overturns Muhammad Ali's draft evasion conviction by an 8–0 decision, with the only black justice, Thurgood Marshall, abstaining.

1972 Munich, Germany, 27 August–10 September: Eighty nations take part in the Olympic Games boxing competition with 354 contestants. Cuban heavyweight Téofilo Stevenson wins his first three bouts by knockout to win his first of three Olympic gold medals.

1973 Kingston, Jamaica, 22 January: In a bout between two former Olympic heavyweight champions, George Foreman knocks Joe Frazier down six times in two rounds and wins the world's heavyweight championship, with referee Arthur Mercante stopping the bout at 2:26 of the second round.

1974 New York, New York, 28 January: In a rematch of their classic 1971 bout, Muhammad Ali wins a hard-fought 12-round unanimous decision over Joe Frazier at Madison Square Garden. Neither fighter is champion at the time, and the bout is billed for the North American Boxing Federation heavyweight championship.

1974 Havana, Cuba, 17–30 August: The Association Internationale de Boxe Amateur (AIBA) holds its first World Championship boxing tournament. Cuban boxers win five of the 11 weight classes, Russian boxers win two, and boxers from Puerto Rico, Uganda, the United States, and Yugoslavia each win one. **Kinshasa, Zaire, 31 October:** Muhammad Ali regains the world's heavyweight championship with an eighth round knockout of George Foreman. The bout, known as "The Rumble in the Jungle," is one of the most unusual heavyweight championship bouts in history and takes place at 4 a.m. to accommodate American television. In an unusual tactic, dubbed the "Rope-a-Dope" by Ali, he leans back against the ropes and, while protecting his head, allows Foreman to throw punches at him. Foreman eventually becomes tired, which allows Ali to knock him out.

1975 Richfield, Ohio, 21 March: Muhammad Ali successfully defends his heavyweight championship against journeyman Chuck Wepner. Wepner, who enters the ring with a record of 30–9–2, puts up a good battle and knocks Ali down in the ninth round before he is stopped at 2:41 of the 15th round. This bout serves as the inspiration for Sylvester Stallone's 1976 film *Rocky*. **Milan, Italy, 4 April:** Franco Udella wins the newly created WBC light flyweight (108 pound) title over Valentín Martínez by disqualification in the 12th round and becomes that division's first world champion. **Manila, Philippines, 1 October:** In a bout dubbed "The Thrilla in Manila," Muhammad Ali stops Joe Frazier after 14 rounds of exceptionally hard-fought action and retains his heavyweight championship.

1976 San Juan, Puerto Rico, 6 March: Wilfred Benítez wins the World Boxing Association (WBA) light welterweight title by a split decision over Antonio Cervantes. Benítez, only 17 years and six months old, becomes the youngest world boxing champion in the history of the sport. **Montreal, Canada, 18–31 July:** The United States and Cuba dominate the Olympic Games boxing tournament. The USA wins seven medals—five gold—and Cuba wins eight medals—three gold. Among the American winners are future professional world champions Sugar Ray Leonard, Michael Spinks, Leon Spinks, and Leo Randolph.

1977 Pensacola, Florida, U.S.S. Aircraft Carrier *Lexington*, 17 January: In an attempt to get more American boxers to challenge for world titles in lower weight divisions, promoter Don King begins his United States Championship tournament with a series of televised eight-round bouts. Sixty boxers are scheduled to take part during the next several months. Future world's heavyweight champion Larry Holmes is one of the winners on the first program. **Los Angeles, California, 28 March:** *Rocky* receives the Academy Award for the Best Picture of 1976. John Avildsen wins an Academy Award as Best Director, and the film receives a third Oscar for Best Film Editing. **Miami Beach, Florida, 16 April:** After six boxing shows in the U.S. Championship tournament have been completed, Don King suspends the tournament due to allegations concerning falsification of records and rankings and possible kickbacks.

1978 Las Vegas, Nevada, 15 February: In a lackluster performance, Muhammad Ali loses his heavyweight title to Olympic champion Leon Spinks by a 15-round split decision. Spinks enters the bout as a 10–1 underdog, having had only seven previous professional bouts. **New Orleans, Louisiana, 15 September:** In a rematch, Muhammad Ali regains his heavyweight title by easily outboxing Leon Spinks in a unanimous 15-round decision.

1979 New York, New York: A syndicate headed by writer and sports memorabilia collector Bert Randolph Sugar purchases *Ring* magazine. Other members of the purchasing group include former professional basketball player Dave DeBusschere, Nick Kladis, and Jim Bukata. Sugar becomes the magazine's editor. **Split, Croatia, 8 December:** Marvin Camel and Mate Parlov meet for the newly created WBC cruiserweight (190 pound) title. Two of the three ring officials score the bout even, and the result is a draw with the title still vacant. Three months later, Camel becomes the first cruiserweight champion when he defeats Parlov in a rematch in Las Vegas, Nevada.

1980 Warsaw, Poland, 14 March: A Polish Airlines flight crashes while attempting to land. All 87 people on board die, including 14 members of the United States amateur boxing team and six coaches, among them 1976 U.S. Olympic team coach Thomas "Sarge" Johnson. **Montreal, Canada, 20**

June: Former world's lightweight champion Roberto Duran defeats previously undefeated Sugar Ray Leonard by a close unanimous decision and wins Leonard's WBC welterweight title. **Moscow, Russia, USSR, 20 July–2 August:** The Olympic Games is boycotted by the United States and more than 60 other countries. Cuba dominates the boxing competition, winning six gold, two silver, and two bronze medals in the 11 weight classes. Heavyweight Téofilo Stevenson wins his third consecutive Olympic gold medal. **Las Vegas, Nevada, 2 October:** Muhammad Ali comes out of retirement to fight undefeated Larry Holmes for Holmes's WBC heavyweight title. Holmes wins every round in a bout that is stopped after 10 rounds. **New Orleans, Louisiana, 25 November:** Sugar Ray Leonard regains the welterweight title by stopping Roberto Durán at 2:44 in the eighth round of their rematch. Durán, frustrated by Leonard's showboating tactics, quits, stating, "No más."

1981 Las Vegas, Nevada, 16 September: WBC welterweight champion Sugar Ray Leonard meets WBA welterweight champion Thomas Hearns in a bout for the undisputed welterweight championship. In a thrilling bout, selected by *Ring* magazine as their "Fight of the Year," Leonard, losing on points, rallies and stops Hearns at 1:45 of the 14th round. **Nassau, Bahamas, 11 December:** Trevor Berbick defeats Muhammad Ali by unanimous decision in Ali's last professional bout.

1982 Las Vegas, Nevada, 13 November: Ray Mancini knocks out Deuk-Koo Kim in the 14th round of their televised WBA lightweight championship bout. Four days later, Kim dies from his injuries. The WBA then changes the length of all future WBA championship bouts from 15 to 12 rounds.

1983 Newark, New Jersey, April: Robert W. Lee Sr., former vice president of the WBA, forms a new boxing sanctioning organization—the United States Boxing Association–International. The organization is renamed the International Boxing Federation (IBF) in 1984 and quickly gains recognition as one of the three leading boxing organizations. **New York, New York, 16 June:** Welterweight Luis Resto defeats previously undefeated Billy Collins Jr. in a preliminary to the Roberto Durán–Davey Moore light middleweight championship bout at Madison Square Garden. Collins is savagely beaten, with both eyes closed by the end of the 10-round bout, which he loses by decision. After the fight, it is disclosed that Resto's trainer, Carlos "Panama" Lewis, had tampered with Resto's gloves, removing padding, and had also soaked Resto's hand wraps in plaster of paris. Three years later, both Resto and Lewis were found guilty of assault and were sentenced to prison.

1984 Los Angeles, California, 29 July–11 August: The Olympic Games are boycotted by 14 communist countries. A super heavyweight class is added, with the heavyweight class being restricted to boxers weighing less than 91 kilograms (201.6 pounds). The United States wins 11 medals—nine gold, one silver, and one bronze—of the 12 boxing events since their two leading rivals in boxing, Cuba and the Soviet Union, are both absent.

1985 Palos Heights, Illinois, 14 December: Heavyweight Craig Bodzianowski makes a successful return to the ring 18 months after having a foot amputated. Bodzianowski, who was fitted for a prosthetic limb, knocks out his opponent, Francis Sargent, in two rounds.

1986 Las Vegas, Nevada, 22 November: Undefeated Mike Tyson (27–0 with 25 knockouts) stops Trevor Berbick at 2:35 of the second round to win the WBC heavyweight championship. Tyson, aged 20, is the youngest man to win the heavyweight title.

1987 Sacramento, California, 9 March: Former heavyweight champion George Foreman returns to the ring after an absence of 10 years with a four-round technical knockout victory over Steve Zouski. Foreman weighs 267 pounds—50 pounds more than when he won the title in 1973. **Bukok, Korea, 14 June:** Kyung-Yung Lee knocks out Masaharu Kawakami at 0:31 of the second round to win the IBF minimumweight (105 pounds) title—the first championship bout for the weight class.

1988 Atlantic City, New Jersey, 22 January: Mike Tyson stops former heavyweight champion Larry Holmes at 2:55 of the fourth round to retain his heavyweight title. **Seoul, South Korea, 17 September–2 October:** The largest field in Olympic boxing history takes part in the tournament—432 boxers from 106 different nations. In a bout between two future professional world's heavyweight champions, British-born Lennox Lewis, representing Canada, stops American Riddick Bowe to win the Olympic super heavyweight gold medal. As a result of a controversial scoring decision favoring Korean boxer Si-Heon Park over American Roy Jones Jr. in a bout in which Jones landed 86 punches to Park's 32, a new system for scoring was implemented for the 1992 Olympic Games.

1989 Canastota, New York: The International Boxing Hall of Fame opens.

1990 Tokyo, Japan, 11 February: In one of boxing's biggest upsets, 42–1 underdog James "Buster" Douglas survives an eighth-round knockdown and comes back to knock out the previously undefeated world's heavyweight champion, Mike Tyson, at 1:22 of the 10th round. **Las Vegas, Nevada, 25 October:** Evander Holyfield knocks out Douglas in the third round and becomes world's heavyweight champion.

1992 Indianapolis, Indiana, 11 February: Former heavyweight champion Mike Tyson is convicted of rape. In March, he is sentenced to 10 years in prison, with the last four years suspended. He is released in 1995 after serving three years. **Barcelona, Spain, 26 July–9 August:** The first Olympic Games since 1972 without countries boycotting the events takes place. A new scoring system is installed whereby the five judges press a computer button when they see an effective punch, but the system still results in controversial decisions. Cuban boxers dominate, winning seven gold medals. Lightweight Óscar De La Hoya wins the only gold medal for the United States.

1993 Mexico City, Mexico, 20 February: The largest paid attendance for a boxing card, 132,247 fans, watch undefeated local hero Julio César Chávez defend his WBC light welterweight title and win his 85th consecutive match with a fifth-round technical knockout over Greg Haugen. **Las Vegas, Nevada, 6 November:** Evander Holyfield defeats Riddick Bowe by majority decision in 12 rounds to win the WBA heavyweight title. The bout is stopped midway through the seventh round as a man (James Jarrett Miller, AKA "Fan Man") who had been circling the bout in a paraglider becomes entangled in the overhead lights and lands on the top rope of the ring. The arena's security people beat on him, and he eventually is taken to a hospital, while ringside fans tear his parachute to shreds for souvenirs.

1994 Las Vegas, Nevada, 5 November: George Foreman, who first won the world's heavyweight championship in 1973, regains the title by knocking out Michael Moorer in the 10th round to win the WBA heavyweight title. Foreman, at 45 years and nine months, becomes the oldest man to win a world's boxing championship.

1996 Atlanta, Georgia, 19 July: Muhammad Ali, the 1960 light heavyweight Olympic gold medalist, lights the Olympic torch to open the 1996 Olympic Games. Ali, visibly shaking from the effects of Parkinson's disease, performs his task without incident, to the delight of millions. **20 July–4 August:** Cuban boxers still dominate the Olympic Games with seven medals. Tonga wins the first Olympic medal in their history in any sport in the boxing tournament. Tongan super heavyweight Paea Wolfgramm defeats a Cuban boxer in a preliminary bout and wins the silver medal, losing his gold medal bout to future world's professional heavyweight champion Wladimir Klitschko.

1997 Las Vegas, Nevada, 28 June: Mike Tyson is disqualified by referee Mills Lane for twice biting Evander Holyfield's ear in the third round of their WBA world heavyweight championship bout.

1998 Phutthamonthon, Thailand, 4 December: Manny Pacquiao knocks out Chatchai Sasakul to win the WBC world flyweight title. Over the next 12 years, Pacquiao will win world championships in five other weight classes.

2000 Sydney, Australia, 16 September–1 October: As boxing becomes more universal, 48 Olympic boxing medals are awarded to boxers from 22 different countries. Russia with seven medals and Cuba with six (four gold) are the dominant nations.

2004 Athens, Greece, 14–29 August: Cuban boxers again dominate the Olympic Games tournament with five gold medals and eight total medals. Only 11 weight classes are held, with the light middleweight eliminated.

2005 Berlin, Germany, 17 December: At the Max Schmeling Halle, seven-foot, two-inch Russian Nikolai Valuev defeats John Ruiz by a majority decision in 12 rounds and wins the WBA heavyweight championship. Valuev is by far the tallest man to become heavyweight champion.

2006 Turmero, Venezuela, 25 February: Edwin Valero wins the WBA Fedalatin super featherweight title with a one-round technical knockout over Whyber Garcia. Valero has won all 18 of his bouts in the first round—an all-time boxing record.

2007 Las Vegas, Nevada, 5 May: Floyd Mayweather Jr. wins a 12-round split decision over Óscar De La Hoya in a bout for the WBC light middleweight title. The bout generates a record $120 million in revenue, including a record live gate of $19 million. De La Hoya earns $52 million and Mayweather $25 million.

2008 Beijing, China, 9–24 August: Boxers from nine different countries win gold medals at the Olympic Games. Chinese boxers Zou Shiming, in the light flyweight class, and Zhang Xiaoping, in the light heavyweight class, win their country's first Olympic boxing gold medals.

2010 Chiang Mai, Thailand, 23 July: Flyweight Liempetch Sor Veerapol stops Lookrak Kiatmungmee with one punch in a bout that was ended in just three seconds—the shortest bout in ring history. **Arlington, Texas, 13 November:** Manny Pacquiao wins a unanimous 12-round decision over Antonio Margarito for the vacant WBC light middleweight title, the sixth different weight class in which Pacquiao has won a world championship.

2011 Montreal, Canada, 21 May: Bernard Hopkins wins a unanimous 12-round decision over Jean Pascal for the WBC light heavyweight championship and becomes the oldest world champion in history at the age of 46 years, four months, and six days.

2012 London, England, 28 July–12 August: The featherweight class is eliminated from the men's Olympic boxing tournament, but three weight classes for women are added. **5 August:** Flyweight Elena Savelyeva of Russia defeats Hye Song Kim of North Korea 12–9, in the first Olympic women's boxing bout. The bout was refereed by a female referee from Algeria, Kheira Sidi Yakoub. **9 August:** Flyweight Nicole Adams of Great Britain, lightweight Katie Taylor of Ireland, and middleweight Clarissa Shields of the United States win the first Olympic gold medals in women's boxing.

Introduction

Boxing is one of the world's oldest sports—if not the oldest. In Nat Fleischer's *Ring Record Book and Boxing Encyclopedia*, he lists the first recorded bout as the biblical Cain vs. Abel. The Romans and Greeks had boxing contests, and in the ancient Olympic Games boxing was one of the three combat events, the other two being wrestling and pankration (a combination of wrestling and boxing similar to modern day mixed martial arts). The famed Greek author Homer wrote about boxing in *The Iliad*. This epic poem was written in the eighth century BC, around the time of the first Olympic Games.

ANCIENT GREEK BOXING

Although no known extensive treatises on early Greek boxing survive, a few facts have been surmised by scholars. The early Greek boxers wore leather straps on their hands. Wrestling in boxing competition was not permitted. (Wrestling was a separate combat sport.) Hitting with the hands and fist were permitted, but eye gouging was not. Hitting below the belt was prohibited. There were no weight classes, although fighters were matched within age groups. A ring was not used, and the boxers could use the entire stadium area. Contests lasted without rounds or time limits until one boxer submitted or was unable to continue. A unique aspect of this was that in some contests that went on too long, the fighters would alternate at punching each other undefended until one submitted. It was also forbidden to kill your opponent—boxers who did so were severely punished.

The ancient Olympic Games began in 776 BC, but hand-to-hand combat sports were not introduced until the 18th Olympiad in 708, when wrestling was first contested. Boxing was not added to the Olympic Games until 688 BC at the 23rd Olympiad. The first Olympic champion boxer was Onomastus of Smyrna. He has also been credited as the author of the first boxing rules. At the 33rd Olympiad in 648 BC, the pankration was added. A few of the early boxing champions were Tissandros of Naxos (winner of four consecutive Olympic championships from 572 to 560 BC), Glaucus of Carystus (winner in 520 BC, and also a celebrated winner at other ancient Greek sports festivals), Euthymos of Locres (three-time winner in 484, 476, and 472 BC), Diagoras of Rhodes (winner in 464 BC; his son Damagetos of Rhodes won the pankration in 448 BC), and Kleitomachus of Thebes (winner in both boxing and pankration in 216 BC). The last known Olympic boxing competition took place in AD 385. Caesar Theodosus I passed a law discontinuing the Olympic Games in AD 393.

ROMAN GLADIATORIAL CONTESTS

The Romans from about the third century BC to the third century AD engaged in many gladiatorial spectacles. There were many different forms of individual combat, and each had strict sets of rules. In some, the gladiators wore protective equipment, while in others they had none. Competition often involved swords, spears, or daggers. One of the forms of combat was similar to boxing, but the fighters wore spiked gloves called cestuses.

BAREKNUCKLE BOXING

For the next 1,400 years, boxing as a form of sport or entertainment did not exist. In the early 1700s, boxing as a method of exercise, self-defense, and entertainment began in England. James Figg, of Thame, Oxfordshire, with the backing of his patron, the Earl of Peterborough, opened a school on 18 September 1719 and taught boxing, fencing, and fighting with cudgels (also known as singlesticks) and quarterstaffs (a longer stick than a cudgel). He claimed the championship of England and is generally regarded as the father of modern boxing. He is listed as the first bareknuckle heavyweight champion and is credited with winning 269 of 270 bouts, although records were not reliably kept then. His only loss was to Ned Sutton in 1724, which he reversed by defeating Sutton in 1725 and again in 1727. Figg retired in 1730 and died in 1734 at the age of 39.

Following Figg's death, George Taylor claimed the championship and took over Figg's boxing amphitheater. Shortly afterward, Jack Broughton defeated Taylor and was recognized as champion. After severely beating George Stevenson in a fight in 1741 in London, to the extent that Stevenson died a few days later, the remorseful Broughton drew up a set of boxing rules to prevent a reoccurrence. The rules were used by Broughton to regulate bouts in his boxing academy. Bouts were fought to a finish until one fighter was unable to continue or surrendered and provided for 30-second rest periods following a knockdown. Broughton's Rules governed the London Prize Ring until superseded by the London Prize Ring Rules of 1838.

Broughton should more rightly be known as the "father of boxing" since he did more to advance boxing than did Figg, who was more of an advocate and teacher of multiple self-defense methods. Broughton, as did his predecessors, ran a boxing academy. His patron was the Duke of Cumberland.

Broughton was succeeded as champion by Jack Slack, who defeated him in 1750. The duke lost a considerable amount of money betting on Broughton and later felt that the bout was not on the level and he had been swindled. As a result, he had Broughton's academy closed and was able to persuade Parliament to ban prizefighting.

Slack fought the first international championship match on 29 July 1754 when he defeated a giant (for those days) six-foot-six-inch, 220-pound Frenchman with the ironic name of Jean Petit (John Little) in seven rounds and 25 minutes. Since prizefighting was illegal, the match was held in a remote area near Norwich, England.

Slack, who claimed to be the grandson of Figg, was notorious for his dirty tactics. It was said that he was the first to use a "rabbit punch" (blow to the back of the neck). In 1760, Slack lost his championship to William Stevens, "The Nailer," in a bout that most likely was fixed. Stevens was uninterested in boxing and sold his title to Slack's protege, George Meggs, in 1761, losing in four rounds in another fixed bout.

Over the next two decades, the quality of the prize ring suffered, and it was not until the mid-1780s that Thomas Jackling, who boxed as "Tom Johnson," restored some honesty to the sport. He was defeated in 1791 by "Big Ben" Brain. Brain died of cirrhosis of the liver in 1794 and was succeeded as champion by Daniel Mendoza, the first Jewish fighter of note. "Gentleman" John Jackson, a well-mannered socialite, defeated Mendoza in 1795 and retired from the ring shortly afterward.

The early part of the 19th century became the golden age of bareknuckle boxing. In 1800, Jem Belcher, known as "The Napoleon of the Prize Ring," claimed the championship. He was followed by Henry Pearce, "The Game Chicken," considered by boxing historians as among the most skillful fighters in the London Prize Ring. Pearce relinquished his championship in 1807 due to ill health and died in 1809 at the age of 31. John Gully, who had been scheduled to fight Pearce, claimed the title in 1807. Gully had an interesting life. A pub owner, he was a bookmaker and then a racehorse owner. He was quite successful and was elected to Parliament in 1832 and served two terms.

Following Gully's short-lived claim as champion, Tom Cribb, one of the all-time greatest bareknuckle fighters, claimed the title in 1808. He retained the championship until his retirement from the ring in 1822. Two of his best-known title defenses were made in 1810 and 1811 against Tom Molineaux, a former slave who after becoming a free man traveled to England to become a prizefighter.

Other English champions following Cribb from 1822 to 1850 include Tom Spring, Tom Cannon, Jem Ward and his brother Nick, Peter Crawley, James "Deaf" Burke, Ben Caunt, and William Thompson, known as "Bendigo."

In 1838, a new set of boxing rules still using bareknuckles was adopted, known as the London Prize Ring Rules, and replaced Broughton's Rules. They were revised in 1853 and governed bareknuckle boxing until the sport was superseded by gloved boxing under the Marquess of Queensberry Rules of 1867. Those rules, written by John Graham Chambers, and sponsored by John Sholto Douglas, the ninth Marquess of Queensberry, required boxers to wear gloves and box for three-minute rounds with a one-minute rest period between rounds. They were gradually adopted and by 1890 were nearly universally used.

Professional boxing in the United States began in 1816 with Jacob Hyer, a New York butcher, meeting Tom Beasley, an English sailor, in a formal bout under English prize ring rules. Hyer suffered a broken arm, but Beasley was badly beaten, and reports vary as to the winner of the bout. Hyer never fought again, but his son, Tom Hyer, claimed to be the first American boxing champion after he defeated Country McCloskey in New York in 1841. Tom Hyer's next fight occurred in 1849, when he defeated Yankee Sullivan in Maryland. The Irish-born John Morrissey succeeded Hyer as American champion and, after retiring from fistic activities, served two terms as a United States congressman.

John Camel (sometimes misspelled Carmel) Heenan was the next American title claimant. He traveled to England in 1860 and fought the English champion, Tom Sayers, in one of that era's most publicized bouts and the first between the English and American champions. The bout was called a draw after rowdy spectators broke into the ring after 42 rounds of boxing. Sayers retired after the bout.

The next English title claimant was Jem Mace, often referred to as the father of "scientific boxing." Although his first recorded bout was in 1849 when he was 18 years old, he did not become a title claimant until 1861 when he defeated Sam Hurst, who had claimed the title after Sayers's retirement. Mace lost to Tom King in 1862, but after King's retirement reclaimed the title and held it until 1871. In 1869, Mace became the first English champion to fight in the United States and toured with Heenan, giving sparring exhibitions. Mace fought Tom Allen, the American champion, in 1870 and, following his victory over Allen, claimed the heavyweight championship of both England and America. He abandoned his title claims in 1871 but continued boxing exhibitions in England and the United States. By 1876, he was fighting under the new Marquess of Queensberry Rules. In 1877, he traveled to Australia and introduced the sport there. He opened a school of boxing and toured Australia and New Zealand. He later returned to the United States and in 1903 went to South Africa, where he opened another boxing school. He continued giving boxing exhibitions into his 60s.

After Mace fought in the United States, the English bareknuckle champion lineage ended and the heavyweight champion was considered the "world's heavyweight champion." Tom Allen filled that role from 1873 to 1876. He was followed by Joe Goss from 1876 to 1880 and by Paddy Ryan from 1880 to 1882. On 7 February 1882, Ryan was defeated by John L. Sullivan, known as the "Boston Strong Boy." From 1882 to 1889, Sullivan fought mostly exhibition bouts but defended his title claim in France against Charley Mitchell in 1888. The last bareknuckle title bout took place in Richburg, Mississippi, on 8 July 1889 when Sullivan knocked out Jake Kilrain in 75 rounds.

BOXING BOOTHS

In the early 1700s, another form of boxing began—the boxing booth. At English country fairs, one of the forms of entertainment was the boxing booth. A large tent was set up, and inside a fighter would take on challenges from the audience. Should there be none, a prearranged opponent would appear from the audience to challenge the fighter. A prize would be offered should the challenger survive a specified period of time with the boxer. Boxing booths lasted from the bareknuckle era through the gloved era and only ceased in the 1970s.

BOXING THROUGHOUT THE WORLD

Boxing, although primarily a sport in England and the United States, soon became popular in other countries. When Commodore Matthew Perry landed in Japan in 1854, American sailors would engage in boxing matches aboard ship. The Japanese soon started engaging in various martial arts competitions. By 1896, a boxing gymnasium was opened in Yokohama. Yujiro Watanabe, known as the father of Japanese boxing, learned his skills in San Francisco. He returned to Japan and founded the Nippon Kento Club in 1921, with the first Japanese national champions crowned in 1922. It was not until 1952 that the first Japanese world champion flyweight, Yoshio Shirai, won a world title. Since then, more than 50 Japanese boxers have been recognized as world champions.

Boxing in the Philippines did not begin until the early part of the 20th century, with Filipino prisoners being taught to box by U.S. guards during the 1890s. Filipino boxing evolved from a Filipino sport called Suntukan, a bare-handed martial arts sport, which in turn evolved from Kali, a Filipino knife-fighting technique. Boxing was first legalized around 1920 in the Philippines. Two American brothers, Eddie and Stewart Tait, were the ones responsible for promoting interest in the sport in the Philippines. Frank Churchill, another American, helped promote fights there as well and later discovered Francisco Guilledo, whom he renamed Pancho Villa. Villa came to the United States and won the world's flyweight championship on 18 June 1923. Boxing has been a popular sport since, and more than 30 world champions have been born in the Philippines, including Manny Pacquiao, a 21st-century boxer who is arguably among the best pound-for-pound fighters in boxing history.

Latin American boxing also began around the turn of the 20th century. The first recorded professional boxing match in Puerto Rico took place on 15 January 1899. Their first Puerto Rico island championship bout took place in 1929, and their first world champion was Sixto Escobar, who won the world's bantamweight title in 1935. Venezuela's first national title bout occurred in 1925. They have produced more than 30 world champions, with junior welterweight Carlos Hernández being their first world champion in 1965. The first Argentinean national championship bout took place in 1915. Shortly afterward, Luis Ángel Firpo came to the United States and fought Jack Dempsey for the world's heavyweight title in 1923. In 1954, flyweight Pascual Pérez became their first world champion, and they have had more than 35 others since.

Mexico has had a long history of boxing, with the first national championship bout occurring in 1913. The first Mexican world champion was Battling Shaw (José Pérez Flores), who won the junior welterweight championship in 1933. Mexico has produced more world champions than any country except the United States, and more than 125 Mexican boxers have won world championships. Cuba's boxing tradition goes back to the early 20th century, with their first national title bout in 1912. Kid Chocolate (Eligio Sardiñias) was their first recognized world champion in 1931. Professional boxing was quite popular in Cuba until the Fidel Castro regime. The professional sport was prohibited in 1960, but amateur boxing thrived, and Cubans have done exceptionally well in Olympic boxing. Since 1960, they have won 67 Olympic medals. They have also produced two three-time Olympic champions, Téofilo Stevenson and Félix Savon.

Continental European boxing also stems from the early 20th century. The French national title began in 1911. Georges Carpentier was one of the first world-renowned French boxers. In 1920, he came to the United States, won the world's light heavyweight championship, and unsuccessfully challenged

Jack Dempsey for the world's heavyweight title. More than 25 Frenchman have since claimed world championships. Italy also has a long tradition of boxing. Their first national championship bout took place in 1910. In 1933, Primo Carnera won the world's heavyweight title. More than 25 Italians since have become world champions. German professional boxing dates back to the same era, with their first national title bout in 1911. Max Schmeling was their first world champion in 1930. Since Schmeling, 18 other Germans have become world champions.

In former Iron Curtain countries, professional boxing was not permitted during most of the 20th century. Many of them, however, had excellent amateur boxing programs, and countries such as Poland, Hungary, and Romania have done well in Olympic competition. Poland first entered the Olympic boxing tournament in 1924 and has since won 43 medals. Romania first competed in the 1936 Olympic Games and has won 25 Olympic medals. Hungarians have won 20 Olympic boxing medals since 1924. The Soviet Union first competed in Olympic boxing in 1952 and won 51 medals through 1988.

Boxing in Africa, with the exception of South Africa, was virtually nonexistent until the 1960s, when many countries gained their independence from colonial rule. Nigeria had a boxing program and had professional national championships as early as 1951, but most of the other African nations had none. Boxing in South Africa began in the late 19th century, and by 1884 there were national championships contested.

Boxing in Australia dates back to the bareknuckle days. Bareknuckle champion Jem Mace traveled there in 1877 and introduced the sport there and in New Zealand, showing his patrons the new Marquess of Queensberry Rules. Among the early Australian boxers of note was Peter Jackson, a black fighter born in the Dutch West Indies but a resident of Australia, who fought Jim Corbett and was regarded as one of the world's best fighters, although he never won a world's championship.

THE EARLY GLOVED ERA, 1890–1908

Boxing, although illegal in most parts of the country, remained popular in the United States. Bouts under Marquess of Queensberry Rules were held in several weight classes with heavyweight being far and away the most popular. One of the places where boxing was legal was New Orleans, Louisiana, and in 1892 a three-day series of bouts, billed as the Carnival of Champions, was held. On 5 September, world lightweight champion Jack McAuliffe knocked out challenger Billy Myer in the 15th round in a world's lightweight championship bout. On the next day, 118-pound George Dixon, a black

Canadian boxer, and 116.5-pound Jack Skelly fought for the world's feather-weight title, with Dixon prevailing on an eighth-round knockout. The main attraction of the carnival occurred on the third day, when John L. Sullivan, the heavyweight champion of the world, made his first title defense under Marquess of Queensberry Rules against challenger Jim Corbett. Corbett won the title by knocking out Sullivan in the 21st round. This bout was a sharp contrast in styles and personalities as the rough, brawling Sullivan was defeated by the scientific boxer Corbett, known as "Gentleman Jim."

One of the innovations in boxing during the 1890s was the use of the newly invented motion picture camera. On 7 September 1894, Corbett and Peter Courtney engaged in an exhibition bout that was recorded on film by Thomas Edison's kinetoscope process. Filming of boxing bouts became popular, and in fact was the only way that most of the country's population ever saw a boxing contest for the next 20 years.

Corbett, as was the custom in that era, only defended his title once—a three-round knockout of Charlie Mitchell in January 1894. Champion boxers capitalized on their titles by boxing exhibitions and appearing on the vaudeville stage and made more money in that way than by accepting challenges for their title. In Corbett's next defense, on 17 March 1897, he was stopped in the 14th round by Bob Fitzsimmons, a gangly 167-pound former middleweight champion.

Fitzsimmons lost the heavyweight title in his first defense two years later in Coney Island, New York, to Jim Jeffries, who outweighed him by nearly 40 pounds. After an unsuccessful attempt to regain the title in 1902, Fitzsimmons then moved up to win the newly created light heavyweight title in 1903 and became the first boxer to win championships in three different weight classes.

Earlier in 1903, on 22 April, Jack Root and Charles "Kid" McCoy met in the first light heavyweight championship bout (175-pound weight limit), which was won by Root in a 10-round decision in Detroit, Michigan. Root's manager, Lou Houseman, created the new division, although some record books claim that several bouts in 1899 won by Joe Choynski, who never claimed the title himself, were light heavyweight title bouts.

Jeffries was more active in the ring than his predecessors and defended his title seven times from 1899 to 1904. In 1905, he retired undefeated, claiming there were no viable challengers for the title. He then selected Jack Root and Marvin Hart to box for the championship and offered his services as referee of that bout. On 3 July 1905, Hart knocked out Root in 12 rounds in Reno, Nevada, to become champion.

Hart was heavyweight champion for barely seven months as he was defeated in February 1906 by Canadian-born Tommy Burns. Burns, only five feet seven inches tall, the shortest heavyweight champion in boxing history, proved to be a fighting champion. He successfully defended his title 11 times over the next 33 months and fought in California, England, Ireland, France, and Australia. On 26 December 1908, in Sydney, Australia, he was defeated by Jack Johnson, a 30-year-old black fighter from Texas. Johnson's reign as champion became one of the low periods in boxing history.

Other significant boxers in the 1890–1908 era who won championships include middleweights Jack Dempsey, "The Nonpareil," and Tommy Ryan; welterweights "Mysterious Billy" Smith, Joe Walcott, and the "Dixie Kid"; lightweights Jack McAuliffe, George "Kid" Lavigne, Joe Gans, and Battling Nelson; featherweights "Torpedo" Billy Murphy, George Dixon, and Terry McGovern; and bantamweight Jimmy Barry. Notable nonchampions of the era include heavyweights Peter Jackson, Joe Jeannette, and Sam Langford and featherweight Jem Driscoll.

THE WHITE HOPE ERA, 1908–1915

Although Jack Johnson was one of the most talented heavyweight boxers in history, with no challenger during his era a match for him, his arrogance in his public life and his penchant for expensive cars, jewelry, and white women were strongly in defiance of the mores of the era. After he successfully defended his title four times in 1909, Johnson's demeanor was such that former champion Jim Jeffries, who had been retired for nearly six years, felt obliged to come out of retirement to challenge Johnson for the heavyweight title to restore it to the Caucasian race. Jeffries lost more than 80 pounds to get into fighting shape and accepted promoter Tex Rickard's offer of a $101,000 purse (which was agreed by the two boxers to be split 60 percent to the winner and 40 percent to the loser) to fight Johnson in Reno, Nevada, on 4 July 1910.

The scheduled 45-round bout took place in a specially constructed arena before 15,760 fans, with Rickard acting as referee after U.S. president William Howard Taft declined the offer to referee the bout. Johnson won when he knocked Jeffries down three times in the 15th round before Jeffries's seconds stepped in to stop the fight. After the results of the fight were spread across the country, race rioting occurred, with at least a dozen people, both black and white, killed and hundreds injured. Subsequently, Congress passed a law prohibiting the transportation of fight films across state lines to minimize the number of people who could see films of a black man beating a white man.

The sports world began to search for a Caucasian boxer who could dethrone Johnson. These boxers were referred to as "white hopes" in the vernacular of that era. Among the boxers considered as "white hopes" were Bill Brennan, Georges Carpentier, Dan "Porky" Flynn, "Fireman" Jim Flynn,

Fred Fulton, Al Kaufman, Luther McCarty, Frank Moran, Carl Morris, Arthur Pelkey, George "Boer" Rodel, Ed "Gunboat" Smith, and Jess Willard. Kaufman, "Fireman" Flynn, and Moran all failed in heavyweight title bouts against Johnson.

With extreme anti-Johnson sentiment guiding the nation's actions, Johnson was arrested on 18 October 1912 for violating the Mann Act for "transporting women across state lines for immoral purposes" since his fiancée at the time, Lucille Cameron, was a white woman accused of being a prostitute. She refused to testify against him, and the case fell apart. The government continued to hound him, and a second offense was found, this time with a former girlfriend of Johnson's, Belle Schreiber. In June 1913, Johnson was convicted by an all-white jury and sentenced to a year and a day in prison. Although the Mann Act was only passed on 25 June 1910, Johnson was convicted for acts committed prior to its passage. Clearly, the government was out to get him to "show him his place."

Johnson skipped bail and fled the country, living and boxing in Europe with successful title defenses in France in 1913 and 1914. On 5 April 1915, "white hope" Jess Willard succeeded by knocking out Johnson in the 26th round of their scheduled 45-round bout in Havana, Cuba, and the era of the white hope ended. Johnson remained a fugitive and lived in Europe and South America before voluntarily returning to the United States in 1920.

Other notable boxers during this era include light heavyweights "Philadelphia" Jack O'Brien and Jack Dillon, middleweights Stanley Ketchel and Billy Papke, welterweight Mike "Twin" Sullivan, lightweights Ad Wolgast and Freddie Welsh, featherweight Abe Attell, bantamweight Johnny Coulon, and flyweight Jimmy Wilde.

THE NO-DECISION ERA, 1911–1920

During the early 20th century, boxing was still illegal in many jurisdictions within the United States. In an attempt to regulate it somewhat, several states passed laws that, while allowing boxing contests to occur, prohibited judges or referees from deciding the winner should the bout last the scheduled number of rounds. In New York State, for example, the Frawley Law was passed in 1911 limiting bouts to 10 rounds and prohibiting decisions. Boxing matches in Pennsylvania during this time were limited to six rounds.

Championships did not change hands unless the bout ended in a knockout. The daily newspapers that covered the bouts would select the fighter they felt had won, and boxing fans would use the newspaper decision to settle their bets. These laws lasted roughly 10 years, with the New York State law being superseded by the Walker Law, which permitted decisions and created a New York State Athletic Commission to regulate the sport.

Boxing was still a popular sport despite these limitations. Significant boxers during this time include light heavyweight Battling Levinsky, middleweight Mike O'Dowd, welterweights Ted "Kid" Lewis and Jack Britton, lightweight Benny Leonard, featherweight Johnny Dundee, and bantamweights Kid Williams and Pete Herman.

THE GOLDEN AGE OF SPORT, 1920–1928

The next decade in U.S. sports history has been referred to as the "Golden Age of Sport." Each of the major sports had star performers who were adulated by the public to a much greater extent than was the case in earlier times. Baseball had Babe Ruth, tennis had Bill Tilden, golf had Bobby Jones, football had Red Grange, and in boxing it was Jack Dempsey, who headlined the decade.

Dempsey won the heavyweight championship by annihilating Willard on 4 July 1919. Willard, although he outweighed Dempsey by 58 pounds, proved to be no match for Jack and was knocked down seven times in the first round. Although Willard survived the knockdowns, he put up little resistance, and the bout was stopped in the third round. Dempsey then made two successful defenses of the title in 1920.

His next bout, against French champion and war hero, Georges Carpentier, was heavily promoted by Tex Rickard and drew more than 80,000 spectators to an arena specially constructed for the bout in Jersey City, New Jersey. The paid attendance of $1,789,238 was the first time that proceeds from a boxing match exceeded one million dollars. The bout itself was anticlimactic, and Dempsey, who outweighed the 172-pound Carpentier by 16 pounds, won by a knockout in the fourth round.

Dempsey's next title defense was another legendary bout. It took place in the small town of Shelby, Montana, on 4 July 1923. The town's leaders, eager to attract attention to their town, where oil had recently been discovered, offered $250,000 to Dempsey and Jack "Doc" Kearns, his manager, to defend the heavyweight title there, with an additional $150,000 promised to Dempsey's opponent, Tommy Gibbons. Local banks put up the money to stage the attraction. Attendance was exceptionally poor though, with only 7,000 fans paying to see the fight and an estimated 13,000 crashing the gate and seeing it for free. Kearns received $200,000 before the fight with a promise of part of the gate receipts. The bout was a relatively dull affair in which Dempsey won a 15-round decision. Immediately after the bout, Kearns and Dempsey left town with the additional $50,000 from the gate receipts. Several Shelby banks failed as a result of the fiasco.

Dempsey's next title defense occurred only two months afterward and was another of Rickard's major promotions. At the Polo Grounds in New York on 14 September 1923, Dempsey met Argentinean Luis Ángel Firpo. The bout turned out to be one of the most exciting in boxing history, as Firpo knocked Dempsey down twice in the first round, the second time through the ropes. After the first knockdown, where Dempsey's knees barely touched the canvas, he got up and knocked Firpo down seven times. After the seventh knockdown, Firpo hit Dempsey with a wild right-hand punch that knocked Dempsey through the ropes. He was helped back into the ring by the newspaper men seated in ringside seats and was ready to continue boxing by the count of nine. In the second round, Dempsey continued his attack and had Firpo down twice more, with the second knockdown being for the 10 count. The first round as well as the entirety of the brief bout appear on many boxing historians' lists as among the greatest rounds and greatest bouts in boxing history.

Dempsey did not fight for three years after that bout. His next bout took place on 23 September 1926 and, through Rickard's promotional efforts, drew 120,557 fans to Philadelphia's Sesquicentennial Stadium—the largest crowd in boxing history to that point. His opponent, Gene Tunney, a former United States marine, won a 10-round decision and the heavyweight championship.

Their rematch one year later on 22 September 1927 at Soldier Field in Chicago was another of boxing's most famous bouts. It drew boxing's first two million dollar gate, with a live attendance of 104,943. Again, Tunney outboxed Dempsey, but in the seventh round Jack knocked Tunney down. A new rule at that time required the boxer scoring the knockdown to go to a neutral corner while the referee counted over the fallen fighter. (Previously the fighter scoring the knockdown could just stand over his fallen foe and knock him down again as soon as he got up.) In the fight with Tunney, Dempsey forgot the rule and stood over his opponent until referee, Dave Barry, made Dempsey move. After Dempsey did so, Barry began to count. Tunney got up at the count of nine, but films of the fight show that he was down for 14 seconds. Tunney continued to stay away from Dempsey and was not down again in the fight. At the end of the scheduled 10 rounds, Tunney was declared the winner. Dempsey retired from the ring after the bout, and Tunney only fought once more before retiring also.

Other of boxing's most noteworthy fighters during this era include light heavyweights Battling Siki (a French boxer from Senegal), Irishman Mike McTigue (who won the title from Siki on St. Patrick's Day in Dublin, Ireland), and Tommy Loughran. Harry Greb and Theodore "Tiger" Flowers were the two top middleweights, and both, ironically, died after minor operations while still active boxers. Other champions of note were welterweights Mickey Walker, Pete Latzo, and Jackie Fields; lightweight Sammy Mandell; featherweights Eugene Criqui and Louis "Kid" Kaplan; bantamweights Joe Lynch, Abe Goldstein, Charley Phil Rosenberg, and Charles "Bud" Taylor; and flyweights Pancho Villa and Frankie Genaro.

Two other important events in boxing history occurred during the 1920s. The first was the founding of *Ring* magazine by Nat Fleischer and Tex Rickard in 1922. For the next 50 years, until his death in 1972, Fleischer exerted significant influence upon boxing's record keeping. His monthly magazine became known as the bible of boxing, with comprehensive results of boxing bouts. He introduced a system of ranking boxers monthly according to recent performances, and in 1942 he began publishing an annual *Ring Record Book* with boxers' records. *Ring* also created a boxing hall of fame and museum in the 1950s. Following Fleischer's death in 1972, *Ring* magazine has continued under several different editors.

The second significant event in boxing history during the 1920s was the introduction of the Golden Gloves tournament for amateur boxers. Begun in Chicago in 1926 by the sports editor of the *Chicago Tribune*, Arch Ward, and begun in New York the following year by the sports editor of the *Daily News*, Paul Gallico, the tournaments grew, and most of the top boxers took part in them. Although amateur boxing in the United States had been going on under the auspices of the Amateur Athletic Union since the 1880s, the Golden Gloves popularized amateur boxing to a much greater extent. In the 21st century, the Golden Gloves remains as a starting point for many boxers' careers.

BOXING BETWEEN THE JACK DEMPSEY AND JOE LOUIS ERAS, 1928–1937

After the retirement of Dempsey and Tunney, boxing did not have one major hero. The sport still thrived, but the heavyweight championship changed hands almost annually from 1928 until 1937.

In 1930, Max Schmeling and Jack Sharkey were selected to fight for the vacant world's heavyweight title. Schmeling won the bout in the fourth round after claiming that Sharkey fouled him with a low blow. This was the first time (and as of 2012 the only time) that the heavyweight championship changed hands via a disqualification. Schmeling successfully defended his title once in 1931 before losing it to Sharkey in 1932 via a split decision. Sharkey lost to Primo Carnera in his first defense in 1933. Carnera, a six-foot-six-inch giant from Italy was not a particularly skillful fighter but had been manipulated by gangsters to a position as a title challenger. The results of many of his bouts including his title victory were questionable as to their legitimacy.

Carnera made two successful title defenses, winning both on 15-round decisions. One was in his native Italy against the Basque fighter Paulino Uzcudun. The other was against Tommy Loughran, a former light heavyweight champion who was outweighed by 84 pounds in his bout with Carnera. On 14 June 1934, Carnera lost his title after being badly beaten by Max Baer and stopped in the 11th round after being down about 10 times (accounts vary as to the exact number). Baer, in turn, lost the title to Jim Braddock in his first defense one year later. Braddock, nicknamed the "Cinderella Man," had been boxing since 1926 with mixed results. From 1929 to 1933, he had lost 19 of 29 bouts and reached a point where he was unable to get bouts and was forced to go on public relief to support his family. Braddock held the title for two years without defending it, and when he did was knocked out by Joe Louis in eight rounds.

During this period, the leading boxers included light heavyweights Slapsie Maxie Rosenbloom (so called for his lack of a strong punch and his slapping attack) and John Henry Lewis; middleweights Marcel Thil and Freddie Steele; welterweights Jimmy McLarnin and Barney Ross; lightweights Tony Canzoneri and Lou Ambers; featherweights Bat Battalino, Kid Chocolate, and Freddie Miller; bantamweights Panama Al Brown and Sixto Escobar; and flyweights Jackie Brown and Benny Lynch.

JOE LOUIS—"A CREDIT TO HIS RACE," 1937–1951

After the Jack Johnson era, black boxers did not get an opportunity to fight for the heavyweight title. Harry Wills, one of the best heavyweights of the 1920s, was avoided by Jack Dempsey. There were black champions in lighter divisions, among them light heavyweight Battling Siki, middleweight Tiger Flowers, and featherweight Kid Chocolate, but although there were competent black heavyweight boxers, they were not afforded the opportunity to compete for the title.

Joe Louis was raised in Detroit and was a Golden Gloves champion. In 1934, he also won the national Amateur Athletic Union light heavyweight title. He was befriended by two Detroit black men, John Roxborough, a successful bookmaker, and Julian Black, a Chicago promoter and onetime speakeasy owner who managed several fighters and knew his way around the fight business. They convinced Louis that a white manager would not work hard to further a black fighter's career. To train Louis, the two men then hired Jack "Chappie" Blackburn, a former lightweight who had been a competent boxer in the early years of the 20th century.

To counter the negative image of black boxers that Jack Johnson had created, Louis's management team insisted on several conditions to enable them to promote Louis successfully and be nonthreatening to white people. He was not to be photographed with white women or with alcohol. He was not to gloat over opponents after victories and was never to flaunt any of the material successes that came his way.

Louis began his professional career in the heavyweight class in 1934, and after he won his first 19 bouts (15 by knockout), white promoter Mike Jacobs made a deal with Louis, Roxborough, and Black and signed a three-year exclusive promotion contract with them. Jacobs had promotional rights at major New York venues such as Madison Square Garden and Yankee Stadium and was also able to help counter the prejudice that Louis faced.

In 1935, Louis easily defeated former heavyweight champion Primo Carnera. After winning four more bouts, including a defeat of former heavyweight champion Max Baer, Louis appeared to be heading for a match with heavyweight champion Jim Braddock.

On 19 June 1936, Louis proved to be not invincible, as he was knocked out by former heavyweight champion Max Schmeling in 12 rounds. This set back plans for a title bout somewhat. Louis then knocked out former heavyweight champion Jack Sharkey in three rounds and won six more bouts against lesser opponents (five by knockout). He then was matched with Jim Braddock for the heavyweight title on 22 June 1937 at Comiskey Park in Chicago. In that bout, Louis was down in the first round but got up and knocked out Braddock in the eighth round to become world's heavyweight champion.

Louis then won three title defenses easily. That set the stage for a return match with the former heavyweight champion, Max Schmeling. The bout took place on 22 June 1938 and was highly anticipated by both Louis and the public. Louis wanted to avenge the only loss in his career. It was built up by the promoters as a match between the Nazi Schmeling and the black American Louis. The bout only lasted two minutes and four seconds as Louis received his revenge. He knocked Schmeling down three times, and referee Arthur Donovan looked at the beaten Schmeling and stopped the bout.

Louis proved to be the most active heavyweight champion in history and defended his title 15 times from 1939 to 1941, although he came close to losing his championship in June 1941 against light heavyweight champion Billy Conn. At the start of the 13th round, Louis was behind on points, and had Conn chosen to box defensively in the last few rounds, he might have defeated Joe. But Conn decided to go for a knockout in the 13th round, and Louis knocked him out with two seconds remaining in that round.

Louis fought one more title defense in 1941, and then one month after the Pearl Harbor attack, Louis defended his title at Madison Square Garden against Buddy Baer, brother of former heavyweight champion Max Baer. Louis donated his entire purse to the Navy Relief Fund. The next day, 10 January 1941, Louis enlisted in the U.S. Army. At one point, he was quoted as saying, "We'll win because we're on God's side." That slogan was later used on recruiting posters with Louis's photo.

Two months later, Private Joe Louis was given leave to defend his title once more at the Garden, against Abe Simon, in a bout for the Army Emergency Relief Fund. Again, Louis donated his entire purse. Ironically, those two bouts would haunt Louis the rest of his life as the Internal Revenue Service claimed he owed income tax on his earnings for the bouts and he was hit with enormous tax bills later in the decade.

While in the army, Louis was a member of the Special Services Division. He traveled to military bases worldwide and boxed exhibitions to entertain the troops. After his discharge, he knocked out Conn in eight rounds in June 1946. Louis again nearly lost his title on 5 December 1947. Jersey Joe Walcott knocked Louis down in both the first and fourth rounds but received a split decision victory in a bout that Louis was sure he had lost. In 1948, Louis knocked out Walcott in the 11th round after trailing throughout most of the fight. On 1 March 1949, Louis announced his retirement from the ring. During his reign, Louis's popularity among both whites and blacks was unsurpassed by any other black athlete. He was widely referred to by whites as "a credit to his race," although sportswriter Jimmy Cannon clarified the statement by stating that Louis was a "credit to his race—the human race."

One of the other most accomplished boxers during Louis's reign was Henry Armstrong, another black fighter. Armstrong was the first fighter to be champion of three weight divisions simultaneously. In 1937, he won the world's featherweight title. He followed that by winning the welterweight title in 1938 and then the lightweight title the same year. In 1940, he nearly won a fourth title as he fought a draw for the middleweight championship.

During World War II, many fighters were drafted or enlisted in the military services, and consequently, champions who served had their boxing titles "frozen for the duration." Among the best fighters during the 1940s were light heavyweights Gus Lesnevich and Englishman Freddie Mills; middleweights Tony Zale, Rocky Graziano, Frenchman Marcel Cerdan, and Jake LaMotta; welterweight Ray Robinson; lightweights Ike Williams, Beau Jack, and Bob Montgomery; featherweight Willie Pep; bantamweight Manuel Ortiz; and British flyweights Scot Jackie Paterson and Irishman Rinty Monaghan. Zale and Graziano fought three exceptionally stirring bouts from 1946 to 1948.

THE INTERNATIONAL BOXING CLUB AND THE TELEVISION ERA, 1949–1960

Following the war, the growing popularity of television played a major role in boxing's history. The sport was one of the easiest to televise since all the action took place in a small area. The fixed duration of rounds and rest periods provided a regular interval for commercial advertising for sponsors. From 1947 to the early 1960s, boxing was one of the highest-rated television shows. Boxing cards were televised nearly every night of the week except Sundays. The result was that while the sport retained its popularity with the fans, individual fight clubs lost patronage as people preferred to stay home and watch the free show on television.

In 1949, James Norris and Arthur Wirtz, owners of several of the major arenas in the country, formed the International Boxing Club (IBC) to promote fights throughout the eastern part of the United States. They acquired promotional rights for New York's Madison Square Garden. They also obtained the contracts of several major fighters. Consequently, the IBC held a virtual monopoly of boxing, especially of nationally televised bouts. They also became involved with a few organized crime figures. While most of these dealings were of little interest to boxing fans, the fighters lost out, with only those who "had connections" able to progress toward championship bouts. In 1959, the IBC was declared a monopoly and ordered to dissolve. The following year, the United States Senate held investigations into organized crime, and several individuals were convicted of extortion.

MARCIANO, PATTERSON, AND ROBINSON, 1950–1960

After the announced retirement of Joe Louis, the two leading contenders, Jersey Joe Walcott and Ezzard Charles, met in June 1949, with Charles winning a unanimous 15-round decision and the world's heavyweight championship. He made four successful title defenses and on 27 September 1950 fought Louis, whose income tax problems necessitated a return to the ring. Louis no longer had his earlier boxing abilities and, while he lasted 15 rounds with Charles, was totally outclassed and outpointed. Charles made four more successful defenses before being knocked out in seven rounds by the 37-year-old Walcott in July 1951. Walcott's reign was brief, as he won a rematch with Charles by decision in June 1952 but was knocked out in the 13th round by the undefeated Rocky Marciano in September 1952. Marciano had previously ended Louis's comeback attempt in October 1951.

From 1953 to 1956, Marciano made six successful title defenses, and then on 27 April 1956, he announced his retirement as undefeated champion. During his relatively brief ring career (1947–1956), he had won all 49 bouts with 43 by knockout. Olympic champion Floyd Patterson, only 21 years old, was selected to fight light heavyweight champion Archie Moore, 39 years old (and possibly older), for the vacant title. Patterson won on a fifth-round knockout and became the youngest fighter to win the heavyweight championship. Patterson's manager, Cus D'Amato, did not want to deal with the IBC and consequently avoided title defenses against the leading contenders of the 1950s. Instead, Floyd fought successful defenses against some of the lesser heavyweights. One of his bouts was against Pete Rademacher, the 1956 Olympic champion, who was making his professional debut in the championship bout with Patterson.

In June 1959, Patterson was knocked out in three rounds by Ingemar Johansson, a Swede who was relatively unknown in the United States, although he was undefeated and the European champion. The following year, Patterson knocked out Johansson and became the first man to regain the heavyweight title.

Two top heavyweights of the 1950s who did not receive title bouts until the 1960s when they were past their prime were Zora Folley and Eddie Machen.

The light heavyweight class during the 1950s was dominated by Joey Maxim and Archie Moore—each of whom figured in a memorable bout of the decade, although not against each other. In June 1952, Maxim successfully defended his title against the middleweight champion "Sugar Ray" Robinson by outlasting him on an exceptionally hot and humid night. In that bout, referee Ruby Goldstein was overcome by the heat and retired after 10 rounds. Robinson lasted until the 13th round before he, too, had to quit. Moore's memorable bout took place in Montreal, Canada, against the French-Canadian challenger Yvon Durelle in December 1958. Moore was knocked down three times in the first round and once in the fourth round. He survived the knockdowns and knocked Durelle down four times, with the last knockdown being for the 10 count, in the 11th round.

The middleweight class in the 1950s featured "Sugar Ray" Robinson, a man called the greatest "pound-for-pound" fighter in ring history. Robinson, a welterweight during the 1940s, moved up to the middleweight class in 1950 and won the middleweight title on five different occasions during the decade, either retiring or losing the title five times. Another of the decade's featured fighters was Carmen Basilio, also a welterweight and middleweight champion, who was featured in *Ring* magazine's "Fight of the Year" five consecutive times. Other welterweights and middleweights of note during the decade include Kid Gavilan, Billy Graham, Gene Fullmer, Ralph "Tiger" Jones, Laszlo Papp, Gaspar Ortega, and Carl "Bobo" Olson.

During this decade, the international nature of the sport became more prevalent, and world champions were no longer only U.S. born. Since 1952, when the Japanese Yoshio Shirai won the flyweight championship from Hawaii-born Dado Marino, that division has rarely been led by a U.S.-born fighter. The bantamweight championship changed hands in 1950 when Mexican American Manuel Ortiz was defeated by South African Vic Toweel. Since then, nearly every bantamweight champion has been born outside the United States, with quite a few being of Mexican birth.

The top fighters in the lighter weights in the 1950s include light welterweight Duilio Loi; lightweights Jimmy Carter, Joe Brown, and Wallace "Bud" Smith; featherweights Willie Pep, Sandy Saddler, and Nigerian Hogan "Kid" Bassey; bantamweights Jimmy Carruthers and Raul Macias; and flyweights Pascual Perez and Pone Kingpetch.

LISTON, CLAY/ALI, AND VIETNAM, 1961–1970

The decade of the 1960s began with heavyweight champion Floyd Patterson regaining his title from Ingemar Johansson in June 1960 and successfully defending it against Johansson in March 1961. Patterson then met Charles "Sonny" Liston, an ex-convict with a terrific knockout punch who had a menacing aura. Liston knocked out Patterson in the first round in September 1962 to win the heavyweight championship and repeated the victory less than one year later in July 1963, needing just four more seconds to again stop Patterson in the first round.

One of the more colorful heavyweight contenders at that time was Cassius Marcellus Clay Jr., the 1960 Olympic light heavyweight champion who was extremely quick in the ring, good looking, loquacious, and a great self-promoter. After beginning his professional career with 19 straight victories, 15 by knockout, he was matched with Liston on 25 February 1964 in Miami Beach, Florida, for Liston's heavyweight title. Although a 7–1 underdog, Clay's speed befuddled Liston, who quit after six rounds, claiming a shoulder injury, but most likely he was just frustrated at his inability to dominate Clay. Following the bout, Clay announced that he had joined the Nation of Islam (popularly known as the Black Muslims) and was renouncing his birth name. He originally called himself Cassius X, but it was quickly changed to Muhammad Ali. This generated much negative publicity among the white public, and finding a suitable venue for his rematch with Liston became problematic as many boxing commissions would not permit it.

The bout finally took place in the small town of Lewiston, Maine, before only 2,434 paid attendees. Liston went down in the first round after a glancing blow and did not get up before the 10 count, although the bout ended in confusion. It has been widely speculated that Liston, for reasons unknown, "took a dive" (deliberately lost).

Ali proved to be a fighting champion, with eight additional successful title defenses from 1965 to 1967 following the Liston rematch. The one complication in Ali's life at this time was his draft status. Although extremely quick-witted and verbal, he was not particularly adept at scholastic subjects. In 1964, he had failed his written test for military service and was classified 1-Y. In 1966, the qualifying grades were lowered, and he was then reclassified 1-A. The Vietnam War was going on then, and Ali resisted the draft, claiming conscientious objector status as a minister of the Nation of Islam with a famous quote: "I ain't got no quarrel with them Viet Congs." On 28 April 1967, in Houston, Texas, after refusing induction into the Armed Forces he was arrested for draft evasion. He also was stripped of his heavyweight title by the New York State Athletic Commission. On 20 June 1967, he was tried and found guilty of draft evasion. A court of appeals upheld the conviction, and in a further appeal the case was advanced to the United States Supreme Court. During the next three years, at the prime of his boxing life, he was not permitted to fight in the ring.

Although most of the focus in the boxing world during the 1960s was on the heavyweights, boxing in the lighter weights also made headlines. The most significant event in boxing during the decade, outside of the heavyweight class, occurred on 24 March 1962. On that date, former welterweight champion Emile Griffith regained his title against Benny "Kid" Paret. In the prefight weigh-in, Paret and Griffith exchanged words, and the Cuban Paret taunted Emile by calling him "maricón," a derogatory Spanish word for homosexual. The slur especially affected Griffith since there was a ring of truth to it, although at the time there was no public awareness of the fact. In the 13th round of their bout, Griffith caught Paret against the ropes and unleashed a savage attack of at least 29 unanswered blows before referee Ruby Goldstein, one of the sport's better referees, was able to separate the two and stop the fight. Paret went into a coma and died 10 days later. The bout was the first nationally televised fight in which a fighter died, and it led to public outcries to ban the savage sport but, as usual, nothing came of it, and the sport continued without major changes.

Among the more notable boxers of the decade were heavyweights George Chuvalo, Ernie Terrell, and Cleveland Williams; light heavyweights Willie Pastrano, José Torres, and Dick Tiger; middleweights Joey Giardello, Rubin Carter, and Nino Benvenuti; welterweights Luis Manuel Rodríguez and Curtis Cokes; lightweights Carlos Ortiz and Carlos Teo Cruz; featherweights

Davey Moore, Ultiminio "Sugar" Ramos, and Vicente Saldivar; bantam-weights Éder Jofre and Masahiko "Fighting" Harada; and flyweights Pone Kingpetch and Charchai Chionoi.

FRAZIER, ALI, FOREMAN, *ROCKY*, AND DON KING, 1971–1980

In August 1970, before the Supreme Court made a decision on Muhammad Ali's appeal on draft-dodging charges, he was granted a boxing license by the Atlanta Boxing Commission, and shortly thereafter also by the New York State Athletic Commission. He stopped Jerry Quarry on cuts in three rounds on 26 October 1970 in Atlanta, and followed that win by stopping Óscar Bonavena on 7 December 1970 in a bout at Madison Square Garden.

While Ali was inactive, the New York State Athletic Commission held a series of bouts, and 1964 Olympic heavyweight champion Joe Frazier emerged as their heavyweight champion. Frazier and Ali, both undefeated heavyweight champions, were matched for the undisputed heavyweight title on 8 March 1971 at Madison Square Garden in a match billed as the "Fight of the Century," with each fighter guaranteed two and a half million dollars—a record for that time. The bout lived up to its billing. For 15 rounds, both fighters traded blows, and Frazier knocked Ali down in the 15th round. Frazier won the unanimous decision, and Ali suffered his first professional loss.

Frazier's reign as champion was relatively short-lived, as after two successful title defenses against relatively unheralded contenders in 1972, he was knocked out in two rounds by 1968 Olympic heavyweight champion George Foreman in January 1973. Foreman then won two championship bouts with one- and two-round knockouts.

Don King, a former successful bookmaker and numbers racketeer, entered the boxing promotion business in the early 1970s, shortly after his release from prison on a manslaughter charge. He helped arrange a heavyweight championship bout between Muhammad Ali and George Foreman to be held in the relatively new African nation of Zaire, which funded the bout, with each fighter guaranteed an unprecedented five million dollars. Ali dubbed the bout the "Rumble in the Jungle," much to the chagrin of Zaire's political leaders, who were trying to promote tourism to their newly independent nation.

At this point in his career, Foreman had a record of 40–0 with 37 knockouts and appeared invincible. The bout took place on 30 October 1974 at 4 o'clock in the morning (so that it could be televised in the United States at 10 p.m.). The fight began with Ali aggressively hitting Foreman on top of the head and dancing away. He then began to use his speed to avoid Foreman's retaliation, but in the second round changed tactics (contrary to his corner's advice) and leaned on the relatively loose ropes, allowing Foreman to throw punches at him while protecting his face in a tactic that Ali dubbed the "rope-a-dope." Foreman's arms grew tired from the continuous punching, and by the eighth round Ali was able to turn the tables and knock out Foreman at 2:58 of the round.

In Ali's first defense of his newly regained title, he chose Chuck Wepner, a journeyman boxer, as his opponent. Wepner surprised the boxing world by nearly lasting the full 15 rounds, being stopped with just 19 seconds to go in the bout. His bravery inspired Sylvester Stallone to write the screenplay for *Rocky*, which won the Academy Award in 1976 as Best Picture, has led to five sequels, and has become a film classic.

After two more title defenses, including one in Kuala Lumpur, Malaysia, Ali fought a rubber match with Joe Frazier in Manila, Philippines, on 1 October 1975, which was another one of boxing's all-time greatest fights. Both fighters were nearly exhausted when Frazier was unable to continue after the 14th round. Ali dubbed this fight "The Thrilla in Manila."

Ali continued as heavyweight champion until February 1978, when he was outpointed in 15 rounds by the 1976 Olympic light heavyweight champion, Leon Spinks, who had had only seven previous professional bouts. Ali relaxed throughout most of the fight and, in one of boxing's biggest upsets, lost a 15-round split decision to Spinks. Ali did not treat Spinks as lightly in their rematch seven months later and became the first man to regain the heavyweight championship twice. Ali retired after the bout but in an ill-fated comeback attempt was defeated by Larry Holmes in 1980.

Another major event in boxing history that occurred during the decade was the aborted United States Championship Tournament. The brainchild of promoter Don King, it was an attempt to capitalize on patriotism following the bicentennial of 1976 and the success of the United States Olympic boxing team that year. Plans were for competition to be held in the six major weight classes, with eight boxers selected for each weight class. Venues were also selected to promote patriotism, with an aircraft carrier and the U.S. Naval Academy being chosen to host fights. King got Roone Arledge, head of the American Broadcasting Company (ABC) television network sports department, to agree to televise the fights and provide the financial backing and *Ring* magazine to provide rankings of the boxers in order to select the best ones in each division. New York State boxing commissioner James Farley was named chairman of the tournament committee. After six cards of boxing from January to April had been completed, the tournament was abruptly discontinued after ABC discovered that the tournament was not completely on the up and up, with some fighters' records falsified and other fighters required to pay kickbacks in order to progress. Although investigations were made, no legal charges were ever filed.

Among the most notable fighters of the 1970s were the following: heavyweights Earnie Shavers and Ron Lyle; light heavyweights Bob Foster and Victor Galindez; middleweights Carlos Monzón and Rodrigo Valdez; welterweights José Napoles, José "Pipino" Cuevas, and Carlos Palomino; lightweights Roberto Durán, Sean O'Grady, and Esteban De Jesus; featherweights Rubén Olivares and Alexis Argüello; bantamweights Carlos Zárate and Alfonso Zamora; and flyweights Miguel Canto and Guty Espadas. In addition, intermediary classes known as "junior" classes became popular, and junior middleweights Koichi Wajima and Eckhard Dagge, junior welterweights Antonio Cervantes and Wilfred Benítez, junior lightweights Ricardo Arredondo and Alfredo Escalera, and junior featherweight Wilfredo Gómez were among the sport's best at their weights.

TYSON, LEONARD, HEARNS, HAGLER, AND DURÁN, 1981–1990

Following the retirement of Muhammad Ali, the heavyweight title lost much of the luster it had had previously. One reason was that the two major sanctioning organizations rarely agreed on who was champion, and for most of the time since Ali's retirement, there has been more than one man recognized as heavyweight champion. After Leon Spinks signed for a rematch with Muhammad Ali, shortly after winning the undisputed title in February 1978, the World Boxing Council (WBC) stripped him of the heavyweight title and named Ken Norton their champion, even though Norton had never won a heavyweight championship bout. He was superseded by Larry Holmes, who defeated Norton. Spinks still remained the World Boxing Association (WBA) champion until he was defeated by Ali in September 1978. From that point on, the WBC and WBA have seldom recognized the same fighter as their heavyweight champion. WBA champions from 1979 to 1987 following Ali's retirement were John Tate, Mike Weaver, Michael Dokes, Gerrie Coetzee, Greg Page, Tony Tubbs, Tim Witherspoon, and James "Bonecrusher" Smith—nearly a new champion every year. During that same time, Larry Holmes was recognized by the WBC as well as by most boxing fans as champion from 1978 to 1984, when the WBC withdrew recognition from Holmes even though he had not been defeated in the ring. The newly created International Boxing Federation (IBF) recognized Holmes as champion though, until he was defeated by Michael Spinks in 1987. The WBC's champions from 1984 to 1987 were Tim Witherspoon, Pinklon Thomas, and Trevor Berbick.

Fortunately for boxing fans, Mike Tyson came along in 1985, and in November 1986, although still only 20 years old, he defeated Berbick to gain WBC recognition. Four months later, he defeated the WBA champion, James

Smith, and five months after that defeated Tony Tucker to gain IBF recognition. From August 1987 to May 1989, there was only one heavyweight champion again. In May 1989, the newly created World Boxing Organization decided to show their independence and rather than recognize Tyson as heavyweight champion selected Italian Francesco Damiani as their champion. Tyson remained champion in the eyes of most of the boxing world, however.

Boxing in the lighter weights throughout the 1980s featured four fighters—Panamanian Roberto Durán and Americans Marvin Hagler, Thomas Hearns, and 1976 Olympic champion "Sugar Ray" Leonard. Leonard won the welterweight title in 1979 and during the 1980s fought memorable bouts with each of the others, defeating all three fighters. During the decade, Leonard became the first man to win championships in five different weight classes—each one from welterweight to light heavyweight.

Durán won the lightweight title in 1974, defeated Leonard for the welterweight title in 1980, won the light middleweight title in 1983, and then gained the middleweight title in 1989. He also fought each of the other three but was only successful once against Leonard. Hearns won the welterweight title in 1980, the light middleweight in 1982, middleweight and light heavyweight in 1987, super middleweight in 1990, and light heavyweight in 1991, bettering Leonard's record by winning titles in six weight classes. Hearns also fought the other three but only defeated Durán and boxed a draw with Leonard. Hagler won the middleweight title in 1980 and shortly afterward legally changed his name to Marvelous Marvin Hagler. He retained his middleweight title against both Durán and Hearns but lost it to Leonard in 1987 and retired shortly after.

Other boxers of note in the 1980s were heavyweight Gerry Cooney; light heavyweights Matthew Saad Muhammad, Dwight Braxton (AKA Dwight Muhammad Qawi), and Bobby Czyz; super middleweight Chong-Pal Park; junior middleweight Mike McCallum; welterweight Donald Curry; junior welterweight Billy Costello; lightweights Livingstone Bramble and Héctor Camacho; junior lightweight Julio César Chávez; featherweights Salvador Sánchez, Barry McGuigan, and Azumah Nelson; junior featherweight Ji-Won Kim; bantamweight Jeff Fenech; junior bantamweight Gilberto Roman; flyweight Santos Laciar; and junior flyweight Jung-Koo Chang.

One of the decade's other major events occurred on 13 November 1982. Lightweight Ray "Boom Boom" Mancini had been carefully brought along by the Columbia Broadcasting System television network as a promising star. His father had been a boxer whose career was curtailed by military service during World War II, and Ray was out to win the championship that had been denied to his father. Mancini gained the championship and in his second defense of the title knocked out the Korean challenger Deuk-Koo Kim in 14 rounds on national television on a Saturday afternoon. Unfortunately, Kim died four days later from brain injuries suffered in the bout. This brought about a new clamor to ban boxing, but the only change to the sport shortly afterward was the reduction of championship bouts in length from 15 to 12 rounds.

FOREMAN, TYSON, AND THE REAL DEAL, 1990–2000

The decade of the 1990s saw some strange events in the heavyweight division. The decade began with the seemingly invincible Mike Tyson losing his title to a 42–1 underdog, James "Buster" Douglas, with the bout stopped by the referee in the 10th round after Tyson had been knocked down. Tyson's career than took a sharp detour after he was imprisoned for rape and spent three years behind bars from 1992 to 1995.

As was the case in the 1980s, with four sanctioning organizations recognizing various fighters as heavyweight champions, a new champion was created annually, and there were 17 men who were called "heavyweight champion" at one time or another during the decade. Of these, only seven received the acclaim previously due to a heavyweight champion—Douglas, Riddick Bowe, George Foreman, Evander Holyfield, Lennox Lewis, Michael Moorer, and Mike Tyson.

Douglas retained his title only until his first defense in October 1990, at which time Evander Holyfield, a former Olympic light heavyweight bronze medalist and professional cruiserweight champion, knocked him out in three rounds. Holyfield proved himself to be "The Real Deal" (his self-appointed nickname) as he made three successful defenses before losing the title by decision to Riddick Bowe in November 1992. Shortly after winning the title and recognition by three of the four sanctioning bodies, Bowe abandoned his WBC title due to a conflict with them over his next opponent. Bowe made two successful defenses and then defended against Holyfield in a rematch on 6 November 1993 that featured one of the most bizarre occurrences ever in a heavyweight championship bout. During the seventh round of the fight, a fan who had been circling the outdoor arena in a powered paraglider lost control of his device and landed in the ring, with the lines from his machine caught in the overhead lights. As he tried to extricate himself, fans in the arena as well as the fighters' seconds began attacking him and knocked him unconscious. After a 21-minute delay, the bout between Holyfield and Bowe resumed, and after 12 rounds Holyfield won the majority decision.

In the first defense of his newly rewon title, Holyfield was outpointed by Michael Moorer, who became the first left-handed boxer to become heavyweight champion. Moorer's reign was short-lived, as he was knocked out in 10 rounds by the 45-year-old George Foreman on 5 November 1994. This was the same George Foreman who had retired from boxing in 1977, three years after losing the heavyweight title to Muhammad Ali in Zaire. After being away from the ring for 10 years, George made a comeback in 1987 and won 27 of 29 fights between 1987 and 1994.

After Tyson was released from prison in 1995, he returned to the ring and in 1996 regained the heavyweight title (WBC version) by stopping Englishman Frank Bruno in three rounds. In November 1996, Tyson was stopped by Holyfield, who won the title for the third time. Their subsequent rematch on 28 June 1997 was another of the decade's bizarre fights. In the third round, Tyson bit Holyfield's right ear so severely that a piece was torn off. Referee Mills Lane stopped the fight, deducted two points from the scorecards for Tyson, and warned Tyson, who claimed the damage was caused by a punch. Tyson then bit Holyfield's left ear and was disqualified.

Englishman Lennox Lewis became the final major heavyweight champion of the decade. In March 1999, he fought a 12-round draw with Holyfield in a bout where most boxing fans thought he should have been awarded the decision. Lewis then won their rematch in November 1999 and ended the decade as heavyweight champion.

Other notable boxers of the 1990s include light heavyweight Virgil Hill; super middleweight Joe Calzaghe; middleweights James Toney and Bernard Hopkins; junior middleweights Julio César Vásquez, Vinnie Pazienza, and Terry Norris; welterweights James "Buddy" McGirt, Pernell Whitaker, and Félix Trinidad; junior welterweights Edwin Rosario, Héctor Camacho, and Julio César Chávez; lightweight Óscar De La Hoya; junior lightweights Genaro Hernández and Tracy Harris Patterson; featherweight Yong-Kyun Park; junior featherweights Wilfredo Vásquez and Kennedy McKinney; bantamweights Naseem Hamed and Orlando Canizales; junior bantamweight Johnny Tapia; flyweights Yuri Arbachakov and Carlos Salazar; junior flyweights Michael Carbajal and Humberto González; and strawweight Ricardo López.

One of the more notable bouts not in the heavyweight division that occurred during the 1990s took place in Mexico City at the Estadio Azteca on 20 February 1993 when 132,247 fans saw their undefeated local hero, Julio César Chávez, successful defend his WBC light welterweight title and win his 85th consecutive bout without a loss with a fifth-round technical knockout over Greg Haugen.

WOMEN ENTER THE RING

For the better part of the 20th century, women's participation in boxing was limited to a few who worked as promoters. In the 1970s, a few became licensed as judges, and a few actually entered the ring as fighters. Cathy Davis was one of the first but soon ran out of opponents.

In the 1990s, more females became professional boxers, and by the end of the century, the Golden Gloves had established a women's division. The daughters of several boxing champions, such as Joe Frazier, Muhammad Ali, George Foreman, and Archie Moore, also took up the sport and boxed professionally. In the 2012 Olympic Games, women's boxing was added for the first time. Women's boxing still does not have the spectator appeal that women's tennis, golf, or basketball have, but the sport is no longer solely limited to males.

21ST-CENTURY BOXING, 2000–2012

The four sanctioning organizations have recognized 19 different men as heavyweight champions in the 21st century. Of these 19, eight are from the former Soviet Union and only seven are U.S. born, with two Englishmen, a South African, and a Nigerian making up the other four. The champions who have held their titles the longest have been the Klitschko brothers, Vitaly and Wladimir. Both brothers have earned PhD degrees from the Kiev University of Physical Science and Sports—the first boxing champions with doctoral degrees. Another notable 21st-century heavyweight champion was the Russian Nikolai Valuev, a seven-foot-tall, 300-pound giant who was recognized by the WBA as world's heavyweight champion from 2005 to 2007 and again from 2008 to 2009. As a result of the fact that the majority of heavyweight champions have been non-Americans and that many of their title defenses have occurred outside the United States, the heavyweight championship no longer has the aura it once had in North America.

Boxing in the lighter weights has been the major 21st-century attraction, as the Filipino Manny Pacquiao has been one of the era's top fighters. He has won world championships in eight different classes, from flyweight to light middleweight. Floyd Mayweather Jr., undefeated in 43 bouts as of 2012, has been another of the best fighters in this century. Óscar De La Hoya, another multidivision champion, has been involved in some of the most lucrative fights and reportedly has a net worth in excess of 175 million dollars.

Other notable 21st-century fighters include heavyweight Roy Jones Jr.; cruiserweight David Haye; light heavyweight Tomasz Adamek; super middleweight Markus Beyer; middleweights Jermain Taylor and Felix Sturm;

welterweights Cory Spinks and Zab Judah; junior welterweights Arturo Gatti, Kosta Tszyu, Micky Ward, and Ricky Hatton; lightweights Edwin Valero and José Luis Castillo; junior lightweight Juan Márquez; featherweight Erik Morales; junior featherweight Óscar Larios; bantamweight Anselmo Moreno; junior bantamweight Martín Castillo; flyweight Eric Morel; junior flyweight Jorge Arce; and strawweight Ivan Calderon.

Although the sport has declined somewhat in popular interest in the United States, with MMA (mixed martial arts) surpassing it in popularity, boxing has survived with most shows taking place at casinos. Pay-per-view television has helped make a handful of modern-day fighters wealthy, and the sport is still followed worldwide, although not to the extent it once was.

A MULTIPLICITY OF SANCTIONING ORGANIZATIONS

For much of boxing's history during the 20th century, the New York State Athletic commission and the National Boxing Association (NBA) were the major governing bodies for the sport, with both seemingly working toward the best interests of boxing. At times, one or the other organization would withdraw recognition from a world champion, but for most of the century this was not the case and world championship claims were usually undisputed. During this time, European boxing was governed by the British Boxing Board of Control in the British Isles and the European Boxing Union on the continent. Asian boxing was governed by the Oriental and Pacific Boxing Federation, and African boxing was under the auspices of the African Boxing Union. Several countries also had their own governing bodies, such as the Japanese Boxing Commission or Italian Boxing Federation, but they restricted their activities to within their nations.

In 1962, the NBA was renamed the World Boxing Association, and in 1963 the World Boxing Council was created. Both were predominantly Latin American, but they quickly gained recognition as the leading influences in the sport. However, they rarely worked together and generally recognized different boxers as division champions. They also began introducing intermediary weight classes, naming them either "junior" or "super," so that instead of the traditional eight weight classes, there soon were 16 of them. Adding to the confusion were two more sanctioning groups—the International Boxing Federation, which began in 1983, and the World Boxing Organization, in 1988. Boxing in the 21st century recognizes these four organizations as "major" ones, but there have been many other minor ones with limited recognition in the boxing world. Although much has been written about these "alphabet organizations," no concrete steps have yet been taken to better organize the sport. Should a change be made so that one organization governs boxing worldwide, the sport will grow in interest substantially.

SHOULD BOXING BE OUTLAWED?

Due to the nature of the activity, boxing has always produced fatalities. Bouts during the Roman era were often fought to a finish. When the Prize Ring era began in England, rules were written in an attempt to minimize severe injury, but nonetheless boxers still occasionally died as a result of their bouts. There have been more than 1,000 ring fatalities from 1725 to 2011. Each time a fighter dies in the ring, there is a public outcry to ban the sport, although it has never succeeded.

In 1983, the *Journal of the American Medical Association* published several articles and editorials on boxing with the position that boxing should be banned in civilized countries. Although these articles created much controversy, boxing has yet to be modified substantially.

In the *Boxing Register*, authors James B. Roberts and Alexander G. Skutt write: "At its best, boxing is an unparalleled physical art. At its worst, it is a killer and maimer of good men." Author Joyce Carol Oates has written that "boxing is not a sport—you play baseball, you don't play boxing."

The sport of boxing will most likely never be prohibited in the next century, but various safeguards will continue to be added to the sport. Recent ones include head guards for amateur boxers, fewer rounds for professional championship bouts, and the mandatory requirement of ringside physicians. Through the years, boxing has provided an outlet for many people in the lower rungs of the economic ladder and has helped to reform the lives of some who had gone astray in their youth. The rigid training requirements for success in the sport have helped many to learn self-discipline and improve their self-esteem. Boxing will continue to provide entertainment for countless fans and hope for many young men (and now young women) as a way out of their current economic situation.

A

ABDUL-AZIZ, MALIK. *See* TYSON, MICHAEL GERARD "MIKE," "IRON MIKE" (aka MALIK ABDUL-AZIZ).

AFRICAN BOXING. Since the 1960s, when many African nations became independent, most African countries have entered the **Olympic Games** boxing competition at least once. **South Africa**, one of the few nations in Africa where boxing was popular during the first half of the 20th century, has had 19 Olympic boxing medalists. Kenya has had seven, Algeria and Nigeria have each had six, Uganda has had four, and Egypt, Ghana, and Morocco have each had three.

There have been quite a few **professional world champions** born in Africa. Probably the most famous was the Nigerian **Dick Tiger**, born Richard Ihetu, who won the world's **middleweight** and **light heavyweight** championships during the 1960s. One of the first Africans to achieve fame in the boxing **ring** was Amadou M'Barick Fall, a native of Senegal who competed in **France** during the 1920s as Battling Siki and won the world's light heavyweight championship in 1922. Siki then made the mistake of defending his title against an Irishman, Mike McTigue, in Dublin, **Ireland**, on St. Patrick's Day in 1923 and lost a 20-**round decision**.

Other central African world champions include Cameroon's Hassan N'Dam N'Jikam; Congo's Anaclet Wamba; Ghana's Joseph Agbeko, Joshua Clottey, Nana Konadu, David Kotei, Alfred Kotey, **Azumah Nelson**, and Ike Quartey; Namibia's Paulus Moses and Harry Simon; Nigeria's Hogan "Kid" Bassey and Samuel Peter; and Uganda's Cornelius Boza-Edwards, Ayub Kalule, John "The Beast" Mugabi, and Kassim Ouma. South Africa has had more than 20 professional champions. North African champions include Algerian-born **Marcel Cerdan** and Alphonse Halimi; Moroccan Khalid Rahilou; and Tunisians Taoufik Belbouli, Kamel Bou Ali, and Victor "Young" Perez.

A few other boxers with ties to Africa are Henry Akinwande, born in **England** but raised in Nigeria, Herbie Hide (Herbert Okechukwu Maduagwu), born in Nigeria but raised in England, and Sumbu Kalambay, born in Zaire but raised in **Italy**.

The most significant boxing match to take place on the African continent did not include any native Africans (although it featured two African Americans, had an African American **referee**, and was promoted by an African American), but was the 30 October 1974 **heavyweight** championship **bout** in Zaire between **Muhammad Ali** and **George Foreman**, refereed by Zach Clayton and promoted by **Don King**, known as the **Rumble in the Jungle**.

AIBA. *See* INTERNATIONAL BOXING ASSOCIATION (AIBA) .

ALI, MUHAMMAD "THE LOUISVILLE LIP," "THE GREATEST" (né CASSIUS MARCELLUS CLAY). B. 17 January 1942, Louisville, Kentucky. At the peak of his career, Muhammad Ali was the person most widely recognized throughout the world. For those who were not alive during the 1960s and 1970s, it is impossible to accurately convey a clear picture of his life and his impact upon the world through words alone.

As a 12-year-old in Louisville, he was steered into a boxing program by police sergeant Joe E. Martin, who reportedly encountered Clay after he was enacting revenge upon a thief who had stolen his bicycle. Clay had an excellent **amateur boxing** career and won six Kentucky **Golden Gloves** titles, the 1959 and 1960 Chicago Golden Gloves Tournament of Champions **light heavyweight** titles, and the 1959 and 1960 Intercity Golden Gloves titles.

His 1959 final **bout** for the Chicago Tournament of Champions light heavyweight title was against a boxer named Jefferson Davis. Clay also won the 1959 and 1960 National **Amateur Athletic Union** light heavyweight title. He won the 1960 **Olympic Games gold medal** in the light heavyweight class, with one of his **preliminary bouts** in the games a victory over **Australian** Tony Madigan, whom he had previously defeated to win the 1959 Intercity Golden Gloves. Clay's amateur record has been reported with various totals ranging from 99–8 to 137–7.

A group of 11 successful Louisville businessmen, headed by William Faversham, who became Clay's manager of record, decided to help Clay establish a professional career and formed the Louisville Sponsoring Group to back Clay as he became a **professional boxer**. His first professional bout was on 29 October 1960 in Louisville, a six- **round decision** over journeyman Tunney Hunsaker, the chief of police of Fayetteville, West Virginia, and a part-time boxer. After this bout, **Angelo Dundee** was hired as Clay's **trainer**.

Clay moved quickly up the **heavyweight** ranks with a combination of his foot and hand speed, unusual boxing style (with hands held low), and cocky loquaciousness (earning him the sobriquet "The Louisville Lip") combining to make him a sought-after attraction in the ring. Before his fights, he often would compose simple poems about the outcome and would predict the round in which the bout would end. Surprisingly, many of his predictions came true.

After winning his first 10 bouts, he fought at **Madison Square Garden** on national television against Lucien "Sonny" Banks, a relatively unknown boxer. Banks surprised Clay and **knocked him down** in the first round. Clay quickly rebounded, knocked Banks down in the second round, and stopped him in the fourth round. Clay won his next four bouts in 1962 and concluded the year by stopping former world's light heavyweight champion **Archie Moore** in four rounds in Los Angeles, California.

In 1963, Clay won all three of his fights, but one, on 13 March 1963 at Madison Square Garden against Doug Jones, proved to be his most difficult to that point in his career. In a fight named "Fight of the Year" by *Ring* **magazine**, Jones rocked Clay in several of the early rounds, but Clay finished strong and won the bout on two of three **judges'** scorecards by a slim 5–4–1 margin, while the **referee** saw it 8–1–1 for Cassius.

Clay's final bout in 1963 was another legendary one and was won through the help of his trainer, Angelo Dundee. On 18 June, Clay fought British heavyweight champion Henry Cooper in London, **England**. Near the end of the fourth round, Cooper staggered Clay with a left **hook** and knocked him down. Clay arose at the count of four, and the bell rang with Clay still groggy. His quick-thinking trainer Dundee, after seeing Clay's reaction to the punch, then enlarged a small nick on Clay's boxing **glove** and called it to the referee's attention. The referee ordered a replacement glove. The resulting interval to find a replacement took nearly another minute, and the additional rest enabled Clay to regain his senses. When he came out for the fifth round, he wasted no time attacking a cut over Cooper's eye. After 2:15 of the round, the bout was stopped with Cooper's face a bloody mess and Clay's undefeated record intact.

Clay's next bout, on 25 February 1964, was with **Charles "Sonny" Liston** in Miami Beach, Florida, for Liston's world's heavyweight title. At the time, Liston appeared invincible, having defeated **Floyd Patterson** twice in one-round **knockouts**. Clay, although undefeated, was not given much chance to win and was a 7–1 underdog. Clay spent much of the time leading up to the bout taunting Liston, going so far as to drive to Liston's house in the middle of the night and wake him up with his car horn to shout insults at him. During the prefight weigh-in, Clay's incessant raving gave Liston the idea that Clay was a lunatic.

Clay started the fight quickly by jabbing Liston and dancing away, but in the fourth round some liniment on Liston's glove got in Clay's eyes, and when he returned to his corner, Cassius shouted at his seconds to cut his gloves off because he was blinded. Again, Dundee came to the rescue by washing Clay's eyes off and pushing him into the **ring** to start the next round, telling him to just stay away from Liston until his eyes cleared. By the sixth round, he was better and continued to hit Liston and dance away. At the end of the sixth round, Liston had had enough, refusing to come out for the seventh round and claiming an injury to his shoulder, and Clay became world's heavyweight champion. Although there was speculation that Liston, who had ties to organized crime, **took a dive**, nothing was ever proved.

After the bout, Clay announced that he was joining the Nation of Islam (popularly known as the Black Muslims) and changing his name to Cassius X. Subsequently, he was given the name Muhammad Ali by Elijah Muhammad, the leader of that organization. Even though Clay defeated an unpopular heavyweight champion in Liston, his own popularity waned as a result of this move since the Black Muslim organization was feared by many of the white, mainstream United States citizens.

A rematch was scheduled for Boston, Massachusetts, in November 1964, but after Ali suffered a strangulated hernia requiring emergency surgery, the bout was postponed for six months. During that time, the Massachusetts Boxing Commission had second thoughts and refused to allow the bout to be held in their state. Arrangements were made for the fight to be held in Lewiston, Maine, at a small auditorium used for minor league hockey. The bout on 25 May 1965 drew only 2,434 fans, the smallest attendance for a heavyweight title fight in history.

The bout itself was another in the strange histories of both Ali and Liston. Shortly after the bout began, Liston went down from what appeared to be a glancing blow to the head. Ali stood over Liston yelling at him to get up and did not go to a **neutral corner** as specified by the rules when a knockdown occurs. Referee **Jersey Joe Walcott** attempted to get Ali to a neutral corner. By the time he finally did so, approximately 20 seconds had passed and Liston then arose and began to resume boxing. But *Ring* magazine publisher **Nat Fleischer**, who was sitting at **ringside**, called Walcott over to tell him that the fight should be over since Liston was down for more than 10 seconds. At that point, Walcott stopped the fight and awarded it to Ali. To add to the confusion, the "official" time of the end of the bout was announced as "one minute of the first round," when in actuality the bout was not ended until 2:12 of the round. Again, most fans believe that Liston took a dive, with various motives suggested ranging from Liston's fear of retaliation from Black Muslims to his owing money to gangsters and betting on himself to be able to pay his debts. But no investigation was ever held.

Ali proved to be a fighting champion, and in an 18 month-span defended his title eight times. On 22 November 1965, in **Las Vegas**, Nevada, he defended against former heavyweight champion Floyd Patterson, who had previously been knocked out twice in the first round by Liston. Since the Liston fights, Patterson had reestablished himself as a viable contender with four consecutive victories. Unfortunately for Patterson, he hurt his back prior to the bout with Ali, was in agony for much of the fight, and was unable to do much in the ring that night before he was stopped in the 12th round by Ali. Prior to the fight, Patterson had refused to refer to Ali by his Muslim name and called him Clay. This caused Ali during the fight to taunt Patterson by shouting, "What's my name?" nearly every time he threw a punch.

Ali's next seven title defenses were less dramatic, and he easily defeated **George Chuvalo** (Toronto, **Canada**, 29 March 1966, **unanimous decision**); Henry Cooper (London, England, 21 May 1966, **technical knockout [TKO]** 6 rounds); Brian London (London, England, 6 August 1966, **knockout** 3); Karl Mildenberger (Frankfurt, **Germany**, 10 September 1966, TKO 12); **Cleveland Williams** (Houston, Texas, 14 November 1966, TKO 3); Ernie Terrell (Houston, Texas, unanimous decision 15); and **Zora Folley** (New York, 6 February 1967, KO 7).

The one complication in Ali's life at this time was his draft status. Although extremely quick-witted and verbal, he was not particularly adept at scholastic subjects (graduating 376th of 391 students in his high school class). In 1964, he had failed his written test for military service and was classified 1-Y (unqualified for duty except in time of declared war or national emergency). In 1966, the qualifying grades were lowered, and he was then reclassified 1-A (available for combat service). The Vietnam War was going on then (although the **United States** never made a formal declaration of war). Ali resisted the draft, claiming conscientious objector status with a famous quote: "I ain't got no quarrel with them Viet Congs." On 28 April 1967, in Houston, Texas, during formal induction ceremonies for the Armed Forces, he refused to step forward when he name was called and was arrested. He also was stripped of his heavyweight title by the **New York State Athletic Commission**. On 20 June 1967, he was tried and found guilty of draft evasion. A court of appeals upheld the conviction, and in a further appeal the case was advanced to the United States Supreme Court.

During the next three years, at the prime of his boxing life, he was unable to pursue his profession. He spent much of the time giving speeches at colleges where opposition to the war was growing and also appeared in a Broadway show, *Big Time Buck White* , which only had seven appearances on Broadway before closing.

In August 1970, before the Supreme Court made a decision on his appeal, he was granted a license by the Atlanta (Georgia) Boxing Commission and shortly thereafter also by the New York State Athletic Commission. He fought his first bout after three and a half years of inactivity and stopped **Jerry Quarry** on cuts in three rounds on 26 October 1970. He followed that win by knocking down Óscar Bonavena three times in the 15th round (an automatic technical knockout) in their 7 December 1970 bout at Madison Square Garden.

While Ali was inactive, the New York State Athletic Commission held a series of bouts, and **Joe Frazier** emerged as their heavyweight champion. Frazier and Ali, both undefeated heavyweight champions, were matched for the undisputed heavyweight title on 8 March 1971 at Madison Square Garden in a match billed as the "Fight of the Century," with each fighter guaranteed two and a half million dollars—a record for that time. The bout lived up to its billing. For 15 rounds, both fighters traded blows, and Frazier knocked Ali down in the 15th round. Frazier won the **unanimous decision**, and Ali suffered his first professional loss.

Ali returned to the ring four months later and defeated former sparring partner and former **World Boxing Association** heavyweight champion Jimmy Ellis on a 12th-round **technical knockout** in a bout billed for the North American Boxing Federation heavyweight championship (a relatively meaningless title).

On 28 June 1971, the Supreme Court reversed Ali's conviction, although it did not elaborate on the merits of the case.

Over the next two years, Ali fought and won nine more bouts against top-flight opposition in venues throughout the world, winning bouts in Canada, Switzerland, **Ireland**, and **Japan** in addition to Las Vegas, New York, and Houston.

On 31 March 1973, he suffered the second defeat of his career—a 12-round **split decision** loss to **Ken Norton** in a bout in which Ali's jaw was broken. In a rematch six months later, Norton again gave Ali a tough time, but this time Ali won the split decision. One month later, Ali traveled to Indonesia, where on 20 October 1973 he easily won a 12-round unanimous decision over Dutchman Rudi Lubbers.

In January 1974, at Madison Square Garden, Ali and Frazier fought again, although this time neither was heavyweight champion. The bout lasted the full 12 rounds, and Ali prevailed on a unanimous decision.

Nine months later, Ali fought **George Foreman** for Foreman's heavyweight championship. In one of boxing's most unusual bouts, it took place in Zaire, Africa, at four o'clock in the morning. Foreman, who had won the title by knocking out Joe Frazier in two rounds and had made two successful title defenses, with both bouts ending in less than two rounds, was the betting favorite. Ali, who dubbed the bout the **Rumble in the Jungle** (much to the dismay of Zaire's President Mobutu, who was attempting to promote tourism to his country), employed an unusual strategy—he simply leaned back against the ropes and let Foreman throw punches at him while blocking them with his arms and elbows. By the eighth round, Foreman was exhausted, and Ali was able to knock him out and regain the championship. Ali dubbed this strategy the "**rope-a-dope.**"

In Ali's first defense of his newly regained title, he chose **Chuck Wepner**, a **journeyman** boxer, as his opponent. Wepner surprised the boxing world by nearly lasting the full 15 rounds, being stopped with just 19 seconds to go in the bout. His bravery inspired Sylvester Stallone to write the screenplay for *Rocky* , which has become a film classic.

After a relatively routine defense against Ron Lyle, Ali traveled to Kuala Lumpur, Malaysia, where he defeated the Hungarian-born Englishman Joe Bugner on a 15-round unanimous decision. That set the stage for a **rubber match** with Joe Frazier. The bout was held in Manila, **Philippines**, on 1 October 1975 and was one of boxing's all-time greatest fights. Both fighters were nearly exhausted when the bout was stopped after 14 rounds by Frazier's trainer, Eddie Futch. As with some of Ali's other fights, he gave this one a nickname, the **Thrilla in Manila**.

Over the next two years, Ali made six more title defenses, winning all six easily, although only two of them did not go the distance. On 15 February 1978, he made another routine title defense against the 1976 Olympic light heavyweight champion, **Leon Spinks**, who had had only seven previous professional bouts. Ali relaxed throughout most of the fight and, in one of boxing's biggest upsets, lost a 15-round split decision to Spinks.

Seven months later, they had a rematch. Ali did not treat Spinks as lightly and easily outpointed him to become the first man to regain the heavyweight championship twice. By now, Ali's skills had begun to erode, and his physician, **Dr. Ferdie Pacheco**, urged him to retire as Pacheco could see physical deterioration beginning in Ali's body, which had absorbed quite a bit of punishment throughout his 18-year professional career.

Ali ignored Pacheco's pleas and on 2 October 1980 fought the undefeated (35–0) **World Boxing Council** heavyweight champion, **Larry Holmes**. In a one-sided mismatch, Ali absorbed a beating for 10 rounds before he was forced to retire. The following year, Ali fought one more fight, against the advice of many, and lost a 10-round unanimous decision to Trevor Berbick in a bout fought in the Bahamas.

In retirement, Ali was still an extremely popular person and made many public appearances, although the physical effects of his 20 years of boxing began to take their toll and he began to noticeably slow down, both in physical movement and in speech. He was first assessed with Parkinson's syndrome, but later it was admitted that he suffered from **pugilistic dementia**.

In 1996, one of the highlights of the Olympic Games in Atlanta was when Ali was chosen to be the last torchbearer for the opening ceremonies and ran up the stairs to light the cauldron. The unannounced surprise of seeing him run with the torch, although physically shaking from the effects of Parkinson's disease, brought chills to many of the spectators.

He continues to be one of the world's great heroes, although his present physical condition in 2012 is a depressing one. He still at times makes public appearances and was part of the 2012 opening ceremonies at the Olympic Games in London. He is truly one of the most remarkable personages of 20th-century sport.

Ali is six foot three inches tall and has a 78-inch **reach**. He fought at weights ranging from 188 to 236 pounds as a heavyweight. In 61 professional bouts, from 1960 to 1981, he won 56 (37 by knockout), lost five (one by knockout), and fought a total of 549 rounds. He was inducted as a member of the inaugural class of the **International Boxing Hall of Fame** in 1990.

ALI–FOREMAN. In 1974, former world's **heavyweight** champion **Muhammad Ali** challenged **George Foreman** for the world's heavyweight title in one of boxing's most unusual **bouts**. It was first referred to as the "**Rumble in the Jungle**" by Ali on 17 July at the opening of his **training** camp in Deer Lake, Pennsylvania, and has since carried that name. The bout was announced in May 1974 when promoter **Don King** convinced the new government of Zaire to put up 10 million dollars to enable the bout to take place, with each of the two fighters receiving five million dollars. Zaire was anxious to promote tourism and felt that this bout would showcase their country. Originally scheduled for 24 September in Kinshasa, Zaire (now known as the Democratic Republic of the Congo), it was postponed on 16 September as Foreman suffered a cut above his eye. It finally took place on 30 October 1974 at four a.m. so that it could be **televised** live in the **United States** at 10 p.m. Foreman, who had won the title in a convincing manner by **knocking down Joe Frazier** six times in two **rounds** in Kingston, Jamaica, on 22 January 1973, appeared to be an invincible champion and entering the fight was undefeated in 40 bouts with 37 **knockouts** (the last eight in two rounds or less).

The fight began with Ali aggressively hitting Foreman on top of the head and dancing away. He then began to use his speed to avoid Foreman's retaliation, but in the second round Ali changed tactics (contrary to his **corner's** advice) and leaned on the relatively loose ropes, allowing Foreman to throw punches at him while protecting his face in a tactic that Ali dubbed the "**rope-a-dope**." Foreman's arms grew tired from the continuous punching, and by the eighth round Ali was able to turn the tables and knock out Foreman at 2:58 of that round. Ali thus became only the second man to regain the **heavyweight** title (**Floyd Patterson** was the first).

ALI–FRAZIER TRILOGY. On 8 March 1971, the undefeated **Muhammad Ali** met the undefeated **Joe Frazier** at **Madison Square Garden** in New York for the world's **heavyweight** title. Ali had been heavyweight champion but had been stripped of his title after being convicted of avoiding the draft. As part of his sentence, he was not permitted to box and was consequently inactive for three and a half years from March 1967 to October 1970. On 26 October 1970, while his case was being appealed, he was granted a boxing license and was able to fight. While he was inactive, Joe Frazier defeated Buster Mathis and became recognized as heavyweight champion.

The **bout** between the two undefeated heavyweight champions was billed as the Fight of the Century and was immediately sold out. Singer Frank Sinatra was unable to get tickets and was only able to see the match by working as a **ringside** photographer.

For 15 **rounds**, Ali and Frazier took turns pounding each other, and although Frazier won a **unanimous decision**, the fight turned out to be even better than advertised. The two champions fought each other twice more in their careers, with Ali winning a 12-round **decision** on 28 January 1974 in New York in what was essentially a **nontitle bout**. Their subsequent fight on 1 October 1975 in Manila, **Philippines**, was for Ali's heavyweight title, which he had regained by knocking out **George Foreman** in Zaire in 1974. The Frazier–Ali **rubber match** in 1975 was a war, with both fighters exchanging solid blows throughout the fight before Frazier was unable to continue after the 14th round in a bout dubbed the "**Thrilla in Manila**." The bout is on most boxing historians' lists as one of the five greatest fights in history.

ALI–MARCIANO. In 1967, Miami radio producer Murray Woroner created a computerized boxing tournament. He had a series of variables about 16 **heavyweight** champions inputted into a NCR-315 computer with 20K of memory and had a computer program analyze the variables. He then created a fictitious tournament among 16 past champions, and the results of each **bout** were broadcast on the radio, with veteran boxing announcer Guy LeBow doing the commentary.

Although **Rocky Marciano** was named the champion and defeated **Jack Dempsey** in the final bout, current champion **Muhammad Ali** was upset that he was eliminated by **Jim Jeffries** in a quarterfinal match and sued Woroner for defamation of character. The suit was settled when Ali agreed to box Marciano in a filmed simulation of a computerized bout between the two of them, with the result to be shown in movie theaters. Ali at the time had been stripped of his heavyweight title and had his license suspended, so he was available. Marciano, who had been retired since 1956, also agreed with the plan. Marciano received a flat fee for his work while Ali signed for a percentage of the profits.

Marciano had to lose about 50 pounds to get into shape for the reenactment and also wore a toupee to cover a bald spot. The two boxed behind closed doors and went through the motions of every possible ending scenario since neither was shown the computerized result.

The film, billed as *The Super Fight*, was shown in about 1,500 motion picture theaters throughout the **United States** and **Canada** on one day only—20 January 1970. All prints of the film but one were supposed to be destroyed, although that was not the case and some theaters kept theirs for additional showings. In the film, Marciano knocks out Ali in the 13th **round**. Ironically, Marciano never saw the completed film nor learned of the ending as he died in a plane crash on 31 August 1969, three weeks after the filming was completed.

AMATEUR ATHLETIC UNION (AAU). The Amateur Athletic Union was founded in 1888 and administered **amateur boxing** (along with most other amateur sports) in the **United States** until 1978. In that year, the United States Congress passed the Amateur Sports Act, which chartered the United States **Olympic** Committee and provided for national governing bodies for each Olympic sport. Prior to that act, the AAU exerted much more influence, at times controversial, over U.S. athletes' international participation.

In 1978, it was superseded by the United States Amateur Boxing Federation, now known simply as USA Boxing. It is the United States' member organization of the **International Boxing Association (AIBA)**.

Since 1888, the AAU and its successor organizations have held annual national amateur boxing championships.

AMATEUR BOXING. Amateur boxing is contested among boxers who do not get paid for their **bouts**. Most boxers begin as amateurs while learning to box. The **Golden Gloves**, which began in 1926 in Chicago and in 1927 in New York, is one of the most famous tournaments for amateur boxers. In the early days of amateur boxing, promoters often awarded small prizes to amateur winners and would buy back the prize from the winner for cash, thus complying with the amateur rules but yet allowing the boxers to earn some money for their efforts.

All sports in the **Olympic Games** were restricted to amateur competitors until the 1980s, when professionals began to be accepted in various sports. Boxing in the Olympic Games is still restricted to amateur boxers, although most other Olympic sports allow professionals to compete. In some communist countries, such as **Cuba** and **Russia**, successful amateur boxers were not allowed to become professional boxers, and consequently some of the best Olympic boxers, such as three-time Olympic **heavyweight** champion **Teófilo Stevenson**, never had the opportunity to compete against champions such as **Muhammad Ali**, **George Foreman**, or **Joe Frazier**.

Amateur boxing is administered worldwide by the **International Boxing Association (AIBA)** and within the **United States** by USA Boxing.

See also BRONZE MEDAL; GOLD MEDAL; SILVER MEDAL.

ARCEL, RAY. B. 30 August 1899, Terre Haute, Indiana. D. 6 March 1994, New York, New York. Ray Arcel was one of boxing's most accomplished and respected **trainers**. His day job was as a purchasing agent for the Meehanite Metal Corporation, but he is best remembered for his work as a boxing trainer.

Although born in Indiana, he was raised in the East Harlem section of New York at a time when the neighborhood housed mixed ethnic groups, although Arcel claimed that his was the only Jewish family there. He claimed he attended Stuyvesant High School in Manhattan—one of the more prestigious schools academically in the city—although his biographer, Donald Dewey, disputes that claim.

He began **training** boxers in the 1920s and continued into the 1950s. During the 1950s, he arranged fights for the American Broadcasting Company television network. Some of the **bouts** competed with those of the **International Boxing Club**, an organization with reputed underworld associations, and on 14 September 1953 he was attacked in Boston, knocked unconscious on the head with a lead pipe, and was in the hospital for 19 days in critical condition. He subsequently dropped out of boxing for two decades but resumed in the 1970s as the trainer of **Roberto Durán**.

He trained boxing champions from the 1920s to the 1980s. The last championship bout he worked was at the age of 82 with **Larry Holmes** in his 1982 defense against **Gerry Cooney**. Among the other champions he handled were Jack "Kid" Berg, **Jim Braddock**, Lou Brouillard, **Ezzard Charles**, Roberto Durán, Sixto Escobar, Alfonso "Peppermint" Frazer, Ceferino Garcia, **Kid Gavilán**, **Frankie Genaro**, Abe Goldstein, Larry Holmes, Bob Olin, Charley Phil Rosenberg, **Barney Ross**, Billy Soose, Freddie Steele, Teddy Yarosz, **Tony Zale**, and **Benny Leonard**, his favorite. He worked with more than 2,000 boxers in his career and claimed that he was the trainer of 14 different opponents of **heavyweight** champion **Joe Louis**.

Boxing writer A. J. Liebling described Arcel as "severe and decisive, like a teacher in a Hebrew school." Arcel favored brains over brawn, and he was quoted as saying, "The name of the game has always been outsmarting the other fighter, not beating him to a pulp. If you can't outsmart him, [if you] don't use your brain, you're going to be a loser."

Arcel was inducted into the **International Boxing Hall of Fame** in 1991.

ARGENTINA. In **amateur boxing**, Argentinean boxers first competed in the 1920 **Olympic Games** and have entered 21 Olympic boxing tournaments—every one except 1980, when Argentina boycotted the games. They have won seven **gold medals**, seven **silver medals**, and 10 **bronze medals** and are in 10th place among all countries in boxing. Their first Olympic gold medals in boxing came in 1928, when Víctor Avendaño won the **light heavyweight** class and Arturo Rodríguez won the **heavyweight** class. Argentina won two more in 1932, with **featherweight** Carmelo Robledo and heavyweight Alberto Lovell. Featherweight Óscar Casanovas in 1936 and **flyweight Pascual Pérez** and heavyweight Rafael Iglesias in 1948 were Argentina's other Olympic gold medalists.

One of the earliest Argentine professional boxers to come to the **United States** was **Luis Ángel Firpo**, who challenged **Jack Dempsey** for Dempsey's heavyweight championship title in 1923 and knocked Dempsey down twice before losing in one of boxing's most memorable **bouts**. There have been more than 35 Argentinean professional world champion boxers. Among the best have been Horacio Accavallo, Juan Martín Coggi, Hugo Corro, Miguel Ángel Cuello, **Víctor Galíndez**, Santos Benigno Laciar, Nicolino Locche, **Carlos Monzón**, Pascual Pérez, and Julio César Vásquez. Other top Argentinean professional boxers include Jorge Ahumada, Óscar Bonavena, Eduardo Lausse, Alejandro Lavorante, Gregorio Peralta, and Víctor Zalazar.

ARGÜELLO, ALEXIS "EL FLACO EXPLOSIVO". B. 19 April 1952, Managua, Nicaragua. D. 1 July 2009, Managua, Nicaragua. Nicaragua, a rather small country in Central America, has produced several accomplished athletes, such as perfect-game major league baseball pitcher Dennis Martínez and seven other major league baseball players, weight lifter Karla Moreno Rodríguez, and soccer players Emilio Palacios and Samuel Wilson. Several other accomplished athletes were born in Nicaragua but were raised in other countries, such as the swimming champion Poll sisters and the taekwondo champion López family. It is in the sport of boxing where Nicaraguans have demonstrated the most success. José Alfaro, Rosendo Álvarez, Eddie Gazo, Eduardo Ray Márquez, Ricardo Mayorga, Juan Palacios, Luis Alberto Pérez, and Adonis Rivas have all captured world championships.

By far the best-known Nicaraguan athlete in history was boxer Alexis Argüello. Nicknamed "El Flaco Explosivo" (the explosive thin man), Argüello fought professionally from 1968 to 1986 and then made a brief two-**bout** comeback attempt in 1994 and 1995. He fought 33 of his first 34 bouts in Nicaragua and compiled a 31–3 record, with 26 fights ending short of the scheduled distance. On 16 February 1974, he was matched with **Panamanian** Ernesto Marcel for Marcel's **World Boxing Association (WBA)** world **featherweight** title but lost a unanimous 15-**round decision**. Later that year

(23 November 1974), Argüello **knocked out Rubén Olivares** at 1:20 of the 13th round in Inglewood, California, and won the WBA world featherweight championship.

Argüello successfully defended that title four times (all with knockout victories) and then abandoned his featherweight title to challenge for the WBA **super featherweight** title. He won that crown by stopping champion Alfredo Escalera on cuts at 2:06 of the 13th round in San Juan, **Puerto Rico**. Argüello made eight successful defenses of that title before abandoning it and moving up in weight to challenge for the **lightweight** title.

On 20 June 1981, Argüello won a **unanimous decision** over Scotsman James Watt in London, **England**, and won his third title. He defended it successfully four times and then challenged WBA **light welterweight** champion Aaron Pryor on 12 November 1982 in Miami, Florida, in an attempt to win a fourth title. Pryor stopped Argüello at 1:06 of the 14th round in one of the most hotly contested fights of the 1980s. In a rematch on 9 September 1983, in **Las Vegas**, Nevada, Pryor again stopped Argüello—this time by knockout at 1:48 of the 10th round. Argüello retired after the bout but made two brief two-bout comebacks. He won both fights by knockout in his first comeback attempt in 1985 and 1986, and then eight years later won a bout by **majority decision** in 1994 but was defeated on 21 January 1995 on a unanimous 10-round decision by **journeyman** Scott Walker.

Argüello had an adventurous life in addition to being one of boxing's greatest champions. He survived the devastating 1972 earthquake in Managua. He was a freedom fighter for the Contras against the Sandinista Liberation Front during the 1980s. He later became active in Nicaraguan politics on the side of the Sandinistas, became vice mayor of Managua in 2004, and in 2008 won a controversial election for mayor. He earned millions of dollars as a boxer yet battled a drug addiction that left him near bankruptcy. Although never an **Olympic** athlete, Alexis Argüello was the flag bearer for Nicaragua at the 2008 Olympics in Beijing.

His death occurred under suspicious circumstances. He allegedly shot himself through the heart, and the death was officially ruled a suicide, but given Argüello's political activities questions still remain.

Argüello was five foot 10 inches tall and had a 72-inch **reach**. He fought at weights ranging from 118 to 143 pounds, from featherweight to light welterweight. In 85 professional bouts from 1968 to 1995, he won 77 (62 by knockout), lost eight (four by knockout), and fought a total of 492 rounds. He was inducted into the **International Boxing Hall of Fame** in 1992.

ARMSTRONG, HENRY "HURRICANE HANK," "HAMMERIN' HANK," "HOMICIDE HANK" (né HENRY JACKSON JR.). B. 12 December 1912, Columbus, Mississippi. D. 22 October 1988, Los Angeles, California. Henry Armstrong was the first man to hold three world championships simultaneously—and the only man to do so, since the rules were changed subsequently, prohibiting a fighter from holding more than one title.

He began boxing under the name "Melody Jackson" and had two pro **bouts** under that name in 1931. He then returned to the **amateur** ranks under the name "Henry Armstrong" in a failed bid to make the 1932 **United States Olympic** team. After he did not succeed in doing so, he began boxing professionally as Henry Armstrong, with his first bout under that name on 30 August 1932 in Los Angeles, California. In an unusual start for a future world champion, he lost his first two bouts boxing as Armstrong. He then won 11 straight bouts before his next defeat.

By 1937, his record was 72–11–7, with most of his bouts on the West Coast and a few in **Mexico**. On 29 October 1937, he fought his first world title bout—something he would do 23 additional times over the next four years. On that date, he knocked out Petey Sarron in six **rounds** and won the world's **featherweight** title. Armstrong never defended this crown and never again made the featherweight limit of 126 pounds for a fight. He relinquished the title shortly after he won his next two titles.

On 31 May 1938, although he only weighed 133 pounds, he won the **welterweight** title (147-pound class) on a **unanimous decision** over **Barney Ross**. In Armstrong's next bout, he won his third title, the **lightweight** title, by winning a **split decision** over Lou Ambers on 17 August 1938. In his next seven fights, he concentrated on defending the welterweight title even though he weighed in under the lightweight limit of 135 pounds for all of them. He defeated Ceferino Garcia (New York, 15-round **decision**); Al Manfredo (Cleveland, **technical knockout** [TKO] 3 rounds); Alberto "Baby" Arizmendi (Los Angeles, 10-round decision); Bobby Pacho (Havana, **Cuba**, TKO 4); Lew Feldman (St. Louis, first-round **knockout**); Davey Day (New York, TKO 12); and Englishman Ernie Roderick (London, **England**, 15-round decision).

On 22 August 1939, Armstrong lost his lightweight title to Lou Ambers in a close fight that Armstrong would have won had he not been penalized five rounds for low blows by **referee** Arthur Donovan.

In 1939 and 1940, Armstrong successfully defended the welterweight title eight times, winning seven times by knockout or technical knockout and fighting in eight different states.

On 1 March 1940, Henry came very close in his attempt to be the first man to win titles in four different weight divisions. On that date in Los Angeles, he went 10 rounds with **middleweight** Ceferino Garcia in a close bout that was ruled a **draw**. Referee George Blake was the sole arbiter of the bout, which many observers thought that Armstrong had won.

Armstrong made four more successful title defenses in 1940 before finally losing his crown to Fritzie Zivic on 4 October 1940 at **Madison Square Garden**. The bout was even going into the final round, but Zivic easily won the round and the title. The two fought a rematch at the Garden three months later, but that time Zivic stopped Armstrong in the 12th round in what would be Henry's final championship bout.

He continued fighting until 1945, winning most of his fights, including victories over future lightweight champion Juan Zurita, Zivic, former lightweight champion Lew Jenkins, and future **junior welterweight** champion Tippy Larkin. He also lost to future welterweight and middleweight champion **"Sugar Ray" Robinson**.

Armstrong's last professional fight was on 14 February 1945, a 10-round loss to Chester Slider. In retirement, Armstrong became an ordained Baptist minister.

Armstrong was five foot five inches tall and had a 67-inch **reach**. He fought at weights ranging from 120 to 148 pounds, from featherweight to welterweight. In 181 professional bouts, from 1931 to 1945, he won 150 (101 by knockout), lost 21 (two by knockout), had 10 draws, and fought a total of 1,156 rounds. He was inducted as a member of the inaugural class of the **International Boxing Hall of Fame** in 1990.

ARUM, ROBERT "BOB". B. 8 December 1931, New York, New York. Bob Arum is a graduate of Erasmus Hall High School in Brooklyn, New York, and holds degrees from New York University and Harvard Law School. He worked as an attorney for the **United States** Department of Justice but became interested in boxing promoting in the 1960s, and since then he, along with rival promoter **Don King**, have been the two major boxing promoters in the United States.

The first world championship **bout** promoted by Arum's organization, Top Rank, was the **Muhammad Ali–George Chuvalo** match on 29 March 1966 in Toronto, **Canada**. Top Rank and Arum promoted a total of 27 of Ali's bouts and have promoted more than 400 world championship bouts. Virtually all of the major boxers since then have appeared in a Top Rank promotion at one time or another.

As with many boxing promoters, he has not been immune from controversy and has sued and been sued, been fined by a state boxing **commission**, and been investigated by the Federal Bureau of Investigation, but he has managed to continue promoting boxing and, as of 2012, is still one of boxing's two major promoters.

He was inducted into the **International Boxing Hall of Fame** in 1999.

ATLANTIC CITY. Atlantic City, a coastal resort city in southern New Jersey, became the site of many major boxing **bouts** in the 1980s as the state of New Jersey legalized **casinos** in 1976 and many of them began to add periodic boxing shows to their offerings. Some of the better-known casinos include Atlantis, Bally's, Caesar's, Resorts, and Trump Casino. Atlantic City has also used the famed Boardwalk Hall, sometimes referred to as the Convention Center, as a site for major boxing events. **Las Vegas**, which also has legal casinos, is Atlantic City's chief competition in the quest to attract boxing's major bouts.

Promoter **Don King** helped popularize the venue by featuring **Mike Tyson** in eight different **cards** during the 1980s as Tyson was rising through the ranks to become world **heavyweight** champion. After Tyson won the championship, he defended the title in Atlantic City against Tyrell Biggs, **Larry Holmes**, **Michael Spinks**, and Carl Williams during that decade.

In recent years, with the rise in legal casinos throughout the **United States**, Atlantic City's prominent role in boxing has diminished somewhat.

ATLAS, THEODORE A. "TEDDY". B. 29 July 1956, Staten Island, New York. Teddy Atlas was the son of an esteemed physician on Staten Island.

As a youth, Teddy was in and out of trouble and has a scar the length of his face that reportedly took 400 stitches to close as a result of a street fight. He also served time for an armed robbery.

He began working with **Cus D'Amato** at D'Amato's gym in upstate New York in 1976 and had several **amateur bouts**, winning the 139-pound championship of the Adirondack **Golden Gloves** tournament. He had to quit boxing due to a back injury and became a **trainer** full-time. While with D'Amato, he worked briefly with a young **Mike Tyson**. He left the D'Amato camp in 1982 after a confrontation with Tyson.

As a trainer, Atlas worked with Simon Brown, Joey Gamache, Kallie Knoetze, Donny Lalonde, **Barry McGuigan**, Michael Moorer, and Alexander Povetkin, as well as the 1980 Swedish Olympic boxing team.

He also worked with dancer-choreographer Twyla Tharp to aid her in a comeback, helped prepare actor Willem Dafoe for his role as a boxer in the film *Triumph of the Spirit*, and choreographed the fight scenes for that picture.

In 1997, in memory of his late father, he founded the Dr. Theodore A. Atlas Memorial Foundation, which is a "community service organization that provides financial, legal and emotional support to individuals and organizations in need, and focuses particularly on the needs of children. In the spirit of Dr. Atlas, who provided free medical care to those who could not afford it and made house calls to give personal care to his patients until he was 80 years old, the Foundation has attempted since its inception to ease the burden of the less fortunate among us. And it accomplishes this in a very human way, in a way which preserves the dignity of the people it helps."

In recent years, he has become a boxing color analyst and is probably best known to the boxing public in that role, although he continues to work as a trainer. In 2006, he coauthored his autobiography with Peter Alson, and in 2010 he coauthored a book with **Bert Randolph Sugar**, *The Ultimate Book of Boxing Lists*.

ATTELL, ABRAHAM WASHINGTON "ABE," "THE LITTLE HE-BREW". B. 22 February 1883, San Francisco, California. D. 7 February 1970, New Paltz, New York. Abe Attell was one of the very few individuals who made a significant impact in the worlds of both boxing and baseball. He was quite successful as a boxer, winning the world's **featherweight** championship and retaining it for a decade. He also became friendly with several professional gamblers and was one of the people responsible for bribing several White Sox major league baseball players to conspire to lose the 1919 World Series. Neither the gamblers nor the baseball players were ever convicted, although eight baseball players were banned from the sport for life.

Attell began his boxing career in 1900 in his native San Francisco but moved to Denver, Colorado, shortly afterward. After only a year as a professional, Attell fought the great **George Dixon**, who had been world's **bantamweight** and featherweight champion. The two fought a 10-**round draw** on 23 August 1901 in Denver, then a 20-round draw two months later in Cripple Creek, Colorado, and just eight days after that **bout**, a third time in St. Louis, Missouri, which was won by Attell on a 15-round **decision**. Following that bout, Attell claimed the world's featherweight championship.

Attell enhanced his title claim by beating Johnny Reagan on 3 September 1903 on a 20-round decision, and after a 10-round draw with Harry Forbes on 4 January 1904 followed by a fifth-round **knockout** of Forbes one month later, he gained universal recognition as world's featherweight champion. Over the next eight years, Attell fought 23 bouts with the title at stake, as well as 84 **nontitle bouts**, all over the country, from Maine to California. Most of the nontitle bouts were **no-decision** bouts in which Attell received the **newspaper decision**.

On 22 February 1912 (Abe's 29th birthday), in Vernon, California, Attell was defeated by decision in a 20-round bout with Johnny Kilbane and lost his championship claim. Attell had also won a title defense on his 23rd birthday in 1906 and might be the only fighter in boxing history to both win and lose a championship on his birthday. Attell continued boxing through 1913, then after a year's retirement fought once in 1915 and twice more in 1917 before permanently retiring from the **ring** after a 29 November 1917 no-decision bout.

After he retired, he owned a shoe store in New York and also worked in vaudeville. In 1919, he allegedly was the "bag man" for gambler Arnold Rothstein, who attempted to fix the outcome of the 1919 baseball World Series. When a grand jury investigated the scandal, Attell was able to convince them that the Abe Attell mentioned by others as part of the conspiracy was actually some one else, and he was never indicted.

Attell was five foot four inches tall and had a 66-inch **reach**. He fought at weights ranging from 116 to 133 pounds, primarily as a bantamweight and featherweight. In 154 professional bouts, from 1900 to 1917, he won 72 (39 by knockout), lost 10 (five by knockout), had 17 draws and two **no contests**, and fought 53 no-decision bouts, in which he was awarded the newspaper decision in 41, was the loser in six, and six others were drawn. He fought a total of 1,487 rounds. He was inducted as a member of the inaugural class of the **International Boxing Hall of Fame** in 1990.

AUSTRALIA. In a country that loves sports, boxing has always played a significant role in Australia, dating back to the 19th century. In **amateur boxing**, Australian boxers first competed in the 1908 **Olympic Games**. That year, Australia and New Zealand sent a combined team as "Australasia." Their representative in the boxing tournament was all-around sportsman **Reginald "Snowy" Baker**, who won the **silver medal** in boxing in addition to competing in the swimming and diving competitions. Australia also entered the 1924 Olympic boxing tournament, and from 1936 to 2012 have competed in boxing in each Olympic Games—one of only four countries to do so, the others being **France**, **Great Britain**, and **Italy**. In addition to Baker, Australian boxers have won four other Olympic medals—**bantamweight** Ollie Taylor, 1956 **bronze**; **light middleweight** Grahame Cheney, 1988 silver; **welterweight** Kevin Hogarth, 1956 bronze; and **light heavyweight** Tony Madigan, 1960 bronze. (Madigan also came to New York in 1959 and won the New York **Golden Gloves** and the Eastern Regional Golden Gloves but was defeated by **Cassius Clay** in the Chicago–New York Intercity Golden Gloves competition.)

Professional **heavyweight** champion **Tommy Burns** fought several fights in Australia, including one on 26 December 1908 in Sydney in which he lost his title to **Jack Johnson** in the 14th **round**.

Australia has produced 16 fighters who have won world championships during their careers. They are Jimmy Carruthers, Billy Dib, Lester Ellis, Johnny Famechon, Jeff Fenech, Daniel Geale, Danny Green, Young Griffo, Jeff Harding, Philip Holiday, Rocky Mattioli, Barry Michael, Anthony Mundine, Lovemore N'Dou, Robbie Peden, and Lionel Rose. Gairy St. Clair was born in Guyana but now boxes out of Australia. In addition, **Russian**-born world champion **Kosta Tszyu** immigrated to Australia in 1992 and has dual citizenship. Among the best Australian professional boxers who did not become world champions have been Les Darcy, **Peter Jackson** (although born in the Dutch West Indies, he was raised in Australia), and indigenous fighters Tony Mundine and Dave Sands.

One of the most knowledgeable and respected Australian boxing personalities (writer, announcer, **judge**) was Ray Mitchell, who has been nominated (but not yet elected) to the **International Boxing Hall of Fame**.

B

BAER, MAXIMILIAN ADELBERT "MAX," "THE LIVERMORE LA-RUPPER," "MADCAP MAXIE". B. 11 February 1909, Omaha, Nebraska. D. 21 November 1959, Hollywood, California. Although Max Baer would not be considered Jewish by Orthodox and Conservative Jews, the fact that his paternal grandfather was Jewish made Max a Jew in the eyes of Reform and Reconstructionist Jews. Although personally a nonsectarian believer, he capitalized on his Jewishness (wearing a Star of David on his trunks) in a **bout** against German **Max Schmeling**, a personal favorite of Adolph Hitler.

Baer, born in the Midwest, moved with his family to California at the age of 13 and settled several years later in Livermore, California. His father, Jacob, was a butcher who raised livestock on a ranch. Max worked for him and built up his body by carrying meat carcasses. He began a **professional boxing** career in 1929, and his first recorded bout was on 16 May in Stockton, California, where he knocked out a fighter billed as "Chief Caribou" in the second **round** of a four-round bout. He continued his **ring** activity and in a little over a year had amassed a record of 23–3 with 19 **knockouts**. On 25 August 1930, Baer knocked out ring veteran Frankie Campbell in five rounds. Campbell died the following day, and this significantly altered Baer's boxing career.

Although he had one of boxing's hardest punches, Baer lost four of his next six bouts because he became afraid of being too aggressive and started to loop his punches. Former **heavyweight** champion **Jack Dempsey** began working with Baer, helping him to redirect his punches. Baer's record improved, and he won 10 consecutive bouts. On 31 August 1932, he won a **majority decision** from Ernie Schaaf, to whom Baer had lost two years previously. Schaaf took a bad beating in that fight, and in a subsequent fight in February 1933 against **Primo Carnera**, not known as a powerful puncher, suffered a brain hemorrhage and died four days later.

Baer's next big fight was on 8 June 1933 against the former world's heavyweight champion Max Schmeling. In *Ring* **magazine's** "Fight of the Year," Baer stopped Schmeling in the 10th round before 53,000 fans at Yankee Stadium.

Baer did not fight again for one year, and when he did he fought the giant Italian Primo Carnera for the world's heavyweight title on 14 June 1934 at the outdoor facility in Long Island City, New York, known as the **Madison Square Garden** Bowl. Baer gave Carnera a savage beating in the bout, knocking him down about 10 times before the bout was stopped in the 11th round.

Baer held the world's heavyweight championship for one year before losing it to **James J. Braddock**, a 10–1 underdog, in one of boxing's biggest upsets. Baer took the challenger lightly and did not train extensively for the bout, while Braddock saw the bout as his chance of a lifetime and trained hard for it.

Baer's next fight, only three months later, was with the undefeated (21–0) **Joe Louis**. Louis knocked Baer down twice in the third round before finishing him for the count in the fourth round. It was later disclosed that Baer fought the bout with a broken right hand that had not healed since the Braddock fight.

After the Louis fight, Baer fought 21 bouts throughout the western **United States** against lesser opposition and won 20, losing only to Willie Davies in a six-round bout billed as an **exhibition**, but one in which the **referee** gave the decision to Davies.

Baer traveled to **England** in 1937 and lost a 12-round decision to British Empire heavyweight champion Tommy Farr but defeated Ben Foord. In 1938, Farr came to the United States, and Baer beat him in a 15-round bout at Madison Square Garden.

Baer continued fighting until 1941 and retired after Lou Nova stopped him in 11 rounds on 4 April 1941.

After he retired, Baer had a nightclub act with former boxer **"Slapsie Maxie" Rosenbloom** and acted in about 20 motion pictures. He also did some refereeing of boxing and wrestling bouts. His brother Buddy Baer was a top heavyweight contender who twice fought Joe Louis unsuccessfully in heavyweight title bouts. Max's son, Max Baer Jr., was also an actor and was best known for his part as Jethro Bodine in *The Beverly Hillbillies* television series. Max Baer died of a heart attack at the age of 50.

Baer was six foot two inches tall and had an 81-inch **reach**. He fought at weights ranging from 190 to 226 pounds as a heavyweight. In 80 professional bouts, from 1929 to 1941, he won 67 (52 by knockout), lost 13 (three by knockout), and fought a total of 426 rounds. He also fought one six-round no-decision bout in which he was awarded the **newspaper decision**. He was inducted into the **International Boxing Hall of Fame** in 1995.

BAKER, REGINALD LESLIE "SNOWY". B. 8 February 1884, Sydney, **Australia**. D. 2 December 1953, Hollywood, California. Reginald "Snowy" Baker was a man for all seasons and competed successfully in more than 20 sports. Called "Snowy" due to his extremely light-colored hair, he won swimming events in high school, played water polo for his club, and competed in athletics events. In 1902, he began service in the military and won prizes for fencing. In 1904, he played for Australia in an international rugby match with **Great Britain**.

He began boxing in 1902 and became New South Wales's **amateur middleweight** champion. He competed in the 1908 London **Olympic Games** boxing tournament and was the only non-British boxing medalist. That year's competition was conducted on only one day, 27 October, and Baker won two **bouts** by **knockout** and one by decision before losing a decision in the final bout and earning the **silver medal**.

That year's Olympic Games events were spread from April through October, and the swimming and diving events were held in July. Baker competed in the springboard diving on 14 July but finished sixth and last in his group in the first round and was eliminated from further competition in the event. Ten days later, he was a member of the Australasian (Australia plus New Zealand) swimming 4 x 200 relay team and helped them win their semifinal heat, but they could only manage fourth place in the final.

After he returned to Sydney, he opened a physical culture company and offered mail-order courses. He wrote for a local newspaper, wrote a book on physical culture, and began publishing a magazine, *Snowy Baker's Magazine*. He also worked as a boxing **referee** and helped Hugh D. McIntosh build boxing stadiums in Australia and helped promote the boxing career of Les Darcy.

Baker began acting in films in Australia with his horse Boomerang and left in 1920 to go to Hollywood to further his film career. Billed as "Rex 'Snowy' Baker," he appeared in about a dozen films in Australia and the **United States** during the 1920s. He was an excellent horseman and trained Hollywood stars in riding. He also acted as technical advisor in Westerns.

An accomplished polo player, he purchased an ownership interest in the Riviera Country Club and spent his time as riding instructor to Hollywood stars as well as playing polo.

He died at the age of 69 of cerebro-vascular disease.

BANTAMWEIGHT. Bantamweight is a boxing weight class with a maximum weight of 118 pounds, although the weight limits in early bantamweight **bouts** varied from 114 to 118 pounds. **George Dixon**, a black boxer from Nova Scotia, **Canada**, is generally considered to be the first bantamweight champion. His 27 June 1890 bout with Edwin "Nunc" Wallace in London in which Wallace retired after 19 **rounds** of their scheduled 30 rounds was advertised for the world 114-pound championship. As with most of the lighter weight classes, the bantamweight class has never been very popular in the **United States**. Among the best bantamweights have been

Jimmy Barry, Panama Al Brown, Gaby Canizales, Orlando Canizales, Jimmy Carruthers, Jeff Chandler, Sixto Escobar, **Masahiko "Fighting" Harada**, **Pete Herman**, **Éder Jofre**, Raúl Macías, Anselmo Moreno, **Rubén Olivares**, **Manuel Ortiz**, Vic Toweel, Alfonso Zamora, and **Carlos Zárate**.

BARBELLA, THOMAS ROCCO. *See* GRAZIANO, ROCKY "THE ROCK" (né THOMAS ROCCO BARBELLA).

BAREKNUCKLES. Prior to the 20th century, the predominant style of boxing was bareknuckle. **Bouts** were conducted initially under Jack Broughton's Rules and then later under the **London Prize Ring Rules**, which stipulated that a **round** would end when one contestant was knocked down and that a 30 second rest period would occur between rounds. Bouts were usually to a finish—when one contestant was unable to continue or surrendered. The institution of the **Marquess of Queensberry Rules** in 1867, which required boxers to wear **gloves**, gradually eliminated bareknuckle contests, and by the 20th century boxing was restricted to gloved bouts.

Englishman James Figg had a school in which he taught various forms of self-defense and from 1719 to 1730 was recognized as the first bareknuckle champion.

Among other of the best-known bareknuckle boxers were Tom Allen, Jem Belcher, **Bendigo**, Ben Brain, Jack Broughton, James "Deaf" Burke, Ben Caunt, Peter Crawley, **Tom Cribb**, Bill Darts, Joe Goss, Thomas Jackling, John Jackson, **Jake Kilrain**, Jem Mace, Daniel Mendoza, **Tom Molineaux**, Tom Paddock, Henry Pearce, Paddy Ryan, Tom Sayers, Harry Sellers, Jack Slack, Tom Spring, **John L. Sullivan**, and Jem Ward. Sullivan concluded his career under Marquess of Queensberry Rules and is generally considered the last bareknuckle **heavyweight** champion.

See also APPENDIXES H, I, and J for early boxing rules.

BARROW, JOSEPH LOUIS. *See* LOUIS, JOE "THE BROWN BOMBER" (né JOSEPH LOUIS BARROW).

BASILIO, CARMINE "CARMEN," "THE UPSTATE ONION FARMER". B. 7 July 1927, Canastota, New York. D. 7 November 2012, Rochester, New York. Carmen Basilio was a boxer who was never afraid to take a punch, and many of his **bouts** were described as "wars" by the boxing press. In five consecutive years, from 1955 to 1959, one of his bouts was selected by *Ring* **magazine** as the "Fight of the Year."

After serving in the U.S. Marine Corps, Basilio began a **professional boxing** career with his first bout on 24 November 1948 in Binghamton, New York. Most of his early bouts were in the Upstate New York cities of Binghamton, Syracuse, Buffalo, Utica, and Rochester. After compiling a record of 19–2–2, he fought his first fight in New York City but lost an eight-round decision to Mike Koballa at the Eastern Parkway Arena in Brooklyn. He then spent several months in New Orleans, Louisiana, where he won three of five bouts with one loss and one **draw**.

By 29 May 1952, Basilio had a not exceptional record of 28–8–3. On that date, in Syracuse, he fought the undefeated (32–0–1) Chuck Davey, an up-and-coming fighter who had been a four-time national collegiate champion. Although Basilio won the decision, it was announced that one of the **judges'** scorecards had been marked incorrectly, and the result was changed to a draw. In their subsequent rematch six weeks later, Davey clearly won a **unanimous decision**.

In 1953, Basilio had two 12-round bouts with **Billy Graham** that were billed for the USA New York State **welterweight** title. Carmen won the first, and the second was a draw. Basilio then challenged **Kid Gavilán** for the world welterweight title but lost a **split decision** in Syracuse on 18 September 1953.

Basilio then won nine of his next 11 bouts with two draws. On 10 June 1955, he won the world's welterweight title by stopping Tony DeMarco in the 12th round in DeMarco's hometown of Boston. The bout earned recognition by *Ring* magazine as the 1955 "Fight of the Year." But in his very first title defense on 14 March 1956 in Chicago, Basilio was outpointed by Johnny Saxton and lost the title. Saxton, at that time, was controlled by underworld figure Frank "Blinky" Palermo, and the decision was questionable. The two had a rematch six months later in Syracuse, and Basilio made sure of the victory by stopping Saxton in the ninth round in a fight that was named "Fight of the Year" by *Ring* magazine. A subsequent rematch in February 1957 was also won by Basilio with a second-round **technical knockout**.

Basilio then set his sights on **"Sugar Ray" Robinson's middleweight** title, and in the 1957 "Fight of the Year" won a split decision over Robinson and gained the middleweight title. Their 1958 rematch was again the "Fight of the Year," but this time Robinson prevailed and rewon the title.

Robinson was stripped of his title by the **National Boxing Association (NBA)** for inactivity (although he was still recognized as champion in New York and Massachusetts), and the NBA sanctioned a bout between **Gene Fullmer** and Basilio on 28 August 1959 for the middleweight title. For the fifth consecutive year, Basilio figured in *Ring* magazine's "Fight of the Year," but he was on the losing end this time, as Fullmer won on a 14th-round technical knockout. The two fought a rematch in 1960, but again Fullmer stopped Basilio—this time in the 12th round.

After two victories in 1961, Basilio once more challenged for the middleweight title, now owned by Paul Pender, but again fell short, losing a unanimous decision.

He retired following the bout and worked for Genesee Brewery in Rochester, New York, and also taught physical education at LeMoyne College in Syracuse. He was also associated with his brother, Paul, in a sausage-making company, Basilio's Sausages.

He was honored by his hometown of Canastota, New York, with a statue and that led to the founding of the **International Boxing Hall of Fame** in Canastota in 1990.

Basilio was five foot six inches tall and had a 67-inch **reach**. He fought at weights ranging from 141 to 159 pounds as a welterweight and middleweight. In 79 professional bouts, from 1948 to 1961, he won 56 (27 by knockout), lost 16 (two by knockout), had seven draws, and fought a total of 634 rounds. He was inducted as a member of the inaugural class of the International Boxing Hall of Fame in 1990.

BBBofC. *See* BRITISH BOXING BOARD OF CONTROL (BBBofC).

BENDIGO (né WILLIAM ABEDNEGO THOMPSON). B. 18 October 1811, Sneinton, **England**. D. 23 August 1880, Beeston, England. William Abednego Thompson, who boxed as "Bendigo," was one of triplets named for the brothers in the Bible—Shadrach, Meshach, and Abednego. He was a **bareknuckle** fighter who indirectly has a city named for him, albeit in **Australia**.

Born into a family of 21 children, at the age of 15 he and his mother were placed in the Nottingham Workhouse upon the death of his father. When he was 18, he began boxing to earn money for his family. After winning his first 12 fights, he faced Ben Caunt on 21 July 1835 and defeated him in 22 **rounds**. (Bareknuckle rounds ended when a fighter went down and bouts were usually fought until one fighter was unable to continue.) Bendigo won another **bout** in 1836, a 52-round bout over John "Brassey" Leachman that was won on a **foul**. Bendigo had two bouts in 1837—a 32-rounder over Young Charles Langan and a 99-rounder over Bill Looney.

In 1838, he again fought Caunt and lost on a foul after 75 rounds, Caunt claiming that Bendigo went down without being hit. Caunt then claimed the **heavyweight** championship. A rematch two months later was canceled. In 1839, Bendigo defeated James "Deaf" Burke and, after winning on a foul after 10 rounds, was given a championship belt of England from former boxer Jem Ward and retired from the ring. He came back six years later on 9 September 1845, when he defeated Caunt on a foul after 93 rounds. Bendigo again claimed the title. His next, and last, recorded bout occurred on 5 June 1850, when he defeated Tom Paddock on a foul in 49 rounds.

After retiring from prizefighting, Bendigo became an alcoholic. In 1872, he happened to attend a sermon and was inspired by it. He joined the Ebenezer Lodge of Good Templars and became an evangelist. Due to his popularity as a fighter, his sermons attracted large crowds.

Bendigo was quite popular among the "fancy," as boxing fans were known in those days, and even inspired Sir Arthur Conan Doyle, creator of Sherlock Holmes and a fight fan, to write a poem about him titled "Bendigo's Sermon."

The city in Victoria, Australia, named Bendigo was indirectly named for him. A 19th-century Australian boxer admired William Thompson and took his nickname of Bendigo. An area in Australia was named Bendigo's Creek after the Australian boxer, and when the gold rush town was built there, it was named Bendigo.

As with most bareknuckle boxers, exact details of his boxing record are sketchy, although the *Ring Record Book* lists 20 bouts with 19 wins and one loss. He was inducted into the **International Boxing Hall of Fame** in 1991.

BENÍTEZ, WILFRED "EL RADAR". B. 12 September 1958, New York, New York. Wilfred Benítez has the distinction of being the youngest person to win a world's **professional boxing** championship. At an age when most aspiring fighters are boxing in **Golden Gloves bouts** as **amateurs**, he was fighting **main events** at **Madison Square Garden**.

Although born in New York City, Benítez was raised in **Puerto Rico**, as his father, Gregorio, took the family to live in Puerto Rico when Wilfred was seven years old. Gregorio built his three sons a gymnasium with a boxing **ring** behind their house in Puerto Rico, and Wilfred and his brothers Gregorio Jr. and Frankie began boxing as amateurs. By the time he was 15 years old, Wilfred had a reported 123–6 record as an amateur.

On 22 November 1973, just two months after his 15th birthday, Wilfred Benítez fought his first professional fight, a first-**round knockout** over Hiram Santiago in San Juan, Puerto Rico. After winning his first 11 bouts (10 by knockouts), all in Puerto Rico and St. Maarten, he came to the mainland and fought in the main event at the **Felt Forum** on 16 September 1974, with his brother Frankie fighting in the semifinal that night.

Wilfred won easily on a fifth-round **technical knockout** over **journeyman** Al Hughes. One month later, Benítez was fighting Terry Summerhays at Madison Square Garden, while his brother Frankie was fighting Johnny Summerhays, Terry's brother, on the same **card**. Both Benítez brothers won, both by sixth-round technical knockouts. After winning one more bout in New York, Wilfred returned to Puerto Rico in 1975, where he won his next 11 bouts, fighting eight times in Puerto Rico, twice on St. Maarten, and once back in New York.

He was then matched with the experienced **Colombian Antonio "Kid Pambelé" Cervantes**, the **World Boxing Association (WBA) light welterweight** champion, on 6 March 1976 in San Juan. To the surprise of many, Benítez won a 15-round **split decision** and the title, becoming the youngest professional world champion in boxing history at the age of 17 years, five months, and 23 days. After two successful title defenses, Benítez was stripped of his title by the WBA for failing to give Cervantes a rematch. Benítez then moved up in class and fought as a **welterweight**. On 2 February 1977, Benítez was held to a **draw** in a 10-round **nontitle bout** against Harold Weston Jr.—the first bout that Benítez did not win.

Benítez then won eight straight bouts to raise his record to 36–0–1 and on 14 January 1979 defeated **Carlos Palomino** on a 15-round split decision in San Juan to win the **World Boxing Council** welterweight title. After one successful defense of that title against Harold Weston Jr., Benítez then fought the 1976 **Olympic** champion, **"Sugar Ray" Leonard**, who was being promoted as the sport's next big star and who had won all of his 25 bouts. The match on 30 November 1979 at Caesars Palace in **Las Vegas** went into the 15th round before Leonard, who was ahead on points, knocked Benítez down late in the round and **referee** Carlos Padilla stopped the fight with just six seconds to go.

After the loss to Leonard, Benítez again moved up in weight class and fought as a **light middleweight**. He won all three of his bouts in this class in 1980, and on 23 May 1981 in Las Vegas he defeated the West Indian British-er Maurice Hope by a 12th-round technical knockout to win the world's light middleweight championship. He became only the eighth man in **professional boxing** history to win world titles in three different weight classes. Benítez successfully defended that title against the previously undefeated (22–0) Carlos Santos and the former **lightweight** and welterweight champion **Roberto Durán**. On 3 December 1982, at the Superdome in New Orleans, Benítez lost his light middleweight crown to **Thomas Hearns** on a 15-round **majority decision**.

Benítez continued boxing through 1986 but lost four of his 11 fights. He made an ill-advised comeback attempt in 1990, winning two and losing two fights.

Although Benítez was managed for much of his career by Bill Cayton and **Jim Jacobs**, two of boxing's most honest and upright men, who then put part of his earnings in a trust fund not to be touched until after his retirement, apparently Benítez's father, Gregorio, was able to access that account and reportedly spent it all. As a result, Benítez was awarded a modest pension by the Puerto Rico government. Since the mid-1990s, Benítez has been ravaged by posttraumatic encephalitis as a result of the head blows he took during his boxing career—an ironic ending for one of boxing's best defensive fighters.

Cared for by his mother until her death in 2008, and now by his sister Yvonne, his current situation is a sad ending to one of boxing's greatest champions.

Benítez is five foot 10 inches tall and has a 70-inch **reach**. He fought at weights ranging from 139 to 160 pounds as a light welterweight, welterweight, and light middleweight. In 62 professional bouts, from 1973 to 1990, he won 53 (31 by knockout), lost eight (four by knockout), had one draw, and fought a total of 485 rounds. He was inducted into the **International Boxing Hall of Fame** in 1996.

BENTON, GEORGE ALLEN "THE PROFESSOR". B. 15 May 1933, Philadelphia, Pennsylvania. D. 19 September 2011, Philadelphia, Pennsylvania. George Benton was one of the best **middleweights** of the 1950s and early 1960s, yet modern-day boxing fans know him primarily as a **cornerman** for some of boxing's greatest fighters, such as **Joe Frazier, Leon Spinks, Pernell Whitaker**, and **Evander Holyfield**.

Benton's first professional **bout** was as a **welterweight** on 18 July 1949 in Philadelphia, Pennsylvania. He won that bout as well as his next six before losing a six-**round** decision to Al Mobley on the **undercard** of the **"Sugar Ray" Robinson**–Robert Villemain middleweight championship bout outdoors at Municipal Stadium in Philadelphia on 5 June 1950.

Fighting as a middleweight during the 1950s, Benton won 27 of his next 29 bouts from 1951 to 1958, with most of the bouts being **main events** and many of them **televised** on the various "Fight of the Week" telecasts.

As an excellent defensive boxer, he was never a crowd-pleaser, even though he won nearly all of his bouts.

He continued to be a top middleweight although he had one stretch from 1958 to 1960 in which he was outpointed in five of 10 bouts. On 6 August 1962, he decisioned **Joey Giardello**, who would become world's middleweight champion the following year. Benton, although the number one rated middleweight, was unable to gain a world's championship bout, possibly because his manager, Herman Diamond, refused to surrender a piece of his contract to make it happen.

The closest he came were two bouts with Johnny Morris for the Pennsylvania State middleweight title in 1963 and 1964, with Morris winning the first and Benton the second. On 30 November 1964, Benton won a close **majority decision** over Jimmy Ellis, then a middleweight who would later become the **World Boxing Association's heavyweight** champion during **Muhammad Ali's** enforced retirement. In 1966, Benton lost all three bouts that year, including the only two in his career that he did not last the scheduled distance. Benton was stopped on cuts in the ninth round by Luis Manuel Rodríguez and did not answer the bell for the 10th round in a bout with Bennie Briscoe.

Benton's last professional bout was on 3 April 1970. His boxing career ended when he was shot in the back, with the bullet lodging near his spine. He began working with **trainer** Eddie Futch and became one of boxing's top trainers. Manager Lou Duva hired Benton, and he trained many of boxing's champions over the next four decades. Benton won the first two Boxing Writers' Association of America Trainer of the Year awards in 1989 and 1990.

Benton was five foot nine inches tall and fought at weights ranging from 146 to 168 pounds, primarily as a middleweight. In 76 professional bouts, from 1949 to 1970, he won 62 (37 by **knockout**), lost 13 (two by knockout), had one **draw**, and fought a total of 501 rounds. He began as a welterweight but fought most of his bouts as a middleweight. He was inducted into the **International Boxing Hall of Fame** in 2001.

BENVENUTI, GIOVANNI "NINO". B. 26 April 1938, Isola d'Istria, **Italy** (now Izola, Slovenia). Nino Benvenuti was undoubtedly Italy's greatest boxer. Not only was he an accomplished **amateur** boxer, winning Italian national amateur championships five straight years from 1956 to 1960, he also won the European **light middleweight** titles in 1957 and 1959 as well as the 1960 **Olympic gold medal** and was awarded the **Val Barker Trophy** as the outstanding boxer in the 1960 Olympic Games. He had a reported amateur record of 119–1.

His first professional **bout** took place on 20 January 1961 in Trieste, Italy, and he won a six-**round** decision over the Tunisian Ben Ali Allala. That year he had 14 fights, all in Italy, and won them all, six by **knockout**. He had 15 more bouts in 1962 and again won all with five knockouts. On 1 March 1963, he won the Italian **middleweight** title with an 11th-round knockout of Tommaso Truppi in Rome. Benvenuti added 12 more wins to his record, with six knockouts, in 1963. He won nine more in 1964 and six others in 1965, for a total record of 65–0, before he challenged Italian Sandro Mazzinghi for Mazzinghi's world light middleweight title in Milan on 18 June 1965. Benvenuti knocked out Mazzinghi in six rounds to become world champion.

Benvenuti added the European middleweight championship on 14 May 1966 when he stopped the German Jupp Elze in the 14th round of their bout in Berlin, **Germany**, Benvenuti's first fight outside of Italy. Benvenuti's next fight outside his homeland was not as successful, as he lost his world light middleweight championship to the **Korean** Ki-Soo Kim in Seoul, Korea, on 25 June 1966 via a 15-round **split decision**.

Returning to Italy, Nino won six straight bouts before going to the United States to fight world middleweight champion **Emile Griffith** at **Madison Square Garden** on 17 April 1967. Benvenuti won a unanimous 15-round decision and added the world's middleweight championship to his resume. This would be the first of three bouts with Griffith over an 11-month period in which they would trade victories. Griffith rewon the title on 29 September 1967 outdoors at Shea Stadium in Flushing, New York, on a **majority decision**, and Benvenuti recaptured it on 4 March 1968 at the new Madison Square Garden in its first boxing program, sharing the billing with the Buster Mathis–**Joe Frazier heavyweight** title fight.

Benvenuti returned to Italy, fought two **nontitle bouts** there, and then came back to North America for two more nontitle bouts, one in Toronto, **Canada**, and one in Akron, Ohio. He was held to a **draw** in the bout in Akron by Doyle Baird and then returned to Italy again for a title defense against Don Fullmer, Gene's brother, on 14 December 1968. Don lasted the 15 rounds but lost a **unanimous decision**.

On 26 May 1969, Benvenuti was defeated in a 10-round nontitle bout on a unanimous decision by former middleweight and **light heavyweight** champion **Dick Tiger** at Madison Square Garden. Nino's next two fights that year were championship defenses in Italy, a seven-round **disqualification** victory over Fraser Scott and an 11th-round knockout of former world **welterweight** champion **Cuban** Luis Manuel Rodríguez. In 1970, Benvenuti traveled to Melbourne, **Australia**, to fight Tom Bethea in a 10-round nontitle bout on 13 March. Although Bethea only had a record of 9–5–1 entering the bout, he was able to knock Benvenuti down in the seventh round and injure his ribs so severely that Benvenuti quit in the eighth round. Benvenuti granted Bethea a rematch for the middleweight title, which took place in Umag, Croatia, and this time he knocked out Bethea in the eighth round.

In Benvenuti's next bout, he and Argentinean **Carlos Monzón** fought *Ring* magazine's "Fight of the Year," and Monzón stopped Benvenuti in the 12th round to win the middleweight championship of the world. After a tune-up fight in Italy four months later in which Benvenuti lost a majority decision to José Roberto Chirino, Monzón and Benvenuti fought a rematch in Monte Carlo, Monaco, on 8 May 1971. This would be Benvenuti's last fight, as Monzón knocked him down in the second and third rounds and Benvenuti's manager, Bruno Amaduzzi, threw in the towel to have the **referee** stop the fight.

In retirement, Benvenuti was a successful businessman in Trieste, owning a first-class restaurant and becoming a television show host. He also entered politics and was elected to the city council.

Benvenuti is five foot 11 inches tall and has a 75-inch **reach**. He fought at weights ranging from 153 to 164 pounds as a middleweight. In 90 professional bouts, from 1961 to 1971, he won 82 (35 by knockout), lost seven (three by knockout), had one draw, and fought a total of 707 rounds. He was inducted into the **International Boxing Hall of Fame** in 1992.

BERARDINELLI, GIUSEPPE ANTONIO. *See* MAXIM, JOEY (né GIUSEPPE ANTONIO BERARDINELLI).

BLUE HORIZON. The Blue Horizon was a small neighborhood boxing arena in Philadelphia, Pennsylvania, that was often referred to as "the Legendary Blue Horizon." Built in 1865 as three four-story private houses, it was renovated in 1914 to be used by a fraternal organization, the Loyal Order of Moose. In 1938, it held its first boxing show. The building was sold in 1961, renovated again, and on 3 November 1961 regular boxing shows were presented there until 1966. After a three-year hiatus, promoter J. Russell Peltz resumed the weekly shows at the 1314 North Broad Street facility. Although its capacity was only 1,500, it usually drew a near-capacity crowd. The matches there were usually made to develop local Philadelphia and Trenton boxers, who would then appear at major arenas such as **Madison Square Garden**. Among the boxers who appeared there were **George Benton**, Benny Briscoe, Gypsy Joe Harris, and Stanley "Kitten" Hayward. The arena, which featured a balcony that nearly overhung the **ring** and placed spectators quite close to the action, was acclaimed by *Ring* **magazine** as "the best place in the **United States** to watch a prizefight."

After a period of disuse, the facility was purchased in 1994 by a group headed by Vernoca L. Michael, who then became the first female black boxing promoter in Pennsylvania. **Bouts** continued to be held on a more infrequent basis, but the facility held its first world championship bout on 2 December 1997 when Philadelphian Charles Brewer successfully defended his **International Boxing Federation super middleweight** title against Joey DeGrandis.

The facility ran into trouble with the Internal Revenue Service in 2010 and was closed. In 2011, a real estate developer purchased the property with plans to convert it into a hotel and restaurant.

See also FELT FORUM; ST. NICHOLAS ARENA; SUNNYSIDE GARDEN.

BOLO PUNCH. The bolo punch is a type of underhanded low punch popularized initially by Filipino **middleweight** Ceferino García during the 1930s. García claimed that as a youth in the **Philippines** he would cut sugar cane with a bolo knife in a motion similar to that which he used for his "bolo punch." **Kid Gavilán** was known for his extensive use of this punch, and **"Sugar Ray" Leonard** occasionally used it as well.

See also COUNTERPUNCH; CROSS; HAYMAKER; HOOK; JAB; UPPERCUT.

BOUT. A boxing contest or match is more commonly known as a bout.

BOWE, RIDDICK LAMONT "BIG DADDY," "SUGAR MAN". B. 10 August 1968, Brooklyn, New York. Riddick Bowe was involved in more strange scenarios in the boxing **ring** than most fighters. His boxing career got off to a good start as he is one of the few boxers to win four New York **Golden Gloves** championships. He won the 1985 **light heavyweight sub-novice** title, the 1986 light heavyweight **open** title, and the 1987 and 1988 **super heavyweight** open class championships. He was also the 1987 Pan American super heavyweight **bronze medalist** and in the 1988 **Olympic Games** was defeated by **Lennox Lewis** in the super heavyweight final and was the **silver medalist**.

He became a professional boxer on 6 March 1989 with a two-round **technical knockout** over Lionel Butler. Bowe won his first 31 fights, 27 by **knockout**. Included among those 31 victims were former world's **heavyweight** champions Pinklon Thomas and Tony Tubbs and 1984 Olympic super heavyweight champion Tyrell Biggs. One of the other fights during that time was the first in several strange fights that Bowe participated in. On 29 October 1991, in a 12-round **bout** with Elijah Tillery for the **World Boxing Council** Continental Americas heavyweight title, toward the end of the first round, Bowe knocked Tillery down. After he arose, the round ended, but Tillery started verbally taunting Bowe (legal if not sportsmanlike). Bowe retaliated by illegally punching Tillery. Tillery retaliated by kicking Bowe, and Bowe continued punching him. Bowe's manager, Rock Newman, then grabbed Tillery, and Bowe knocked Tillery over the ropes. When the **referee** finally separated everyone, he ruled that Tillery was **disqualified** for kicking Bowe.

On 13 November 1992, Bowe fought another former Olympic champion, **Evander Holyfield**, who was then the world's heavyweight champion. Bowe won a unanimous 12-round decision and became the new world's champion in one of the year's most exciting bouts, which was named the "Fight of the Year" by *Ring* **magazine**. After successfully defending his title against another former heavyweight champion, Michael Dokes, via a first-round stoppage, Bowe knocked out Jesse Ferguson in 12 rounds in his second title defense.

On 6 November 1993, Bowe then fought a rematch with Holyfield but this time lost a 12-round **majority decision**. This fight was unusual in that during the seventh round of the fight, a fan who had been circling the outdoor arena in a powered paraglider lost control of his device and landed in the **ring**, with the lines from his machine caught in the overhead lights. As he tried to extricate himself, fight fans in the arena as well as the fighters' seconds began attacking him and knocked him unconscious. After a 21-minute delay, the bout between Holyfield and Bowe resumed.

In his next fight, on 13 August 1994, Bowe engaged in another one of his strange fights. In the fourth round of his bout with Buster Mathis Jr., the previously undefeated (14–0) Mathis, who had been holding his own, got hit with a few hard punches by Bowe and knelt down in order to clear his head. This action is interpreted as a **knockdown**, and Bowe should have gone to a neutral **corner** while the **referee** counted. Instead, he inexplicably hit Mathis while he was down. This should have resulted in a disqualification, but referee Arthur Mercante simply ruled the bout "**no contest**."

Bowe's next opponent was Larry Donald. In the prefight press conference, typically each fighter will brag about what he will do to his opponent in an effort to build fan interest in the fight. Bowe took this approach one step too far, and after verbally insulting Donald, he then threw two solid **bareknuckle** punches that landed on Donald's head. The subsequent fight the following day proved to be a dull 12-round bout won by Bowe. In Bowe's next fight, on 11 March 1995, he knocked out Herbie Hide in six rounds and won the **World Boxing Organization** world heavyweight title—the least prestigious of the four major sanctioning organizations. Bowe made a successful title defense against the previously undefeated (23–0) Jorge Luis González, knocking him out in six rounds. Bowe then fought a third fight with Holyfield and this time stopped him in the eighth round.

Bowe's next two fights were with Andrew Gołota, a Polish heavyweight who had been the **bronze medalist** in the heavyweight class in the 1988 Olympics and had accumulated a 28–0 record as a professional, with 25 knockouts. These two fights added to Bowe's legacy of weird ring happenings. The first bout took place on 11 July 1996 at **Madison Square Garden**. Bowe underestimated Gołota's ability and was knocked down in the second round. Bowe then knocked Gołota down in the fourth round, and Gołota knocked Bowe down in the fifth. Gołota, though, had thrown several low blows. In the seventh round, Gołota received his third warning for low blows and was told that he would be disqualified if it repeated the infraction. Gołota landed several legal blows and appeared to have staggered Bowe but then threw a blatantly low blow that floored Bowe. Gołota was then disqualified by **referee** Wayne Kelly, and a riot broke out at the Garden as Bowe's supporters entered the ring to fight with Gołota and his handlers.

A Bowe–Gołota rematch five months later in **Atlantic City** had similar results, minus the postbout riot. Gołota, although leading on the scorecards with knockdowns of Bowe in the second and fifth rounds, had a point deducted in the second round for an intentional headbutt, another one for a low blow in the fourth round, and finally lost on a disqualification in the ninth round after another low blow.

Bowe retired after the Gołota bouts but ran into trouble of another sort. He first attempted to join the U.S. Marine Corps but quit after three days of basic training at Parris Island, South Carolina. He then was accused of beating his sister and later was accused of assault and battery on his wife. He then kidnapped his wife and children and eventually served 17 months in federal prison. He attempted a comeback in 2004 and fought three times, in 2004, 2005, and 2008, but even though he won all three bouts, he no longer had the abilities he once had and, as of 2012, has not fought since.

Bowe is six foot five inches tall and has an 81-inch **reach**. He fought at weights ranging from 218 to 280 pounds as a heavyweight. In 45 professional bouts, from 1989 to 2008, he won 43 (33 by knockout), lost one by decision, had one no contest bout, and fought a total of 195 rounds.

BOXING BOOTHS. From the 18th century up to the mid-20th century, fairs in **England** often featured boxing booths in which spectators would pay a small admission fee to enter a tent where a boxer would challenge all comers to brief boxing **bouts**. Boxers employed by boxing booths would often have several bouts in a day, and it was not uncommon for some of the more successful ones to have 500 or more such fights in their lifetimes. Results of booth boxing are unrecorded. Quite a few boxers who later became world champions in the regular prize **ring** got their start in booths, among them **Jimmy Wilde**, Jem Mace, Tommy Farr, and Randy Turpin.

BOXING DAY. Boxing Day is celebrated in **Great Britain** and in other British Commonwealth nations on December 26. Although it has nothing to do with the sport of boxing, because it is a bank holiday many sporting events are traditionally held on that day—boxing matches as well.

The term probable arises from the British custom of presenting servants with a box of Christmas gifts. It recent years, it has become a day for shopping comparable to the day after Thanksgiving in the United States.

BOXING FILMS. Shortly after the invention of motion pictures, boxing became one of the most popular subjects for films. During the early 20th century, the only way that most people could see championship boxers was on film. Consequently, unlike most other sporting activities of that era, many early boxing matches have been captured on film. Although boxing was illegal in many states, showing films of actual boxing matches was not.

After **Jack Johnson** won the **heavyweight** championship, his arrogant behavior antagonized people and race riots occurred, causing the **United States** government in 1912 to outlaw transporting boxing films across state lines for purposes of public exhibition—a law that was not repealed until 1940.

Jim Jacobs, one of heavyweight champion **Mike Tyson's** early managers, became a collector of boxing films, and his library at the time of his death in 1987 totaled more than 20,000 films.

BRADDOCK, JAMES WALTER "JIM," "JAMES J." "CINDERELLA MAN". B. 7 June 1905, New York, New York. D. 29 November 1974, North Bergen, New Jersey. Jim Braddock was one of the least-likely **heavyweight** champions. His rags-to-riches story earned him the nickname "Cinderella Man" from sportswriter Damon Runyon after he reappeared as a heavyweight title contender in 1935.

Born in the Hell's Kitchen area of Manhattan's west side, Braddock moved with his family to North Bergen, New Jersey, as a youth. He began boxing as an **amateur** at the age of 16. Although Braddock's given name was James Walter, he began boxing as James J. Braddock in emulation of earlier heavyweight champions **James J. Corbett** and **James J. Jeffries**. Braddock's first recorded professional fight was on 13 April 1926 in Union, New Jersey. It was a four-**round no-decision bout** that was scored a **draw** by the newspapers. He then won his next 11 bouts by **knockout**, fighting in various cities in New Jersey. Of his next 14 bouts, Braddock won 12 and had two draws. After his first 26 bouts, his record on 27 May 1927 stood at 23–0–3. Over the next 11 years, he would only win 28 while losing 26. One of those victories, however, brought him the world's heavyweight championship.

Victories over former **light heavyweight** champion Jimmy Slattery and Gerald "Tuffy" Griffiths in 1928 and 1929 gained Braddock a shot at Tommy Loughran's world's light heavyweight title on 18 July 1929 at Yankee Stadium. Braddock could not capitalize on this opportunity, and Loughran won a 15-round decision. Braddock's career then took a tailspin, and he lost 19 of his next 29 bouts from 1929 to 1933. Braddock had sensitive hands, and he broke them several times during his fights. During this time, work was scarce, both in the **ring** and out, and in order to support his family he worked on the docks as a longshoreman but eventually got to the point where he was accepting public relief.

In 1934, after not having been able to get a match for nearly nine months, he was matched with an up-and-coming boxer, John "Corn" Griffin, merely as a "name" opponent. Braddock surprised Griffin and the boxing world by stopping him in the third round. Braddock's next match, five months later, was with another up-and-coming fighter, John Henry Lewis, who would later become world's light heavyweight champion. Braddock knocked Lewis down in the fifth round and won a 10-round decision. In March 1935, Braddock won a 15-round decision over Art Lasky, another top contender.

By virtue of these three victories, Braddock was selected as the next opponent for heavyweight champion Max Baer, who saw Braddock as an "easy" opponent. Baer hardly trained for the bout, while Braddock saw this as a great opportunity and trained hard but was still a 10–1 underdog on the day of the fight. In one of boxing's biggest upsets, Braddock won a **unanimous decision** on 13 June 1935 and became world's heavyweight champion.

Braddock was scheduled to defend against former heavyweight champion **Max Schmeling** in 1936, but the fight did not place due to an alleged hand injury to Braddock. Instead, Braddock's manager signed a contract for Braddock to fight **Joe Louis**, a black fighter who was one of the top contenders but who had recently lost to Schmeling. The terms of the contract provided for Braddock to receive 10 percent of Louis' ring earnings over the next 10 years regardless of who won the Braddock–Louis match.

On 22 June 1937, Braddock and Louis met in the ring in Comiskey Park in Chicago. Braddock knocked Louis down in the first round, but Louis got up and was able to knock out Braddock in the eighth round to win the heavyweight title.

Braddock only fought one more bout in his career, a 10-round **split decision** victory over Welshman Tommy Farr, the British Empire heavyweight champion, at **Madison Square Garden** on 21 January 1938. He retired after that bout.

During World War II, Braddock enlisted in the U.S. Army and became a first lieutenant. After the war, he invested well and had several successful businesses. He also repaid the government the money they paid him while he and his family were on relief and spent much of the remainder of his life devoting his efforts to helping various relief organizations.

Braddock was six foot two inches tall and had a 75-inch **reach**. He fought at weights ranging from 163 to 199 pounds as a light heavyweight and heavyweight. In 76 professional bouts, from 1926 to 1938, he won 46 (26 by knockout), lost 24 (two by knockout), had four draws, and fought a total of 509 rounds. He also had 10 no-decision bouts, in which he received the newspaper decision in five, lost two, and drew three times and fought 88 rounds in those bouts.

BRAMBLE, LIVINGSTONE (aka RAS-I-ALUJAH BRAMBLE). B. 3 September 1960, St. Kitts and Nevis. Possibly the only world-class boxer to own a pet snake, Livingstone Bramble often played up his **Caribbean** island background and did not discourage rumors of his practicing witchcraft before his **bouts**.

He began his **professional boxing** career on 16 October 1980 in New Jersey with a first-**round knockout** of Jesús Serrano. After a four-round **draw** in his next bout, he won his next six bouts before losing an eight-round **majority draw** to the undefeated Anthony Fletcher. Bramble then won 13 consecutive bouts and was matched with **Ray Mancini** for the **World Boxing Association (WBA) lightweight** title on 1 June 1984 in Buffalo, New York. Coming into the bout, Mancini had a record of 29–1 and Bramble was at 20–1–1, with all of Bramble's bouts occurring in New Jersey.

In an upset, Bramble stopped Mancini in the 14th round and became the WBA world lightweight champion. After winning a **nontitle bout**, Bramble met Mancini in a rematch held on 16 February 1985 in Reno, Nevada. Again Bramble prevailed, this time on a 15-round **unanimous decision**. Bramble successfully defended his title exactly one year later also in Reno with a 13th-round **stoppage** of Tyrone Crawley.

On 26 September 1986, Bramble met Edwin Rosario in an outdoor match in Miami Beach. Rosario, who had 24 knockouts among his 28 victories and had been previously been the **World Boxing Council** world lightweight champion, caught Bramble with a knockout punch that ended the fight at 2:28 of the second round.

Bramble continued fighting for another 17 years, but although he won the North American Boxing Federation **light welterweight** title and defended it once successfully, he never again challenged for a major title. During this period, he fought quite a few competent fighters, such as Roger Mayweather, **Kosta Tszyu**, and James "Buddy" McGirt, but he was always on the losing end of the bout. His record prior to the Rosario fight was 24–1–1, and his record afterward was 16–25–2. During the 1990s, he changed his name to Ras-I-Alujah Bramble, but the name change had little effect on the outcome of his bouts.

He never officially announced his retirement from the **ring**, but his last bout was on 27 June 2003. He is the only world champion boxer to be born in the Caribbean island nation of St. Kitts and Nevis. He had a small part in the *Rocky* film and runs a fitness studio with his son, Alujah, in Saugerties, New York, a small town 45 miles south of Albany on the Hudson River.

Bramble is five foot eight inches tall and has a 74-inch **reach**. He fought at weights ranging from 129 to 156 pounds as a lightweight and light welterweight. In 69 professional bouts, from 1980 to 2003, he won 40 (25 by knockout), lost 26 (five by knockout), had three draws, and fought a total of 498 rounds.

BRAMBLE, RAS-I-ALUJAH. *See* BRAMBLE, LIVINGSTONE (aka RAS-I-ALUJAH BRAMBLE).

BRAZIL. In a country where soccer is the number one sport by far and motor sports, tennis, and basketball are quite a bit behind in popularity, boxing is quite far down the list, although there have been several outstanding Brazilian boxers.

In **amateur boxing**, Brazil first competed in the 1948 **Olympic Games** and has entered each of the Olympic boxing tournaments since, with the exception of the 1984 games—a total of 16 tournaments. Although they have won a total of 108 Olympic medals in all sports, they have only won four in boxing. Servilio de Oliveira won their first in 1968—a **bronze medal** in the **flyweight** class, losing his semifinal **bout** to the eventual winner, Ricardo Delgado. This was Brazil's only Olympic boxing medal until 2012, when they won three more. Brothers Esquiva and Yamaguchi Florentino both won medals that year—Esquiva a **silver medal** in the **middleweight** class and Yamaguchi a bronze medal in the **light heavyweight** class. Adriana Araújo also won a bronze medal in the **women's light welterweight** class in 2012. Brazil will be the host country for the 2016 Olympic Games and most likely will win a few more Olympic boxing medals at the games in Rio de Janeiro.

Brazil has also had several outstanding professional boxers, with world **bantamweight** and **featherweight** champion **Éder Jofre** being their best boxer by far. Acelino Freitas, Miguel de Oliveira, and Valdemir Pereira are Brazil's other professional world champions. Among other outstanding Brazilian boxers are Waldemar Adão, George Arias, Giovanni Andrade, Everaldo Costa Azevedo, Francisco de Jesús, Paulo de Jesús, Vicente dos Santos, João Henrique, Luis Faustino Pires, Adilson Rodrigues, and Patrick Teixeira.

BRENNER, THEODORE "TEDDY". B. 25 April 1917, Brooklyn, New York. D. 7 January 2000, New York, New York. Teddy Brenner was the matchmaker for boxing in New York for more than 30 years. His interest in boxing began as a teenager, and in 1934 he was a **cornerman** for a friend in the New York **Golden Gloves** tournament. He also worked as a shirt salesman.

After returning from serving in the U.S. Navy during World War II, he did some work arranging matches for boxing manager Irving Cohen at a small arena in New Brunswick, New Jersey. In 1947, he was hired as the assistant matchmaker at **Madison Square Garden**. He also worked at several other smaller New York area boxing venues, such as Laurel Gardens, Long Beach Stadium, Eastern Parkway Arena, Coney Island Velodrome, and **St. Nicholas Arena**. He later became the chief matchmaker at the Garden and remained there until 1973. He was promoted to president of Madison Square Garden Boxing Inc. but was fired from that position in 1978 for refusing to do business with promoter **Don King**. Brenner was later hired as an advisor by **Bob Arum**.

His most famous match was the 8 March 1971 fight between the two undefeated **heavyweight** champions **Joe Frazier** and **Muhammad Ali**. In 1971, Brenner received the James J. Walker Memorial Award "for long and meritorious service in boxing" from the Boxing Writers Association of New York.

He was inducted into the **International Boxing Hall of Fame** in 1993.

BRESLIN, WILLIAM J.. *See* BRITTON, JACK "BOXING MARVEL" (né WILLIAM J. BRESLIN).

BRITISH BOXING BOARD OF CONTROL (BBBofC). The British Boxing Board of Control is an organization that is sorely lacking in the **United States**—a national governing body that administers and regulates boxing in the country. The BBBofC was established in 1929 from its predecessor, the **National Sporting Club**. One of the unique aspects of BBBofC matches is that **judges** are not used, and the **referee** is the sole determinant of the **bout's** winner, which he does by raising the winner's hand immediately after the conclusion of the bout.

The organization is based in Cardiff, **Wales**, and, among its duties, sanctions matches in each of the weight classes for the British championship. Winners receive the Lonsdale Belt. Champions who successfully defend their belt on three occasions against a British challenger earn the right to keep the belt.

BRITTON, JACK "BOXING MARVEL" (né WILLIAM J. BRESLIN). B. 14 October 1885, Clinton, New York. D. 27 March 1962, Miami, Florida. Jack Britton is one of a very few boxers with more than 300 recorded professional **bouts** (although he claimed to have more than 400). During his career, he also fought the same opponent, Ted "Kid" Lewis, 20 times—another rare feat.

He began his **professional boxing** career on 11 November 1904 with a six-**round decision** victory over Jack Nolan in Milwaukee, Wisconsin. His next two recorded bouts were losses. Beginning in 1906 with his fourth recorded bout, the vast majority of his fights over the next three years occurred in the eastern part of the **United States** in either New York, Philadelphia, or Delaware and were **no-decision** bouts that went the six-round distance. In December 1909, he moved to Georgia, where 15-round bouts that reached a decision were permitted. He fought primarily in the South in 1909 through 1911.

On 30 January 1911, he fought the undefeated (56–0–4) Packey McFarland to a 10-round **draw** in Memphis, Tennessee. Britton then spent most of the next two years fighting in the San Francisco area. He came back east in July 1912, fighting in New York's **St. Nicholas Arena** and **Madison Square Garden** (the second version of the Garden, then still located in Madison Square). In March 1913, he lost the **newspaper decision** in a rematch to McFarland in New York.

On 26 March 1915, Britton faced the English fighter born Gershon Mendelhoff but known in the **ring** as Ted "Kid" Lewis uptown in New York at the 135th Street Athletic Club in the first of boxing's longest series of bouts between two foes. The bout, a no-decision affair, found Britton on the winning end of most newspapers' reporters.

On 22 June 1915, Britton defeated Mike Glover on a 12-round decision in Boston and won recognition as the world's **welterweight** champion. In Britton's next fight, on 31 August 1915, he had a rematch with Lewis in Boston, and as Lewis won the 12-round decision, he became world's welterweight champion. The two fought again one month later in Boston, and Lewis successfully defended his title. The next meeting between the two occurred in January 1916 in Buffalo and was a no-decision bout that most newspapers saw as a draw. The two fought again in February in Brooklyn and on 24 April 1916 in New Orleans. The latter fight went 20 rounds to a decision, and Britton officially regained the welterweight title.

Britton fought five more fights in 1916 before meeting Lewis twice more in Boston in October and November. He received the decision in the first fight, but the second was called a draw. The two combatants then did not see each other for the next four months but kept busy fighting other boxers—Britton had nine fights and Lewis seven. On 26 March 1917, they met in Cincinnati and before the year ended had fought each other four more times—in Toronto in May and St. Louis, New York, and Dayton, Ohio, in June, with the latter fight and title going to Lewis via a 20-round decision.

The pair met four more times in 1918, twice more in 1919, and on 7 February 1921 in Madison Square Garden under the new Walker Law, which permitted bouts to a decision. Britton won the bout, the 20th in their series. Britton regained the title in their 17 March 1919 bout in Canton, Ohio, by knocking out Lewis in the ninth round—the only one of their 20 bouts not to go the scheduled distance.

Britton defeated world **lightweight** champion **Benny Leonard**, who was attempting to win Britton's welterweight championship, in a controversial bout on 26 June 1922 in the Bronx, New York, when Leonard **fouled** Britton in the 13th round and was disqualified. Four months later, on 1 November at **Madison Square Garden**, Britton lost his welterweight championship to **Mickey Walker** on a 15-round **unanimous decision**.

Britton continued to fight all over the **United States** before finally retiring following his 29 July 1930 loss to Rudy Marshall in Stamford, Connecticut. After retiring from the ring, Britton worked as a boxing instructor in New York.

Britton was five foot eight inches tall and had a 70-inch **reach**. He fought at weights ranging from 133 to 153 pounds, primarily as a welterweight. In 346 professional bouts, from 1904 to 1930, he had 159 that went to a decision. Of these he won 104 (30 by **knockout**), lost 28 (one by knockout), and had 20 draws. He fought a total of 1,469 rounds in those bouts. He also fought 187 no-decision bouts, in which he received the newspaper decision in 135 bouts, lost 27, and drew 25. He fought 1,649 rounds in those bouts. He was inducted as a member of the inaugural class of the **International Boxing Hall of Fame** in 1990.

BRONZE MEDAL. In international amateur boxing competitions, such as the **Olympic Games**, the third-place boxer in the tournament is awarded a bronze medal. Through the 1948 games, the two losers in the semifinal round would box each other, and the winner of that match would receive the bronze medal. In Olympic Games competition since 1952, duplicate medals are awarded to the two semifinal losers, and an additional **bout** is not held.

BRUSSO, NOAH. *See* BURNS, TOMMY "LITTLE GIANT OF HAN-OVER" (né NOAH BRUSSO).

BULGARIA. Boxing is not a major sport in Bulgaria, but as with many of the former Iron Curtain countries, they have produced excellent **amateur boxing** teams that competed in the **Olympic Games**. The Bulgarian Boxing Association administers the sport there.

Bulgaria first competed in Olympic boxing competition in 1952. Since then, they have had entrants in 15 Olympic Games—every one except 1984, when they boycotted the games. They have won 18 medals—15th best among all nations—and have won four **gold**, five **silver**, and nine **bronze**.

Their gold medalists were **light flyweights** Ismail Mustafov in 1988 and Daniel Bozhinov in 1996 and **flyweights** Georgi Kostadinov in 1972 and Petar Lesov in 1980. Mustafov and Bozhinov were also multiple medalists, as Mustafov also won the 1980 light flyweight bronze medal and Bozhinov also won the 1992 light flyweight silver medal.

Bulgaria has not had a lot of professional boxers, but a few who have done well include Borislav Abadjiev, Stiliyan Kostov, Martin Krastev, Alexey Ribchev, Konstantin Semerdjiev, Spas Spassov, and Asan Yuseinov.

BURNS, TOMMY "LITTLE GIANT OF HANOVER" (né NOAH BRUSSO). B. 17 June 1881, Normanby Township, Ontario, **Canada**. D. 10 May 1955, Vancouver, Canada. Tommy Burns holds the distinction of being the shortest (five foot seven inches tall) world's **heavyweight** champion and one of the lightest, weighing only 175 pounds when he won the title and 168 when he lost it. Burns was also the first heavyweight champion to defend his title all over the world, fighting in **Australia**, **England**, **Ireland**, **France**, and Canada as well as the **United States**.

Burns began boxing professionally in Detroit in 1902, with his first recorded fight a five-record **technical knockout** on 16 January over Fred Thornton. After winning his first 12 **bouts**, he lost a 10-**round decision** to Mike Schreck exactly one year later. Burns won his next five bouts and then defeated Jack Hammond via a three-round **knockout** in Sault Ste. Marie, Michigan, to win the Michigan State **middleweight** title. Undefeated in his next 12 bouts, although four of them were scored as draws, Burns met **Philadelphia Jack O'Brien** on 7 October 1904 and lost a six-round decision to the man who had once been recognized as the world's middleweight champion.

Burns's next bout of significance was on 7 March 1905 in Tacoma, Washington, where he fought a 20-round **draw** with Jack "Twin" Sullivan for the world's middleweight title. Two months following that bout, Burns won a 20-round decision in Tacoma over Dave Barry in a bout billed for the Pacific Coast middleweight title. Barry, 22 years later, would figure significantly in a heavyweight title bout as the **referee** who gave **Gene Tunney** a "long count" in his championship bout with **Jack Dempsey**. Burns then fought a 10-round draw with Hugh Kelly for Kelly's claim to the middleweight title.

After fighting rematches with Kelly (a 20-round draw), Barry (20-round technical knockout), and Sullivan (20-round loss), Burns met **Marvin Hart** for Hart's world heavyweight championship. Weighing only 175 pounds to Hart's 195 pounds, Burns was awarded the decision after 20 rounds in Los Angeles.

Less than two months later, Burns won two one-round knockouts in the same day in Los Angeles in bouts billed for Burns's world heavyweight title, although some boxing historians treat these two bouts as **exhibitions**. Burns then took six months off to enjoy his title before coming back on 2 October 1906 to knock out Fireman Jim Flynn in 15 rounds. Burns next faced Philadelphia Jack O'Brien in a 20-round bout that was called a draw by the referee, former world's heavyweight champion **Jim Jeffries**. In a rematch six months later, Burns received the 20-round decision. Both O'Brien fights were held in Los Angeles.

After knocking out **Australian** Bill Squires in 2:09 of the opening round on 4 July 1907 in Colma, California, Burns traveled to London and began a world tour that saw him defend his title successfully seven times, all seven fights lasting less than the scheduled distance. He knocked out Gunner Moir and Jack Palmer in London; Jem Roche in 1:28 of the first round in Dublin, **Ireland**; Jewey Smith and Bill Squires in Paris, **France**; Squires again in Sydney, Australia; and Bill Lang in Melbourne, Australia.

Burns remained in Australia and fought the black fighter **Jack Johnson** on 26 December 1908—a day that, in the minds of some, will live in infamy. Johnson, at six feet tall and 192 pounds, easily dominated the fight over the five-foot-seven-inch, 168-pound Burns. The bout was stopped by police intervention in the 14th round as Burns was taking a beating from Johnson. Johnson's arrogance and lifestyle made him one of the most hated figures over the next seven years and occasioned boxing promoters to search for a Caucasian fighter as a "**white hope**" to return the heavyweight title to the white race.

After the Johnson fight, Burns only fought a few more times, but in his next bout, 16 months later, he defeated Bill Lang in Sydney and won the British Empire and Australian heavyweight championships on a 20-round decision. Burns's next recorded fight was two years later when he won the Canadian heavyweight title on a six-round technical knockout over Bill Rickard. Burns fought one bout each in 1913, 1914, and 1918 before fighting his last professional fight on 16 July 1920, when he retired in the seventh round of his bout with Joe Beckett for the British Empire heavyweight title in London.

In retirement, Burns was involved in several ventures and lived in several countries. He was a boxing promoter and owned a clothing store in Calgary, **Canada**. He promoted boxing in New Orleans, Louisiana, and owned a pub in Newcastle-upon-Tyne, **England**. He is also reported as running a speakeasy in New York City and, after losing his fortune in the Wall Street crash of 1929, working as an insurance salesman and security guard. Toward the end of his life he was ordained as a minister in 1948 and worked as an evangelist preacher in Coalinga, California. He died of a heart attack while visiting a friend in Vancouver, Canada, and is buried in nearby Burnaby.

Burns was five foot seven inches tall and had a 73-inch **reach**. He fought at weights ranging from 156 to 190 pounds, primarily as a heavyweight. In 60 professional bouts, from 1902 to 1920, he won 46 (34 by knockout), lost five (one by knockout), had eight draws, and had one no-decision bout that was called a **draw** by **newspaper decision**. He fought a total of 497 rounds. He was inducted into the **International Boxing Hall of Fame** in 1996.

BUTTERBEAN "KING OF THE FOUR ROUNDERS" (né ERIC SCOTT ESCH). B. 3 August 1966, Bay City, Michigan. Eric Esch, better known simply as "Butterbean," has a unique place in boxing history. The 300-pound man began boxing in "**tough man**" contests in the 1990s in Texas and made his **professional boxing** debut on 15 October 1994 in Birmingham, Alabama, winning a four-**round decision**. Esch had a powerful **knockout** punch but little stamina and only boxed four-round **bouts**, billing himself as "the king of the four rounders." He won his first 15 bouts, nine by knockout or **technical knockout**, before appearing at New York's **Madison Square Garden** on 15 December 1995, where he was stopped in two rounds by Mitchell Rose, a boxer who had won only one of his nine previous fights. Butterbean then went undefeated in his next 51 bouts (all but one scheduled for four rounds), with three draws and 39 knockouts, and entered the **ring** on

19 August 2001 with a record of 63–1–3. He lost a **majority decision** to Billy Zumbrun on that night. Two fights later, Butterbean fought his first bout scheduled for 10 rounds.

He was matched with former world's **heavyweight** champion **Larry Holmes** on 27 July 2002 at the Scope in Norfolk, Virginia. The 52-year-old Holmes, who weighed 45 pounds more than when he won the heavyweight title 24 years previously, was still outweighed by 80 pounds (334 to 254) and fought a very defensive fight. He still won most rounds on the **judges'** scorecards though, and won a **unanimous decision**, although Butterbean knocked him down in the 10th round.

After the Holmes fight, Butterbean continued his **ring** career, although with several more losses than in his first few years. His popularity was such that he fought bouts in Beijing, China, and **Australia** in 2005. On 9 March 2007, Butterbean fought and won a four-round bout in Worcester, Massachusetts, and his son, Brandon (aka Babybean), also appeared in a bout on the same **card** but was knocked out in the first round. As of 2012, this was Brandon's only professional boxing match.

Butterbean branched out into other combat sports while he continued to box and has participated in **kickboxing** and **mixed martial arts**. He has also taken part in some professional wrestling exhibitions. Although he announced his retirement in 2009, he still fought one bout in 2012. In June 2013, he fought one bout in Newcastle, Australia, but retired after two rounds due to a shoulder injury

Butterbean is five foot 11 inches tall and has a 78-inch **reach**. As one of the heaviest fighters in the heavyweight class, his lightest recorded weight was 280 (in 1995), and his heaviest was 417 (in 2007). His lightest opponent was 193, and his heaviest 340. In 90 professional bouts, from 1994 to 2012, he won 77 (58 by knockout), lost nine (one by knockout), had four draws, and fought a total of 260 rounds. Only three of his 90 bouts were scheduled for more than four rounds..

BYE. A bye occurs when the number of boxers in a tournament draw will not allow each boxer to fight a match in every **round**, and a boxer receives a free pass into the next tournament round. In a tournament in which 48 boxers are entered, 32 of them will be matched in the first round, with the winners advancing to meet the remaining 16 contestants, who receive a bye into the second round.

C

CALZAGHE, JOSEPH WILLIAM "JOE," "THE PRIDE OF WALES," "THE ITALIAN DRAGON". B. 23 March 1972, Hammersmith, London, **England**. Joe Calzaghe is one of a small number of boxing **world champions** to retire without ever losing a single **professional bout**. He was raised in Newbridge, **Wales**, and began boxing at an early age, eventually winning seven British **amateur** championships. He won his last **Amateur Boxing** Association of England title in 1993 (the **middleweight** championship) and then became a professional boxer. His first professional fight was 1 October 1993 in Cardiff, Wales, when he stopped Paul Hanlon in the first **round**.

After winning his first 13 bouts (12 by **knockout**), the **southpaw** Calzaghe was matched with Stephen Wilson for the **vacant** British **super middleweight** title on 28 October 1995 at Royal Albert Hall in London. Calzaghe stopped Wilson in the eighth round of their scheduled 12-round bout. On 11 October 1997, Calzaghe won the **World Boxing Organization** super middleweight championship on a **unanimous decision** in Sheffield, England. He held that title until 26 September 2008, when he vacated it after having successfully defended it 21 times—one of the longest championship reigns in boxing history. All of those 21 bouts, save one in Copenhagen, Denmark, in 2001, were held in the United Kingdom, either in Wales or England.

On 4 March 2006, Calzaghe also won the **International Boxing Federation (IBF)** super middleweight title by defeating Jeff Lacy on a unanimous decision, and on 3 November 2007, he won the **World Boxing Association** and **World Boxing Council** super middleweight titles by defeating Mikkel Kessler in Wales, although by then he had given up his IBF title.

In 2008, Calzaghe came to the **United States** for his first bout there. He defeated former middleweight champion **Bernard Hopkins** in a **nontitle bout** on 19 April in **Las Vegas** on a 12-round **split decision**, despite being **knocked down** in the first round. Calzaghe's final bout was in **Madison Square Garden** on 8 November 2008, when he defeated former **light heavy-**

weight champion **Roy Jones Jr.** on a unanimous decision in a 12-round nontitle bout in which Calzaghe was again knocked down in the opening round.

Calzaghe announced his retirement from the **ring** on 5 February 2009 and was only the 12th world champion to retire undefeated. He has since joined with his father, Enzo, as a boxing promoter.

Calzaghe is five foot 11 inches tall and has a 73-inch **reach**. His weight has been almost constant and ranged only from 166 to 174 pounds during his professional career as a super middleweight. In 46 professional bouts, from 1993 to 2008, Joe Calzaghe won all 46 (32 by knockout) and fought a total of 262 rounds.

CAMACHO MATÍAS, HÉCTOR LUIS "MACHO". B. 24 May 1962, Bayamon, **Puerto Rico**. D. 24 November 2012, Bayamon, Puerto Rico. Héctor "Macho" Camacho was one of the most colorful boxers of his generation and would approach the **ring** with his entourage shouting, "What time is it? It's Macho time." He often entered the ring wearing outlandish costumes, and in his nearly 30 years of boxing, he became one of the few boxers in ring history to compete while his son was also an active boxer.

Born in Puerto Rico but raised in New York City, Héctor Camacho Sr. began boxing as an **amateur** in the New York **Golden Gloves**. He won the 1978 **flyweight sub-novice** championship and the 1979 and 1980 **bantam-weight open** titles. He was also the 1979 intercity bantamweight champion and the 1980 intercity **featherweight** champion. He claimed an amateur record of 96–4.

His first **professional bout** was on 12 September 1980 in New York, and he won a four-round **decision**. After winning his first 21 bouts, mostly in the New York area (although he did fight one bout in Anchorage, Alaska), he defeated Rafael "Bazooka" Limón in five rounds and won the **World Boxing Council (WBC) super featherweight** title on 7 August 1983 in San Juan, Puerto Rico. After only one defense of that title (Rafael Solís, 18 November 1983, KO round 5), he moved up in weight and won the WBC **lightweight** title on a 12-round decision over José Luis Ramírez on 10 August 1985.

He defended that title successfully twice, winning decisions over Edwin Rosario and Cornelius Boza-Edwards. He again moved up in class and on 6 March 1989 won the **World Boxing Organization light welterweight** title with a **split decision** victory over **Ray Mancini**. In 1990, he successfully defended that title twice with victories over **Vinny Pazienza** and Tony Baltazar before losing it on a split decision to Greg Haugen on 23 February 1991 in **Las Vegas**.

Camacho quickly regained it three months later by defeating Haugen on a split decision. On 12 September 1992, Camacho suffered his second loss, a 12-round decision to WBC light welterweight champion **Julio César**

Chávez. After winning his next three fights, Camacho challenged **Félix Trinidad** for the **International Boxing Federation welterweight** title but lost a 12-round **unanimous decision** on 29 January 1994. Camacho then won his next four bouts in 1994.

On 14 January 1995, Camacho won his fourth title with a victory over Todd Foster for the less-prestigious **International Boxing Council (IBC) welterweight** title, stopping Foster in five rounds. After winning 10 of his next 11 bouts, with a **draw** with Sal Lopez the only nonwinning bout, Camacho fought former multiple champion **Roberto Durán** for the **vacant** IBC **middleweight** title. Camacho won a 12-round unanimous decision and added his fifth title to his collection, albeit another minor one.

The Macho Man then took on another of boxing's legends, **"Sugar Ray" Leonard**, who had come out of retirement for the fifth time and had not boxed for six years. Camacho easily won the one-sided bout by stopping the 40-year-old Leonard in the fifth round and causing Leonard to finally retire permanently.

Camacho then fought a much younger fighter who would become one of the greatest of his generation, the 24-year-old undefeated (25–0) **Óscar De La Hoya**, WBC welterweight champion. De La Hoya won nearly every round on all three scorecards and knocked Camacho down in the fifth round en route to a unanimous decision.

The 36-year-old Camacho continued fighting and on 11 August 1998 won yet another minor title, the vacant IBC **light middleweight** title on a 12-round unanimous decision over Tony Menefee. Three years later, Camacho became the first fighter to win titles in seven different weight classes (although four of them were from minor sanctioning bodies) as he defeated the 50-year-old Roberto Durán for the **National Boxing Association super middleweight** title.

In 2005, Camacho was arrested for burglary and two years later was sentenced to seven years in prison, but a lenient judge suspended all but one year of the sentence and then gave Camacho probation. Camacho continued fighting until 2010, although at the time of his death he had plans for another bout in 2013.

In 2011, Camacho was shot at but the assailants missed. On 20 November 2012, while seated in a parked car, he was shot at again, and this time they did not miss. After several days in critical condition on life support systems, his family gave the hospital permission to remove them, and Camacho died on 24 November 2012.

Camacho's son, Héctor "Machito" Camacho Jr., born in 1978 when Héctor Sr. was just 16 years of age, began a professional boxing career before Héctor Sr. was finished with his. Machito had his first fight on 1 October 1996 in Fort Lauderdale, Florida, on the same **card** as his father, with both father and son winning their bouts. Through 2012, Machito had a record of 54–5–1 and had won several minor titles in divisions ranging from **light welterweight** to middleweight.

Camacho was five foot six inches tall and had a 69-inch **reach**. He fought at weights ranging from 127 to 161 pounds, from super featherweight through middleweight. In 88 professional bouts, from 1980 to 2010, he won 79 (38 by knockout), lost six (none by knockout), had three draws, and fought a total of 673 rounds.

CANADA. Boxing is not a major sport in Canada, although through the years the country has produced several **amateur** and **professional** champions. In amateur boxing, Canadian boxers first competed in the 1920 **Olympic Games** and have entered 21 Olympic boxing tournaments—every one except 1980, when they boycotted the games. They have done well with 17 medals—three **gold medals**, seven **silver medals**, and seven **bronze medals**. Bert Schneider won their first Olympic boxing gold medal in the **welterweight** class in 1920. Horace "Lefty" Gwynne, a prospective jockey, won their second in the **bantamweight** class in 1932. Future professional world's **heavyweight** champion British-born **Lennox Lewis** won their third in 1988 in the **super heavyweight** class.

Among the best Canadian professional boxers have been champions Trevor Berbick, Lou Brouillard, **Tommy Burns**, Jackie Callura, Johnny Coulon, Jack Delaney, **George Dixon**, brothers Dave and Matthew Hilton, Donny Lalonde, Eric Lucas, Steve Molitor, and Jean Pascal. Irish-born **Jimmy McLarnin**, welterweight champion, was raised in Canada, as was Italian-born **Arturo Gatti**. Haitian-born Joachim Alcine and Jamaican-born Otis Grant are other champions who were raised in Canada. Other top Canadian boxers include Albert "Frenchy" Belanger, **George Chuvalo**, Robert Cleroux, Willie DeWit, Yvon Durelle, Fernando Gagnon, Larry Gains, Les Gillis. Clyde Gray, Wilfie Greaves, Johnny Greco, Gaetan Hart, Ryan Henney, Shawn O'Sullivan, Donato Paduano, Donovan "Razor" Ruddock, Armand Savoie, and Gary Summerhays. **Mysterious Billy Smith** and **Sam Langford** were born in Canada but spent most of their lives in the **United States**, and promoter **Aileen Eaton** was also a Canadian who was raised in the United States.

Several important **bouts** in boxing history took place in Canada, including **Muhammad Ali**'s 29 March 1966 heavyweight title defense against George Chuvalo in Toronto; **Archie Moore's light heavyweight** title defense against Yvon Durelle on 10 December 1958 in Montreal, when both Moore and Durelle were each knocked down four times in one of boxing's greatest bouts; and the 20 June 1980 bout between **Roberto Durán** and **"Sugar Ray" Leonard** in which Durán outpointed Leonard to win the world's **welterweight** title.

See also McLAGLEN, VICTOR ANDREW DE BIER EVERLEIGH "SHARKEY".

CANVAS. The floor of the **ring** is made of canvas material. When a boxer is **knocked down**, he is said to "hit the canvas." The phrase "canvasback" is sometimes used in a derogatory fashion to describe a boxer who often gets **knocked out**.

CANZONERI, TONY. B. 6 November 1908, Slidell, Louisiana. D. 9 December 1959, Staten Island, New York. Tony Canzoneri was one of boxing's first three-division world champions and one of very few fighters prior to 1960 to fight championship **bouts** at four different weights.

He was born in Louisiana but raised in Staten Island, New York. He began boxing **professionally** at the age of 16 on 24 July 1925. After going undefeated in his first 30 bouts, with three **draws**, he suffered his first loss to Davey Abad by **decision**. After seven more bouts without a loss, Canzoneri challenged Charles "Bud" Taylor for the **National Boxing Association (NBA)** world's **bantamweight** title in Chicago on 26 March 1927. The boxers went 10 rounds to a draw decision, and three months later in a rematch, also in Chicago, Taylor won a close but **unanimous decision**.

Canzoneri won his first world's championship on 24 October 1927 at **Madison Square Garden** when he decisioned Johnny Dundee in 15 rounds to win the New York State version of the **featherweight** title. He then also won the NBA featherweight title on a **split decision** over Benny Bass on 10 February 1928. Less than eight months later, Canzoneri lost his titles to Frenchman Andre Routis in a close 15-round decision at Madison Square Garden. Canzoneri won a rematch in 1929 in a **nontitle bout**.

Canzoneri then moved up in weight class and challenged world **lightweight** champion Sammy Mandell on 2 August 1929 in Chicago. Mandell retained his title on a close 10-round split decision.

Canzoneri won his next two world titles, the lightweight and **junior welterweight**, on 24 April 1931 when he knocked out Englishman Jack "Kid" Berg in Chicago in three rounds. In 1931, he successfully defended the junior welterweight title against Cecil Payne, both titles in a rematch with Berg, the junior welterweight title against Philly Griffin, and the lightweight title against **Kid Chocolate**.

On 18 January 1932, Canzoneri lost his junior welterweight title to Johnny Jadick on a 10-round unanimous decision in Philadelphia but successfully defended the lightweight title against Billy Petrolle. After Jadick lost the junior welterweight title to Battling Shaw, Canzoneri regained it by defeating Shaw in New Orleans on 21 May 1933.

One month later, on 23 June 1933, **Barney Ross** defeated Canzoneri in Chicago on a close 10-round **majority decision** and won both titles from Tony. Ross retained both titles in a rematch on 12 September 1933 on a 15-round split decision at the Polo Grounds in New York.

After Ross vacated the title to move up to the **welterweight** class, Canzoneri and Lou Ambers fought for the **vacant** title, which Tony won on a unanimous 15-round decision on 10 May 1935 in Madison Square Garden. He defended it successfully once against Al Roth before losing a rematch to Ambers on 3 September 1936. In a **rubber match** with Ambers eight months later, Canzoneri again failed to recapture the title.

Canzoneri retired from the **ring** after being **stopped** by Al "Bummy" Davis in three rounds on 1 November 1939—the only time in his boxing career that he failed to go the distance.

In retirement, Tony became a successful restauranteur in New York City until he died of a heart attack in 1959.

Canzoneri was five foot four inches tall and had a 65-inch **reach**. He fought at weights ranging from 117 to 144 pounds, primarily as a lightweight, junior welterweight, and welterweight. In 175 professional bouts, from 1925 to 1939, he won 137 (44 by **knockout**), lost 24 (one by knockout), had 10 draws, and fought four no-decision bouts, in which he won the **newspaper decision** in all four. He fought a total of 1,385 rounds. He was inducted as a member of the inaugural class of the **International Boxing Hall of Fame** in 1990.

CARBAJAL, MICHAEL "MANITAS DE PIEDRA". B. 17 September 1967, Phoenix, Arizona. Michael Carbajal was the first **junior flyweight** to gain popularity in the **United States**. His hard punching power earned him the nickname "Manitas de Piedra"—Little Hands of Stone—after his idol, **Roberto Durán**, who was the original Manos de Piedra. In his **amateur boxing** career, Carbajal won **light flyweight** championships at the 1986 National **Golden Gloves** and 1988 United States national amateur championships. In international competition, he was the 1987 Pan American Games **silver medalist** and the 1988 **Olympic Games** silver medalist.

Trained and managed by his brother Danny, Michael became a professional boxer on 24 February 1989 in **Atlantic City**, New Jersey, on a **card** that featured four other 1988 Olympians and won a **split-decision** four-**round bout**. After winning his first 14 bouts, with eight **knockouts**, he won the **International Boxing Federation (IBF)** light flyweight championship by stopping Muangchai Kittikasem in seven rounds on 29 July 1990 in Phoenix, Arizona. He successfully defended the title six times. He then fought the **World Boxing Council (WBC)** light flyweight champion Humberto González on 13 March 1993 in **Las Vegas** in the **main event** on the card—a rarity for boxing in the United States for a light flyweight bout to be the headline attraction. Although Carbajal was knocked down twice, he got up from the **canvas** and knocked out González in the seventh round. Carbajal was named the "Fighter of the Year" for 1993 by *Ring* **magazine**—the first fighter at his weight to be so honored.

Carbajal defended the dual titles twice and then fought González in a rematch in Inglewood, California, on 19 February 1994. For that match, which was **televised** on pay-per-view, Carbajal was paid one million dollars, and he became the first light flyweight to earn that much for one fight. González, though, won Carbajal's titles on a split decision.

After winning one more match against a lesser opponent, Carbajal won the **World Boxing Organization (WBO)** light flyweight title on 15 July 1994 in Phoenix by defeating WBO champion Josue Camacho on a 12-round **unanimous decision**. Four months later, Carbajal again challenged González for the WBC and IBF titles but lost a **majority decision** in Mexico City.

After seven **nontitle** victories with six knockouts, Carbajal rewon the IBF light flyweight title by defeating Melchor Cob Castro on a unanimous decision in Las Vegas on 16 March 1996. He made two successful defenses but then lost the title to Mauricio Pastrana on 18 January 1997 on a split decision. Carbajal fought twice more in 1997, winning and losing the **International Boxing Association** light flyweight title (a title not highly regarded). He retired but then made a brief comeback in 1999, winning all four of his comeback fights before permanently retiring.

In retirement, Michael Carbajal owns and operates the Ninth Street Gym in Phoenix. In 2007, he and his brother Danny had a falling out, with Michael claiming that Danny as manager stole two million dollars from him. Danny was sentenced to four years in prison for fraud and theft in 2008.

Carbajal is five foot five inches tall, relatively tall for his weight, and has a 63-inch **reach**. His weight has been quite constant and has only varied from 106 to 113 pounds, as he has boxed as a light flyweight and **flyweight**. In 53 professional bouts, from 1989 to 1999, he won 49 (33 by knockout), lost four (one by knockout), and fought a total of 367 rounds. He was inducted into the **International Boxing Hall of Fame** in 2006 along with his former adversary, Humberto González.

CARD. An evening's schedule of several boxing matches is often referred to as a boxing card.

CARIBBEAN BOXING. As many Caribbean nations gained their independence during the 1960s, they began entering **Olympic** boxing competition. **Puerto Rico** (which is a member of the International Olympic Committee although not strictly an independent nation) first sent a boxing team to the Olympic Games in 1960. **Cuba**, the strongest Caribbean nation in boxing and one of the strongest in the world, has competed since 1960 and has won 34 **gold medals** and 67 total medals. The **Dominican Republic** first sent a team to the Olympics in 1964 and have won two medals—a **bronze** in 1984 and a gold in 2008. The island of Bermuda, although not strictly in the Caribbean, has also produced an Olympic boxing medalist—**heavyweight** Clarence Hill, the 1976 bronze medal winner. Bermuda is the least populous country (53,500 people) to win an Olympic medal.

Among professional champion boxers from the Caribbean are Elisha Obed from the Bahamas, Gilbert Delé from the French island of Guadeloupe, Joachim Alcine (born in Haiti but raised in Canada), Otis Grant (born in Jamaica but raised in **Canada**), O'Neil Bell, Simon Brown, Uriah Grant, Glen Johnson and Mike McCallum from Jamaica, **Livingston Bramble** from St. Kitts and Nevis, Claude Noel and Leslie Stewart from Trinidad and **Emile Griffith** from the **United States** Virgin Islands. Gairy St. Clair was born in the South American Caribbean nation of Guyana and competed for them in the Olympic Games but moved to **Australia** and now represents that country. The original **Joe Walcott**, although born in South America in British Guiana, was raised on the island of Barbados. **Peter Jackson** was born in the Dutch West Indies but moved with his family to Australia at a young age and was an Australian resident when his boxing career began.

Two major boxing **bouts** have been held in the Caribbean area. **George Foreman** won the world's heavyweight championship on 22 January 1973 by stopping **Joe Frazier** in two rounds in Kingston, Jamaica, and **Muhammad Ali's** final bout (a loss to Trevor Berbick) occurred in Nassau, Bahamas, on 11 December 1981.

CARNERA, PRIMO "THE AMBLING ALP". B. 26 October 1906, Sequals, Udine, **Italy**. D. 29 June 1967, Sequals, Italy. Although Primo Carnera was the biggest **heavyweight** champion in the 20th century, he was the least competent. Budd Schulberg's great story *The Harder They Fall* is a thinly disguised biography of Carnera.

At the age of 14, Primo moved to **France** on his own, worked at various jobs, and wound up in a circus as a strongman when he was 16. He was noticed by a boxer, Paul Journée, who talked Carnera into becoming a boxer with Journée's associate, Léon Sée, as Carnera's manager. Carnera's first recorded **professional** fight was on 12 September 1928 in Paris, and he won easily in two **rounds**. As would be the case for most of Carnera's fights, he outweighed his opponent in that match, this time by 70 pounds—266 to 196.

After winning 14 of 15 fights, he faced heavyweight contender Young Stribling in London on 18 November 1929. Stribling at that time was a veteran with more than 200 fights. The result was a four-round **disqualifica-**

tion win for Carnera, although some boxing historians claim the fight was fixed. That accusation would be true for many of Carnera's subsequent fights.

After a rematch with Stribling in Paris that ended with Carnera being disqualified in four rounds and a six-round **technical knockout** of Franz Diener in London, Carnera was brought to the **United States** in early 1930. He was not a competent boxer, but his huge size of six foot five inches and 270 pounds made him an attraction. Shortly after his arrival in the United States, the gangster Owney Madden managed to obtain Carnera's contract, using American boxing manager Walter Friedman and Carnera's European manager Léon Sée as fronts. From that point on, no one could be sure of the legitimacy of Carnera's matches. Some of Carnera's opponents might have honestly been afraid of the huge Carnera, who usually had a 60- to 70-pound advantage, but others were probably afraid of the underworld connections surrounding Carnera.

Carnera won his first 22 **bouts** in 1930, 21 by **knockout** (often in the first or second round) and one by disqualification. His streak was stopped on 7 October 1930 with a 10-round **decision** loss to Jim Maloney. Carnera then won his next nine bouts, seven by knockout and decision victories over Maloney and the Basque Paulino Uzcudun.

On 12 October 1931, Carnera lost a 15-round decision to future heavyweight champion **Jack Sharkey**. Carnera then won two more bouts in the United States and in 1932 returned to Europe. Carnera won seven bouts in Europe, fighting in France, **Germany**, Italy, and **England**, before losing a 10-round decision to Canadian Larry Gains before 70,000 people in London.

Returning to the United States, Carnera won three bouts and then lost a 10-round decision to Stanley Poreda in Newark, New Jersey. After the bout, New Jersey **Commissioner** George E. Keenen suspended **referee** Joe Mangold indefinitely for what Keenen termed "an unpardonable decision." Carnera won his next 14 bouts in 1932.

In his first bout in 1933, on 10 February in **Madison Square Garden**, Carnera faced Ernie Schaaf, one of the leading heavyweights and a good friend and protege of Jack Sharkey. Schaaf had been badly beaten by **Max Baer** in August 1932 but since then had fought three bouts and won two of the three. Carnera knocked out Schaaf in the 13th round, and Schaaf died four days later. There was much speculation that Schaaf's death was caused by previous injuries and not by Carnera's fists.

In Carnera's next bout, on 29 June 1933, he fought Jack Sharkey for the world's heavyweight title and won it by knocking out Sharkey in six rounds. Sharkey later claimed that during the fight he saw visions of Schaaf and could not concentrate on the fight. Carnera then defended his title in Rome against Paulino Uzcudun and won a 15-round **unanimous decision**. In his next title defense, Carnera, weighing 270 pounds, won another unanimous decision over former **light heavyweight** champion Tommy Lougran, who weighed in at just 186 pounds. The 84-pound weight difference was the greatest in a championship bout in **ring** history and was unsurpassed until the seven-foot-tall **Nikolai Valuev** became heavyweight champion.

On 14 June 1934, Carnera was badly beaten by Max Baer and lost his heavyweight championship. Carnera was down as many as 10 times (reports differ as to the exact number), with the bout finally being stopped in the 11th round.

Six months later, he traveled to South America and won three bouts in **Argentina** and **Brazil**. In 1935, Carnera faced an opponent nearly his own size in the six-foot-seven-inch, 258-pound Ray Impelletiere at Madison Square Garden and stopped Impelletiere in the ninth round. On 15 June 1935, Carnera faced the undefeated (19–0) **Joe Louis**, who was rapidly rising as the country's top heavyweight but had not yet fought for the title. Louis easily defeated Carnera, knocking him down three times before the fight was stopped in the sixth round.

After the Louis fight, Carnera fought eight more times, losing three, with his last bout on 4 December 1937 in Budapest, **Hungary**. In 1938, he had a kidney removed. World War II intervened, and Carnera was on the side of the anti-Fascists and was wounded by the Nazis in 1943.

After the war, Carnera, needing money, made a brief comeback, fighting in Italy five times in 1945 and 1946 and losing his last three bouts. He then turned to professional wrestling and had a relatively successful career there, wrestling until 1962. He became a U.S. citizen in 1953 and lived in Los Angeles, where he owned a restaurant and liquor store.

He appeared in several feature films, including the 1933 *The Prizefighter and the Lady*, which featured him in a bout against Max Baer, ironically just one year before the two actually fought in the ring. Carnera returned to Italy in the 1960s and died at the age of 60 in his native city of Sequals from complications of diabetes.

Carnera was six foot five inches tall and had an 85-inch **reach**—one of the largest among heavyweight champions. He fought at weights ranging from 260 to 284 pounds as a heavyweight. In 103 professional bouts, from 1928 to 1946, he won 88 (72 by knockout), lost 14 (five by knockout), had one no decision in which he was awarded the **newspaper decision**, and fought a total of 529 rounds.

CARNIVAL OF CHAMPIONS. In 1892, a three-day series of championship **bouts** took place in New Orleans, Louisiana, from 5 to 7 September. On the first day, world **lightweight** champion Jack McAuliffe **knocked out** challenger Billy Myer in the 15th **round** in a bout billed for the world's lightweight championship, even though both fighters weighed in over the 133-pound lightweight limit. On the second day, **George Dixon** and Jack

Skelly fought for the world **featherweight** title, with Dixon prevailing on an eighth-round knockout. The main attraction of the Carnival occurred on the third day, when **John L. Sullivan**, the **heavyweight** champion of the world, defended his claim for the first time in a bout under **Marquess of Queensberry Rules** against challenger **Jim Corbett**. Corbett won the title by knocking out Sullivan in the 21st round. Professor John Duffy was the **referee** for all three of the bouts.

On 23 September 1937, promoter **Mike Jacobs** put on a boxing **card** at the Polo Grounds in New York that featured four world championship bouts and billed the event as the "Carnival of Champions." The title bouts were each scheduled for 15 rounds and were contested along with a four-round **preliminary bout**.

The bouts resulted in two new champions. Harry Jeffra dethroned champion Sixto Escobar by a **unanimous decision** for the world's **bantamweight** title. In a **middleweight** title bout that was recognized by the International Boxing Union (but not the **New York State Athletic Commission**), Fred Apostoli stopped champion Marcel Thil at 0:44 of the 10th round due to a cut over Thil's right eye. (This would be Thil's final professional bout.)

The two champions who successfully defended their titles were world **welterweight** champion **Barney Ross**, who despite breaking his left hand during the bout won a unanimous decision over challenger Ceferino Garcia, and world lightweight champion Lou Ambers, who won a **majority decision** over challenger Pedro Montañez.

There were no **knockdowns** in any of the 55 rounds of championship boxing. The results were disappointing for promoter Jacobs, as the paid attendance was just 30,969 in the 60,000-seat outdoor arena, and the gross receipts were only $209,076.

The title "Carnival of Champions" was also used for a **Don King** promotion on 3 December 1982 that featured two **main events—World Boxing Council (WBC)** bantamweight champion Lupe Pintor against WBC **super bantamweight** champion **Wilfredo Gómez** and former welterweight champion **Thomas Hearns** versus WBC **light middleweight** champion **Wilfred Benítez**. Gomez won a 14th-round technical knockout, and Hearns won a 15-round majority decision. There were also nine preliminary bouts and a scheduled total of 96 rounds of boxing.

CARPENTIER, GEORGES "THE ORCHID MAN". B. 12 January 1894, Liévin, Pas-de-Calais, France. D. 28 October 1975, Paris, **France**. Georges Carpentier is possibly the only boxer who fought successfully in each of the eight divisions from **flyweight** to **heavyweight**. It was in a heavyweight **bout** (although he only weighed 172 pounds for it) that he engaged in his most memorable fight.

He began boxing as a **professional** at the age of 14, with his first recorded bout on 1 November 1908—a win by **disqualification** in 13 **rounds** over Ed Salmon. In his second fight, a rematch with Salmon, Carpentier was stopped in the 18th round. One of Carpentier's early victories was a 15-round decision over the previously undefeated Charles Ledoux in a **bantamweight** bout. Ledoux would later win the European bantamweight title and would receive recognition by the **National Sporting Club** in London as world's bantamweight champion.

In June 1911, Carpentier won the French **welterweight** title and, in September of that year, the European welterweight title. Less than a year later, he became European **middleweight** champion as well. By virtue of his win over Jim Sullivan on 29 February 1912, Carpentier claimed the world's middleweight championship as well as the European title. After two defenses of the two titles, Carpentier was defeated by Frank Klaus on 24 June in Dieppe, France, on a 19th-round disqualification. On 23 October 1912, Carpentier lost to another of the middleweight title claimants, Billy Papke, on an 18th-round **technical knockout** due to a bad cut over his eye.

The following year, Carpentier, who was just 19 years old and still growing, won the European **light heavyweight** title with a second-round **knockout** of Bandsman Dick Rice. Four months later, he won the European heavyweight title (although he weighed only 168 pounds) by knocking out Bombardier Billy Wells in four rounds. He defended that successfully once and then lost a 15-round bout to the veteran boxer **Joe Jeannette**.

During this era, the heavyweight champion was **Jack Johnson**, a black man whose deportment left much to be desired. Promoters searched for a white fighter who could possibly dethrone him and labeled them "**white hopes.**" Carpentier was labeled as one of the "white hopes." Ironically, Carpentier (although 20 years old at the time) acted as the **referee** for Johnson's heavyweight title bout with Frank Moran in Paris on 27 June 1914. On 16 July 1914, in London, **England**, Carpentier fought Ed "Gunboat" Smith for the so-called "white" heavyweight championship of the world and defeated Smith on a six-round disqualification. After one more bout 10 days later, Carpentier went off to war.

He served as an aviator for France from 1914 to 1918 and won two of France's highest military honors, the *Croix de Guerre* and the *Médaille Militaire*. He resumed boxing in July 1919 and defended his European heavyweight title twice that year.

In October 1920, he came to the **United States** and defeated Battling Levinsky on a fourth-round knockout to win the world's light heavyweight title. Promoter **Tex Rickard** then matched Carpentier with the world's heavyweight champion, **Jack Dempsey**.

Rickard originally wanted the bout to take place in New York City, but the governor of New York State, Nathan Lewis Miller, opposed boxing and would not allow it. Rickard accepted a proposal from the mayor of Jersey City, across the river from New York City. An 80,000-seat wooden outdoor arena was constructed in Jersey City, which became known as Boyle's Thirty Acres (after John P. Boyle, a paper manufacturer who sold the land to Jersey City). The bout was highly promoted, and the gate exceeded one million dollars for the first time in boxing history. The bout was relatively anticlimactic, as Dempsey easily defeated Carpentier on a fourth-round knockout.

Carpentier returned to Europe and knocked out **Australian** heavyweight George Cook in four rounds on 12 January 1922 in London, England. He followed that bout with a one-round, one-punch knockout in defense of his **light heavyweight** and European heavyweight titles against Ted "Kid" Lewis, former world **welterweight** champion, who weighed only 157 pounds for the bout.

In Carpentier's next bout, he lost his world's light heavyweight and European titles on a sixth-round knockout by the Senegalese Frenchman Battling Siki. Although the bout was originally ruled a disqualification victory for Carpentier, the French Boxing Federation overruled the **ringside judges** and awarded the titles to Siki.

Carpentier returned to the United States in 1924 and lost a 10-round **newspaper decision** to Tommy Gibbons. In his next bout, future heavyweight champion **Gene Tunney** stopped Carpentier in the 15th round at the Polo Grounds in New York. Carpentier did not fight for two years and then finished his career with four bouts in 1926. His last bout was a three-round knockout against a **journeyman** boxer in Coeur d'Alene, Idaho, on 15 September 1926.

In retirement, Carpentier was extremely popular in Europe. He made several motion pictures, both silent and sound, did some work as a **referee**, appeared in vaudeville, and owned an upscale bar, Chez Georges Carpentier, in Paris.

Carpentier was five foot 11 inches tall and fought at recorded weights ranging from 146 to 175 pounds, primarily as a light heavyweight and heavyweight. When he first began professional boxing, he competed as a flyweight and moved his way up through the various weight divisions, although his weight for his early bouts was not recorded. In 109 professional bouts, from 1908 to 1926, he won 88 (57 by knockout), lost 14 (nine by knockout), had six **draws**, and fought one no-decision bout that was called a draw by the newspapers. He fought a total of 860 rounds and was inducted into the **International Boxing Hall of Fame** in 1991.

CARTER, RUBIN "HURRICANE". B. 6 May 1937, Clifton, New Jersey. Rubin "Hurricane" Carter is remembered most for one fight—his fight with the judicial system to prove his innocence after being convicted of murder. In his lifetime, he has spent more years in prison than he did as a boxer.

A troubled youth, he was sentenced to a reformatory after he was accused of assault and robbery when he was 14 years old. He escaped from that institution a few years later and joined the U.S. Army. After serving in the army for 21 months, he was found out, discharged, and sentenced for an additional nine months for his escape. He was released after serving five of the nine months but was arrested again for another series of crimes and sent to a maximum-security prison, where he spent four more years.

After his release from that prison in 1961, he became a **professional boxer**, having learned the skill while in the army. His first professional **bout** was on 22 September 1961, and he won a **split decision** in a four-round bout.

Carter compiled a record of 12–2, with 10 **knockouts**, and on 27 October 1962 was matched with top **middleweight** contender Florentino Fernández at **Madison Square Garden**. Fernández, who had lost a close 15-round split decision to **Gene Fullmer** in a world's middleweight championship bout the previous year, was **knocked out** in the first round by Carter.

The following year, Carter knocked out **welterweight** champion **Emile Griffith** in the first round of a **nontitle bout**. In his next bout, Carter won a **unanimous decision** over future **heavyweight** champion Jimmy Ellis, who was fighting as a middleweight at that point in his career and had won 14 of his 16 previous fights.

These victories provided Carter with the biggest opportunity of his life—a shot at the world's middleweight title against **Joey Giardello**, another fighter who had served time earlier in his life. In a relatively close fight, Giardello, who was cut earlier in the bout, was able to use his **ring** experience and outbox Carter to win a unanimous 15-round decision.

Carter lost his next bout, a 10-round decision to contender Luis Manuel Rodríguez, and then traveled to Europe, where he won one bout in **France** and split two bouts in **England**. In May 1965, Carter lost a 10-round unanimous decision to future middleweight and **light heavyweight** champion **Dick Tiger** at Madison Square Garden in a bout in which Rubin was knocked down twice.

After the Tiger fight, Carter fought only nine more bouts as a professional boxer, winning four, losing four, and drawing one. His last bout was on 6 August 1966.

On 6 June 1966, a triple murder was committed at a bar in New Jersey. Carter's car matched the description of the getaway car, and he was questioned by police and released. Later, after an eyewitness to the murder claimed that Carter was one of the perpetrators, Carter was arrested on 17 October 1966. Although Carter maintained his innocence, his past series of convictions worked against him, and he was sentenced to life imprisonment for the crime. In 1974, Carter's accusers recanted their confessions accusing Carter and a new trial was sought, but a New Jersey judge denied the motion for a new trial.

The case now took on added publicity as heavyweight champion **Muhammad Ali** pledged his support and singer-songwriter Bob Dylan wrote a song about the story. A second trial was eventually granted, but the original conviction was upheld. In 1985, a further legal process resulted in Carter's release from prison. Carter moved to **Canada** and worked for the Canadian organization Association in Defence of the Wrongly Convicted.

A 1999 movie, *The Hurricane*, starred Denzel Washington as Carter, although some parts of the film were fictionalized. Joey Giardello later sued for the way he was depicted in the film, with the suit being settled out of court.

Carter is five foot eight inches tall and fought at weights ranging from 154 to 165 pounds as a middleweight. In 40 professional bouts, from 1961 to 1966, Carter won 27 (19 by knockout), lost 12 (one by knockout), had one **draw**, and fought a total of 256 rounds.

CASINO BOXING. Since the mid-1960s, casinos have replaced the small **fight clubs** as the venues for regularly scheduled nonchampionship **bouts**. They have also replaced the big ballparks as the site of major championship fights. Some of the first casinos to recognize the potential for hosting boxing were Atlantis, Bally's, Caesar's, Resorts, and Trump Casino in **Atlantic City**, New Jersey, and Caesar's Palace, Dunes, Harrah's, MGM Grand, the Mirage, and the Riviera Hotel in **Las Vegas**, Nevada.

Many others have since followed suit, as casinos in the United States have grown to the point where nearly every state has a legalized casino (albeit mostly on Indian reservations to avoid state gambling laws). Some of the more popular ones include Foxwoods Resort in Mashantucket, Connecticut; Hollywood Casino in Bay St. Louis, Mississippi; Miccosukee Gaming Resort in Miami, Florida; Mohegan Sun Casino in Uncasville, Connecticut; and Turning Stone Resort Casino in Verona, New York.

CATCHWEIGHTS. Although boxing matches are usually made with fixed maximum weights for the combatants, in the early days of boxing, on occasion, **bouts** would be arranged at "catchweights," meaning that the fighters could weigh in at whatever weight they chose and not be bound by the normal weight limits for their class.

In modern terminology, boxers occasionally agree to box at a specified weight that might be in between the traditional maximum weight for the class. For example, a **welterweight** (normal limit of 147 pounds) might agree to fight a junior **middleweight** (normal limit of 154 pounds) at a catchweight of 150 pounds.

CERDAN, MARCELLIN "MARCEL," "THE CASABLANCA CLOUTER". B. 22 July 1916, Sidi-Bel-Abbès, Algeria. D. 28 October 1949, São Miguel Island, Azores, Portugal. Marcel Cerdan is one of sport's participants whose premature death has raised him to legendary status. He began boxing professionally in North Africa at the age of 18, with his first recorded **bout** (a six **round decision**) in Meknès, Morocco, on 4 November 1934. After winning his first 28 bouts in Morocco and Algeria, he was brought to Paris, **France**, in October 1937. He continued his undefeated streak and, on 21 February 1938, defeated Omar Kouidri by decision in 12 rounds for the French **welterweight** title. With an undefeated record of 45–0, he was matched with Harry Craster at the **National Sporting Club** in London, **England**, where he met his first defeat—by **disqualification** in the fifth round.

On 3 June 1939, Cerdan became the European welterweight champion when he defeated Saverio Turiello in Milan, **Italy**, on a 15-round decision. After two successful defenses of that title, Cerdan joined the armed forces. While serving his country in the Allied Forces, he also boxed in military bouts and won the Inter-Allied welterweight and **middleweight** championships.

Returning to civilian life, he **knocked down** Assane Diouf six times in three rounds to capture the French middleweight championship on 30 November 1945. After two successful defenses of that title, he defeated Holman Williams on 7 July 1946 in Paris and attracted the attention of North American fight promoters. Cerdan was brought to New York in December 1946 and defeated George Abrams by **unanimous decision** at **Madison Square Garden**. He returned to Paris and won the European middleweight title on 2 February 1947 with a one-round **knockout** of Léon Fouquet. In 1947 and 1948, he successfully defended that crown twice in Paris and also made several trips to North America, where he remained in the public eye as a viable contender for the world middleweight title. In May 1948, he lost the European middleweight title to Cyrille Delannoit in Brussels by 15-round decision, but regained it less than two months later in a rematch, also in Brussels.

On 21 September 1948, Cerdan was matched with world middleweight champion **Tony Zale** in a championship bout at Roosevelt Stadium in Jersey City, New Jersey. The match was voted the "Fight of the Year" by *Ring* **magazine** as Cerdan stopped Zale at the end of 11 rounds of their scheduled 15-round bout.

Cerdan's final bout was a world middleweight championship title defense against **Jake LaMotta** on 16 June 1949 in Detroit, Michigan. LaMotta stopped Cerdan in the 10th round of that bout after Cerdan had dislocated his shoulder. A rematch was scheduled for November 1949, but the flight from Paris to New York carrying Cerdan never reached its destination, as it crashed in the Azores while landing for a scheduled refueling stop, and all 48 passengers and crew were killed.

A 1983 film, *Edith et Marcel*, by Academy Award–winning French film-maker Claude Lelouch, tells the story of Cerdan's love affair with famed French singer Édith Piaf. Cerdan's son, Marcel Jr. (also a professional box-er), played the role of his father in that film.

Cerdan was five foot eight inches tall and fought at weights ranging from 145 to 164 pounds, primarily as a welterweight and middleweight. In 115 professional bouts, from 1934 to 1949, he won 111 (65 by knockout), lost four (one by knockout), and fought a total of 756 rounds. He was inducted into the **International Boxing Hall of Fame** in 2001.

CERVANTES REYES, ANTONIO "KID PAMBELÉ". B. 23 December 1945, San Basilio de Palenque, **Colombia**. Arguably, the greatest fighter that Colombia ever produced was Antonio Cervantes, more popularly known by his nickname, Kid Pambelé. He began his **professional boxing** career on 31 January 1964 in Cereté, Colombia, and won his first 18 **bouts** before being held to an eight-**round draw** by Reynaldo López in Cartagena on 29 July 1966.

After fighting his first 60 fights in Colombia and **Venezuela** and compil-ing a record of 49–8–3, Cervantes was invited to box in the **United States**, and on 6 November 1970 he defeated Jorge Rodríguez on an eighth-round **knockout** in San Jose, California. After two more **technical knockout** wins in Los Angeles and three wins by **decision** in Venezuela, Cervantes was matched with the Argentine Nicolino Locche for Locche's **World Boxing Association (WBA)** world **light welterweight** title in Buenos Aires, **Argen-tina**, on 11 December 1971. In a one-sided fight, Locche won every one of the 15 rounds on all three of the **judges'** scorecards. Three months later, Locche lost his title to the **Panamanian** Alfonso "Peppermint" Frazer.

Cervantes knocked out Frazer in the 10th round on 28 October 1972 in Panama and became the new WBA light welterweight champion. Cervantes then successfully defended that title 10 times over the next three years throughout Latin America and Asia. He defeated Puerto Rican Josue

Márquez in **Puerto Rico**, Locche in Venezuela, Frazer in a rematch in Panama, Carlos Maria Giménez in Colombia, Lion Furuyama in Panama, Changkil Lee in Colombia, Victor Ortiz in Colombia, Shinichi Kadota in **Japan**, Esteban de Jesús in Panama, and Héctor Thompson in Panama.

On 6 March 1976, he faced the 17-year-old undefeated (25–0) Puerto Rican **Wilfred Benítez** and lost a close 15-round **split decision** to Benítez in Puerto Rico. After the WBA declared the title **vacant**, Cervantes fought Carlos Maria Giménez for the title on 25 June 1977 in Venezuela, stopped Giménez in six rounds, and recaptured the light welterweight championship. Over the next three years, Cervantes again traveled the world in defense of that crown. He defeated Adriano Marrero in Venezuela, Tongta Kiatvayupakdi in **Thailand**, Norman Sekgupane in **South Africa**, Miguel Montilla in New York, Kwang-min Kim in South **Korea**, and Montilla in Colombia.

Cervantes finally lost his title to Aaron Pryor by a fourth-round knockout on 2 August 1980 in Cincinnati, Ohio. He retired after the fight but made a brief comeback and fought five more times, winning four and retiring from the **ring** after a 10-round loss by **unanimous decision** to Danny Sánchez in Miami on 9 December 1983.

Cervantes is five foot nine inches tall and has a 72-inch **reach**. He fought at weights ranging from 121 to 141 pounds, primarily as a light welterweight. In 106 professional bouts, from 1964 to 1983, he won 91 (45 by knockout), lost 12 (two by knockout), had three draws, and fought a total of 797 rounds. He was inducted into the **International Boxing Hall of Fame** in 1998.

CHARLES, EZZARD MACK "THE CINCINNATI COBRA". B. 7 July 1921, Lawrenceville, Georgia. D. 28 May 1975, Chicago, Illinois. Ezzard Charles came by his unusual first name in a novel way—he was named for the physician that delivered him—Dr. Webster Pierce Ezzard. Charles moved with his family to Cincinnati, Ohio, at the age of nine and became the most famous boxer from that city. In fact, one of the city's streets bears his name—Ezzard Charles Drive—as does an apartment complex.

He began boxing as an **amateur** and won the national **Amateur Athletic Union middleweight** championship in 1939. On 12 March 1940, he began his **professional boxing** career with a four-**round knockout** victory over Melody Johnson in Middletown, Ohio. Charles won his first 15 **bouts** and was matched with Ken Overlin on 9 June 1941 in an outdoor bout at Crosley Field in Cincinnati. The veteran boxer Overlin, who had begun boxing professionally in 1931, had fought 147 bouts and been recognized as world middleweight champion in 1940. Charles was **knocked down** in the second round of their bout and lost a **unanimous decision**, his first defeat as a professional. Within the next nine months, Charles defeated former champions Teddy Yarosz and Anton Christoforidis before gaining a **draw** in a rematch with Overlin. Later in 1942, Charles won two **decisions** over future world's **light heavyweight** champion **Joey Maxim**.

Charles's only two bouts in 1943 resulted in bad losses for him; he was knocked down seven times in a bout with Jimmy Bivins and was knocked down eight times by Lloyd Marshall before the **referee** stopped the bout in the eighth round. Charles served in the military during World War II and won the Inter-Allied light heavyweight championship in 1944 in Rome, **Italy**.

After being discharged, Charles resumed boxing in 1946 and won all 10 of his bouts that year, including victories over Marshall and future world's light heavyweight champion **Archie Moore**. Charles again defeated Moore in 1947 and had another successful year with 11 victories in 12 bouts—the only loss coming on a controversial **split decision** against Elmer Ray. Even though Charles continued to win nearly all his bouts (eight more in 1948 and another defeat of Moore), he was not selected to compete for a world championship.

After world **heavyweight** champion **Joe Louis** announced his retirement on 1 March 1949, the title was declared **vacant**, and the **National Boxing Association (NBA)** on 22 June matched Charles with **Jersey Joe Walcott** for the vacant title. Despite weighing only 181 pounds and being outweighed by Walcott by 14 pounds, Charles won a unanimous decision and became NBA world heavyweight champion. He successfully defended that title three times—against Gus Lesnevich, Pat Valentino, and Freddie Beshore.

In 1950, Joe Louis came out of retirement and fought Charles for the undisputed world's heavyweight championship on 27 September 1950 at Yankee Stadium in New York. Charles gave away 34 pounds but easily outboxed Louis and won universal recognition as champion. (Author's note—this was the first boxing match I ever saw. It was on our one-month-old 16-inch Philco black-and-white television set, and my father let me, a seven-year-old second grader, stay up past my bedtime to see the "great" Joe Louis.)

Charles was an active champion and defended his title four times within 12 months, stopping Nick Barone and Lee Oma and winning decisions over Jersey Joe Walcott and Joey Maxim. On 18 July 1951, Charles lost his title to Walcott when he was stopped in the seventh round. Nearly a year later, Charles faced Walcott in a rematch on 5 June 1952 but again lost—this time by a close but unanimous 15-round decision. A sidelight of that bout was that referee Zach Clayton became the first African American to referee a world's heavyweight championship bout.

Charles continued to be one of the top-ranked contenders and was given another chance at the world's heavyweight championship by then champion **Rocky Marciano** on 17 June 1954 at Yankee Stadium. Charles put up a good battle but lost the unanimous decision. He was rewarded with a rematch just three months later (17 September 1954 at Yankee Stadium), and the resulting contest was voted "Fight of the Year" by *Ring* **magazine**. Although Charles severely cut Marciano's nose, Marciano knocked Charles down in the second and eighth round before knocking him out in the eighth round to retain his title.

After the second Marciano bout, Charles continued fighting until 1959 but lost more than he won—losing 13 of 23 bouts against opponents of lesser quality. His health began to decline, and he contracted amyotrophic lateral sclerosis, succumbing to that disease in 1975.

Charles was six feet tall and had a 73-inch **reach**. He fought at weights ranging from 157 to 204 pounds, primarily as a light heavyweight and heavyweight. In 119 professional bouts, from 1940 to 1959, he won 93 (52 by knockout), lost 25 (seven by knockout), had one **draw**, and fought a total of 960 rounds. He was inducted as a member of the inaugural class of the **International Boxing Hall of Fame** in 1990.

CHÁVEZ GONZÁLEZ, JULIO CÉSAR "J. C.," "EL CÉSAR DEL BOXEO," "EL GRAN CAMPEÓN MEXICANO". B. 12 July 1962, Obregón, Sonora, **Mexico**. **Julio César Chávez** was one of the greatest fighters in boxing history and arguably the greatest Mexican fighter of all time. Among the records he holds are most title fights, most title fight victories, most successful consecutive title defenses, and longest undefeated streak.

He began boxing in Mexico in his hometown of Culiacán on 5 February 1980 as a **bantamweight**. After winning his first 43 **bouts**, 37 by **knockout** and nearly all of them in Mexico, he defeated Mario Martínez on an eighth-round **technical knockout** on 13 September 1984 in Los Angeles, California, for the **vacant World Boxing Council (WBC) super featherweight** championship. Chávez then made 10 successful defenses of that title from 1985 to 1987 fighting in **France**, Monaco, and Mexico, in addition to California, New York, and Nevada.

On 21 November 1987, he moved up in weight class and won the **World Boxing Association lightweight** title by stopping Edwin Rosario in the 11th round. He made one successful defense of that title and then added the WBC lightweight championship on 29 October 1988 on an 11th-round **technical decision** victory over José Luis Ramírez in a bout that was stopped due to a cut on Ramírez, caused by an accidental headbutt.

In his next bout, Chávez won his third title, the WBC **light welterweight** championship, when champion Roger Mayweather retired after the 10th round of their bout. Chávez would remain in that weight class (140 pounds) for most of the rest of his career. He successfully defended that title 12 consecutive times. On 17 March 1990, Chávez nearly lost the title to previously undefeated (24–0–1) **International Boxing Federation** light welterweight champion Meldrick Taylor in a bout named "Fight of the Year" by **Ring** magazine. Losing the bout going into the 12th round, Chávez staggered Taylor with 28 seconds to go and then knocked him down. After Taylor arose at the count of five, **referee** Richard Steele looked at him and stopped the fight with just two seconds remaining.

On 12 September 1992, Chávez defeated former triple champion **Héctor Camacho** on a 12-round **unanimous decision** in defense of his WBC light welterweight title. He followed that defense with a five-round technical knockout over former lightweight champion Greg Haugen on 20 February 1993 in an outdoor bout at the huge Estadio Azteca in Mexico City before 132,247 spectators—the largest paid attendance in boxing history.

On 10 September 1993, Chávez's winning streak was ended after 87 consecutive victories. The bout with **Pernell Whitaker** for Whitaker's WBC **welterweight** title ended in a 12-round **majority draw** (two **judges** scoring it as a **draw** and one judge voting for Whitaker), although most spectators thought that Whitaker had won the fight.

Two bouts later, on 29 January 1994, Chávez lost the first bout of his career, and also his light welterweight title, on a 12-round **split decision** to Frankie Randall. Less than four months later, Chávez avenged that defeat and recaptured the title by stopping Randall in eight rounds due to a cut caused by an accidental butt, with Chávez being awarded the technical decision. In his first title defense, Chávez stopped Meldrick Taylor in eight rounds on 17 September 1994. He then made three more successful title defenses before losing his title to **Óscar De La Hoya** on 7 June 1996 via a fourth-round **technical knockout** due to a cut over Chávez's eye.

After De La Hoya vacated the title to move up to the welterweight class, Chávez fought Miguel Ángel González for the **vacant** WBC light welterweight title on 7 March 1998 in the bullring in Mexico City. The close 12-round bout was ruled a draw, and the title remained vacant. Chávez then attempted to win De La Hoya's WBC welterweight title on 19 September 1998 but was unable to come out for the eighth round.

Chávez fought one more world championship bout in his career—on 29 July 2000 for **Kostya Tszyu's** WBC light welterweight title—but again fell short, with the bout being stopped in the sixth round in favor of Tszyu.

After one more **nontitle bout** in 2001 Chávez began a series of retirements from the **ring**. He came back for one fight in 2003, had another in 2004 and two more in 2005, with a fourth-round stoppage by Grover Robinson on 17 September 2005 being Chávez's final ring appearance.

In retirement, he has devoted his efforts to furthering the boxing career of his son, Julio César Chávez Jr., who held the WBC **middleweight** title from 4 June 2011 to 15 September 2012 and from 2003 to 2012 compiled a record of 46–1–1, with one **no-contest** bout. Chávez Sr.'s other son, Omar Chávez, is also a professional boxer, with a record of 28–2–1 from 2006 to 2012.

Chávez Sr. is five foot seven inches tall and has a 66-inch **reach**. He fought at weights ranging from 116 to 152 pounds, from **featherweight** to welterweight classes. In 115 professional bouts, from 1980 to 2005, he won 107 (86 by knockout), lost six (four by knockout), had two draws, and fought a total of 633 rounds. He was inducted into the **International Boxing Hall of Fame** in 2011.

CHOCOLATE, KID "THE CUBAN BON BON" (né **ELIGIO SARDIÑAS MONTALVO**). B. 6 January 1910, Cerro, Havana, **Cuba**. D. 8 August 1988, Havana, Cuba. Kid Chocolate, nicknamed the "Cuban Bon Bon" by sportswriters, was one of the first boxers from Cuba to attain popularity in the **United States**, and before his career ended, he became the first Cuban world champion.

Although he claimed an undefeated **amateur** record of 100 victories, with 86 by **knockout**, that was most likely due to the imagination of his manager, Luis "Pincho" Gutiérrez. As with most professional boxers of that era, his amateur record remains undocumented and unknown, although Cuban boxing historian Enrique Encinosa has found 21 amateur **bouts** for Chocolate— all victories.

Kid Chocolate's first professional bout took place in Havana, Cuba, on 3 March 1928, a bout he won easily with a first-**round** knockout. After winning five more bouts in Cuba, he came to New York, where he would spend much of the rest of his boxing career. He won 25 of his first 26 bouts, with a 10-round **draw** against Joey Scalfaro on 30 November being his only non-victory. Chocolate returned to Havana in February 1929 and defeated Chick Suggs in a bout billed as the "colored world **featherweight** championship." Even though boxing by that time was fully integrated, the bout's promoters attempted to capitalize on the fact that both boxers were black. Chocolate did not suffer his first loss until 7 August 1930, when he lost a 10-round **split decision** to the British fighter Jack "Kid" Berg at the Polo Grounds in New York. Although Berg was recognized as the world's **junior welterweight** champion at that time, it was a **nontitle bout**, even though both boxers were under the weight limit for the fight.

On 12 December 1930, Chocolate fought his first world's title bout but was defeated on a 15-round **decision** by Christopher "Battling" Battalino in a bout recognized by the **New York State Athletic Commission (NYSAC)** for the world's **featherweight** championship. Seven months later, Chocolate became the first Cuban to win a world title when he stopped Benny Bass in the seventh round on 15 July 1931 at Shibe Park in Philadelphia to win the **National Boxing Association junior lightweight** (now often called **super featherweight**) title. His first title defense was one of the **quickest** world championship bouts in history, when he stopped Joey Scalfaro in just 39 seconds of the first round on 1 October 1931 in Long Island City, New York.

In the next six weeks, Chocolate fought four **nontitle bouts** before challenging champion **Tony Canzoneri** for the world's **lightweight** title at **Madison Square Garden**, losing a 15-round split decision.

Chocolate lost only the fifth bout in his career on 18 July 1932 when, in his 82nd professional bout, a nontitle 15-rounder, he was defeated on a split decision by Jack "Kid" Berg in Long Island City. On 13 October 1932, Chocolate won a second championship when he defeated Lew Feldman in a bout billed by the NYSAC for the **vacant** featherweight championship. Chocolate successfully defended both titles (featherweight and junior lightweight) twice. He won a majority 15-round decision over Fidel LaBarba at Madison Square Garden on 9 December 1932 and a unanimous 15-round decision over Seaman Tommy Watson on 19 May 1933, also at the Garden. Chocolate then made his first, and only, trip to Europe as a boxer, winning two nontitle bouts in **Spain** and one in **France**. He then finished his travels by winning another nontitle bout in **Canada**.

On 24 November 1933, Kid Chocolate was stopped for the first time in his career. Tony Canzoneri knocked him out at 2:30 of the second round in their nontitle bout at Madison Square Garden. One month later, on Christmas Day in Philadelphia, Chocolate was stopped in the seventh round by Frankie Klick and lost his junior lightweight title, although he still retained the featherweight title. On 20 February 1934, Chocolate lost that crown also as the NYSAC stripped him of the title for insufficient title defenses.

Chocolate continued boxing for the next four years, winning nearly all his bouts and spending most of 1935 and 1936 in Cuba and **Venezuela** before returning to the United States in 1937. After two bouts in Cuba in 1938, he announced his retirement from the **ring** on 19 December 1938.

To show how much Chocolate was respected as a champion, there have been more than 50 boxers who subsequently adopted the name "Kid Chocolate," including Peter Quillin, who, as Kid Chocolate, from 2005 to 2012 has compiled an undefeated record of 28–0 and has won the **World Boxing Organization middleweight** title. Writer Clifford Odets in his classic 1937 boxing drama (and 1939 film) *Golden Boy* named one of his characters Chocolate Drop, in homage to Kid Chocolate.

Chocolate was five foot six inches tall and had a 65-inch **reach**. He fought at weights ranging from 118 to 133 pounds, primarily as a featherweight and junior lightweight. In 152 professional bouts, from 1927 to 1938, he won 135 (51 by knockout), lost 10 (two by knockout), had six draws, and fought one no-decision bout in which he was awarded the **newspaper decision**. He fought a total of 1,188 rounds. He was inducted into the **International Boxing Hall of Fame** in 1991.

CHUVALO, GEORGE LOUIS (né JURE ČUVALO). B. 12 September 1937, Toronto, **Canada**. George Chuvalo was one of the toughest fighters of all time and could take a punch better than most men. He was never **knocked down** in his 22 years of **professional boxing** and was rated by boxing historian **Bert Randolph Sugar** as the fighter with the "best chin" in boxing history.

Chuvalo won the Canadian national **amateur heavyweight** championship in 1955. His first recorded professional **bout** was in a Canadian heavyweight novice tournament in Toronto on 23 April 1956. He won four bouts that night, all by **knockout** in the first or second round, to win the tournament. In his next bout, on 11 June 1956, he was featured in the **main event** at Maple Leaf Gardens in Toronto. In that bout, he won a unanimous eight-round decision over former **South African** heavyweight champion and 1948 **Olympic bronze medalist** Johnny Arthur. In October 1956, Chuvalo suffered his first professional loss—a 10-round **split decision** to Howard King. He avenged that loss by knocking out King in two rounds in 1958.

On 15 September 1958, Chuvalo won the Canadian heavyweight championship by stopping James J. Parker in the first round by knocking him down three times in two minutes. After losing a 10-round **unanimous decision** to Pat McMurtry in **Madison Square Garden**, in his first fight outside of Ontario, Chuvalo successfully defended his Canadian title with a 12th-round knockout of Yvon Durelle, who had given **light heavyweight** champion **Archie Moore** a tough battle the previous year in a bid for Moore's title.

Chuvalo lost his Canadian title to Bob Cleroux on a split decision in Montreal on 16 August 1960 but rewon it on a unanimous decision in a rematch on 23 November 1960. In the **rubber match** of their series, on 8 August 1961, Cleroux again won by split decision. Chuvalo continued meeting most of the era's top heavyweights and lost a 10-round unanimous decision to **Zora Folley** in 1964.

After Cleroux retired in 1963, Chuvalo won the then **vacant** Canadian heavyweight championship on 18 March 1964 with a first-round knockout of Hugh Mercier (a **journeyman** boxer with only five bouts to his credit). Chuvalo then stopped one of the top heavyweight contenders, Doug Jones, in the 11th round and was matched with former heavyweight champion **Floyd Patterson**. Patterson won a close, but unanimous, decision at Madison Square Garden on 1 February 1965.

After **Muhammad Ali** was no longer recognized as world's heavyweight champion by the **World Boxing Association (WBA)**, the WBA matched Chuvalo with Ernie Terrell for their version of the heavyweight championship. The 15-round bout took place at Maple Leaf Gardens in Toronto on 1 November 1965, and Terrell won a unanimous decision. On 29 March 1966, Chuvalo again fought for the world's heavyweight title—this time against

Ali, who was still recognized by most organizations as the heavyweight champion. Again, Chuvalo went the 15 round distance and lost a unanimous decision. From that date until 19 July 1967, Chuvalo kept busy and had 14 bouts, winning 13 (all by knockout or **technical knockout**) and losing only to Óscar Bonavena by majority 10-round decision.

On 19 July 1967, Chuvalo faced the 1964 Olympic heavyweight champion, **Joe Frazier**, who as a professional had won all 16 of his bouts, 14 by knockout. Frazier became the first man to stop Chuvalo, who lost on a technical knockout in the fourth round, although he was never knocked down in the bout. Chuvalo's only other bout in which he lost short of the scheduled distance occurred on 4 August 1970, when another former Olympic champion and undefeated professional, **George Foreman**, stopped Chuvalo in three rounds. In 1972, Chuvalo against faced Muhammad Ali, who at that time was no longer champion. Chuvalo again went the distance but lost a 12-round unanimous decision. Chuvalo continued boxing until 1978 and in his last fight, on 11 December, ended his **professional boxing** career with a three-round technical knockout over George Jerome in a bout billed for the Canadian heavyweight title. Altogether in Chuvalo's 22-year boxing career, he fought 12 bouts billed for the Canadian heavyweight championship and won 10 of them, losing only to Bob Cleroux twice. He fought seven fights with five Olympic champions and one Olympic **bronze medalist** and seven fights with six men recognized at one time or another as world's heavyweight champions.

In retirement, Chuvalo has had a somewhat tragic life, losing a son to suicide in 1985, a second son to a drug overdose in 1993, losing his wife to suicide after that, and losing a third son to a drug overdose in 1996. He currently lectures on drugs and does extensive charity work, for which he was recognized by being made a member of the Order of Canada in 1998. He was inducted into the Canadian Sports Hall of Fame in 1990 as well as the Canadian Boxing Hall of Fame. He has also appeared as an actor in 13 films and television series from 1977 to 2005.

Chuvalo is six feet tall and has a 76-inch **reach**. He fought at weights ranging from 192 to 249 pounds as a heavyweight. In 93 professional bouts, from 1956 to 1978, he won 73 (64 by knockout), lost 18 (two by knockout), had two draws, and fought a total of 507 rounds.

CLANCY, GILBERT THOMAS "GIL". B. 30 May 1922, Rockaway Beach, New York. D. 31 March 2011, Lynbrook, New York. Gil Clancy was raised in the Rockaway section of New York City. While serving in the U.S. Army, he became interested in boxing and did a little **amateur boxing**. After being discharged, he attended New York University and received both bachelor's and master's degrees. He worked as a teacher in the New York City school system, ran a gymnasium (which he later owned) on West 28th Street, and worked with amateur boxers for the New York Parks Department. One of his pupils, **Emile Griffith**, did well in the New York **Golden Gloves** tournament, reaching the **welterweight sub-novice** final in 1957 and winning the 1958 **open** championship, the 1958 eastern regionals championship, and the 1958 intercity championship.

When Griffith decided to become a professional boxer in 1958 following the Golden Gloves, Clancy became his **trainer** and comanager. Griffith's career rose, and before he retired in 1977, he had won both the world's welterweight and **middleweight** titles. Clancy became respected in the boxing world for his abilities as a trainer and worked at various times with champions **Muhammad Ali**, **Joe Frazier**, **George Foreman**, Rodrigo Valdés, Juan LaPorte, Ken Buchanan, and contenders **Ralph "Tiger" Jones**, **Jerry Quarry**, and **Gerry Cooney**.

He was voted as the "Manager of the Year" by the Boxing Writers Association of America in 1967 and 1973 and a decade later received their Sam Taub Award for Excellence in Broadcasting Journalism.

In 1978, he became the matchmaker for **Madison Square Garden** Boxing. In 1981, he turned to broadcasting and worked for the Columbia Broadcasting System, Home Box Office, and the Madison Square Garden Network.

He retired as a **cornerman** in 1990 but in 1997 came out of retirement to work with **Óscar De La Hoya**, remaining with him until 1999.

He was elected to the **International Boxing Hall of Fame** in 1993.

In the latter years of his life, he lived at an assisted living facility on Long Island and died at the age of 88 in 2011.

CLARK, LAMAR F. B. 1 December 1933, Cedar City, Utah. D. 5 November 2006, West Jordan, Utah. LaMar Clark is a boxer whose career might have gone completely differently had his manager been more careful in selecting an opponent.

Clark attended Cedar City High School and excelled in sports, playing basketball, football, and baseball. He was selected to Utah high school all-state teams in both basketball and football and received an athletic scholarship to the College of Southern Utah, where he was a fullback on their football team. His biggest claim to fame in the sports world occurred in boxing. He had an estimable **amateur boxing** career, won a regional **Golden Gloves** championship, and claimed an amateur record of 25–2.

Managed by Merv Jenson, who also managed **Gene Fullmer**, Clark became a professional boxer on 4 January 1958 with a six-round decision victory over John Hicks. This would be the only one of Clark's 46 **bouts** to go the distance. Fighting once a week at first and then once a month afterward, Clark won his first 12 bouts—11 by **knockout**. Jenson then sought publicity for Clark and had him fight twice in one night, scoring two first-round knockout wins on 13 October 1958. He bettered this feat on his next appearance by stopping three opponents on 10 November 1958. He then took part in the "Intermountain **Heavyweight**" tournament from 28 November to 1 December, scoring two knockouts on 28 November, one on 29 November, and then six on 1 December—five in the first round (one in seven seconds and one in 22 seconds).

Clark continued building up his remarkable record and by April 1960 had compiled a record of 42–0, with 41 knockouts (28 in the first round), although the quality of his opposition was poor. He made his national television debut against Bartolo Soni on 8 April 1960, and this choice of opponent was Jensen's (and Clark's) big mistake. Soni was a tough **journeyman** boxer with a 12–2–1 record who had never been knocked out and who was able to take Clark's best shots. Clark tired late in the fight and was stopped in the ninth round.

After that bout, Clark's career virtually came to an end. Clark met former **Olympic** champion **Pete Rademacher** on 29 June 1960 and was again stopped—this time in the 10th round. The following year, Clark knocked out Chuck Wilburn in two rounds and then met the undefeated **Cassius Clay**. Clay (later, the world's heavyweight champion and known as **Muhammad Ali**), in only his fifth professional bout, easily won by knockout at 1:27 of the second round, and Clark's **professional boxing** career ended.

Clark then returned to his life as a Utah chicken farmer and family man, but his name remains in boxing's record books for his 42 consecutive knockouts (some sources claim 44) and his six knockouts in one night.

Clark was five foot 10 inches tall and fought at weights ranging from 175 to 187 pounds as a heavyweight. In 46 professional bouts, from 1958 to 1961, he won 43 (42 by knockout), lost three (all three by knockout), and fought a total of 90 rounds.

CLAY, CASSIUS MARCELLUS, JR. *See* ALI, MUHAMMAD "THE LOUISVILLE LIP," "THE GREATEST" (né CASSIUS MARCELLUS CLAY).

CLINCH. When boxers are fighting close to one another, a boxer will often hold his opponent's **gloves** under his own arms as a defensive move to prevent the opponent from throwing punches. Such action will result in the **referee** issuing the command to "break," at which time both fighters are required to release contact with their opponent and take a step back. Failure to do so, or hitting when the break command is given, can result in a warning, loss of points, or even **disqualification**.

COHEN, HOWARD WILLIAM. *See* COSELL, HOWARD WILLIAM (né COHEN, HOWARD WILLIAM).

COLLEGE BOXING. At one time, collegiate boxing was a major collegiate sport administered by the National Collegiate Athletic Association (NCAA). National championships were held most years from 1924 to 1960. Schools that won more than one national championship were Wisconsin (eight titles), Penn State (five titles), Navy (four titles), Idaho (three titles), San Jose State (three titles), Idaho State (two titles), and Michigan State (two titles).

Among the boxers who won individual championships were Chuck Davey and Chuck Spieser of Michigan State, Ellsworth "Spider" Webb of Idaho State, and Tony DiBiase (all four becoming successful professional boxers), **Mills Lane** of Nevada (who became a well-known **referee**), Chuck Drazenovich of Penn State (who went on to a 10-year career in the National Football League), and Herbert Odom of Michigan State (who lost one professional **bout** then went on to a successful career as a dentist and tried his hand at **professional boxing** again at the age of 46, winning all six of his bouts before quitting the **ring** at the age of 50).

In 1961, however, following the 17 April 1960 death of University of Wisconsin college boxer Charlie Mohr in the 1960 NCAA national championships, the NCAA discontinued its association with boxing by eliminating its national collegiate boxing championship tournament, and most colleges dropped the sport. In 1976, the National Collegiate Boxing Association (NCBA) was formed, and in 2012 more than 35 member schools competed under its auspices. From 1976 to 2011, competition has been dominated by the service academies, with the **United States** Air Force Academy winning 18 NCBA national titles, the United States Naval Academy winning five national titles, and the United States Military Academy winning four national titles. The University of Nevada has also won four national titles.

See also COLLEGIANS WHO BOXED PROFESSIONALLY.

COLLEGIANS WHO BOXED PROFESSIONALLY. The overwhelming majority of **professional boxers** have minimal formal education and have found boxing a way to progress economically. But there have been a few who have attended college and found boxing a challenging sport to the extent that they have boxed professionally. In addition to the boxers who boxed on **college boxing** teams, such as Chuck Davey, Chuck Spieser, Ellsworth "Spider" Webb, and Tony DiBiase, there have been several other boxers with college educations who have become successful as professional boxers. Perhaps the most accomplished collegians/boxers are the **Klitschko brothers**—

Vitaly and Wladimir. Both earned PhD degrees in their native **Ukraine** at the Kiev University of Physical Science and Sports, and both also won the world's heavyweight championship.

James "Bonecrusher" Smith, who received a bachelor's degree in business administration from Shaw University in 1975, became a professional boxer in 1981 and won the **World Boxing Association** world's **heavyweight** championship in 1986. He compiled a record of 44–17–1 before retiring in 1999.

Carlos Palomino, who won the **welterweight** championship, attended Orange Coast College, a junior college in California, and later transferred to California State University, Long Beach, where he received a degree in recreational administration.

Other collegians with professional success include **Pete Rademacher**. In 1948, he enrolled at Washington State University, played on their football team, and continued **amateur boxing**. Following graduation with a bachelor of science degree in animal husbandry, he served in the U.S. Army at Fort Benning, Georgia, and then won the 1956 **Olympic** heavyweight title. In his first **bout** as a professional, he challenged **Floyd Patterson** for the world's heavyweight title but after scoring a **knockdown** in the second round was stopped in the sixth round. He continued boxing as a professional for several years before embarking on a successful business career.

Several other boxers in recent years have combined college and boxing. Among them are welterweight and **light middleweight** champion Vernon Forrest (University of Northern Michigan—business administration); Peter McNeeley, son of heavyweight title challenger Tom McNeeley (Bridgewater State College—political science); **World Boxing Organization middleweight** champion **Canadian** Otis Grant (Concordia University—recreation and leisure services); heavyweight title challenger Calvin Brock (University of North Carolina, Charlotte—finance); John DuPlessis (Southern University—psychology, master's degree in social work); British Olympic **gold medalist** and European Boxing Union heavyweight champion Audley Harrison (Brunel University, London—sport sciences); and **Tommy Hearns's** son, Ronald Hearns, who is a graduate of American University with a degree in criminal justice.

See also COLLEGE BOXING.

COLOMBIA. Although boxing is not one of the favorite sports in Colombia, since the 1960s the country has produced a significant amount of outstanding boxers. The sport is administered by the Comisión Nacional de Boxeo de Colombia.

In **amateur boxing**, Colombian boxers first competed in the 1972 **Olympic Games** and have entered 10 Olympic boxing tournaments—every one except 1980, when they boycotted the games. Their best year was their first year, 1972, when Clemente Rojas won the **featherweight** bronze medal and Alfonso Pérez won the **lightweight** bronze medal. Their only other Olympic boxing medalist was Jorge Julio in 1988. He won a bronze medal as a **bantamweight**.

Colombia has fared much better in **professional boxing**. They have produced 33 boxers who were world champions. The best, by far, was **Antonio Cervantes**, known as **Kid Pambelé**, who was inducted into the **International Boxing Hall of Fame** in 1998. Other Colombian world champions include Elvis Álvarez, Miguel Barrera, Fidel Bassa, Alejandro Berrio, Rodolfo Blanco, Prudencio Cardona, Ricardo Cardona, Jesús Geles, Harold Grey, Kermin Guardia, Ener Julio, Jorge Eliécer Julio, Miguel Lora, Carlos Maussa, Beibis Mendoza, Luis Enrique Mendoza, Harold Mestre, Tomas Molinares, Irene Pacheco, Rubén Darío Palacios, Mauricio Pastrana, Juan Polo Pérez, Yonnhy Pérez, Rafael Pineda, Daniel Reyes, Jorge Julio Rocha, Bebis José "Sugar Baby" Rojas, Carlos Tamara, Francisco Tejedor, Ricardo Torres, Juan Urango, and Rodrigo Valdéz.

COMMISSION. In most states in the **United States**, boxing is regulated by a state athletic commission, which licenses boxers, managers, seconds, and **referees**. Some state athletic commissions have gained considerable power in the boxing world, and for much of the 20th century, the **New York State Athletic Commission** was a leader in determining world champion boxers.

COMPUBOX. Compubox is a computerized punch counting system that was invented in 1984 by Jon Gibbs and initially promoted and operated by Bob Canobbio and Logan Hobson. It has been used under various names, such as Punchstat and FightStat. Two individuals, each following one of the two boxers in a match, press computer keys each time they see a punch thrown and punch connect. They also at times keep track of **jabs** or power punches. The system, although computerized, is limited by the sight and ability of its operators and, although widely used for **televised** fights, is far from perfect.

CONN, WILLIAM DAVID "BILLY," "THE PITTSBURGH KID". B. 8 October 1917, Pittsburgh, Pennsylvania. D. 29 May 1993, Pittsburgh, Pennsylvania. Billy Conn could have been the first world's **light heavyweight** champion to win the heavyweight title had he been more patient.

He began his **professional boxing** career on 20 July 1934 at the age of 16. After winning his first three fights, mostly in the Pittsburgh area, he then had a stretch in which he only won five of 11 **bouts**. His fortunes (and his skills) improved, and from 9 September 1935 until 13 August 1937, he won 27 of 28 bouts, with a **draw** in the other bout. Included in that streak were victories over future champion Fritzie Zivic and former champions Vince Dundee, Eddie "Babe" Risko, and Teddy Yarosz. His winning streak was stopped by former champion Young Corbett III, but Conn avenged that defeat three months later. In 1938 and 1939, Conn twice defeated **middleweight** champion Fred Apostoli in **nontitle** matches and also won twice against Solly Krieger, who was then recognized by the **National Boxing Association** as middleweight champion.

On 13 July 1939, Conn defeated Melio Bettina at **Madison Square Garden** on a 15-**round decision** and became world's light heavyweight champion. After three successful title defenses, one in a rematch with Bettina and two with future light heavyweight champion Gus Lesnevich, Conn decided to move up to the heavyweight class.

On 18 June 1941, at the Polo Grounds in New York, Conn fought **Joe Louis** for the world's heavyweight title. Conn only weighed 174 pounds to Louis' 199 and a half pounds. For most of the bout, Conn outboxed Louis and through 12 rounds was ahead on the scorecards of two of the officials, with the third official scoring the bout even. Had Conn been content to box with Louis for the next three rounds, most likely he would have won the heavyweight title. But Conn decided that he would go for a **knockout** in the 13th round. The tables turned on him, and Louis knocked him out with just two seconds remaining in the round.

After the fight, Conn won three more bouts, including a decision over future middleweight champion **Tony Zale**, and then went into the U.S. Army. Louis also served in the army.

In 1946, after both Louis and Conn had been discharged from the service, they met again on 19 June 1946 in a highly anticipated bout at Yankee Stadium. The fight was the first heavyweight championship bout to be **televised**. Before the fight, it was mentioned to Louis that Conn might outpoint him due to his speed. Louis's reply was the classic, "He can run, but he can't hide." True to his word, Louis attacked from the opening bell and knocked out Conn in the eighth round.

Conn fought only two more bouts, both in November 1948, and won both by knockouts in the ninth round.

Conn was six foot one inch tall and had a 72-inch **reach**. He fought at weights ranging from 135 to 190 pounds, primarily as a light heavyweight and heavyweight. In 76 professional bouts, from 1934 to 1948, he won 64 (15 by knockout), lost 11 (three by knockout), had one draw, and fought a total of 646 rounds. He was inducted as a member of the inaugural class of the **International Boxing Hall of Fame** in 1990.

COONEY, GERRY "GENTLEMAN GERRY". B. 4 August 1956, New York, New York. At the height of his career, Gerry Cooney was billed by promoters as a "**White Hope**." He attended Walt Whitman High School in

Huntington Station, New York, in Suffolk County on Long Island and began boxing for the Huntington Athletic Club. He won the 1973 New York **Golden Gloves middleweight sub-novice** championship. His brother, Tom, also competed in the Golden Gloves that year and reached the **heavyweight** final but was defeated. Gerry Cooney entered again in 1974, losing in the **light heavyweight open** quarterfinal round. In 1975, Gerry again lost as a light heavyweight but reached the final round. The following year, he moved up to the heavyweight class and won that championship.

Gerry Cooney became a professional boxer in 1977, winning his first fight with a one-**round knockout** against Bill Jackson at **Sunnyside Garden** on 15 February. By the end of 1978, he had won 15 straight **bouts**, 12 by knockout, often by virtue of his powerful left **hook**. In 1979, he began fighting scheduled 10-round bouts, usually as the semifinal or cofeatured bout at the **Felt Forum** or **Madison Square Garden**.

On 4 May 1980, Cooney fought Jimmy Young, a top-rated heavyweight who had lost a 15-round decision with **Muhammad Ali** in a heavyweight title bout and had also gone the distance with **George Foreman**, **Ron Lyle**, **Ken Norton**, and **Earnie Shavers**, some of boxing's hardest punchers. Cooney opened a bad cut over Young's eye and stopped him in four rounds. In his next fight, on 24 October 1980, Cooney knocked out Lyle at 2:49 of the first round.

Cooney was then matched with former heavyweight champion Ken Norton on 11 May 1981 and stopped him in only 54 seconds of the first round. At this point, the Caucasian Irish-American Cooney became one of boxing's hottest attractions in a sport in which the heavyweight division had been dominated by African American boxers. Promoter **Don King** latched on to this aspect and matched Cooney with heavyweight champion **Larry Holmes**, promoting Cooney as "the Great White Hope." Cooney, a pleasant personality with the nickname "Gentleman Gerry," disdained the publicity.

Cooney's managers, Dennis Rapaport and Mike Jones, shrewdly did not allow Cooney to fight again until the bout with Holmes, which took place on 11 June 1982 in **Las Vegas**. The highly promoted bout set Las Vegas attendance records and surprisingly lived up to expectations. Cooney, who entered the **ring** undefeated with a record of 25–0, was knocked down in the second round but came back strong. Holmes retained his undefeated record, winning his 40th consecutive bout, when he finally stopped Cooney in the 13th round.

Although Cooney fought and won twice in 1984 and once in 1986 against lower-caliber opponents, alcohol abuse contributed to his downfall. He never regained his aura and concluded his career by being stopped in five rounds by former heavyweight champion **Michael Spinks** in 1987 and in two rounds by former heavyweight champion **George Foreman** in 1990.

After retiring from ring activity, Cooney founded an organization called F.I.S.T. (Fighters Initiative for Support and **Training**) to help retired boxers. He has also cohosted a weekly radio boxing program and appeared in the 1998 Hollywood film *Mob Queen*. He has worked with boys at a youth home in Paterson, New Jersey, counseling them as well as teaching them boxing.

Cooney is six foot six inches tall and has an 81-inch **reach**. He fought at weights ranging from 208 to 238 pounds as a heavyweight. In 31 professional bouts, from 1977 to 1990, he won 28 (24 by knockout), lost three (all three by knockout), and fought a total of 113 rounds.

CORBETT, JAMES JOHN "JIM," "GENTLEMAN JIM". B. 1 September 1866, San Francisco, California. D. 18 February 1933, Bayside, New York. Gentleman Jim Corbett was a new breed of prizefighter in the late 19th century. Unlike many of the other fighters of that day, he came from a middle-class home, was a graduate of Sacred Heart High School in San Francisco, and worked as a bank teller after graduation. He did not learn his boxing skills by street fighting but rather from Professor William Watson, an Englishman, at the Olympic Sporting Club in San Francisco. Corbett was known for his scientific approach to boxing.

Corbett's first recorded professional fight took place in Salt Lake City, Utah, and Corbett, boxing under the name of Jim Dillon, won a four-**round bout** by **disqualification**. Over the next two years, Corbett had 13 fights on his record, the most notable being a win over top **heavyweight** Joe Choynski in a bout that began on 30 May 1889 in Fairfax, California, that was stopped by police after four rounds and continued on 5 June on a barge in the Fairfax harbor to avoid police intervention. Corbett **knocked out** Choynski in the 27th round of that battle. Corbett also won a six-round **decision** over **Jake Kilrain** on 18 February 1890 in New Orleans, Louisiana. Kilrain had previously gone 75 rounds with heavyweight champion **John L. Sullivan** in 1889 in the last **bareknuckle** heavyweight title bout.

On 21 May 1891, Corbett fought another of the era's best fighters, the black **Australian Peter Jackson**, in San Francisco. After 61 rounds, the bout was called "**no contest**" by **referee** Hiram Cook. On 7 September 1892, in the first heavyweight championship bout under **Marquess of Queensberry Rules**, Corbett faced the previously undefeated John L. Sullivan in New Orleans, Louisiana. Corbett knocked him out in the 21st round and became the new world's champion.

Over the next few years, Corbett appeared on the stage and boxed **exhibitions**. He only made one defense of his title, knocking out Charlie Mitchell in three rounds in Jacksonville, Florida, on 25 January 1894. Later that year, on 7 September 1894, he boxed an exhibition with Peter Courtney that was one of the first boxing matches ever filmed.

On 17 March 1897, in Carson City, Nevada, Corbett lost his championship to **Bob Fitzsimmons**, a former **middleweight** champion who only weighed 167 pounds on that day to Corbett's 184 pounds. The state of Nevada had recently passed a law legalizing the bout, and to ensure fair play, famed lawman Wyatt Earp and four others armed with six-shooters were in Corbett's **corner**, and Fitzsimmons had a similar amount of guardians. Fitzsimmons knocked Corbett down with a solid blow to the solar plexus, and Corbett was not able to get up by the count of 10.

Corbett had four more bouts in his boxing career. On 22 November 1898, he was losing a bout with Tom Sharkey in New York City when one of Corbett's seconds jumped into the **ring** in the ninth round. The referee, Honest John Kelly, had no choice but to disqualify Corbett and award the bout to Sharkey.

Corbett two years later challenged Fitzsimmons's conqueror, **James J. Jeffries**, for the world's heavyweight title on 11 May 1900 at Coney Island, New York, and was winning the bout when Jeffries caught him with a short left-hand punch to the jaw, knocking him out in the 23rd round of their scheduled 25-round bout.

In Corbett's next bout, he won by a fifth-round knockout over **Charles "Kid" McCoy** in a bout that was suspected of being deliberately lost by McCoy. Corbett's final bout of his ring career was a rematch with Jeffries on 14 August 1903 in San Francisco, but Corbett was stopped in the 10th round.

In retirement, Corbett returned to the stage and films. He and his second wife (the actress Jessie Taylor) lived in Bayside, New York (a section of the Borough of Queens in New York City), and lived on Corbett Road—a road that still bears his name in the 21st century. He died at his home at the age of 67. Jim's brother, Joe Corbett, was a major league baseball player.

Corbett was six foot one inch tall and had a 73-inch **reach**. He fought at weights ranging from 178 to 188 pounds as a heavyweight. In 24 professional bouts, from 1886 to 1903, he won 11 (five by knockout), lost four (three by knockout), had three draws, had three **no-contest** bouts, and fought three bouts in which he was awarded a **newspaper decision**. He fought a total of 252 rounds and was inducted as a member of the inaugural class of the **International Boxing Hall of Fame** in 1990.

CORNER. Boxers are assigned to opposite corners of the **ring**. The two other corners of the ring are referred to as neutral corners, and when a boxer scores a **knockdown**, he must go to a neutral corner while the **referee** counts over his fallen opponent.

CORNERMAN. Boxers generally have two or three individuals to attend to them during the intervals between **rounds**. They are known as seconds or cornermen. One usually specializes in repairing physical damage due to cuts or abrasions and is known as a **cutman**. The other is usually the boxer's **trainer** or manager, who attempts to impart strategic advice.

CORTEZ, JOE. B. 13 October 1945, New York, New York. Although born in New York, Joe Cortez was raised in **Puerto Rico** and is bilingual in English and Spanish, an accomplishment that has been quite useful in his career as a boxing **referee**. He began boxing as an **amateur** in New York and did well in the New York **Golden Gloves**. He represented the Boys Club of New York and won the 1960 **flyweight sub-novice** and the 1961 **open**, eastern regionals, and intercity **bantamweight** titles. In 1962, he was defeated in the New York Golden Gloves finals. His brother, Mike, was also an exceptional amateur boxer during those three years, winning the 1960 **featherweight** sub-novice, 1961 open, eastern regionals, and intercity **lightweight** titles and also losing in the 1962 lightweight finals.

Joe became a professional boxer on 3 December 1962 and won his first **bout** as a bantamweight on a second-round **knockout** over Tony Salgado in Bakersfield, California. In his third bout, he lost a six-round decision to George Foster. From 1963 to 1966, Cortez had eight bouts in the featherweight class, winning all by decision. His final bout was on 28 February 1970 in San Juan, Puerto Rico—another winning effort.

In 1969, he moved with his family to Puerto Rico and began working in the hotel industry, moving up from front desk clerk to executive assistant manager. He returned to New York in 1976 and continued working for the hotel's parent corporation. In New York, he began his alternate career as a referee. By the 1980s, he was refereeing and judging world championship bouts. In 1982, he purchased a delicatessen in Yonkers and began working in the community for the Police Athletic League.

He became one of the most widely sought-after officials during the next 30 years and by the time of his retirement on 15 September 2012 had worked 170 world championship bouts as a referee. His catchphrase, "I'm fair but I'm firm," has become a copyrighted trademark.

In retirement, he plans on working on a project he calls Cortez 2020, which will elevate the position that the **ringside judges'** view a fight from to enable them to have a better view of the action.

Although he claims to have had 19 professional bouts (winning all but one), only 11 are recorded on Boxrec. In those 11 professional bouts, from 1962 to 1970, he won 10 (only one by knockout), lost one (by decision), and fought a total of 51 rounds, primarily in the featherweight class. For his work as a referee and judge, he was inducted into the **International Boxing Hall of Fame** in 2011 in the nonparticipant category.

COSELL, HOWARD WILLIAM (né COHEN, HOWARD WILLIAM).

B. 25 March 1918, Winston-Salem, North Carolina. D. 23 April 1995, New York, New York. Howard Cosell "never played the game," as one of his books was titled, yet he was one of the major factors in the rise of interest in professional football during the 1970s.

Born in North Carolina, he was raised in Brooklyn, New York, and graduated from Alexander Hamilton High School in Brooklyn. He continued his education at New York University (NYU) earning a bachelor's degree in English, and followed that with a law degree also from NYU.

He served in the U.S. Army Transportation Corps during World War II and achieved the rank of major when he was discharged. He began practicing law, specializing in union law.

In 1953, he was offered a nonpaying job by the American Broadcasting Company (ABC) as a host of a radio show about Little League baseball. After three years, he decided he enjoyed radio more than law and convinced the head of ABC to give him a full-time radio position. He was able to later parlay his radio broadcasting into television work for ABC and was a sports anchorman from 1961 to 1974.

During that time, boxer Cassius Clay came into prominence, and Cosell befriended him. When Clay converted to Islam and changed his name to **Muhammad Ali**, Cosell was one of the few sportscasters to use the name Ali. Cosell also took a strong stand in favor of Ali when Ali was stripped of his **heavyweight** championship for his stand on the Vietnam War and refusal to serve in the military. After Ali won his Supreme Court battle and returned to boxing, Cosell was the primary announcer for many of Ali's fights. When in 1970 ABC began an experiment televising football in prime time, Cosell was chosen along with Keith Jackson and Don Meredith to host Monday Night Football. The thrust of the show was to be entertaining, and Cosell was selected for his opinionated persona. The show turned out to be successful far beyond the expectations of ABC producer Roone Arledge and NFL commissioner Pete Rozelle. The chemistry between Cosell and the laid-back Meredith provided many memorable moments, and Monday Night Football became mandatory watching for much of the United States' male population. Although Cosell came across as pompous and arrogant at times, and was voted as the favorite sports broadcaster by some and the least favorite by others, he definitely had people watching. During the height of his career, he hosted an entertainment show, *Saturday Night Live with Howard Cosell*, for several weeks during 1975. He also worked other sports, including baseball, and was one of the commentators during the massacre at the 1972 **Olympic Games** in Munich.

During the 1980s, Cosell became disenchanted with much of professional sports and withdrew from announcing boxing. The final straw for Cosell was the 26 November 1982 heavyweight championship **bout** between Randall

"Tex" Cobb and **Larry Holmes**. The bout was extremely one-sided, with Cobb absorbing punishment in each of the 15 **rounds**. As the fight progressed, Cosell became more and more adamant that referee Steve Crosson should stop the bout and finally said words to the effect that if the bout was not stopped that he would never broadcast boxing again.

He continued to do *Monday Night Football*, but after criticizing ABC in one of his books, *I Never Played the Game*, he was dropped by the network. He is best remembered for his voice, for his deliberate delivery, and for "telling it like it is." He was inducted into the **International Boxing Hall of Fame** in 2010 in the category of observer.

COUNTERPUNCH. A counterpunch is a punch thrown immediately after an opponent throws a punch and is meant to exploit the opening left by the original punch. Among the best counterpunchers were **Roy Jones Jr.**, **Floyd Mayweather Jr.**, Eddie Mustafa Muhammad, **José Nápoles**, **Salvador Sánchez**, **James Toney**, **Jersey Joe Walcott**, and **Pernell Whitaker**.

See also BOLO PUNCH; CROSS; HAYMAKER; HOOK; JAB; UPPERCUT.

CREAM, ARNOLD RAYMOND. *See* WALCOTT, JERSEY JOE (né ARNOLD RAYMOND CREAM).

CRIBB, TOM. B. 8 July 1781, Bristol, **England**. D. 11 May 1848, London, England. After Tom Cribb completed service in the British Navy, he turned to **bareknuckle** prizefighting, with his first recorded **bout** occurring on 7 January 1805—a 76-**round** defeat of George Maddox in a battle lasting two hours and 12 minutes. Following that bout, he won twice more in 1805 before losing in July to George Nichols in 52 rounds and one and a half hours.

In October 1805, Cribb, in a bout lasting one and a half hours, defeated Bill Richmond, a former slave who reportedly was one of the hangmen involved with the death of Nathan Hale, captured as a spy by the British in 1776.

Cribb's next reported bout was not until 1807, when he stopped Jem Belcher in 41 rounds. The following year, Cribb defeated George Horton in May and on 25 October 1808 defeated Bob Gregson in 23 rounds and claimed the championship of England. Cribb kept that title until 1822, when he retired from the **ring**.

He defended it in 1809 against Belcher, in 1810 and again in 1811 against **Tom Molineaux**, another former slave who became a prizefighter, and in several less-documented fights.

In his career as a prizefighter, Cribb was one of the first to actually train for upcoming fights. He was also known for "milling on the retreat"—striking a blow and then backing up to avoid a **counterpunch**.

On 18 May 1822, Cribb announced his retirement from the ring. In retirement, he was a coal merchant and opened a pub. In London today, there is still a Tom Cribb pub located in the general area of Cribb's original establishment.

He was inducted into the **International Boxing Hall of Fame** in 1991.

CROSS. A cross, usually referred to as a right (or left) cross, is a type of straight punch that is thrown directly across a boxer's body. It is usually one of the more powerful punches and can often cause a **knockdown** or **knockout**.

See also BOLO PUNCH; COUNTERPUNCH; HAYMAKER; HOOK; JAB; UPPERCUT.

CRUISERWEIGHT. Cruiserweight is a boxing weight class. In Britain, the term *cruiserweight* was formerly synonymous with **light heavyweight**, but in 1979 the **World Boxing Council** created a division with a maximum weight limit of 190 pounds and called it "cruiserweight." Through the years, the weight limit has been gradually raised from 190 pounds to its present-day 200-pound limit in 2012 and has been referred to at times by some sanctioning organizations as "junior heavyweight."

On 12 August 1979, Marvin Camel and Mate Parlov met in Split, Croatia, in the first world's cruiserweight championship match in a rare fight between two **southpaws**. Ironically, the two **judges** and the **referee** split their votes, with the referee voting for Parlov but the two judges calling the **bout** even. Consequently, the bout was ruled a **draw**, and there was no champion selected. In the rematch, held on 31 March 1980 in **Las Vegas**, Nevada, Camel won a **unanimous decision** and became the division's first champion.

Among the division's best champions have been Tomasz Adamek, O'Neil Bell, Juan Carlos Gómez, Bobby Czyz, Carlos de León, David Haye, Virgil Hill, **Evander Holyfield**, Orlin Norris, Dwight Muhammad Qawi, and **James Toney**.

CUBA. Boxing has long been a popular sport in Cuba. Prior to the Fidel Castro administration, quite a few Cuban professional boxers appeared among the ranked boxers, and several were world champions. When Cuba became a communist country, it, as did most of the European Iron Curtain countries, placed emphasis on **amateur boxing**, and since 1960, Cuba has continually furnished the top boxing teams in world competition.

Cuba first competed in the 1960 **Olympic Games** and has entered 12 Olympic boxing tournaments. They boycotted both the 1984 and 1988 games but still are in second place with a total of 67 Olympic boxing medals—34 **gold**, 19 **silver**, and 14 **bronze**. They have won gold medals in every weight class save **light heavyweight**. **Teófilo Stevenson** and **Félix Savon**, both heavyweights, each have won three Olympic gold medals. The only other man to win three Olympic gold medals in boxing was the **Hungarian László Papp**. In 1980, Cuba won 10 medals in the 11 weight divisions (although that year many countries boycotted the games). But in 1992, when all nations competed, they won nine medals in 12 divisions, eight of 11 in 2004, and eight of 10 in 2008. In fact, in the five Olympic Games from 1992 to 2008, Cuba medaled in 38 of the 57 boxing events.

Cuban Olympians who won more than one gold medal in addition to Stevenson and Savon are Guillermo Rigondeaux (2000 and 2004 **bantamweight**), Mario Kindelán (2000 and 2004 **lightweight**), Ángel Herrera (1976 **featherweight** and 1980 lightweight), Héctor Vinent (1992 and 1996 **light welterweight**), and Ariel Hernández (1992 and 1996 **middleweight**). Other Cuban boxers with multiple Olympic medals include Maikro Romero (1996 **flyweight** gold and 2000 **light flyweight** bronze), Andrés Aldama (1976 light welterweight silver and 1980 **welterweight** gold), Roniel Iglesias (2008 light welterweight bronze and 2012 gold), Juan Hernández (1992 and 1996 welterweight silver), and Rolando Garbey (1968 **light middleweight** silver and 1976 bronze).

Emilio Correa won the 1972 welterweight gold medal, and his son, Emilio Jr., won the 2008 middleweight silver medal.

Although Cuba today does not permit their top amateur boxers to become **professional**, in recent years this prohibition has been relaxed, and several Cuban boxers have left Cuba and boxed professionally, including world champions Joel Casamayor, Yuriorkis Gamboa, Juan Carlos **Gómez**, Yoan Pablo Hernández, Diosbelys Hurtado, and Guillermo Rigondeaux. Prior to Cuba becoming a communist country in 1959, there were quite a few good Cuban world champions, such as **Kid Chocolate**, **Kid Gavilán**, José Legrá, **José Nápoles**, the ill-fated **Benny "Kid" Paret**, Ultiminio "Sugar" Ramos, and Luis Manuel Rodríguez. Other exceptional Cuban professional boxers include Omelio Agramonte, Black Bill, Orlando Echeverria, Florentino Fernández, Ángel Robinson García, Isaac Logart, Jesús "Chico" Varona, Doug Vaillant, Niño Valdés, and Orlando Zulueta.

CUTMAN. A cutman is a boxer's second who specializes in patching cuts between **rounds** so that a boxer is able to continue. Some of the techniques used are placing an icebag or a piece of cold metal (called enswell) on the injured area, rubbing petroleum jelly to prevent additional damage, and applying cotton swabs treated with various medications to the injury. Among the best cutmen have been Eddie Aliano, Pedro "Pellin" Ávila, Milt Bailey, "Whitey" Bimstein, Chuck Bodak, Freddie Brown, Ralph Citro, **Angelo Dundee**, Al Gavin, Jimmy Glenn, Adolph "Ace" Marotta, and Joe Souza.

ČUVALO, JURE. *See* CHUVALO, GEORGE LOUIS (né JURE ČUVALO).

D

D'AMATO, CONSTANTINE "CUS". B. 17 January 1908, Bronx, New York. D. 4 November 1985, Catskill, New York. Cus D'Amato was one of boxing's great managers and **trainers**. He, along with partner Jack Barro, opened the Empire Sporting Club at the Gramercy Gym on 14th Street in New York City. D'Amato was extremely dedicated to **training** young boxers and actually lived at the gym for a time. His first big success was **Floyd Patterson**, whom he helped win the 1951 and 1952 New York **Golden Gloves** and 1952 **Olympic Games gold medal**. After Patterson became a **professional** boxer, D'Amato helped guide him to the world's **heavyweight** championship.

D'Amato taught his fighters the "peek-a-boo" style of defense, in which the boxer holds both hands up high to protect his face and uses his elbows to protect the body.

He was a very honest man who mistrusted many in the world of boxing, especially those in the International Boxing Club (IBC), the organization with underworld ties that ran boxing in the 1950s. As a result of this mistrust, after Patterson won the championship, D'Amato very carefully selected his opponents to avoid dealing with the IBC.

Another of D'Amato's prize pupils was **José Torres**, who after winning the 1956 Olympic Games and the 1958 New York Golden Gloves, won the world's professional **middleweight** and **light heavyweight** championships. After Patterson and Torres retired, they each became commissioners of the **New York State Athletic Commission**.

In the 1960s, D'Amato moved from the city to the country, relocating in upstate Catskill, New York, about 30 miles south of Albany near the Hudson River. He continued running a gym there and was assisted at times by trainers Kevin Rooney and **Teddy Atlas**. One of his pupils was **Mike Tyson**, who had been in a nearby reform school. D'Amato became a father figure to Tyson and helped to bring him along as a professional fighter but died about one year before Tyson won the heavyweight championship. One of the great tragedies in Tyson's life was the death of D'Amato and the subsequent death two years later of Tyson's comanager, **Jim Jacobs**. Tyson had turned his life around from a background as a troubled youth and was living the life of a model citizen and being groomed as one of boxing's future great fighters, but after the passing of D'Amato and Jacobs, Tyson came under the influence of promoter **Don King** and, although still a good fighter, his behavior changed drastically.

After D'Amato moved upstate, he became an avid fisherman. He had some unusual quirks. One of them was that when getting dressed he always jumped into his pants with two feet at the same time so that when someone would use the old adage and say to him, "You're no different than me; you put your pants on one leg at a time," D'Amato could just smile at him.

He was inducted into the **International Boxing Hall of Fame** in 1995.

DE LA HOYA, ÓSCAR "GOLDEN BOY". B. 4 February 1973, East Los Angeles, California. Óscar De La Hoya has been one of the most successful boxers in history—both in the **ring** and out. He has won an **Olympic gold medal** and **professional** championships in six different weight classes and reportedly has a net worth in excess of 175 million dollars.

Of Mexican American descent, he was raised in the largely Hispanic East Los Angeles section of Los Angeles, California, and is a graduate of Garfield High School. As an **amateur** boxer, he claimed a record of 234–6 (although some sources say 223–5). He won the 1989 National **Golden Gloves feather-erweight** title, the 1990 **United States** amateur featherweight championship, the 1990 Goodwill Games featherweight gold medal, the 1991 United States amateur **lightweight** title, and 1992 Olympic lightweight gold medal.

He fought his first professional **bout** on 23 November 1992, winning easily on a one-**round knockout**. After winning his first 11 bouts, 10 by knockout, he fought Jimmi Bredahl, a Danish fighter who was also undefeated (16–0) at that time for the **World Boxing Organization** (WBO) **super featherweight** title on 5 March 1994 in Los Angeles. De La Hoya won the first of his many professional titles when Bredahl retired after the 10th round.

After one defense of that title, De La Hoya won the **vacant** WBO **lightweight** title by knocking out Jorge Páez, the colorful former circus clown, on a second-round knockout. De La Hoya defended that title six times successfully and then moved up in weight class to the **light welterweight** division.

On 7 June 1996, he fought the legendary **Julio César Chávez**, the **World Boxing Council (WBC)** light welterweight champion, who had lost just once in 98 bouts. De La Hoya stopped Chávez on cuts in the fourth round and gained his third title. After just one defense of that title, De La Hoya again moved up in weight and fought **Pernell Whitaker**, also a former Olympic champion, for Whitaker's WBC **welterweight** title. Óscar won a 12-round **unanimous decision** and gained his fourth title in less than four years of boxing as a professional.

De La Hoya defended the WBC welterweight title seven times successfully, including victories over former multiple-division champion **Héctor Camacho** and a rematch eighth-round stoppage of Chávez.

On 18 September 1999, De La Hoya suffered the first defeat of his professional career and the loss of his title when the undefeated (35–0) **Félix Trinidad** won a close 12-round **majority decision**. After Trinidad vacated the title to move up in weight class, in 2000 De La Hoya fought another undefeated (34–0) fighter, Shane Mosley, for the vacant WBC welterweight championship. De La Hoya was stymied again as he lost a **split decision** to Mosley. Óscar then stopped **Arturo Gatti** (another ex-champion, who was also between championships at the time) in a **nontitle bout**.

In De La Hoya's next fight, he won his fifth championship. He won a 12-round unanimous decision over Javier Castillejo on 23 June 2001 and became WBC **light middleweight** champion. In his first title defense, he stopped Fernando Vargas and in the process gained the **World Boxing Association** light middleweight title also. After defending those titles once, he then took on Shane Mosley and again lost to Mosley, along with the light middleweight titles.

In 2004, De La Hoya again moved up in weight and won a title in a sixth different weight class. He won a 12-round unanimous decision over Felix Sturm for the WBO **middleweight** title. He only held it for three months, as he was knocked out by **Bernard Hopkins** in nine rounds on 18 September 2004 in a failed attempt to unify the four middleweight titles. With the victory, Hopkins then claimed all four belts.

After a brief hiatus of 18 months, De La Hoya was back in the **ring** on 6 May 2006 and regained the WBC light middleweight title by stopping Ricardo Mayorga in six rounds. He lost that title in his first defense, nearly one year later, to **Floyd Mayweather Jr.** on a 12-round split decision.

On 6 December 2008, De La Hoya faced another super champion, **Manny Pacquiao**, in a nontitle match that was one of the most widely seen pay-per-view contests in boxing history, generating $70 million in revenue.

De La Hoya retired from the bout after the eighth round and retired from boxing following the fight.

De La Hoya has been involved in a variety of enterprises. In 2007, his company Golden Boy Enterprises acquired ownership of several boxing publications, including the historic *Ring* **magazine**. In 2008, he purchased a part ownership in the professional soccer team the Houston Dynamo. In 2010, he began promoting boxing shows with his company Golden Boy Productions.

De la Hoya is five foot 10 inches tall and has a 73-inch **reach**. He fought at weights ranging from 128 to 160 pounds in weight classes from super featherweight to middleweight. In De La Hoya's professional career, he fought 45 bouts, and only 16 were nontitle bouts—including 11 at the beginning of his career and three at the end of it. Of course, with the proliferation of sanctioning organizations and weight classes, this was much easier to accomplish in the 1990s and early 21st century than it would have been in earlier generations of boxing history. In those 45 professional bouts, from 1992 to 2008, he won 39 (30 by knockout), lost six (two by knockout), and fought a total of 308 rounds.

DEATH IN THE RING. *See* FATALITIES.

DECISION. When a **bout** reaches the end of the scheduled number of **rounds**, the winner is determined by the decision of the **referee** and/or **judges**. In most modern-day professional bouts, three judges are used. In some jurisdictions, the referee casts a vote along with two judges. In **England**, historically, only the referee determines the victor. In some **amateur boxing** matches, five judges are used. During the early 20th century, some jurisdictions did not permit decisions to be rendered for bouts that went the scheduled distance, although most newspapers covering the bout gave their opinion as to the winner.

See also DRAW; MAJORITY DECISION; MAJORITY DRAW; NEWSPAPER DECISION; SPLIT DECISION; TECHNICAL DECISION; UNANIMOUS DECISION.

DEMPSEY, JACK "THE NONPAREIL" (né JOHN EDWARD KELLY). B. 15 December 1862, Curran, County Kildare, **Ireland**. D. 2 November 1895, New York, New York. In the words of the incomparable **Bert Randolph Sugar** in his book *The 100 Greatest Boxers of All Time*, "We tend to forget that there were two Jack Dempseys. Without the second one, the original might well have enjoyed timeless fame as one of the greatest fighters of all time; instead, he is known only as the second greatest fighter named Jack Dempsey, if he is known at all."

Born in Ireland, Dempsey was raised in New York City and worked as a cooper (barrel maker). He began boxing in the days when **bareknuckle** fighting was still an acceptable method, and his early fights include bareknuckle **bouts** as well as ones fought under the **Marquess of Queensberry Rules**. His first recorded bout was on 3 September 1883 in the Coney Island section of Brooklyn, New York. On 6 March 1884, he stopped Bill Dacey in nine rounds and claimed the **lightweight** championship of New York.

Later that year, in a bout in Philadelphia, Pennsylvania, he boxed a six-round **draw** with Jimmy Ryan. In a situation typical of the era, the bout was rather a tame one, and the fans demanded that the fighters box an additional round so that they would feel they had received their money's worth of action. The two boxers obliged, and the result was recorded as a seven-round draw.

In 1885, Dempsey traveled to California and engaged in several bouts in San Francisco and Los Angeles, including at least one bareknuckle bout. After spending a year out west, he returned to New York in 1886. One of his victories that year was a four-round defeat of Professor Mike Donovan, one of the foremost boxing instructors of the era, father of famed **referee** Arthur Donovan, and grandfather of hall of fame professional football player Art Donovan.

As Dempsey was undefeated, he began referring to himself as "the nonpareil," from the French words meaning "without equal."

On 14 March 1886, in Larchmont, New York (a suburb of New York City), Dempsey defeated George LaBlanche in 13 rounds and claimed the American **middleweight** title as a result. On 9 April 1887, Dempsey suffered his first loss after 44 fights. It occurred in a four-round bout with Billy Baker and was only due to the prefight agreement that Baker would be the winner should he last all four rounds.

On 13 December 1887, Dempsey engaged in another bout peculiar to that era. He met John Reagan for the middleweight championship of America in a bareknuckle bout under **London Prize Ring Rules** wearing skintight **gloves**. The bout was held on the shore of Long Island Sound in Manhasset, and spectators reached the venue via tugboat. After 15 minutes of fighting, a rising tide caused the bout to be relocated 25 miles away. Reagan retired after the 44th round.

In 1889, Dempsey traveled west again and fought LaBlanche in San Francisco on 27 August in a **"fight to the finish."** LaBlanche was losing that fight, but in the 32nd round he closed his eyes and pivoted on one foot with his arm extended. His punch hit Dempsey flush on the jaw and knocked him out. The punch, labeled a "pivot punch," was subsequently ruled to be an illegal blow and forbidden in future fights, although the result of the LaBlanche–Dempsey bout was allowed to stand. As Dempsey's title was not at stake in the bout, he remained middleweight champion.

On 18 February 1890, in San Francisco, Dempsey successfully defended his title against Billy McCarthy with a 28th-round **technical knockout** of McCarthy. The following year in New Orleans, Louisiana, on 14 January 1891, Dempsey lost his title to **Bob Fitzsimmons** via a 13th-round retirement.

Dempsey went into semiretirement and did not fight for two years. His next bout was a four-round bout in 1893 in which he was outweighed by 42 pounds, 190 to 148, but won the decision over Billy Keough. Dempsey fought only two more bouts—a 20-round **draw** with Billy McCarthy in New Orleans in 1894 and a three-round technical knockout at the hands of **Tommy Ryan** in Coney Island on 18 January 1895.

Dempsey died of tuberculosis on 2 November 1895 at the age of 32. After he died, he was buried in an unmarked grave that inspired a Portland, Oregon, man to write a poem about Dempsey.

Dempsey was five foot eight inches tall and fought at weights ranging from 134 to 164 pounds in weight classes from lightweight to middleweight. In 67 professional bouts, from 1883 to 1895, he won 49 (23 by **knockout**), lost five (three by knockout), had 11 draws and two **no-contest** bouts, and fought a total of 474 rounds. He was inducted into the **International Boxing Hall of Fame** in 1992.

See also APPENDIX M.

DEMPSEY, WILLIAM HARRISON "JACK," "THE MANASSA MAULER". B. 24 June 1895, Manassa, Colorado. D. 31 May 1983, New York, New York. Although he only fought a comparatively few fights, Jack Dempsey's most memorable ones occurred during the "Golden Age of Sport," and consequently his name is place alongside those of Babe Ruth, Red Grange, Bill Tilden, and Bobby Jones as that era's sports heroes.

Dempsey began boxing in Colorado mining towns, often challenging men in local saloons to **bouts**. He claimed to have first fought **professionally** in 1913 as "Kid Blackie," but records of those fights have not yet been found. His first recorded bout was on 18 August 1914 in Colorado Springs, Colorado, and it was ruled a six-**round draw**. He then has recorded bouts in Utah, Idaho, and Nevada in 1914 and 1915. After winning most of his early bouts by **knockout**, he came to New York City in 1916. He won his first two bouts in New York and then fought John Lester Johnson, a tough black opponent. Johnson broke two of Dempsey's ribs with hard body blows in the 10-round **no-decision** fight, which was ruled a draw by the newspapers. As a result of that bout, Dempsey learned the importance of body punching and subsequently became one of the sport's best body punchers.

He returned west and after winning four bouts met "Fireman" Jim Flynn in Murray, Utah, on 13 February 1917. Flynn had been one of the better **heavyweights** but was then 37 years old and past his prime. Dempsey was knocked out by Flynn in just a few seconds of the opening round, although it has been speculated that Dempsey **took a dive**. Dempsey then traveled to California, where he fought a series of four-round bouts. It was during this time in California that Dempsey met **Jack "Doc" Kearns**, who became his manager.

In 1917, Dempsey fought Willie Meehan, a relatively short (five foot nine inch), fat fighter who defeated Dempsey in one bout, fought draws with him in two others, and lost only one of four bouts to Dempsey. With Kearns's help Dempsey began establishing a reputation and defeated contenders Ed "Gunboat" Smith, Bill Brennan, Carl Morris, and, in a return bout, "Fireman" Jim Flynn, whom Dempsey knocked out in one round. In 1918, Dempsey scored five consecutive one-round knockouts.

Kearns's promotion of Dempsey earned Jack a shot at **Jess Willard's** heavyweight title on 4 July 1919 in Toledo, Ohio. Reportedly, Kearns bet a huge sum of money on Dempsey to win by knockout in the first round. Although Dempsey was outweighed by 58 pounds by Willard and was five inches shorter, Willard was no match for Dempsey, who knocked Willard down seven times in the first round. Unfortunately for Kearns and Dempsey, Willard got up each time and survived until the third round, when the bout was finally stopped.

Dempsey's first defense of his title was on 6 September 1920 against Billy Miske in a 10-round no-decision fight in Benton Harbor, Michigan. Miske had previously fought a 10-round draw and a six-round no decision bout with Jack, but by then he had contracted Bright's disease and was no match for Dempsey, who knocked him out in three rounds.

In Dempsey's next title defense, he stopped Bill Brennan in 12 rounds on 14 December 1920 at **Madison Square Garden**. On 21 July 1921, promoter **Tex Rickard** established boxing's first million-dollar gate when he scheduled Dempsey (who had incurred some public animosity as a "slacker" during the World War when he did not serve in the U.S. Armed Forces) versus the decorated French war hero and **light heavyweight** champion **Georges Carpentier**. The bout drew 80,183 people, who paid $1,789,238, to an arena specially constructed for the bout in Jersey City, New Jersey. The bout proved to be a relatively one-sided one, with Dempsey knocking out Carpentier in the fourth round.

Dempsey's next major bout occurred in the small town of Shelby, Montana, on 4 July 1923. The town's leaders, eager to attract attention to their town, where oil had recently been discovered, offered $250,000 to Kearns and Dempsey to defend the heavyweight title there, with an additional $150,000 promised to Dempsey's opponent, Tommy Gibbons. Local banks put up the money to stage the attraction. Attendance was exceptionally poor though, with only 7,000 fans paying to see the fight and an estimated 13,000 fans crashing the gate and seeing it for free. Kearns received $200,000 before the fight, with a promise of part of the gate receipts. The bout was a relatively dull affair in which Dempsey won a 15-round **decision**. Immediately after the bout, Kearns and Dempsey left town with the additional $50,000 from the gate receipts. Several Shelby banks failed as a result of the fiasco.

Dempsey's next title defense occurred only two months afterward and was another of Rickard's major promotions. At the Polo Grounds in New York on 14 September 1923, Dempsey met Argentinean **Luis Ángel Firpo**. The bout turned out to be one of the most exciting in boxing history, as Firpo knocked Dempsey down twice in the first round, the second time through the ropes. After the first knock down, where Dempsey's knees barely touched the **canvas**, he got up and knocked Firpo down seven times. After the seventh **knockdown**, Firpo hit Dempsey with a wild right-hand punch that knocked

Dempsey through the ropes. He was helped back into the **ring** by the newspaper men seated in **ringside** seats and was ready to continue boxing by the count of nine. In the second round, Dempsey continued his attack and had Firpo down twice more, with the second knockdown being for the 10 count.

The first round as well as the brief bout appear on many boxing historians' lists as among the greatest rounds and greatest bouts in boxing history.

Kearns and Dempsey split acrimoniously in 1925 after Dempsey's wife accused Kearns of withholding monies due to Dempsey.

Dempsey did not fight for three years after that bout. In one of boxing's most famous bouts, he defended his title against **Gene Tunney**, a former U.S. Marine. The bout, another Rickard promotion, drew 120,557 fans to Philadelphia's Sesquicentennial Stadium—the largest crowd in boxing history to that point. It was scheduled for only 10 rounds due to Pennsylvania law, and Tunney won the decision and the heavyweight championship.

In 1927, Dempsey fought **Jack Sharkey**, a future heavyweight champion on 21 July in a bout to determine Tunney's next challenger. Dempsey knocked out Sharkey in the seventh round to set up a rematch with Tunney for the title. That bout took place just two months later on 22 September 1927 in Chicago at Soldier Field. It drew boxing's first two-million-dollar gate with a live attendance of 104,943. Dempsey was behind on points but in the seventh round knocked Tunney down. A new rule at that time required the boxer scoring the knockdown to go to a neutral **corner** while the **referee** counted over the fallen fighter. (Previously, the fighter scoring the knockdown could just stand over his fallen foe and knock him down again as soon as he got up—Dempsey's seven knockdowns of Willard occurred in this manner.) In the fight with Tunney, Dempsey forgot the rule and stood over his opponent until referee Dave Barry made Dempsey move.

After Dempsey did so, Barry began to count. Tunney got up at the count of nine, but films of the fight show that he was down for 14 seconds. Tunney continued to stay away from Dempsey and was not down again in the fight. At the end of the scheduled 10 rounds, Tunney was declared the winner.

Dempsey retired after the fight, claiming problems with his eye, although he continued to box **exhibitions** for several years afterward. He also worked as a referee for both boxing and professional wrestling and owned a popular restaurant on Broadway in New York City. During World War II, he served in the New York State Guard and in the U.S. Coast Guard reserve.

Dempsey was six foot one inch tall and had a 77-inch **reach.** He fought at weights ranging from 181 to 200 pounds as a heavyweight. In 83 professional bouts, from 1914 to 1927, he won 61 (50 by knockout), lost six (one by knockout), and had nine draws, one **no-contest**, and six no-decision bouts, in which he was awarded the **newspaper decision** four times and drew two other. He fought a total of 350 rounds. He was inducted as a member of the inaugural class of the **International Boxing Hall of Fame** in 1990.

DEMPSEY–TUNNEY. On 23 September 1926, in Sesquicentennial Stadium, Philadelphia, Pennsylvania, before a record crowd of 120,557, **Gene Tunney** challenged **Jack Dempsey** for the world's **heavyweight** championship and surprised the boxing world by winning a **unanimous decision** in a **bout** scheduled for only 10 rounds (the mandatory state limit in Pennsylvania at the time). A rematch was held one year later on 22 September 1927 in Soldier Field in Chicago, Illinois. That bout was also only scheduled for 10 rounds and also drew an attendance in excess of 100,000 (104,957 was the announced figure). In the rematch, Tunney won most of the first six rounds, but in the seventh round Dempsey knocked Tunney down but did not immediately go to a neutral **corner**, as the rules specified. **Referee** Dave Barry did not begin counting for several seconds, and Tunney was actually down on the **canvas** for 14 seconds. He subsequently recovered and retained his title on a unanimous decision in the 10-round bout. This bout was dubbed the battle of the long count, and there has been much speculation among boxing fans as to whether Tunney could have arisen before the count of 10. Dempsey retired following the bout, and Tunney, after one title defense in 1928, also retired.

DIGENNARO, FRANK. *See* GENARO, FRANKIE (né FRANK DIGENNARO).

DISQUALIFICATION. A boxing match can end by disqualification if in the **referee's** opinion one boxer is repeatedly using **foul** tactics such as low blows, holding and hitting, biting, or thumbing. A referee will also disqualify a boxer if he feels that the boxer is not being aggressive enough or if the boxer's seconds enter the **ring** prior to the end of a **round**. Usually a referee will warn a boxer for foul tactics several times before disqualifying him.

Several well-known disqualifications include **Ingemar Johansson** being disqualified in the 1952 **Olympic Games** final for not being aggressive enough; **Mike Tyson** being disqualified in his 1997 **heavyweight** title **bout** with **Evander Holyfield** for biting Holyfield's ear; and the 1941 heavyweight title bout between **Joe Louis** and Buddy Baer, which was awarded to Louis when Baer's manager, Ancil Hoffman, refused to leave the ring at the start of the seventh round while arguing with referee Art Donovan.

See also NO CONTEST.

DIVE. *See* TAKE A DIVE.

DIXON, GEORGE "LITTLE CHOCOLATE". B. 29 July 1870, Halifax, Nova Scotia, **Canada**. D. 6 January 1908, New York, New York. George Dixon was the first black professional world champion boxer. A small man, he weighed slightly more than 100 pounds for many of his early **bouts** but eventually moved up to around 120—the **featherweight** class. He began boxing in his native Nova Scotia in 1886, with his first recorded bout on 1 November 1886. His next recorded bout was the following year in Boston, Massachusetts.

Dixon's first title claim (the American 115-pound title) came after he knocked out Eugene Hornbacher in two **rounds** on 27 December 1889 in New London, Connecticut. After fighting a 70-round **draw** with Cal McCarthy in Boston on 7 February 1890, Dixon claimed the American featherweight title (even though the fighters only weighed 114 pounds).

Dixon then traveled to London, **England**, and on 27 June 1890 defeated Edwin "Nunc" Wallace, the English title claimant at 114 pounds, stopping Wallace in 19 rounds to win the world's 114-pound championship. Back in the United States, Dixon defended that title four months later by knocking out Johnny Murphy in the 40th round in Providence, Rhode Island.

Dixon's next bout was a rematch with McCarthy in Troy, New York, and after he knocked McCarthy down seven times in the 22nd round, McCarthy did not come out for the next round. This bout was billed for the world featherweight title, although the combatants weighed only about 114 pounds. After two more victories in bouts billed for the "world **bantamweight** title," Dixon took part in the three-day "**Carnival of Champions**" series of championship fights in New Orleans, Louisiana. His bout was on the middle day of the event, and he knocked out Jack Skelly in eight rounds in defense of his world featherweight title. This might have been the last interracial boxing match in Louisiana for 50 or more years, as a near riot took place following the victory of the black man, Dixon, over his white opponent.

Dixon made two title defenses in 1893, both in Coney Island, New York. He stopped Eddie Pierce in three rounds in August and Solly Smith in seven rounds in September. Dixon won his next bout in a rather unusual manner. In the third round, as **referee** James Stoddard attempted to separate Dixon from his opponent, Torpedo Billy Murphy, Murphy turned and hit the referee. Stoddard retaliated with a couple of blows of his own on Murphy, and soon Murphy and Stoddard were having their own battle. At that point, the police stepped in and terminated the bout, awarding the decision to Dixon via **disqualification**.

On 27 November 1896, with the world's featherweight title at stake and both fighters weighing under the 122-pound limit, Dixon was defeated by Frank Erne on a 20-round decision in New York City. Even though he lost, Dixon still continued to claim the title, and his next bout on 22 January 1897 with Murphy, won by Dixon on a six-round knockout, was billed for the title.

On 24 March 1897, Dixon defeated Erne (who was eight pounds overweight) on a 25-round decision and reestablished his claim to the featherweight title. Dixon lost the title in his first defense to Solly Smith on a 20-

round decision in San Francisco on 4 October 1897. Smith was subsequently defeated by Dave Sullivan, and Dixon rewon the title on 11 November 1898 on a 10th-round disqualification.

Dixon defended the title nine times over the next two years before losing it to **Terry McGovern** on 9 January 1900 on an eighth-round **technical knockout.**

In 1902, Dixon traveled to England and spent the next three years fighting there. On 9 November 1903 in Newcastle, he defeated Pedlar Palmer by decision over 20 rounds and appropriated Palmer's claim to the world's 120-pound title. Dixon returned to the United States in 1905 and fought five more times, with his last bout on 10 December 1906.

In retirement, Dixon's penchant for alcohol caught up with him, and he wound up in the alcohol treatment ward at a New York hospital in 1908, where he died on 6 January. As Dixon himself put it, he could defeat most competitors in the **ring**, but John Barleycorn did him in.

Dixon was five foot three inches tall and had a 66-inch **reach**. He fought at weights ranging from 105 to 128 pounds as a **bantamweight** and feather-weight. As can be seen by a look at his boxing record, boxing matches in his era were often called draws by referees attempting to not antagonize either side's backers. In 167 professional, bouts from 1886 to 1906, he won 69 (38 by **knockout**), lost 29 (six by knockout), and had 52 draws, six **no contests**, and 11 no-decision bouts, in which he had a record of six wins, one loss, and four draws by **newspaper decision**. He fought a total of 1,739 rounds. He was inducted as a member of the inaugural class of the **International Boxing Hall of Fame** in 1990.

DOMINICAN REPUBLIC. Boxing is one of the more popular sports in the Dominican Republic, and the country has produced more than their share of **professional** world champions. In **amateur** boxing, it first competed in the **Olympic Games** boxing tournament in 1968 and since 1976 has had at least one competitor in each Olympic tournament. It is one of 31 countries to enter in both 1980 and 1984, years in which many nations boycotted the games. Its only two Olympic medalists were Félix Díaz, who won the 2008 **light wel-terweight gold medal**, and Pedro Nolasco, bronze medalist in 1984 as a **bantamweight**.

There are 13 professional world champions native to the Dominican Re-public. Carlos Teo Cruz, who died in a plane crash while still an active boxer, was the best-known champion and was also the Domincan Republic's first world champion. Others include Leonardo Cruz (brother of Carlos Teo Cruz), Julio Gervacio, Joan Guzmán, Juan Antonio Guzmán, Eleoncio Mer-cedes, César Polanco, Francisco Quiroz, Elio Rojas, Agapito Sánchez, Héctor Acero Sánchez, Luis Santana, and Rafael Torres. Other top Dominican fighters who did not win championships include Dario Hidalgo, Darling Jiménez, Rogelio Martínez, and Julio Soto Solano.

DOUGLAS, JOHN SHOLTO. *See* MARQUESS OF QUEENSBERRY (né JOHN SHOLTO DOUGLAS).

DRAW. One of the legitimate possible outcomes of a **professional boxing bout** is a draw. This can occur in several ways. If the **referee** is the sole arbiter of the bout and in his opinion neither fighter dominated, he can raise the hands of both boxers and call it a draw. If the bout is judged by three **judges** (or two judges and the referee) and two of the three scorecards show the fighters even, the bout is called a **majority draw**. A draw also results if one judge scores the bout even and the other two judges split their votes— each voting for a different fighter.

Since most **amateur boxing** is contested in tournament structures, draws seldom occur in amateur bouts. Officials in tournaments (such as the **Golden Gloves**, **World Championships**, or **Olympic Games**) are instructed to cast their vote for one of the two fighters. In amateur tournament boxing during the early part of the twentieth century, if the fight was even after the scheduled number of rounds (usually three), the boxers would be required to box an additional round. This tiebreaking procedure was also tried briefly in professional bouts in the second half of the twentieth century but was abandoned as not being a satisfactory solution.

See also DECISION.

DRISCOLL, JAMES "JEM," "PEERLESS JIM". B. 15 December 1880, Cardiff, **Wales**. D. 30 January 1925, Cardiff, Wales. Jem Driscoll was one of the greatest boxers of all time and one of the few on that list who was never a world champion. He grew up in an impoverished family in Cardiff, as his father was killed in an industrial accident before Jem was one year old. While still a young boy, Jem worked as an apprentice for a local Cardiff newspaper. He also began boxing in the **boxing booths** in Wales to earn money for his family.

He might have had as many as 500 or 600 **bouts** in the booths before becoming a prizefighter and fighting in regular boxing clubs. His first recorded bout was in 1902, although specific details do not exist. He is credited with 15 wins in 1901 and 1902 before he boxed a 10-**round draw** on 29 September 1902. Fourteen more victories, one draw, and one **no-contest** bout appear on his record for 1903 and 1904 before his first loss, to Harry Mansfield on 29 August 1904.

By the time he faced Joe Bowker for the British Empire **featherweight** title on 28 May 1906 at the **National Sporting Club** in London, Driscoll's record stood at 38–1–3. Driscoll won a 15-round **decision** and the title. In a 1907 title defense rematch with Bowker, Driscoll won on a 17th-round **knockout**. A 24 February 1908, 15-round decision over Charlie Griffin earned Driscoll the British Empire featherweight championship.

Driscoll traveled to the **United States** in 1908 and remained there through 1909. While there, his bouts that went the distance were not permitted to be judged, and in this era of "no-decision" bouts, fans went by the decisions rendered by newspapers to settle boxing bets. Driscoll fought 10 bouts, meeting such fighters as Leach Cross, Grover Hayes, and Matty Baldwin and was adjudged the victor in all. His last fight in 1909 was against world featherweight champion **Abe Attell** in a **nontitle bout**. After winning the **newspaper decision** and being unable to get Attell to agree to a bout with the championship at stake, Driscoll returned to **England**, where he was unofficially recognized as world champion.

After defending his British Empire featherweight title by knockout in two bouts, Driscoll made another trip to the United States but was beaten by a German American fighter known as Philadelphia Pal Moore on a six-round newspaper decision on 25 May 1910. Driscoll, who had been ill, returned to England and did not fight again until December, when he took on Freddie Welsh for the European Boxing Union (EBU) **lightweight** title. In that bout, Driscoll was knocked down in the fourth round and was disqualified in the 10th round for headbutting.

Driscoll had only one recorded fight in each of the next three years—each one held at the National Sporting Club in London. In January 1911, he successfully retained his British featherweight title against Spike Robson on a seventh-round **technical knockout**. In June 1912, he knocked out Jean Poesy and won the EBU featherweight title. In January 1913, he defended all three of his featherweight titles by fighting a 20-round **draw** with Owen Moran.

He served in the Armed Forces during World War I as a physical **training** instructor and did not fight again until 1919. That year he knocked out Pedlar Palmer in four rounds, fought a 20-round draw with Francis Rossi, and ended his career by retiring after 16 rounds in his bout with Charles Ledoux for the EBU featherweight title. During this time, his health began to fail and he died of tuberculosis in 1925.

Driscoll was five foot four inches tall and fought at weights ranging from 119 to 127 pounds, primarily as a featherweight. In 74 professional bouts, from 1901 to 1919, he won 55 (36 by knockout), lost three (one by knockout), and had six draws, two **no contests**, and eight no-decision bouts, in which he was awarded the newspaper decision in seven of them. He fought a total of 575 rounds. He was inducted as a member of the inaugural class of the **International Boxing Hall of Fame** in 1990.

DUNDEE, ANGELO (né ANGELO MIRENA). B. 30 August 1921, Philadelphia, Pennsylvania. D. 1 February 2012, Tampa, Florida. Angelo Dundee's was one of boxing's greatest **trainers**. As a **cornerman** for both **Muhammad Ali** and **"Sugar Ray" Leonard**, he worked many of boxing's greatest **bouts** in the latter half of the 20th century.

After serving in the Army Air Force during World War II, he went to New York to work at **Stillman's Gym** with some of the best trainers in boxing. There he learned his craft from men like **Ray Arcel**, Whitey Bimstein, and Charlie Goldman. His older brother, Chris Dundee, a manager and a trainer, opened a gymnasium in Miami Beach, Florida, during the 1950s, and Angelo went with him to work as a trainer there.

Known for being able to bring out the most in a boxer's ability, Dundee was able to subtly influence a boxer by making the boxer think that Dundee's suggestions were the boxer's own ideas. He was also responsible in at least two of Ali's fights for turning a potential loss into a victory. In Ali's first fight with Englishman Henry Cooper on 18 June 1963 in London, **England**, Cooper knocked Ali down in the fourth round. After Ali arose but was still wobbly, Dundee noticed a small slit in Ali's glove, which he enlarged and then brought to the attention of the **referee**, who requested that a substitute glove be used. A delay occurred as a replacement glove could not be found immediately. This delay in the bout enabled Ali to clear his head and stop Cooper in the next round.

In Ali's first fight with **Sonny Liston** for the **heavyweight** title on 25 February 1964 in Miami Beach, during the rest period between rounds four and five, Ali complained that a foreign substance had gotten in his eyes and he could not see. He wanted Dundee to tear his **gloves** off and end the fight. Dundee wiped Ali's eyes and pushed him out into the **ring** to begin the next round, telling him to run from Liston until his vision improved. Two rounds later, Liston quit and Ali was champion.

In addition to Ali and Leonard, Angelo also worked with champions **Carmen Basilio**, Jimmy Ellis, Ralph Dupas, Slobodan Kačar, **José Nápoles**, Michael Nunn, Pinklon Thomas, Willie Pastrano, Luis Manuel Rodríguez, and Ultiminio "Sugar" Ramos. During **George Foreman's** comeback, Dundee worked in his corner for the Michael Moorer fight in which Foreman rewon the heavyweight championship.

Dundee was named Manager of the Year by the Boxing Writers Association of America in 1968 and again in 1979. In 1996, he also received the James J. Walker Award for Long and Meritorious Service. He was inducted into the **International Boxing Hall of Fame** in 1992.

DUNPHY, DON. B. 5 July 1908, New York, New York. D. 22 July 1998, New York, New York. Don Dunphy was a graduate of Manhattan College. While in school, he worked as a correspondent reporting on the college's sports activities for several New York newspapers. He became a radio broadcaster shortly after graduation, broadcasting ice hockey, baseball, football, and wrestling. In 1937, he became the sports director of radio station WINS in New York. In 1939, he added boxing to the sports that he covered.

In 1941, he was hired by the Gillette Safety Razor Company for their weekly boxing series and was their voice for the next 19 years. One of his first fights was the **Joe Louis–Billy Conn heavyweight** championship fight in 1941. In 1960, he switched to television and called the fights for the American Broadcasting Company television network for four years. By the 1970s, he had retired from network television but still occasionally was the announcer for closed circuit television of some of the major fights and was the announcer for the first **Ali–Frazier** fight and the **Ali–Foreman** fight. One of his last fights was the **"Sugar Ray" Leonard–Thomas Hearns** bout in 1981.

He was inducted into the **International Boxing Hall of Fame** in 1993.

DURÁN SAMANIEGO, ROBERTO CARLOS "MANOS DE PIE-DRA". B. 16 June 1951, El Chorrillo, **Panama**. Roberto Durán was one of hardest-hitting **lightweights** in the history of boxing and one of its toughest competitors. He was voted by the Associated Press as the greatest lightweight of the 20th century and is included on some boxing historians' lists among the 10 greatest fighters of all time regardless of weight. Yet, ironically, he is remembered by many fans for uttering two words, *No más* (no more), in a **bout** later in his career. In his 25 November 1980 rematch against **"Sugar Ray" Leonard** in the Superdome in New Orleans, Louisiana, Leonard realizing he could not just slug with Durán, attempted to box him and dance around him. Leonard also began showboating and in the seventh **round** windmilled his right hand to attract Durán's eye and then hit him when a straight left hand. Durán, frustrated with these tactics, abruptly quit in the middle of the eighth round, telling **referee** Octavio Meyrán, "No más," and walked to his **corner**.

Durán was raised in the slums in his native Panama and began boxing as a **professional** in 1968 at the age of 16. His first recorded bout was on 23 February 1968 in Colón, Panama. After winning his first 24 fights (21 by **knockout**) in Panama and **Mexico**, he came to New York, where he knocked out Benny Huertas in one round at **Madison Square Garden** on the **undercard** of the Ismael Laguna–Ken Buchanan world lightweight championship bout.

After three victories in Panama, including a seventh-round knockout of former **super featherweight** champion Hiroshi Kobayashi, he returned to the Garden on 26 June 1972 and won the world lightweight title by stopping Buchanan in the 13th round. In his next fight in the Garden, Durán suffered his first loss after 31 consecutive victories when Esteban de Jesús knocked him down in the first round and then won a 10-round **unanimous decision** in a **nontitle bout**.

Over the next six years, Durán defended his lightweight title 12 times in addition to winning 20 nontitle bouts without a loss. He defeated Jimmy Robertson, Héctor Thompson, Guts Ishimatsu, Esteban de Jesús twice, Masataka Takayama, Ray Lampkin, Leoncio Ortiz, Lou Bizzaro, Alvaro Rojas, Vilomar Fernández, and Edwin Viruet in title defenses. In January 1979, Durán vacated the lightweight title to move up to **welterweight**.

As a welterweight, Durán won eight bouts, including a decision over former welterweight champion **Carlos Palomino**, and then challenged "Sugar Ray" Leonard for the **World Boxing Council (WBC)** welterweight title on 20 June 1980 in Montreal, **Canada**. In a closely contested bout, Durán won a unanimous decision and the world welterweight title. In their rematch on 25 November 1980, Durán lost the title when Leonard's tactics completely frustrated him and he quit in the eighth round in the infamous "No Más" bout.

Durán's next major fight was on 30 January 1982, when he fought **Wilfred Benítez** for the WBC **light middleweight** title held by Benítez. In a close bout, Benítez prevailed on a unanimous decision.

In Durán's next bout (4 September 1982, Detroit, Michigan), he lost for only the fourth time in 78 bouts in one of that year's major upsets to Kirkland Laing on a 10-round decision. Laing, a Jamaican, was making his first fight outside of **England**, and although he had held the British welterweight title, he was relatively unknown in the **United States**.

Durán won his next two bouts, one of them a fourth-round **technical knockout** over former **World Boxing Association (WBA)** welterweight champion Pipino Cuevas, and then was successful in another bid for the light middleweight title by defeating WBA champion Davey Moore on an eighth-round technical knockout.

Durán's next fight was another of the 1980s' megabouts, as he attempted to win his fourth title. On 10 November 1983, he narrowly missed doing so, as he lost a very close decision to **Marvelous Marvin Hagler** for the world's **middleweight** title. After 15 rounds, the **judges'** scorecards read 144–143, 144–142, and 146–145, all for Hagler.

Seven months later, Durán was stopped for only the second time in his career as **Thomas Hearns** knocked him down twice in the first round and once in the second round before the fight for Hearns's WBC light middleweight title was stopped. Durán then fought sporadically, but on 24 February 1989 he defeated Iran Barkley by **split decision** and won the WBC middleweight title in *Ring* **magazine's** "Fight of the Year." That victory gained Durán his fourth title in four different weight classes. He attempted to make it five titles on 7 December 1989 when he fought "Sugar Ray" Leonard for the WBC **super middleweight** championship. The bout was held outdoors on 7 December 1989 in **Las Vegas** in 37 degree weather. Leonard dominated the fight and won a 12-round unanimous decision.

Durán continued to box until 2001, fighting his last bout at the age of 50. From 1989 to 2001, he unsuccessfully challenged **Vinny Pazienza** in 1994 and again in 1995 for the less highly regarded International Boxing Council super middleweight title, **Héctor Camacho** for that title in 1996, and William Joppy in 1998 for the WBA middleweight title, losing unanimous decisions to Pazienza and Camacho and being stopped by Joppy in three rounds.

On his 49th birthday (16 June 2000), Durán defeated Pat Lawlor in Panama for the **National Boxing Association** super middleweight title, which although not one of boxing's more highly regarded titles, was still quite an accomplishment. One year later, Durán lost that title to Héctor Camacho in what proved to be Durán's last fight.

On 4 October 2001, while in Buenos Aires, **Argentina**, he was involved in a bad auto accident as a passenger and, although he survived, decided that his boxing days were over and announced his retirement in January 2002. In retirement, he has recorded salsa CDs and works with DRL Promotions as a boxing promoter.

Durán is five foot seven inches tall and has a 66-inch **reach**. He fought at weights ranging from 119 to 176 pounds in all classes from **featherweight** to super middleweight. In 119 professional bouts, from 1968 to 2001, he won 103 (70 by knockout), lost 16 (four by knockout), and fought a total of 822 rounds. He was inducted into the **International Boxing Hall of Fame** in 2007.

EATON, AILEEN GOLDSTEIN LEBELL. B. 5 February 1909, Vancouver, **Canada**. D. 15 November 1987, Los Angeles, California. Aileen Goldstein, although born in Canada, was raised in Los Angeles, California, and attended Los Angeles High School. Shortly after graduation, she married Maurice LeBell, who became an osteopath. They had two sons, Gene and Mike. Maurice died in 1941 after becoming paralyzed following a near drowning.

She worked for the California Military Academy, handling their advertising in exchange for tuition for her two boys at the school. One of her accounts was the Los Angeles Athletic Club, owner of the Olympic Auditorium. She introduced the owner of the club to Alvah "Cal" Eaton, then an inspector for the California State Athletic **Commission**, and he took over promotion for the auditorium.

She and Cal were married in 1947. She worked as the business manager with him in his promoting ventures and upon his death in 1966 took over the business. She held weekly boxing shows at the Olympic Auditorium in Los Angeles and put on more than 2,500 fight **cards**. In 1982, she was named to the California State Athletic Commission.

Her son Gene LeBell was a national **Amateur Athletic Union** judo champion in 1954 and 1955 and became a **professional** wrestler. He also has worked as a stuntman or stunt coordinator for Hollywood films and has written more than 10 books on judo and martial arts. Aileen's other son, Mike LeBell, is a professional wrestling promoter.

She was inducted into the **International Boxing Hall of Fame** in 2002 and as of 2012 is the only female enshrined in the hall. She was also inducted into the National Wrestling Alliance Hall of Fame in 2011.

ENGLAND. England can be thought of as the cradle of boxing. Although the Greeks and Romans had various types of boxing contests, modern boxing records stem from Jim Figg in 1719 when he first established his boxing school in Thame, Oxfordshire, England.

Bareknuckle boxing was popular for much of the next two centuries, and it was first codified with Broughton's Rules in 1743 and then modified with the **London Prize Ring Rules** of 1838 and revised in 1853. In 1867, the **Marquess of Queensberry Rules** were promoted, which called for **gloves** and a fixed time limit for rounds. Boxing has continued to be popular in England throughout the 20th and 21st centuries.

In **amateur boxing**, English boxers first competed in the 1908 **Olympic Games** in London and have entered 23 Olympic boxing tournaments as part of the **Great Britain** team. Of the 53 Olympic boxing medals (17 **gold**, 12 **silver**, and 24 **bronze**), 43 were won by English boxers (all 16 gold, nine silver, and 18 bronze).

England has had many top-notch professional boxers. Many of the early professional championships, especially in the lighter weights, were first claimed by English boxers. Among the best English champions have been Terry Allen, Dennis Andries, Nigel Benn, Jack "Kid" Berg, Frank Bruno, John Conteh, Terry Downes, Chris Eubank, **Bob Fitzsimmons**, **Naseem Hamed**, Len Harvey, Ricky Hatton, David Haye, Herbie Hide, Lloyd Honeyghan, Maurice Hope, Amir Khan, **Lennox Lewis**, Ted "Kid" Lewis, Charlie Magri, Duke McKenzie, Freddie Mills, Alan Minter, Owen Moran, John H. Stracey, and Randy Turpin.

Some of the better English boxers who did not win championships include Jack Bodell, Joe Bugner, Joe Bygraves, Dave Charnley, Don Cockell, Henry Cooper, Pat Cowdell, Richard Dunn, Joe Erskine, Chris Finnegan, Dave "Boy" Green, William "Iron" Hague, Brian London, Jock McAvoy, James "Gunner" Moir, Dick Turpin (Randy's brother), Bombardier Billy Wells, and Bruce Woodcock. **Victor McLaglen**, who became better known for his acting than his boxing ability, was also an Englishman.

See also BENDIGO (né WILLIAM ABEDNEGO THOMPSON); BOXING BOOTHS; BOXING DAY; CRIBB, TOM; GREAT BRITAIN; NATIONAL SPORTING CLUB.

ESCH, ERIC SCOTT. *See* BUTTERBEAN "KING OF THE FOUR ROUNDERS" (né ERIC SCOTT ESCH).

EXHIBITION. Champion boxers have occasionally performed in exhibition **bouts** in which they demonstrated their skills in the **ring** against a lesser opponent (often a **sparring partner**) before a paying audience eager to see the champion in person. Protective headgear is usually worn, and the **rounds** are not scored. Usually, the exhibition is for only a few rounds, and the rounds are often shorter than the normal three minutes.

F

FATALITIES. Due to the nature of the activity, boxing has always produced fatalities. **Bouts** during the Roman era were often **fought to a finish**. When the Prize Ring era began in **England**, rules were written in an attempt to minimize severe injury, but nonetheless boxers still occasionally died as a result of their bouts. The Boxrec website lists 643 boxers who were killed in the **ring**. Historian Miguel Velázquez has a website (cited in the Bibliography) in which he documents more than 1,000 ring fatalities from 1725 to 2011. Among the more publicized fatalities are the following:

Boxers killed by former or future world champions in nontitle bouts:

> Con Riordan died after a 15 November 1894 bout with **Bob Fitzsimmons**.
> Joe Devitt died after a 27 April 1898 bout with Young Griffo.
> Tom Lansing died after a 15 November 1898 bout with Jack Root.
> Harry Tenny died after a 28 February 1906 bout with Frankie Neil.
> Mike Ward died after a 15 November 1906 bout with Harry Lewis.
> Tommy McCarthy died after a 29 April 1910 bout with Owen Moran.
> Jack "Bull" Young died after a 22 August 1913 bout with **Jess Willard**.
> Frankie Jerome died after an 11 January 1924 bout with Charles "Bud" Taylor.
> Clever Sencio died after a 19 April 1926 bout with Charles "Bud" Taylor.
> Steve Adams died after a 1 June 1927 bout with Sammy Mandell.
> Frankie Campbell died after a 25 August 1930 bout with **Max Baer**.
> Sam Terrin died after an 11 March 1931 bout with John Henry Lewis.
> Ernie Schaaf died after a 10 February 1933 bout with **Primo Carnera**.
> Tony Scarpati died after a 17 March 1936 bout with Lou Ambers.
> Sam Baroudi died after a 20 February 1948 bout with **Ezzard Charles**.
> Walt Ingram died after a 24 October 1959 bout with José Becerra.
> Jupp Elze died after a 12 June 1968 bout with Juan Carlos Durán.
> Angelo Jacopucci died after a 19 July 1978 bout with Alan Minter.
> Charles Newell died after a 9 January 1980 bout with Marlon Starling.
> Young Ali died after a 14 June 1982 bout with **Barry McGuigan**.
> Jacob Morake died after a 2 November 1985 bout with Brian Mitchell.

Champions who died in the ring:

Benny "Kid" Paret died after a 24 March 1962 bout with **Emile Griffith**.

Davey Moore died after a 21 March 1963 bout with Sugar Ramos.

Pedro Alcázar died after a 22 June 2002 bout with Fernando Montiel.

Challengers who died in the ring in world championship fights:

Andy Bowen died after a 14 December 1894 bout with George "Kid" Lavigne.

Walter Croot died after a 6 December 1897 bout with Jimmy Barry.

Jimmy Doyle died after a 24 June 1947 bout with **Ray Robinson**.

Johnny Owen died after a 19 September 1980 bout with Lupe Pintor.

Deuk-Koo Kim died after a 13 November 1982 bout with **Ray Mancini**.

Francisco "Kiko" Bejines died after a 1 September 1983 bout with Alberto Davila.

Jimmy García died after a 6 May 1995 bout with Gabriel Ruelas.

Leavander Johnson died after a 17 September 2005 bout with Jesús Chávez.

Boxers involved with multiple fatalities include Sam Baroudi, whose bout on 15 August 1947 resulted in the death of Newton Smith and who died himself after his 20 February 1948 bout with Ezzard Charles. Charles "Bud" Taylor had two opponents die after bouts with him: Frankie Jerome after an 11 January 1924 bout and Clever Sencio after a 19 April 1926 bout. Ironically, **bantamweight** Taylor was not known for an exceptional **knockout** punch and only had 37 knockouts in 165 bouts. Ultiminio "Sugar" Ramos also won two bouts in which his opponents died—José Blanco died after his 8 November 1958 bout with Ramos, and on 21 March 1963 Ramos won the **featherweight** title by knocking out Davey Moore, who died two days later.

Notable amateur boxers who died in the ring include Charlie Mohr of the University of Wisconsin, who died following his 9 April 1960 bout with Stu Bartell for the National Collegiate Athletic Association **middleweight** title. The New York **Golden Gloves** has had two fatalities in its 85 years of existence and more than 40,000 bouts. In 1947, 16-year-old Anthony Sconzo died following his bout with Stanley Smolken in the 118-pound **sub-novice** class, and in 1979 25-year-old Francisco Rodríguez died after his bout with Francis Riccotilli in the **heavyweight** sub-novice class. On 3 April 2005, 34-year-old Becky Zerlentes became the first female to die after a boxing match. She was competing in a Denver Golden Gloves bout in Fort Collins, Colorado.

FEATHERWEIGHT. Featherweight is a boxing weight class with a maximum weight of 126 pounds, although in the early years of the division the weight limits varied from 120 to 126 pounds. Unlike some other weight classes, there is no one clearly recognized as the first champion in this class as several **bareknuckle** boxers were claimants. "Torpedo" Billy Murphy is generally credited as the first gloved featherweight champions after his defeat of Ike Weir in San Francisco on 13 January 1890. Many boxers begin their careers in this class and as they age and gain weight move up to **lightweight** or **welterweight**. Among the best featherweights have been **Alexis Argüello, Abe Attell, Kid Chocolate, George Dixon, Jem Driscoll**, Johnny Dundee, **Wilfredo Gómez, Naseem Hamed**, Harry Jeffra, **Éder Jofre**, Johnny Kilbane, Danny "Little Red" Lopez, **Terry McGovern, Barry McGuigan, Azumah Nelson, Willie Pep, Sandy Saddler**, Vicente Saldivar, **Salvador Sánchez**, and **Pernell Whitaker**.

See also TIBBS, TOMMY.

FELT FORUM. When **Madison Square Garden** was rebuilt in 1968, several other sports facilities were included in the structure, among them a bowling alley and a small arena seating approximately 5,000 that was called the Felt Forum (named for Irving Mitchell Felt, president of Madison Square Garden). By that time, nearly all the small **fight clubs** in the New York City area had closed, and this arena (plush by fight club standards) was often used for lesser **professional boxing** shows as well as **Golden Gloves** amateur **bouts**. Occasionally, a world championship **bout** would be held, usually featuring a New York–area fighter such as Mark Medal, Howard Davis, or James "Buddy" McGirt. Quite a few future world champions got their start in boxing **cards** at the forum, including **Mike Tyson**, Iran Barkley, Mike McCallum, and Saoul Mamby. Barkley, in fact, fought in the forum nine times in 1985 and 1986. The arena has undergone several name changes and is currently known as the Theater at Madison Square Garden.

See also BLUE HORIZON; ST. NICHOLAS ARENA; SUNNYSIDE GARDEN.

FIGHT CLUBS. For the first half of the 20th century, boxing in the **United States** occurred on most nights in small (1,000–2,000 capacity) arenas. The featured boxers often included ones who resided in the neighborhood of the arena. Among the more popular ones in New York City were **St. Nicholas Arena** in Manhattan, Eastern Parkway Arena in Brooklyn, and Ridgewood Grove and **Sunnyside Garden** in Queens.

Philadelphia's main fight club was the **Blue Horizon** (which was still being operated in the 21st century and was referred to then as "the legendary Blue Horizon." Olympic Auditorium in Los Angeles, Laurel Garden in Newark, and War Memorial Auditorium in Syracuse were some of the others.

As **televised boxing** gradually put an end to local boxing shows, **casinos** supplanted the local fight club, although not with the same color or frequency of shows.

See also FELT FORUM.

FIGHT TO THE FINISH. In the early days of boxing, under the various sets of **bareknuckle** rules, matches were usually contested as "fights to the finish." When the **Marquess of Queensberry Rules** became prevalent, matches occasionally were still scheduled as "fights to the finish." Rather than a specified number of **rounds**, the **bout** would be continued until one fighter was either knocked out or retired. This practice was discontinued around 1910, and all bouts since have been scheduled for a specific number of rounds.

In the early part of the 20th century, bouts were occasionally scheduled for 20, 25, or as many as 45 rounds, with the last scheduled 25-round bout on 27 August 1941 in Washington, DC, between **heavyweights** Bill Poland and Eddie Blunt. To the disappointment of spectators at that bout, Poland scored a four-round **knockout**. Since then, championship bouts have usually been scheduled for 15 rounds, with **nontitle main event** bouts being scheduled for 10 or 12 rounds and **preliminary bouts** scheduled for four, six, or eight rounds. Since 1988, as a direct result of the **Ray Mancini**–Deuk Koo Kim tragedy, championship bouts have been limited to 12 rounds by the major sanctioning organizations, although an occasional 15-round bout has been sanctioned by one of the minor organizations.

FIRPO, LUIS ÁNGEL "THE WILD BULL OF THE PAMPAS". B. 11 October 1894, Junín, Buenos Aires, **Argentina**. D. 7 August 1960, Buenos Aires, Argentina. Luis Ángel Firpo is remembered more for one of the four **bouts** that he lost than for any of the 31 bouts that he won. His first recorded professional bout took place in his native Argentina in 1917 and was a six-**round no-decision** bout. He was overmatched in his second recorded professional bout and was opposed by Ángel Rodríguez, an undefeated boxer with 25 wins. Rodríguez knocked Firpo down four times and knocked him out in the first round in a bout that took place in Uruguay.

Firpo resumed his boxing career against lesser-quality opposition and won 13 of his next 15 bouts—all in South America. He was brought to the **United States** in 1922 and won eight consecutive bouts by **knockout**. He was then matched on 12 July 1923 with former world's **heavyweight** champion **Jess**

Willard, who at 42 years of age was no longer the fighter he once was. Firpo stopped Willard in eight rounds and was then seen as a potential challenger for **Jack Dempsey**—the world's heavyweight champion.

The bout with Dempsey took place on 14 September 1923 at the Polo Grounds in New York, and the 80,000 spectators who were there saw one of the most memorable bouts in boxing history. Although the bout only lasted three minutes and 57 seconds, there were 11 **knockdowns**. In the first round, Firpo staggered Dempsey at the beginning of the fight, and Dempsey's knees hit the **canvas**. He arose and knocked Firpo down—the first of seven knockdowns of Firpo in the round. After the seventh knockdown, Firpo threw a wild right that knocked Dempsey through the ropes. He was pushed back in by the sportswriters who were at **ringside** and beat the 10 count, although he was staggering when the bell sounded to end the round. At the beginning of the second round, Dempsey rushed out and after a few seconds knocked Firpo down again. Firpo was up at the count of two and promptly was knocked down again. This time he rose at the count of five. Dempsey was back on top of him, and this time a left to the jaw followed by a hard right hand knocked Firpo out. The time was 57 seconds of the second round.

In 1950, an Associated Press Poll of sportswriters named this bout as the top sports drama of the first half-century. The bout also heads many historians' lists as the greatest fight in boxing history.

After the Dempsey fight, Firpo returned to Argentina. He won three bouts there and returned to the United States, where he met **Harry Wills**, the great black heavyweight that Dempsey avoided fighting. Wills won a 12-round **newspaper decision** over Firpo on 11 September 1924 in Jersey City, New Jersey. Firpo's next bout two months later, also in Jersey City, was another newspaper decision loss, this time to Charlie Weinert.

Firpo returned to Argentina and retired. He fought once more in 1926, winning a 12-round **decision** in Buenos Aires, and then 10 years later made a brief comeback, winning two bouts before being knocked down nine times and stopped in the fourth round by Chilean Arturo Godoy in Buenos Aires. Godoy would later fight **Joe Louis** twice in heavyweight championship bouts, losing a **split decision** in February 1940 and then being stopped by Louis in eight rounds of their rematch in June 1940.

Firpo retired to his ranch in Argentina and became a multimillionaire and one of the most famous men in Argentina. A first-class soccer team, one of the country's best, in El Salvador is named for him.

Firpo was six foot two inches tall and fought at weights ranging from 214 to 227 pounds as a heavyweight. In 37 professional bouts, from 1917 to 1936, he won 31 (26 by knockout), lost four (three by knockout), had two **no contests** and two no-decision bouts (both newspaper decision losses), and fought a total of 228 rounds.

FITZSIMMONS, ROBERT JAMES "BOB," "RUBY ROBERT," "THE FRECKLED WONDER". B. 26 May 1863, Helston, Cornwall, **England**. D. 22 October 1917, Chicago, Illinois. Bob Fitzsimmons was the first boxer to win world championships in three different weight divisions. He also looked less like a professional boxer than most of his successors. He was balding and lanky, with spindly legs but a powerful upper torso. In his career, he often fought boxers bigger than himself, and when he was once asked about this disparity, he replied with the classic line, "The bigger they are, the harder they fall." The phrase was later used in part for one of the best novels about boxing, *The Harder They Fall* by Budd Schulberg.

Although born in England, he was raised in New Zealand, having moved with his family there as a youth. He worked for his brother as a blacksmith as a teenager. He became interested in boxing while living in New Zealand and is recorded as having competed in two "Jem Mace" tournaments in 1881. (Mace was an English **bareknuckle** fighter in the 1860s and was considered to be the father of the modern school of British scientific boxing.) Details of Fitzsimmons's early fights have been lost, but he most likely engaged in several bareknuckle **bouts**.

By 1885, he was established in **Australia** as a professional boxer. In 1890, he fought a scheduled 20-**round** bout with Jim Hall for the Australian **middleweight** title but was **knocked out** in the fourth round.

In the spring of 1890, he came to the **United States**, and after two fights in San Francisco, he traveled to New Orleans, Louisiana, where on 14 January 1891 he stopped the original **Jack Dempsey**, known as the Nonpareil, in the 13th round of their scheduled 20-round bout and won the world's middleweight championship. The following year, he stopped Peter Maher in the 12th round of a bout that was scheduled as a "**fight to the finish**," meaning it would continue until one of the fighters surrendered or was unable to continue.

From New Orleans, he traveled to Newark, New Jersey, where he advertised a prize of $50 to anyone who could last four rounds with him in the ring. From 26 April through 29 April 1892, he is recorded as having five bouts, with none of his opponents lasting more than three rounds.

On 8 March 1893, he knocked out Jim Hall in four rounds in New Orleans in a bout listed as being for the world middleweight title and scheduled as a "fight to the finish." During the rest of that year, Fitzsimmons toured the eastern United States taking on all comers in four-round bouts with a prize for those boxers who could last all four rounds. Fighting in Indianapolis, Chicago, Baltimore, Philadelphia, Boston, and Newark, he won 12 of 13 bouts inside the four-round limit, with only one man lasting the full four rounds.

Fitzsimmons's next major bout with an opponent of significance was on 18 June 1894 in Boston, when he stopped **heavyweight** Joe Choynski in five rounds. On 26 September 1894 in New Orleans, Fitzsimmons successfully defended his middleweight title with a second-round knockout of Dan Creedon.

On 21 February 1896, in a town in **Mexico** just across the Texas border, Fitzsimmons knocked out Peter Maher in the first round in a bout billed for the world's heavyweight title, although **Jim Corbett** also claimed that title by virtue of his defeat of **John L. Sullivan** in 1892. In Fitzsimmons's next bout, he was disqualified by the **referee**, the famed lawman Wyatt Earp, for an alleged low blow in the eighth round of his bout with Tom Sharkey, which was advertised for the heavyweight championship of the world.

On 17 March 1897 in Carson City, Nevada, Fitzsimmons knocked out Corbett in the 14th round and gained undisputed possession of the world's heavyweight championship. Fitzsimmons only weighed 167 pounds for the bout and remains the lightest man in boxing history to win the heavyweight championship. But in his first title defense, two years later on 9 June 1899 in Coney Island, New York, he was knocked out by **James J. Jeffries** in the 11th round and lost his title.

Fitzsimmons then won his next five fights by knockout—each in six rounds or less. Included among those five victims were top contenders Gus Ruhlin, Ed Dunkhorst, and Tom Sharkey.

On 25 July 1902 in San Francisco, Fitzsimmons was knocked out in the eighth round of a rematch with Jeffries for the heavyweight title. The following year, Fitzsimmons defeated George Gardner in San Francisco on 25 November 1903 via a 20-round decision and won the newly created **light heavyweight** title—Fitzsimmons's third title in three different weight classes.

Fitzsimmons fought only one bout in 1904, stopping **Philadelphia Jack O'Brien** in six rounds. The following year, the two met again, and this time O'Brien caused Fitzsimmons to retire in the 13th round and claimed the **light heavyweight** championship as a result.

Fitzsimmons only fought one bout in each of the next four years, but his fight in 1907 was with the future world's heavyweight champion, **Jack Johnson**, who knocked out Bob in two rounds. Fitzsimmons returned to **Australia** for one bout in 1909 and was knocked out in the 12th round by Bill Lang in a bid for the Australian heavyweight title.

In 1914, at the age of 50, Fitzsimmons fought his last two bouts, both **newspaper decisions**. In retirement, he went into vaudeville, as did many of his contemporaries, and later became an evangelist. He died in 1917 of pneumonia and never saw his son box professionally.

His son, who boxed as Young Bob Fitzsimmons, fought as a professional from 1919 to 1931. He was not nearly as competent as his father and compiled a record of 26–14–1, with 18 additional no-decision bouts.

Fitzsimmons Sr. was five foot 11 inches tall and had a 71-inch **reach**. He fought at weights ranging from 148 to 175 pounds in weight classes from middleweight to heavyweight. In 99 professional bouts, from 1885 to 1914, he won 66 (59 by knockout), lost eight (seven by knockout), and had four draws, 19 **no-contest** bouts, and two no-decision bouts, in which he was awarded the newspaper decision in both. He fought a total of 403 rounds and was inducted as a member of the inaugural class of the **International Boxing Hall of Fame** in 1990.

FLEISCHER, NATHANIEL STANLEY "NAT". B. 3 November 1887, New York, New York. D. 25 June 1972, New York, New York. For nearly 50 years, Nat Fleischer was "Mr. Boxing." A 1908 graduate of City College of New York, he worked for the *New York Press*, later becoming its sports editor. In 1922, along with promoter **Tex Rickard**, he began publishing *Ring* **magazine**, which became known as the bible of boxing. By 1929, he was the sole owner of the magazine. He remained owner and editor-in-chief until his death in 1972.

During that time, he wrote more than 50 books on boxing, including an annual boxing record book. The publication first appeared in 1942 as *Nat Fleischer's All-Time Ring Record Book* and contained historical records of past fighters as well as those active in 1941. Through the years, this annual publication became the standard reference book for boxers, managers, and promoters. In 1953, he expanded the book with an encyclopedic section on **ring** history, and the title then became *Nat Fleischer's Ring Record Book and Boxing Encyclopedia*.

He also acted as a boxing **judge** and **referee** and was one of the founders of the Boxing Writers Association of America. He received their award for "long and meritorious service" in 1943 and again in 1966. A present-day award, the Nat Fleischer Award, was inaugurated after his death in 1972 and is presented for "excellence in boxing journalism."

In 1965, he figured significantly in the outcome of a world's **heavyweight** championship **bout**. On 25 May 1965, **Muhammad Ali** defended his newly won heavyweight title in a rematch with **Charles "Sonny" Liston** in a small arena in Lewiston, Maine. In the first **round**, Liston went down from a seemingly innocuous punch. Ali stood over him, shouting at him to get up. Referee **Jersey Joe Walcott** did not begin counting (although the **knock-down timekeeper** did) and instead attempted to get Ali to go to a neutral **corner**. Liston eventually got up, but Fleischer, sitting **ringside**, called Walcott over and told him that the timekeeper had reached the count of 10 and the fight should be over. Walcott took Fleischer's advice and stopped the bout, declaring Ali the victor. In an added bit of confusion the "official" time of the ending was announced as one minute of the first round when in actuality the bout took two minutes and 12 seconds.

Upon Fleischer's death in 1972, ownership of *Ring* was transferred to his son-in-law and editor, Nat Loubet. Fleischer was inducted as a member of the inaugural class of the **International Boxing Hall of Fame** in 1990.

FLYWEIGHT. Flyweight is a boxing weight class with a maximum weight of 112 pounds. The division was first recognized in **England** in 1911 and until 1975 was the lightest weight division in **professional boxing**. In that year, the **World Boxing Council** established a **light flyweight** class of 108 pounds, and in 1987 the **International Boxing Federation** created an even lighter weight class known variously as **strawweight**, **minimumweight**, or **mini flyweight** with a 105-pound limit. Englishman Sid Smith, in 1913, was the first flyweight to achieve recognition as division champion. As with most of the lightest weight classes, it has never been very popular in the **United States**. Among the best flyweights have been Yuri Arbachakov, Miguel Canto, Chartchai Chionoi, Sot Chitalada, **Frankie Genaro**, **Masahiko "Fighting" Harada**, Peter Kane, Pone Kingpetch, Fidel LaBarba, Ricardo López, Benny Lynch, Rinty Monaghan, Small Montana, **Pascual Pérez**, Shoji Oguma, Masao Ohba, **Pancho Villa**, **Jimmy Wilde**, and Midget Wolgast.

FOLLEY, ZORA BELL. B. 27 May 1931, Dallas, Texas. D. 9 July 1972, Tucson, Arizona. Zora Folley moved with his family from Dallas to Chandler, Arizona, in 1942. Although underage, he joined the U.S. Army in 1948 and served during the **Korean** War, earning five battle stars. He became a boxer while in the army and won the 1952 All-Army **heavyweight** championships but was defeated in the trials for the 1952 **Olympic** team. He became a **professional** boxer shortly after his discharge from the service in 1953 and had his first professional **bout** in Los Angeles, California, on 22 September 1953, winning a four-**round decision** over Jimmy Ingram. Folley won 18 of his first 19 **bouts**, with a four-round **draw** being his only setback.

On 23 June 1955, he lost his first fight when, after being **knocked down** by Johnny Summerlin, he retired in the sixth round due to a possible broken jaw. His second loss came later that year when Young Jack Johnson stopped him in five rounds. Folley then won his next 18 bouts, with victories over Niño Valdés and Wayne Bethea (twice) among his better outings. He became the second-rated contender in the heavyweight rankings and was matched with the number one ranked heavyweight, **Eddie Machen**. The fight did not live up to expectations and was ruled a 12-round draw.

After a four-round **knockout** victory over former Olympic heavyweight champion **Pete Rademacher**, in Rademacher's second professional fight, Folley traveled to London, **England**, and lost a decision to Englishman Henry Cooper. Folley remained in England and one month later knocked out Joe Bygraves, another top British boxer. Folley won his next nine bouts, including a 12-round unanimous decision over Machen. On 18 July 1960, Folley suffered another setback as he was knocked out by **Sonny Liston** in three rounds. After two more victories, Folley was stopped by Alejandro Lavorante in seven rounds.

Folley then won his next nine bouts, including a two-round knockout of Henry Cooper in London. On 15 December 1962, Doug Jones stopped Folley, who then won 12 of his next 15 bouts, with a **unanimous decision** loss to future heavyweight champion Ernie Terrell and two draws the only non-winning outings. Included in those 12 victories were ones over Óscar Bonavena (his first loss) and **George Chuvalo**.

On 22 March 1967, Folley finally got his chance at the heavyweight title after being one of the division's top contenders for over a decade, but **Muhammad Ali** knocked him out in seven rounds in Ali's last bout before Ali's problems with the draft board caused him to be inactive for three and a half years.

Folley continued boxing for the next three years with no notable matches. On 29 September 1970, he was knocked out in the first round by Mac Foster and was down six times in the round.

In retirement, he became a member of the Chandler, Arizona, City Council and raised a family of nine children. He died under unusual circumstances. He drowned in a hotel swimming pool in Tucson, Arizona, but with bruises on his head. Coming on the heels of the controversial deaths of two other major heavyweight contenders of the era, Charles "Sonny" Liston and Eddie Machen, his death remains suspicious to this day, although officially listed as an accident.

Folley was six foot one inches tall and had a 77-inch **reach**. He fought at weights ranging from 187 to 228 pounds as a heavyweight. In 96 professional bouts, from 1953 to 1970, he won 79 (44 by knockout), lost 11 (seven by knockout), had six draws, and fought a total of 669 rounds.

FOREMAN, GEORGE EDWARD "BIG GEORGE". B. 10 January 1949, Marshall, Texas. George Foreman has had two public lives. In the first, he was a nearly invincible **Olympic** champion and world's **professional** champion with one of the best **knockout** punches in boxing history. In the second, he was a kindly former minister and television pitchman who returned to his previous life's work and proved that age for an athlete is often just a mental block, not a physical one.

Raised in his native Texas, he got into trouble as a youth and eventually joined the Job Corps. He moved to California and began **amateur boxing** at the age of 18. He won the 1968 national **Amateur Athletic Union heavyweight** title and the 1968 **United States** Olympic trials. He competed in the 1968 Olympic Games and won the heavyweight **gold medal**, winning three of his four **bouts** in less than the scheduled three **rounds**. At a time of protest during the Olympics by U.S. black athletes, he won public acclaim by waving a small American flag in the **ring** following his final bout.

He had his first professional bout in New York's **Madison Square Garden** on 23 June 1969, stopping his opponent in three rounds. Ironically, the **referee** for that bout was Zach Clayton, who would later be the referee in George's most famous bout, the "**Rumble in the Jungle.**"

After winning his first 37 bouts, 34 by knockout, he fought **Joe Frazier** for the world's heavyweight title in Kingston, Jamaica, on 22 January 1973. In that bout, he knocked Frazier down three times in the first round and three more times in the second round before the fight was stopped by referee Arthur Mercante at 2:26 of that round. One of the more famous lines in boxing history was uttered by broadcaster **Howard Cosell**, who kept saying, "Down goes Frazier . . . down goes Frazier."

Foreman then made two successful defenses of his title, traveling to **Japan**, where he knocked out José "King" Roman in one round, and to Caracas, **Venezuela**, where he stopped **Ken Norton** in two rounds after knocking Norton down three times.

At this point in his career, Big George had a record of 40–0 with 37 knockouts and appeared invincible. A title defense with former champion **Muhammad Ali** was scheduled. Promoter **Don King** was able to arrange for each fighter to receive five million dollars each. The government of the country of Zaire was anxious to publicize their country and helped with the financial arrangements. After a month's delay due to an injury suffered by Foreman while **training** for the bout, it finally took place on 30 October 1974 at 4 o'clock in the morning (so that it could be **televised** in the **United States** at 10 p.m.).

The fight began with Ali aggressively hitting Foreman on top of the head and dancing away. He then began to use his speed to avoid Foreman's retaliation, but in the second round Ali changed tactics (contrary to his **corner's** advice) and leaned on the relatively loose ropes and allowed Foreman to throw punches at him while protecting his face in a tactic that Ali dubbed the "**rope-a-dope.**" Foreman's arms grew tired from the continuous punching, and by the eighth round Ali was able to turn the tables and knock out Foreman at 2:58 of the round. Ali thus became only the second man to regain the heavyweight title (**Floyd Patterson** was the first).

Foreman did not fight in 1975 but in 1976 announced that he was making a comeback with the intention of gaining a rematch with Ali. In his first fight since the Rumble in the Jungle with Ali, Foreman knocked out **Ron Lyle** in five rounds on 24 January 1976. He then stopped Frazier in five rounds five months later. Foreman won three more bouts by knockout against lesser opposition, but on 17 March 1977 in San Juan, **Puerto Rico**, he lost a 12-round decision to Jimmy Young in a bout in which George was knocked down in the 12th round. The bout was named "Fight of the Year" by *Ring* **magazine**. This was the fourth time in five years that one of Foreman's fights was voted as "Fight of the Year"—the others being the ones with Frazier in 1973, Ali in 1975, and Lyle in 1976.

In the dressing room after the Young fight, Foreman became ill with heat stroke and exhaustion and believed he had a near-death experience. He prayed to God and felt that God's reply was for Foreman to change his life.

Foreman then became an ordained minister, opened a youth center in Texas, and abandoned boxing, devoting himself to his family and these other pursuits.

In 1987, after not boxing for 10 years, the 38-year-old Foreman announced that he was making a ring comeback to prove that age was not a factor. Although he had gained more than 50 pounds from the 217 pounds he weighed when he won the title, he went on a diet and worked out rigorously to get into fighting shape. The first bout he had in his comeback attempt was on 9 March 1987 in Sacramento, California. Foreman, at 267 pounds, easily defeated **journeyman** Steve Zouski and stopped him in the fourth round. For his next fight four months later, Foreman had trimmed down to 247 pounds. He got down as low as 235 pounds in 1988 for a bout with former **light heavyweight** and **cruiserweight** champion Dwight Muhammad Qawi but then settled on a weight of about 250 pounds for the rest of his comeback bouts.

Foreman won the first 18 bouts in his comeback by knockout before he won a 10-round **unanimous decision** over Everett "Big Foot" Martin on 20 July 1989. In his next fight, Foreman stopped former contender **Gerry Cooney** in two rounds. After four more wins by knockout, Foreman was ready to challenge heavyweight champion **Evander Holyfield** for the world's heavyweight title. In his comeback, Foreman had won 24 straight bouts, all but one by knockout.

On 19 April 1991, in **Atlantic City**, New Jersey, Holyfield, although outweighed by 49 pounds, won a unanimous decision over the 42-year-old Foreman. George just considered this a minor setback in his attempt to recapture the heavyweight title and was back in the ring later that year.

After winning three more bouts, he again fought for the heavyweight title. On 7 June 1993, he was matched with Tommy Morrison for the **vacant World Boxing Organization** heavyweight title. He again came up short, as Morrison won a 12-round unanimous decision.

Eighteen months later, Foreman made one more attempt at recapturing the heavyweight title and this time was successful, as he knocked out Michael Moorer, the **left-handed World Boxing Association** and **International Boxing Federation** heavyweight champion, on 5 November 1994 in **Las Vegas** and regained the championship 20 years after he had lost it to Ali. Foreman, then aged 45, became the oldest man in **ring** history to win the heavyweight title. He defended it successfully in 1995 against Axel Schulz, winning a **majority decision**, but then was stripped of the title for not giving Schulz a rematch.

Foreman had three more fights in his career—a 12-round unanimous decision over Crawford Grimsley in **Japan** in 1996, a 12-round **split decision** over Lou Savarese in 1997, and a 12-round majority decision loss to Shannon Briggs on 22 November 1997.

His unprecedented successful comeback inspired several other fighters to continue boxing into their late 40s and also was the model for the sixth film in Sylvester Stallone's **Rocky** series, *Rocky Balboa*.

When Foreman began his comeback in 1987, he attributed it to healthy eating. He then became a spokesman for a fat-reducing grill dubbed the George Foreman Lean Mean Fat-Reducing Grilling Machine. That grill has sold more than 100 million units since it was first introduced, and Foreman has earned substantially more from its sales than he did in all his years of boxing. In 1999, he received $137 million for the rights to his name for that device.

One other interesting aspect to Foreman is his devotion to his large family. He has 11 children, with all five boys named George. George III, nicknamed Monk, has become a professional heavyweight boxer and has compiled a record of 16–0 with 15 knockouts from 2009 to 2012. Foreman's daughter Freeda George Foreman boxed briefly as a **middleweight** from 2000 to 2001 and won her first five bouts before losing a split decision. In retirement, George has worked as a commentator for **televised** boxing.

Foreman is six foot three inches tall and has an 82-inch **reach**. He fought at weights ranging from 212 to 267 pounds as a heavyweight. As a result of his dual boxing careers, he had quite a few more bouts than his heavyweight contemporaries. In 81 professional bouts, from 1969 to 1997, he won 76 (68 by knockout), lost five (one by knockout), and fought a total of 349 rounds. He was inducted into the **International Boxing Hall of Fame** in 2003.

FOSTER, ROBERT LLOYD "BOB". B. 27 April 1938, Albuquerque, New Mexico. **Bob Foster** was one of the best **light heavyweights** in his era, but he should have been contented with that. Every time he attempted to move up into the **heavyweight** class, he was badly beaten.

Foster began boxing as a member of the U.S. Air Force in 1957. He served four years and claims to have had more than 100 **amateur bouts**, losing just three. He was an air force champion and also was the 1959 Pan American Games **middleweight silver medalist**. After his discharge in 1961, he became a professional boxer with his first fight on 27 March 1961, a two-**round knockout** of Duke Williams in Washington, DC. After winning his first nine bouts, Foster was named as a last-minute substitute against heavyweight contender Doug Jones and was stopped in the eighth round on 20 October 1962 at **Madison Square Garden**. Foster won two more bouts before losing a 10-round decision to Peruvian light heavyweight Mauro Mina in Lima, Peru, on 7 November 1963, with the bout being fought in the heavyweight class as both fighters weighed in at slightly more than the light heavyweight limit. Foster's next loss came when he again attempted to fight a ranked heavyweight and Ernie Terrell knocked him out in seven rounds on 10 July 1964. Foster won his next seven fights, six by knockout, before his next loss—this time to heavyweight contender **Zora Folley** on 6 December 1965 in New Orleans, Louisiana. Folley won nearly every round and a 10-round **unanimous decision**.

On 24 May 1968, Foster faced world light heavyweight champion **Dick Tiger** at Madison Square Garden, Tiger's favorite venue. Foster caught Tiger with a left **hook** in the fourth round, and Tiger was counted out. Ring historian **Bert Randolph Sugar** in his book *The 100 Greatest Boxers of All Time* describes the blow as "a picture-perfect punch the likes of which had never been seen before." Foster then demonstrated his superiority as a light heavyweight by winning his next 11 bouts, all short of the distance, including four title defenses.

He then made the mistake of challenging **Joe Frazier** for the world's heavyweight title and was knocked out in two rounds by Frazier on 18 November 1970 in Detroit. Foster returned to fighting light heavyweights and won his next eight bouts, including seven title defenses—seven by knockout or **technical knockout**. His next mistake was to challenge **Muhammad Ali**, who at that time was in between stints as heavyweight champion but still a dangerous fighter. Foster lasted until the eighth round this time but was knocked out at 0:40 of that round in Stateline, Nevada, on 21 November 1972.

After two more title defenses, both decisions over Pierre Fourie, Foster's mother passed away in December 1973 and he lost his interest in boxing. He had a lackluster performance in a title defense against Jorge Ahumada in

Foster's hometown of Albuquerque on 17 June 1974. Foster thought he had lost but was given a hometown decision that called the bout a **draw**. Foster announced his retirement in September 1974.

He began a career in law enforcement with the sheriff's department in Albuquerque but then attempted a halfhearted comeback in 1975 against lower-caliber opposition. He won five straight bouts before being stopped twice in 1978 and retiring permanently.

In retirement, he worked full-time in the Albuquerque sheriff's department and occasionally worked with prospective fighters, including his son, Tony.

Foster was unusually tall for a light heavyweight at six foot three inches and has an exceptional 79-inch **reach**. He fought at weights ranging from 170 to 186 pounds, primarily as a light heavyweight and heavyweight. In 65 professional bouts, from 1961 to 1978, he won 56 (46 by knockout), lost eight (all in the heavyweight division; six by knockout), had one draw, and fought a total of 353 rounds. He was inducted as a member of the inaugural class of the **International Boxing Hall of Fame** in 1990.

FOUL. Hitting a boxer below the beltline, hitting him when he is down, punching behind the neck (known as rabbit punching), headbutting, and holding with one hand and hitting with the other are all considered foul tactics. The **referee** usually will warn the offender the first time a foul is committed and instruct the **judges** to penalize the offender one point on the scorecards for the second offense. Subsequent offenses can result in the loss of additional points or even in the **bout** being terminated and the offender **disqualified**.

FRANCE. In **amateur boxing**, French boxers first competed in the 1908 **Olympic Games** and have entered each one of the 22 subsequent Olympic boxing tournaments. Only France and **Great Britain** have done so. France has won 19 Olympic boxing medals (four **gold**, seven **silver**, and eight **bronze**), which is tied with **South Africa** for 13th best. Their four gold medalists are Brahim Asloum, 2000 **light flyweight**; Paul Fritsch, 1920 **featherweight**; Jean Despeaux, 1936 **middleweight**; and Roger Michelot, 1936 **heavyweight**. Jérôme Thomas, a **flyweight** who won the bronze medal in 2000 and the silver medal in 2004, is the only Frenchman to win two Olympic boxing medals.

France has had quite a few professional champions. The most notable were **Georges Carpentier**, a **light heavyweight** champion who lost a **bout** to **Jack Dempsey** for the heavyweight title in 1921, and **Marcel Cerdan**, a middleweight champion who died in a plane crash in 1949 while en route to the **United States** for a championship bout with **Jake LaMotta**. Other French world champions include Brahim Asloum, Fabrice Benichou, Laurent

Boudouani, Hacine Cherifi, Robert Cohen, Eugene Criqui (a boxer who served in the French Army in World War I, had his jaw shattered by a bullet, and after surgery, resumed his boxing career and won the world's featherweight title in 1923), Gilbert Delé, Bruno Girard, Alphonse Halimi, René Jacquot, Thierry Jacob, Daniel Londas, Julian Lorcy, Souleymane M'Baye, Salim Medkoune, Jean Baptiste Mendy, Jean-Marc Momeck, Mahyar Monshipour, Hassan N'Dam N'Jikam, Andre Routis, Mehdi Sahnoune, brothers Christophe and Fabrice Tiozzo, Marcel Thil, Anaclet Wamba, and Battling Siki, born in French Senegal as Amadou M'Barick Fall.

Frenchmen elected to the **International Boxing Hall of Fame** are Georges Carpentier, Marcel Cerdan, Eugene Criqui, and Marcel Thil.

FRAZIER, JOSEPH WILLIAM "JOE," "SMOKIN' JOE". B. 12 January 1944, Beaufort, South Carolina. D. 7 November 2011, Philadelphia, Pennsylvania. Joe Frazier is remembered mainly for his three classic battles with **Muhammad Ali**. Nearly forgotten is the fact that he, too, along with **Floyd Patterson**, Muhammad Ali, and **George Foreman**, was an **Olympic** champion.

Frazier had a successful amateur career and won the Middle Atlantic **Golden Gloves heavyweight** championship in 1962, 1963, and 1964. He lost a close decision to the 295-pound Buster Mathis in the 1964 Olympic trials but was named to the **United States** Olympic team when Mathis suffered a broken thumb. Frazier won his first three Olympic **bouts** by **technical knockout** (or in **amateur boxing** parlance, **Referee** Stops Contest) but broke his thumb in the semifinal bout. He did not disclose the injury and won his final bout on a 3–2 decision while boxing with a broken thumb.

Frazier was known for his relentless style and powerful left **hook**. His first professional bout was on 16 August 1965 in Philadelphia, when he stopped Woody Goss in the first **round**. After winning his first 11 bouts by **knockout**, Frazier faced the durable Argentinean Óscar Bonavena at **Madison Square Garden** on 21 September 1966 and won a 10-round **majority decision**. In his next bout, Frazier stopped the former number one heavyweight contender **Eddie Machen** in the 10th round. A sixth-round knockout of Doug Jones was Frazier's next bout. After stopping Jefferson Davis in five rounds, Joe had to go the distance for only the second time as a professional but won a **unanimous decision** over George "Scrap-Iron" Johnson, a short, stocky boxer with a physique similar to that of Frazier. Joe then knocked out tough **George Chuvalo** in four rounds, the first time in his career that Chuvalo was stopped. Frazier's next two bouts were technical knockouts of Tony Doyle and Marion Conner.

On 4 March 1968, Frazier met his old nemesis, Buster Mathis, in a bout sanctioned by the **New York State Athletic Commission** for the world's heavyweight title, formerly held by Muhammad Ali, who was stripped of the crown for refusing induction into the U.S. Army and subsequently convicted of draft-dodging. Frazier was outweighed by nearly 40 pounds (even though Mathis had slimmed down from 295 to 243) and stopped Mathis in the 11th round of the bout—the first **main event** held at the new Madison Square Garden.

Over the three years from 1968 to 1970, Frazier defended his heavyweight championship six times and along the way gained recognition as champion by both the **World Boxing Association (WBA)** and **World Boxing Council**. Included in those six defenses were well-known contenders such as Bonavena, **Jerry Quarry**, Jimmy Ellis, world's **light heavyweight** champion **Bob Foster**, and relatively unknown fighters Manuel Ramos and Dave Zyglewicz.

After Ali was reinstated, he and Frazier met on 8 March 1971 at Madison Square Garden in a bout between two undefeated heavyweight champions that was billed as the Fight of the Century. The bout lived up to expectations and was exciting from start to finish. Frazier won a unanimous but close decision and the undisputed heavyweight championship. He then defended his title twice more against lesser competition—Terry Daniels, whom he stopped in four rounds, and Ron Stander, who lasted into the fifth round.

Frazier, with an undefeated record of 29–0 with 25 knockouts, next fought another former Olympic champion, George Foreman, who won the Olympic heavyweight **gold medal** in 1968 and since turning professional had won 37 straight bouts, 34 by knockout. Foreman had stopped his last five opponents in the second round, and Frazier became his sixth straight as he knocked Frazier down three times in the first round and three times in the second round before **referee** Arthur Mercante stopped the bout at 2:26 of the round, in a bout held outdoors in Kingston, Jamaica, on 22 January 1973.

Six months later, Frazier resumed his boxing career with a 12-round decision over the **Hungarian**-born British boxer Joe Bugner in London. Frazier and Ali then fought for the second time. This time neither held the world championship, but they still put on a tough battle at Madison Square Garden. Ali won a unanimous decision this time in their 12-round fight on 28 January 1974. In Frazier's next bout, he stopped Jerry Quarry in five rounds in a bout refereed by former heavyweight champion **Joe Louis**. In March 1975, Frazier traveled to **Australia**, where he stopped former WBA heavyweight champion Jimmy Ellis in nine rounds.

Frazier's next bout was one that appears on many boxing historians' lists of the greatest fights in boxing history and is known as the **Thrilla in Manila**. He fought a third match with Muhammad Ali—this time as the challenger for Ali's heavyweight championship, which he had rewon the previous year by defeating George Foreman in Zaire. The bout took place in Manila, **Philippines**, at 10:45 in the morning to fit the television schedule for the **United States**. Ali and Frazier went toe-to-toe for 14 rounds in the humid heat of

Manila, but Frazier had the worst of it, and after the 14th round his **trainer**, Eddie Futch, refused to allow Frazier to continue. Unbeknownst to them, Ali was also telling his **corner** that he had had enough, but the referee stopped the bout before Ali could surrender.

Frazier fought Foreman once more eight months later but was again stopped—this time in five rounds. He retired following the bout but was coaxed into one final bout five years later. Frazier and Floyd "Jumbo" Cummings fought to a 10-round **draw**, and Frazier never boxed again. At the time of his fight with Frazier, Cummings had recently been paroled after a murder conviction. After the draw with Frazier, he lost his next five fights and then was sentenced to 12 years in prison for armed robbery. In 2002, he was convicted of a third major crime and was sentenced to life in prison.

Frazier had owned and operated a boxing gymnasium in Philadelphia since 1968, and when he retired, he helped train his sons, Marvis Frazier and Joe Frazier Jr. and his daughter, Jacqui. Marvis had a respectable **ring** career from 1980 to 1988, winning 19 of 21 bouts, but his two losses were in high-profile bouts against **Larry Holmes** and **Mike Tyson**, and both ended in one-round knockouts. Joe Frazier Jr., much smaller than his father and brother, fought as a **light middleweight** and had a respectable career from 1983 to 1992, although he never reached the top echelon and retired with a record of 23–7–4. Their sister, Jacqui Frazier-Lyde, won 13 of 15 bouts from 2000 to 2004 and had one bout with Muhammad Ali's daughter, Laila Ali, which Jacqui lost on a **majority decision**.

Joe Frazier Sr. was diagnosed with liver cancer in September 2011 and died two months later. Frazier was five foot 11 inches tall and had a 73-inch **reach**. He fought at weights ranging from 197 to 229 pounds as a heavyweight. In 37 professional bouts, from 1965 to 1981, he won 32 (27 by knockout), lost four (three by knockout), had one draw, and fought a total of 214 rounds. He was inducted as a member of the inaugural class of the **International Boxing Hall of Fame** in 1990.

FRIDAY NIGHT FIGHTS. For 14 years, the Gillette Cavalcade of Sports, known to boxing fans as the "Friday Night Fights," were one of the most popular **televised** sporting events. Each week from 1946 until 1960, a 10-round **main event** was televised by the National Broadcasting Company, often from New York's **Madison Square Garden** but also from other cities. The sponsor was the Gillette Safety Razor Company. *New York Daily News* sportswriter Jimmy Powers was the announcer, and **Don Dunphy** did the radio broadcast.

FULLMER, GENE "CYCLONE". B. 21 July 1931, West Jordan, Utah. Gene Fullmer is best remembered as a boxer whose relentless head-first style resulted in quite a few **bouts** in which headbutting by both fighters was the order of the day.

After compiling a reported 70–4 **amateur** record, Fullmer became a **professional** boxer. His first professional bout was on 9 June 1951 in Logan, Utah, and Fullmer won easily by **knocking down** his opponent three times in the first **round**. He won his first 11 bouts by **knockout** before being required to go the distance—10 two-minute rounds on 25 September 1951—a **majority-decision** victory against the tough veteran **middleweight** contender Garth Panter. A stint in the U.S. Army interrupted Fullmer's professional career, and he was only able to fight two bouts in 1952 and none in 1953.

Fullmer won his first 24 bouts (19 by knockout) in the western part of the country, and nearly all in Utah, before heading east and fighting Jackie LaBua in Brooklyn, New York, on 8 November 1954, winning a 10-round **decision**. From this point in his career until he retired in 1963, all but one of Fullmer's bouts was against a top contender or champion with a winning record.

Fullmer suffered his first loss on 4 April 1955 on a 10-round decision to Gil Turner but avenged the defeat two months later in his hometown of West Jordan, Utah. After decision victories over Del Flanagan and Al Andrews, Gene lost decisions to Bobby Boyd and Eduardo Lausse. He then won his next five bouts, decisioning top contenders Rocky Castellani, Gil Turner, **Ralph "Tiger" Jones**, and Charles Humez and knocking out Moses Ward.

On 2 January 1957 at **Madison Square Garden**, Fullmer met the great **"Sugar Ray" Robinson** for Robinson's world middleweight championship. At the time of the fight, Robinson had a record of 139–4–2 versus Fullmer's 37–3. Fullmer won a **unanimous decision** and the middleweight title. After two **nontitle** victories, Fullmer met Robinson again, this time in Chicago Stadium on 1 May 1957. Robinson regained his title with a fifth-round knockout of Fullmer.

Fullmer won his next nine bouts and on 28 August 1959 in the Cow Palace in Daly City, California, fought **welterweight** and middleweight champion **Carmen Basilio** for the **vacant National Boxing Association** middleweight title. In a bout that *Ring* magazine called the "Fight of the Year," Fullmer stopped Basilio in the 14th round and rewon the championship.

Fullmer then made seven consecutive successful defenses of his title. He decisioned Ellsworth "Spider" Webb, fought a **draw** with **Joey Giardello**, stopped Basilio in 12 rounds, fought a draw with "Sugar Ray" Robinson and then won a decision over him, won a **split decision** over the hard-hitting **Cuban** Florentino Fernández in a bout in which Fullmer hurt his elbow, and then stopped the ill-fated **Benny "Kid" Paret** in 10 rounds after knocking him down three times in the final round. This was to be Paret's next-to-last fight, as he died at the hands of **Emile Griffith** four months later in their welterweight title bout.

On 23 October 1962 in Candlestick Park in San Francisco, Fullmer fought the first of three bouts with the Nigerian middleweight **Dick Tiger**. Tiger won the bout, and the middleweight title, on a unanimous decision. In their first rematch on 23 February 1963 in **Las Vegas**, Nevada, the two fought to a 15-round draw. A second rematch on 10 August 1963 in Ibadan, Nigeria, saw Fullmer's manager, Merv Jenson, ask to have the bout stopped after seven rounds with Tiger well ahead in the bout.

Fullmer's two younger brothers, Don and Jay, were both boxers. Don fought as a middleweight from 1957 to 1973 and compiled a record of 54–20–5. He challenged **Nino Benvenuti** for the middleweight title on 14 December 1968 and scored a **knockdown** of Benvenuti but lost a unanimous decision. Jay fought from 1956 to 1960 as a **lightweight** and had a record of 20–5–2.

Fullmer is five foot eight inches tall and has a 69-inch **reach**. He fought at weights ranging from 148 to 167 pounds, primarily as a middleweight. In 64 professional bouts, from 1951 to 1963, Gene Fullmer won 55 (24 by knockout), lost six (two by knockout), had three draws, and fought a total of 508 rounds. He was inducted into the **International Boxing Hall of Fame** in 1991.

G

GALENTO, DOMENICO ANTONIO "TONY," "TWO-TON TONY".
B. 12 March 1910, Orange, New Jersey. D. 22 July 1979, Orange, New
Jersey. "Two-Ton" Tony Galento will never be inducted into a boxing hall of
fame, but if ever a hall of fame were created for boxing's greatest characters,
he would be among the first to be enshrined.

He was five foot nine inches tall and for most of his boxing career usually
weighed around 225 pounds. Had there been **toughman competitions** in his
era, he would have been one of its star performers. He owned a bar in New
Jersey and worked as a bartender when he wasn't fighting. He was known for
his powerful left **hook** and lack of defense.

There are many legends surrounding Galento, who reportedly trained on
beer and hot dogs. His nickname supposedly originated when he was late for
a **bout** and told his manager that he had "two tons of ice" to deliver, although
his physique could also have been the source of the nickname. In various
publicity stunts, he allegedly wrestled an octopus and boxed a kangaroo and
a bear. He trained at night after closing his bar at two in the morning because,
in his words, "I fight at night." Before one bout, he allegedly ate 52 hot dogs
on a bet and then could not close his trunks. He spoke (and was quoted) in his
Brooklynese accent, and one of his familiar sayings when asked about a
future opponent was, "I'll moider da bum."

He fought his first recorded professional bout on 12 March 1928 in Newark, New Jersey, and won with a third-**round knockout**. He was quite active
during the 1930s and would win some and lose some but always put on an
entertaining show with his roughhouse brawling tactics. He fought some of
the better **heavyweights** during that era and recorded one-round knockout
victories over Natie Brown, Don "Red" Barry, and Jorge Brescia, among
others. He knocked out Nathan Mann in two rounds and stopped Harry
Thomas in three rounds. He also lost 10-round decisions to Paul Cavalier,
Johnny Risko, Ernie Schaaf, and Arturo Godoy.

His most famous battle was with heavyweight champion **Joe Louis** for the
world's heavyweight title on 28 June 1939 at Yankee Stadium in the Bronx,
New York. Galento, who outweighed Louis by 33 pounds but was at least

five inches shorter, staggered Louis in the first round. Louis retaliated by knocking Galento down in the second round, reportedly the first time in his career that he was knocked off his feet. Galento got up and in the third round scored a **knockdown** of Louis with a wild left hook. That appeared to anger Louis, and in the fourth round he unleashed an assault that the defenseless Galento could not contain, and **referee** Arthur Donovan stopped the bout at 2:29 of the fourth round.

Galento's next bout against heavyweight contender Lou Nova was one of the dirtiest fights in history, with Galento stopping Nova in the 14th round of their scheduled 15-round **nontitle bout**. Galento then fought former heavyweight champion **Max Baer** and was stopped in the eighth round. Baer's brother, Buddy, was Galento's opponent one month later, but Galento quit in the seventh round, claiming a broken hand. Galento's last legitimate fight was on 1 June 1943 when he knocked out Herbie Katz in just 25 seconds of the first round.

Galento then became a professional wrestler and had two boxing bouts in 1943 with professional wrestlers Fred Blassie and Jack Suzek, both quick knockouts. He also wrestled and acted as referee in professional wrestling bouts for the next decade. He appeared in several films and television shows. A true-life Damon Runyon character, he had a bit part in *Guys and Dolls* and more substantial parts in *On the Waterfront*, *The Best Things in Life Are Free*, and *Wind Across the Everglades*.

Galento fought at weights ranging from 183 to 247 pounds as a heavyweight. In 112 professional bouts, from 1928 to 1944, he won 80 (57 by knockout), lost 26 (six by knockout), had five draws and one **no contest**, and fought a total of 662 rounds.

GALÍNDEZ, VICTOR EMILIO "EL LEOPARDO DE MORÓN". B. 2 November 1948, Vedia, Buenos Aires, **Argentina**. D. 25 October 1980, Veinticinco de Mayo, Buenos Aires, Argentina. Victor Galíndez was one of the best fighters in Argentina's history. As an **amateur** boxer, he was the **light middleweight silver medalist** at the 1967 Pan American Games, losing his final **bout** to the great **Cuban** boxer Rolando Garbey, who won the first of his three Pan American Games **gold medals** by defeating Galíndez. In the 1968 **Olympic Games**, Galíndez lost his first-round light middleweight bout to the **Italian** boxer Aldo Bentini.

Galíndez fought his first bout as a **professional** on 10 May 1969, defeating Ramón Ruiz on a fourth-**round knockout** in Buenos Aires. His early career was not exceptional, and after his first 22 bouts, most of them in Buenos Aires, his record only stood at 11–6–3 with two **no contests**. In 1972, he defeated Juan Aguilar on a 12-round decision to win the Argentine **light heavyweight** championship and three months later won the South American light heavyweight title.

On 7 December 1974 in Buenos Aires, Galíndez stopped Len Hutchins in the 13th round to win the **vacant World Boxing Association** light heavyweight title. He made his first title defense on 7 April 1975, winning a 15-round **unanimous decision** over **South African** Pierre Fourie in Johannesburg, South Africa—Galíndez's first fight outside of his native Argentina. He then defeated countryman Jorge Ahumada by unanimous decision at **Madison Square Garden** in New York on 30 June 1975. In September 1975, Galíndez made a return visit to South Africa and won a **split decision** in a rematch with Fourie.

In 1976, Galíndez started his year by knocking out previously undefeated Norwegian Harald Skog in three rounds in one of the two world championship bouts ever to take place in Norway, which five years later banned the professional sport. After a **nontitle** split decision win over Jesse Burnett in Copenhagen, Denmark, Galíndez made another title defense in Johannesburg, this time knocking out Richie Kates in the 15th round. In October 1976, Galíndez returned to his home away from home, Johannesburg, where he defeated South African Kosie Smith on a unanimous decision in his sixth title defense and fourth in South Africa.

In 1977, Galíndez made three successful defenses of his light heavyweight title—all by 15-round unanimous decisions and all in **Italy**. He first defeated Kates in a rematch in Rome in June, then Mexican American Alvaro "Yaqui" López in September also in Rome, and Eddie Mustafa Muhammad (formerly known as Eddie Gregory) in Torino in November. After winning a nontitle bout in Buenos Aires in April 1978, he returned to Italy in May for a return bout with López in Viareggio, which Galíndez again won on a unanimous decision.

On 15 September 1978, on the **undercard** of the **Muhammad Ali–Leon Spinks** return bout in the Superdome in New Orleans, Louisiana, Galíndez lost his title to Mike Rossman on a 13th-round **technical knockout**. They had a rematch in April 1979, also at the Superdome, and Galíndez regained his title by stopping Rossman in nine rounds. On 30 November 1979, in the first title defense of his newly reacquired title, Galíndez was knocked out in the 11th round by Marvin Johnson. Galíndez's final bout took place in Anaheim, California, on 14 June 1980, and fighting at 190 pounds, the heaviest of his career, he lost a 12-round unanimous decision to Jesse Burnett.

Galíndez retired following the bout and was ready to pursue another of his childhood dreams—motor racing. In his first race in the Turismo Carretera circuit in Buenos Aires on 25 October 1980, Galíndez stopped in the pits for repairs. While there, he was hit by an out-of-control car and killed instantly.

Galíndez was five foot nine inches tall and had a 72-inch **reach**. He fought at weights ranging from 171 to 190 pounds, primarily as a light heavyweight. In 70 professional bouts, from 1969 to 1980, he won 55 (34 by knockout), lost nine (three by knockout), had four draws and two **no contests**, and fought a total of 603 rounds. He was inducted into the **International Boxing Hall of Fame** in 2002.

GALLICO, PAUL WILLIAM. B. 26 July 1897, New York, New York. D. 15 July 1976, Monte Carlo, Monaco. Paul Gallico is known by most people as an award-winning author whose works include *The Snow Goose, The Poseidon Adventure, The Adventures of Hiram Holliday,* and *Mrs. 'Arris Goes to Paris.*

A 1919 graduate of Columbia University, he began as a sportswriter for the *New York Daily News* and is the man responsible for creating the New York **Golden Gloves** boxing tournament in 1927 and writing daily articles on the tournament's progress. During his career as a sportswriter, he challenged several athletes at their own sports so that he could better appreciate their efforts. He sparred with **heavyweight** champion **Jack Dempsey**, played golf with Bobby Jones, swam against Johnny Weismuller, and batted against baseball pitchers Herb Pennock and Dizzy Dean. Writer George Plimpton acted similarly during the 1960s and boxed **Archie Moore** and played football with the Detroit Lions and ice hockey with the Boston Bruins.

Gallico left the sports desk of the *Daily News* in 1936 to concentrate on writing fiction. From 1938 until 1974, he wrote more than 40 books and numerous short stories, several of which were later made into films or television series. The 1952 film *Lili,* starring Leslie Caron, was based on one of his short stories, which was later turned into a book by Gallico. *Lili* later became the Broadway musical *Carnival.*

He was inducted into the **International Boxing Hall of Fame** in 2009.
See also APPENDIX K.

GANS, JOE "THE OLD MASTER" (né JOSEPH GANT). B. 25 November 1874, Baltimore, Maryland. D. 10 August 1910, Baltimore, Maryland. Joe Gans was one of the first black boxers to be successful in the **ring**. In 1960, he was considered by ring historian **Nat Fleischer** to be the best **lightweight** of all time.

Details of his early life are sketchy, and his birth name might have been Gant or Gaines or Gantz. There is even mention that he was born Joseph Saifuss Butts and took the name of his adopted mother, Gant. His birthdate is also unknown, with Gans himself stating that he did not know it. Regardless, he boxed as Joe Gans and in his time was one of the best lightweights.

His first recorded **bout** was 23 October 1893 in Baltimore. He boxed almost exclusively in Baltimore until 1896, when he fought his first bout in New York City. His popularity grew, and he then fought in San Francisco, Philadelphia, Cleveland, and other cities that allowed boxing, with bouts scheduled for four to 25 **rounds**, depending on the laws of the venue. On 27 September 1897 in Brooklyn, New York, he fought Bobby Dobbs, another black fighter, for the so-called colored lightweight title but was outpointed by Dobbs in 20 rounds.

On 23 March 1900 in New York City, Gans fought the white fighter Frank Erne for the world's lightweight title but was stopped in the 12th round of their scheduled 25-round bout due to a cut. On 11 October 1900 in Leadville, Colorado, Gans fought two bouts, scoring a first-round **knockout** in one and a fourth-round **technical knockout** in the second. On 13 December 1900 in Chicago, Illinois, Gans fought **featherweight** champion **Terry McGovern** in a **nontitle bout** and was knocked out in the second round by the champion.

In a bout typical of the terms of matches in that era, on 13 December 1901 Gans met Bobby Dobbs in Baltimore. The agreement between the two fighters was that Gans had to stop Dobbs within 10 rounds or else Gans would only receive the loser's end of the purse, 25 percent, and in addition would have to pay Dobbs $50 for each round after 10 that Dobbs continued without being knocked out or retiring. Dobbs lasted until the 14th round of the 20-round bout before giving up.

On 2 May 1902, Gans fought Erne in a rematch for the world's lightweight championship. Gans knocked out his opponent after only 1:40 of the first round and became the first black world champion born in the United States. (Canadian-born George Dixon was the first black world champion.) Gans defended the title successfully 15 times all over the country. He fought George "Elbows" McFadden (27 June 1902, San Francisco, TKO round 3); Rufe Turner (24 July 1902, Oakland, California, KO 15); Kid McPartland (13 October 1902, Fort Erie, Ontario, **Canada**, KO 5); Charley Sieger (14 November 1902, Baltimore, TKO 14); Gus Gardner (1 January 1903, New Britain, Connecticut, disqualified 11); Steve Crosby (11 March, Hot Springs, Arkansas, TKO 11); Frank "Buddy" King (4 July 1903, Butte, Montana, KO 5); Willie Fitzgerald (12 January 1904, Detroit, Michigan, decision 10); Jimmy Britt (31 October 1904, San Francisco, disqualified 5); Dave Holly (23 July 1906, Seattle, Washington, decision 20); Battling Nelson (3 September 1906, Goldfield, Nevada, disqualified 42—fight to a finish); Kid Herman (1 January 1907, Tonopah, Nevada, KO 8); Jimmy Britt (9 September 1907, San Francisco, TKO 6); George Memsic (27 September 1907, Los Angeles, decision 20); and Rudy Unholz (14 May 1908, San Francisco, TKO 11). In addition to these bouts for the world title, he fought numerous nontitle bouts in this period and defeated Jack Blackburn (**Joe Louis's** future **trainer**) and future **welterweight** and **middleweight** champion Harry Lewis. He also drew with **Joe Walcott** and lost to **Sam Langford**.

On 19 January 1906, he also won the world's welterweight title by knocking out Mike "Twin" Sullivan in 15 rounds in San Francisco but never defended that title and continued boxing as a lightweight.

He finally lost the lightweight championship to Battling Nelson on 4 July 1908 in Colma, California, on a knockout in the 17th round of their scheduled 45-round bout. In a rematch in Colma on 9 September, Nelson again knocked out Gans—this time in the 21st round of a scheduled 45-round bout.

Gans's final bout was on 12 March 1909, when he knocked down Jabez White four times en route to a 10-round **newspaper decision** in New York City. He died of tuberculosis in 1910 but might have contracted it as early as 1907 and fought his last few years with the disease.

Gans was five foot six inches tall and had a 71-inch **reach**. He fought at weights ranging from 124 to 143 pounds, primarily as a lightweight. In 196 professional bouts, from 1893 to 1909, he won 145 (100 by knockout), lost 10 (five by knockout), and had 16 draws. He had 20 no-decision bouts in which he received the newspaper decision in 14, lost twice, and had four draws. He fought a total of 1,608 rounds. He was inducted as a member of the inaugural class of the **International Boxing Hall of Fame** in 1990.

GANT, JOSEPH. *See* GANS, JOE "THE OLD MASTER" (né JOSEPH GANT).

GATTI, ARTURO "THUNDER". B. 15 April 1972, Cassino, **Italy**. D. 11 July 2009, Ipojuca, **Brazil**. Arturo Gatti fought in several of the most highly contested **bouts** during the 1990s and early 21st century. Four of his bouts were selected by *Ring* **magazine** as the "Fight of the Year"—his 1997 bout with Gabriel Ruelas, his 1998 bout with Ivan Robinson, and two bouts with Micky Ward in 2002 and 2003.

Born in Italy but raised in **Canada**, Gatti was a member of the Canadian **Olympic** team but passed up a chance to compete in the 1992 Olympic Games by becoming a **professional** boxer on 10 June 1991. He won 23 of his first 24 bouts, with 20 **knockouts**, 14 in the first **round**. His only loss was a six-round **split decision** in 1992.

On 15 December 1995, he won the **International Boxing Federation super featherweight** title on a 12-round **decision** over Tracy Harris Patterson at **Madison Square Garden**. Over the next two years, he defended it successfully three times, including a rematch with Patterson and a bout with Gabriel Ruelas that was the *Ring* magazine "Fight of the Year" for 1997. After that bout, he vacated the title to move up in weight class to the **lightweight** division.

His first three bouts as a lightweight were exciting if not successful. He was stopped on a cut in the eighth round by Ángel Manfredy, lost a split decision to Ivan Robinson in the 1998 *Ring* magazine "Fight of the Year," and lost a **unanimous decision** to Robinson in a rematch. He then came back with a first-round **technical knockout** of Reyes Muñoz in which Muñoz left the **ring** on a stretcher, and then he stopped former super featherweight and lightweight champion Joey Gamache in two rounds in a bout that ended Gamache's career.

Gatti's next major opponent was the legendary **Óscar De La Hoya**, who at the time of the fight with Gatti was in between titles, having just lost the **welterweight** title in his last fight and winning the **light middleweight** title in his next fight. De La Hoya stopped Gatti in the fifth round to win their **nontitle bout** on 24 March 2001 in **Las Vegas**.

After a four-round technical knockout of Terron Millett, Gatti fought Micky Ward in the first of three consecutive fights between the two. Their first fight on 18 May 2002 was won by Ward on a **majority decision** and was voted *Ring* magazine's "Fight of the Year." Their next battle on 23 November 2002 was nearly as exciting and was won by Gatti. The two fought their last fight on 7 June 2003, which was also won by Gatti and was the 2003 *Ring* magazine "Fight of the Year." Ward retired from the **ring** following that fight.

In 2004, Gatti won the **vacant World Boxing Council (WBC) light welterweight** title on 24 January by defeating the previously undefeated (32–0–1) Italian Gianluca Branco by a 12-round unanimous decision. Arturo successfully defended against Leonard Dorin with a second-round knockout and Jesse James Leija with a fifth-round knockout. He lost his title to the undefeated (33–0) **Floyd Mayweather Jr.** on 25 June 2005 when he retired after the sixth round of a one-sided fight. Gatti won the vacant **International Boxing Association** welterweight title (not one of the major ones) in 2006. He then challenged Carlos Manuel Baldomir for the more prestigious WBC welterweight title on 22 July 2006 but was knocked down twice in the ninth round before the bout was stopped. In his final bout, on 14 July 2007, Gatti was stopped in the seventh round by Alfonso Gómez and retired from the ring in the dressing room after the bout.

In 2009, Gatti was on a vacation with his second wife, a Brazilian, in Ipojuca, Pernambuco, Brazil. He was found dead in his hotel room. Initially, the death was ruled a homicide and his wife was suspected, then it was changed to a suicide and she was released. Investigations have continued into the death, but as of 2012 there have been no definitive results.

Gatti was five foot seven inches tall and had a 70-inch **reach**. He fought at weights ranging from 126 to 149 pounds in weight classes from **featherweight** to welterweight. In 49 professional bouts, from 1991 to 2007, he won 40 (31 by knockout), lost nine (five by knockout), and fought a total of 253 rounds. He was inducted as a member of the **International Boxing Hall of Fame** in 2013.

GAVILÁN, KID "THE CUBAN HAWK" (né GERARDO GONZÁLEZ). B. 6 January 1926, Berrocal, Camagüey, **Cuba.** D. 13 February 2003, Miami, Florida. Kid Gavilán was one of the mainstays of **televised boxing** in the 1950s. A flashy boxer known for his **bolo punch**, he appeared in **main events** on national television more than 30 times and was a fan favorite.

Born Gerardo González, he was named Kid Gavilán by his first manager, Fernando Balido, who owned a restaurant called "El Gavilán" (The Hawk) in Cuba. The Kid, as he became known in the United States, began boxing **professionally** in Cuba on 5 June 1943 and won his first 14 fights and the Cuban **lightweight** title. He traveled to **Mexico** in 1945, and it was there that he lost his first **bout**, a 10-**round** decision to Mexican Carlos Malacara. Gavilán's second loss in 1946 was also by decision to a Mexican fighter in Mexico.

Gavilán came to the **United States** toward the end of 1946 and made his United States debut at **Madison Square Garden** on 1 November, winning a six-round bout by **technical knockout** in five rounds. He would spend most of the remainder of his boxing career in the United States.

On 27 February 1948, Gavilán lost a close decision to then lightweight champion **Ike Williams** in a 10-round **nontitle bout** at the Garden. Later that year, Gavilán fought the **welterweight** champion, **"Sugar Ray" Robinson** (who had an 87–1–1 record at the time), in a 10-round nontitle bout at Yankee Stadium and lost another close decision. The year 1949 proved to be an interesting one for the Hawk. In January, he won a nontitle rematch with the still-champion Williams and in April defeated him again in a nontitle bout. Gavilán also fought his first world championship bout that year on 11 July but was outpointed by "Sugar Ray" Robinson in a bid for the world's welterweight championship. After decisioning contender Rocky Castellani in September, Gavilán then defeated the former lightweight champion Beau Jack in November.

He began 1950 by losing a close **split decision** to welterweight contender **Billy Graham**. Gavilán also was defeated that year by Frenchman Robert Villemain in Montreal, **Canada**, George Costner, and Gene Hairston and drew with Tommy Ciarlo. He did win 10 of his 15 bouts that year, including a rematch with Graham in November.

After winning his first five bouts in 1951, Gavilán won the world welterweight championship by decisioning Johnny Bratton in 15 rounds on 18 May at Madison Square Garden. Gavilán successfully defended the title against Graham (29 August 1951, split decision); Bobby Dykes (4 February 1952, split decision); Gil Turner (7 July 1952, TKO round 11); Graham (5 October 1952, **unanimous decision**); Chuck Davey (11 February 1953, TKO 10); **Carmen Basilio** (18 September 1953, split decision); and Bratton (13 November 1953, unanimous decision).

On 2 April 1954, Gavilán challenged **Carl "Bobo" Olson** for the world's **middleweight** title but lost a close 15-round **majority decision**. Gavilán lost his welterweight title to Johnny Saxton on a 15-round unanimous decision in Philadelphia on 20 October 1954. Saxton was managed by mobster Frank "Blinky" Palermo, and before the fight it was rumored that Gavilán would have to win by **knockout** if he intended to retain his championship. Gavilán won the fight in the eyes of 20 of 22 **ringside** journalists, but Saxton received the decision.

Gavilán continued as a professional boxer until 18 June 1958 and fought in South America and Europe in 1955 and 1956 before returning to the United States. From 1955 to 1958, he fought 26 bouts but could only win 10 of them, although they each went the full 10 rounds. He was never stopped or knocked out in his career.

Gavilán was five foot 10 inches tall and had a 71-inch **reach**. He fought at weights ranging from 121 to 156 pounds, primarily as a welterweight. In 143 professional bouts, from 1943 to 1958, he won 108 (28 by knockout), lost 30 (none by knockout), had five draws, and fought a total of 1,342 rounds. He was inducted as a member of the inaugural class of the **International Boxing Hall of Fame** in 1990.

GENARO, FRANKIE (né FRANK DIGENNARO). B. 26 August 1901, New York, New York. D. 27 December 1966, Staten Island, New York. At five foot one inch tall and 110 pounds, Frank DiGennaro was built to be a jockey. He did get a job as a stable boy but decided that he would rather be a boxer. He began boxing as an **amateur** in 1917 and in 1920 won the **Olympic Games gold medal** in the **flyweight** class.

He became a **professional** boxer shortly afterward and fought his first professional **bout** on 15 October 1920—a three-**round disqualification** victory over Joe Colletti at **Madison Square Garden**. The two boxers fought three more times in 1921, with each fighter winning one and one bout ending in a **draw**.

In 1922, Genaro defeated future world's **bantamweight** champion Charley Phil Rosenberg on a 12-round **decision** and would beat him again in a subsequent rematch the following year. On 6 July 1922, Genaro decisioned the future world's flyweight champion **Pancho Villa** in 12 rounds—the first of three bouts they would have in 1922 and 1923. After Genaro won a 10-round rematch with Villa, the two fought for a 15-round bout won by Genaro. It was billed for the "American flyweight title" as Englishman **Jimmy Wilde** was then the world's flyweight champion.

Although Genaro fought 13 more bouts in 1923, winning 12, only one of those fights was in defense of his "American flyweight title." Genaro won six of eight bouts in 1924, with two draws, and in none of them was that title on the line.

On 12 August 1925, Genaro defended the title against the 1924 Olympic flyweight champion, Fidel La Barba, in a bout that was also for the **vacant** world's flyweight championship. LaBarba won the 10-round decision and became recognized as world champion.

After winning most of his bouts over the next few years, Genaro got another chance at a world title. On 6 February 1928, he defeated French Canadian Albert "Frenchy" Belanger on a 10-round decision and won recognition by the **National Boxing Association (NBA)** as world flyweight champion. He successfully defended the NBA title three times in 1928—twice against Steve Rocco (although one of the two bouts was a draw) and once in a rematch with Belanger.

On 2 March 1929, in Paris, **France**, Genaro scored one of the **quickest knockouts** in a championship bout when a solid body punch knocked out the European flyweight champion Émile "Spider" Pladner in 47 seconds of the first round and consequently gave Genaro universal recognition as world flyweight champion. In a return bout, also in Paris the next month, Pladner was disqualified in the fifth round.

Genaro made eight more successful defenses of his world title, fighting internationally in his opponents' home countries in most of the bouts. He defeated Englishman Ernie Jarvis (17 October 1929, London, **England**, 15-round decision); Frenchman Yvon Trèvédic (18 January 1930, Paris, **technical knockout**, 12 rounds); Canadian "Frenchy" Belanger (12 June 1930, Toronto, **Canada**, 10-round decision); Midget Wolgast (26 December 1930, New York, 15-round draw); Spaniard Victor Ferrand (25 March 1931, Barcelona, **Spain**, 15-round draw); Chilean Routier Parra (16 July 1931, North Adams, Massachusetts, fourth-round knockout); Jackie Harmon (30 July 1931, Waterbury, Connecticut, sixth-round knockout); and Frenchman Valentin Angelmann (3 October 1931, Paris, 15-round decision).

He lost his title to Tunisian Frenchman Victor "Young" Perez on 26 October 1931 in Paris on a 15-round decision. After one more bout in France, which Genaro lost by **disqualification**, he returned to the **United States** and, boxing primarily as a **bantamweight**, fought nine more fights over the next three years. He won only five of those bouts, but one was a decision over future world's **featherweight** champion Joey Archibald.

On 21 February 1934 in Oakland, California, Genaro was stopped in eight rounds by Little Pancho and retired from the ring.

Flyweights in the 1920s often had interesting **ring** names, which make them sound like they could have been extras in *The Wizard of Oz*. Over the course of his 15-year professional career, Genaro met Little Pancho, Young Speedy Dado, Young Tommy, Young Perez, Midget Wolgast, Little Jeff Smith, Newsboy Brown, Kid Williams, Kid Wolfe, and Jockey Joe Dillon.

Genaro had a 63-inch **reach** and fought at weights ranging from 108 to 118 pounds, primarily as a flyweight. In 128 professional bouts, from 1920 to 1934, Genaro won 76 (17 by knockout), lost 22 (four by knockout), and had eight draws and 22 no-decision bouts in which he was awarded the **newspaper decision** in 19 and lost three. He fought a total of 1,186 rounds. He was inducted into the **International Boxing Hall of Fame** in 1998.

GERMANY. Boxing has always been quite popular in Germany, and **Max Schmeling**, world **heavyweight** champion from 1930 to 1932 and one of Germany's all-time favorite sports heroes, was inducted into the **International Boxing Hall of Fame** in 1992. The sport had a resurgence in the 1990s, with many world championship **bouts** taking place there.

In **amateur boxing**, German boxers first competed in the 1928 **Olympic Games** and have entered 13 Olympic boxing tournaments. From 1968 to 1988, the divided Germany competed in six Olympic boxing tournaments with the Federal Republic of Germany (West Germany) team and six tournaments with the German Democratic Republic (East Germany) team. West Germany boycotted the 1980 games, and East Germany boycotted the 1984 games. West Germany won six medals—one **gold** and five bronze. East Germany won 13 medals—five gold, two **silver**, and six bronze. The undivided nation of Germany has won 28 medals—five gold, 12 silver, and 11 bronze for seventh place among all nations in Olympic boxing competition.

Dieter Kottysch was West Germany's gold medalist. He won the 1972 **light middleweight** class in his home country in Munich. East Germany's boxing gold medalists were Rudi Fink, 1980 **featherweight**; Andreas Zülow, 1988 **lightweight**; Manfred Wolke, 1968 **welterweight**; Jochen Bachfeld, 1976 welterweight; and Henry Maske, 1988 **middleweight**. The united Germany's five gold medalists in Olympic boxing were Willi Kaiser, 1936 **flyweight**; Wolfgang Behrendt, 1956 **bantamweight**; Andreas Tews, 1992 featherweight; Torsten May, 1992 **light heavyweight**; and Herbert Runge, 1936 heavyweight. The only German to win multiple medals in Olympic boxing was Richard Nowakowski, the 1976 featherweight silver and 1980 lightweight bronze medalist who fought for East Germany.

There have been 19 Germans who claimed professional world championships, with Schmeling, by far, being the best and most popular. Other German world champions include Firat Arslan, Markus Beyer, Markus Bott, Jürgen Brähmer, Eckhard Dagge, Marco Huck, Henry Maske, Darius Michalczewski, Sven Ottke, Graciano Rocchigiani and his brother Ralf, Dimitri Sartison, Bert Schenck, Felix Sturm, Robert Stieglitz, Sebastian Sylvester, Vitali Tajbert, and Sebastian Zbik. Other notable German boxers who did not win world championships include Willi Besmanoff, Jurgen Blin, Gustav

Eder, Jupp Elze, Gerhard Hecht, Willi Hoepner, Karl Mildenberger, Peter Mueller, Heinz Neuhaus, Walter Neusel, Willi Quatuor, Gustav "Bubi" Scholz, Axel Schulz, Hein Ten Hoff, Albert Westphal, and Gerhard Zech.

On 10 September 1966, **Muhammad Ali** defended his world's heavyweight title against Karl Mildenberger in Frankfurt, Germany, with a 12th-round **technical knockout**.

German boxing promoter Wilfried Sauerland was inducted into the **International Boxing Hall of Fame** in 2010.

GIARDELLO, JOEY (né CARMINE ORLANDO TILELLI). B. 16 July 1930, Brooklyn, New York. D. 4 September 2008, Cherry Hill, New Jersey. Carmine Tilelli officially became Joe Giardello in 1945 when he borrowed a birth certificate from a cousin so that he could enlist in the U.S. Army although underage at 15 years old. After serving briefly as a paratrooper, he was found out by his parents and discharged from the service. He moved to Philadelphia and began his **professional boxing** career in Trenton, New Jersey, in 1948. Although he stopped 16 opponents in his first 31 professional **bouts**, the quality of his opposition during this time was mediocre. (After his fast start, in his next 104 bouts over the remainder of his career Giardello only scored 17 **knockouts**.)

He became one of the top **middleweight** contenders during the 1950s and was often featured in the **televised** "Fight of the Week." One reason that made him attractive to television sponsors was that he rarely knocked out his opponents, and television would be assured of a competitive bout that would last the 10-**round** distance.

Giardello was in line for an opportunity to box for the middleweight title in 1954, but a series of unfortunate occurrences prevented that. On 8 August 1954, he was involved in an auto accident in New Jersey. He suffered only minor cuts and contusions but injured his left knee as well. The knee injury was not severe enough to prevent him from fighting **Ralph "Tiger" Jones** on 24 September 1954 and winning a unanimous 10-round **decision**, but afterward the knee required surgery for cartilage removal, which took place on 6 October. He was scheduled to fight **Carl "Bobo" Olson** for the middleweight championship on 15 December 1954 in San Francisco even though Giardello was still on crutches recovering from the surgery. In a bizarre twist of fate, Giardello was arrested along with three companions on 27 November. He was charged with assault on a gas station attendant in Philadelphia on 29 October. Giardello, still on crutches, was accusing of hitting the attendant with his crutch. Although the Olson title fight never took place, Giardello returned to the **ring** in January 1955 and fought and won three bouts from January through March. On 16 March 1955, he was convicted and on 9 June was sentenced to six to 18 months in prison on charges of riot and conspiracy to riot. On 22 July 1955, he began his prison sentence and on 11 November was paroled.

He returned to the ring in February 1956 and again worked his way back to being one of the top contenders in the middleweight class. He was among the top 10 middleweights during most of the 1950s yet did not get an opportunity to fight for a title until 20 April 1960, when he challenged world middleweight champion **Gene Fullmer** in Bozeman, Montana, for the **National Boxing Association** title. After a close 15-round fight in which both fighters committed numerous infractions, the decision was a **draw** (a rarity in title fights) and Fullmer retained his title.

Giardello finally became a champion at the age of 33 when he outboxed **Dick Tiger** on 7 December 1963 for the undisputed world middleweight title in **Atlantic City**, New Jersey, and was awarded the decision by **referee** Paul Cavalier, the sole arbiter of the bout. Giardello successfully defended that title against **Rubin "Hurricane" Carter** in 1964 before losing a unanimous 15-round decision in a rematch with Tiger on 21 October 1965 at **Madison Square Garden** in New York.

During his 20-year boxing career, Giardello figured in a couple of memorable bouts in addition to his title bouts. On 19 March 1954, he faced Willie Troy at Madison Square Garden on the **televised Friday Night Fights** in the first boxing match to be televised in color. Troy had an outstanding record of 26–1, and Giardello knocked him down three times in the first two rounds before winning the bout on a **technical knockout** at 0:39 in the seventh round when referee Al Berl stopped the bout.

Giardello's bout with **Billy Graham** on 19 December 1952 at Madison Square Garden is memorable for a different reason. The 10-round bout was won by Giardello on a **split decision**, with the referee and one **judge** (Joe Agnello) voting for Giardello and the other judge for Graham. New York State Boxing **Commissioner** Bob Christenberry, sitting at **ringside**, had the scorecards reviewed and changed two rounds on Agnello's scorecard and awarded the bout to Graham. (Christenberry had heard rumors that the fight was "fixed" and in an earnest effort to do right took this action.) Giardello sued, and the case was decided in a New York state court with the judge, Bernard Botein, ruling for Giardello, stating that the Boxing Commission, while acting in what it thought was the "best interests of boxing," nonetheless overstepped its bounds in changing judge Agnello's scorecard.

In 1957, Giardello was involved in another bout in which the official decision as announced in the ring was reversed. On 27 March 1957 in Kansas City, Missouri, Giardello lost a split decision to Willie Vaughn in a 10-round bout. After the bout, it was disclosed by the Missouri Athletic Commission that the referee inadvertently used a different scoring system than that used by the two judges, and the bout was ruled a **"no contest,"** even though a recalculation of the referee's scorecard under the correct scoring system would not have changed his vote and Vaughn still would have been the victor.

After retiring from boxing, Giardello resumed using his birth name, Carmine Tilelli, and worked as an insurance salesman and then as an inspector for the New Jersey Department of Weights and Measures. His son, Carman Tilelli, was born with Down Syndrome in 1955, and Giardello spent much of his postboxing career working with the Special Olympics and raising money for the St. John of God School in Westville Grove, New Jersey, which his son had attended.

In 1999, a film was made about Rubin "Hurricane" Carter's life in which one scene featured his bout with Giardello. In the film, it was depicted that the bout was much closer than it actually was, with a punch-drunk, bloodied Giardello winning the decision due to racial prejudice against Carter. Giardello sued the Hollywood filmmakers and won an out-of-court settlement.

Giardello was five foot 10 inches tall and fought at weights ranging from 151 to 173 pounds, primarily as a middleweight. In 135 professional bouts, from 1948 to 1967, he won 100 (33 by knockout), lost 26 (four by knockout), had eight draws and one no contest, and fought a total of 1,062 rounds. He was inducted into the **International Boxing Hall of Fame** in 1993.

GLOVES. Since the late 19th century, contestants in all boxing **bouts** are required to wear large gloves weighing from six to eight ounces, depending on the boxers' weight class. Heavier gloves of 12 to 16 ounces are sometimes used in **amateur** bouts or in **sparring** sessions. The main purpose of the gloves is to protect the boxers' hands. In the 1980s, thumbless gloves were introduced in an effort to protect against eye injuries from a boxer's thumb making contact with his opponent's eye—often a deliberate, although illegal, act.

GOLD MEDAL. In international amateur boxing competition, such as the **Olympic Games** and **World Championships**, the tournament winner is awarded a gold medal.

GOLDEN GLOVES. The Golden Gloves is an **amateur boxing** tournament that was created by Arch Ward, the sports editor of the *Chicago Tribune*, in 1926. The *New York Daily News*, under the auspices of sports editor **Paul Gallico**, instituted a similar tournament in 1927. The *Daily News* tournament in 1927 lasted just two and a half weeks, from 11 to 28 March, but for its time was considered to be a mammoth tournament with nearly 500 boxers in

16 weight classes. The finals held at **Madison Square Garden** drew a capacity crowd of over 20,000 fans, and the tournament was proclaimed a huge success.

In 1928, an intercity series of **bouts** was held between the New York and Chicago Golden Gloves champions. That too was a huge success. Other midwestern newspapers began sponsoring Golden Gloves tournaments, and following the Chicago Golden Gloves tournament, a Chicago Regional tournament was held, with boxers from Detroit and Cleveland invited.

By 1936, the New York Golden Gloves tournament had grown to the point where over 1,400 boxers entered and participated, and the tournament lasted from 27 January until 23 March. Following that year's huge tournament, it was decided to lower the number of entrants by encouraging other newspapers in the New York metropolitan area to hold their own tournaments, with the winners competing in a special Tournament of Champions.

That first regional Tournament of Champions began with 57 bouts in 16 weight divisions and was held in three **rings** simultaneously on the afternoon of 22 February 1937. That evening, 56 more bouts were conducted in a similar fashion. Ticket prices for the events ranged from 40 to 75 cents for the afternoon show and 55 cents to $2.20 for the evening's bouts. Ads for the extravaganza read, "A penny a bout—100 punches a minute," and they were not misleading. Winners of that tournament were named to the New York team that fought the Chicago team a few weeks later in the Intercity Golden Gloves competition.

Through the years, the three tournaments continued to do well. The New York Tournament of Champions was renamed the Eastern Regionals, while the one in Chicago became the Western Regionals. During the war years, the number of entrants understandably decreased, but the tournaments continued. In 1961, the regional tournament was discontinued, as was the intercity competition, but the intercity bouts resumed in 1977.

Changes to the tournament occurred in the next decade, and in the 1990s a newspaper strike canceled the 1991 tournament. In 1995, a **women's** division was added.

In 1962, the Chicago Golden Gloves tournament became the National Golden Gloves and was taken over by the Golden Gloves of America Inc.

Among the many professional boxers who got their start in the sport boxing as amateurs in Golden Gloves tournaments are **Muhammad Ali**, **Riddick Bowe**, **Héctor Camacho**, Paddy DeMarco, **Emile Griffith**, **Sonny Liston**, **Rocky Marciano**, **Floyd Patterson**, **Ray Robinson**, **Barney Ross**, Johnny Saxton, **José Torres**, **Chuck Wepner**, and **Tony Zale**.

See also ATLAS, THEODORE A. "TEDDY"; AUSTRALIA; BENÍTEZ, WILFRED "EL RADAR"; BRENNER, THEODORE "TEDDY"; CARBAJAL, MICHAEL "MANITAS DE PIEDRA"; CLANCY, GILBERT THOMAS "GIL"; CLARK, LAMAR F; COONEY, GERRY "GENTLEMAN GER-

RY"; CORTEZ, JOE; D'AMATO, CONSTANTINE "CUS"; DE LA HOYA, ÓSCAR "GOLDEN BOY"; FATALITIES; FELT FORUM; FRAZIER, JOSEPH WILLIAM "JOE," "SMOKIN' JOE"; GOLDSTEIN, REUVEN "RUBY," "THE JEWEL OF THE GHETTO"; GRAHAM, WILLIAM WALTER, JR., "BILLY"; HANDICAPPED BOXERS; HEARNS, THOMAS "TOMMY," "HIT MAN," "MOTOR CITY COBRA"; HOLYFIELD, EVANDER "THE REAL DEAL"; JONES, ROY LEVESTA, JR; LAMOTTA, GIACOBBE "JAKE," "THE BRONX BULL"; LEONARD, RAY CHARLES "SUGAR RAY"; LOUIS, JOE "THE BROWN BOMBER" (né JOSEPH LOUIS BARROW); MAXIM, JOEY (né GIUSEPPE ANTONIO BERARDINELLI); MAYWEATHER, FLOYD JOY, JR., "PRETTY BOY," "MONEY" (né FLOYD JOY SINCLAIR); O'GRADY, SEAN "THE BUBBLE-GUM KID"; OPEN; ORTIZ, MANUEL; QUARRY, JERRY "IRISH," "THE BELLFLOWER BOMBER"; QUICKEST KNOCKOUTS; RADEMACHER, THOMAS PETER "PETE"; SHAVERS, EARNIE "THE ACORN," "THE BLACK DESTROYER" (né EARNIE DEE SHAVER); SHOMO, VINCENT O'NEAL "VINCE"; SPINKS, MICHAEL "JINX"; STEWARD, EMANUEL "MANNY"; SUBNOVICE; SUNNYSIDE GARDEN; TIGER, DICK (né RICHARD IHETU); TYSON, MICHAEL GERARD "MIKE," "IRON MIKE" (aka MALIK ABDUL-AZIZ); WALCOTT, JERSEY JOE (né ARNOLD RAYMOND CREAM); WALLACE, COLEY; WILLIAMS, IKE; WOMEN IN BOXING.

GOLDSTEIN, REUVEN "RUBY," "THE JEWEL OF THE GHETTO". B. 10 October 1907, New York, New York. D. 23 April 1984, Miami Beach, Florida. Ruby Goldstein, while a most competent boxer, became more well known to boxing fans as the third man in the **ring** for many of boxing's most important **bouts** during his 20-year career as a **referee**.

He was raised on the Lower East Side of New York City, home for many immigrants in the early 20th century. He began boxing at the Henry Street Settlement House and also at the Educational Alliance and claimed an amateur record of 19–0. Had he been a few years younger, he undoubtedly would have been among the first New York **Golden Gloves** participants when that tournament began in March 1927.

His first professional bout took place on 30 December 1924 in New York, and Goldstein, boxing as a **featherweight**, won by a **knockout** in two **rounds**. He won his first 23 bouts, gradually moving from featherweight to the **lightweight** class before he was knocked out by Ace Hudkins in the fourth round on 25 June 1926 in Brooklyn. In his next bout, he sprained his ankle and had to retire after five rounds. Goldstein then won six straight bouts, including a six-round decision over former lightweight champion Jimmy Goodrich. In his next bout, Goldstein **knocked down** his opponent, Sid

Terris, in the first round, but after Terris got up and Goldstein went to attack him, Terris landed a solid right hand to the jaw of Goldstein and knocked him out in the first round.

Fighting as a **junior welterweight** and then **welterweight**, Goldstein won his next 10 bouts, eight by knockout, but was then knocked out by future welterweight champion **Jimmy McLarnin** in two rounds at **Madison Square Garden**. Goldstein continued to be one of the top boxers but never received a chance to box for a world title. He retired in 1933, made a brief comeback in 1937, won all four bouts, and then retired permanently.

He enlisted in the U.S. Army in 1942 and began refereeing bouts while in the service, including many of **Joe Louis's exhibition** bouts. He became licensed as a referee by New York State and from 1944 to 1964 was one of the most active referees.

In 1946, he refereed his first world title bout—Allie Stolz versus Bob Montgomery for the lightweight championship. He was the referee for the first **Tony Zale–Rocky Graziano** bout in 1946. He refereed the Joe Louis–**Jersey Joe Walcott** bout in 1947 and was the only one of the three officials who saw that bout in favor of Walcott—a bout that even Joe Louis thought Walcott had won.

One of the most memorable bouts that he worked as a **referee** was on 25 June 1952 when **middleweight** champion **"Sugar Ray" Robinson** challenged **Joey Maxim** for the latter's **light heavyweight** title. The bout took place on an extremely hot, humid night, and Goldstein was overcome by the 104 degree heat and had to retire as referee after the 10th round. Robinson, though ahead on points, had to retire after the 13th round due to the heat.

Goldstein refereed bouts involving nearly all the major champions in the 1950s and was in the **ring** with **Archie Moore**, **Rocky Marciano**, Joe Louis, **Ezzard Charles**, **Floyd Patterson**, **Willie Pep**, **Sandy Saddler**, **Carmen Basilio**, **Gene Fullmer**, and Robinson, among others. He even worked one of **Cassius Clay's** early bouts in 1962.

Goldstein was also the referee in the **Emile Griffith–Benny "Kid" Paret** world welterweight championship bout on 24 March 1962 at Madison Square Garden. In that bout, Griffith had Paret leaning on the ropes in the 12th round and kept pounding him. Goldstein, inexplicably, did not stop the fight until Griffith had landed more than a dozen unanswered punches. Paret went into a coma and died 10 days later, and Goldstein was distraught. He was exonerated by the **New York State Athletic Commission** but could not bring it upon himself to referee again. Somehow, he decided to referee one more bout two years later, a 10-round bout on 20 March 1964 between Luis Manuel Rodríguez and Holley Mims. In 1968, he worked as a **judge** for two bouts but never judged again.

Goldstein also worked as a liquor salesman for Schenley Distillers. He retired to Miami Beach and died of cancer on 23 April 1984.

Goldstein was five foot four inches tall and fought at weights ranging from 125 to 148 pounds at weight classes from **featherweight** to **light welterweight**. In 60 professional bouts, from 1924 to 1937, he won 54 (38 by knockout), lost six (all six by knockout), and fought a total of 219 rounds. He was inducted into the **International Boxing Hall of Fame** in 1994 as a nonparticipant in recognition of his refereeing.

GÓMEZ, WILFREDO "BAZOOKA". B. 29 October 1956, San Juan, **Puerto Rico.** Wilfredo Gómez had one of the most powerful punches in boxing history, although he was only five foot five inches tall and weighed just 122 pounds for most of his fights. As a 15-year old **amateur** boxer, he lost in the first round of the 1972 **Olympic Games flyweight** competition, although he was technically underage and should not have been allowed to enter. In the 1974 **World Amateur Boxing Championships**, he won the **bantamweight gold medal**. He claimed an amateur record of 96–3.

His first professional **bout** was on 16 November 1974. He boxed a six-**round draw** with Jacinto Fuentes in **Panama** City. He did not go the scheduled distance again for the next 10 years and 41 bouts. By 21 May 1977, Gómez had won 15 straight bouts, all by **knockout**. On that date, he fought the **Korean** Dong-Kyun Yum in Hato Rey, Puerto Rico, for the newly created **World Boxing Council (WBC)** world's **super bantamweight** championship. Although Gómez was **knocked down** in the first round, he got up to knock out Yum in the 12th round of their scheduled 15-round bout.

Over the next one and a half years, Gómez defended the title five times and won all five bouts by knockout, fighting in **Thailand** and **Japan** as well as in Puerto Rico. On 28 October 1978, the undefeated Gómez (21–0–1) made a title defense against the legendary world bantamweight champion **Mexican Carlos Zárate**, also undefeated with 52 victories in 52 bouts and 51 knockouts. Gómez proved to be the better of the two fighters and knocked Zárate down three times before the bout was stopped in the fifth round.

Gómez won his next 10 bouts by knockout, seven title defenses and three **nontitle bouts**. He then got ambitious and challenged **featherweight** champion **Salvador Sánchez** on 21 August 1981 in **Las Vegas**. Although the bout was fought at 126 pounds—only four pounds more than Gómez's usual 122-pound super bantamweight limit, Sánchez easily took the measure of Gómez and knocked him down in both the first and eighth rounds before the bout was stopped at 2:09 of the eighth round.

Gómez then won his next eight bouts by knockout—four title defenses and four nontitle bouts. After the August 1982 death of Sánchez in an auto accident, Puerto Rican Juan LaPorte won the **vacant** featherweight title. Gómez decided to challenge him and on 31 March 1984 in Hato Rey, Gómez won a 12-round **unanimous decision** and the WBC world featherweight title. This was the first time in 10 years as a professional boxer that Gómez won a bout by decision and only the second time he had had to go the distance.

He did not keep that title for long, as in his first defense of the featherweight title he was knocked out by **Azumah Nelson** in the 11th round of their bout on 9 December 1984 in San Juan, Puerto Rico. Gómez again moved up in weight for his next bout and challenged **World Boxing Association super featherweight** champion Rocky Lockridge on 19 May 1985. Gómez won a close **majority decision** in 15 rounds and his third championship. Gómez then was inactive for a year and in his first fight lost his super featherweight title to Alfredo Layne on a ninth-round **technical knockout**.

Gómez retired after the bout but made a brief two-bout comeback, winning one bout in each of 1988 and 1989 by knockout.

In retirement, after combating drug problems, he worked as a **trainer** for Héctor Camacho Jr.

Gómez fought at weights ranging from 118 to 138 pounds, primarily as a super bantamweight and featherweight. In 48 professional bouts, from 1974 to 1989, he won 44 (42 by knockout), lost three (all three by knockout), had one draw, and fought a total of 265 rounds.

GONZÁLEZ, GERARDO. *See* GAVILÁN, KID "THE CUBAN HAWK" (né GERARDO GONZÁLEZ).

GRAHAM, WILLIAM WALTER, JR., "BILLY". B. 9 September 1922, New York, New York. D. 22 January 1992, West Islip, New York. Billy Graham, the evangelist, was four years older than Billy Graham, the boxer. But during most of the 1940s and 1950s, in the public's eye the name Billy Graham meant the boxer.

Although he boxed some as an **amateur** in New York, he was denied entrance to the prestigious New York **Golden Gloves** tournament because of a heart murmur. His **professional** career suffered as underworld figures controlled much of boxing during Graham's career, and his refusal to do business with them might have cost him a few decisions.

He began boxing professionally as a **featherweight** on 14 April 1941 with a fourth-**round technical knockout** victory at **St. Nicholas Arena** in New York. Over the next four years, he was undefeated in 58 **bouts** with six **draws**. He lost his first bout on 11 September 1945 to Tony Pellone on a 10-round **split decision**. Graham won his next seven bouts before losing again to Pellone. After three more victories, Graham was next defeated by junior **welterweight** champion Tippy Larkin in a **nontitle bout**. Graham won 14 straight bouts and traveled to London, **England**, where he lost a 10-round decision to the Welshman Eddie Thomas. After losing to future world **light-**

weight champion Paddy DeMarco, Graham won 13 straight bouts, including a victory over future welterweight champion **Kid Gavilán** and another over his former nemesis Pellone.

Gavilán won a **majority decision** in a rematch in 1950 and then on 29 August 1951 fought Graham in a bout for the world's welterweight title. Gavilán kept his title by a narrow margin, winning a split-decision 15-round bout. Graham's next eight bouts saw six victories for him and two draws.

From August 1952 to July 1953, Graham fought eight bouts against some of the best welterweights of the era. He began on 4 August 1952 by losing a split decision to future **middleweight** champion **Joey Giardello**. Graham then won a **unanimous decision** over future welterweight and middleweight champion **Carmen Basilio**. On 5 October 1952, in Havana, **Cuba**, Graham lost a rematch with Gavilán for the world's welterweight title.

Graham's next bout was with Giardello, on 19 December 1952 at **Madison Square Garden**. The 10-round bout was won by Giardello on a split decision, with the **referee** and one **judge** (Joe Agnello) voting for Giardello and the other judge for Graham. New York State Boxing **Commissioner** Bob Christenberry, sitting at **ringside**, had the scorecards reviewed and changed two rounds on Agnello's scorecard and awarded the bout to Graham. (Christenberry had heard rumors that the fight was "fixed" and in an earnest effort to do right took this action.) Giardello sued, and the case was decided in a New York state court with Judge Bernard Botein ruling for Giardello, stating that the boxing commission, while acting in what it thought was the "best interests of boxing," nonetheless overstepped its bounds in changing judge Agnello's scorecard.

After the loss to Giardello, Graham rebounded by defeating top contender Art Aragon, followed that with a 12-round decision over Giardello, and then fought two 12-round bouts with Basilio that were billed for the "New York State welterweight title," losing the first and drawing the second.

Graham fought six more fights in his professional career, winning the first two and losing the last four. He retired after his 1 April 1955 loss to Chico Vejar.

In retirement, Graham became a boxing judge and referee. Graham was five foot seven inches tall and had a 68-inch **reach**. He fought at weights ranging from 128 to 156 pounds at weight classes from junior lightweight to welterweight. In 126 professional bouts, from 1941 to 1955, he won 102 (27 by **knockout**), lost 15 (none by knockout), had nine draws, and fought a total of 908 rounds. He was inducted into the **International Boxing Hall of Fame** in 1992.

GRAZIANO, ROCKY "THE ROCK" (né THOMAS ROCCO BAR-BELLA).

B. 1 January 1919, New York, New York. D. 22 May 1990, New York, New York. Rocky Graziano fought three memorable **bouts** with **Tony Zale**, two of which were named "Fight of the Year" by *Ring* magazine, yet he became better known in his post-**ring** career as a television personality.

Rocky Graziano was raised on the Lower East Side of New York and as a youth was constantly in trouble and spent time in various reformatories. As a teenager, he entered a local **amateur boxing** tournament and won the Metropolitan **Amateur Athletic Union** championship. In 1941, after being released from one stretch in prison and placed on parole, his parole officer was the famed baseball player Lou Gehrig, who in his last months of life had been given the job of parole officer in 1939 by kindly New York City mayor Fiorello LaGuardia. Gehrig died on 2 June 1941 of amyotrophic lateral sclerosis (now known as Lou Gehrig's disease).

After being released from Rikers Island prison in New York in 1941, it was suggested by the authorities that Graziano enlist in the U.S. Army. His lack of respect for authority saw him punch an officer at Fort Dix, New Jersey, and then go AWOL. He was later captured by the military authorities and spent time at a military prison on Governors Island in New York Harbor.

When he finally was released, he began boxing **professionally** in New York. He disliked **training** and seldom devoted much time to it. He had a brawling style of fighting and a powerful **knockout** punch. His first recorded professional bout was 31 March 1942.

After compiling a record of 38–6–5, with most of his fights in the New York City area, Graziano was matched with **welterweight** champion Freddie "Red" Cochrane in a **nontitle bout** at **Madison Square Garden** on 29 June 1945 that earned *Ring* magazine's award as the "Fight of the Year." Graziano lost most of the early rounds but caught Cochrane in the ninth round and knocked him down. In the 10th, Graziano finished Cochrane with a knockout punch. In a rematch six weeks later, Graziano again knocked out Cochrane in the 10th round.

After Marty Servo won the **welterweight** title from Cochrane on 1 February 1946, Graziano knocked out Servo in two rounds in a nontitle bout on 29 March 1946. This earned Rocky a shot at the world's middleweight title, then held by Tony Zale. In another *Ring* magazine "Fight of the Year," Zale retained his title by stopping Rocky in the sixth round on 27 September 1946 at Yankee Stadium. Graziano was down in the first round, and Zale was down in the second round.

On 7 February 1947, the **New York State Athletic Commission** suspended Graziano and revoked his license for failure to report a bribe attempt, even though Graziano did not take any bribes. Fortunately for boxing history's sake, the **National Boxing Association (NBA)** did not go along with the suspension, and a Zale–Graziano rematch was held in Chicago on 16 July

1947. This bout proved to be every bit as entertaining as their first meeting. Graziano was down in the third round and recovered to stop Zale in the sixth round and win the NBA version of the world's middleweight championship.

Zale and Graziano met in a **rubber match** on 10 June 1948 in Newark, New Jersey. This time Zale had the upper edge and knocked out Graziano in the third round. Graziano continued boxing in 1949 and over the next four years won 20 of 21 bouts, 17 by knockout, a **draw** with contender Tony Janiro being the only nonwinning bout.

On 16 April 1952, Graziano challenged **"Sugar Ray" Robinson** for the world's middleweight title. Robinson retained his championship with a third-round knockout of Graziano. Rocky's last fight was on 17 September 1952 against the undefeated Chuck Davey. Rocky went 10 rounds with Davey but lost a **unanimous decision** and retired shortly thereafter.

In retirement, Rocky Graziano became a popular television personality, generally playing himself and appeared quite often on *The Martha Raye Show*, playing her boyfriend whom she affectionately called "her Goombah." A 1956 film starring Paul Newman based on Rocky's autobiography titled *Somebody Up There Likes Me* was a quite popular film and helped keep Rocky in the spotlight after his retirement. He also opened a pizzaria on New York's East Side. He was one of the most popular ex-champions and in his later years became an accomplished painter and had his work shown in several New York art galleries.

Graziano was five foot seven inches tall and had a 68-inch **reach**. He fought at weights ranging from 144 to 165 pounds, primarily as a welter-weight and middleweight. In 83 professional bouts, from 1942 to 1952, he won 67 (52 by knockout), lost 10 (three by knockout), had six draws, and fought a total of 412 rounds. He was inducted as a member of the inaugural class of the **International Boxing Hall of Fame** in 1990.

GREAT BRITAIN. In international **amateur** competition, fighters from **England**, **Scotland**, **Wales**, and **Northern Ireland** compete as Great Britain, even though the name *Great Britain* properly consists only of the island that contains England, Scotland, and Wales and does not include Northern Ireland.

The team's first **Olympic** competition occurred in the 1908 games, which were held in London. An oddity of that competition was that all **bouts** were contested on just one day, 27 October 1908. Of the 42 boxers entered in the tournament, one was **Australian**, two were Danish, seven were French, and the remaining 32 were British. Understandably, Great Britain won 14 of the 15 medals awarded that year.

Teams from Great Britain have entered each one of the 22 Olympic boxing tournaments since 1908—a feat matched only by **France**. Great Britain has won 53 medals—17 **gold**, 12 **silver**, and 24 **bronze**. This total is the third best among all nations. Harry Mallin is the only British boxer to win two gold medals. He won the **middleweight** championship in both 1920 and 1924, although his second medal at the Olympics in Paris was quite controversial as he apparently outboxed his French opponent, Roger Brousse, but the hometown decision was given to Brousse. After the bout, Mallin showed officials teeth marks on his arms and chest and a protest was lodged. The protest was successful, Brousse was disqualified for biting, and Mallin was allowed to remain in the tournament. He then won semifinal and final bouts and became the first Olympic champion to successfully defend his title.

Great Britain's only other boxer with multiple medals was Richard McTaggart, a Scotsman from Dundee. He won the **lightweight** gold medal in 1956 and the lightweight bronze medal in 1960. He also boxed in the 1964 **Olympic Games** as a **light welterweight** but lost in his third-round bout to the eventual winner, Jerzy Kulej.

The other Olympic gold medalists from Great Britain are Terry Spinks, 1956 **flyweight**; Harry Thomas, 1908 **bantamweight**; Luke Campbell, 2012 bantamweight; Richard Gunn, 1908 **featherweight**; Frederick Grace, 1908 lightweight; John Douglas, 1908 middleweight; Chris Finnegan, 1968 middleweight; James DeGale, 2008 middleweight; Harry Mitchell, 1924 **light heavyweight**; Albert Oldman, 1908 **heavyweight**; Ron Rawson, 1920 heavyweight; Audley Harrison, 2000 super heavyweight; Anthony Joshua, 2012 super heavyweight; and Nicola Adams, 2012 **women's** flyweight.

GREB, EDWARD HENRY "HARRY," "THE PITTSBURGH WIND-MILL". B. 6 June 1894, Pittsburgh, Pennsylvania. D. 22 October 1926, **Atlantic City**, New Jersey. Harry Greb had nearly 300 recorded **bouts**, yet in more than half of them there was no official winner. He fought during the era of "**no decision**" bouts, in which state law prohibited an official **decision** if the fight lasted the scheduled distance. Newspaper reporters in their coverage of the bout would usually select the fighter who they thought outpointed their opponent, and bets would be settled in this manner.

According to an article in the 31 May 1913 issue of the *Pittsburgh Press* cited on the Harry Greb website, www.harrygreb.com, Greb began boxing as an **amateur** in the beginning of 1913. Five of his amateur bouts (all victories) have been documented by researchers, but as his first recorded professional bout was 29 May 1913, it is unlikely that he had very many amateur bouts.

His professional career, on the other hand, was quite extensive, with 299 recorded bouts and possibly another 100 or so that have not been documented. He fought nearly all the top **middleweights** of his era and also quite a few **light heavyweights** and **heavyweights**. He often was outweighed by 20 or more pounds.

Greb was accused by some of being a dirty fighter, while others admired his nonstop aggressive style and called him "The Pittsburgh Windmill." Among the fighters who were **world champions** at one point of their careers that Greb defeated were **Gene Tunney, Mickey Walker, Maxie Rosenbloom**, Johnny Wilson, Tommy Loughran, Jimmy Slattery, Tiger Flowers, Mike McTigue, Battling Levinsky, Al McCoy, and Jack Dillon.

On 23 May 1922, Greb handed Gene Tunney, future heavyweight champion, his only defeat on a 15-round **unanimous decision** for the "American light heavyweight championship." On 30 January, Greb defeated future light heavyweight champion Tommy Loughran in defense of his American light heavyweight title. The following month, Greb was defeated by Tunney in a rematch on a **split decision**.

On 31 August 1923, Greb won the world's middleweight championship by 15-round decision over Johnny Wilson. He retained that title with four successful defenses. In defense of that title, he defeated Brian Downey (3 December 1923, 10-round unanimous decision); Johnny Wilson (18 January 1924, 15-round unanimous decision); Ted Moore (26 June 1924, 15-round unanimous decision); and Mickey Walker (2 July 1925, 15-round unanimous decision).

On 26 February 1926, Greb was defeated by Theodore "Tiger" Flowers on a 15-round decision at **Madison Square Garden** and lost his middleweight title. Greb's final bout was an unsuccessful rematch with Flowers on 19 August 1926.

Greb died on the operating table after minor surgery on his nose on 22 October 1926. While undergoing that surgery, it was found that Greb had been blind in one eye for the latter part of his career. In a bit of irony, Greb's last opponent, Flowers, died on the operating table after minor surgery to remove scar tissue on 16 November 1927.

Greb was five foot eight inches tall and had a 71-inch **reach**. He fought at weights ranging from 150 to 178 pounds, primarily as a middleweight and light heavyweight. In 299 professional bouts, from 1913 to 1926, he won 104 (48 by **knockout**), lost eight (two by knockout), had three draws, and fought 183 no-decision bouts in which he was awarded the newspaper decision in 157, lost 12, and drew 14. He fought a total of 2,590 rounds. He was inducted as a member of the inaugural class of the **International Boxing Hall of Fame** in 1990.

GRIFFITH, EMILE ALPHONSE. B. 3 February 1938, St. Thomas, **United States** Virgin Islands. D. 23 July 2013, Hempstead, N. Y. Emile Griffith was one of the few champions who killed a man in the ring. Although he continued boxing, since in his words, "I would have quit, but I didn't know how to do anything else but fight," he was never quite the same. In his fights prior to that momentous night, he won about 40 percent of them short of the distance, while afterward it was closer to 20 percent.

He was born in the U.S. Virgin Islands and came to New York City as a teenager. He worked in a hat factory in New York's garment district, and one day the factory's owner, Howard Albert, noticed Griffith's muscular physique. Albert brought Griffith to a nearby gymnasium run by **Gil Clancy**, and Clancy worked with Emile and entered him in the New York **Golden Gloves**. Griffith did well in that tournament, reaching the **welterweight subnovice** finals in 1957 and winning the 1958 welterweight championship, the 1958 Eastern Regionals championship, and the 1958 intercity championship. Ironically, in his 14 Golden Gloves **bouts**, only his first one did not go the distance.

He became a **professional** boxer shortly afterward, with his first bout on 2 June 1958 at **St. Nicholas Arena** in New York, which he won by **decision** in four **rounds**. After winning his first 13 bouts, Griffith lost a **split decision** to Randy Sandy, a competent fighter who had also been a triple champion in the New York Golden Gloves. Griffith then won decisions over **Gaspar Ortega**, Denny Moyer, Jorge Fernández, Florentino Fernández, Willie Toweel, and Luis Manuel Rodríguez, some of the best welterweights of the era.

On 1 April 1961 in Miami Beach, Florida, Griffith knocked out **Benny "Kid" Paret** in the 13th round and won the world's welterweight championship. In his first defense, just two months later, Griffith stopped Gaspar Ortega in the 12th round, the first time in Ortega's 81-bout career to that point in which he failed to go the distance. After a nontitle victory over the mellifluously named Yama Bahama, Griffith fought a rematch with Paret. On 30 September 1961 at **Madison Square Garden**, Griffith lost his title to Paret on a close split decision, although many observers thought that Griffith had earned the victory.

Griffith then won three more bouts before the fateful **rubber match** with Paret on 24 March 1962 at Madison Square Garden. In the prefight **weigh-in**, Paret and Griffith had words, and the **Cuban** Paret taunted Griffith by calling him "maricón," a derogatory Spanish word for homosexual.

The slur especially affected Griffith since there was a ring of truth to it, although at the time there was no public awareness of the fact. Griffith was ready to fight Paret right then but was held back. During the hard-fought bout, Griffith was knocked down in the sixth round, but he got up and was leading the bout. In the 13th round, Griffith caught Paret against the ropes and unleashed a savage attack of at least 29 unanswered blows before **referee Ruby Goldstein**, one of the sport's better referees, was able to separate the two and stop the fight. Paret went into a coma and died 10 days later.

The bout was the first nationally **televised** fight in which a fighter died, and it led to public outcries to ban the savage sport. But no major changes occurred, and the sport continues to this day.

Griffith was deeply affected by the incident but felt he had no choice but to continue his boxing career. In later years, he was quoted as saying, "After that fight, I did enough to win. I would use my **jab** all the time. I never wanted to hurt the other guy." Less than four months later, Griffith was back in the **ring** and won a 15-round decision over Ralph Dupas in a welterweight title defense.

On 17 October 1962, Griffith defeated Ted Wright in Vienna, Austria, on a 15-round decision in a bout billed for the "world **light middleweight** title," although it was not recognized by other sanctioning bodies outside of Austria. (The Austrian organization was slightly ahead of its time, as three days later the **World Boxing Association** recognized the winner of the Denny Moyer–Joey Giambra bout in the **United States** as the first world's light middleweight champion.)

After defeating Jorge Fernández in defense of his welterweight title, Griffith defeated the Dane Chris Christensen in Copenhagen, Denmark, in defense of his light middleweight title claim.

On 21 March 1963 in Los Angeles, Griffith lost his welterweight title to Luis Manuel Rodríguez on a close 15-round **unanimous decision**. Griffith quickly regained it on a **split decision** less than three months later in **Madison Square Garden**. After several **nontitle bouts**, Griffith successfully defended his title against Rodríguez in **Las Vegas**, winning on a close split decision on 12 June 1964. After three more successful defenses, against Brian Curvis, José Stable, and Manuel González, Griffith vacated his title to move up in weight class.

On 25 April 1966, Griffith gained the world **middleweight** title by winning a close but unanimous decision over **Dick Tiger** at Madison Square Garden. He defended it successfully twice over Joey Archer and then lost it to **Nino Benvenuti** on 17 April 1967 on a unanimous decision in a bout in which each fighter was down once and was named the "Fight of the Year" by *Ring* **magazine**. Their rematch, held outdoors at Shea Stadium in Flushing, New York, was nearly as thrilling, and Griffith regained the title on a **majority decision**. This set up a **rubber match** on 4 March 1968, which was the first bout to be held at the new Madison Square Garden and was the cofeatured bout to the **Joe Frazier**–Buster Mathis **heavyweight** title fight. Benvenuti knocked Griffith down in the ninth round and won the close bout by a unanimous decision.

After winning six of seven bouts as a middleweight over the next year, Griffith lost nearly 10 pounds and fought **José Nápoles** for the world welterweight title on 17 October 1969 but lost the 15-round decision in a one-sided bout. Griffith then won his next 10 bouts and fought **Carlos Monzón** on 25

September 1971 in Monzón's home country of Argentina. Monzón won the bout by stopping Griffith in the 14th round. On 2 June 1973, the two boxers fought a rematch in Monte Carlo, Monaco, which was won by Monzón on a 15-round unanimous decision.

Over the next three years, Griffith kept active, although his boxing skills were diminishing, and in 13 bouts he won six, lost six, and had one draw. He had one more attempt at a world title when at the age of 38 he fought Eckhard Dagge in Dagge's native **Germany** on 18 September 1976 and nearly pulled off an upset but lost a 15-round majority decision for the light middleweight title. Griffith finally retired from the ring following a 10-round loss to future middleweight champion Alan Minter in Monaco on 30 July 1977.

In retirement, Griffith worked as a corrections officer in the Secaucus, New Jersey, juvenile detention facility. In 1992, he was savagely beaten after leaving a gay bar in New York and was hospitalized for four months afterward. He eventually became a victim of **pugilistic dementia** and as of 2012 resided at a full-care nursing facility in Hempstead, New York, until his death on July 23, 2013.

In 2005, an excellent documentary on Griffith was produced—*Ring of Fire: The Emile Griffith Story*.

Griffith was five foot seven inches tall and had a 72-inch **reach**. He fought at weights ranging from 144 to 165 pounds as a welterweight and middleweight. In 112 professional bouts, from 1958 to 1977, he won 85 (23 by **knockout**), lost 24 (two by knockout), had two draws and one **no-contest** bout, and fought a total of 1,122 rounds. He was inducted as a member of the inaugural class of the **International Boxing Hall of Fame** in 1990.

GUILLEDO, FRANCISCO VILLARUEL. *See* VILLA, PANCHO (né FRANCISCO VILLARUEL GUILLEDO).

GULOTTA, PETER. *See* HERMAN, PETE "KID" (né PETER GULOTTA).

H

HAGEN, JOSEPH FRANCIS ANTHONY. *See* O'BRIEN, PHILADEL-
PHIA JACK (né JOSEPH FRANCIS ANTHONY HAGEN).

**HAGLER, MARVELOUS MARVIN (né MARVIN NATHANIEL HA-
GLER).** B. 23 May 1954, Newark, New Jersey. Marvin Hagler was such an
outstanding boxer that he was nicknamed "Marvelous Marvin." He liked that
appelation so much that he legally changed his name to Marvelous Marvin
Hagler in 1982. Reportedly, this occurred because he was not introduced as
"Marvelous Marvin" prior to a **televised** fight on the American Broadcasting
Company television network, and he did this to ensure that he would be
addressed by that name for future fights.

Marvin Hagler was born in Newark, New Jersey, but after the riots in the
city in 1967, his family moved to Brockton, Massachusetts. As an **amateur**
boxer, he claimed a record of 52–2 with 43 **knockouts**. He won the 1973
National **Amateur Athletic Union middleweight** championship. Basically
ambidextrous, he boxed as a **southpaw**.

He began his **professional boxing** career on 18 May 1973 in Brockton
with a two-**round** knockout. He won his first 14 **bouts**, 12 by knockout, and
was matched with the undefeated (21–0) 1972 **Olympic** champion "Sugar
Ray" Seales. Hagler extended his winning streak with a 10-round **decision**
over Seales. In a rematch three months later, the two fought to a **draw**—the
first nonwinning effort in Hagler's professional career. On 13 January 1976,
Hagler suffered his first loss after 26 bouts, a 10-round **majority decision** to
Bobby "Boogaloo" Watts in Watts's hometown of Philadelphia. After a two-
round knockout victory, Hagler lost his second fight—also by decision in
Philadelphia to a Philadelphia fighter—Willie "The Worm" Monroe.

After the loss to Monroe, Hagler won 20 consecutive fights, including two
knockouts of Monroe. Hagler than was matched with the **Italian** American
Vito Antuofermo for the **World Boxing Council** and **World Boxing Association** middleweight titles on 30 November 1979 in **Las Vegas**. Although
Hagler was winning most of the early rounds, he got cautious in the last five

rounds. Most observers thought Hagler won, but the **judges** scored the bout a draw—a rarity in title fights—and Vito retained his championship. In his next bout, Antuofermo lost his title to Englishman Alan Minter.

Hagler then traveled to London, England, where on 27 September 1980 he stopped Minter in the third round on a badly cut eye and became middleweight champion. A minor riot ensued as Minter's fans became upset at the stoppage.

From 1981 to 1986, Hagler successfully defended his title 12 times against some of the era's best middleweights. He beat Fulgencio Obelmejias twice (17 January 1981, TKO round 8; 30 October 1982, TKO 5); Vito Antuofermo (13 June 1981, TKO 4); Mustafa Hamsho twice (3 October 1981, TKO 11; 19 October 1984, TKO 3); William "Caveman" Lee (7 March 1982, TKO 1); Tony Sibson (11 February 1983, TKO 6); Wilford Scypion (27 May 1983, KO 4); **Roberto Durán** (10 November 1983, **unanimous decision** 15); Juan Domingo Roldán (30 March 1984, TKO 10); **Thomas Hearns** (15 April 1985, TKO 3); and John Mugabi (10 March 1986, KO 11). The Hearns fight was one of the best of the decade. *Ring* **magazine** voted it "Fight of the Year" for 1985 and called round one "the greatest round in boxing history."

On 6 April 1987, Hagler lost his title to **"Sugar Ray" Leonard** in Las Vegas on a **split decision** in a close bout. Leonard, who came out of retirement for the bout, had had just one fight in the previous five years.

Hagler retired from the **ring** after Leonard refused to grant him a rematch. In retirement, he moved to Italy and has starred in several Italian films.

Hagler is five foot nine inches tall and has a 75-inch **reach**. He fought at weights ranging from 156 to 163 pounds as a middleweight. In 67 professional bouts, from 1973 to 1987, he won 62 (52 by knockout), lost three (none by knockout), had two draws, and fought a total of 399 rounds. He was inducted into the **International Boxing Hall of Fame** in 1993.

HAGLER, MARVIN NATHANIEL. *See* HAGLER, MARVELOUS MARVIN (né MARVIN NATHANIEL HAGLER).

HAMED, NASEEM "PRINCE," "NAZ". B. 12 February 1974, Sheffield, **England**. Prince Naseem Hamed was one of boxing's most colorful athletes, although he had a relatively short time in the limelight. He was a talented boxer and a fan favorite and was known for his spectacular entrances to the ring. An Englishman of Yemeni extraction, he became a professional boxer in 1992. At only five foot four inches and 114 pounds, he did not pose a threat physically, but the **southpaw** boxer had a powerful punch.

After winning his first 11 fights, 10 by **knockout**, he won nearly every **round** on all three officials' scorecards en route to a 12-round **decision** over Vincenzo Belcastro and won the European Boxing Union **bantamweight** championship on 11 May 1994 in Sheffield, England. Two fights later, on 12 October 1994 in Sheffield, he added the **World Boxing Council (WBC)** International **super bantamweight** title by stopping Freddy Cruz in six rounds.

After five successful defenses of the WBC title, all by knockout within four rounds or less, he moved up in weight and won the **World Boxing Organization (WBO) featherweight** title in the rain in Cardiff, **Wales**, on 30 September 1995 by stopping Steve Robinson in eight rounds. Hamed then successfully defended the WBO title four times. In his fifth defense, on 8 February 1997 in London, he added the **International Boxing Federation** featherweight title when he stopped Tom Johnson in eight rounds.

Hamed made three more successful title defenses in England, and on 19 December 1997 Hamed fought his first **bout** in the **United States**. There he knocked out Kevin Kelley in four rounds at **Madison Square Garden**. After winning six more title defenses, alternating venues between England and the United States, the 35–0 Hamed suffered his first loss. On 7 April 2001 in **Las Vegas**, Marco Antonio Barrera won a 12-round **unanimous decision** over Hamed. More than one year later, Hamed fought his last fight, winning a 12-round unanimous decision over Miguel Calvo in London.

He retired after that bout, citing hand injuries and the dislike of not seeing his family while spending weeks in **training** camps. He later rejoined the boxing world as a manager of Scottish contender Callum Johnson.

Hamed has a 64-inch **reach** and fought at weights ranging from 114 to 126 pounds as a bantamweight and featherweight. In 37 professional bouts, from 1992 to 2002, Hamed won 36, (31 by knockout), lost one (none by knockout), and fought a total of 185 rounds.

HANDICAPPED BOXERS. Although many boxers have fought through **bouts** after incurring an injury such as a broken hand or severe cuts, there have been several boxers who entered the **ring** each time with physical limitations.

The excellent website Boxrec lists 39 **professional** boxers who were deaf. Among them was the English **bareknuckle** fighter James "Deaf" Burke, who was one of the sport's leading boxers from 1828 to 1843. **Italian** Mario D'Agata was the world's **bantamweight** champion from 1956 to 1957. Eugene Hairston was one of the leading **middleweight** contenders in the 1940s and 1950s and was a 1947 New York **Golden Gloves** and Intercity Golden Gloves champion. As a professional, he fought a **draw** with **Jake LaMotta** and defeated Paul Pender and **Kid Gavilán**, all champions at one time in their careers. Hairston had a professional record of 45–13–5 from 1947 to 1952.

Italian Carlo Orlandi was another accomplished deaf fighter. He won the 1928 **Olympic Games lightweight gold medal** and as a professional boxer won the European lightweight championship as well as the Italian lightweight and **welterweight** titles. His professional record from 1929 to 1944 was 97–19–9.

Thai bantamweight boxer Thanomchit Sukhotai, another deaf boxer, fought during the 1970s. He held the Thai bantamweight title, twice fought draws for OPBF titles, fought former world champion Rolando Navarrete to a **draw** in Navarrete's native **Philippines**, and once challenged Alfonso Zamora for the **World Boxing Association** bantamweight championship but was stopped in the fourth **round**.

Spanish lightweight Kid Tano, who fought during the 1970s, won both the Spanish **featherweight** and Spanish lightweight titles and challenged twice unsuccessfully for the European lightweight championship.

Federico Mesa, a Mexican American **light welterweight** who boxed as Fred "Dummy" Mahan in the 1920s and had a record of 31–12–1 with 10 no-decision bouts, was a deaf boxer with an interesting if tragic story. He had apparently regaining some hearing after parachuting, and on 24 February 1930 he went parachuting again in the hope it would cure his deafness. On that day, though, his chute did not open, and he fell to his death.

Mike "Dummy" Rowan, 1900s **light heavyweight**, and his brother John "Silent" Rowan, 1900s featherweight, were brothers who were both deaf. Mike reportedly had two fights with another deaf boxer, "Deafy" Thompson, the only known case of two deaf fighters opposing each other.

Other deaf boxers were the 1920s Scottish featherweight "Deaf" Burke, 1950s Canadian middleweight Ossie Farrell and Jimmy Anest, 1940s welterweight; Eddie Butts, 1940s lightweight; Mike Caminiti, 1980s middleweight; Dick Collie, 1940s middleweight; David Davis, 1980s light heavyweight; "Dummy" Deputy, 1910s lightweight; Frankie Duran, 1960s bantamweight; Lloyd "Silent" Escobar, 1940s middleweight; Hilton "Fitzie" Fitzpatrick, 1940s **heavyweight**; Curtis Fulmer, 1940s middleweight; "Silent" Joe Hill, 1940s heavyweight; Mike Jacon, 1930s welterweight; Ben Lee, 1950s welterweight; Jimmy Lubash, 2000s middleweight; Thomas "Silent" Martin, 1920s middleweight; Willie McCloskey, 1920s middleweight; Joey McLaughlin, 1950s middleweight; Glen "Silent" McNeish, 1920s featherweight; Art Moore, 1940s welterweight; Leroy Pate, 1940s light heavyweight; Emmet "Silent" Puryear, 1920s heavyweight; "Silent" Ramponi, 1940s welterweight; "Dummy" Robinson, 1930s light heavyweight; Jimmy Santora, 1940s lightweight; Pete Tamalonis, 1930s heavyweight; "Dummy" Thomas, 1920s featherweight; Deafy Thompson, 1900s welterweight; and Dallas Vargas, 2000s **cruiserweight**. There was an opponent of **Charles "Kid" McCoy** in the 1890s who was simply listed in his record as "Deaf Mute."

One of the more unbelievable stories is that of Illinois heavyweight Craig Bodzianowski. He began boxing in 1982 and won his first 13 bouts, 11 by **knockout**. On 31 May 1984, the motorcycle he was riding was hit by a car and his foot severely injured. Nine days later, doctors amputated it. He was fitted with a prosthetic limb and resumed his boxing career 18 months later on 14 December 1985. He won the **World Boxing Association (WBA)** Continental Americas cruiserweight championship in 1989 and challenged for the WBA world cruiserweight title in 1990, losing by 12-round decision. He continued boxing until 1993 and for his career had a record of 31–4–1 with 23 knockouts.

Frenchman Eugene Criqui is another remarkable story about courage. He began boxing in 1910, won the French **flyweight** title, and challenged unsuccessfully for the European and International Boxing Union world flyweight title in 1913 and again in 1914. He served in the French Army during World War I and was shot, with his jaw being shattered. Doctors rebuilt the jaw with a silver plate, and he resumed his boxing career. He boxed until 1928 and won the French featherweight title in 1921, European featherweight title in 1922, and world featherweight championship in 1923.

There have been several instances of boxers missing digits. The 1964 Italian Olympic flyweight **gold medalist** Fernando Atzori was missing part of a finger. The 1924 Olympic middleweight **silver medalist** Englishman John Elliott was missing a thumb due to an accident on a naval ship during World War I. Welshman Howard Winstone won the **World Boxing Council** world featherweight championship in 1968 and boxed from 1959 to 1968 despite losing the tops of three fingers on his right hand. Scotsman Gary Jarvie, who was born without three fingers on his left hand, won 54 of 60 amateur bouts but was denied a **professional boxing** license in 2001 by the **British Boxing Board of Control**, who claimed that Jarvie could not make a proper fist. He cited the case of Englishman Alex Romeo, who boxed professionally from 1982 to 1989 also minus three fingers.

Heavyweight champion **Primo Carnera**, a diabetic, had a kidney removed in 1938 yet returned to the **ring** seven years later and fought five bouts.

Several champion boxers fought the last few years of their career blind in one eye—**Harry Greb**, **Sam Langford**, and **Pete Herman** were three of them. Gypsy Joe Harris, though not a champion, compiled a record of 24–1 during the 1960s, but in 1968 a physical examination disclosed the fact that Harris had been competing while blind in one eye.

HANDLER. *See* TRAINER.

HARADA, MASAHIKO "FIGHTING". B. 23 April 1943, Tokyo, **Japan**. Masahiko "Fighting" Harada is one of the greatest Japanese boxers of all time. He is not to be confused with Masahiko "Happy" Harada, a Japanese Olympic ski jumper. Fighting Harada began boxing as a **flyweight**, but by the time he ended his **professional** career, he was competing in the **feather-weight** class. He fought his first professional **bout** on 21 February 1960 and stopped Isami Masui in Tokyo in four **rounds**. Harada won his first 25 bouts, nine by **knockout**, all in Japan. On 14 June 1962, he suffered his first loss, a 10-round **split decision** to Edmundo Esparza. Four months later, Harada defeated the Thai Pone Kingpetch on an 11th round knockout in Tokyo and became the **World Boxing Association** world flyweight champion.

In a subsequent rematch on 12 January 1963 in **Thailand**, Harada lost a 15-round **majority decision**, and Kingpetch reclaimed the flyweight title. Harada moved up to the **bantamweight** class, won 11 of his next 12 bouts, and challenged the world bantamweight champion, **Éder Jofre**, in a title bout on 18 May 1965 in Nagoya, Japan. In a very close bout, **refereed** by former welterweight champion **Barney Ross**, Harada prevailed via a split decision and gained his second world title. He successfully defended that title four times, including a rematch with Jofre. Jofre only lost two bouts in a 78-bout career, but they were both to Harada. Masahiko finally lost his bantam-weight title on 27 February 1968 in Tokyo to **Australian** Lionel Rose on a 15-round **unanimous decision**.

Harada then moved up to the **featherweight** class and won four of his next five fights in the 126-pound weight division. On 28 July 1969, Harada fought only his third fight outside of Japan. He met the Australian Frenchman Johnny Famechon in Sydney, Australia, for Famechon's **World Boxing Council** featherweight title. The bout was extremely close, and referee **Willie Pep**, the former featherweight champion and sole arbiter of the bout, scored the bout a draw. After Famechon's fans raised a protest, Pep said that he had miscalculated and that the final result was six rounds for Famechon, five for Harada, and four even. On 6 January 1970, Famechon had a rematch with Harada in Tokyo and proved his superior boxing skills on that day, rallying from a 10th-round **knockdown** to end Harada's boxing career with a knock-out in the 14th round.

In 2002, Harada became the president of the Japanese Boxing **Commission**.

Harada is five foot three inches tall and has a 64-inch **reach**. He fought at weights ranging from 110 to 127 pounds in weight classes from flyweight to featherweight. In 62 professional bouts, from 1960 to 1970, he won 55 (22 by knockout), lost seven (two by knockout), and fought a total of 501 rounds. He was inducted into the **International Boxing Hall of Fame** in 1995.

HART, MARVIN "THE FIGHTIN' KENTUCKIAN," "THE LOUIS-VILLE PLUMBER". B. 16 September 1876, Louisville, Kentucky. D. 17 September 1931, Fern Creek, Kentucky. Until the 1990s, when multiple sanctioning organizations recognized multiple champions, **Marvin Hart** was probably the least known of all the men recognized as world's **heavyweight** champion.

Called "The Louisville Plumber," he was a tradesman before he began **professional boxing** in 1899. His first recorded **bout** was on 12 December of that year. From 1899 to 1901, he won his first 14 bouts, one by **disqualifica-tion** and the rest by **knockout**, with all 14 bouts taking place in Louisville. He suffered his first lost on 17 December 1901 when he was knocked out in the first **round** by Wild Bill Hanrahan. Hart won his next three bouts by knockout, with the third bout being a victory over Kid Carter in nine rounds. Following that bout, Hart claimed Carter's American 170-pound title. On 10 November 1902, Hart suffered his second loss, a six-round decision to Jack Root. Hart followed that bout with a six-round **draw** with **Philadelphia Jack O'Brien**.

In 1903, Hart lost to George Gardner in 12 rounds, fought a draw with Joe Choynski, and stopped Carter in 15 rounds. In 1904, he drew with Gardner and John Wille and defeated Sandy Ferguson in a 20-round bout. The year 1905 was clearly Hart's best as a fighter. He began the year by decisioning future heavyweight champion **Jack Johnson** in 20 rounds. Heavyweight champion **Jim Jeffries** had retired as undefeated champion, citing lack of competition, and named Hart and Jack Root to fight for the heavyweight title. The bout took place in Reno, Nevada, on 3 July 1905 with Jeffries as **referee**. There was no scheduled number of rounds, but the fight was to be to the finish under **Marquess of Queensberry Rules**. Hart knocked out Root in the 12th round and claimed the heavyweight championship.

After winning a bout with Pat Callahan in January 1906 via a two-round knockout, Hart took on **Tommy Burns** on 23 February in Los Angeles. Burns won a 20-round decision and the title. Hart continued boxing for four more years but won only five of 11 bouts, with one bout a draw. His last fight took place on 20 December 1910.

After retiring from boxing, Hart ran a tavern in Louisville and worked as a referee.

Hart was five foot 11 inches tall and had a 74-inch **reach**. He fought at weights ranging from 165 to 212 pounds as a **light heavyweight** and heavy-weight. In 48 professional bouts, from 1899 to 1910, he won 29 (21 by knockout), lost seven (four by knockout), had four draws, and fought seven no-decision bouts in which he was awarded the **newspaper decision** in two, lost two, and drew three. He fought a total of 394 rounds.

HAYMAKER. A haymaker is a colloquial term for a powerful punch that **knocks down** or **knocks out** a fighter.

See also BOLO PUNCH; COUNTERPUNCH; CROSS; HOOK; JAB; UPPERCUT.

HEARNS, THOMAS "TOMMY," "HIT MAN," "MOTOR CITY CO-BRA". B. 18 October 1958, Memphis, Tennessee. Thomas Hearns became known as "The Hit Man" due to his powerful punch. During his career, he fought some of boxing's top fighters in some of the era's most memorable **bouts**. He became the first boxer to win titles in four different weight divisions as well as the first to win titles at five different weight divisions. Hearns actually won titles in a sixth weight class although the sanctioning organizations, the World Boxing Union (WBU) and the International Boxing Organization (IBO), are not highly regarding by the boxing world.

An extremely tall fighter at six foot one inch for his weight, he claimed an outstanding **amateur** record of 155–8. In 1977, he won both the **light welterweight** national **Amateur Athletic Union** and national **Golden Gloves** championships. As an amateur, he was an effective but light-hitting boxer. When he began boxing under the tutelage of **Emanuel Steward** at the Kronk Gym in Detroit, Michigan, Steward changed Hearns's style, making him into one of the hardest hitters of his era. Hearns fought his first **professional** bout on 25 November 1977 and won a two-round **knockout**.

By March 1979, he had won 17 straight bouts, all by knockout. His first bout that lasted the scheduled distance was on 3 April 1979 when Alfonso Hayman lasted the full 10 rounds, although Hearns won every round on each of the three officials' scorecards for a **unanimous decision**.

On 2 August 1980, Hearns, with a record of 28–0 with 26 knockouts, added one more victory to his credit by stopping José "Pipino" Cuevas in the second round to win the **World Boxing Association (WBA) welterweight** championship. After three successful title defenses, Hearns met the **World Boxing Council (WBC)** welterweight champion, **"Sugar Ray" Leonard**, on 16 September 1981 in an outdoor arena at Caesar's Palace in **Las Vegas**. Although Hearns was ahead on points, Leonard came from behind to stop Hearns in the 14th round in a bout that was voted "Fight of the Year" by *Ring* magazine.

After winning three **nontitle bouts**, Hearns stepped up in weight and won the WBC **light middleweight** title on a **majority decision** over **Wilfred Benítez** in the Superdome in New Orleans on 3 December 1982. Hearns successfully defended that title three times, including a second-round **technical knockout** over former three-division champion **Roberto Durán** on 15 June 1984.

On 15 April 1985, Hearns attempted to move up to the **middleweight** division and fought **Marvelous Marvin Hagler** for Hagler's WBC, WBA, and **International Boxing Federation middleweight** titles. In one of the sport's greatest three-round fights, Hagler, although badly cut, stopped Hearns in the third to retain his titles. The first round of the bout has been called by some the greatest round in boxing history. Hearns broke his hand in that round but still was able to continue the fight.

After three more bouts, including a WBC light middleweight title defense, Hearns again moved up in weight and stopped Dennis Andries on 7 March 1987 in the 10th round to win the WBC **light heavyweight** title. Leonard retired on 27 May, and his WBC middleweight title became **vacant**. Hearns was matched with Juan Domingo Roldán on 29 October 1987 for the vacant title and knocked out Roldán in four rounds to become the first boxer to win championships in four different weight classes.

On 6 June 1988, Hearns lost his WBC middleweight title in an upset to Iran Barkley on a third-round stoppage after Barkley, a 4–1 underdog, bleeding badly from cuts, caught Hearns with a right hand, knocked him down once, and the second time knocked him through the ropes.

In Hearns's next fight, he won a championship in a fifth different weight class on a majority decision over James Kinchen for the **World Boxing Organization (WBO) super middleweight** title. He had now won championships in five divisions—**welterweight** (147-pound limit), light middleweight (154 pounds), middleweight (160 pounds), super middleweight (168 pounds), and light heavyweight (175 pounds).

Hearns then fought Leonard again. At the time, Leonard was the WBC super middleweight champion and Hearns had the WBO super middleweight belt. The bout ended in a 12-round **draw**, with both fighters retaining their respective titles.

Hearns was not through in his quest for additional titles, and after a successful title defense and two victories in nontitle bouts, he took on former **Olympic silver medalist** Virgil Hill for Hill's WBA light heavyweight title on 3 June 1991. Hearns added that title to his collection on a 12-round **unanimous decision**, but then lost it to Barkley via **split decision** in his first defense on 20 March 1992.

Hearns continued to move up in weight and now competed as a **cruiserweight**. On 31 March 1995, he stopped Lenny LaPaglia in the first round to win the WBU (one of boxing's lesser sanctioning organizations) cruiserweight title. It was, however, the sixth different weight class in which he had won a title—the first man to win in six different classes.

He then went into semiretirement and fought just once in each of the next five years. His 1999 bout earned him the IBO cruiserweight title, which he then lost in his only bout of 2000. He came back in 2005 and had one bout that year and one bout in 2006 at the age of 47.

His son, Ronald Hearns, a college graduate, has boxed from 2004 to 2012 and has a record of 26–4. Tommy's younger brother, Billy, also briefly boxed professionally during the 1980s and retired undefeated after eight bouts.

Hearns has a 78-inch **reach** and fought at weights ranging from 144 to 191 pounds in weight classes from welterweight to cruiserweight. In 67 professional bouts, from 1977 to 2006, he won 61 (48 by knockout), lost five (four by knockout), had one draw, and fought a total of 380 rounds. He was inducted into the **International Boxing Hall of Fame** in 2012.

HEAVYWEIGHT. Heavyweight is a **professional boxing** class with unlimited weight. It has traditionally been the most popular with boxing fans and the most lucrative. For the better part of the 20th century, a heavyweight championship **bout** was an infrequent occurrence and ranked with other extra-special sports events such as the Kentucky Derby in horse racing, the Rose Bowl in college football, and the World Series in baseball. With the rise of multiple boxing sanctioning organizations in the latter part of the 20th century, the heavyweight championship has lost much of its luster and rarely attracts the attention it once did.

John L. Sullivan was the last **bareknuckle** heavyweight champion and first recognized heavyweight champion in the gloved era. Among the best heavyweights have been **Muhammad Ali**, **Jack Dempsey**, **George Foreman**, **Joe Frazier**, **Larry Holmes**, **Jack Johnson**, **Sam Langford** (although not a champion), **Sonny Liston**, **Joe Louis**, **Rocky Marciano**, Sullivan, and **Gene Tunney**.

In **amateur boxing**, heavyweight was the unlimited weight class until 1981, at which time the unlimited class was renamed "**super heavyweight**" and the phrase "heavyweight" was restricted to a weight class with a 91-kilogram (200.6 pound) limit.

See also BAER, MAXIMILIAN ADELBERT "MAX," "THE LIVERMORE LARUPPER," "MADCAP MAXIE"; BOWE, RIDDICK LAMONT "BIG DADDY," "SUGAR MAN"; BRADDOCK, JAMES WALTER "JIM," "JAMES J." "CINDERELLA MAN"; BURNS, TOMMY "LITTLE GIANT OF HANOVER" (né NOAH BRUSSO); BUTTERBEAN "KING OF THE FOUR ROUNDERS" (né ERIC SCOTT ESCH); CARNERA, PRIMO "THE AMBLING ALP"; CHARLES, EZZARD MACK "THE CINCINNATI COBRA"; CHUVALO, GEORGE LOUIS (né JURE ČUVALO); CLARK, LAMAR F; COONEY, GERRY "GENTLEMAN GERRY"; CORBETT, JAMES JOHN "JIM," "GENTLEMAN JIM"; FIRPO, LUIS ÁNGEL "THE WILD BULL OF THE PAMPAS"; FITZSIMMONS, ROBERT JAMES "BOB," "RUBY ROBERT," "THE FRECKLED WONDER"; FOLLEY, ZORA BELL; GALENTO, DOMENICO ANTONIO "TONY," "TWO-TON TONY"; HART, MARVIN "THE FIGHTIN' KENTUCK-

IAN," "THE LOUISVILLE PLUMBER"; HOLYFIELD, EVANDER "THE REAL DEAL"; JACKSON, PETER "THE BLACK PRINCE," "PETER THE GREAT"; JEANNETTE, JEREMIAH "JOE"; JEFFRIES, JAMES JACKSON "JIM," "THE BOILERMAKER"; JOHANSSON, JENS INGEMAR "INGO"; KLITSCHKO, VITALY VOLODOMYROVICH "DR. IRONFIST"; KLITSCHKO, VOLODOMYR VOLODOMYROVICH "WLADIMIR," "DR. STEELHAMMER"; LEWIS, LENNOX CLAUDIUS "THE LION"; LYLE, RON; MACHEN, EDWARD MILLS "EDDIE"; McLAGLEN, VICTOR ANDREW DE BIER EVERLEIGH "SHARKEY"; NORTON, KENNETH HOWARD SR; PATTERSON, FLOYD; QUARRY, JERRY "IRISH," "THE BELLFLOWER BOMBER"; RADEMACHER, THOMAS PETER "PETE"; SAVON FABRE, FÉLIX "NIÑOTE"; SCHMELING, MAXIMILLIAN ADOLPH OTTO SIEGFRIED "MAX," "THE BLACK UHLAN OF THE RHINE"; SHARKEY, JACK "THE BOSTON GOB" (né JOSEPH PAUL ZUKAUSKAS); SHAVERS, EARNIE "THE ACORN," "THE BLACK DESTROYER" (né EARNIE DEE SHAVER); SPINKS, LEON "NEON LEON"; SPINKS, MICHAEL "JINX"; STEVENSON LAWRENCE, TEÓFILO; TYSON, MICHAEL GERARD "MIKE," "IRON MIKE" (aka MALIK ABDUL-AZIZ); VALUEV, NIKOLAI SERGEYEVICH "THE RUSSIAN GIANT," "THE BEAST FROM THE EAST"; WALCOTT, JERSEY JOE (né ARNOLD RAYMOND CREAM); WALLACE, COLEY; WEPNER, CHARLES "CHUCK," "THE BAYONNE BLEEDER"; WILLARD, JESS "THE POTTAWATOMIE GIANT"; WILLIAMS, CLEVELAND T. "BIG CAT"; WILLS, HARRY "THE BLACK PANTHER"; APPENDIX G for a list of professional world's heavyweight champions.

HERMAN, PETE "KID" (né PETER GULOTTA). B. 12 February 1896, New Orleans, Louisiana. D. 13 April 1973, New Orleans, Louisiana. Peter Gulotta was a shoeshine boy as a teenager. As a youth, he got into many scraps with other boys in the French Quarter of New Orleans. When he found out that people actually got paid for fighting, he decided to become a **professional** prizefighter. He adopted the name Kid Herman after a fighter he had read about and admired.

His first recorded professional **bout** occurred when he was just 16 years old on 30 September 1912 in New Orleans, and it went into the books as a **draw**. Only five foot two inches tall, he began fighting in the **flyweight** class and later moved up to **bantamweight**. In his first two years, fighting primarily in and around New Orleans, with occasional trips up the Mississippi River to Memphis, he compiled a record of 18–5–4. His first well-known opponent was Kid Williams, the world's bantamweight champion. They first fought on 30 June 1914 in a 10-round no-decision bout in which Herman held his own but Williams was awarded the **newspaper decision**.

Two years later, after recording victories over some of the era's better bantamweights, such as Eddie Campi, Young Zulu Kid, Eddie Coulon, and a fighter known simply as "Louisiana," Herman fought Williams in a return bout on 7 February 1916 in New Orleans—this time with Williams's world bantamweight title at stake. The bout resulted in a 20-round draw, and Williams retained his title. One year later, on 9 January 1917, the two met for a third time. This time, Herman knocked Williams down in the fifth and 12th rounds of their 20-round bout and won the decision and the world's bantamweight title. Later that year, the two met for a fourth time in a nontitle no-decision bout in Philadelphia, and Williams won a six-round newspaper decision.

Champions in that era fought often, but in the majority of their bouts their title was not at stake. Herman made his first title defense on 5 November 1917, winning a 20-round decision over Frankie Burns. Although Herman kept active, with 47 bouts in the next three years, none were in defense of his title. Nearly all were no-decision bouts, although in several of them his title was technically on the line should he not have lasted the scheduled distance since both fighters were under the bantamweight limit.

Toward the end of 1920, Herman signed a contract to fight the world's flyweight champion, Jimmy Wilde, in London in January 1921. Before that bout, though, he made a title defense on 22 December 1920 against his friend Joe Lynch at New York's **Madison Square Garden**. The bout resulted in Lynch winning a 15-round decision and Herman losing his title. The following month, Herman traveled to London, **England**, for the bout with Wilde. It was a 20-round **nontitle bout** since Herman no longer had the bantamweight title and could not get down to the flyweight limit. Herman surprised Wilde and stopped him in the 17th round.

On 25 July 1921, Herman easily regained the world's bantamweight title in a return bout with Lynch on a 15-round decision at Ebbets Field in Brooklyn, New York. There was some speculation that Herman had allowed his friend Lynch to win their first bout in order for the title to remain in the United States and not be in jeopardy when he fought Wilde, but Herman denied the speculation.

On 23 September, Herman lost the title to Johnny Buff at Madison Square Garden on a 15-round decision. He continued fighting until 24 April 1922, when he defeated Roy Moore and retired afterward.

Somewhere near the end of his career, Herman got thumbed in the eye while boxing an **exhibition** with Gussie Lewis and for the last few years fought while blind in one eye and with failing vision in the other. He retired at the age of 26 when he was nearly totally blind.

In retirement, he owned a bar in the French Quarter of New Orleans and was appointed to the Louisiana State Athletic **Commission**.

Herman had a 63-inch **reach** and fought at weights ranging from 110 to 124 pounds, primarily as a flyweight and bantamweight. In 143 professional bouts, from 1912 to 1922, he won 62 (20 by **knockout**), lost 13 (one by knockout), had seven draws, and fought 61 no-decision bouts in which he was awarded the newspaper decision in 39, lost 16, and had six draws. He fought a total of 1,386 rounds. He was inducted into the **International Boxing Hall of Fame** in 1997.

HOLMES, LARRY "THE EASTON ASSASSIN". B. 3 November 1949, Cuthbert, Georgia. Larry Holmes is best remembered for his **jab**—one of the best in **ring** history. Although Holmes was born in Georgia, his family moved to Easton, Pennsylvania, where he was raised and still lives. As an **amateur** boxer, he claimed a record of 19–3, with one of those losses to Duane Bobick during the 1972 **Olympic** trials. He became a **professional** boxer in 1973, with his first professional **bout** on 21 March in Scranton, Pennsylvania. He won his first 48 professional bouts, one shy of **Rocky Marciano's** streak of 49.

On 9 June 1978, after Holmes won his first 27 bouts, he won the **World Boxing Council (WBC) heavyweight** title on a **split decision** over **Ken Norton** in **Las Vegas**. He then successfully defended the title 20 consecutive times—more than any heavyweight champion with the exception of **Joe Louis**. Those 20 opponents were Alfredo Evangelista, Ossie Ocasio, Mike Weaver, **Earnie Shavers**, Lorenzo Zanon, Leroy Jones, Scott LeDoux, **Muhammad Ali**, Trevor Berbick, **Leon Spinks**, Renaldo Snipes, **Gerry Cooney**, Randall "Tex" Cobb, Lucien Rodríguez, Tim Witherspoon, Scott Frank, Marvis Frazier (son of **Joe Frazier**), James "Bonecrusher" Smith, David Bey, and Carl Williams. Ali, Berbick, Smith, Spinks, Weaver, and Witherspoon all owned heavyweight titles at one point in their careers.

On 21 September 1985, Holmes was involved in boxing history as he lost his title on a 15-**round unanimous decision** to **Michael Spinks**, the **light heavyweight** champion. Spinks became the first light heavyweight champion to win the heavyweight championship. (**Bob Fitzsimmons** also held the two titles but won the light heavyweight title after losing the heavyweight title.)

Seven months later, Spinks and Holmes fought a rematch, and Spinks won on a split decision. After Spinks was stripped of his title, **Mike Tyson** became heavyweight champion. Holmes challenged Tyson on 22 January 1988 but was stopped in the fourth round—his only loss short of the distance in his career. Holmes announced his retirement after the bout.

Three years later, Holmes came out of retirement. After winning five bouts against mediocre opposition Holmes won a 12-round decision over the previously undefeated (18–0) Ray Mercer, the 1988 Olympic heavyweight champion. On 19 June 1992, Holmes again attempted to regain the world's heavyweight title but lost a 12-round decision to **Evander Holyfield**. Holmes then won seven more bouts against lower-caliber opposition, and on 8 April 1995 the 45-year old Holmes challenged the WBC heavyweight champion, Oliver McCall, in yet another attempt at regaining the title. Once more Holmes was stymied, as he lost a 12-round unanimous decision. Undaunted, Holmes won four more bouts and then in one final attempt fought the undefeated (31–0) Dane Brian Nielsen in Copenhagen, Denmark, on 24 January 1997 in a bout billed for the International Boxing Organization heavyweight championship. Holmes once more was defeated, although on a close split decision. Although Holmes was then 47 years old, he continued boxing. In 1999, at the age of 49, he stopped the former heavyweight champion James "Bonecrusher" Smith, then 46 years old, in eight rounds. The following year, Holmes, two weeks past his 51st birthday, defeated another former heavyweight champion, the 49-year-old Mike Weaver, on a sixth-round **technical knockout**.

In Holmes's final bout on 27 July 2002, he faced the 334-pound Eric Esch, known as **Butterbean**, in a 10-round bout. Butterbean had never fought more than six rounds in a bout previously. Due to his massive size, he specialized in four-round bouts and billed himself as the "king of the four rounders." Holmes and Butterbean went the full 10 rounds, and Holmes won a unanimous decision even though he was knocked down in the 10th round.

Holmes has not fought since that bout and has devoted his time to managing his multiple business interests in his hometown of Easton. In addition to two restaurants and a nightclub, Holmes owns an office complex, a gymnasium, a snack food bar, and slot machines. He was one of the few boxers who invested wisely and consequently is quite well off financially.

Holmes is six foot three inches tall and has an 81-inch **reach**. He fought at weights ranging from 196 to 255 pounds as a heavyweight. In 75 professional bouts, from 1973 to 2002, he won 69 (44 by knockout), lost six (one by knockout), and fought a total of 581 rounds. He was inducted into the **International Boxing Hall of Fame** in 2008.

HOLYFIELD, EVANDER "THE REAL DEAL". B. 19 October 1962, Atmore, Alabama. During his boxing career, Evander Holyfield has been involved in some of boxing's strangest happenings.

Raised in Atlanta, Georgia, he began boxing at the age of 12. As a **light heavyweight**, he won the **silver medal** at the Pan American Games in 1983 and the National **Golden Gloves** in 1984. At the **Olympic Games** in Los Angeles, he won his first three **bouts** by **knockout** but in a controversial decision in the semifinal bout was **disqualified** for hitting on the break and had to settle for the **bronze medal**. Holyfield claimed a record of 160–14 as an **amateur** boxer.

He fought his first **professional** bout at **Madison Square Garden** on 15 November 1984 on a **card** that featured six Olympians making their professional debuts. After winning his first 11 fights, eight by knockout, Holyfield won the **World Boxing Association (WBA) cruiserweight** title by defeating Dwight Muhammad Qawi on a 15-round **split decision** in a closely fought battle on 12 July 1986 in Atlanta. Holyfield successfully defended that title five times, all by knockout. His unfortunate opponents were Henry Tillman, Rickey Parkey, Ossie Ocasio, Qawi, and Carlos de León.

Holyfield then moved up to the **heavyweight** division and won six more bouts by knockout. On 25 October 1990, he knocked out James "Buster" Douglas and gained the heavyweight championship of the world. Douglas, who had won the title eight months earlier by knocking out **Mike Tyson** in one of the biggest upsets in boxing history, was making the first defense of his title. On 19 April 1991, Holyfield won a 12-round **unanimous decision** over the 42-year-old former heavyweight champion **George Foreman**, who had won 24 straight bouts, 23 by knockout, in a comeback attempt after being out of the **ring** for 10 years.

Holyfield then defeated Bert Cooper and former heavyweight champion Larry Holmes in title defenses before losing his title to **Riddick Bowe** on 13 November 1992 on a 12-round unanimous decision. One year later, Holyfield regained the heavyweight title on a 12-round **majority decision** over Bowe in a weird bout that was suspended for 21 minutes in the seventh round after a man, known as Fanman, circled above the ring in a motorized paraglider, crashed into the overhead ring lights, and was stuck there. The scoring of the bout was quite close, with the three **judges** voting 115–114, 115–113, and 114–114 for Holyfield.

In Holyfield's next fight, he again lost the heavyweight title. Michael Moorer won a 12-round majority decision to take the title from Holyfield. After defeating Ray Mercer in a nontitle fight, Holyfield was stopped by Riddick Bowe in the eighth round—the first time in his career that Evander was stopped. He rebounded in his next fight with a fifth-round **technical knockout** over Bobby Czyz.

On 9 November 1996, Holyfield won the heavyweight title for the third time in his career when he stopped Mike Tyson in the 11th round. The two fought a rematch on 28 June 1997 that was another bizarre affair.

In the third round Tyson bit Holyfield's right ear so severely that a piece was torn off. **Referee Mills Lane** stopped the fight, deducted two points from the scorecards for Tyson, and warned Tyson, who claimed the damage was caused by a punch. Tyson then bit Holyfield's left ear and was disqualified.

Holyfield then successfully defended against Moorer and Vaughn Bean. On 13 March 1999, he fought **Lennox Lewis** to a 12-round **draw** in one of boxing's worst decisions. In a rematch on 13 November 1999, Lewis won a 12-round unanimous decision, and Holyfield lost the heavyweight championship for the third time.

Holyfield was not without a title for long since in his next bout on 12 August 2000 he defeated John Ruiz on a 12-round unanimous decision and won the WBA heavyweight title. He became the first man to win a heavyweight title four times. In his first defense, Holyfield also became the first man to lose the heavyweight title four times, as Ruiz won a 12-round decision to regain the title. The two boxers then fought a third match that ended in a draw.

Holyfield was not ready to retire from the ring and after defeating Hassan Rahman fought Chris Byrd for the **International Boxing Federation** heavyweight title on 14 December 2002 but lost a 12-round unanimous decision. Although 40 years old, Holyfield continued fighting and was defeated by **James Toney** in 2003 and Larry Donald in 2004. He then did not fight in 2005 but came back in 2006 and won two fights and won two more in 2007.

On 20 December 2008, at the age of 46, Holyfield challenged the seven-foot-tall **Nikolai Valuev** for the **World Boxing Organization** heavyweight title. Although 10 inches shorter, 96 pounds lighter, and 11 years older, Holyfield put up a good fight but lost on a **majority decision**.

After another year off, Holyfield stopped Frans Botha in the eighth round on 10 April 2010 and, at the age of 47, won the lightly regarded **World Boxing Federation** heavyweight championship.

Holyfield's most recent fight was on 7 May 2011, a 10th-round **technical knockout** over Brian Nielsen in Nielsen's hometown of Copenhagen, Denmark.

Holyfield is six foot two inches tall and has a 78-inch **reach**. He fought at weights ranging from 176 to 226 pounds as a **cruiserweight** and heavyweight. In 57 professional bouts, from 1984 to 2011, he won 44 (29 by knockout), lost 10 (two by knockout), had two draws and one no decision, and fought a total of 443 rounds.

HOOK. A hook is a type of boxing punch, usually designated by the hand with which it is thrown as a right hook or a left hook. Rather than being thrown directly, it is thrown with a looping motion.

See also BOLO PUNCH; COUNTERPUNCH; CROSS; HAYMAKER; JAB; UPPERCUT.

HOPKINS, BERNARD HUMPHREY, JR., "THE EXECUTIONER". B.

15 January 1965, Philadelphia, Pennsylvania. Bernard Hopkins was 23 years old when he began boxing **professionally** and 25 years later is still going strong. Along the way, he has set records for being the oldest champion in boxing history.

He got his late start as a professional because when he was 17 years old he was sentenced to 18 years in prison for nine felonies, including armed robbery. He learned to box in prison, and when he was released in 1988 after serving five years, he became a professional boxer.

His first **bout** was 11 October 1988 in **Atlantic City**, and he was defeated by Clinton Mitchell on a **majority decision**. Hopkins then did not lose again for four and a half years, winning 22 straight bouts, 16 by **knockout**.

On 22 May 1993, Hopkins fought **Roy Jones Jr.** for the **vacant International Boxing Federation (IBF) middleweight** title but lost a 12-**round unanimous decision** to Jones. In 1994, Hopkins again fought for that title, this time traveling down to Quito, Ecuador, to take on Segundo Mercado in a bout held in a bullring. Hopkins suffered his first professional **knockdown** in the bout but was able to hang on and receive a **draw** decision for his efforts. In a rematch four months later, on 29 April 1995 in Landover, Maryland, Hopkins won the IBF middleweight title by stopping Mercado in the seventh round.

Hopkins then made an unprecedented 20 successful defenses of that championship over the next 10 years. Along the way, he also won the middleweight title of each of the other three major sanctioning organizations.

He added the **World Boxing Council (WBC)** middleweight title on 14 April 2001 when he won a unanimous decision over Keith Holmes at **Madison Square Garden**. In Hopkins's next fight on 29 September 2001, also at the Garden, he stopped **Félix Trinidad** in the 12th round and gained **World Boxing Association (WBA)** recognition as a "Super" world champion—a title they bestow on titleholders who own championships of the other sanctioning organizations in addition to their own WBA title.

Hopkins won the fourth sanctioning organization's middleweight title when on 18 September 2004 he added the **World Boxing Organization** title by knocking out **Óscar De La Hoya** in the ninth round in **Las Vegas**. He successfully defended the four titles just once before losing them to the undefeated (23–0) Jermain Taylor on 16 July 2005 in Las Vegas on a **split decision**. A subsequent rematch on 3 December 2005 resulted in a close but unanimous decision for Taylor.

Hopkins then moved up to the **light heavyweight** class and won the lightly regarded International Boxing Organization (IBO) light heavyweight championship against a formidable opponent, the 1996 **Olympic bronze medalist** Antonio Tarver, on a 12-round unanimous decision.

After winning a unanimous decision over former **light middleweight** champion Ronald "Winky" Wright in a **nontitle bout**, Hopkins then faced the **super middleweight** champion **Joe Calzaghe**, an undefeated (44–0) Welshman who was making his first fight outside the British Isles. Calzaghe kept his undefeated streak alive, as he got up off the **canvas** in round one to outpoint Hopkins on a close split decision in Las Vegas on 19 April 2008.

On 3 April 2010, Hopkins, age 45, fought **Roy Jones Jr.**, age 41, in a rematch of their 1993 fight. The bout was scheduled for 12 rounds even though no title was at stake. This time Hopkins avenged his loss of 17 years previous by winning at 12-round unanimous decision.

Later in 2010 in Montreal, **Canada**, Hopkins fought a 12-round **draw** with Haitian Canadian Jean Pascal for the WBC and IBO light heavyweight titles. In their rematch on 21 May 2011, also in Montreal, Hopkins became the oldest man to win the light heavyweight championship when he won a 12-round unanimous decision. Hopkins was 46 years, four months, and six days old and surpassed **Archie Moore's** record.

Hopkins retained that title until 28 April 2012, when he was defeated by Chad Dawson on a **majority decision** in **Atlantic City**. Prior to his loss on that day, Hopkins, age 47 years, three months, and 13 days, was the oldest man to hold a world championship title.

Hopkins plans to keep fighting until age 50. On 9 March 2013, he defeated Tavaris Cloud on a unanimous decision and won the IBF light heavyweight title.

Hopkins is six foot one inch tall and has a 75-inch **reach**. He has fought at weights ranging from 156 to 177 pounds as a middleweight and light heavyweight. In 62 professional bouts, from 1988 to 2012, he won 52 (32 by knockout), lost six (none by knockout), had two draws and two **no contests**, and fought a total of 458 rounds.

HUNGARY. Boxing in Hungary, as with most of the Iron Curtain countries prior to the fall of communism, was done only at the **amateur** level. The country had good boxing programs and fared well in the **Olympic Games**. It first competed in the Olympic boxing tournament in 1924 and has taken part in 20 games—all save 1984, when it joined the **Soviet** boycott. In this time, the country has won 20 medals—10 **gold**, two **silver**, and eight **bronze**—and is tied for 11th place among all nations in Olympic boxing. Only five countries have won more Olympic gold medals in boxing, and all five of them have populations in excess of Hungary's 10 million.

László Papp was one of the greatest Olympic boxers of all-time and is one of only three men (the others—**Cubans Teófilo Stevenson** and **Félix Savon**) to win three Olympic boxing gold medals. He won the 1948 **middleweight** and 1952 and 1956 **light middleweight** classes. Hungary's other Olympic boxing gold medalists include György Gedó, who won the Olympic **light**

flyweight title in 1972 and competed in four Olympic Games—the first man to do so; Antal Kocsis, 1928 **flyweight**; István Énekes, 1932 flyweight; Gyula Török, 1960 flyweight; István Kovács, 1996 **bantamweight**, who also won a bronze in 1992 as a flyweight; Tibor Csík, 1948 bantamweight; and Imre Harangi, 1936 **lightweight**.

Papp was one of the few Hungarian boxers allowed to box professionally and from 1957 to 1964 won all 27 of his **bouts** and the European Boxing Union middleweight championship. Since **professional boxing** was illegal in Hungary at that time, he fought all his bouts in European countries outside his homeland. Since the fall of communism, István Kovács, Károly Balzsay, and Zsolt Erdei have all won professional world championships. Stefan Redl, born in Hungary but residing in New Jersey, had a modicum of success as a **welterweight** during the 1950s and early 1960s and had the distinction of headling the final **card** at the venerable **St. Nicholas Arena** in New York on 28 May 1962.

I

IHETU, RICHARD. *See* TIGER, DICK (né RICHARD IHETU).

INTERNATIONAL BOXING ASSOCIATION (AIBA). The International Boxing Association was originally known as Association Internationale de Boxe Amateur and still retains the abbreviation AIBA. It was created in November 1946 and administers **amateur boxing** worldwide. It sponsors a **world championship** tournament that was first contested in 1974, then repeated quadrennially, then in 1989 and 1991, and is now held biannually. The International Boxing Association is the sports federation that is associated with the International Olympic Committee and controls boxing in the **Olympic Games**. In 2013, it plans to expand and have a division devoted to **professional boxing**.

INTERNATIONAL BOXING ASSOCIATION (IBA). The International Boxing Association was founded in 1998 by former major league baseball player and boxing promoter Dean Chance in Wooster, Ohio. It should not be confused with the **amateur boxing** association of the same name. The Ohio-based IBA sanctions **professional bouts** and is similar to the other professional sanctioning organizations, such as the **World Boxing Council, World Boxing Association, World Boxing Organization**, and **International Boxing Federation**, although its championships are not valued as highly as are ones from those four major sanctioning organizations.

INTERNATIONAL BOXING CLUB. *See* NORRIS, JAMES DOUGAN.

INTERNATIONAL BOXING COUNCIL (IBC). The International Boxing Council is one of numerous boxing sanctioning organizations that have been established since the mid-1980s. Its titles carry little weight in the boxing world.

INTERNATIONAL BOXING FEDERATION (IBF). The International Boxing Federation is a boxing sanctioning organization based in New Jersey that has become recognized as one of the four major such groups. It originated in 1983 when Robert W. "Bob" Lee Sr., then president of the **United States** Boxing Association, lost in a bid to become president of the **World Boxing Association** and decided to form a competing organization. It was originally called USBA–International, but later that year the name was changed to its present one.

On 4 November 1999, Lee was indicted on 33 counts of racketeering for soliciting and accepting bribes to manipulate the organization's ratings of boxers. His son, Robert W. Lee Jr., was also indicted on nine counts. Lee Sr. was later acquitted on the bribery charges but was found guilty on six of the 33 other counts, including tax evasion, money laundering, and interstate travel in aid of racketeering, and sentenced to 22 months in prison. Lee Jr. was acquitted on all nine counts. An appeal was made to the Supreme Court of the United States, but that court declined to review the case.

INTERNATIONAL BOXING HALL OF FAME. The International Boxing Hall of Fame is located in Canastota, New York, a small town 30 miles east of Syracuse in Upstate New York. It was founded in 1990 by Ed Brophy. Since then, it has inducted nearly 400 people in five categories—modern boxers, oldtime boxers, pioneer (**bareknuckle**) boxers, nonparticipants (promoters, **referees**, **trainers**, managers), and observers (journalists and broadcasters).

Its annual induction weekend is generally the second weekend in June, and four days of activities are held, including a golf tournament, 5K run, **ringside** lectures, cocktail hour, induction dinner, parade, and induction ceremonies.

Its museum and library is open to the public daily.

See also APPENDIX A for a list of inductees.

INTERNATIONAL BOXING RESEARCH ORGANIZATION (IBRO). The International Boxing Research Organization was founded in May 1982 by boxing historian John Grasso and *Ring* **magazine** writer Herbert G. Goldman for the express purpose of establishing an accurate history of boxing, compiling complete and accurate boxing records, facilitating the dissemination of boxing research information, and cooperating in safeguarding the individual research efforts of its members by application of the rules of scholarly research. It was created based on a suggestion by *Ring* magazine editor **Bert Randolph Sugar** that boxing historians worldwide should pool their research efforts.

There were 15 charter members of the organization, and by 2012 the membership had grown to 150. A periodic newsletter and annual journal were published. By 2012, the organization has expanded to include a website. Since 2000, Dan Cuoco has been IBRO's director.

IRELAND. The citizens of Ireland have always appreciated a good fight, and Irish boxers have done well in the **ring**. In **amateur boxing**, Irish boxers first competed in the 1924 **Olympic Games** and have entered 20 Olympic boxing tournaments. Irish boxers have won 16 Olympic medals—two **gold**, five **silver**, and nine **bronze**—18th best among all nations. Paddy Barnes is the only Irish boxer to win two Olympic medals—both bronze in the **light flyweight** class in 2008 and 2012. Michael Carruth, 1992 **welterweight**, and Katie Taylor, 2012 **women's light welterweight**, are the two Irish Olympic gold medalists. The silver medalists were **bantamweights** John McNally, 1952, Wayne McCullough (Belfast native who competed for Ireland), 1992, and John Joe Nevin, 2012; welterweight Fred Tiedt, 1956; and **light heavyweight** Kenny Egan, 2008. In addition to Barnes's two bronze medals, other Irish Olympic bronze medalists were **flyweights** Johnny Caldwell, 1956, Hugh Russell, 1980, and Michael Conlan, 2012; bantamweight Freddie Gilroy, 1956; **lightweights** Tony Byrne, 1956, and Jim McCourt, 1964; and **middleweight** Darren Sutherland, 2008.

In **professional boxing**, there have been eight Irish world champions. **Barry McGuigan** and Mike McTigue are two of the best-known ones. Other Irish world champions are Steve Collins, Bernard Dunne, George Gardiner, Dave "Boy" McAuley, and **Tommy Ryan**. Other top-rated Irish boxers include **bareknuckle** boxer Dan Donnelly, Christy Elliott, Cathal O'Grady, and Gary Sullivan. There have been scores of top Irish American boxers as well as quite a few boxers born in Ireland but raised in North America. Among the latter are **Jack "Nonpareil" Dempsey**, Peter Maher, Jack McAuliffe, **Jimmy McLarnin**, and bareknuckle boxers Owney Geoghegan and Paddy Ryan. Irish American world champions born in the **United States** include Jimmy Barry, **James J. Braddock**, Paddy Duffy, **Jack Dempsey**, **John L. Sullivan**, and **Gene Tunney**.
See also NORTHERN IRELAND.

ITALY. Boxing has always been a popular sport in Italy, with a substantial number of Italian world champions both in **amateur** and **professional boxing**. In addition, there have been many Italian American top-notch boxers.

In amateur boxing, Italian boxers first competed in the 1920 **Olympic Games** and have entered 22 Olympic boxing tournaments. Their 47 medals in Olympic boxing is fifth best among all nations, and their total of 15 **gold medals** is fourth best, as is their 15 **silver medals**. They also have won 17

bronze medals. Roberto Cammarelle is one of just nine boxers to have won three Olympic medals and is the only one of the nine to win one of each—gold, silver, and bronze. Italian gold medalists were Fernando Atzori, 1964 **flyweight**; Vittorio Tamagnini, 1928 **bantamweight**; Ulderico Sergo, 1936 bantamweight; Maurizio Stecca, 1984 bantamweight; Ernesto Formenti, 1948 **featherweight**; Francesco Musso, 1960 featherweight; Giovanni Parisi, 1988 featherweight; Carlo Orlandi, 1928 **lightweight**; Aureliano Bolognesi, 1952 lightweight; Patrizio Oliva, 1980 **light welterweight**; **Nino Benvenuti**, 1960 **welterweight**; Piero Toscani, 1928 **middleweight**; Cosimo Pinto, 1964 **light heavyweight**; and Clemente Russo, who won silver medals in both the 2008 and 2012 **heavyweight** classes.

In professional boxing, Italy has claimed 28 world champions. Among the most notable have been Vito Antuofermo, Bruno Arcari, Carmelo Bossi, Silvio Branco, Salvatore Burruni, **Primo Carnera**, Mario D'Agata, Francesco Damiani, Sumbu Kalambay, **Duilio Loi**, Sandro Lopopolo, Sandro Mazzinghi, Patrizio Oliva, Giovanni Parisi, Gianfranco Rosi, and Maurizio Stecca. **Arturo Gatti**, born in Italy, moved to **Canada** at a young age and boxed professionally as a Canadian. Other notable Italian boxers include Dante Cane, Piero del Papa, Tiberio Mitri, Giulio Rinaldi, Piero Rollo, Giuseppe "Bepi" Ros, Paolo Rosi, Italo Scortichini, Bruno Visintin, and Franco Zurlo. There have been many Italian American boxers. World champions among them are **Carmen Basilio**, Sal Bartolo, **Tony Canzoneri**, Paddy DeMarco, Tony DeMarco, **Rocky Graziano**, Fidel LaBarba, **Jake LaMotta**, **Rocky Marciano**, **Vinny Pazienza**, and Lou Salica.

Quite a few Italian American boxers anglicized their names—Lou Ambers (Luigi D'Ambrosio), Sammy Angott (Samuel Engotti), Frankie Conley (Francesco Conte), Young Corbett III (Rafaelle Capobianco Giordano), Johnny Dundee (Giuseppe Carrora), Vince Dundee (Vincent Lazzaro), Fireman Jim Flynn (Andrew Chiariglione), Joe Grim (Saverio Giannone), Harry Jeffra (Ignacius Pasquale Guiffi), Hugo Kelly (Ugo Micheli), Tippy Larkin (Antonio Pilleteri), **Joey Maxim** (Giuseppe Antonio Berardinelli), Packey O'Gatty (Pasquale Agati), **Willie Pep** (Guglielmo Papaleo), Mike Rossman (Michael Albert DePiano), Johnny Wilson (Giovanni Panica), and Benny Yanger (Frank Angone).

Giuseppe Ballarati was the **Nat Fleischer** of Italian boxing. His annual work *La Bibbia di Pugilato* was one of the most esteemed boxing record books. He has been inducted into the **International Boxing Hall of Fame**, as has Umberto Branchini, one of Italy's most noted fight managers, and Rodolfo Sabbatini, the leading boxing promoter in Italy.

J

JAB. A jab is a type of boxing punch that is a short straight punch, usually without much power behind it, that is used to keep an opponent from getting too close.

See also BOLO PUNCH; COUNTERPUNCH; CROSS; HAYMAKER; HOOK; UPPERCUT.

JACKSON, HENRY, JR. *See* ARMSTRONG, HENRY "HURRICANE HANK," "HAMMERIN' HANK," "HOMICIDE HANK" (né HENRY JACKSON JR.).

JACKSON, PETER "THE BLACK PRINCE," "PETER THE GREAT". B. 3 July 1861, Christiansted, Danish West Indies. D. 13 July 1901, Roma, Queensland, **Australia**. Peter Jackson, like several other excellent 19th-century boxers, was born the wrong color. Had he had white skin, he most likely would have been the world's **heavyweight** champion.

He was born in the West Indies but at the age of 12 immigrated with his family to Australia. After three years, the family returned to the West Indies, but Jackson remained in Australia and became a sailor. His boss, ship owner Clay Callahan, found that Jackson had a talent for boxing and brought him to Larry Foley, a former boxer and Australia's foremost boxing instructor, operating out of his White Horse Saloon in Sydney.

Jackson's earliest recorded **bouts** occur in 1882 in Sydney. In 1884, he fought Bill Farnan for the Australian heavyweight championship under **Marquess of Queensberry Rules** but was stopped in four **rounds**. Two months later, he again fought Farnan, but the bout was called a **draw** after six rounds. On 25 September 1886, Jackson became the Australian heavyweight champion when he stopped Tom Lees in the 30th round of their bout in Sydney.

In April 1888, Jackson was brought to the **United States** and was based in San Francisco. He attempted to arrange a bout with Joe McAuliffe but was rebuked by McAuliffe, who said he would not fight a black fighter. Jackson then fought George Godfrey on 24 August 1888 for the "colored heavyweight title" and stopped Godfrey in the 19th. McAuliffe then had a change of heart, feeling that a defeat of Jackson would further his career, and agreed to meet him on 28 December 1888. Jackson knocked him out in the 24th round in a bout billed for the "Heavyweight Championship of the Pacific Coast." After his victory, Jackson became a hero in the black community.

In his next bout, Jackson stopped Patsy Cardiff in 10 rounds in San Francisco. Feeling that he would find better competition in the eastern part of the country, he began traveling, fighting in several cities along the way. He ended up in New York City but then decided to go to London, **England**, in hopes of meeting Jem Smith, the English champion. He fought Smith on 11 November 1889 in London in front of an audience that included the Marquess of Queensberry himself. After Jackson dominated the first round, in the second round he was wrestled down to the floor and hit, as one Australian newspaper quaintly described it, "in a part of the body that may be hinted at but not named in newspaper phraseology." The fight was immediately stopped and Jackson was awarded the victory.

After winning seven more bouts against lesser opposition in November and December 1889 Jackson defeated Peter Maher in Dublin, **Ireland**, on 24 December in three rounds and then returned to the United States in his quest to meet the world's **heavyweight** champion, **John L. Sullivan**. Although several North American promoters made offers to stage a fight between the two, Sullivan was adamant in his refusal to fight a black fighter. His famous words were: "I will not fight a Negro. I never have and I never will."

Unable to get a match with Sullivan, Jackson returned to **Australia** after just a few months in the **United States** and a few more victories. On 20 October 1889, he fought Joe Goddard for the Australian heavyweight title in Melbourne, but the bout was ruled a **draw** after eight rounds.

Jackson did get a match with **James J. Corbett**, one of the leading heavyweights of the time and soon-to-be conqueror of John L. Sullivan and world's champion. Jackson returned to San Francisco, and on 21 May 1891 the two fought defensively for 61 rounds before the **referee** ruled it "**no contest**" and stopped the fight without naming a winner. Corbett was then viewed with admiration by boxing fans for having lasted so long with Jackson while Jackson was seen as being past his prime.

Jackson then traveled back to London and on 30 May 1892 defeated the previously undefeated (30–0–5) Paddy Slavin on a 10th-round **knockout** and won the British Empire heavyweight championship.

Jackson fought once more in 1892, once in 1895, and on 22 March 1898 was stopped in three rounds by **James J. Jeffries**, another future world's champion. Jackson's last bout was on 23 August 1899, when he was stopped in four rounds by Jim Jeffords in Vancouver, **Canada**.

After returning to Australia, he was stricken with tuberculosis and died on 13 July 1901 at the age of 40. His epitaph at the Toowong Cemetery in Brisbane, Australia, reads simply, "This was a man."

Jackson was six foot one inch tall and had a 77-inch **reach**. He fought at weights ranging from 189 to 200 pounds as a heavyweight. In 100 professional bouts, from 1882 to 1899, he won 44 (30 by knockout), lost three (all three by knockout), and had four draws, 48 no contests, and one no-decision bout in which he was awarded the **newspaper decision**. He fought a total of 468 rounds. He was inducted as a member of the inaugural class of the **International Boxing Hall of Fame** in 1990.

An excellent biography of Jackson by David K. Wiggins can be found in the North American Society for Sport History's *Journal of Sport History*, vol. 12, no. 2 (Summer 1985).

JACOBS, JAMES LESLIE "JIM". B. 18 February 1930, St. Louis, Missouri. D. 23 March 1988, New York, New York. For about 15 years, Jim Jacobs was the best handball player in the world. (The handball he played is the North American game hitting a ball against a wall—not the European team game that is a cross between basketball and soccer.) He was raised in Los Angeles and was a versatile athlete as a youth, playing baseball, football, and basketball as well as handball. He served in the U.S. Army during the **Korean** conflict and was awarded a Purple Heart. In 1955, he won the American four-wall singles handball championship. Over the next 15 years, he won six national singles and six national doubles handball titles.

He started collecting **boxing films** in the late 1940s and over time amassed the largest collection in the world. In 1959, he became partners with Bill Cayton, another collector, and they formed Big Fights Inc. The two worked on restoring fight films. In 1974, they purchased the **Madison Square Garden** collection of fight films.

They also dabbled in managing boxers and in 1978 became managers of **Wilfred Benítez**, **light welterweight** champion, and managed him until 1983. They also managed Edwin Rosario. They then joined with an old friend, boxing **trainer Cus D'Amato**, and managed the early career of future heavyweight champion **Mike Tyson**.

Jacobs also had an extensive comic book collection of more than 500,000 comics. After his death from leukemia in 1988, Cayton was the sole owner of the film collection, which he sold to the Entertainment and Sports Programming Network in 1998 for a reported $100 million.

Jacobs was inducted into the **International Boxing Hall of Fame** in 1993.

JACOBS, MICHAEL STRAUSS "MIKE". B. 17 March 1880, New York, New York. D. 24 January 1953, Miami, Florida. Mike Jacobs was the leading boxing promoter in the 1930s and 1940s as well as the manager of **heavyweight** champion **Joe Louis**.

An ambitious youngster, he sold candy and newspapers on excursion boats in New York harbor in the 1890s. He progressed to selling tickets for the boats and then became a ticket speculator or scalper (a legal practice then), reselling theater, opera, and sports event tickets. He then started backing various promotions and after meeting promoter **Tex Rickard** began working with him.

After Rickard died in 1929, Jacobs began promoting boxing at the Hippodrome in New York City. In 1933, he joined with sportswriters Damon Runyon, Ed Frayne, and Bill Farnsworth to found the Twentieth Century Sporting Club to promote boxing in opposition to **Madison Square Garden**.

In 1935, Jacobs worked out a deal with Joe Louis and promised him a shot at the world's heavyweight title. Jacobs then negotiated with Madison Square Garden to rent their facility as well as the outdoor facility they owned in Long Island City, the Madison Square Garden Bowl. This effectively removed Madison Square Garden from boxing promotion in New York, and Jacobs capitalized on the opportunity.

In 1938, he bought out his three sportswriter partners and became the sole owner of the Twentieth Century Sporting Club. He then became the major boxing promoter in New York City.

In 1946, he suffered a cerebral hemorrhage and was incapacitated for the rest of his life. He sold his organization to **Madison Square Garden** in 1949 and died in 1953. He was inducted into the **International Boxing Hall of Fame** in 1990.

JAPAN. Boxing is one of the more popular sports in Japan, although Japanese fighters' physiques tend to restrict them to the lighter weight classes. The organization controlling Japanese boxing is the Japan Boxing **Commission**, founded in 1952.

In **amateur boxing**, Japanese boxers first competed in the 1928 **Olympic Games** and have entered 18 Olympic boxing tournaments. They have won two **gold medals**; Takao Sakurai won Japan's first Olympic boxing gold medal at the Tokyo Olympics in 1964 in the **bantamweight** class, and Ryota Murata won the 2012 **middleweight** gold medal. Their three other Olympic boxing medalists, all **bronze medal** winners, are flyweight Kinoshi Tanabe, 1960, and bantamweights Eiji Morioka, 1968, and Satoshi Shimizu, 2012.

The first Japanese **professional** world champion was **flyweight** Yoshio Shirai, who defeated Dado Marino in Tokyo on 19 May 1952 by **unanimous decision** to win the world's flyweight championship. Other excellent Japanese boxers include **International Boxing Hall of Fame** inductee **Masahiko "Fighting" Harada** (world's flyweight and bantamweight champion, 1962–1967); Hiroyuki Ebihara (world's flyweight champion, 1963–1964); Yoko Gushiken (**World Boxing Association [WBA] light flyweight** champion, 1976–1981, 14 successful title defenses); Shoji Oguma (world's flyweight champion, 1974–1975, 1980–1981); Masao Ohba (WBA flyweight champion, 1970–1973, died in an automobile accident while still champion); "Guts" Ishimatsu Suzuki (**World Boxing Council [WBC] lightweight** champion, 1974–1976); Masamori Tokuyama (WBC **super flyweight** champion, 2000–2106); and Jiro Watanabe (WBA super flyweight champion, 1982–1986, made 11 successful title defenses).

Joe Koizumi has been Japan's most noted boxing writer and has been elected to the International Boxing Hall of Fame. Promoter Akihiko Honda was also elected to that hall.

JEANNETTE, JEREMIAH "JOE". B. 26 August 1879, North Bergen, New Jersey. D. 2 July 1958, Weehawken, New Jersey. Had Joe Jeannette lived at another time or had his skin been another color, he might be remembered as one of the great boxing champions. As it is, though, being black at the beginning of the 20th century limited his options as a professional boxer.

His first recorded professional **bout** was on 11 November 1904, a four-**round** no-decision **newspaper decision** loss to Morris Harris. Although records of boxers in that era, especially black boxers, are notoriously incomplete, his next fights were also losses. In his fourth recorded bout, he went three rounds with the future **heavyweight** champion **Jack Johnson**, and the bout was called a draw.

Most of Jeannette's bouts were against other black fighters, and he fought fighters such as Harris, Johnson, Black Bill, George Cole, **Sam Langford**, Young Peter Jackson, Sam McVey, **Harry Wills**, and Battling Jim Johnson numerous times.

In 1909, Jeannette traveled to Europe and won seven of eight fights in London and Paris. His only loss was to Sam McVey in Paris on 20 February on a 20-round decision. The two combatants were rematched on 17 April in a **fight to the finish**. The bout, one of the all-time greatest in **ring** history, saw Jeannette knocked down 27 times in the early rounds but recover and knock McVey down 11 times before McVey finally had enough and retired in the 49th round. The total of 38 combined **knockdowns** has been printed in various sources, but a modern attempt at locating contemporary sources has been unable to find enough details to corroborate the knockdown figure. The bout, though, was a classic, with both fighters giving their all. As a result of the victory, Jeannette claimed the "colored world heavyweight title." This designation was ironic, insofar as the world's heavyweight championship was owned by a black man, **Jack Johnson**, but as he refused to defend his title against the top black heavyweights it was felt to be justified.

Jeannette faced Sam Langford at least 14 times, winning three, losing four, drawing two, and fighting five no-decision bouts. He also faced Jack Johnson nine times (all prior to Johnson winning the title), winning one, losing two, and fighting two draws and five no-decision bouts.

Jeannette did fight a few white fighters and scored victories over Porky Dan Flynn, Al Kubiak, George "Boer" Rodel, Bartley Madden, Arthur Pelkey, Tony Ross, and future **light heavyweight** champion **Georges Carpentier.**

Jeannette's last recorded bout occurred on 1 June 1922, a six-round draw. In retirement, he owned a gymnasium in Union City, New Jersey, and helped to train young boxers, one of them being future heavyweight champion **Jim Braddock.** Jeannette also owned a rental limosine and taxi company and occasionally worked as a boxing **referee.**

Jeannette was five foot 10 inches tall and fought at weights ranging from 180 to 204 pounds as a heavyweight. In 166 professional bouts, from 1904 to 1922, he won 81 (68 by **knockout**), lost 10 (two by knockout), had 10 draws, and fought seven **no contests** and 58 no-decision bouts, in which he was awarded the newspaper decision in 34, lost 15, and drew nine. He fought a total of 1,232 rounds. He was inducted into the **International Boxing Hall of Fame** in 1997.

JEFFRIES, JAMES JACKSON "JIM," "THE BOILERMAKER". B. 15 April 1875, Carroll, Ohio. D. 3 March 1953, Burbank, California. James J. Jeffries is regarded as one of the greatest **heavyweight** champions in history, yet he is largely remembered today for the only loss he suffered in his boxing career.

He was born in Ohio, but as a youth his family moved to Los Angeles, California, where he was raised. A strong six-foot-tall 200-pounder as a teenager, he worked at jobs that took advantage of his sturdy physique.

He worked in neighboring mining camps, shoveled coal for the Santa Fe railroad, and worked as a boilermaker, fabricating steel for use in industry. He did some boxing with coworkers as a hobby.

In September 1895, he met Hank Griffin, an itinerant boxer who traveled to mining camps offering to box anyone. Jeffries was encouraged to try his skill against Griffin but found Griffin much too cagey for him. Jeffries, though, landed a lucky punch and won the fight and the winner's share of the purse.

Encouraged by this, he decided to try his luck in the prize **ring** and traveled to San Francisco, where there was more of an opportunity. There he fought 20-**round draws** with two of the best fighters of the era, Joe Choynski and Gus Ruhlin. In 1898, Jeffries defeated the black **Australian** fighter **Peter Jackson**, another of the era's great fighters. After **knockout** victories over Mexican Pete Everett and Tom Sharkey, Jeffries went to New York.

In New York, after defeating Bob Armstrong, Jeffries fought heavyweight champion **Bob Fitzsimmons** in a title **bout**. Jeffries, at 205 pounds, knocked out the much smaller Fitzsimmons (167 pounds) on 9 June 1899 in Coney Island and became world's heavyweight champion. Jeffries made his first title defense in November, winning a 25-round decision over Tom Sharkey.

Jeffries's next defense was against Jack Finnegan in Detroit, Michigan, on 6 April 1900. Finnegan was no match for Jeffries, who knocked him down with the first blow of the fight and knocked him out at 0:55 of the first round.

One month later, on 11 May in Coney Island, Jeffries defended against the former heavyweight champion **Jim Corbett**. In an evenly contested bout with Corbett holding a slight advantage, Jeffries caught Corbett in the 23rd round and knocked him out.

Jeffries then returned to San Francisco and stopped Gus Ruhlin in five rounds in November 1905 and knocked out Fitzsimmons in a rematch on 25 July 1902. The following year, he again defeated Corbett, this time stopping him in the 10th round. One year after that, on 26 August 1904, he knocked out Jack Munroe in just 45 seconds of the second round.

Feeling that there was no competition left, Jeffries retired as undefeated champion and named **Marvin Hart** and Jack Root to fight for the heavyweight title, with Jeffries acting as **referee**. On 3 July 1905, that bout took place in Reno, Nevada, with Hart winning on a 12th-round knockout.

Hart lost the title to **Tommy Burns** and Burns lost to **Jack Johnson**. Johnson, a black man, flaunted many of the mores of integrated society of the era, and while an exceptional boxer, had many people clamoring for a white man to defeat him, looking for a "**white hope**," in the terminology of the day.

Jeffries felt it incumbent upon himself to take up this challenge. Although out of shape, weighing nearly 300 pounds, and out of competition for nearly six years, he accepted promoter **Tex Rickard's** offer of a $101,000 purse (which was agreed by the two boxers to be split 60 percent to the winner and 40 percent to the loser) to fight Johnson in Reno, Nevada, on 4 July 1910.

The scheduled 45-round bout took place in a specially constructed arena before 15,760 fans, with Rickard acting as referee after U.S. President William Howard Taft declined the offer to referee the bout. Johnson won when he knocked Jeffries down three times in the 15th round before Jeffries's seconds stepped in to stop the fight.

Jeffries retired to his alfalfa farm in California and later bred prize cattle. He set up a boxing ring in a barn, worked as a **trainer**, and promoted bouts. He also refereed quite a few. He ran into financial difficulties in 1923 and declared bankruptcy. He also toured in vaudeville with Tom Sharkey, giving boxing **exhibitions**. His barn was later moved to the Knott's Berry Farm amusement park in California and for a time housed a boxing museum. Upon the death of the museum's director, the facility reverted to a china doll display, with just a small plaque on the wall reminding visitors that this was once Jim Jeffries's barn.

Jeffries was six feet tall and had a **reach** of 76 inches. He fought at weights ranging from 201 to 240 pounds as a heavyweight. In 23 professional bouts, from 1895 to 1910, he won 19 (16 by knockout), lost one by knockout, had two draws and one **no contest**, and fought a total of 215 rounds. He was inducted as a member of the inaugural class of the **International Boxing Hall of Fame** in 1990.

JOE PALOOKA. The comic strip *Joe Palooka* began in 1930. It was a creation of cartoonist Hammond Edward "Ham" Fisher and featured the clean-living, good-looking, all-American boxer Joe Palooka from Wilkes-Barre, Pennsylvania. Fisher apparently had met fighter Pete Latzo in Wilkes-Barre and, impressed by his personality, a big, good-natured prizefighter who didn't like to fight, modeled his cartoon character after him. Other regulars in the strip included Joe's manager Knobby Walsh, Joe's fiancée society girl Ann Howe (whom Joe later married), and Joe's friend but one-time **ring** opponent, the 500-pound blacksmith Humphrey Pennyworth from West Wokkington Falls, Ohio, who rode around in a special vehicle called the Humphreymobile—a three wheeled motorized vehicle with a small square building behind the driver's seat where Humphrey kept his snacks.

The strip was one of the era's most successful and during the 1930s appeared in more than 600 newspapers with more than 50 million readers. It also resulted in a 1934 feature film, a series of nine short films, 11 more feature films, a radio series, and a 1954 television series. Although Fisher died in 1955, the strip was continued by his associates and lasted until 1984.

JOFRE, ÉDER ZUMBANO "GALINHO DE OURO," "JOFRINHO". B. 26 March 1936, São Paulo, **Brazil**. Éder Jofre is Brazil's greatest boxer, and many boxing authorities consider him to be the greatest **bantamweight** of all time. He is also rated by some as the second best pound-for-pound boxer in history, second only to **"Sugar Ray" Robinson**.

He was born into a boxing family as his father owned a gymnasium in São Paulo and his mother supervised the facility. Éder reportedly had a dozen **relatives** who were involved in boxing or wrestling. As an amateur boxer, he claimed 150 fights with only two losses. One came when he competed for Brazil in the 1956 **Olympic Games** bantamweight class and after winning one **bout** was defeated in the quarterfinal round by Chilean Claudio Barrientos, who would win the **silver medal**. Four years later, as a professional boxer, Jofre avenged that defeat with an eighth-round **technical knockout** of Barrientos.

Éder made his **professional boxing** debut on 28 March 1957 with a fifth-round **knockout** of Raúl López in São Paulo. After winning his first seven bouts, Jofre fought two 10-round draws with Ernesto Miranda. Jofre's record after his first 31 bouts was 28–0–3, and on 19 January 1960 he won the South American bantamweight championship by defeating Miranda on a 15-round **unanimous decision** in São Paulo. He knocked out Miranda in three rounds in a rematch three months later and then came to the **United States**. After defeating Joe Medel in Los Angeles on 18 August 1960 on a 10th-round knockout, he fought the Mexican Eloy Sánchez for the **vacant National Boxing Association** world bantamweight championship on 18 November 1960 in Los Angeles. Jofre knocked out Sánchez in the sixth round and became champion.

Over the next four and a half years, Jofre had 12 bouts and won them all by knockout, including eight title defenses. He defended his title against Piero Rollo in Brazil, Ramón Arias in **Venezuela**, Johnny Caldwell in Brazil, Herman Marques in California, Joe Medel in Brazil, Katsutoshi Aoki in **Japan**, Johnny Jamito in the **Philippines**, and Bernardo Caraballo in **Colombia**.

On 31 May 1966, Jofre lost his title on a **split decision** to **Masahito "Fighting" Harada** in Tokyo, Japan. One year later, Harada gave Jofre a rematch and retained his title on a unanimous decision in Tokyo. Jofre then retired from the ring.

Three years later, on 29 August 1969, Jofre came out of retirement at the age of 33. He won 14 straight bouts over the next three years, fighting exclusively in São Paulo. On 5 May 1973, he won the **World Boxing Council featherweight** championship on a 15-round majority over the **Cuban Spaniard** José Legrá in Brasilia, Brazil. He only defended it once (against Vicente Saldivar on 21 October 1973 in Brazil) and then retired, surrendering his title. He made another brief comeback in 1975 and 1976, winning seven fights in Brazil before permanently retiring. In retirement, he has worked as a **trainer** and has investments in Brazil.

Jofre is five foot four inches tall and has a **reach** of 66 inches. He fought at weights ranging from 116 to 125 pounds as a bantamweight and featherweight. In 78 professional bouts, from 1957 to 1976, he won 72 (50 by knockout), lost two (none by knockout), had four draws, and fought a total of 554 rounds. He was inducted into the **International Boxing Hall of Fame** in 1992.

JOHANSSON, JENS INGEMAR "INGO". B. 22 September 1932, Gothenburg, Sweden. D. 30 January 2009, Kungsbacka, Sweden. Ingemar Johansson is one of the very few Scandinavian boxers to leave a lasting legacy. Although he had only 28 **professional bouts**, with only three in the **United States**, those three contributed strongly to boxing history.

Johansson is one of the few fighters whose **amateur** career is well documented. Details of each of his 71 amateur fights (61 wins, 10 losses) are listed in the appendix to his 1960 autobiography *Seconds Out of the Ring*. His amateur record included a second place in the 1952 **Olympic Games heavyweight** competition. That bout had a controversial ending as Johansson was disqualified by the **referee** in the second **round** of his bout with Ed Sanders for not being aggressive. Johansson later claimed that the referee misunderstood his tactics as he planned to have Sanders tire himself out by chasing him for two rounds before Johansson would then attack his tired opponent. As a result of his **disqualification**, Johansson did not receive the **silver medal**. (Thirty years later, it was finally given to him.)

Although Johansson considered quitting the sport, he was talked into becoming a professional by boxing promoter Edwin Ahlqvist, who became his manager. Johansson's first professional fight took place on 5 December 1952, and he knocked out Robert Masson in four rounds in his hometown of Gothenburg. In his fourth fight, Johansson won the Scandinavian heavyweight championship on a six-round decision over Erik Jensen in Copenhagen, Denmark. This was one of only six fights that Johansson fought outside of Sweden. Johansson continued winning and with a record of 14–0 faced Franco Cavicchi for the European Boxing Union (EBU) heavyweight championship on 30 September 1956 in Bologna, **Italy**. He knocked out Cavicchi in 13 rounds and became EBU heavyweight champion. He successfully defended his title with a fifth-round **knockout** of Englishman Henry Cooper in 1957 and 13th round **technical knockout** of Welshman Joe Erskine in 1958.

On 14 September 1958, Johansson fought the top-rated **Eddie Machen**, who was then undefeated with a record of 24–0–1. Johansson knocked Machen down three times in the first round, with the final **knockdown** being for the 10 count. This brought Johansson worldwide attention, he was named "Fighter of the Year" by *Ring* **magazine**, and he was matched with heavyweight champion **Floyd Patterson** in a title bout on 26 June 1959 at Yankee Stadium in New York.

He came to New York to train for the fight, and his easygoing, casual manner of **training** in contrast to the spartan-style employed by Patterson caused sportswriters to not give him much of a chance. He entered the **ring** as a 5–1 underdog. To everyone's surprise, he caught Patterson in the third round with a sharp right hand and floored him. Patterson got up and was knocked down six more times in that round before the fight was halted by referee **Ruby Goldstein** at 2:03 of the third round.

The good-looking Johansson enjoyed his celebrity status and was featured on several magazine covers and television shows in the United States. He appeared in a televised dramatic production of *The Killers*, a remake of a 1946 film starring Burt Lancaster about a Swedish ex-boxer based on an

Ernest Hemingway short story. Johansson, naturally, played "The Swede," one of the leading roles in the story. Johansson also had a minor part in a 1960 Hollywood war film, *All the Young Men.*

He fought a rematch with Patterson almost one year to the day after their first fight, also outdoors in New York, but this time at the Polo Grounds. The result was entirely different, as Patterson caught Johansson with a left **hook** in the fifth round and knocked him out unconscious to become the first man to regain the heavyweight championship.

Patterson promised him a rematch, which took place on 13 March 1961 in Miami Beach. In this bout, both fighters had their chances. Johansson knocked Patterson down twice in the first round, but Patterson recovered and knocked Johansson down at the end of that round. Patterson then knocked out Johansson in the sixth round and retained his title.

Johansson had four more fights in Sweden in 1962 and 1963, including a defense of his European Boxing Union heavyweight title with an eight-round knockout of Dick Richardson. In his final bout, on 21 April 1963, against Brian London, he was leading throughout the fight but was knocked down with four seconds remaining in the fight. He was awarded the victory on points but the next day retired from the ring.

In retirement, he did well for himself, promoting several fight **cards** and owning a fishing boat and a bar. He also became quite friendly with Patterson, and they would socialize fairly often. During the 1970s, he became interested in marathon running and ran several, including the Boston and New York marathons. He even had Patterson join him in the Stockholm marathon in 1982 and 1983. Ironically, both he and Patterson became afflicted with Alzheimer's disease toward the end of the century and succumbed to its effects, Patterson in 2006 and Johansson in 2009.

Johansson was six feet tall and had a **reach** of 72 inches. He fought at weights ranging from 193 to 206 pounds as a heavyweight. In 28 professional bouts, from 1952 to 1963, he won 26 (17 by knockout), lost two (both by knockout), and fought a total of 173 rounds. He was inducted into the **International Boxing Hall of Fame** in 2002.

JOHNSON, JOHN ARTHUR "JACK," "LI'L ARTHUR," "GALVESTON GIANT". B. 31 March 1878, Galveston, Texas. D. 10 June 1946, Raleigh, North Carolina. Jack Johnson did more to set back racial progress than anyone else in history. His flamboyant style and his flaunting of the customs of his era antagonized the white public and had nearly all of them rooting against him.

As was the case for most of the black boxers of the early 20th century, many of his **bouts** were not well documented. His first recorded bout was on 1 November 1897 in Galveston and was billed for the Texas State **middle-**

weight title. Johnson knocked out Charley Brooks in two **rounds**. The following year, Johnson was stopped in five rounds in Chicago by a fighter known as Klondike, who then claimed the "colored **heavyweight** title."

In 1901, Johnson was knocked out in three rounds by white heavyweight Joe Choynski in Galveston. After the bout, the two men were arrested for taking part in an illegal prizefight. While they were in jail, the sheriff had the two men spar for the benefit of local citizens, who gathered nightly to watch these sessions. After three weeks, the two were released. Johnson later claimed that this is where he developed his boxing abilities.

In 1902, Johnson traveled to California, and among his victories there was a five round **knockout** of Jack Jeffries, the brother of future heavyweight champion **Jim Jeffries**. Among Johnson's wins in California were ones over George Gardner, Denver Ed Martin (as a result of which Johnson claimed the "colored heavyweight title"), and Sam McVey.

In 1905, Johnson lost a 20-round decision to **Marvin Hart**. Hart would win the world's heavyweight title four months later. Over the next few years, Johnson scored victories over former heavyweight champion **Bob Fitzsimmons**, Fireman Jim Flynn, **Sam Langford**, Young Peter Jackson, and **Joe Jeannette**. He defeated Jeannette four times in seven bouts.

In December 1908, Johnson traveled to **Australia** for a bout that would change the course of boxing history. On **Boxing Day** (26 December), he won the world's heavyweight championship by defeating **Tommy Burns** in a bout that was stopped by police in the 14th round. Since Johnson was ahead on the referee's scorecard, he was awarded the **decision** and the title.

Johnson made his first title defense against **Philadelphia Jack O'Brien** in Philadelphia in May 1909. The bout went the six-round no-decision limit and was labeled a **draw** by the newspapers. His next defense, one month later, was also a six-round no-decision bout with Tony Ross, in which Johnson received the **newspaper decision**. Johnson then went west to California and fought a 10-round no-decision bout with Al Kaufman.

On 16 October 1910, Johnson faced former middleweight champion **Stanley Ketchel** in Colma, California. Reportedly, the two had agreed before the bout to box the full 20 rounds so that the films of the bout would draw more paying fans to see them. In the 12th round, however, Ketchel thought he spotted an opening and knocked down Johnson. Johnson rose angered and with a three-punch combination knocked out his adversary.

Johnson's arrogance in his public life and his penchant for expensive cars, jewelry, and white women were strongly in defiance of the mores of the era, and a public demand for a "**white hope**" to restore the heavyweight championship to the Caucasian race led former undefeated heavyweight champion Jim Jeffries to come out of retirement and challenge Johnson for the title. Although out of shape, weighing nearly 300 pounds, and out of competition for nearly six years, he accepted promoter **Tex Rickard**'s offer of a

$101,000 purse (which was agreed by the two boxers to be split 60 percent to the winner and 40 percent to the loser) to fight Johnson in Reno, Nevada, on 4 July 1910.

The scheduled 45-round bout took place in a specially constructed arena before 15,760 fans, with Rickard acting as referee after U.S. President William Howard Taft declined the offer to referee the bout. Johnson won when he knocked Jeffries down three times in the 15th round before Jeffries's seconds stepped in to stop the fight. After the results of the fight were spread across the country, race rioting occurred with at least a dozen people, both black and white, killed and hundreds injured. Another result of the fight was that Congress passed a law prohibiting the transportation of fight films across state lines to minimize the number of people who could see films of a black man beating a white man.

Johnson did not fight for two years, with his next defense against Fireman Jim Flynn in Las Vegas, New Mexico, on 4 July 1912. The bout was stopped by police in the ninth round with Johnson ahead.

Over the next few months, Johnson's life would change dramatically. With extreme anti-Johnson sentiment guiding the nation's actions, he was arrested on 18 October 1912 for violating the Mann Act for "transporting women across state lines for immoral purposes" since his fiancée at the time, Lucille Cameron, was a white woman accused of being a prostitute. She refused to testify against him, and the case fell apart. The government continued to hound him, and a second offense was found, this time with a former girlfriend of Johnson's, Belle Schreiber. In June 1913, Johnson was convicted by an all-white jury and sentenced to a year and a day in prison. Although the Mann Act was only passed on 25 June 1910, Johnson was convicted for acts committed prior to its passage. Clearly, the government was out to get him to "show him his place."

Johnson skipped bail and fled the country, living in Europe and later South America, and did not return until 1920. In the meantime, he continued boxing and was still recognized as the world's heavyweight champion.

Ironically, while some white boxers in that era drew the color line and refused to defend their title against a black boxer, so did Johnson, who claimed that a fight between two black men would not draw fans to see it. Johnson thus never allowed several of that era's top fighters, such as **Sam Langford**, **Joe Jeannette**, or Sam McVey, to fight for the title, even though he had fought all three prior to his winning the title.

On 19 December 1912 in Paris, **France**, he did make his only title defense against another black fighter, Battling Jim Johnson. The fight went the 10-round distance and was called a **draw**, although Jack apparently broke a bone in his arm early in the bout and neither man did much in the **ring** afterward. Remaining in France, Johnson made one more title defense in Europe, winning a 20-round decision over Frank Moran in Paris on 27 June in a bout **refereed** by the 20-year old future **light heavyweight** champion **Georges Carpentier**.

Johnson's career turned again in 1915. He agreed to defend his title against the six-foot-six-inch, 238-pound giant **Jess Willard** outdoors in Havana, **Cuba**, in a scheduled 45-round bout on 5 April. Johnson appeared to be well ahead in the bout but in the 26th round was knocked down and counted out. In later years, he claimed that he threw the bout, although his claim has not been taken seriously by boxing historians.

Johnson remained away from the **United States** and fought several bouts in **Spain** and **Mexico** before surrendering to U.S. authorities at the Mexican border on 20 July 1920. He served time at the Leavenworth, Kansas, federal penitentiary and was released on 9 July 1921. While in prison, he created some modifications to a wrench and successfully patented it in April 1922.

He continued boxing sporadically in Cuba, **Canada**, Mexico, and the midwestern United States until 28 April 1931, although the caliber of opponents was poor and the bouts were often not much more than **sparring exhibitions**. His last appearance in the ring was on 27 November 1945, when at the age of 67 he sparred three one-minute rounds on a benefit **card** for U.S. War Bonds. He died on 10 June 1946 in an automobile crash near Raleigh, North Carolina, after being refused service at a local diner.

Several excellent stories have been made of his life. The 1967 Tony Award–winning play *The Great White Hope* was made into a 1970 film. In 2005, filmmaker Ken Burns produced an excellent documentary about Johnson entitled *Unforgivable Blackness: The Rise and Fall of Jack Johnson*.

Johnson was six feet tall and had a **reach** of 74 inches. He fought at weights ranging from 168 to 242 pounds as a heavyweight. In 93 recorded professional bouts, from 1897 to 1931, Johnson won 53 (34 by knockout), lost 11 (six by knockout), had nine draws, had three **no contests**, and fought 17 no-decision bouts, in which he was awarded the newspaper decision in 14 and drew in three. He fought a total of 815 rounds. He was inducted as a member of the inaugural class of the **International Boxing Hall of Fame** in 1990.

JONES, RALPH "TIGER". B. 14 March 1928, Brooklyn, New York. D. 17 July 1994, Jamaica, New York. Ralph "Tiger" Jones was one of the mainstays of **televised boxing** during the 1950s. He possibly appeared on network television more than any other fighter during that time. He was a steady, unspectacular fighter without a **knockout** punch who met all the top **middleweights** and would put on 10 **rounds** of action.

He made his **professional** debut on 27 May 1950, winning a four-round **bout** by **decision**, and was undefeated in 1950, winning all nine of his fights. His scorecard for 1951 was eight victories in 11 bouts with one **draw**. In his first bout that year, he lost on a first-round **technical knockout** when he suffered a badly cut eye early in the bout. This would be his only loss short of the distance in his 13-year career. In 1952, he also fought 11 bouts with seven wins, three losses, and one draw. Included among his victories that year was a 10-round decision over former world's **welterweight** champion Johnny Bratton. The next year, 1953, saw Jones fight nine times, winning six, boxing one draw, and losing to Rocky Castellani and welterweight champion **Kid Gavilán** in a **nontitle** match.

After four years of boxing and 40 bouts, Jones had a record of 30–7–3. Over the next nine years, his record would be almost even, with 22 victories, 25 losses, and two draws, but he fought virtually every top contender during that time.

He began 1954 with one of his most dramatic victories. After being well behind in points against Bobby Dykes, Jones rallied and knocked Dykes down twice in the 10th round and scored one of his rare knockouts when the bout was stopped at 2:12 of that round. After winning a decision in his next bout, Jones finished the year by losing five consecutive decisions, with future middleweight champion **Joey Giardello** being one of Jones's victorious opponents.

The biggest win of Jones's career came in his next bout. After losing five straight decisions, he met **"Sugar Ray" Robinson**, one of the greatest boxers in **ring** history. Going into the fight, Robinson had a record of 132–3–2. Jones won nearly every round of the bout (with the officials' scorecards reading 100–88, 99–94, and 98–89) and won a **unanimous decision**. This was only the fourth loss in Robinson's career.

In Jones's next fight, however, he was nearly shut out as middleweight champion **Carl "Bobo" Olson** won nearly every round of their nontitle bout. Later that year, former welterweight champion Johnny Saxton won a unanimous decision over Jones, and the following year future middleweight champion **Gene Fullmer** did likewise. Jones did win a disputed **split decision** over European middleweight champion Charles Humez in 1956. In 1957, Jones lost return bouts to both Fullmer and Giardello. In 1958, Jones split two bouts with Kid Gavilán. In 1959, he fought only four bouts, but one was a unanimous decision over Giardello and another was a loss to future middleweight champion Paul Pender. Jones continued his boxing career until 21 March 1961, when **Olympic** triple **gold medalist** and European middleweight champion László Papp defeated him in Vienna, Austria, in a bout in which Jones was knocked down three times but on his feet at the end of 10 rounds.

Jones never took part in a world championship bout, although he fought eight fighters, Johnny Bratton, Kid Gavilán, Johnny Saxton, Joey Giardello, Ray Robinson, Bobo Olson, Gene Fullmer, and Paul Pender, who were world champions at one point of their careers.

In retirement, Jones was a taxicab driver and worked for a canning company.

Jones was five foot eight inches tall and fought at weights ranging from 149 to 162 pounds as a middleweight. In 89 professional bouts, from 1950 to 1962, he won 52 (13 by knockout), lost 32 (one by knockout), had five draws, and fought a total of 751 rounds.

JONES, ROY LEVESTA, JR. B. 16 January 1969, Pensacola, Florida. Roy Jones Jr. holds several unique distinctions among boxers. He is the only man to play **professional** basketball during the afternoon and compete in a boxing match that same night. He is also the only fighter since **Bob Fitzsimmons** in the 19th century to win both the **middleweight** and **heavyweight** championships.

Roy is a graduate of Washington High School in Pensacola and attended Pensacola Junior College. Roy's father, Roy Jones Sr., was a former professional boxer who had a gym in Pensacola and led his son into the world of boxing. As an **amateur** boxer, Roy Jr. won the 1984 **United States** National Junior Olympics and the 1986 and 1987 National **Golden Gloves** titles, moving up in weight class from **bantamweight** in 1984 to **light middleweight** in 1987. He was the **United States** light middleweight entrant in the 1988 **Olympic Games** and won a **silver medal**. He lost in the final to **Korean** Park Si-Heon in one of the worst decisions in Olympic boxing history. In the unofficial **Compubox** punch count, Jones outpunched his opponent 86 to 32 and threw 303 punches to Park's 188. Three **judges** voted for Park and only two for Jones, but one of the three judges who voted for Park was quoted as saying, "The American won easily, so easily, in fact, that I was positive my four fellow judges would score the fight for the American by a wide margin. So I voted for the Korean to make the score only 4–1 for the American and not embarrass the host country." Jones won the **Val Barker Trophy** as the most outstanding boxer of the Olympic Games, only the third non-**gold medalist** to win the award. As a result of the **bout**, the scoring system was changed for the 1992 Olympic boxing tournament.

Jones began boxing as a professional on 6 May 1989 in Pensacola, Florida. After winning his first 21 bouts (20 by **knockout**, including his first 17 bouts), he won a 12-round **unanimous decision** over **Bernard Hopkins** for the **International Boxing Federation (IBF)** middleweight title on 22 May 1993 in Washington, DC. After one successful defense of that title, Jones then won the IBF **super middleweight** title by a unanimous decision over **James Toney** on 18 November 1994 in **Las Vegas**. Jones then defended that title five times.

In the summer of 1996, Jones played minor league professional basketball for the Jacksonville Barracudas, and on 15 June 1996 he scored six points in an afternoon game and that evening successfully defended his IBF super middleweight title with an 11th-round **technical knockout** of Eric Lucas.

On 22 November 1996, he defeated Mike McCallum on a unanimous 12-round decision to win the **World Boxing Council (WBC)** interim **light heavyweight** title. In his next fight, with Montell Griffin for the outright WBC light heavyweight title, Jones was disqualified in the ninth round for hitting Griffin while Griffin had one knee on the **canvas**. The two fought a rematch on 7 August 1997, and Jones knocked out Griffin in the first round to win the WBC light heavyweight championship.

Jones then knocked out former light heavyweight champion Virgil Hill in a **nontitle bout** and made 11 successful title defenses, picking up recognition from five other organizations in the process.

On 1 March 2003, Jones made boxing history by defeating John Ruiz for the **World Boxing Association** heavyweight title on a 12-round unanimous decision, even though he was outweighed by Ruiz 226 to 193. Jones became the first former middleweight champion to win the heavyweight championship since Fitzsimmons did it on 17 March 1897.

After winning that title, Jones returned to the light heavyweight division and defeated Antonio Tarver on 8 November 2003 to recapture the light heavyweight championship. Six months later, Jones suffered the first knockout loss in his career when Tarver stopped him in the second round to regain the light heavyweight title. Jones lost his next two fights—a ninth-round knockout at the hands of Glen Johnson for the IBF light heavyweight title and a 12-round unanimous decision loss to Tarver.

Jones rebounded and won his next three bouts, all nontitle, including a 12-round decision over former three-division champion **Félix Trinidad**. He then lost a 12-round nontitle decision to super middleweight champion **Joe Calzaghe**, won two bouts and then was stopped in the first round by Danny Green on 2 December 2009 in Sydney, **Australia**, for the International Boxing Organization **cruiserweight** title. Jones was then defeated by **Bernard Hopkins** on a 12-round **unanimous decision** in a nontitle bout and lost his third in a row when he was knocked out in the 10th round by Denis Lebedev in Moscow, **Russia**.

Jones continued to box and won a 10-round decision in 2011 and another split-round decision in Łódź, **Poland**, on 30 June 2012 at the age of 43.

Jones has also recorded several rap albums and has worked as a color analyst for **televised** fights.

Jones is five foot 11 inches tall and has a 74-inch **reach**. He has fought at weights ranging from 154 to 198 pounds in weight classes from middle-weight to heavyweight. In 64 professional bouts, from 1989 to 2012, he won 56 (40 by knockout), lost eight (four by knockout), and fought a total of 434 rounds.

JOURNEYMAN. A journeyman in boxing terminology is a fighter who has mediocre abilities and loses nearly as many fights as he wins. He usually has a crowd-pleasing style and lasts 10 or more years as a **professional** boxer, although he is seldom good enough to qualify for a championship **bout**. He is not in the category of "**palooka**" or "stiff" or "opponent," as those are terms for fighters who seldom win.

Tommy Tibbs, with a career record of 60 wins and 78 losses in 24 years of **professional boxing**, was a perfect example of the word.

The British fighter Peter Buckley could be considered a journeyman by some, but his won–loss record more accurately places him in the category of "opponent." Buckley competed in exactly 300 bouts from 1989 to 2008, winning just 32, losing 256, and drawing 12 in bouts from **featherweight** to **welterweight**. After his first two years of boxing, he had an acceptable record of 17–10–4 and won the **British Boxing Board of Control** Midlands Area **super featherweight** title, but then he went 15–246–8 over his next 18 years. He retired on 31 October 2008 after winning his last bout, the 300th total professional bout in his career. His last win prior to that bout was five years earlier, and he had been winless in his last 88 bouts with losing streaks of 37 and 47 interrupted by a **draw** decision.

JUDGES. Most boxing **bouts** are scored by a series of judges who sit at **ringside** and evaluate each boxer's skill. They keep a scorecard and assign points to each boxer after each round depending on the boxer's effective punching and defensive abilities. **Professional** bouts are usually scored by two judges and the **referee** or, in some jurisdictions, three judges. In bouts governed by the **British Boxing Board of Control**, only the referee scores the bout. **Amateur** bouts can be scored by as many as five judges.

See also SCORING SYSTEMS.

JUNIOR BANTAMWEIGHT. *See* SUPER FLYWEIGHT.

JUNIOR FEATHERWEIGHT. *See* SUPER BANTAMWEIGHT.

JUNIOR FLYWEIGHT. *See* LIGHT FLYWEIGHT.

JUNIOR LIGHT HEAVYWEIGHT. *See* SUPER MIDDLEWEIGHT.

JUNIOR LIGHTWEIGHT. *See* SUPER FEATHERWEIGHT.

JUNIOR MIDDLEWEIGHT. *See* LIGHT MIDDLEWEIGHT.

JUNIOR WEIGHT CLASSES. With the rise of boxing sanctioning organizations during the last half of the 20th century, additional weight classes have been added to the traditional eight weight classes. Weight limits in between those of the traditional ones have been used, and the classes have been termed "junior" classes. For example, a class with a 130-pound limit was added between the 126-pound **featherweight** division and the 135-pound **lightweight** division and was named "junior lightweight." Some boxing organizations do not use the term "junior" and prefer to call them "super" divisions, so the 130-pound class is known as "**super featherweight**" by those organizations.

See also APPENDIX D for a list of weight classes.

JUNIOR WELTERWEIGHT. *See* LIGHT WELTERWEIGHT.

K

K.O. *See* KNOCKOUT.

KAYO. *See* KNOCKOUT.

KAZAKHSTAN. Kazakhstan was one of the former Soviet Socialist Republics, and as such its athletes competed for the **Union of Soviet Socialist Republics** until 1992. It has since competed as an independent nation and sent boxing teams to the **Olympic Games** in each of the five tournaments from 1996 to 2012, winning medals in each of the five years.

During those five years, Kazakhstan has had one of the best Olympic boxing teams and won 17 medals—six **gold**, five **silver**, and six **bronze**. It has also had three individuals who won the **Val Barker Trophy** as the outstanding boxer in the Olympic Games. The gold medalists were Bekzat Sattarkhanov, 2000 **featherweight**, who was killed at the end of that year in an automobile accident; Bakhtiyar Artiyev, 2004 **welterweight**; Bakhyt Sarsekbayev, 2008 welterweight; Serik Sapiyev, 2012 welterweight; Yermakhan Ibramov, 2000 **light middleweight** and also 1996 bronze medalist; and Vasily Zhirov, 1996 **light heavyweight**. Other outstanding Kazakh Olympic boxers include Bolat Zhumadilov, who won silver medals in 1996 and 2000 as a **flyweight**, and Marina Volnova, who won a bronze medal in the **women's** light heavyweight class in 2012. Val Barker winners were Vassiliy Jirov, 1996; Bakhtiyar Artiyev, 2004; and Serik Sapiyev, 2012.

Professional Kazakh boxers who have won world championships are Anatoly Alexandrov, Gennady Golovkin, Vassiliy Jirov, and Beibut Shumenov

KEARNS, JACK "DOC" (né JOHN LEO McKERNAN). B. 17 August 1882, Waterloo, Michigan. D. 7 July 1963, Miami, Florida. Jack "Doc" Kearns lived an adventurous life. His father, John Philip McKernan, was also an adventurer and owned a gold mine in Montana, was a scout for General Custer, had a ranch in North Dakota, and moved his family, including young Jack, to Washington State via wagon train.

At the age of 15, Jack left home and went to the Klondike, where gold had just been discovered. He did not prospect but instead worked weighing gold dust and keeping accounts. Among his contemporaries also involved in the gold rush were writers Rex Beach and Jack London, lawman Wyatt Earp, and promoter **Tex Rickard**.

After returning to the continental **United States**, he worked as a ranch-hand, allegedly helped smuggle Chinese immigrants into the country, and boxed **professionally** as "Young Kid Kearns." In 1904, he got into a street brawl in Washington and spent a year in prison. He then went into the sand and gravel business.

In 1917, he met **Jack Dempsey**, then a raw unpolished boxer. Kearns became his manager and guided Dempsey to the world's **heavyweight** title. He remained with Dempsey for the million-dollar gate fight with **Georges Carpentier** and engineered a heavyweight title **bout** with Tommy Gibbons in Shelby, Montana, on 4 July 1923. Kearns got a $200,000 guarantee for Dempsey for the bout and $50,000 additional from the gate receipts. The town of Shelby could not come up with the money, and several banks closed as a result of the fiasco.

In 1925, Kearns signed a contract to manage **welterweight** champion **Mickey Walker**. The following year, Kearns and Dempsey had a falling out, and Kearns was able to concentrate his efforts on Walker and on Jackie Fields, another champion. Kearns also briefly managed **Benny Leonard** during Leonard's comeback in 1931.

In the 1940s and 1950s, Kearns managed **light heavyweight** champion **Joey Maxim** and then Maxim's successor as champion, **Archie Moore**.

Kearns died in his sleep in 1963 at the home of his son Jack, who in speaking of his father said, "He had the mind of a 21-year-old, but 80 years of living to the hilt gave him the body of a man of 125."

Kearns was inducted as a member of the inaugural class of the **International Boxing Hall of Fame** in 1990.

KELLY, JOHN EDWARD. *See* DEMPSEY, JACK "THE NONPAREIL" (né JOHN EDWARD KELLY).

KETCHEL, STANLEY "THE MICHIGAN ASSASSIN" (né STANIS-LAUS KIECAL). B. 14 September 1886, Grand Rapids, Michigan. D. 15 October 1910, Springfield, Missouri. During his relatively short life, Stanley Ketchel was one of the toughest, hardest-hitting **middleweights** and was not afraid to tackle much heavier fighters. He was voted by **ring** historian **Nat Fleischer** as the "best middleweight champion in history."

Ketchel had a difficult childhood and ran away from home as an adolescent, ending up in Montana. There he had various odd jobs, including one as a bouncer in a local saloon in Butte. He also reportedly took on all comers in barroom brawls. His first recorded **professional bout** occurred on 2 May 1903 in Butte, Montana, a bout that he won on a one-**round knockout**.

In 1907, he traveled to California, where he fought Joe Thomas in three successive bouts. The first in Marysville on 4 July was a 20-round draw. After the second, on 2 September in Colma, he claimed the **welterweight** title after knocking out Thomas in the 32nd round of their scheduled 45-round bout. The third bout was held on 12 December in San Francisco, and following a 20-round **decision**, Ketchel claimed the middleweight title as well.

In 1908, Ketchel defended his middleweight title claim by defeating both Sullivan twins in bouts in Colma. He knocked out Mike in one round on 22 February and Mike's twin brother, Jack, in 20 rounds on 9 May. He then traveled to Milwaukee, Wisconsin, where he defeated Billy Papke on 4 June on a 10-round decision in defense of his title. Returning to San Francisco, he knocked out Hugo Kelly in three rounds on 31 July in another bout with the title on the line.

Ketchel lost his middleweight title to Papke on 7 September 1908 in Vernon, California, when Papke stopped him in the 12th round in a bout **refereed** by former world's **heavyweight** champion **James J. Jeffries**. In a rematch two months later, on 26 November in Colma, Ketchel recaptured the middleweight title by knocking out Papke in 11 rounds.

In 1909, Ketchel fought four **nontitle bouts**, including two with **light heavyweight** champion **Philadelphia Jack O'Brien**. The bouts, while no-decision ones, ended with Ketchel receiving the **newspaper decision** in the first bout after knocking down O'Brien four times in the last two rounds. O'Brien was actually knocked out in the 10th round but was saved by the bell ending the fight. In their second meeting, Ketchel stopped O'Brien in three rounds. After a 20-round decision over Papke in defense of his middleweight title, Ketchel took on the world's heavyweight champion, **Jack Johnson**, in Colma on 16 October 1909.

The two boxers were friends and had a tacit agreement to box the full 20 rounds so that the films of the fight would have interest to the boxing public and earn them additional money. Ketchel, outweighed by Johnson 170 to 205 and four inches shorter, thought he saw an opening in the 12th round and knocked Johnson down. Johnson quickly rose in anger and proceeded to batter Ketchel with blows and knocked him out.

Ketchel had five bouts in 1910. He won three by knockout and fought no-decision bouts with future middleweight champion Frank Klaus and **Sam Langford**, losing the newspaper decision in the Langford bout and receiving a **draw** decision with Klaus.

Ketchel's hard-living life ended when he was shot in the back and killed on a farm in Conway, Missouri. Details of the story have never been completely clear, but it is known that a farmhand named Walter Dipley shot and killed Ketchel presumably in a dispute over a woman.

Ketchel was five foot nine inches tall and fought at weights ranging from 154 to 170 pounds in weight classes from middleweight to heavyweight. In 64 professional bouts, from 1903 to 1910, he won 51 (48 by knockout), lost four (two by knockout), and had four draws, one **no contest**, and four no-decision bouts, in which he received the newspaper decision in two, lost one, and drew one. He fought a total of 528 rounds and was inducted as a member of the inaugural class of the **International Boxing Hall of Fame** in 1990.

KICKBOXING. Kickboxing is a combat sport in which the contestants are permitted to use their bare feet to deliver blows.

See also MIXED MARTIAL ARTS; MUAY THAI; SAVATE.

KIECAL, STANISLAUS. *See* KETCHEL, STANLEY "THE MICHIGAN ASSASSIN" (né STANISLAUS KIECAL).

KILLION, JOHN JOSEPH. *See* KILRAIN, JAKE (né JOHN JOSEPH KILLION).

KILRAIN, JAKE (né JOHN JOSEPH KILLION). B. 9 February 1859, Greenpoint, New York. D. 22 December 1937, Quincy, Massachusetts. Jake Kilrain provides a bridge in **heavyweight** boxing history between **bareknuckle** fighting and the **Marquess of Queensberry Rules** of gloved fighting. He moved as a teenager to Somerville, Massachusetts, and worked in a mill. He was a champion oarsman and won the 1883 National **Amateur** Junior Sculling championship, although he later forfeited the award when it was found out that he had boxed **professionally**.

As with many bareknuckle boxers, exact details of many of their fights are unknown, but it was recorded that Kilrain knocked out Jack Daley early in 1879 in Somerville.

Richard K. Fox, owner and editor of the *National Police Gazette*, an influential boxing publication of the era, proclaimed Kilrain world's heavyweight champion in 1887, but this was primarily a ploy to draw **John L. Sullivan**, another title claimant, into a fight with Kilrain.

On 8 July 1889 in Richburg, Mississippi, the fight took place, and Kilrain and Sullivan fought in a bareknuckle **bout** under **London Prize Ring Rules**. Kilrain lost in 75 rounds over two hours and 16 minutes. After the fight, which was illegal in Mississippi at the time, the principles and **referee** were arrested and fined. This was the last heavyweight championship bout with bareknuckles.

Kilrain continued fighting gloved fights under Marquess of Queensberry Rules and lost a six-round bout in 1890 to **James J. Corbett**, future heavyweight champion and conqueror of Sullivan. On 13 March 1891, Kilrain defeated George Godfrey in 44 rounds in San Francisco, California. Kilrain's last recorded bout was on 20 October 1899 in Baltimore, when he was stopped in the fifth round by Steve O'Donnell.

In retirement, Kilrain owned a saloon in Baltimore and later became good friends with Sullivan.

Kilrain was five foot 10 inches tall and fought at weights ranging from 175 to 220 pounds as a heavyweight. In 48 professional bouts, from 1879 to 1899, he won 29 (17 by **knockout**), lost five (four by knockout), had 11 **draws** and three **no-contest** bouts, and fought a total of 337 rounds. He was inducted into the **International Boxing Hall of Fame** in 2012.

KING, DONALD "DON". B. 20 August 1931, Cleveland, Ohio. Don King has become one of boxing's most powerful men and is one of the top two boxing promoters (the other being **Bob Arum**), who have virtually controlled boxing during the last 30 years of the 20th century and first 10 years of the 21st century.

Before he got into boxing, he had built a substantial (if illegal) business as a bookmaker in Cleveland and controlled the numbers racket in that city. In 1954, he killed a man who had attempted to rob him and was set free as it was judged a justifiable homicide. In 1967, he killed another gambling associate and this time was sentenced to jail for manslaughter.

After serving nearly four years of his time, he was released in September 1971. In 1972, he arranged for **Muhammad Ali** to box an exhibition in Ohio to raise money for a black hospital that was in financial difficulties. The success of that promotion intrigued King, and he began promoting boxing in Ohio on a regular basis.

In 1974, he was a copromoter of the **Ali–Foreman heavyweight** title fight in Zaire, and after that success his promoting career spiraled. He promoted the 1975 **Ali–Frazier** title fight in the **Philippines** dubbed the **Thrilla in Manila**.

In 1977, one of his promotions backfired as he organized the **United States Championship Tournament**, presumably to give young American fighters a chance to progress to championship level. The tournament was abandoned, though, after four months when the American Broadcasting Company television network discovered that the tournament was not completely on the up and up. Some fighters' records were falsified, and other fighters were required to pay kickbacks in order to progress. Although investigations were made, no legal charges were ever filed, and although the tournament was abandoned, King continued to be a major boxing promoter.

In his dealings, he has always looked to gain the edge in negotiations. One example of his technique was a boxing **card** at **Madison Square Garden** in the mid-1980s. He advertised that one dollar of every ticket sold would go to help a particular charity. He then raised the normal admission prices so that $25 tickets were sold for $26 and $50 tickets had a price of $51.

As a result of always looking for a competitive advantage for himself, quite of a few of the boxers who have dealt with him have sued him. The list of fighters who have sued King reads like a who's who of boxing's best fighters during King's era. Among them are Muhammad Ali, **Larry Holmes**, **Mike Tyson**, Tim Witherspoon, Terry Norris, **Lennox Lewis**, and Chris Byrd.

Although many of the boxers who have had dealings with King have felt cheated by him, there is no denying the fact that he has helped to bring about multimillion-dollar **bouts** and that nearly 100 boxers have each earned in excess of a million dollars as a result of King's promotions.

King was also accused of tax evasion by the Internal Revenue Service in 1985, was accused of insurance fraud by Lloyds of London in 1995, and was investigated in 1992 by the United States Senate for alleged organized crime activities. Through it all, King has emerged unscathed. His secretary went to prison for the tax evasion charge, the Lloyds of London indictment ended in a hung jury, and the Senate investigation disclosed nothing.

In his 40 years of promoting boxing, King has promoted more than 500 world championship fights. He was inducted into the **International Boxing Hall of Fame** in 1997.

KLITSCHKO, VITALY VOLODOMYROVICH "DR. IRONFIST". B. 19 July 1971, Belovodsk, Kirghiz SSR, **Union of Soviet Socialist Republics**. Vitaly Klitschko is the older of two brothers who were recognized as world's **heavyweight** champions in the 21st century. He and his brother are also the only world champions to have received a PhD. He earned his in sports science from the Kiev University of Physical Science and Sports in 2000. In addition, he is also an avid chess player and is a friend of world chess champion Vladimir Kramnik.

The six-foot-seven-inch, 240-pound Klitschko first began as an **amateur** in the sport of **kickboxing**. He did well as an amateur boxer and claimed an amateur record of 195–15. He won the **super heavyweight gold medal** at the 1995 World Military Championships and the **silver medal** at the 1995 **World Championships** in the same class. He was a member of the **Ukraine** national boxing team but tested positive for a banned steroid in 1996 and was not allowed to compete with them in the 1996 **Olympic Games**. He was replaced on the team by his brother, **Wladimir Klitschko**, who then won the Olympic gold medal.

Vitaly's first professional **bout** took place on 16 November 1996 in Hamburg, **Germany**. As would be the case with his next 27 bouts, it was won by Klitschko via **knockout**. On 24 October 1998, Klitschko won the **vacant** European Boxing Union heavyweight title by stopping Mario Schiesser in the second **round** of their bout in Hamburg. He defended that title twice successfully and then won the **World Boxing Organization** heavyweight title by knocking out Herbie Hide in the second round in London, **England**, on 26 June 1999. In his third defense of that title, Klitschko suffered his first loss, as he retired after the ninth round due to a shoulder injury in his 1 April 2000 bout with Chris Byrd in Berlin, Germany.

In his next fight, Klitschko went the distance for the first time and won the European Boxing Union title by **decisioning** the previously undefeated (22–0) Timo Hoffmann in 12 rounds. After four more knockout victories, during which time he won the **World Boxing Association** Inter-Continental title, he fought **Lennox Lewis** in Los Angeles, California, on 21 June 2003 for the more respected **World Boxing Council (WBC)** heavyweight championship. Klitschko, ahead on points, suffered a very badly cut eye that required 60 stitches to repair when the fight was stopped after the sixth round. Lewis retired after that bout, and the title became vacant. On 24 April 2004 in Los Angeles, Klitschko stopped Corrie Sanders in the eighth round and won the WBC heavyweight title.

After one successful title defense, Klitschko underwent knee surgery and announced his retirement on 9 November 2005. The WBC named him "Champion Emeritus," which meant that should he desire to return to the **ring**, he would receive a championship bout.

Klitschko made a comeback in 2008 and defeated WBC champion Samuel Peter via retirement after eight rounds to regain his WBC title on 11 October in Berlin. Klitschko has since made nine successful title defenses through 2012.

Klitschko has a 79-inch **reach** and has fought at weights ranging from 232 to 252 pounds as a heavyweight. In 47 professional bouts, from 1996 to 2012, he won 45 (41 by knockout), lost two (two by retirement), and fought a total of 235 rounds.

KLITSCHKO, VOLODOMYR VOLODOMYROVICH "WLADI-MIR," "DR. STEELHAMMER". B. 25 March 1976, Semipalatinsk, Kazakh SSR, **Union of Soviet Socialist Republics**. Wladimir Klitschko is the younger brother of **Vitaly Klitschko**. Both boxers have won recognition as world's **heavyweight** champions and both have earned PhD degrees, with Wladimir obtaining his in sports science from the Kyiv University of Physical Science and Sports in 2001, one year after his brother.

Their father, Vladimir Rodinovich Klitschko, was an officer in the Soviet Union Air Force. He was one of the men responsible for cleaning up the effects of the 1986 Chernobyl nuclear disaster and died of cancer in 2011 after seeing both sons become heavyweight champions.

Wladimir had an outstanding amateur career and claims a record of 134–6. He won the **gold medal** in the heavyweight class at the 1993 Junior European Championships and 1995 World Military Championships. He was the heavyweight **silver medalist** at the 1994 Junior European Championships, the **super heavyweight** silver medalist at the 1996 European Championships, and won the 1996 **Olympic** gold medal in the super heavyweight class.

The six-foot-six-inch 220-pounder became a **professional** boxer on 16 November 1996 in Hamburg, **Germany**, with his brother also making his debut on the same **card**. Wladimir won his first 24 **bouts** with 21 **knockouts**, two **disqualifications**, and only one by **decision**. Included in those 24 bouts was one in which he won the **World Boxing Council (WBC)** International heavyweight title—a minor title.

He suffered his first loss on 5 December 1998 when he was stopped in the 11th **round** by Ross Puritty, a fighter with only a 24–13 record at the time. Klitschko rebounded and won his next four bouts by knockout. On 25 September 1999 in Cologne, Germany, he stopped Axel Schulz in eight rounds and won the European heavyweight title.

On 14 October 2000 in Cologne, he won the **World Boxing Organization (WBO)** heavyweight title on a 12-round **unanimous decision** over Chris Byrd. He then made five defenses of that title before Corrie Sanders stopped him in the second round. After two wins by knockout, Klitschko challenged Lamon Brewster on 10 April 2004 for the WBO title only to be stopped in the fifth round.

Through July 2013, Klitschko has won 18 straight bouts and has not lost since the Brewster bout. On 22 April 2006, he defeated Chris Byrd on a seventh-round **technical knockout** to win the **International Boxing Federation** heavyweight title. He added the WBO title on 23 February 2008 with a 12-round decision win over Sultan Ibragimov. With Klitschko's 12-round decision victory over David Haye on 2 July 2011, he captured the **World Boxing Association (WBA)** title and was called the WBA super world heavyweight champion since he was champion of three of the four major sanctioning organizations. His brother, Vitaly has been the WBC heavyweight champion since 11 October 2008, so all four heavyweight championships have belonging to the Klitschko brothers since July 2011. In 2012, Wladimir made three successful defenses of the multiple titles.

Klitschko has an 81-inch **reach** and has fought at weights ranging from 220 to 249 pounds as a heavyweight. In 62 professional bouts, from 1996 to 2012, he won 59 (50 by knockout), lost three (all three by knockout), and fought a total of 307 rounds.

KNOCKDOWN. If any portion of a boxer's body (except his **gloves**) touches the **canvas** during a round as a result of a blow by his opponent, the result is a knockdown. The scorekeepers (**referee** and/or **judges**) of a professional **bout** will usually credit the boxer knocking down his opponent with more points for the round, although under most **scoring systems** such action is not mandatory. (In recent years, the practice has been to penalize the boxer who was knocked down by deducting a point so that a close round will be scored 10–8 rather than 10–9). In **amateur boxing**, a knockdown is just considered an effective punch, and there is not a scoring premium as a result. Under many boxing jurisdictions, if a boxer is knocked down three times in one round, the match is automatically terminated.

KNOCKDOWN TIMEKEEPER. The **knockdown** timekeeper is a **ring** official whose main duty is to use a stopwatch and count to 10 in a loud voice (in modern-day fights using a microphone) when a fighter is knocked down and to ring a bell to indicate the start and end of each round. Usually, he also gives a warning 10 seconds prior to the start of a round via a whistle. One of the most famous was Fred Abbatiello, who worked most matches at **Madison Square Garden** for more than 30 years and has even been nominated to the **International Boxing Hall of Fame**.

KNOCKOUT. A knockout occurs in a boxing match when one boxer is knocked down and does not arise before the **referee** counts to 10. This is often written as Kayo or just K.O.
See also TECHNICAL KNOCKOUT (TKO).

KOREA. Boxing is one of the more popular sports in Korea. In **amateur boxing**, Korean boxers first competed in the 1948 **Olympic Games** and have entered 16 Olympic boxing tournaments—every one except 1980, when they boycotted the games. They have won 20 Olympic boxing medals, which places them in 12th among all nations in Olympic boxing. Both Kim Jeong-Ju (2004, 2008 **welterweight bronze**) and Lee Seong-Bae (1992 **middleweight** bronze and 1996 **light heavyweight silver**) have won two medals. Seoul, Korea, was the site of the 1988 Olympic Games and was the Olympic boxing tournament with the most entrants, 432, and the most countries, 106.

Other Korean medalists are **gold medalists** Kim Gwang-Seon, 1988 **fly-weight**; Park Si-Heon, 1988 **light middleweight**; and Sin Jun-Seop, 1984 middleweight. Silver medalists were Ji Yong-Ju, 1968 **light flyweight**; Song Sun-Cheon, 1956 **bantamweight**; Jeong Sin-Jo, 1964 bantamweight; Han Sun-Cheo, 2012 **lightweight**; An Yeong-Su, 1984 welterweight; and Baek Hyeon-Man, 1988 **heavyweight**. The other bronze medalists were Han Su-An, 1948 flyweight; Gang Jun-Ho, 1952 bantamweight; Jang Sun-Gil, 1968 bantamweight; Lee Jae-Hyeok, 1988 **featherweight**; Jo Seok-Hwan, 2004 featherweight; Jeon Chil-Syeong, 1984 lightweight; and Hong Syeong-Sik, 1992 lightweight.

There have been more than 40 Korean professional world champions. Among the best were In-Jin Chi, Yong-Soo Choi, Soo-Hwan Hong, Ki-Soo Kim (first Korean professional world champion), Sung-Kil Moon, Chan-Hee Park, Chong-Pal Park, Choi Yo-Sam, and **International Boxing Hall of Famers** Jung-Koo Chang and Myung-Woo Yuh.

L

LAMOTTA, GIACOBBE "JAKE," "THE BRONX BULL". B. 10 July 1921, Bronx, New York. Jake LaMotta was the first boxer to defeat **"Sugar Ray" Robinson** in a **professional bout**. That one victory would prove to be the exception, as Robinson won the other five bouts they had.

LaMotta began as a professional boxer on 3 March 1941. He won that fight and 12 of his next 13 fights, with a **draw** being the only nonwin. On 24 September 1941, he lost his first bout, a 10-round **split decision** to Jimmy Reeves in Cleveland, Ohio. LaMotta was way behind on points after the first seven **rounds**, but in the last three rounds the fight changed significantly. Reeves was **knocked down** in round nine and four times in round 10. After the decision was announced in favor of Reeves, a near riot broke out among the fans. One month later, the two fought a rematch, and Reeves more easily won a **unanimous decision**. The rest of that year and in 1942, LaMotta won most of his bouts and by 2 October 1942 had compiled a record of 25–4–2. On that day he fought the undefeated (35–0) two-time New York **Golden Gloves** champion "Sugar Ray" Robinson at **Madison Square Garden**. Robinson outboxed LaMotta and won a 10-round decision. The two boxers had a rematch a few months later in Detroit, Michigan, on 5 February 1943, and LaMotta handed Robinson his first professional defeat after 40 victories by winning a unanimous 10-round decision and knocking down Robinson in the eighth round. Less than one month later, on 26 February 1943 and again in Detroit, Robinson won the third match in their series by unanimous decision.

In June 1943, LaMotta began a series of bouts with the former world champion Fritzie Zivic. Over the course of seven months, the two met four times, with LaMotta winning a 10-round split decision on 10 June, losing a 15-round split decision on 12 July, winning a 10-round split decision on 12 November, and finally winning a unanimous decision on 14 January 1944.

LaMotta and Robinson fought for the fourth time on 23 February 1945, and Robinson won a 12-round unanimous decision.

After winning 12 of his next 14 fights, with a draw with Jimmy Edgar and a loss to Cecil Hudson the only nonwinning efforts, LaMotta fought "Blackjack" Billy Fox on 14 November 1947 at Madison Square Garden. Fox won on a fourth-round **technical knockout**. Prior to the fight, a fix was rumored, and betting odds changed drastically. Although the **New York State Athletic Commission** investigated the bout, no concrete evidence was found, and the fighters were exonerated. In subsequent years, LaMotta admitted he threw the fight, as he was promised a title bout if he did so.

On 16 June 1949, LaMotta received that title opportunity against **Marcel Cerdan**, a Frenchman who had recently won the title from **Tony Zale**. LaMotta stopped Cerdan in the 10th round and became world **middleweight** champion. The bout was Cerdan's last, as he was killed on 27 October 1949 in an airplane crash while en route to the United States for a rematch.

On 12 July 1950, LaMotta made the first defense of his title, winning a 15-round decision over Tiberio Mitri. On 13 September 1950, LaMotta was featured in the *Ring* **magazine** "Fight of the Year" when, losing a middleweight championship bout on points to French Canadian Laurent Dauthuille, he rallied and knocked out Dauthuille with just 13 seconds remaining in the bout.

In LaMotta's next bout, he fought Robinson again—this time with his middleweight title on the line. LaMotta took a beating in this fight, held in Chicago on 14 February 1951, which was finally stopped in the 13th round. The bout was subsequently referred to as the "St. Valentine's Day massacre." Over the next three years, LaMotta fought primarily as a **light heavyweight** but won just five of 10 bouts, losing four and drawing one.

His last fight was on 14 April 1954, when he lost a split decision to Billy Kilgore in Miami Beach.

In retirement, LaMotta remained in Miami Beach, where he ran a nightclub. He also became a stand-up comedian and appeared in over a dozen movies and television shows. His autobiography, *Raging Bull: My Story*, was published in 1970, and in 1980 a feature film starring Robert DeNiro based on the book and also titled *Raging Bull* was produced. The film is considered one of the best boxing movies and won the Academy Award for DeNiro. In 2008, the American Film Institute named it the best sports movie of all time.

LaMotta has remained active and in 2012 at the age of 91 appeared in an off-Broadway show about his career.

LaMotta's younger brother, Joey, boxed professionally in 1945 and 1946 and had a record of 32–5–2.

LaMotta is five foot eight inches tall and has a 67-inch **reach**. He has fought at weights ranging from 157 to 175 pounds, primarily as a middleweight. In 106 professional bouts, from 1941 to 1954, Jake LaMotta won 83 (30 by **knockout**), lost 19 (four by knockout), had four draws, and fought a total of 870 rounds. He was inducted as a member of the inaugural class of the **International Boxing Hall of Fame** in 1990.

LANE, MILLS BEE, III. B. 12 November 1936, Savannah, Georgia. Mills Lane, although a competent boxer, is best remembered as the **referee** in more than 90 world championship **bouts** and for his familiar phrase after giving the boxers their instructions, "Let's get it on!"

His grandfather founded the largest bank in Georgia, and his uncle was also a bank president. Lane was sent to the Middlesex School, a private secondary school in Massachusetts, but upon graduation in 1956 chose to enlist in the U.S. Marine Corps. He began boxing in the Marines and after being discharged enrolled at the University of Nevada, where he fought on their National Collegiate Athletic Association boxing team. He won the 1960 **welterweight** championship and became a **professional** boxer in 1961.

Although he won nine of his first 10 bouts, he decided to pursue other ventures and after graduating in 1963 with a business degree enrolled in law school at the University of Utah.

He began refereeing in 1964 in Nevada. He refereed his first world championship bout in 1971 when the **World Boxing Council (WBC)** sent him to Maracaibo, **Venezuela**, to officiate the Erbito Salavarria–Betulio González world's **flyweight** championship bout. Later that year, he worked the **Muhammad Ali–Bob Foster** bout in Nevada. On 9 June 1978, he refereed his first **heavyweight** world championship bout when **Larry Holmes** defeated **Ken Norton** for the WBC heavyweight title.

Lane then received more and more officiating assignments, resulting in his refereeing nearly 100 world championship bouts over the next 20 years.

In 1979, he was named the chief deputy sheriff of investigative services at the Washoe County Sheriff's Office in Nevada. In 1982, he was elected district attorney and in 1990 was elected district judge. As a judge, he became a television personality, and his court show, *Judge Mills Lane*, was televised from 1998 to 2001. He refereed his last bout on 6 November 1998 and concentrated on his court activity. He also began Let's Get It On Promotions but after promoting one boxing **card** suffered a major stroke in March 2002 and has been incapacitated since then. His sons Terry and Tommy have since continued the promotional venture.

Lane fought at weights ranging from 139 to 145 pounds as a welterweight. In 11 professional bouts, from 1961 to 1967, he won 10 (six by **knockout**), lost one (by knockout), and fought a total of 47 **rounds**. He was inducted as a member of the **International Boxing Hall of Fame** in 2013 as a nonparticipant.

LANGFORD, SAMUEL E. "SAM," "BOSTON TAR BABY". B. 4 March 1883, Weymouth Falls, Nova Scotia, **Canada**. D. 12 January 1956, Cambridge, Massachusetts. Sam Langford is often cited as the greatest boxer never to hold a world's championship. He fought at a time when black boxers did not often fight white fighters and whites often used the color barrier to avoid good black fighters. Langford was not a particularly big man, about five and a half feet tall, and when he began boxing was only a **lightweight**, although he gradually moved up to **heavyweight** with age.

As with many of the black boxers of his generation, not all of his fights have been well documented, and even though 317 of his **bouts** have been recorded, he most likely had quite a few more.

He fought most of his early fights in New England, with his first recorded bout on 11 April 1902 in Boston, Massachusetts. On 8 December 1903, he defeated another black fighter, lightweight champion **Joe Gans**, on a 15-**round decision** in a **nontitle bout**. On 29 July 1904, he knocked out the white fighter George "Elbows" McFadden in two rounds.

Langford's one opportunity to fight for a world title occurred on 5 September 1904 when he met the black fighter **Barbados Joe Walcott** for the world's **welterweight** title, owned by Walcott. The 15-round bout was scored a **draw**, and Walcott retained his title.

Langford, six inches shorter and 30 pounds lighter than his opponent, the future world's heavyweight champion **Jack Johnson**, fought for the "colored heavyweight title" but lost a 15-round decision on 26 April 1906.

In 1908, Langford traveled to **England** and fought Welshman James "Tiger" Smith in a bout billed for the "world's 158-pound **middleweight** title" at the **National Sporting Club** in London. Langford knocked out Smith in four rounds. He won a second bout while in England before returning to the **United States**.

Back in Massachusetts, Langford fought a 10-round no-decision bout with Larry Temple for the "colored 158-pound middleweight title." Three months later, Langford won a 20-round decision over Young Peter Jackson for that same title.

While Langford was mainly fighting other black boxers, on occasion he was matched with a white fighter. On 21 December 1908, he knocked out Fireman Jim Flynn in one round. Seven years later, Flynn knocked out **Jack Dempsey, the Nonpareil**, although there was some speculation as to the legitimacy of the Dempsey bout.

In 1909, Langford again traveled to London. On 24 May 1909, he knocked out a white Englishman William "Iron" Hague and won the "English heavyweight title." In 1910, Langford fought Fireman Jim Flynn twice, losing a **newspaper decision** in the first bout and knocking him out in one round in their second bout. Later that year, Langford won a six-round newspaper decision over former middleweight champion **Stanley Ketchel**.

In 1911, Langford defeated another of that era's great fighters, scoring a **technical knockout** over former world's **light heavyweight** champion **Philadelphia Jack O'Brien** in five rounds. In December of that year, Langford traveled to **Australia** along with Sam McVey. On **Boxing Day** (26 December) 1911, McVey won a 20-round decision over Langford for the Australian heavyweight title as well as the "colored heavyweight title." In April 1912, Langford defeated McVey on a 20-round decision and claimed those two titles. The two fought four more times in Australia in 1912 and 1913, and Langford won three with one draw.

Returning to the United States, Langford continued fighting frequently, although more often than not against other black fighters. Although the world's heavyweight champion at the time was Jack Johnson, another black fighter, he refused to give Langford a shot at the title, claiming that the public would not pay to see two black men fight for the world's heavyweight title. In reality, it was because he feared that Langford would defeat him.

In 1922, he went to **Mexico** and remained there for two years. On 31 March 1923, Langford knocked out Jack Savage in the first round and won the Mexican heavyweight title. He remained in Mexico until early 1924, then fought in California. His final recorded professional bout was on 2 August 1926, when he was stopped in the first round. In the last few years of his career, he was nearly blind and relied on fighting close to his opponents.

When he retired he was completely blind. He wound up living in Harlem in New York City in poverty. In 1944, a newspaper reporter found him and wrote about his plight. As a result, fans donated money, and his last few years were spent more comfortably in a nursing home in Massachusetts.

Over the course of his career, he fought many fights with the top few black boxers and faced **Harry Wills** at least 23 times, Sam McVey 15 times, **Joe Jeannette** 14 times, Jim Barry 12 times, and Jeff Clarke 11 times.

Langford was five foot seven inches tall and had a 72-inch **reach**. He fought at weights ranging from 140 to 206 pounds in weight classes from **welterweight** to heavyweight. In 317 professional bouts, from 1902 to 1926, he won 180 (129 by **knockout**), lost 30 (nine by knockout), and had 40 draws, six **no contests**, and 61 no-decision bouts, in which he was awarded the newspaper decision in 32, lost 14, and drew 15. He fought a total of 2,566 rounds and was inducted as a member of the inaugural class of the **International Boxing Hall of Fame** in 1990.

LAS VEGAS. Las Vegas, Nevada, has become the site of most of the major championship **bouts** since the last half of the 20th century. Several **casinos**, such as Caesar's Palace, Dunes, Harrah's, MGM Grand, the Mirage, and the Riviera Hotel, have found that staging boxing has increased their casino patronage and have thus been able to offer substantial amounts of money to attract the top fighters.

The **Bob Fitzsimmons–Jim Corbett heavyweight** championship bout was the first to be held in the state of Nevada—in Carson City on 17 March 1897. The second **Sonny Liston–Floyd Patterson** bout on 22 July 1963 was the first world heavyweight championship bout to take place in Las Vegas. It was held at the Convention Center. **Muhammad Ali** also defended his title against Floyd Patterson at that venue in 1965, but it was not until the late 1970s that Las Vegas casinos began to dominate as the site of major boxing activity, with virtually every North American world champion defending their titles in Las Vegas.

See also ATLANTIC CITY.

LEFT-HANDED BOXERS. Most boxers do not like to face a left-handed opponent, since they seldom see them and are not used to an opponent that throws punches in a different style. Consequently, it is often more difficult for a left-hander to obtain matches, and quite a few aspiring left-handers have been taught to box right-handed in order to further their **ring** careers. Until recently, left-handed boxers have been quite rare, but the former prejudice against left-handed boxers seems to be decreasing and they have become more prevalent.

According to Boxrec's figures, there have been 228 southpaw world champions, although only five **heavyweight** champions. Michael Moorer was the first left-handed heavyweight champion, and he has been followed by Chris Byrd, Corrie Sanders, Ruslan Chagaev, and Sultan Ibragimov. Southpaw champions at other weight classes include Horacio Accavallo, Elvis Álvarez, Bruno Arcari, Paulie Ayala, Billy Backus, René Barrientos, Melio Bettina, Markus Beyer, Cornelius Boza-Edwards, Lou Brouillard, Johnny Bumphus, Lucian Bute, **Joe Calzaghe**, **Héctor Camacho**, Marvin Camel, Jimmy Carruthers, Joel Casamayor, Young Corbett III, Hiroyuki Ebihara, Gabriel "Flash" Elorde, Crisanto España, Tiger Flowers, twins Khaokor and Khaosai Galaxy, twins Ramón and Raúl García, Juan Carlos **Gómez**, Otis Grant, Yoko Gushiken, **Marvelous Marvin Hagler**, **Naseem Hamed**, Maurice Hope, Luis Ibarra, John David Jackson, Marc Johnson, Marvin Johnson, Reggie Johnson, Zab Judah, Ayub Kalule, Koki Kameda, Kevin Kelley, Ki-Soo Kim, Joe Knight, Cecilio Lastra, Pete Latzo, Rafael "Bazooka" Limón, Sergio Martínez, Henry Maske, Al McCoy, Freddie Miller, Alan Minter, Sharmba Mitchell, Michael Moorer, Saengsak Muangsurin, Welcome Ncita, George Nichols, Michael Nunn, Shoji Oguma, Victor Ortiz, **Manny Pacquiao**, Mate Parlov, Jackie Paterson, José Luis Ramírez, Graciano Rocchigiani, Vicente Saldivar, Agapito Sánchez, Ratanapol Sor Vorapin, Netrnoi Sor Vorasingh, Cory Spinks, Antonio Tarver, Arnold Taylor, **Edwin Valero**, Julio César Vásquez, Bernabe Villacampo, Ben Villaflor, Jiro Watanabe, Jim Watt, **Pernell Whitaker**, Johnny Wilson, Ronald "Winky" Wright, Hilario Zapata, Daniel Zaragoza, and Juan Zurita.

A few other notable left-handed boxers who did not win world championships are Francie Barrett, Ever Beleño, Jack Bodell, Larry Bonds, Tyrone Everett, Horace Gwynne, Ronnie Harris, Audley Harrison, Joe Hipp, Kenny Lane, **Mills Lane**, Eduardo Lausse, Karl Mildenberger, Irish Bob Murphy, **László Papp**, Piero Rollo, Lew Tendler, and William "**Bendigo**" Thompson.

LEINER, BENJAMIN. *See* LEONARD, BENNY "THE GHETTO WIZARD" (né BENJAMIN LEINER).

LEONARD, BENNY "THE GHETTO WIZARD" (né BENJAMIN LEINER). B. 17 April 1896, New York. D. 18 April 1947, New York, New York. Benny Leonard was a **lightweight** champion who died in the **ring**—not as a boxer but as a **referee**.

He was raised on the Lower East Side of New York and began boxing there as a youth. He is one of the few boxing champions who lost his first **bout**. His first recorded **professional** fight was on 14 October 1911 when he was just 15 years old. In that bout, he suffered a severe nosebleed, and the bout was stopped in the third **round**. He was stopped twice more in 1912 but won nearly all his other bouts by **knockout**. His early career was quite spotty, and in his first 50 bouts (through April 1914) he won only 29 and lost 15, with two draws and four **no-contest** bouts.

His career began to improve, and on 31 March 1916 he fought Freddie Welsh for the world's lightweight title at **Madison Square Garden** in a 10-round no-decision bout. Although Leonard won the unofficial **newspaper decision**, he was not awarded the championship. On 28 May 1917, Leonard again fought Welsh. This time he stopped Welsh in the ninth round and won the world's lightweight title. Leonard then held that title for eight years before retiring as undefeated champion in 1925.

As champion, he defended successfully against Leo Johnson (21 September 1917, **technical knockout** [TKO] round 1); Young Erne (21 May 1919, KO 6); Lockport Jimmy Duffy (17 November 1919, TKO 2); Joe Welling (26 November 1920, TKO 14); Richie Mitchell (14 January 1921, TKO 6); Rocky Kansas twice (10 February 1922, **unanimous decision** 15; 4 July 1922, TKO 8); and Lew Tendler twice (27 July 1922, newspaper decision 12; 24 July 1923, unanimous decision 15).

On 23 September 1918, Leonard attempted to move up to the **welterweight** class and fought an eight-round no-decision newspaper decision **draw** with Ted "Kid" Lewis for the welterweight title. Leonard made another attempt at the welterweight title on 26 June 1922 against **Jack Britton** but was **disqualified** in the 13th round in a bout in which he was well behind on the scorecards for hitting Britton who was on one knee at the time.

On 15 January 1925, Leonard announced his retirement as undefeated lightweight champion. Leonard suffered financially after the 1929 stock market crash and returned to the ring on 6 October 1931. He was quite out of shape, and his opponent in the first comeback fight was alleged to have taken a dive in the second round. Leonard won 19 of 20 bouts during his comeback, with a draw the only nonwinning bout.

On 7 October 1932, Leonard was stopped in the sixth round in a one-sided bout by future welterweight champion **Jimmy McLarnin** and permanently retired.

He did remain active in boxing as a referee. He interrupted his refereeing activities to serve in the U.S. Maritime Service during World War II. On 18 April 1947, after refereeing the first six bouts at **St. Nicholas Arena** in New York, he suffered a heart attack and died in the ring.

Leonard was five foot five inches tall and had a 69-inch **reach**. He fought at weights ranging from 126 to 153 pounds in weight classes from lightweight to welterweight. In 219 professional bouts, from 1911 to 1932, he won 90 (70 by knockout), lost six (five by knockout), and had one draw, four **no-contest** bouts, and 118 no-decision bouts, in which he was awarded the newspaper decision in 93, lost 18, and drew seven. He fought a total of 1581 rounds and was inducted as a member of the inaugural class of the **International Boxing Hall of Fame** in 1990.

LEONARD, RAY CHARLES "SUGAR RAY". B. 17 May 1956, Rocky Mount, North Carolina. "Sugar Ray" Leonard capitalized on his **Olympic Games** championship, his good looks, and his charisma and parlayed them to become boxing's top attraction during the late 1970s and early 1980s.

Named Ray Charles Leonard after the popular singer, Leonard began boxing in 1969 at the Palmer Park, Maryland, recreation center, following in the footsteps of his older brother, Roger. Ray had an excellent **amateur boxing** career and won the 1973 National **Golden Gloves lightweight** championship, the 1974 National Golden Gloves **light welterweight** championship, the 1974 and 1975 National **Amateur Athletic Union** light welterweight titles, and the 1975 Pan American Games light welterweight and 1976 Olympic Games light welterweight **gold medals**. He claimed a record of 145–5 as an amateur boxer.

He originally planned on attending the University of Maryland but was guided into **professional boxing** by a family friend, Janks Morton, who introduced Leonard to attorney Mike Trainer. Leonard did not want to become a professional and be under the influence (and financial captivity) of a boxing manager. Trainer created a corporation of which Leonard was the sole shareholder. Trainer also put together a group of men to back Leonard financially at the start of his career. A physically attractive, well-spoken boxer, Leonard was heavily promoted by television and was paid $10,000 for his first professional **bout** plus an additional $30,000 for his share of the gate. He then was able to pay off his backers and was in control of his own destiny.

Trainer then hired famed **cornerman Angelo Dundee**, who had helped guide **Muhammad Ali's** career, to work with Leonard in the ring as well as select future opponents. With this backing, Leonard was able to negotiate independently and not be subject to either **Don King** or **Bob Arum**, the two major boxing promoters.

In his first fight, nationally **televised**, Leonard won a six-**round decision** over Luis Vega on 5 February 1977. After winning his first 25 bouts, Leonard challenged **Wilfred Benítez** for the **World Boxing Council (WBC) welterweight** title on 30 November 1979 in **Las Vegas**. Leonard stopped Benítez with just six seconds to go in the bout and became welterweight champion. After one successful defense of the title against Dave "Boy" Green, Leonard fought former lightweight champion **Roberto Durán** in Montreal, **Canada**, on 20 June 1980. Durán surprised Leonard and outfought him, handing Leonard his first professional loss in a close but **unanimous decision**.

In their rematch five months later in the Superdome in New Orleans, Louisiana, which was prefaced by his namesake, Ray Charles, singing the national anthem, Leonard outsmarted Durán by boxing rather than attempting to slug with him, frustrating and confusing Durán. In the seventh round, Leonard started taunting Durán and, in one famous moment, whirled his right hand around, and when Durán's eyes followed that action, Leonard threw a sharp **left-handed jab** at Durán. Finally, Durán had had enough of the teasing and just turned his back to Leonard and told the **referee** the famous words "No más."

After one successful defense of his newly rewon title, Leonard defeated the Ugandan Ayub Kalule and won the **World Boxing Association (WBA) middleweight** title. Rather than defend that crown, Leonard went back to the **welterweight** ranks and on 16 September 1981 fought WBA welterweight champion **Thomas Hearns**, who at that point in his career was undefeated with 32 victories. In a fight that was named the "Fight of the Year" by *Ring* **magazine**, Leonard, who was losing, caught Hearns in the 14th round and had him on the ropes when the referee stopped the bout.

After a fairly easy defense against Bruce Finch in 1982, Leonard announced his retirement from the **ring** on 9 November 1982 after discovering he had a detached retina.

On 10 December 1983, Leonard announced that he would be returning to the **ring** as he had received clearance from his physician. On 11 May 1984, Leonard stopped Kevin Howard in nine rounds, although Howard had knocked Leonard down in the fourth round. After the fight, Leonard announced his retirement for a second time, saying that he just did not have the ability he formerly had.

On 1 May 1986, he announced that he would come back to fight **Marvelous Marvin Hagler**. That fight took place nearly a year later on 6 April 1987 in **Las Vegas** for Hagler's middleweight title. Leonard won a 12-round **split decision** and his third title. This fight also was a *Ring* magazine "Fight of the Year." Although Hagler wanted a rematch, it did not take place and Hagler retired. On 27 May 1987, Leonard retired for the third time.

Leonard again came out of retirement when he was offered a chance to make boxing history and be the first boxer to win titles in five different weight divisions (although Thomas Hearns, three days prior to Leonard's attempt, actually became the first five-division champion). Leonard signed to meet Donny Lalonde, the WBC **light heavyweight** champion. The WBC also put the **vacant super middleweight** title on the line as both fighters had no trouble making the 168-pound limit. Leonard weighed in at 165 pounds wearing a warm-up suit and reportedly with silver dollars in his pockets so that he would appear heavier. Although he was knocked down in the fourth round, Leonard came back to stop Lalonde in the ninth round of their bout on 7 November 1988 and became the second five-division champion.

A rematch with Thomas Hearns was scheduled next. Although the super middleweight limit was 168 pounds, neither fighter was that heavy, and a **catchweight** limit of 164 pounds was agreed upon. The 12-round fight appeared to be won by Hearns, who knocked Leonard down twice, but the official decision of the 12 June 1989 bout was a **draw**.

Leonard's next bout was on 7 December 1989, a **rubber match** with Roberto Durán, who at that time was the WBC middleweight champion. The bout turned out to be a lackluster affair, with Leonard outboxing Durán and winning nearly every round to defend his WBC super middleweight title.

In January 1990, Leonard gave up his super middleweight title, unsure as to whether he would continue fighting. He offered Hagler a rematch, but Hagler decided to remain retired. A possible rematch with Hearns was suggested by Hearns, who could no longer fight at a weight low enough for a competive bout with Leonard.

On 9 February 1991, after 14 months of inactivity, Leonard moved down to 154 pounds and fought Terry Norris for Norris's WBC **light middleweight** title. In possibly the worst fight of his career, Leonard was knocked down twice and was thoroughly outpointed in the 12-round bout. After the decision was announced in the ring, Leonard took the microphone and said, "This is my last fight."

In 1997, Leonard, who had been inactive for more than five years and therefore eligible for induction, was inducted into the **International Boxing Hall of Fame**. He could not resist fighting one more time, though, and on 1 March 1997 fought former multiple-division champion **Héctor Camacho**. Camacho knocked him down in the fifth round, and referee **Joe Cortez** stopped the fight.

In retirement, Leonard has been active in several charitable organizations.

Leonard is five foot 10 inches tall and has a 74-inch **reach**. He fought at weights ranging from 141 to 165 pounds in weight classes from welterweight to super middleweight. In 40 professional bouts, from 1977 to 1997, he won 36 (25 by **knockout**), lost three (one by knockout), had one draw, and fought a total of 306 rounds. He was inducted into the International Boxing Hall of Fame in 1997.

LEWIS, LENNOX CLAUDIUS "THE LION". B. 2 September 1965, West Ham, London, **England**. Lennox Lewis, although born in England, was raised in Kitchener, Ontario, **Canada**, and after discovering the sport of boxing represented Canada in international competition. He attended Cameron Heights Collegiate Institute in Kitchener, where he played Canadian football, basketball, and soccer. He preferred boxing and did well, claiming a 94–11 record as an **amateur** boxer. He won the 1983 **heavyweight** junior world championship, lost in the 1984 **Olympic Games super heavyweight** quarterfinal **round** to Tyrell Biggs, and won the 1987 Pan American Games super heavyweight **silver medal** and the 1988 Olympic Games super heavyweight **gold medal**.

After the Olympic Games, he returned to England and had his first **professional** fight on 27 June 1989 in London, knocking out Al Malcolm in the second round. After winning his first 13 **bouts** (11 by **knockout**), he was matched with Jean-Maurice Chanet for the European Boxing Union heavyweight title in London on 31 October 1990 and stopped him in the sixth round on cuts. In Lewis's next bout, he stopped the previously undefeated (35–0) Gary Mason in seven rounds and added the **British Boxing Board of Control** heavyweight title to his collection. On 30 April 1992, he stopped Derek Williams in the third round and was also named Commonwealth heavyweight champion.

Lewis was one of the taller (six foot five inches) and heavier (weight range 221–256 pounds) **ring** champions. On 31 October 1992, Lewis knocked down Donovan "Razor" Ruddick three times in two rounds in a bout scheduled as an elimination bout for the **World Boxing Council (WBC)** heavyweight championship. Shortly afterward, Lewis was acclaimed the WBC heavyweight champion as **Riddick Bowe** refused to meet him in a title bout. On 8 May 1993, Lewis defended his new title by winning a 12-round **unanimous decision** over Tony Tucker with two **knockdowns** of his opponent. After defeats of Frank Bruno and Phil Jackson, Lewis lost his title to Oliver McCall on 24 September 1994 in London via a second-round **technical knockout**.

On 7 October 1995, Lewis stopped Tommy Morrison in six rounds and won the lightly regarded **International Boxing Council** world's heavyweight title. Lewis had only one bout in 1996, a 10-round **majority decision** victory over Ray Mercer. On 7 February 1997, Lewis won a more widely recognized title in a bizarre rematch with McCall for the WBC heavyweight title. McCall apparently had a nervous breakdown and stopped throwing punches in the fourth round. In the fifth round, he continued his effortless bout, and the fight was stopped by **referee Mills Lane**.

Lewis then defended his WBC heavyweight championship nine times from 1997 to 2000, adding the **World Boxing Association**, **International Boxing Federation**, and International Boxing Organization titles as a result of his 13 November 1999 defeat of **Evander Holyfield** by 12-round unanimous decision. On 22 April 2001, Hasim Rahman knocked out Lewis in five rounds but in a rematch on 17 November 2001 Lewis knocked out Rahman to regain his title. Lewis then made two more title defenses—an eight-round knockout of **Mike Tyson** in 2002 and a sixth-round stoppage of **Vitali Klitschko** due to cuts—before retiring from the ring.

In retirement, Lewis has remained in the public eye. He has appeared in music videos and the *Celebrity Apprentice* television show, played twice in the World Series of Poker, and worked as a color commentator for **televised boxing** shows.

Lewis has an 84-inch **reach**. In 44 professional bouts, from 1989 to 2003, he won 41 (32 by knockout), lost two (both by knockout), had one **draw**, and fought a total of 225 rounds. He was inducted into the **International Boxing Hall of Fame** in 2009.

LIGHT FLYWEIGHT. Light **flyweight** (sometimes called junior flyweight) is a boxing weight class in which the contestants cannot exceed 108 pounds. The **World Boxing Council** was the first sanctioning organization to recognize this class, and their first champion in this division was the Italian Franco Udella, who defeated Valentin Márquez of **Mexico** on 4 April 1975 in Milan, **Italy**, by a 12th-**round disqualification** to win the title. Among the best light flyweights have been Iván Calderón, **Michael Carbajal**, Jung-Koo Chang, Humberto González, Yoko Gushiken, Ricardo López, Ulises Solís, Saman Sorjaturong, and Myung-Woo Yuh.

LIGHT HEAVYWEIGHT. Light heavyweight is a boxing weight class in which the contestants cannot exceed 175 pounds. It originated in 1903 and was one of the traditional eight weight classes throughout the first half of the 20th century. The first light heavyweight champion was Jack Root, a man born as Janos Ruthaly in what is now the Czech Republic who resided in Chicago, Illinois. His manager, Lou Houseman, conceived of a boxing class for fighters who exceeded the **middleweight** limit, then 158 pounds, but were not big enough to compete with **heavyweights**, who then usually were in excess of 175 pounds. Root, weighing 168 pounds, defeated the 173-pound **Charles "Kid" McCoy** on 22 April 1903 in Detroit, Michigan, in the first match billed for the "light heavyweight championship."

The division has never been one of the more popular classes, as many boxers who could make the 175-pound limit preferred to fight as heavyweights since that division was more attractive financially. Among the better light heavyweights have been **Georges Carpentier**, **Ezzard Charles**, **Billy Conn**, Jack Delaney, **Bob Foster**, **Victor Galíndez**, Harold Johnson, **Roy Jones Jr.**, Gus Lesnevich, John Henry Lewis, Tommy Loughran, **Joey Maxim**, **Archie Moore**, **Philadelphia Jack O'Brien**, **Maxie Rosenbloom**, Battling Siki, **Michael Spinks**, and **José Torres**.

LIGHT MIDDLEWEIGHT. Light **middleweight** (more commonly known throughout boxing history as junior middleweight and now often termed super welterweight) is a boxing class in which the contestants cannot exceed 154 pounds.

The **World Boxing Association** was the first sanctioning organization to recognize this class, and their first champion in the division was Denny Moyer, who defeated Joey Giambra by a **unanimous decision** in 15 **rounds** on 20 October 1962 in Moyer's hometown of Portland, Oregon. **Sonny Liston**, the newly crowned world's **heavyweight** champion, acted as **referee**.

Among the best boxers in this division have been **Wilfred Benítez**, **Óscar De La Hoya**, **Tommy Hearns**, Ayub Kalule, Ki-Soo Kim, Sandro Mazzinghi, Mike McCallum, Terry Norris, Verno Phillips, Gianfranco Rosi, Cory Spinks, and Koichi Wajima.

LIGHT WELTERWEIGHT. Light **welterweight** (more commonly known throughout boxing history as junior welterweight and now often termed super **lightweight**) is a boxing weight class in which the contestants cannot exceed 140 pounds. The class was first recognized (as junior welterweight) when the **National Boxing Association** (forerunner of the present-day **World Boxing Association**) awarded the title of world junior welterweight champion to Myron "Pinky" Mitchell by acclamation on 15 November 1922. The division continued until 1935, when champion **Barney Ross** vacated it in pursuit of the **welterweight** championship.

The division was resurrected briefly in 1946 when Tippy Larkin defeated Willie Joyce and claimed the title but never defended it. On 12 June 1959, the division resurfaced when **Carlos Ortiz** defeated Kenny Lane in a **bout** billed for the world junior welterweight championship. It has been contested continuously since then.

Among the division's best have been **Héctor Camacho, Tony Canzoneri, Antonio Cervantes, Julio César Chávez**, Juan Martín Coggi, Ricky Hatton, Zab Judah, Nicolino Locche, **Duilio Loi**, Eddie Perkins, Aaron Pryor, Frankie Randall, and **Kostya Tszyu**.
See also GATTI, ARTURO "THUNDER".

LIGHTWEIGHT. Lightweight is a boxing weight class in which the contestants cannot exceed 135 pounds. It is one of the eight traditional weight classes. Its first recognized champion was Jack McAuliffe, who began fighting in the **bareknuckle** era and then finished his **ring** career in the gloved era.

Some of the best professional lightweights have been Lou Ambers, **Alexis Argüello, Henry Armstrong**, Joe Brown, **Héctor Camacho, Tony Canzoneri, Julio César Chávez**, Carlos Teo Cruz, **Roberto Durán**, Joe Gans, **Benny Leonard, Floyd Mayweather Jr., Carlos Ortiz, Barney Ross, Edwin Valero, Pernell Whitaker**, and **Ike Williams**. Many lightweight champions have moved up in weight and also won titles in heavier divisions. Benny Leonard is usually regarded as the best champion in this weight class.

See also BRAMBLE, LIVINGSTONE (aka RAS-I-ALUJAH BRAMBLE); MANCINI, RAY "BOOM BOOM" (né RAYMOND MICHAEL MANCINO); O'GRADY, SEAN "THE BUBBLE-GUM KID"; PAZIENZA, VINCENZO EDWARD "VINNY," "THE PAZMANIAN DEVIL" (aka VINNY PAZ).

LISTON, CHARLES L. "SONNY". B. ?, Sand Slough, Arkansas. D. 30 December 1970, **Las Vegas**, Nevada. Charles "Sonny" Liston claimed a birthdate of 8 May 1932, although it was thought that he was quite a bit older. The most recent research into his birthdate based on **United States** census information of 1930 and 1940 indicates that he was probably born in 1929 or 1930. Regardless, in his prime Liston appeared to be much older than he probably actually was. In a period of two and a half years, **Sonny Liston** was involved in four **heavyweight** championship **bouts**—each memorable in different ways and three of which each lasted less than one **round**.

He was born in rural Arkansas and was one of his mother's 11 children and his father's 25 children. Beaten often as a child by his father, he left with his mother to live in St. Louis when he was about 13 years old. As a youth, he led a life of crime and in 1950 was sentenced to five years in prison for armed robbery. While in prison, he learned to box and was counseled by a Catholic priest, who helped Liston receive parole in 1952.

He began boxing as an **amateur** and won the 1953 Chicago **Golden Gloves** and New York–Chicago Intercity Golden Gloves. In September 1953, he fought his first **professional** fight. After winning his first seven bouts, although only two by **knockout**, he was winning a bout against **journeyman** Marty Marshall on 7 September 1954 when he got hit with a punch while apparently laughing at his opponent, resulting in a broken jaw for Liston. Although he lasted the eight-round distance, he lost a **split decision**. This would prove to be his only loss until 1964, when he lost the world's heavyweight championship.

Liston won his next seven bouts, including a rematch with Marshall, which Liston won on a 10-round **unanimous decision** on 6 March 1956. He then did not fight until 1958, as he was sentenced to nine months in prison for assaulting a police officer while resisting arrest in 1956 (he served six of the nine months) and was banned from boxing in 1957.

Liston resumed his professional career in January 1958 and won eight bouts that year, six by knockout. He began to be featured on network **television** as he started fighting some of the top contenders in the heavyweight ranks. In four bouts in 1959, he defeated Mike DeJohn, **Cleveland Williams** (one of the hardest-hitting fighters of the era), Niño Valdés, and Willi Besmanoff, all by knockout or **technical knockout**. He continued this streak in 1960, stopping Howard King, Williams again, Roy Harris, **Zora Folley**, and **Eddie Machen**—the latter two boxers being the number one and number two rated heavyweights, with only Machen lasting the distance.

By now, he appeared unbeatable and was looked at as the top challenger for heavyweight champion **Floyd Patterson's** title, although his criminal background and association with underworld figures had many people not wanting him to get that opportunity. In 1960, he was denied a license to box in New York State for those reasons. After two more knockout victories in 1961 against lesser-ranked opponents, Liston was signed for a bout with Floyd Patterson on 25 September 1962 at Comiskey Park in Chicago.

The bout lasted just two minutes and six seconds of the first round, as Liston floored Patterson with a couple of left **hooks** and Patterson was counted out in the first round. Their rematch on 22 July 1963 in **Las Vegas** lasted just four seconds longer, as Liston again caught Patterson early and knocked him down three times in the first round.

Liston was not a particularly huge man (only six feet tall and 210–215 pounds) , although he did have the largest hands (15-inch fist measurement) of any heavyweight champion and an extraordinary **reach** of 84 inches. He did have a menacing glare, and that, coupled with his prison background for violent crimes, made him an imposing figure as heavyweight champion.

His first title defense was against a young heavyweight named Cassius Clay, who had won the 1960 Olympic **light heavyweight gold medal** and had won his first 19 professional bouts. Although taller and heavier than Liston, he did not appear to have much of a chance and was a 7–1 underdog.

Clay was much faster than Liston and also antagonized Liston prior to the fight with extraordinary actions, including near hysteria at their prefight **weigh-in**, and when the bout began, Liston thought that he was fighting a crazy man. The bout on 25 February 1964 in Miami Beach, Florida, began with Ali using his speed and footwork to frustrate Liston. In the fourth round, Clay got a foreign substance in his eyes and between rounds was ready to surrender. Only after Clay's **trainer, Angelo Dundee**, rubbed his eyes and pushed him out into the **ring** did he continue. Clay was able to dance around in the fifth round, and after his eyes cleared he resumed his attack on Liston. After a frustrating sixth round, Liston told his **cornermen** he would not continue the bout, claiming an injury to his shoulder, and Cassius Clay became the new world's heavyweight champion. After the bout, Clay announced he had joined the Nation of Islam (more popularly known as the Black Muslims) and was changing his name to Cassius X. He later changed it to **Muhammad Ali.**

Their rematch, originally scheduled for Boston on 16 November 1964, was postponed when Ali suffered a hernia. The rematch was then scheduled for 25 May 1965, but the Massachusetts **commission** had second thoughts and refused to sanction the bout. It was eventually set for Lewiston, a small town in the state of Maine, and was held at St. Dominic's Hall, with the result that the paid attendance was only 2,412, the smallest live attendance for any heavyweight championship bout in history.

In another strange happening, after just a brief few seconds of **sparring**, Ali threw a very short right hand, and Liston, who did not appear to be hit hard by the punch, went down. Ali danced around the ring taunting the downed Liston. **Referee Jersey Joe Walcott**, an excellent former champion but who proved to be an incompetent referee, did not begin to count over Liston. Finally, Liston got up and was ready to continue, but *Ring* **magazine** publisher **Nat Fleischer**, at **ringside**, called to Walcott and told him that the timekeeper had reached the count of 10 and the fight should be over. Walcott then raised Ali's hand, and the fight was terminated. The "official" time was announced as "one minute" even though subsequent films of the bout showed that it lasted two minutes and 12 seconds. Most people in the boxing world believe that Liston threw the fight, either from pressure from the underworld or from fear of the Muslims, although nothing was ever proved.

After a year off, Liston resumed boxing, traveling to Sweden, where he won four bouts by knockout against opponents of lesser quality in 1966 and 1967. In 1968, he won seven more bouts by knockout—six in the **United States** and one in **Mexico**. He won three more by knockout in 1969 against journeymen but on 6 December 1969 was himself knocked out by former National **Amateur Athletic Union** and Chicago Golden Gloves champion Leotis Martin, a competent boxer with a 30–5 record. Martin, unfortunately, suffered a detached retina in that bout and never fought again.

Liston fought one bout in 1970, a ninth-round **technical knockout** of **Chuck Wepner** who was stopped on cuts. Wepner later became the inspiration for the *Rocky* movies after his valiant 1975 bout with Ali for the heavyweight title.

As with his birth, Liston's death is shrouded in mystery. His wife found him dead on the floor of their home on 5 January 1971. The cause of death was officially ruled a heroin overdose, and the estimated date of death was 30 December 1970. Liston had no history of drug use and was afraid of needles, so he most likely was not a heroin user. In addition, there were no other signs of heroin paraphernalia. Speculation has been that Liston was murdered, possibly by his underworld connections. Within a two-year period, both **Zora Folley** and **Eddie Machen**, two of that era's top heavyweights and both previous foes of Liston, also died under suspicious circumstances, with their deaths also officially treated as accidents.

Liston fought at weights ranging from 198 to 226 pounds as a heavyweight. In 54 professional bouts, from 1953 to 1970, he won 50 (39 by knockout), lost four (three by knockout) , and fought a total of 267 rounds.

He was inducted into the **International Boxing Hall of Fame** in 1991.

LOI, DUILIO. B. 19 April 1929, Trieste, Friuli-Venezia Giulia, **Italy**. D. 20 January 2008, Treviso, Italy. Duilio Loi is a name unknown to most fight fans, especially North American ones, yet he compiled one of the best records of any **professional lightweight** boxer in history. A boxer without a **knockout** punch, he fought all but 13 of his 126 **bouts** in his home country of Italy but met all comers, was never **knocked down**, and suffered only three losses.

He began his professional boxing career on 1 November 1948 in Genoa, Italy, with a six-**round decision** over Nino Frangioni. After winning 25 and boxing two **draws** in his first 27 bouts, he defeated Gianluigi Uboldi on 18 July 1951 in Milan, Italy, on a 12-round decision to win the Italian lightweight championship. One year later, on 17 August 1952, Loi lost the first bout of his career, a 15-round decision for the European Boxing Union (EBU) lightweight title to Jurgen Johansen in Johansen's native city of Copenhagen, Denmark. In a rematch on 6 February 1954 in Milan, Loi won a 15-round decision and became EBU lightweight champion—a title he did not lose until 1959, when he abandoned it to move up to the **welterweight** class. Loi fought and won three bouts in **Australia** in 1954 and his first bout in the **United States** that same year, defeating Glen Flanagan in Miami Beach before returning to Italy.

Loi gained the EBU welterweight title on 19 April 1959 when he defeated Emilio Marconi in Milan on a 15-round decision. Loi's second boxing venture to the **United States** was to challenge world lightweight champion **Carlos Ortiz**. Loi lost a close 15-round **split decision** to Ortiz on 15 June 1960 at the Cow Palace in Daly City, California. Less than three months later in Milan on 1 September 1960, Loi defeated Ortiz by 15-round **majority decision** in a bout for the world **light welterweight** title and became champion. He defended that title once, boxing a **draw** with Eddie Perkins on 21 October 1961 in Milan, before losing the title in a rematch with Perkins on 14 September 1962. Loi lost a unanimous 15-round decision despite the fact that he knocked Perkins down twice in the bout. Shortly after regaining the title from Perkins by 15-round decision in their **rubber match** on 15 December 1962 in Milan, Loi announced his retirement from the ring.

Loi was five foot four inches tall and had a 69-inch **reach**. He fought at weights ranging from 133 to 146 pounds, primarily as a lightweight and light welterweight. In 126 professional bouts, from 1948 to 1962, he won 115 (26 by knockout), lost three (none by knockout), had eight draws, and fought a total of 1,222 rounds. He was inducted into the **International Boxing Hall of Fame** in 2005, although by then he was suffering from Alzheimer's disease and was unable to personally accept the honor.

LONDON PRIZE RING RULES. The London Prize Ring Rules were formulated in 1838 and revised in 1853 and were used until the 1890s, when **bareknuckle** prizefighting was largely replaced by boxing with **gloves** under the **Marquess of Queensberry Rules.**
See also APPENDIX I.

LONG COUNT. *See* DEMPSEY–TUNNEY.

LOUIS, JOE "THE BROWN BOMBER" (né JOSEPH LOUIS BARROW). B. 13 May 1914, Lafayette, Alabama. D. 12 April 1981, Paradise, Nevada. "A credit to his race"—if you ask any boxing fan what person this phrase describes, chances are they will answer Joe Louis. Never mind the fact that there have been many, many African American boxers who have led exemplarly lives both in and out of the ring, Joe Louis was described in that manner on many occasions.

Louis was raised in Detroit, Michigan, and as a teenager began **amateur boxing.** Fighting in the **light heavyweight** class, he won the 1933 and 1934 Detroit **Golden Gloves** tournaments and the 1934 Chicago Tournament of Champions. He was ineligible to compete against the New York team in the Intercity Chicago–New York Golden Gloves contests due to a rule prohibiting the Chicago team from using Detroit or Cleveland winners. In 1934, he also won the National **Amateur Athletic Union** light heavyweight title.

He was befriended by two Detroit black men, John Roxborough, a successful bookmaker, and Julian Black, a Chicago promoter and one-time speakeasy owner who managed several fighters and knew his way around the fight business. They convinced Louis that a white manager would not work hard to further a black fighter's career. To train Louis, the two men then hired Jack "Chappie" Blackburn, a former **lightweight** boxer who had fought **Joe Gans**, **Sam Langford**, and **Philadelphia Jack O'Brien** and was a competent boxer in the early years of the 20th century.

To counter the negative image of black boxers that **Jack Johnson** had created, Louis's management team insisted on several conditions to enable them to promote Louis successfully as nonthreatening to the white population. He was not to be photographed with white women or with alcohol. He was not to gloat over opponents after victories and was never to flaunt any of the material successes that came his way.

Louis began his professional career in the **heavyweight** class on 4 July 1934 and won via a first-**round knockout** when he knocked his opponent, Jack Kracken, through the ropes. After winning his first 19 **bouts** (15 by knockout), including victories over contenders such as Adolph Wiater, Stanley Poreda, Lee Ramage, Patsy Perroni, and Natie Brown, white promoter **Mike Jacobs** made a deal with Louis, Roxborough, and Black and signed a three-year exclusive promotion contract with them. Jacobs had promotional rights at major New York venues such as **Madison Square Garden** and Yankee Stadium and was also able to help counter the prejudice that Louis faced as a result of the actions of Jack Johnson, an earlier black heavyweight champion who flaunted the law and had many white people not wanting to see another black heavyweight champion.

In his next bout, Louis was matched with **Primo Carnera**, the six-foot-six-inch, 260-pound former heavyweight champion, on 25 June 1935 at Yankee Stadium. Louis thoroughly dominated the bout and knocked Carnera down three times before it was stopped in the sixth round.

After defeating Carnera, Louis beat King Levinsky, former heavyweight champion **Max Baer**, Paulino Uzcudun, and Charley Retzlaff, four formidable opponents, and won all four bouts by knockout or **technical knockout**, each within four rounds. Louis appeared to be heading for a bout with heavyweight champion **Jim Braddock**.

On 19 June 1936, Louis proved to be not invincible, as he was knocked out by former heavyweight champion **Max Schmeling** in 12 rounds. This set back plans for a title bout somewhat. Louis then knocked out former heavyweight champion **Jack Sharkey** in three rounds and won six more bouts against lesser opponents (five by knockout). He then was matched with Jim Braddock for the heavyweight title on 22 June 1937 at Comiskey Park in Chicago. In that bout, Louis was down in the first round but got up and knocked out Braddock in the eighth round to become world's heavyweight champion.

Louis then won three title defenses against Tommy Farr (30 August 1937, **unanimous decision** round 15), Nathan Mann (23 February 1938, KO 3), and Harry Thomas (1 April 1938, KO 5). That set the stage for his return match with the German Schmeling. The bout took place on 22 June 1938 and was highly anticipated, both by Louis and the United States public. Louis wanted to avenge the only loss in his career. It was built up by the promoters as a match between the Nazi Schmeling and the black American Louis. Prior to the bout, Louis was encouraged by President Franklin D. Roosevelt, who told Joe, "We need muscles like yours to beat **Germany**." The bout drew 70,043 to New York's Yankee Stadium and was broadcast worldwide. The bout only lasted two minutes and four seconds, as Louis received his revenge. Louis knocked Schmeling down three times, and after the third **knockdown**, Schmeling's **corner** threw in the towel and **referee** Arthur Donovan looked at the beaten Schmeling and stopped the bout.

Louis proved to be the most active heavyweight champion in history and defended his title four times in 1939, four times in 1940, and seven times in 1941. From December 1940 to June 1941, he fought one title bout each month, and some sportswriters labeled this his "Bum of the Month" campaign, although in actuality Louis was fighting the best heavyweights available and avoiding no one. His opponents all had substantial winning records. In those 17 bouts, he won 15 by knockout, one by **disqualification**, and only one, against Arturo Godoy, by decision.

On 18 June 1941, Louis came close to losing his championship when he fought **light heavyweight** champion **Billy Conn**. Going into the 13th round, Louis was behind on points, and had Conn chosen to box defensively in the last few rounds, he might have defeated Joe. But Conn decided to go for a knockout in the 13th round, and Louis knocked him out with two seconds remaining.

Louis fought one more title defense in 1941, and then one month after the Pearl Harbor attack, Louis defended his title at Madison Square Garden against Buddy Baer, brother of former heavyweight champion Max Baer. Louis donated his entire purse to the Navy Relief Fund. The next day, 10 January 1941, Louis enlisted in the U.S. Army. At one point, he was quoted as saying, "We'll win because we're on God's side." That slogan was later used on recruiting posters with Louis's photo.

Two months later, Private Joe Louis was given leave to defend his title once more at the Garden, against Abe Simon, in a bout for the Army Emergency Relief Fund. Again Louis donated his entire purse. Ironically, those two bouts would haunt Louis the rest of his life because the Internal Revenue Service (IRS) claimed he owed income tax on his earnings for the bouts, and he was hit with enormous tax bills later in the decade.

While in the army, Louis was a member of the Special Services Division. He traveled to military bases worldwide and boxed **exhibitions** to entertain the troops. He was eventually promoted to sergeant and received the Legion of Merit for contribution to the general morale. On 1 October 1945, he was discharged.

His first bout after his discharge was not until 19 June 1946 when he and Conn fought a highly anticipated rematch. Prior to the bout, Louis came out with another of his pithy quotations. When asked about Conn's speed and elusiveness, Louis replied, "He can run, but he can't hide." The bout was somewhat anticlimactic, as Conn was nowhere as effective as he had been in their first bout, and Louis knocked him out in the eighth round.

After a one-round knockout of Tami Mauriello in September 1946, Louis faced **Jersey Joe Walcott** on 5 December 1947 at Madison Square Garden. In this bout, Louis was down in both the first and fourth rounds. At the end of the 15-round bout, Louis was sure that he had lost and was surprised when it was announced that he won a **split decision**. In their rematch in June 1948, Louis was knocked down briefly in the third round but, although trailing on the scorecards of two of the three officials, caught Walcott in the 11th and knocked him out. The following year, on 1 March 1949, Louis announced his retirement from the ring.

His retirement was short lived, as the IRS kept after him and he returned to the **ring** in 1950 to help pay off his debts. On 27 September 1950, he fought **Ezzard Charles**, who was then recognized as heavyweight champion. The 36-year-old Louis was no match for Charles, and although he lasted the full 15 rounds, he lost nearly every round on the **judges'** scorecards.

Louis continued his comeback, as he needed the money, and won his next eight bouts. On 26 October 1951, he went up against the future heavyweight champion **Rocky Marciano**, who at that point in his career had a record of 37–0 with 32 knockouts. Marciano, nine years younger than the 37-year-old Louis, dominated the fight and knocked Louis through the ropes in the eighth round, when referee **Ruby Goldstein** stopped the bout.

In retirement, Louis did some work as a referee, **cornerman**, and promoter and even briefly worked as a professional wrestler and wrestling referee. He also did some television work as a color commentator, although he was not extremely verbal. During the 1960s, he started to develop various physical and mental ailments and for much of the next two decades worked as a greeter at Caesar's Palace in **Las Vegas**, where he was given free rein to pursue his golf addiction. In 1993, he was the first boxer to be honored on a **United States** commemorative stamp.

Louis was six foot two inches tall and had a 76-inch **reach**. He fought at weights ranging from 181 to 218 pounds as a heavyweight. In 70 professional bouts, from 1934 to 1951, he won 66 (52 by knockout), lost three (two by knockout), had one **no contest**, and fought a total of 428 rounds. He was inducted as a member of the inaugural class of the **International Boxing Hall of Fame** in 1990.

LOUIS–SCHMELING. From 1934 to 1936, **heavyweight Joe Louis** won 24 straight **bouts**, 20 by **knockout**, and appeared headed for a match for the heavyweight championship. In preparation for a somewhat routine match with former heavyweight champion German **Max Schmeling**, Louis trained at a resort in Lakewood, New Jersey. There he was introduced to the game of golf, which quickly became almost an obsession to him. Consequently, he was not adequately prepared for his 19 June 1936 bout with Schmeling at Yankee Stadium. Conversely, Schmeling had studied Louis and noticed that Louis would drop his left hand at times after throwing a punch. Although Louis entered the **ring** as a 10–1 favorite, Schmeling caught Louis in the fourth **round** and knocked him down. In the 12th round, Schmeling again connected, and Louis was counted out by **referee** Arthur Donovan at 2:29 of the round in a fight named "Fight of the Year" by *Ring* **magazine**.

Louis went on to win the heavyweight title in 1937 but still felt that he needed to avenge his loss. In the two years since their first fight, the Nazi party had gained strength in **Germany** with their platform of Aryan supremacy. The highly anticipated return match took place on 22 June 1938 and was built up by the promoters as a match between the Nazi Schmeling and the black American Louis, even though Schmeling was not a member of the Nazi Party. Prior to the bout, Louis was encouraged by President Franklin D. Roosevelt, who told Joe, "We need muscles like yours to beat Germany." The bout drew 70,043 to New York's Yankee Stadium and was broadcast worldwide. The bout only lasted two minutes and four seconds, as Louis received his revenge. Louis knocked Schmeling down three times, and after the third knockdown, Schmeling's **corner** threw in the towel and **referee** Arthur Donovan looked at the beaten Schmeling and stopped the bout.

The reaction in the **United States**, especially in the black communities, was one of great joy coupled with relief. As a result of that bout, and Louis's service to the country during World War II, he became the first truly nationwide African American hero in the United States. Ironically, in later years Schmeling and Louis became good friends, and Schmeling was a pallbearer at the funeral of Louis in 1981.

LYLE, RON. B. 12 February 1941, Dayton, Ohio. D. 26 November 2011, Denver, Colorado. Had Ron Lyle's youth been different, he might never have become a world-class boxer. On the other hand, he might have become the **heavyweight** champion of the world. Raised in Denver, Colorado, in a family of 19 children, when Lyle was only a teenager he participated in a gang fight that resulted in the shooting death of a 21 year old. Lyle was convicted of second-degree murder and sentenced to 15 to 25 years in the Canon City State Penitentiary in Colorado. While serving his term, he was knifed and underwent a seven-hour operation to save his life. He was then introduced to boxing by the prison's athletic director, and as a boxer he excelled, winning all but one of his prison boxing matches.

He was paroled on 22 November 1969 after serving seven and a half years of his sentence. He began boxing as an **amateur**, with the intention of becoming a **professional**. As an amateur, he compiled a record of 25–4 and won the 1970 National **Amateur Athletic Union** heavyweight championship and boxed for the **United States** team in two dual meets with the **Soviet Union**, winning one of two **bouts**.

He became a professional boxer on 23 April 1971 when he was 30 years old, an exceptionally old age for a professional boxing debut. After winning his first 19 bouts, 17 by **knockout**, he was matched with **Jerry Quarry** at **Madison Square Garden** on 9 February 1973. Quarry outboxed Lyle and easily won a 12-**round unanimous decision**. Lyle then won 11 of his next 13 bouts, with one **draw** and one unanimous-decision loss, and was matched with **Muhammad Ali** for the world's heavyweight championship.

On 16 May in **Las Vegas**, Nevada, Ali stopped Lyle after 11 rounds, although Lyle had been ahead on the scorecards at the time of the stoppage. In Lyle's next bout, he defeated **Earnie Shavers** on a **technical knockout** in the sixth round. Lyle then faced former heavyweight champion **George Foreman** in a 12-round bout billed for the **vacant** North American Boxing Federation title. Foreman knocked out Lyle in the fifth round of that bout.

Lyle continued boxing, although the quality of his opponents diminished slightly, and he retired after being knocked out by **Gerry Cooney** in the first round on 24 October 1980. Fifteen years later, Lyle made a brief four-bout return to the **ring** at the age of 54 in an attempt to get a rematch with Foreman, who had recently become heavyweight champion at the age of 45. Although Lyle won all four bouts by knockout against mediocre opposition, he was unable to get the Foreman rematch and then retired permanently.

In retirement, Lyle worked as a security guard in Las Vegas, ran a boxing club in Denver, and trained young boxers.

Lyle was six foot three inches tall and had a 76-inch **reach**. He fought at weights ranging from 209 to 240 pounds as a heavyweight. In 51 professional bouts, from 1971 to 1995, he won 43 (31 by knockout), lost seven (four by knockout), had one draw, and fought a total of 324 rounds.

M

MACHEN, EDWARD MILLS "EDDIE". B. 15 June 1932, Redding, California. D. 8 August 1972, San Francisco, California. Eddie Machen was the number-one-rated **heavyweight** at one time in the 1950s. His career turned on one **bout**, and he was never quite the same. He attended Shasta Union High School in Redding and played on its football and basketball teams. He began boxing and was taught by his uncle, Dave Mills, who had fought **professionally** 40 years earlier, had defeated the great Argentinean **Luis Ángel Firpo**, and claimed the heavyweight championship of South America.

Machen only had a few **amateur** bouts (one biography claims three—two **knockouts** and a **draw**) before he was convicted of armed robbery in 1952 and served three years in prison. After he was released, he began his professional boxing career with his first recorded bout on 22 March 1955 in Sacramento, California. The six-foot-tall, 195-pound Machen won his first 24 fights with 15 knockouts. Included in those victories were wins over contenders Niño Valdés, Julio Mederos, John Holman, Johnny Summerlin, Bob Baker, Tommy "Hurricane" Jackson, and former **light heavyweight** champion **Joey Maxim**.

By 1958, he was the number one rated heavyweight and was matched with **Zora Folley**, the number two rated heavyweight. The highly anticipated bout on 9 April 1958 at the Cow Palace in Daly City, California, was instead a boring defensive fight that was scored a draw. Still undefeated, Machen then traveled to Sweden to fight the undefeated European heavyweight champion, Ingemar Johansson, on 14 September 1958, with the winner of the bout to face heavyweight champion **Floyd Patterson** for the world's title. In one of the biggest disappointments in Machen's career, he was caught in the first **round** by Johansson's powerful punches and **knocked down** three times, with the third time being for the 10 count.

Machen resumed boxing in 1959 and won seven bouts over slightly lesser opposition. On 18 January 1960, he and Folley had a rematch, but Folley won a 12-round **decision**. After three more wins in 1960, Machen met future heavyweight champion Charles "Sonny" Liston in a 12-round bout in Seattle, Washington. At the time of the bout, Liston, another former convict, had a record of 30–1 and had won his last nine bouts by knockout, including a three-round knockout of Folley. Machen surprisingly lasted the full 12 rounds, but Liston won a **unanimous decision**. Two years later, Liston would win the world's heavyweight championship with a one-round knockout of Floyd Patterson.

Machen continued to defeat top-rated heavyweights and won eight of his next nine bouts, losing only a close 10-round decision to former light heavyweight champion Harold Johnson. He then fought a 10-round draw with another hard-hitting fighter, **Cleveland Williams**, in July 1962. Although he kept boxing and defeating most of the top-ranked heavyweights, Machen was unable to get a shot at the title.

In the fall of 1962, Machen threatened suicide and was hospitalized for clinical depression. He did not resume boxing for over a year, and then it was against mediocre opposition. After winning five bouts by **knockout**, Machen finally got to fight Floyd Patterson, but by then Patterson was no longer champion, having been twice knocked out by Liston. Patterson still was a capable fighter and won a 12-round decision in a bout held in Solna, Sweden.

On 5 March 1965 in Chicago, Machen finally got a chance to fight for the heavyweight title. After Cassius Clay had successfully defended his heavyweight championship by knocking out Liston in one round in a rematch, he announced that he had joined the Nation of Islam (also known as the Black Muslims). This frightened some people, and the **World Boxing Association** decided to remove their recognition of him as heavyweight champion and declared the title **vacant**. They selected Ernie Terrell and Eddie Machen to fight for the vacant title. Terrell won the 15-round decision, and Machen's career was virtually ended.

He continued boxing and had nine more fights in the next two years but only won three of them. Included in those wins was a decision over undefeated **Jerry Quarry**. One of the losses was a knockout by future heavyweight champion **Joe Frazier**, also undefeated at the time.

Machen's last fight was 26 May 1967, a three-round knockout by Boone Kirkman. After that bout, he worked as a longshoreman until his death in August 1972. Although he allegedly fell to his death from a window, he along with Folley in July 1972 and Liston in 1970 all died under suspicious circumstances, but nothing was ever proved and all three deaths are listed as "accidents."

Machen was six feet tall and had a 75-inch **reach**. He fought at weights ranging from 190 to 200 pounds as a heavyweight. In 64 professional bouts, from 1955 to 1967, he won 50 (29 by knockout), lost 11 (three by knockout), had three draws, and fought a total of 497 rounds.

MADISON SQUARE GARDEN. Madison Square Garden in New York, New York, bills itself as "the world's most famous arena." The building that now stands atop Penn Station between Seventh and Eighth Avenues and 31st and 33rd Streets is the fourth building to bear that name and was opened in 1968. Its predecessor, located at Eighth Avenue and 50th Street, was built in 1925, operated until 1968, and housed many professional championship **bouts** in its lifetime. At a time when boxing was the most popular sport in the **United States** contested indoors, the Garden, with a seating capacity of approximately 20,000 for boxing, featured most of the top boxing shows in the country. **Heavyweight** champion **Joe Louis** fought nine of his title fights there as well as his final one, a **nontitle bout** against **Rocky Marciano.** Although many of the major fights during this era were conducted in outdoor venues such as baseball stadiums Yankee Stadium and the Polo Grounds due to their larger seating capacities (70,000 or more), the Garden featured the top shows throughout the winter months. With the advent of **televised boxing** in the late 1940s, the Garden featured a weekly boxing show that was often the site of the **Friday Night Fights** throughout the 1940s and 1950s.

When the new Garden opened in 1968, its first boxing **card** was **Joe Frazier** versus Buster Mathis for the newly **vacant** world's heavyweight title after **Muhammad Ali** had been stripped of his title for refusing to enter the U.S. Army. The co-featured event was a rematch between **Nino Benvenuti** and **Emile Griffith** for Griffith's world **middleweight** title. Frazier's first title defense, three months later, was also at the Garden, and when Ali had been reinstated following a successful appeal of his charge of draft evasion, the **Ali–Frazier** bout between two undefeated heavyweight champions took place on 8 March 1971 at the Garden. A Frazier–Ali nontitle rematch in 1974 was also held there. Ali also made his last successful title defense at the Garden against **Earnie Shavers** in 1977.

As **casinos** began to get more of the major fights in the 1980s and 1990s, boxing at the Garden declined and fight cards became rare. The facility is still the home of the New York Knickerbockers professional basketball team and New York Rangers ice hockey team, and many other events such as concerts, the circus, and ice shows are still held there.

See also FELT FORUM.

MAIN EVENT. The featured **bout** on a boxing **card** is referred to as the main event. It is generally scheduled for 10 **rounds** and, in the case of championship bouts, 12 or 15 rounds. In addition to the main event, a boxing card usually has additional bouts scheduled for less than 10 rounds that are referred to as **preliminary bouts.**

MAJORITY DECISION. A majority decision is one in which two of the three officials scoring the **bout** vote for one boxer while the other official scores the bout as a **draw**.

See also MAJORITY DRAW; SPLIT DECISION; UNANIMOUS DECISION.

MAJORITY DRAW. A majority **draw** is a **bout** in which two of the three officials scoring the bout vote for a draw while the third official votes for one of the boxers as the winner. The result of the bout is a draw.

See also MAJORITY DECISION; SPLIT DECISION; UNANIMOUS DECISION.

MANCINI, RAY "BOOM BOOM" (né RAYMOND MICHAEL MANCINO). B. 4 March 1961, Youngstown, Ohio. Ray "Boom Boom" Mancini helped fulfill his father's dream. Lenny "Boom Boom" Mancini was a capable **lightweight** contender who had a record of 37–6–3 and appeared headed for a shot at the lightweight title. His plans were changed though as he entered the U.S. Army in 1944 during World War II. On 10 November 1944, he was wounded in battle in **France**. After his discharge from the service, he resumed his boxing career, but his war injuries limited his effectiveness, and although he fought **professionally** until 1947, he never had the opportunity to fight for the lightweight championship.

He brought his son, Ray, to a gym and taught him boxing skills. Ray proved to be quite competent and in 1979 began his professional boxing career. After winning his first 20 fights, 15 by **knockout**, he challenged **Alexis Argüello** for the **World Boxing Council** world's lightweight title on 3 October 1981 in **Atlantic City**, New Jersey. Although he put up a game battle, he was stopped in the 14th **round**. After two more victories, he then challenged the **World Boxing Association (WBA)** lightweight champion, Arturo Frias, on 8 May 1982 in **Las Vegas**, Nevada. Frias caught Mancini with a powerful punch right at the beginning of the fight and soon had Mancini cut. But Mancini retaliated and stopped Frias at 2:54 of the first round to win the title.

After a successful title defense, stopping challenger Ernesto España in the sixth round, Mancini made his second defense on 13 November 1982 in Las Vegas in a **bout** that completely changed his life. He faced the **Korean** challenger Deuk-Koo Kim on nationwide television and fought a highly competitive bout against the comparatively unknown Kim, who was knocked out at 0:19 of the 14th round and died four days later from brain injuries incurred during the bout. The tragic ending affected Mancini deeply, and although he continued boxing until 1992, he was never quite the same. The **referee** of the bout, Richard Green, was one the more competent Las Vegas officials of the era and had refereed several world championship bouts, including three of **Larry Holmes's** title defenses. Seven months after the bout, Green committed suicide.

Mancini attempted to continue his boxing career and three months after the Kim fight traveled to **Italy** for a **nontitle bout** in which he won a 10-round **decision**. He defended his title in September 1983 with a ninth-round knockout of previously undefeated (30–0–1) Orlando Romero. On 14 January 1984, Mancini knocked out the **super featherweight** champion Bobby Chacon in three rounds in another defense of his WBA **lightweight** title. This would be Mancini's last winning boxing match.

On 1 June 1984, Mancini lost his title when he was stopped in the 14th round in a tough battle with **Livingstone Bramble**, after which Mancini needed 71 stitches to close cuts near his eyes. In a rematch with Bramble on 16 February 1985, Mancini lost a **unanimous decision** in an extremely close bout in which he lost by only one point on each of the three officials' scorecards. After retiring, Mancini came back four years later and lost a 12-round **split decision** to **Héctor Camacho** for the **World Boxing Organization light welterweight** title. Mancini's final bout came three years after the Camacho bout, and he was stopped in seven rounds by Greg Haugen on 3 April 1992.

In the aftermath of the Mancini–Kim fight, the various sanctioning organizations reduced the limit of future championship bouts from 15 to 12 rounds under the theory that most severe boxing injuries occurred from the 13th to 15th rounds.

Mancini in retirement has done well for himself, as his **ring** earnings were invested wisely. He has become an actor, appearing in more than 20 films, and owns a cigar company, two movie production companies, and a wine-tasting shop.

Mancini is five foot four inches tall and has a 65-inch **reach**. He fought at weights ranging from 134 to 140 pounds as a lightweight and light welterweight. In 34 professional bouts, from 1979 to 1992, he won 29 (23 by knockout), lost five (three by knockout), and fought a total of 201 rounds.

MANCINO, RAYMOND MICHAEL. *See* MANCINI, RAY "BOOM BOOM" (né RAYMOND MICHAEL MANCINO).

MARCHEGIANO, ROCCO FRANCIS. *See* MARCIANO, ROCKY "THE BROCKTON BLOCKBUSTER" (né ROCCO FRANCIS MARCHEGIANO).

MARCIANO, ROCKY "THE BROCKTON BLOCKBUSTER" (né **ROCCO FRANCIS MARCHEGIANO**). B. 1 September 1923, Brockton, Massachusetts. D. 31 August 1969, Newton, Iowa. Rocky Marciano became a legend because he knew when to quit. He retired as undefeated world's **heavyweight** champion and was smart enough to avoid attempting a comeback.

He was the son of Italian immigrant parents, was raised in Brockton, Massachusetts, and attended Brockton High School, where he played football and baseball. He was a good enough catcher on the baseball team to be offered a tryout by the Chicago Cubs but not quite good enough to be offered a baseball contract. After he dropped out of school following the 10th grade, he worked as a ditch digger, delivery man for an ice and coal company, and shoemaker. He was drafted into the U.S. Army in 1943 and served for three years.

While in the army, he began boxing as an **amateur**. He fought his first professional fight on 17 March 1947 in Holyoke, Massachusetts, under the name of Rocky Mack and defeated Lee Epperson on a third-round **knockout**. In an unusual move, he returned to amateur boxing and won the 1948 Lowell, Massachusetts, **Golden Gloves** heavyweight championship. This qualified him to compete in the Eastern Regional Golden Gloves tournament in New York City. In his first **bout** there, competing under his given name of Rocco Marchegiano, he lost a close three-round decision to the New York Golden Gloves champion, **Coley Wallace**. He returned to Massachusetts and won the New England **Amateur Athletic Union** tournament.

He resumed his **professional boxing** career on 12 July 1948 with a one-round knockout of Harry Bilazarian in Providence, Rhode Island. Fighting almost exclusively in New England, Marciano won his first 22 bouts, 20 by knockout, and was booked in New York's **Madison Square Garden** in the semifinal event on 2 December 1949. Marciano easily defeated Pat Richards on a two-round **technical knockout**. After another win in Providence, Marciano was back at the Garden on 30 December in the **main event** against Carmine "Bingo" Vingo. Although Marciano won on a sixth-round knockout, he later described the bout as the "toughest of my career." It was also the toughest in Vingo's career, as he suffered a brain hemorrhage, was hospitalized in critical condition, and although he recovered was never able to fight again.

In Marciano's next fight (24 March 1950 at Madison Square Garden), he faced former New York Golden Gloves champion Roland LaStarza, who was undefeated with 37 consecutive victories. It was the closest that Marciano came to losing a professional fight. The scoring at the end of the 10-round bout was 5–4–1 for LaStarza, 5–4–1 for Marciano, and the **referee** Harry Watson voted 5 rounds for each fighter. But under the scoring system used by New York State, a supplemental point system was used in the event of an even scorecard. Using the supplemental point score of 9–6 in favor of Marciano, he became the winner on a **split decision**.

Marciano then won his next nine fights in New England against lesser-quality opponents before returning to the Garden on 12 July 1951. On that date, he knocked out Rex Layne in six rounds. Layne had a record of 34–1 at the time of the bout. After a four-round knockout of Freddie Beshore in Boston, Marciano on 26 October 1951 fought the former heavyweight champion **Joe Louis**, who had been attempting a comeback and had won eight fights since retiring after losing his title to **Ezzard Charles**.

The fight with Louis became one-sided, and Marciano knocked Louis down twice in the eighth round—the second time through the ropes. Referee **Ruby Goldstein** stopped the bout without a count, and Louis's **ring** career was over. In later years, Marciano said that he decided to quit boxing while still on top after seeing Louis end his career in this manner.

Marciano won four more bouts and then on 23 September 1952 won the world's heavyweight championship by knocking out **Jersey Joe Walcott** in the 13th round in Philadelphia. Marciano had been far behind on points up to that time and had been knocked down for the first time in his career in the first round. *Ring* **magazine** voted this bout the "Fight of the Year." A rematch with Walcott seven months later saw Marciano knock out Walcott in just 2:25 of the first round.

After he won the title, he often made ring appearances as a guest referee and worked more than 30 bouts in that capacity. After his retirement from the ring, he continued in that role and in 1965 was the referee for the **Carlos Ortiz**–Ismael Laguna world **lightweight** title bout.

Marciano's second title defense in 1953 was with his former nemesis LaStarza. This was the *Ring*'s "Fight of the Year" for 1953 and was won by Marciano with an 11th-round **technical knockout** after LaStarza had been knocked through the ropes.

Marciano's first defense in 1954 was against former heavyweight champion Ezzard Charles, who became the only boxer to go the 15-round distance with Marciano. In a relatively close contest, Marciano prevailed by **unanimous decision**. Their rematch three months later was a different story. Although Charles was knocked down in the second round, he inflicted a severe cut on Marciano's nose and the fight was nearly stopped in Charles's favor. But Marciano knocked Charles down again in the eighth round and then knocked him out in that round. This fight also was voted "Fight of the Year" by *Ring*.

Marciano's next defense was in San Francisco in 1955 against the British heavyweight champion Don Cockell and was won by Marciano on a ninth-round technical knockout.

Marciano's final bout of his career occurred on 21 September 1955 when **light heavyweight** champion **Archie Moore** challenged him for the heavyweight title. Moore scored a second-round **knockdown**, but Marciano retaliated by knocking Moore down five times before the bout was stopped in the ninth round.

On 27 April 1956, Marciano announced his retirement. His refusal to make a comeback was influenced in part by his ending **Joe Louis's** career. Marciano did make a comeback of sorts in 1969 when he took part in a filmed simulation of a computer bout between himself and **Muhammad Ali**. Although he and Ali simulated various possible endings, neither was aware of the result of the film as it was shown. Marciano never found out that he defeated Ali, according to the computer, as he was killed just three weeks after they finished filming.

His untimely death occurred one day before his 46th birthday when a small plane in which he was a passenger crashed in a cornfield near Newton, Iowa, as he was en route to Des Moines for a speaking engagement. He had been a guest at the home of auto racing car owner Andy Granatelli in Chicago the day before his flight.

Marciano was five foot 11 inches tall and had an unusually short 67-inch **reach**. He fought at weights ranging from 178 to 192 pounds as a heavyweight. In 49 professional bouts, from 1947 to 1955, he won all 49 (43 by knockout) and fought a total of 241 rounds. He was inducted as a member of the inaugural class of the **International Boxing Hall of Fame** in 1990.

MARQUESS OF QUEENSBERRY (né JOHN SHOLTO DOUGLAS). B. 20 July 1844, Florence, **Italy**. D. 31 January 1900, London, **England**. The title Marquess of Queensberry is a title in the Peerage of **Scotland** and was created in 1682. The man who was the ninth Marquess of Queensberry, John Sholto Douglas, was educated at the Royal Naval College in Greenwich, England, and at the age of 12 was a midshipman in the Royal Navy. He was promoted to lieutenant by age 15.

As a patron of sport and a boxing enthusiast, he helped found the Amateur Athletic Club in 1866. In 1867, the club published a set of rules governing boxing, written by John Graham Chambers and sponsored by Douglas, which became known as the **Marquess of Queensberry Rules**.

From 1872 to 1880, he served in the House of Lords. In 1895, he became involved in a lawsuit with author and playwright Oscar Wilde over Wilde's homosexuality, which eventually resulted in Wilde being sentenced to prison.

The marquess was inducted into the **International Boxing Hall of Fame** in 1990.

MARQUESS OF QUEENSBERRY RULES. The Marquess of Queensberry Rules were written in 1865 by John Graham Chambers and published in 1867. The rules were sponsored by John Sholto Douglas, the ninth **Marquess of Queensberry**, and have since been known by that name. The rules superseded the revised **London Prize Ring Rules** and require boxers to wear **gloves** and box three-minute **rounds** with a one-minute rest period between rounds. The Marquess of Queensberry Rules continue to govern boxing in the 21st century.

See also APPENDIX J.

MAXIM, JOEY (né GIUSEPPE ANTONIO BERARDINELLI). B. 28 March 1922, Cleveland, Ohio. D. 2 June 2001, West Palm Beach, Florida. Joey Maxim is best remembered as the man who outlasted both his opponent and the **referee**. On 25 June 1952, in a world's **light heavyweight** championship fight outdoors at Yankee Stadium in the Bronx, New York, in 104 degree weather, referee **Ruby Goldstein** succumbed to the heat and had to quit after the 10th **round**, and Maxim's opponent, **"Sugar Ray" Robinson**, quit at the end of the 13th round, even though he was well ahead on points. This was the only **bout** in Robinson's 200-bout professional career in which he failed to go the distance.

Maxim was quite successful as an **amateur** boxer in Cleveland and in 1940, as a **middleweight**, won the local **Golden Gloves** tournament, the Chicago Tournament of Champions, and the Intercity (Chicago vs. New York) Golden Gloves championship. He also won the National **Amateur Athletic Union** championship.

He fought his first **professional** bout on 13 January 1941, winning a four-round **decision** in the light heavyweight class. Not a heavy puncher, Maxim did not score a **knockout** victory until his 10th bout, although he entered that fight with a record of eight wins in his first nine bouts. After winning 20 of his first 25 bouts, Maxim faced future **heavyweight** champion **Ezzard Charles** on 27 October 1942 but was easily defeated on a 10-round **unanimous decision**. A rematch five weeks later produced the same result. Undaunted, Maxim continued to be one of the nation's better light heavyweights. On 28 August 1946, he defeated **Jersey Joe Walcott**, another future heavyweight champion, on a 10-round decision, but Walcott defeated Maxim twice in 1947.

By 23 May 1949, Maxim had compiled a record of 63–16–4 and was matched with Gus Lesnevich in Cincinnati, Ohio, for the **vacant National Boxing Association** light heavyweight championship. Maxim won a unanimous 15-round decision and became recognized by some as champion. A 10th-round knockout win over Freddie Mills in London on 24 January 1950 gave Maxim universal recognition as champion. Maxim was not a particularly active champion, and while he fought and won seven **nontitle bouts** over the next 12 months, he did not defend his title during that time.

Instead, he challenged Ezzard Charles for the world heavyweight title on 30 May 1951 and lost a unanimous decision. Maxim made his first title defense three months later, defeating Bob Murphy in 15 rounds at **Madison Square Garden**. On 25 June 1952, the aforementioned bout with "Sugar Ray" Robinson was Maxim's second title defense. The 30-year-old Maxim lost his title on 17 December 1952 to the 36-year-old **Archie Moore** in St. Louis on a unanimous decision. Two rematches with Moore for the light heavyweight championship on 24 June 1953 and 27 January 1954 also resulted in victories for Moore. Maxim continued fighting in the heavyweight class until 17 May 1958 but lost eight of his final 11 bouts—all by 10-round decision against quality opponents for the most part.

After retiring from boxing, Maxim worked as a stand-up comedian and nightclub greeter in hotels and **casinos** in **Las Vegas**.

Maxim was six foot one inch tall and had a 71-inch **reach**. He fought at weights ranging from 167 to 192 pounds as a light heavyweight and heavyweight. In 115 professional bouts, from 1941 to 1958, he won 82 (21 by knockout), lost 29 (one by knockout), had four **draws**, and fought a total of 1,052 rounds. He was inducted into the **International Boxing Hall of Fame** in 1994.

MAYWEATHER, FLOYD JOY, JR., "PRETTY BOY," "MONEY" (né FLOYD JOY SINCLAIR). B. 24 February 1977, Grand Rapids, Michigan. Floyd Mayweather Jr. is arguably the greatest **professional** boxer of the 21st century. Through July 2013, he has won all 44 of his **bouts** and has won major championships in five different weight divisions. He is considered by many experts to be among the greatest pound-for-pound fighters in boxing history.

The son of former boxer Floyd Mayweather Sr., he had an extensive **amateur** career with a record of 84–6 and won three National **Golden Gloves** championships—1993 **light flyweight**, 1994 **flyweight**, and 1996 **featherweight**. He also won the **United States** national amateur featherweight title in 1995 and won the featherweight **bronze** medal at the 1996 **Olympic Games**, losing a highly controversial decision in his semifinal bout that the United States delegation protested to no avail.

He fought his first professional bout on 11 October 1996 in **Las Vegas**, easily winning on a second-round **technical knockout**. After winning his first 17 bouts, he defeated Genaro Hernández on 3 October 1998 on an eighth-round retirement and won the **World Boxing Council (WBC) super featherweight** title.

He successfully defended that title eight times and then moved up to the **lightweight** class. On 20 April 2002, Mayweather defeated José Luis Castillo and became the WBC lightweight champion. He defended that title three times, including a rematch with Castillo, and moved up in weight class again. As a **light welterweight**, he fought and won two bouts before stopping **Arturo Gatti** in six rounds to win the WBC light welterweight title. After a **nontitle** technical knockout over Sharmba Mitchell, Mayweather won the **International Boxing Federation** and International Boxing Organization **welterweight** titles by decisioning Zab Judah. In his next bout, Mayweather added the WBC welterweight title with a decision over Carlos Manuel Baldomir.

On 5 May 2007, Mayweather took on the celebrated **Óscar De La Hoya** in a WBC **light middleweight** championship match and added that championship on a narrow **split decision**. Mayweather then stopped the previously undefeated (43–0) Ricky Hatton in 10 rounds and rewon the WBC welterweight title, which he had vacated after winning the light middleweight title. He then retired briefly but returned to the **ring** in September 2009, winning a **nontitle bout** with Juan Manuel Márquez. A prospective $50-million fight with multiple champion **Manny Pacquiao** was talked about but never consummated.

Mayweather then fought only once in each of the next three years but rewon the WBC welterweight title in 2011 and won the **World Boxing Association** light middleweight title in 2012.

His career was interrupted in 2012 as he served a prison term from 1 June to 3 August for domestic abuse.

Mayweather is five foot eight inches tall and has a 72-inch **reach**. He has fought at weights ranging from 129 to 151 pounds in weight classes from **super featherweight** to light middleweight. In 43 professional bouts, from 1996 to 2012, he won all 43 (26 by **knockout**) and fought a total of 315 rounds.

McCOY, CHARLES "KID," "THE CORKSCREW KID" (né NORMAN SELBY). B. 13 October 1872, Moscow, Indiana. D. 18 April 1940, Detroit, Michigan. To say that Norman Selby, who fought as Charles "Kid" McCoy, was a character is an understatement. Much of the lore associated with him might be apocryphal, but then again it might be true.

The phrase "real McCoy" is attributed to him since he apparently did not always give his best in a fight and spectators wondered if the man in the **ring** was ready to fight and was the "real McCoy." He also allegedly invented the "corkscrew punch" in which he twisted his fist as he applied the blow to give it more sting. He supposedly also invented the tactic of telling an opponent his shoelace was untied and, when the opponent looked down, hitting him in the face.

He began boxing in the midwestern **United States**, with his first recorded **bout** on 2 June 1891 in St. Paul, Minnesota. He won nearly all his early bouts, with a one-round **knockout** in 1894 by Billy Steffers being the only loss on his record from 1891 until November 1895. During that time, he recorded 30 victories (19 by knockout) and seven **draws**, fighting throughout the eastern United States from Massachusetts to Louisiana. In November 1895, he traveled to London, **England**, where he lost his second bout, a 10-**round decision** to Ted White.

On 2 March 1896, McCoy knocked out **Tommy Ryan** in 15 rounds in New York and claimed the world's **middleweight** title. In May, McCoy defeated **"Mysterious Billy" Smith** by **disqualification** and in December on **Boxing Day** found himself in **South Africa**, where he won the "South African middleweight title" by knocking out Bill Doherty in nine rounds.

On 17 December 1897, McCoy stopped Dan Creedon in 15 rounds in New York in a bout billed for the world's middleweight title. Afterward, McCoy stated that he would be boxing as a **heavyweight** and not defending the middleweight title. Ryan seized the opportunity and claimed the title for himself.

In one of McCoy's first heavyweight bouts, he defeated top contender Gus Ruhlin on a 20-round decision on 20 May 1898 in Syracuse, New York. After losing to Tom Sharkey via a 10-round knockout in New York in January 1899, McCoy won a 20-round decision over Joe Choynski in San Francisco two months later. In Brooklyn in 1900, McCoy scored knockout victories over Peter Maher and Joe Choynski within a two-week period in January. In August 1900, McCoy lost to former heavyweight champion **Jim Corbett** in five rounds in a bout that was suspected of being a fake with McCoy deliberately losing to win a bet.

In 1901, McCoy traveled back to London and is recorded as having won three bouts on the same day, 2 December, winning all three by knockout. On 22 April 1903 in Detroit, Michigan, McCoy lost a 10-round decision to Jack Root in the first world's **light heavyweight** championship bout. Legendary Western lawman Bat Masterson was the bout's **referee**.

McCoy fought a six-round **draw** with **Philadelphia Jack O'Brien** in 1904 and won a 20-round decision over Jack "Twin" Sullivan later that year. He boxed sporadically after that and scored a two-round knockout over Peter Maher in 1908. He had a few bouts in 1911 and traveled to **France** toward the end of that year for four bouts from November 1911 to February 1912. One bout in London, England, in 1914 and one in Texas in 1916 round out his career.

In 1911, he was reported to have opened a detective agency in New York with a partner. He traveled to California and worked in more than a dozen Hollywood films under his given name, Norman Selby. On 14 August 1924, a married woman that he had been living with was shot and killed in Los

Angeles. He was later charged with the crime and sentenced to prison at San Quentin beginning 11 April 1925. He was eventually paroled in August 1932 and worked as a physical education instructor for Ford Motor Company in Dearborn, Michigan.

During his lifetime, he was married nine or 10 times (accounts differ). On 18 April 1940, he committed suicide at a Detroit hotel by an overdose of sleeping pills, leaving behind a note that said, in part, "Sorry I could not endure this world's madness."

McCoy was five foot 11 inches tall and had a 76-inch **reach**. He fought at weights ranging from 142 to 173 pounds in weight classes from **welterweight** to heavyweight. In 116 professional bouts, from 1891 to 1916, he won 87 (65 by knockout), lost seven (four by knockout), and had 10 draws, five **no contests**, and seven no decision bouts, in which he was awarded the **newspaper decision** in five, lost one, and drew one. He fought a total of 680 rounds. He was inducted into the **International Boxing Hall of Fame** in 1992.

McGOVERN, JOSEPH TERRENCE "TERRY," "TERRIBLE TER-RY". B. 9 March 1880, Johnstown, Pennsylvania. D. 22 February 1918, Brooklyn, New York. Terry McGovern was one of the fiercest fighters for his size and one of the first to win world championships in two weight classes. Born in Pennsylvania, he was raised in Brooklyn and claimed never to have gone to school. After several fights with coworkers at the lumberyard where he was employed, he was encouraged to become a **professional** fighter.

He had his first recorded **bout** on 3 April 1897 in Brooklyn. It went into the books as a four-round **disqualification** loss for McGovern. After winning 16 of his first 20 bouts, he lost another fight on a disqualification for hitting during a **clinch** after being warned several times for the infraction. He then won 14 of his next 15 bouts, 11 by **knockout**, and was matched with the previously undefeated (23–0–1) Thomas "Pedlar" Palmer for Palmer's world **bantamweight** title on 12 September 1899 in Tuckahoe, New York (a suburb of New York City). McGovern knocked out Palmer in 2:32 of the first round and won the title. After nine consecutive knockouts, eight in **nontitle bouts** and a second round knockout of Harry Forbes in a title defense, McGovern took on the black Canadian **George Dixon** for Dixon's world **featherweight** title on 9 January 1900 in New York, although both fighters weighed in under the bantamweight limit. McGovern stopped Dixon in the eighth round of their scheduled 25-round bout and became world featherweight champion.

McGovern never defended his bantamweight title and concentrated on bouts in the featherweight division. He successfully defended his featherweight title against Eddie Santry on 1 February in Chicago with a fifth-round

technical knockout, and one month later on 9 March in New York, he knocked out Oscar Gardner in three rounds. The Gardner bout was controversial in that McGovern was knocked down in the first round and while down held on to Gardner's leg for six seconds while Gardner attempted to pull away and only then did the **referee** begin counting.

After several nontitle bouts, McGovern next defended against Tommy White on 12 June 1900 in Brooklyn. Again, McGovern won easily with a three-round knockout. Two weeks later, McGovern won a six-round nontitle bout from Dixon. His next title defense was in Louisville, Kentucky, on 2 November 1900—a seven-round knockout of Joe Bernstein.

McGovern scored a two-round knockout over future **lightweight** champion **Joe Gans** on 13 December 1900, but Gans later claimed to have **taken a dive** in that bout. McGovern's next title defense was 30 April 1901 in San Francisco—a rematch with Gardner, whom Terry knocked out in four rounds. Remaining in San Francisco, McGovern then took on Aurelio Herrera for the featherweight title on 29 May. Although Herrera was stopped in five rounds, he later claimed he was doped by one of his own seconds.

McGovern lost his featherweight title to Young Corbett II on 28 November 1901 in Hartford, Connecticut, when he was knocked out in the second round. They fought a rematch in San Francisco on 23 March 1902, but McGovern lost again—this time by a knockout in the 11th round.

In the next six years, McGovern did not fight any more world championship fights but did knock out Harlem Tommy Murphy in one round in 1905, lose a **newspaper decision** to Battling Nelson in 1906, and fight newspaper decision draws with Jimmy Britt and Young Corbett II in 1906. His last bout was on 26 May 1908—a newspaper decision **draw** with Englishman Frank "Spike" Robson in New York City.

McGovern's health, both mental and physical, began to decline, and he spent much of his last 10 years in various sanatoriums. He collapsed while refereeing at an army camp and died soon after from pneumonia and kidney failure at the age of 37.

He was selected by boxing historian **Nat Fleischer** as the greatest featherweight of all time.

McGovern was five foot three inches tall and had a 65-inch **reach**. He fought at weights ranging from 110 to 130 pounds, primarily as a bantamweight and featherweight. In 80 professional bouts, from 1897 to 1908, he won 59 (44 by knockout), lost five (two by knockout), and had four draws, one **no contest**, and 11 no-decision bouts, in which he was awarded the newspaper decision in six, lost one, and drew four. He fought a total of 541 rounds. He was inducted as a member of the inaugural class of the **International Boxing Hall of Fame** in 1990.

McGUIGAN, FINBARR PATRICK "BARRY," "THE CLONES CYCLONE". B. 28 February 1961, Clones, Ireland. Barry McGuigan near-ly united Ireland and Northern Ireland. Born in and residing in Clones, County Monaghan, a small town in Ireland on the border of Northern Ireland, he represented Northern Ireland in the 1978 Commonwealth Games in Edmonton, Alberta, Canada, yet fought for Ireland in the 1980 Moscow Olympic Games. He was the gold medalist in the bantamweight class in Edmonton but lost in the third round in Moscow after winning his first bout.

McGuigan is the son of Irish tenor, Pat McGuigan, a former Eurovision contestant known for his rendition of "Danny Boy." Barry began amateur boxing in 1976 and had a reported amateur record of 21–2 with 19 knockouts.

He had his first professional bout in Dublin, Ireland, on 10 May 1981, a second-round technical knockout of Selvin Bell. After winning his next bout, McGuigan lost an eight-round decision to Peter Eubank in his third bout. He then won his next 11 bouts (nine by knockout). In one of these fights (14 June 1982 in London), he scored a sixth-round knockout of a Nigerian fighter known as Young Ali, who fell into a coma following the fight and remained incapacitated until he died five months later. This bout almost ended McGuigan's career, as he felt extreme remorse over the incident. Although he resumed boxing, McGuigan remained upset over the tragedy and, after his career ended, unsuccessfully attempted to locate Ali's widow in Nigeria.

McGuigan was able to resume on 12 April 1983 and stopped Vernon Penprase in the second round and won the British Boxing Board of Control featherweight championship. Later that year (16 November 1983), McGuigan won the European Boxing Union (EBU) featherweight title with a sixth-round knockout of Italian Valerio Nati in Belfast. After three successful defenses of the EBU title, McGuigan fought the World Boxing Association (WBA) featherweight champion Panamanian Eusebio Pedroza for Pedroza's crown in London on 8 June 1985. Winning a 15-round unanimous decision, McGuigan became WBA world featherweight champion.

He defended that title twice, in Belfast against Bernard Taylor (28 September 1985, technical knockout [TKO] round 8) and in Dublin against Danilo Cabrera (15 February 1986, TKO 14). For his next defense, he traveled to Las Vegas, where the oppressive heat caused McGuigan to become dehydrated (requiring hospitalization after the bout) , and he lost his title to Steve Cruz via a 15-round close but unanimous decision on 23 June 1986. The fight was named "Fight of the Year" by *Ring* magazine.

Barry lost his father in 1987, and that, coupled with loss of his title, caused him to retire. He made a brief comeback, winning three bouts in 1988, but retired permanently following a bout on 31 May 1989 in Manchester against Jim McDonnell in which McGuigan was stopped in the fourth round due to cuts.

In retirement from the ring, McGuigan has done some television reporting of boxing, appeared in a film, managed boxers, and in 2007 established an organization called Professional Boxers Association, which attempts to provide education and counseling to prospective boxers.

McGuigan is five foot six inches tall and has a 70-inch **reach**. He fought at weights ranging from 124 to 130 pounds as a featherweight. In 35 professional bouts, from 1981 to 1989, he won 32 (28 by knockout), lost three (one by knockout), and fought a total of 198 rounds. He was inducted into the **International Boxing Hall of Fame** in 2005.

McKERNAN, JOHN LEO. *See* KEARNS, JACK "DOC" (né JOHN LEO McKERNAN).

McLAGLEN, VICTOR ANDREW DE BIER EVERLEIGH "SHAR-KEY". B. 11 December 1883, Tunbridge Wells, Kent, **England**. D. 7 November 1959, Newport Beach, California. Victor McLaglen is the only man to win an Academy Award as well as fight the world's **heavyweight** champion. One of his most memorable screen fights was against ex-boxer Trooper Thorn (played by John Wayne) in the 1952 film *The Quiet Man*.

McLaglen was born in England but raised partially in South Africa, where his father, Andrew, was a clergyman. During his teens, the six-foot-three-inch, 195-pound Victor went to **Canada** and traveled the country as a wrestler and boxer. He also worked with a circus and would take on all comers in the ring. Two of his six brothers (Fred, who boxed as Fred Mackay, and Arthur) were also itinerant boxers, and his brother Leopold worked as a wrestler.

On 10 March 1909, McLaglen faced the new heavyweight champion **Jack Johnson** in a six-round **bout** in Vancouver, Canada, that has been variously reported as a championship bout or an **exhibition**. In either case, McLaglen lasted six rounds in the **ring** with the world's heavyweight champion.

At times, McLaglen boxed as "Sharkey" McLaglen and, in an exhibition bout with future heavyweight champion **Jess Willard** in 1911, was known as Fred Romano. McLaglen's recorded bouts were primarily in the Pacific Northwest, both in the **United States** and Canada, but in 1913 he had three bouts in New York City and from 1915 to 1920 had several bouts in London,

England. Among his more notable opponents were Denver Ed Martin, Sailor White, Dan McGoldrick, and Arthur Townley. McLaglen's last recorded bout was against Townley on 11 October 1920 in London.

McLaglen began his acting career in England in 1920 and appeared in 19 British films from 1920 to 1924. In 1924, he was offered the leading role in an American film, *The Beloved Brute*. His Hollywood career progressed from the silent film era to sound films, and one of the highlights of his Hollywood career was the 1935 film *The Informer*, for which he won the Academy Award as best actor. He continued working in Hollywood until the time of his death in 1959 as one of Hollywood's top performers and is credited with appearances in 122 films.

McLaglen was six foot three inches tall and fought at weights ranging from 199 to 210 pounds as a heavyweight. In 19 recorded professional bouts as a boxer, from 1908 to 1920, he won 11 (10 by **knockout**), lost six (four by knockout), had one **draw** and one **no-contest** bout, and fought a total of 94 rounds.

McLARNIN, JAMES "JIMMY," "BABY-FACED ASSASSIN". B. 19 December 1907, Hillsborough, County Down, **Ireland**. D. 28 October 2004, Richland, Washington. Jimmy McLarnin, although born in Ireland, was raised in **Canada**. An **amateur boxing** champion in British Columbia, he began boxing **professionally** in Vancouver in 1923, with his first recorded **bout** a one-**round knockout** of Young Fry on 19 December 1923. After winning a second fight that month, he moved to the San Francisco area in 1924. He was undefeated in 17 bouts that year, with 15 victories and two draws. The draws were with **Olympic flyweight** champion Fidel La Barba (whom he had previously defeated) and future Hall of Famer Memphis Pal Moore. McLarnin suffered his first loss on 2 June 1925, a 10-round **decision** to future world's **bantamweight** champion Charles "Bud" Taylor.

In his next bout, McLarnin won a 10-round decision over world flyweight champion **Pancho Villa** in a **nontitle bout**. The bout would be Villa's last, as he developed an infection in his throat from a tooth extraction and died 10 days later. McLarnin then defeated another Olympic champion—Jackie Fields, the 1924 Olympic **featherweight gold medalist**. McLarnin knocked out Fields in two rounds. McLarnin followed up that accomplishment with two bouts with Taylor—a second-round **disqualification** victory and a 10-round decision loss.

On 18 October 1927, McLarnin knocked out Louis "Kid" Kaplan, a former world's bantamweight champion, after being knocked down himself twice in the bout. In his first bid for a world's title, McLarnin lost a 15-round decision to Sammy Mandell on 21 May 1928 in a world's **lightweight** championship contest held outdoors at the Polo Grounds in New York. McLarnin defeated Mandell in two return bouts in 1929 and 1930, but by then Mandell was no longer the lightweight champion.

In his next fight in 1930, McLarnin defeated another future champion, Young Jack Thompson (future world's **welterweight** champion). McLarnin won a 10-round decision despite breaking his hand in the first round. McLarnin was out of action for five months following the Thompson bout and returned to score a three-round knockout over Al Singer, a former lightweight champion. McLarnin then fought three bouts (losing the first and winning the next two—all 10-round decisions) with Billy Petrolle, a tough welterweight who never won a championship but was elected to the **International Boxing Hall of Fame**.

McLarnin, who always fought the top contenders, then fought his next four bouts against men who either were or would be world champions and won three of the four bouts. He lost the first, a 10-round decision to Lou Brouillard (former welterweight champion), then stopped former lightweight champion **Benny Leonard** in six rounds, knocked out **junior welterweight** champion Sammy Fuller in a nontitle bout, and finally on 29 May 1933 stopped Young Corbett III in 2:37 of the first round and won the world's welterweight title with that victory.

Unfortunately for McLarnin, his next bout was also with a future world's champion, **Barney Ross**, who won the world's championship by winning a **split-decision** 15-round bout with McLarnin on 28 May 1934. McLarnin kept his streak alive of fighting world champions by winning a rematch with Ross on a split decision on 17 September. The two fighters had their third consecutive bout exactly one year to the day after their first bout, and this time Ross rewon the welterweight title on a 15-round **unanimous decision**. This was the 12th straight welterweight title bout in which the champion lost his title.

McLarnin concluded his professional boxing career with three bouts against past, present, or future world champions. He faced lightweight champion **Tony Canzoneri** in a nontitle bout but lost a unanimous 10-round decision on 8 May 1936. They had a rematch on 5 October 1936 won by McLarnin, but by then Canzoneri had lost his title to Lou Ambers. McLarnin then defeated Ambers in a nontitle bout on 20 November 1936.

In the last 10 bouts of his professional boxing career, McLarnin had faced nothing but champions and won six of the bouts.

In retirement, he settled in Washington State, opened an electrical goods store, became a quite competent golfer often playing with Hollywood celebrities, invested wisely, and led a comfortable life.

He was one of the oldest living former boxers when he finally succumbed to Alzheimer's disease at the age of 96.

McLarnin was five foot six inches tall and had a 67-inch **reach**. He fought at weights ranging from 121 to 147 pounds, primarily as a lightweight and welterweight. In 68 professional bouts, from 1923 to 1936, he won 54 (21 by knockout), lost 11 (one by knockout), had three draws, and fought a total of 453 rounds. He was inducted into the International Boxing Hall of Fame in 1991.

MEXICO. Boxing is one of the most popular sports in Mexico. In **amateur boxing**, Mexican boxers first competed in the 1928 **Olympic Games** and have entered 19 Olympic boxing tournaments. Compared to their results in **professional boxing**, Mexico has not fared exceptionally well in amateur competition. They have won 12 Olympic boxing medals (two **gold**, three **silver**, seven **bronze**), which places them in 23rd place overall. But in professional boxing, Mexican boxers have won more world championships than fighters from any other nation except the **United States**.

Their Olympic champions were Ricardo Delgado, 1968 **flyweight**, and Antonio Roldán, 1968 **featherweight**—both champions at the games held in Mexico City. Silver medalists were Francisco Cabañas, 1932 flyweight; Alfonso Zamora, 1972 **bantamweight**; and Héctor López, 1984 bantamweight. Bronze medalists were Mario González, 1988 flyweight; Fidel Ortíz, 1936 bantamweight; Juan Fabila, 1964 bantamweight; Juan Paredes, 1976 featherweight; Cristian Bejarano, 2000 **lightweight**; Agustín Zaragoza, 1968 middleweight; and Joaquín Rocha, 1968 **heavyweight**.

There have been 128 Mexican world champions through 2012 (and more than 40 Mexican American world champions). The bantamweight class has been their primary division, with 19 Mexican world bantamweight champions. Mexican world champions elected to the **International Boxing Hall of Fame** are Miguel Canto, **Julio César Chávez**, José "Pipino" Cuevas, Humberto González, Ricardo López, **Rubén Olivares**, **Carlos Palomino**, Ultiminio "Sugar" Ramos, Vicente Saldivar, **Salvador** Sánchez, Albert "Chalky" Wright, Daniel Zaragoza, and **Carlos Zárate**. Hall of Famer **José Nápoles** was born in **Cuba**, but after the communist government banned boxing there, he moved to Mexico, where he was based for much of his boxing career.

Other notable Mexican fighters, most of whom have won championships, include Romeo Anaya, Alberto "Baby" Arizmendi, brothers René and Ricardo Arredondo, Kid Azteca, Marco Antonio Barrera, Victor Burgos, Chango Carmona, Jesús "Chucho" Castillo, Julio César Chávez Jr. (son of the Hall of Famer), Guty Espadas and his son Guty Jr., twins Raúl and Ramón García Hirales, Miguel Ángel González, Rafael "Bazooka" Limón, Alvaro "Yaqui" López, Raúl Macías, brothers Juan Manuel and Rafael Márquez, Fernando

Montiel, Erik Morales, Armando Muñiz, **Gaspar Ortega**, Jorge Páez, Isidro Pérez, Lupe Pintor, Lauro Salas, Clemente Sánchez, Battling Shaw, Efren Torres, and Alfonso Zamora.

The largest paid attendance for a boxing card, 132,247 fans, occurred in Mexico City on 20 February 1993 at Estadio Azteca as undefeated **World Boxing Council (WBC) light welterweight** champion Julio César Chávez won his 85th consecutive match with a fifth-round technical knockout over Greg Haugen.

The WBC has its offices in Mexico, and its president since 1975 has been the Mexican José Sulaiman. He was elected to the International Boxing Hall of Fame in 2007, and Mexican **trainer** Ignacio "Nacho" Beristáin was elected to the Hall in 2011.

MIDDLEWEIGHT. Middleweight is a boxing weight class in which the contestants cannot exceed 160 pounds. It is one of the oldest boxing weight classes as well as one of the most popular ones. Many **welterweights** move up in weight and compete as middleweights. The first middleweight champion was **Jack Dempsey, the Nonpareil**. Most of his **bouts** were **bareknuckle** bouts. **Bob Fitzsimmons** succeeded Dempsey and later also won the **light heavyweight** and **heavyweight** titles.

Some of the best professional middleweights have been **Carmen Basilio**, **Nino Benvenuti**, **Marcel Cerdan**, Jack "Nonpareil" Dempsey, Theodore "Tiger" Flowers, **Rocky Graziano**, **Harry Greb**, **Emile Griffith**, **Marvelous Marvin Hagler**, **Bernard Hopkins**, **Stanley Ketchel**, **Jake LaMotta**, **Carlos Monzón**, **"Sugar Ray" Robinson**, **Dick Tiger**, **Mickey Walker**, and **Tony Zale**. Robinson is generally regarded as the best champion in this weight class.

See also BAKER, REGINALD LESLIE "SNOWY"; CARTER, RUBIN "HURRICANE"; FULLMER, GENE "CYCLONE"; GIARDELLO, JOEY (né CARMINE ORLANDO TILELLI); JONES, RALPH "TIGER"; JONES, ROY LEVESTA, JR; McCOY, CHARLES "KID," "THE CORKSCREW KID" (né NORMAN SELBY); NAPOLES, JOSÉ ANGEL "MANTEQUILLA"; O'BRIEN, PHILADELPHIA JACK (né JOSEPH FRANCIS ANTHONY HAGEN); OLSON, CARL ELMER "BOBO," "THE HAWAIIAN SWEDE"; PAPP, LASZLO "LACI"; RYAN, TOMMY (né JOSEPH YOUNGS); TONEY, JAMES NATHANIEL "LIGHTS OUT"; TORRES, JOSÉ "CHEGÜI"; TRINIDAD GARCÍA, FÉLIX JUAN, JR., "TITO".

MINI FLYWEIGHT. *See* STRAWWEIGHT.

MINIMUMWEIGHT. *See* STRAWWEIGHT.

MIRENA, ANGELO. *See* DUNDEE, ANGELO (né ANGELO MIRENA).

MIXED MARTIAL ARTS. Mixed martial arts is a relatively new combat sport that combines, boxing, **kickboxing**, and wrestling. It is contested in an octagon-shaped **ring** and in the 21st century has become the most popular combat sport, although many boxing purists do not approve of the sport and it is not licensed in all jurisdictions that license boxing—New York State being one such place.

See also KICKBOXING; MUAY THAI; SAVATE.

MOLINEAUX, TOM. B. 1784, Virginia. D. 4 August 1818, Dublin, **Ireland**. Tom Molineaux was a former slave who demonstrated prowess in the boxing **ring**. He was given his freedom and traveled to **England**, where he engaged in several notable **bareknuckle** boxing matches. In England, he was trained by Bill Richmond, another former slave.

On 24 July 1810, he defeated Jack Burrowes in about one hour. He followed that match with an eight-**round** win over Tom Blake on 21 August. On 18 December 1810, he fought **Tom Cribb** for the **heavyweight** championship in a memorable battle but was defeated after 33 rounds. Cribb apparently collapsed from exhaustion, and various records list the number of rounds as 33, 39, or 40. A rematch on 28 September 1811 also favored Cribb, as he knocked out Molineaux in 11 rounds. Molineaux had several more fights from 1812 to 1815.

Molineaux was well thought of by the leading boxing writer of the time, Pierce Egan, who described him "as courageous a man as ever an adversary contended with."

After his last recorded **bout** in 1815, Molineaux became an alcoholic and spent some time in debtor's prison. He died from liver failure in 1818 at the age of 34.

He was inducted into the **International Boxing Hall of Fame** in 1997.

MONZÓN LEDESMA, CARLOS ROQUE "ESCOPETA". B. 7 August 1942, San Javier, Santa Fe, **Argentina**. D. 8 January 1995, Santa Rosa de Calchines, Argentina. Carlos Monzón was world **middleweight** champion for eight years during the 1970s. He retired undefeated, but the violent streak developed during his youth in the slums became his undoing.

He began boxing as an **amateur** in 1959 and claimed a record of 73–6–8. On 6 February 1963, he became a **professional boxer**, winning his first **bout** by second-**round knockout** in Rafaela, Argentina. In his first 21 bouts in 1963 and 1964, he won 17 (14 by knockout) and lost three. Those three losses would be his only losses as a professional boxer, as he would then fight until 1977 without losing again, ending his career with a 31-bout winning streak.

He captured the Argentine middleweight title in 1966 and the South American middleweight championship in 1967. He did not fight outside of Argentina or **Brazil** until 7 November 1970, when he met the world's middleweight champion Italian **Nino Benvenuti** in Rome, **Italy**. Monzón stopped Benvenuti in the 12th round of a bout selected by *Ring* **magazine** as the "Fight of the Year."

From 1971 to 1977, Monzón defended his world's middleweight championship 14 times all over the world in venues ranging from Monte Carlo, Monaco, to Copenhagen, Denmark. Only one fight was in the **United States**. His title defenses were against Benvenuti (8 May 1971, Monte Carlo, Monaco, **technical knockout** [TKO] round 3); **Emile Griffith** (25 September 1971, Buenos Aires, Argentina, TKO 14); Denny Moyer (4 March 1972, Rome, TKO 5); Jean-Claude Bouttier (17 June 1972, Paris, **France**, TKO 13); Tom Bogs (19 August, 1972, Copenhagen, Denmark, TKO 5); Bennie Briscoe (11 November 1972, Buenos Aires, **unanimous decision** 15); Griffith (2 June 1973, Monte Carlo, unanimous decision 15); Bouttier (29 September 1973, Paris, unanimous decision 15); **José Nápoles** (9 February 1974, Hauts-de-Seine, France, TKO 6); Tony Mundine (5 October 1974, Buenos Aires, knockout [KO] 7), Tony Licata (30 June 1975, **Madison Square Garden**, New York, TKO 10); Gratien Tonna (13 December 1975, Paris, KO 5); Rodrigo Valdéz (26 June 1976, Monte Carlo, unanimous decision 15); and Valdéz again in Monaco on 30 July 1977, another unanimous 15-round decision.

He retired after the second Valdéz bout. His life as a womanizer and his violent attitude in private life received much public attention, especially from paparazzi. He appeared in several films and moved in social circles far removed from those of his poverty-stricken past. In 1988, he argued with his second wife, who then fell from a balcony and died. Monzón was accused of murder and, in a trial that was front-page news in Argentina for months, was convicted and sentenced to 11 years in prison. In 1995, while driving home for a weekend furlough from prison, he drove his car off the road and was killed.

Monzón was five foot 11 inches tall and had a 76-inch **reach**. He fought at weights ranging from 157 to 163 pounds as a middleweight. In 100 professional bouts, from 1963 to 1977, he won 87 (59 by knockout), lost three (none by knockout), had nine draws and one **no-contest** bout, and fought a total of 762 rounds. He was inducted as a member of the inaugural class of the **International Boxing Hall of Fame** in 1990.

MOORE, ARCHIE "THE OLD MONGOOSE" (né ARCHIBALD LEE WRIGHT). B. 13 December 1916, Benoit, Mississippi. D. 9 December 1998, San Diego, California. Archie Moore had one of the longest boxing careers and only became a world champion at the age of 36. Raised in the St. Louis, Missouri, area by an aunt and uncle, he spent a brief time in reform school, where he learned to box.

His early **professional** record is sketchy, and not all his **bouts** have been found. His first recorded professional fight was as a **welterweight** on 3 September 1935 in Poplar Springs, Missouri (a suburb of St. Louis). He won that by a **knockout**, and before he retired from the **ring** 28 years later, he compiled a record total of knockouts variously listed as 131 or 141.

By 1939, he had a record of 33–2–2 and on 20 April 1939 fought Teddy Yarosz, a former **middleweight** champion. In that bout, Moore showed promise but was outboxed by the veteran Yarosz and lost a 10-**round decision**. In 1940, Moore traveled to **Australia**, where he won all seven of his bouts, six by knockout. After returning to the **United States**, he resided in San Diego, California, and fought most of his bouts there over the next few years, winning the California State middleweight title in 1943 by defeating Jack Chase.

In 1944, he came east and boxed for the first time in New York City, winning a 10-round bout over Nate Bolden at **St. Nicholas Arena** on 18 December 1944. During the next few years, he boxed all over the country and defeated some of the better middleweights of the era, such as the Cocoa Kid, Lloyd Marshall, and Holman Williams, but came up short against Charley Burley, Jimmy Bivins, and future **heavyweight** champion **Ezzard Charles**. Later, he defeated Bivins four times, three by knockout.

By the late 1940s, Moore was boxing primarily as a **light heavyweight** and in 1949 handed future light heavyweight champion Harold Johnson his first loss, ending a 24-bout winning streak for Johnson.

In 1951, Moore traveled to South America, where he won seven of eight bouts by knockout with one draw. After defeating Johnson two more times but losing to him once, Moore fought **Joey Maxim** for the world's light heavyweight championship on 17 December 1952 in St. Louis. Moore, who had just turned 36 years old four days previously, won a 15-round **unanimous decision** and became the oldest man to win a world's title.

Moore successfully defended his title in two rematches with Maxim—24 June 1953 in Ogden, Utah, and 27 January 1954 in Miami, Florida, both by 15-round unanimous decisions. In his next title defense on 11 August 1954, Moore stopped Harold Johnson in 14 rounds. On 22 June 1955, Moore knocked out middleweight champion **Carl "Bobo" Olson** in three rounds for yet another successful light heavyweight title defense.

In September 1955, Moore attempted to move up to heavyweight and fought **Rocky Marciano** for the world's heavyweight title on 21 September. Although Moore scored a **knockdown** in the second round, Rocky got up and knocked Moore down five times before the bout was ended in the ninth round. Following the bout, Marciano retired as undefeated world champion.

Moore weighed 188 pounds for the bout and for the rest of his career campaigned almost exclusively as a heavyweight.

After winning eight **nontitle bouts** in the heavyweight ranks, Moore defended his light heavyweight title against Trinidad native Yolande Pompey in London, **England**, on 5 June 1956, winning on a 10th-round **technical knockout**. In order for Moore to make the 175-pound limit for his light heavyweight bouts, he would go on a special diet that he claimed was taught to him by an Australian aborigine. It was later disclosed that he would chew meat and digest the juices but then spit it out. It apparently worked, as several times in his career he would trim down from his usual weight of 190 pounds to meet the 175-pound limit.

On 30 November 1956, Moore again tried for the heavyweight title. With the retirement of Marciano, the title was **vacant**, and the nearly 43-year-old Moore was matched with the 21-year-old **Floyd Patterson** for the title. Youth prevailed, and Patterson became the youngest heavyweight champion in history with a fifth-round knockout of Moore.

On 20 September 1957, Moore again used his secret diet to trim down and defended his light heavyweight title by knocking out challenger Tony Anthony in the seventh round. After the bout, Moore reverted to heavyweight and won 11 straight bouts before being held to a 10-round **draw** by Howard King. On 10 December 1958, Moore again made a light heavyweight title defense, losing 15 pounds in order to do so. The bout against French Canadian Yvon Durelle became one of boxing's greatest fights, as Durelle knocked Moore down three times in the first round and once in the fourth round before Moore caught him and knocked Durelle down four times, with the last one being for the 10 count in the 11th round. Their rematch on 3 August 1959 was less competitive, and Durelle was knocked out in three rounds in that bout.

Moore did not defend his title in 1960 and was stripped of it by the **National Boxing Association**, although the **New York State Athletic Commission** still recognized his claim. Moore's last title defense came on 10 June 1961 at **Madison Square Garden** against Giulio Rinaldi, an Italian boxer who had previously decisioned Moore in a 10-round bout in Rome, **Italy**, eight months earlier. This time, the 47-year-old Moore won a 15-round decision.

After two more knockout victories and a draw, Moore fought the up-and-coming heavyweight prospect Cassius Clay (later known as **Muhammad Ali**) on 15 November 1962. The nearly 49-year-old Moore was no match for the not-yet-21-year-old Clay, and Moore was knocked down three times in the fourth round before the fight was stopped.

Moore then did some work as a professional wrestling **referee** and in a so-called grudge match fought professional wrestler "Iron Mike" DiBiase in a boxing match scheduled for 10 rounds on 15 March 1963 in Phoenix, Arizona. DiBiase was not a skilled boxer and lasted only until the third round before the bout was stopped due to cuts over DiBiase's eyes. Moore retired following that bout.

In retirement, Moore accomplished many things. He had starred in the 1960 film *Huckleberry Finn*, in which he had given an excellent performance, and after he retired permanently, appeared in over a dozen films and television series. He also worked with both Muhammad Ali and **George Foreman** as a **trainer**. Moore created an organization called "ABC—Any Boy Can" to work with young boys.

Moore was five foot 11 inches tall and had a 75-inch **reach**. He fought at weights ranging from 145 to 206 pounds in weight classes from middleweight to heavyweight. In 219 professional bouts, from 1935 to 1963, he won 185 (131 by knockout), lost 23 (seven by knockout), had 10 draws and one **no contest**, and fought a total of 1,474 rounds. He was inducted as a member of the inaugural class of the **International Boxing Hall of Fame** in 1990.

MUAY THAI. Muay Thai is a style of boxing that originated in **Thailand** in which the boxers are barefoot and are permitted to kick their opponent. Many of the **professional boxing** world champions from Thailand, such as Khaosai Galaxy, Kaokor Galaxy, Saengsak Muangsurin, and Sot Chitalada, began as Muay Thai fighters. As with Thai boxers, most contestants use **ring** names that are different from their given names, and it is not uncommon for a Muay Thai boxer to use a different name from the one he uses as a traditional ring boxer. **World Boxing Council flyweight** champion Sot Chitalada, for example, is the traditional boxing ring name of Chaovalit Wongcharoean, but he began his professional combat career as the Muay Thai competitor known as Chaovalit Sithphrabrahma—quite confusing to a Westerner.

Other combat disciplines in which kicking is permitted have evolved from this sport, such as **mixed martial arts**, popular in the 21st century.

See also KICKBOXING; MIXED MARTIAL ARTS; SAVATE.

N

NAPOLES, JOSÉ ANGEL "MANTEQUILLA". B. 13 April 1940, Santiago, **Cuba**. **José Nápoles** was both a Cuban and a Mexican and for the better half of the 1970s was the best **welterweight** boxer in the world. As an amateur boxer, he claimed a record of 113–1.

He began **professional boxing** in his native Cuba as a **featherweight**, with his first recorded **bout** on 2 August 1958 in Havana. He won 20 of his first 21 fights, all in Havana, with the sole loss to Hilton Smith on an eight-**round decision** on 22 August 1959.

In 1961, the Castro government banned professional boxing in Cuba, so Napoles left the country and settled in **Mexico**, where the sport of boxing thrived. He resumed his boxing career, fighting primarily in Mexico City. By this time, he had filled out into a **lightweight**. He continued winning, fighting all over Mexico but with an occasional bout in **Venezuela** and **Japan**. In 1968, he fought his first bout in the **United States**, on 14 June in Inglewood, California. By this time, he had built a record of 54–4. After five more wins, two in California and three in Mexico, he fought world welterweight champion Curtis Cokes for the title in Inglewood, California, on 18 April 1969. Napoles stopped Cokes in the 13th round and became world welterweight champion. For the next six years (with the exception of a brief six-month period), Napoles retained his championship.

Nicknamed "Mantequilla" ("butter" in Spanish) for his smooth boxing style, he defended his title successfully in 1969 against Cokes in a rematch and against former welterweight and **middleweight** champion **Emile Griffith**. In 1970, Napoles beat Ernie Lopez in a title fight, won two **nontitle bouts**, but then lost his title to Billy Backus on 3 December 1970 in Syracuse, New York, when bad cuts over his eyes caused a stoppage in the fourth round. After a nontitle victory in Mexico, Napoles rewon the title from Backus at the Forum in Inglewood on 4 June 1971 when cuts to Backus's eye caused the fight to be stopped in the eighth round.

After six title defenses in California, **England**, Mexico, and **France**, Napoles challenged **Carlos Monzón** for the world middleweight title on 9 February 1974 in Hauts-des-Seine, France. Monzón proved to be too much for

Napoles and easily won on a sixth-round **technical knockout**. Napoles returned to the welterweight class, and after winning four more title defenses, he was stopped in the sixth round by Englishman John H. Stracey on 12 June 1975 in Mexico City in a bout in which Stracey was knocked down in the first round but recovered to defeat Napoles. Napoles retired after the bout and did not attempt a comeback.

Napoles is five foot seven inches tall and has a 72-inch **reach**. He fought at weights ranging from 124 to 153 pounds in weight classes from featherweight to middleweight. In 88 professional bouts, from 1958 to 1975, he won 81 (54 by **knockout**), lost seven (four by knockout), and fought a total of 585 rounds. He was inducted as a member of the inaugural class of the **International Boxing Hall of Fame** in 1990.

NATIONAL BOXING ASSOCIATION (NBA) (1921–1962). *See* WORLD BOXING ASSOCIATION (WBA).

NATIONAL BOXING ASSOCIATION (NBA) (1984–2012). The National Boxing Association was formed in 1984 and is one of boxing's lesser sanctioning organizations. It should not be confused with an earlier organization of the same name that was one of the two major North American sanctioning organizations from 1921 to 1962 and was renamed the **World Boxing Association** in 1962.

NATIONAL SPORTING CLUB. The National Sporting Club was founded in London, **England**, in 1891. One of its founders was Hugh Cecil Lowther (1857–1944), the fifth Earl of Lonsdale. He donated the Lonsdale Belt to be awarded to British champion boxers in each weight class. The National Sporting Club was superseded by the **British Boxing Board of Control** in 1929, which still awards the Lonsdale Belt to British boxing champions.

In 1990, Lord Lonsdale was inducted into the **International Boxing Hall of Fame**.

NELSON, AZUMAH "THE PROFESSOR". B. 19 July 1958, Accra, Ghana. Azumah Nelson was not Ghana's first boxing world champion (David Kotei holds that distinction) but was recognized as champion for nearly 10 years and is arguably Ghana's greatest fighter. As an **amateur** boxer, he won the **featherweight gold medal** at the 1978 Commonwealth Games. He became a **professional** boxer on 1 December 1979 with an eight-**round decision** win in his first **bout** in Accra, Ghana. After winning his first eight bouts in Africa and winning the featherweight championship of Ghana, he came to the **United States** and fought his first bout there on 18 August 1981, a three-round **technical knockout** over Miguel Ruiz in Bakersfield, California.

He returned to Africa and won the Commonwealth featherweight title by stopping Brian Roberts in Accra on 26 September 1981. He won three more bouts in Ghana, including two title defenses, and was matched with **World Boxing Council (WBC)** featherweight champion **Salvador Sánchez** at **Madison Square Garden** on 21 July 1982 for Sánchez's championship. Sánchez won a closely fought bout on a technical knockout at 1:49 of the 15th and final round. Nelson remained in the United States for his next four bouts, winning three of the four by **knockout**. He returned to Africa, where he defended his Commonwealth title in Nigeria with a ninth-round knockout over Nigerian Kabiru Akindele. Returning to the United States, he defeated Héctor Cortez in **Las Vegas** and then fought Puerto Rican **Wilfredo Gómez** in San Juan, **Puerto Rico**, on 8 December 1984 for Gómez's WBC featherweight championship. Nelson knocked out **Gómez** in the 11th round and became the new WBC world's featherweight champion.

Over the next 14 years, Nelson had 26 fights, and in 24 of them a title was at stake. He successfully defended his featherweight title seven times from 1985 to 1987. On 29 February 1988, he won the **vacant** WBC **super featherweight** title on a 12-round **split decision** over Mario Martínez. He made four successful defenses of that title and attempted to move up in weight class. He challenged **Pernell Whitaker** for the WBC and **International Boxing Federation lightweight** titles on 19 May 1990 in Las Vegas, but Whitaker defeated Nelson on a 12-round **unanimous decision**.

From 1990 to 1993, Nelson successfully defended the super featherweight title six times, although two of the bouts (against Jeff Fenech and Jesse James Leija) were draws. In his rematch against the **Australian** Fenech, the former **bantamweight**, **super bantamweight**, and featherweight champion, Nelson stopped Fenech in eight rounds on 1 March 1992 in Melbourne, Australia.

In Nelson's rematch with Leija on 7 May 1994, Nelson lost his title on a 12-round unanimous decision. Leija then lost to Gabriel Ruelas in his first title defense and Nelson was able to rewin the title by stopping Ruelas in five rounds on 1 December 1995. Nelson then defended it successfully against Leija but lost the title to Genaro Hernández on 22 March 1997 on a split decision.

Nelson's fourth bout with Leija was for the **International Boxing Association** lightweight title, and Leija won that bout on a unanimous decision on 11 July 1998. Nelson retired after the bout but 10 years later was talked into a return bout with Fenech in Melbourne, Australia. The 44-year-old Fenech, who had been out of the **ring** since 1996, won a **majority decision** over the 49-year-old Nelson, who had been idle since 1998.

Nelson is five foot five inches tall and has a 68-inch **reach**. He fought at weights ranging from 124 to 134 pounds, primarily as a featherweight and lightweight (although, in his comeback fight with Fenech in 2008, he weighed 152 to Fenech's 151—more than 20 pounds more than in their classic battles 17 years earlier). In 47 professional bouts, from 1979 to 2008, he won 39 (28 by knockout), lost six (one by knockout), had two draws, and fought a total of 398 rounds. He was inducted into the **International Boxing Hall of Fame** in 2004.

NEUTRAL CORNER. *See* CORNER.

NEW YORK STATE ATHLETIC COMMISSION (NYSAC). The New York State Athletic Commission is the organization that governs boxing in New York State. It was created in 1920 when the Walker Law legalized boxing in the state. It historically has been one of the more respected state commissions. For much of the 20th century, the two major boxing sanctioning organizations were the **National Boxing Association** (later the **World Boxing Association**) and the New York State Athletic Commission.

In the words of the commission, "the New York State Athletic Commission (SAC) is authorized to regulate professional boxing and wrestling contests, matches, and exhibitions within the state of New York pursuant to Title 25 of the Unconsolidated Laws. Comprised of three members appointed by the governor, in addition to a physician, a Medical Advisory Board, and staff, SAC administers licenses, enforces rules and regulations, and ensures that medical and safety standards are being met. It provides training seminars for referees, judges, and inspectors, oversees hundreds of events annually across the state, and is committed to promoting and maintaining the health, safety, and integrity of its regulated athletic activities."

Among the men who have served as chairmen of the NYSAC are John Branca, Bob Christenberry, Edward Eagan, James A. Farley, James A. Farley Jr. (son of the first commissioner), Randy Gordon, Melvin Krulewitch, **Floyd Patterson**, and **José Torres**. In 2008, Melvina Lathan was appointed chairperson of the NYSAC. She is the first African American female to hold that post. She had been licensed as a boxing **judge** in New York since 1991.

NEWSPAPER DECISION. During the early 20th century, many jurisdictions did not permit boxing matches that did not end in a **knockout** or submission to award a victory to a boxer based on a **referee's** or **judges'** **decision**. Those matches were recorded as "no decision," although to satisfy the boxing fans' gambling needs, most newspapers that covered the **bouts** awarded the victory to one of the combatants. Although **Nat Fleischer** in his *Ring Record Books* listed the results simply as "no decision," modern-day boxing historians have researched the newspapers and have recorded the newspaper decision in their records.

NO CONTEST. A **bout** can be determined "no contest" for a variety of reasons. If the bout is stopped within the first few **rounds** due to a cut caused by an accidental headbutt, it is called "no contest." If a bout was determined to have been scored incorrectly by **judges** using the wrong scoring system, it has been recorded as "no contest." There have also been instances where a bout has been interrupted by unruly fans and terminated prior to its scheduled distance, and those bouts have also been called "no contest."

See also DISQUALIFICATION.

NO DECISION. *See* NEWSPAPER DECISION.

NONTITLE BOUT. A nontitle **bout** is one that involves a boxing champion whose title is not at stake during the bout. One or both of the competitors will normally exceed the weight limit for the class.

NORRIS, JAMES DOUGAN. B. 6 November 1906, Chicago, Illinois. D. 25 February 1966, Chicago, Illinois. James D. Norris was a powerful man who exerted much influence on **professional boxing** in the 1940s and 1950s, yet he can hardly be described as one of the illustrious names from boxing's past.

Raised in Chicago, he served in the U.S. Navy during World War II. He was a partner in a brokerage firm and also worked for his father, who owned the Detroit Red Wings of the National Hockey League (NHL). The Norris family also had ownership interests in Chicago Stadium, New York's **Madison Square Garden**, and Detroit's Olympia Auditorium. In 1946, Norris and several partners purchased the Chicago Black Hawks team in the NHL. He also was involved in thoroughbred horse racing and was one of the owners of Spring Hill Farms, a horse breeder.

From 1949 to 1958, Norris was the president of the International Boxing Club of New York (IBC). The organization was founded in 1949 by Norris and Arthur Wirtz, his business partner in several other ventures, ostensibly to promote boxing in several of the major arenas, such as Madison Square Garden, the Polo Grounds, and Yankee Stadium in New York and the two Norris-owned facilities, Chicago Stadium and the Detroit Olympia. The IBC quickly became the sport's leading promoter and controlled most of **televised boxing** in that era. It was accused of being a monopoly, and the courts later forced the IBC to dissolve.

In 1960, a U.S. Senate investigation into organized crime disclosed that the IBC had close dealings with several major organized crime figures, included Frankie Carbo and Frank "Blinky" Palermo. It was also disclosed that Norris played a direct role in the fixing of several **bouts** dating back to the 1940s.

A summary of Norris's impact on boxing can be observed from the titles of the following magazine and Internet articles all dealing with Norris: "The 10 Worst Boxing Moments in History," "Jim Norris Is Part of Boxing's Dirty Business," "The Mob, Murder, Inc., and Madison Square Garden," and "Boxing's Tale of Corruption." Even the title of his 1964 biography by Barney Nagler hints at this, *James Norris and the Decline of Boxing*.

Norris died in Chicago at the age of 59 after suffering his second heart attack. It is extremely unlikely that he will ever be inducted into the **International Boxing Hall of Fame**, although his influence on professional hockey was not as inauspicious and he was inducted into the Hockey Hall of Fame in 1962.

NORTHERN IRELAND. Northern Ireland is a country that is part of the United Kingdom, although its athletes compete internationally with those of **England**, **Wales**, and **Scotland** as part of the **Great Britain** team. There has yet to be an Olympic boxing medalist from Northern Ireland who boxed for Great Britain. (Wayne McCullough, born in Belfast, won a **silver medal** boxing for the team from **Ireland** in the 1992 Olympics.) As with the other countries of the United Kingdom, boxing has been quite popular since the 19th century.

Professional world champions from Northern Ireland include Eamonn Loughran, Wayne McCullough, Rinty Monaghan, and Ike Weir. Venezuela-born Crisanto España relocated to Northern Ireland early in his professional career and won the **World Boxing Association** world **welterweight** title while a resident of Belfast. Other top boxers from Northern Ireland included Johnny Caldwell, Edward "Bunty" Doran, Des Rea, and Jimmy Warnock.

NORTON, KENNETH HOWARD SR. B. 9 August 1943, Jacksonville, Illinois. Ken Norton was an excellent fighter who is the answer to the trivia question, "What **heavyweight** champion never won a world's heavyweight championship **bout**?" Norton was an all-around athlete at Jacksonville High School—a member of the Illinois state champion football team and also a member of their track and field team. Reportedly, his coach entered him in eight different events in a track meet, and he won all eight. As a result of his performance, the state instituted the "Ken Norton" rule, limiting a high school athlete to just three events at one meet.

He received a football scholarship to Northeast Missouri State University and majored in elementary education. He joined the U.S. Marine Corps in 1963 and served with them through 1967. In the Marines, he began to box and won the All-Marine heavyweight championship three times.

After his discharge, he became a **professional** boxer, with his first bout on 14 November 1967 in San Diego, California. He won his first 16 fights, all but one by **knockout**, before being knocked out by José Luis García on 2 July 1970 in Los Angeles, California. Norton then won his next 13 bouts and was matched with former heavyweight champion **Muhammad Ali** on 31 March 1973 in San Diego. In a surprising turn of events, Norton broke Ali's jaw en route to winning a 12-**round split decision**. After Ali's jaw healed, they had a rematch on 3 September at the Forum in Inglewood, California. This time Ali prevailed on another split decision. After the bout, Ali said that Norton was the best fighter he had ever fought with the exception of **Joe Frazier**.

George Foreman, then the world's heavyweight champion, gave Norton a shot at his title in a bout that took place in Caracas, **Venezuela**, on 26 March 1974. This was the first heavyweight championship bout in boxing history to take place in South America. The six-foot-three-inch, 210-pound Norton matched up well physically with the six-foot-three-inch, 220-pound Foreman, but George caught Norton early in the second round and knocked him down three times before the bout was stopped.

After winning his next seven bouts by knockout, including a return bout with José Luis García, the fighter who gave Norton his first loss, Norton met Ali in a third bout—this time for Ali's heavyweight title. As with the other two bouts in their series, it was a closely contested affair. Ali won a close but **unanimous decision** by the score of eight rounds to seven on the scorecards of two of the **judges** and 8–6–1 on **referee** Arthur Mercante's card.

In his next bout, Norton ended the 38-bout unbeaten streak of heavyweight hopeful Duane Bobick by stopping him in just 58 seconds of the first round. After a five-round knockout of Italian Lorenzo Zanon, Norton was matched with Jimmy Young on 15 November 1977 in **Las Vegas** in an elimination bout to determine the next challenger for the **World Boxing Council (WBC)** heavyweight title. Norton outboxed Young, won a 15-round split decision, and was ready to box again in a heavyweight championship bout. Ali lost his title to **Leon Spinks** in February 1978, and Norton was the WBC number one challenger scheduled to receive a shot at Spinks. Spinks decided to fight a more lucrative rematch with Ali, and consequently the WBC stripped him of the title and awarded Norton the WBC championship belt by acclamation.

In Norton's first defense of the title, he lost a 15-round split decision in a very close bout to the undefeated (27–0) **Larry Holmes**. That made Norton 0–3 in heavyweight title fights—the only heavyweight champion that never won a heavyweight championship bout.

Norton fought five more times in his professional career, defeating Randy Stephens and Randall "Tex" Cobb, boxing a **draw** with Scott LeDoux, and being knocked out in the first round by **Earnie Shavers** and stopped after just 54 seconds of the first round by **Gerry Cooney**.

Norton retired after the Cooney bout and became a member of the *Sports Illustrated* speakers bureau. He also appeared in more than a dozen films, continuing a film career that began in the mid-1970s when he was still an active fighter.

His role as a public speaker was curtailed, though, after he was in a near-fatal auto accident in 1986 that left him with slurred speech.

Ken Norton is an intelligent, well-spoken man who was quoted as saying, "Of all the titles that I've been privileged to have, the title of 'Dad' has always been the best." His son Ken Norton Jr. was also an outstanding athlete and played linebacker in the National Football League from 1988 to 2000 and was the first player to win Super Bowl rings in three consecutive years, winning with the Dallas Cowboys in 1993 and 1994 and San Francisco 49ers in 1995. His other son, Keith Norton, is a sports announcer in Houston, Texas.

Norton is six foot three inches tall and has an 80-inch **reach**. He fought at weights ranging from 202 to 225 pounds as a heavyweight. In 50 professional bouts, from 1967 to 1981, Ken Norton Sr. won 42 (33 by knockout), lost seven (four by knockout), had one draw, and fought a total of 314 rounds. He was inducted into the **International Boxing Hall of Fame** in 1992.

O

O'BRIEN, PHILADELPHIA JACK (né JOSEPH FRANCIS ANTHO-NY HAGEN). B. 17 January 1878, Philadelphia, Pennsylvania. D. 12 November 1942, New York, New York. Philadelphia Jack O'Brien began boxing **professionally** in the 1890s, with his first recorded **bout** taking place in Philadelphia on 14 December 1896. Through the end of 1900, he had compiled a record of 24–2–9 with 30 no-decision or **no-contest** bouts in addition. Not feeling appreciated in the **United States**, he headed for **England** early in 1901, where he felt he could find better opposition and make a name for himself. While in England, he fought 19 bouts throughout the country, fighting in Newcastle, Liverpool, London, and Leeds and two bouts in **Scotland** as well. He won all 19 with 15 **knockouts** and four by **disqualification**. After each bout, he would send a glowing report of his latest victory back to the newspapers in Philadelphia. When he arrived home in February 1902, his ship was met at the dock by the mayor of Philadelphia and a large crowd of fans.

On 22 December 1903, he defeated Jack "Twin" Sullivan in 20 **rounds** and claimed the **middleweight** championship. He defended that title in a rematch with Sullivan on 14 April 1904 and won on a three-round knockout. Later that year in **nontitle bouts**, O'Brien fought a six-round **draw** with former middleweight champion **Charles "Kid" McCoy**, was stopped in six rounds by former **heavyweight** champion **Bob Fitzsimmons**, and defeated future heavyweight champion **Tommy Burns** on a six-round **decision**.

After several no decision bouts in 1904 and 1905, O'Brien defended his middleweight title twice against Young Peter Jackson in 1905. In the first bout, Jackson knocked out O'Brien in the second round but lost the bout when the **referee** ruled that the punch was thrown after he commanded the boxers to break when they were in a **clinch**. O'Brien won their rematch on a 10-round decision.

On 24 April 1905 in Indianapolis, Indiana, O'Brien lost his claim to the middleweight title when he lost a 10-round decision to Hugo Kelly. In San Francisco on 20 December 1905, O'Brien knocked out Bob Fitzsimmons in the 13th round. Fitzsimmons at that time was the holder of the world's **light heavyweight** title, which O'Brien then claimed although he never defended it.

O'Brien set his sights on the world's heavyweight title and fought a 20-round draw in Los Angeles on 28 July 1906 with champion Tommy Burns in pursuit of it. Six months later, the two fought a rematch, also in Los Angeles, but Burns this time won a 20-round decision. After Burns lost his title to **Jack Johnson**, O'Brien made one more attempt at the heavyweight title and fought a six-round no-decision bout with Johnson in Philadelphia on 19 May 1909, which was ruled a draw by most newspapermen.

O'Brien continued fighting until 1912, with his last bout, a six-round no-decision fight, taking place on 17 June in Philadelphia.

In retirement, he managed a gymnasium in New York City and worked as **Jack Dempsey's** second for Dempsey's heavyweight title defense with **Gene Tunney** in 1926.

O'Brien was five foot 10 inches tall and fought at weights ranging from 140 to 170 pounds in weight classes from middleweight to heavyweight. In 194 professional bouts, from 1896 to 1912, he won 92 (56 by knockout), lost nine (five by knockout), and had 14 draws, five no contests, and 74 no-decision bouts, in which he was awarded the **newspaper decision** in 53, lost seven, and drew 14. He fought a total of 1,215 rounds. He was inducted into the **International Boxing Hall of Fame** in 1994.

O'GRADY, SEAN "THE BUBBLE-GUM KID". B. 10 February 1959, Austin, Texas. Sean O'Grady was a good-looking youth who began boxing **professionally** in his parents Jean and Pat O'Grady's boxing promotions in Oklahoma at the age of 15. He had 63 **bouts** before he was 20 years old, winning 62 of them.

He began boxing as an **amateur** at the age of six. Since his mother, Jean, was a boxing promoter, and his father, Pat, a promoter–**trainer**–manager, and the state of Oklahoma had no state boxing **commission**, his parents were able to begin using him on their professional shows one month before his 16th birthday. They matched him with opponents with very little boxing skills, and by his 17th birthday, Sean, boxing as a **bantamweight** and **featherweight**, had compiled a record of 29–0 with 25 **knockouts**—14 in the first **round**. In his first fight outside of his home area, on 5 February 1976, after just turning 17, he faced his first big test, Danny "Little Red" Lopez, a ranked featherweight who later that year would win the **World Boxing Council (WBC)** world featherweight championship. Lopez stopped O'Grady in four rounds.

O'Grady returned to Oklahoma and for the next year and a half went back to knocking out nonentities, adding 18 consecutive knockouts to his record. He then received a spot on a **card** at **Madison Square Garden** against a local favorite, Davey Vásquez, a former two-time New York **Golden Gloves** champion and **Olympic** boxer. O'Grady outpointed Vásquez for his first victory against a competent opponent. After four more Oklahoma knockouts, O'Grady fought his first fight in **Las Vegas**. There, he stopped Eddie Freeman in one round. Freeman had a record of 21–1, but like O'Grady, it was at the expense of lesser-quality opponents.

After one more first-round knockout in Oklahoma, O'Grady fought Romeo Anaya in Los Angeles on 15 April 1978. Anaya had been the WBC world bantamweight champion in 1973 but was on the downward side of his career and had lost 10 of his last 15 bouts, being stopped in six of them. O'Grady knocked him out in three rounds. O'Grady then won 12 straight bouts (11 knockouts) in the Oklahoma area against minor opposition and on 12 October 1979 won a 15-round **decision** over Arturo León for the **United States** Boxing Association **lightweight** title—not one of the major titles though. After five more victories over nondescript opponents, O'Grady, with a record of 73–1, traveled to Glasgow, **Scotland**, to fight WBC lightweight champion Jim Watt on 1 November 1980. O'Grady was cut badly, and the bout was stopped in the 12th round and awarded to Watt.

On 12 April 1981, O'Grady again fought for a world lightweight championship. This time it was the **World Boxing Association (WBA)** version against Hilmer Kenty in **Atlantic City**, New Jersey. O'Grady easily won a unanimous 15-round decision and at the age of 22 became a world champion.

His championship reign did not last long as the WBA wanted him to defend against Claude Noel but O'Grady's father and manager did not want that match. Consequently, the WBA stripped Sean of his title shortly afterward. Undaunted, Sean's father–manager, Pat O'Grady, created his own sanctioning organization, the World Athletic Association (WAA), and Sean remained champion under that jurisdiction. On 31 October 1981, Sean defended his WAA title in Little Rock, Arkansas, but was upset by unheralded Andy Ganigan, who knocked O'Grady down three times in the second round to win the fight and O'Grady's title.

O'Grady fought seven more bouts but after being stopped by John Verderosa on 23 March 1983 in Chicago decided to retire. Even though he was just 24 years of age, he had fought 86 professional bouts (more than many fighters have in their careers). Unlike many fighters, he wisely never attempted a comeback.

He went into television and was a color announcer for the weekly *Tuesday Night Fights* boxing show on the USA television network with announcer Al Albert. After that series, he continued as a color commentator with other networks. He has since become a real estate broker for commercial properties in Oklahoma.

O'Grady is five foot 10 inches tall and has a 70-inch **reach**. He fought at weights ranging from 120 to 148 pounds, primarily as a featherweight and lightweight. In 86 professional bouts, from 1975 to 1983, he won 81 (70 by knockout), lost five (four by knockout), and fought a total of 327 rounds.

OLIVARES, RUBÉN "EL PÚAS". B. 14 January 1947, Mexico City, **Mexico**. Rubén Olivares was one of the hardest-punching **bantamweights** of all time and a man who won nearly three-quarters of all his **bouts** by **knockout**.

He began his **professional boxing** career on 4 January 1965 in Cuernavaca, Mexico, with a one-**round** knockout of Isidro Sotelo.

Olivares won his first 24 fights by knockout before being required to go the distance. After winning that bout, he had two more knockouts and then was held to a 10-round **draw** on 29 July 1967 by Germán Bastidas. Olivares then won his next 25 bouts, with 24 knockouts and one **disqualification**.

He was matched with **Australian** Lionel Rose for the world bantamweight title on 22 August 1969 at the Forum in Inglewood, California. Going into the fight, Olivares had a record of 52–0–1 with 50 knockouts as against Rose's record of 34–2. Olivares knocked out Rose in the fifth round to become the new bantamweight champion. He then won his next eight bouts, with two of them being title defenses against Alan Rudkin and Jesús "Chucho" Castillo.

On 16 October 1970, Olivares fought a rematch with Castillo, and with the bout even through 13 rounds, Olivares suffered a bad cut over his left eye that caused the bout to be stopped in the 14th round and the loss of his title.

The two Mexican warriors fought a **rubber match** on 2 April 1971, again at the Forum, and this time Olivares prevailed on a hard-fought **unanimous decision** in 15 rounds. He defended it successfully against the **Japanese** fighter Kanuyoshi Kanazawa in Tokyo, winning on a 14th-round knockout, and against Jesús Pimentel at the Forum with an 11-round **technical knockout**.

Olivares suffered only the second loss of his career on 19 March 1972 in Mexico City when he was knocked out in eight rounds by fellow Mexican Rafael Herrera, who then became the sixth Mexican to win the bantamweight world championship. Olivares lost his third bout eight months later in a nontitle rematch with Herrera on a 10-round **majority decision**.

Olivares moved up into the **featherweight** classification, won five of six bouts, and fought Zensuke Utagawa for the **vacant World Boxing Association (WBA)** world featherweight title. He knocked out Utagawa in seven rounds at the Forum and was the new WBA world featherweight champion. In his first defense of that crown on 23 November 1974, he was knocked out by **Alexis Argüello** in 13 rounds. The following year, on 20 June 1975, Olivares won the **World Boxing Council** version of the featherweight championship by knocking out Bobby Chacon in two rounds. He did not hold that title long either, as he lost it in his first defense to the Ghanaian David Kotey on a **split decision** at the Forum on 20 September 1975.

Olivares fought one more world title bout. On 21 July 1979, he challenged WBA world featherweight champion Eusebio Pedroza but was stopped in the 12th round. After the Pedroza bout, Olivares fought four more bouts against lesser-quality opponents but could only win two of them and retired in 1981. Like many other fighters, he made an ill-advised comeback attempt, fighting a four-round **draw** in 1986 and losing via a knockout in four rounds in 1988.

Olivares is five foot five inches tall and has a 67-inch **reach**. He fought at weights ranging from 112 to 133 pounds, primarily as a bantamweight and featherweight. In 104 professional bouts, from 1965 to 1988, he won 88 (77 by knockout), lost 13 (nine by knockout), had three draws, and fought a total of 596 rounds. He was inducted into the **International Boxing Hall of Fame** in 1991.

OLSON, CARL ELMER "BOBO," "THE HAWAIIAN SWEDE". B. 11 July 1928, Honolulu, Hawaii. D. 16 January 2002, Honolulu, Hawaii. In an era when only sailors sported tattoos, Carl "Bobo" was one of the few non-sailors, and few boxers, to be tattooed. He was also one of the few boxers born in Hawaii to become a world champion.

He began **professional boxing** when only 16 using false identification and had his first professional **bout** on 19 August 1944 when he scored a two-**round knockout** over Bob Correa in Honolulu. He won two more bouts in Hawaii and then did not fight for more than one year. He moved to San Francisco in 1945, won eight bouts in 1945 and 1946, and returned to Hawaii. After winning his first 21 bouts, he was matched with George Duke on 4 July 1947 in a bout billed for the "Hawaiian territory middleweight title." Duke gave Olson his first loss by winning a 10-round **decision**. The two fighters were rematched a month later, and Olson was the victor in that bout, also by 10-round decision. Olson lost that title in his next bout to a Filipino boxer named Boy Brooks, and then followed Brooks to the **Philippines**, where Olson had his next three bouts. After winning three bouts in the Philippines, including a rematch with Brooks, Olson returned to Hawaii and continued to build his **ring** record there.

In March 1950, Olson traveled to **Australia**, where he faced the veteran Dave Sands, holder of the British Empire middleweight championship. Sands won a 12-round decision over Olson. Later that year, Olson fought the great **"Sugar Ray" Robinson** for the world's middleweight title as recognized by the state of Pennsylvania but was knocked out by Robinson in the 12th round of their scheduled 15-round bout.

One year later, on 3 October 1951 in Chicago Stadium, Olson lost a 10-round rematch to Sands in a bout that was the first fight **televised** coast-to-coast in the **United States**. On 13 March 1952 in San Francisco, Olson again challenged Robinson for the world's middleweight title—but by this time Robinson had gained universal recognition as champion. Olson went the 15-round distance but lost a **unanimous decision**. Olson continued to be one of the busier fighters on television and won seven more fights in 1952.

In December 1952, Robinson announced his retirement from boxing and the middleweight title became **vacant**. Olson was matched with Englishman Randy Turpin for the vacant title. (Turpin had defeated Robinson in 1951 and was middleweight champion for two months until Robinson defeated him in a rematch.) On 21 October 1953, Olson outpointed Turpin at **Madison Square Garden** and became world's middleweight champion. For his accomplishments, Olson was named *Ring* **magazine's** "Fighter of the Year" for 1953. He successfully defended his title against **Kid Gavilán** in April 1954, Rocky Castellani in August 1954, and Pierre Langlois in December 1954. After a win over **Joey Maxim**, former **light heavyweight** champion, Olson challenged **Archie Moore** for the world's light heavyweight title on 22 June 1955 at the Polo Grounds in New York. Moore proved to be too much for Olson and knocked him out in the third round.

Olson fought Robinson twice more. On 9 December 1955, Robinson reclaimed his middleweight title by knocking out Olson in the second round in their bout in Chicago. Robinson won the rematch on a fourth-round knockout in Los Angeles on 18 May 1956. After that bout, Olson no longer could meet the 160-pound middleweight limit and fought as a light heavyweight and occasionally as a **heavyweight**, weighing 187 in June 1956 for a bout with Joey Maxim. Although he met most of the top light heavyweights from 1956 to 1966, he was unable to get another match for that division's title. His final bout was 28 November 1966, when he lost a **majority-decision** 10-round bout to Don Fullmer.

After retiring, Olson worked as a public relations officer for the Teamsters' Union.

Olson was five foot 10 inches tall and had a 70-inch **reach**. He fought at weights ranging from 128 to 187 pounds, primarily as a middleweight and light heavyweight. In 115 professional bouts, from 1944 to 1966, he won 97 (47 by knockout), lost 16 (seven by knockout), had two draws, and fought a total of 870 rounds. He was inducted into the **International Boxing Hall of Fame** in 2000.

OLYMPIC GAMES. Boxing was one of the sports contested at the ancient Olympic Games. When the modern Olympic Games were instituted in 1896 in Athens, Greece, although the sport of boxing was popular in **England** and the **United States** then, it was not in Europe and was not one of the nine sports that were contested. It was not until 1904 when the games were held in the United States, in St. Louis, that a boxing tournament was added to the program.

In that year, a two-day Olympic boxing program was held on 21–22 September with 18 different boxers competing in seven weight classes (all but **light heavyweight**). Six boxers entered two different weight classes, and Oliver Kirk won both the **bantamweight** and **featherweight gold medals**.

The 1908 Olympic Games, held in London, England, also had a boxing event, and it was nearly as bizarre as the 1904 one. There, the entire tournament of five weight classes and 42 boxers, representing four nations, was contested on just one day, 27 October 1908. Several boxers fought three **bouts** each and two, Fred Spiller and **Australian Reginald "Snowy" Baker**, fought four bouts, although both lost their final bout.

The 1912 Olympic Games did not include boxing among the 16 events (plus art competitions) since the games were held in Stockholm, Sweden, and boxing was illegal in that country at that time. Ironically, other combat sports such as fencing and wrestling were included.

The 1916 games were not held due to World War I, but the 1920 games in Antwerp featured a full slate of boxing, with 116 participants from 12 countries competing in eight weight classes.

For the next 32 years, boxing was held in all eight weight classes in each Olympic Games, and the number of entrants and countries continued to grow. In 1936, the **Val Barker Trophy** was first awarded to the outstanding boxer in the Olympic Games and has been in each subsequent Olympic tournament.

In 1952, two additional weight classes were added, **light welterweight** and **light middleweight**. In 1968, a **light flyweight** class was added, and in 1984 a **super heavyweight** one was added also. Competition continued to grow, and by 1988 there were 432 boxers from 106 countries competing in the 10 weight classes in the Olympic Games held in Seoul, **Korea**. There were so many bouts that boxing was held in two **rings** simultaneously.

In 1992, two major changes were instituted. First, only a limited number of entrants were allowed to compete, a maximum of 32 in a weight class, with qualifying tournaments held prior to the Olympic Games. Second, since boxing judging had had many previous instances of outrageous, improper decisions based on nationality, with the 1988 games having some of the most egregious scoring results, a new system was used whereby a computer was used and **judges** pressed a button when they saw a punch land. The fighter with the most punches landed at the end of the bout was declared the winner. This system was not foolproof either, and there were still some unjust decisions.

Changes to Olympic boxing since 1992 have included the removal of the light middleweight class from 2004 to 2012 and **featherweight** class in 2012. In 2012, however, **women's** boxing was added to the program, and 36 women from 23 countries competed in **flyweight**, light welterweight, and light heavyweight classes.

There have been only three men who have won three Olympic **gold medals** in boxing—Hungarian **László Papp**, who was 1948 **middleweight** and 1952 and 1956 light middleweight champion, and **Cubans Teófilo Stevenson** and **Félix Savon**. Stevenson won the **heavyweight** class in 1972, 1976, and 1980, while Savon won the heavyweight class in 1992, 1996, and 2000. When Stevenson won his medals, the heavyweight was the unlimited class, but when Savon won, the heavyweight class had a limit of 200 pounds and super heavyweight was the unlimited class. Both Stevenson and Savon might have won a fourth gold medal had Cuba not boycotted both the 1984 and 1988 games.

See also ALI, MUHAMMAD "THE LOUISVILLE LIP," "THE GREATEST" (né CASSIUS MARCELLUS CLAY); ARGÜELLO, ALEXIS "EL FLACO EXPLOSIVO"; BENVENUTI, GIOVANNI "NINO"; BOWE, RIDDICK LAMONT "BIG DADDY," "SUGAR MAN"; CARBAJAL, MICHAEL "MANITAS DE PIEDRA"; DE LA HOYA, ÓSCAR "GOLDEN BOY"; FOREMAN, GEORGE EDWARD "BIG GEORGE"; FRAZIER, JOSEPH WILLIAM "JOE," "SMOKIN' JOE"; GENARO, FRANKIE (né FRANK DIGENNARO); GÓMEZ, WILFREDO "BAZOOKA"; HOLYFIELD, EVANDER "THE REAL DEAL"; JOFRE, ÉDER ZUMBANO "GALINHO DE OURO," "JOFRINHO"; JOHANSSON, JENS INGEMAR "INGO"; JONES, ROY LEVESTA, JR; KLITSCHKO, VOLODOMYR VOLODOMYROVICH "WLADIMIR," "DR. STEELHAMMER"; LEONARD, RAY CHARLES "SUGAR RAY"; LEWIS, LENNOX CLAUDIUS "THE LION"; MAYWEATHER, FLOYD JOY, JR., "PRETTY BOY," "MONEY" (né FLOYD JOY SINCLAIR); McGUIGAN, FINBARR PATRICK "BARRY," "THE CLONES CYCLONE"; PALOMINO, CARLOS; PATTERSON, FLOYD; PÉREZ, PASCUAL NICOLÁS "EL LEÓN MENDOCINO," "EL PEQUEÑO GIGANTE"; RADEMACHER, THOMAS PETER "PETE"; SPINKS, LEON "NEON LEON"; SPINKS, MICHAEL "JINX"; TORRES, JOSÉ "CHEGÜI"; WHITAKER, PERNELL "SWEET PEA"; APPENDIX B for a list of Olympic Games boxing champions.

OPEN. In **amateur boxing** tournaments such as the **Golden Gloves**, a tournament class in which amateur boxers with previous boxing experience compete is designated the open class.

See also SUB-NOVICE.

ORTEGA, GASPAR "EL INDIO". B. 31 October 1935, Mexicali, Baja California, **Mexico**. Gaspar Ortega was one of the busiest fighters during the 1950s and 1960s. He averaged more than one fight a month for 13 years during a time when most top-notch fighters had only four or five **bouts** a year. Although most of his bouts in Mexico were against lower-class opponents and often ended in **knockouts** (58 of his 69 knockouts), by contrast his fights in the **United States** nearly always went the distance, and he could be counted on for a full ten **rounds** of action.

He began his **professional boxing** career on 1 January 1953 with a first-round knockout of Miguel Ocaña in San Luis Rio Colorado, Sonora, Mexico and by the end of that year Ortega had fought and won 20 bouts. On 25 August 1954, he was brought to **Madison Square Garden** and won a four-round **preliminary bout** there. He continued fighting as a **welterweight**, both in Mexico and in the United States, and by March 1956 was being featured in the **televised main event** at the Garden. For the next few years, he became one of the most televised fighters since he always put up a good show and usually went the distance.

Among his best victories were two over former welterweight champion Tony DeMarco in 1956, former welterweight champion **Kid Gavilán** in 1957, and future welterweight champion **Benny "Kid" Paret** in 1959 and 1961. During his career, he faced most of the top welterweights and **middleweights** of the era, although he was outpointed in many of the bouts. Among the world champions he fought were **Carmen Basilio, Emile Griffith**, Benny "Kid" Paret, Denny Moyer, Ralph Dupas, Don Jordan, Kid Gavilán, Tony DeMarco, Sandro Mazzinghi, and **Nino Benvenuti**. On 3 June 1961, he fought Emile Griffith for the world's welterweight championship but was stopped in the 12th round after being **knocked down** twice earlier in the bout.

Ortega is five foot nine inches tall and has a 73-inch **reach**. He fought at weights ranging from 138 to 158 pounds, primarily as a welterweight. In 176 professional bouts, from 1953 to 1965, he won 131 (69 by knockout), lost 39 (two by knockout), had six draws, and fought a total of 1,295 rounds.

His son, Mike Ortega is a **referee**.

ORTIZ, CARLOS JUAN. B. 9 September 1936, Ponce, **Puerto Rico**. Carlos Ortiz, like many other boxers, was born in Puerto Rico but raised in New York City. As a youth in New York, he got into a little trouble and was told to join the Madison Square Boys Club, which had a boxing program under the auspices of the Police Athletic League. He found that he enjoyed the sport and worked out in the gym daily.

He began his **professional boxing** career as a **lightweight** on 14 February 1955 by knocking out Harry Bell in the first **round** at the venerable **St. Nicholas Arena** in New York City. After winning his first 16 fights (eight by **knockout**) in New York and Boston, he traveled to Los Angeles, where he continued his winning streak with two more victories.

He returned to New York and on New Year's Eve 1956 met the **Canadian** Gale Kerwin, a rising contender with a record of 22–3–1. Although Ortiz was knocked down for the first time in his career, he got up off the **canvas** to win nearly every round and a **unanimous decision**. Ortiz then became a popular figure on the weekly **televised bouts** and appeared on them from Hollywood, California, Chicago, and Miami Beach as well as New York.

After winning his first 26 bouts, Ortiz lost a close 10-round **split decision** to lightweight contender Johnny Busso at **Madison Square Garden** on 27 June 1958. In a subsequent rematch at the Garden three months later, Ortiz won a unanimous decision. One month later, Ortiz faced the British contender Dave Charnley in London, **England**, and won that bout. After a **majority decision** loss to Kenny Lane and a **technical knockout** over Len Matthews, Ortiz and the **southpaw** Lane were rematched at Madison Square Garden for the newly resurrected **junior welterweight** title. This time Ortiz knocked Lane down in the second round, and bad cuts to Lane's eye and nose caused a halt to the fight in that round.

Ortiz's first defense of that title was against the undefeated (31–0, 24 knockouts) Mexican José Raymundo "Battling" Torres, a fighter with a good knockout punch but an inability to take a punch. Ortiz knocked him out in the 10th round. Ortiz's second title defense came against a man with an even more impressive record than Torres—Italian **Duilio Loi**, who at that time in his career had lost only one bout of 110. Ortiz handed him his second defeat—a 15-round split decision at the Cow Palace in Daly City, California, on 15 June 1960. In a rematch in Milan, **Italy**, three months later, Loi was the victor on a 15-round majority decision and became the new junior welterweight champion. The following year, Ortiz and Loi fought again in Milan for the junior welterweight title, now owned by Loi, and Loi won convincingly with a sixth-round **knockdown** of Ortiz and a 15-round unanimous decision.

Ortiz returned to the **United States** and, after two 10-round unanimous decision wins over top **lightweight** contenders Doug Vaillant and Paolo Rosi, challenged world lightweight champion Joe Brown for his title. The bout was held at the Convention Center in **Las Vegas** and was one of the first world championship bouts to be held in that city. Ortiz won a 15-round unanimous decision and became the first Puerto Rican to win two world championships.

Ortiz then began six years of world travel that saw him fight lightweight championship bouts in **Japan**, **Puerto Rico**, the **Philippines**, **Panama**, **Mexico**, the **Dominican Republic**, and Pittsburgh. He also fought **nontitle bouts** in England, Hawaii, and **Argentina**. He knocked out the Japanese Teruo Kosaka in five rounds in Tokyo in 1962, stopped **Cuban** Doug Vaillant in 13 rounds in San Juan in 1963, stopped the Filipino Gabriel "Flash" Elorde in 14 rounds in Manila in 1964, and won a **unanimous decision** over Kenny Lane in San Juan in 1964. On 10 April 1965, Ortiz lost his title via a majority decision to Panamanian Ismael Laguna in Panama City but regained it on a unanimous decision in their 13 November 1965 rematch in San Juan. In 1966, Ortiz stopped Italian American Johnny Bizzarro in 12 rounds in Pittsburgh, stopped Cuban Mexican Ultiminio "Sugar" Ramos in four rounds in San Juan, and knocked out Elorde in the 14th round at **Madison Square Garden**.

In 1967, Ortiz fought only two bouts. He stopped Ramos in four rounds in San Juan and won a unanimous decision over Laguna at Shea Stadium, the new baseball park in Flushing, New York. In his only bout in 1968, Ortiz was dethroned by Dominican Carlos Teo Cruz on a 15-round **split decision** in Santo Domingo. Ortiz then retired briefly but returned in 1969 and won 10 consecutive bouts before losing to Ken Buchanan on 20 September 1972 on a sixth-round **technical knockout** at Madison Square Garden. He retired from the **ring** shortly afterward.

Ortiz is five foot seven inches tall and has a 70-inch **reach**. He fought at weights ranging from 133 to 145 pounds as a lightweight and junior welterweight. In 70 professional bouts, from 1955 to 1972, he won 61 (30 by knockout), lost seven (one by knockout), had one draw and one **no contest**, and fought a total of 575 rounds. He was inducted into the **International Boxing Hall of Fame** in 1991.

ORTIZ, MANUEL. B. 2 July 1916, Corona, California. D. 31 May 1970, San Diego, California. Manuel Ortiz features in a bit of boxing trivia. In the outstanding Internet boxing database Boxrec, Ortiz was the first boxer to be entered and thus bears the Boxrec identification number 1. An American of Mexican heritage, Ortiz began boxing as an amateur in 1937 and won a **Golden Gloves** title. His first professional **bout** was on 25 February 1938, when he lost a four-**round decision** to Benny Goldberg at Legion Stadium in Hollywood, California.

In his first year as a **professional**, Ortiz fought 18 bouts, winning 14 and progressing from four-round preliminaries to **main events** by the end of the year. Two of those victories were over Richie Lemos, who would become the **National Boxing Association** world's **featherweight** champion in 1941.

Ortiz was also quite active in 1939 with 11 bouts, although he lost five of them. Included among those defeats were decision losses to future world **bantamweight** champion Lou Salica and former world **flyweight** champion Small Montana. Ortiz fared better in 1940, winning five of seven bouts. On 8 August 1941, Ortiz lost a 10-round decision to Tony Olivera in a bout billed for the California State bantamweight championship. Ortiz then won that title in a rematch five months later. On 7 August 1942, Ortiz again met Salica, who at this time was world bantamweight champion. Ortiz gained that title with a 12-round **unanimous decision** in Legion Stadium in Hollywood. He successfully defended it 15 times, including one bout with Benny Goldberg, the boxer who had defeated him in his first professional bout. Ortiz finally lost his title to Harold Dade on a 15-round unanimous decision in San Francisco on 6 January 1947. Dade was only bantamweight champion for two months, as Ortiz defeated him on a 15-round unanimous decision on 11 March 1947 in Los Angeles. After four more successful title defenses, Ortiz met **South African** Vic Toweel in Toweel's native land on 31 May 1950 in Johannesburg. By that time, Ortiz had grown into a **lightweight** and had fought several previous **nontitle bouts** weighing over 130 pounds. Although he was within the bantamweight limit (118 pounds) for the Toweel bout, he lost his title on a 15-round decision. It also proved to be his last fight weighing less than 124 pounds. Ortiz continued boxing until 1955 but lost six of his last 12 bouts.

Ortiz was five foot four inches tall and had a 64-inch **reach**. He fought at weights ranging from 110 to 137 pounds in weight classes from flyweight to featherweight. In 132 professional bouts, from 1938 to 1955, he won 101 (55 by **knockout**), lost 28 (one by knockout), had three draws, and fought a total of 1,111 rounds. He was inducted into the **International Boxing Hall of Fame** in 1996.

OTHER WEIGHT CLASSES. In addition to the eight traditional weight classes and the newer intermediary classes (known as **junior** or **super**), boxing at times has had other class designations, although not widespread in popularity. High school boxing had "gnat weight" (85-pound maximum), "mosquito weight" (92-pound maximum), and "flea weight" (100-pound maximum). It also had a class between **welterweight** and **middleweight** that was called "senior welterweight," and referred to the traditional **heavyweight** class as "unlimited."

Modern-day **amateur boxing** in the **Philippines** has an antweight class at just 32 kilograms (71 pounds), minimumweight class at 34 kilograms (75 pounds), and classes known as light mosquito weight (38 kilograms, 83 pounds), mosquito weight (40 kilograms, 88 pounds), light paperweight (42 kilograms, 93 pounds), and pin weight (46 kilograms, 101 pounds).

See also PAPERWEIGHT; APPENDIX D for a list of weight classes.

PACHECO, FERDIE "THE FIGHT DOCTOR". B. 8 December 1927, Tampa, Florida. Ferdie Pacheco, a true renaissance man, is an accomplished pharmacist, physician, author, television commentator, and painter as well as **cornerman** for the world's **heavyweight** champion for 15 years.

A boxing fan, he received his undergraduate degree (BS in pharmacy) from the University of Florida in 1951 and his medical degree from the University of Miami in 1958. In addition to maintaining a private medical practice, he also worked with boxers with **trainer Angelo Dundee** at Chris Dundee's Fifth Street Gym in Miami. In 1962, he started working with Angelo's protege Cassius Clay (later to be known as **Muhammad Ali**) and became Clay's private physician as well as cornerman, working in the corner of Clay's fights along with Dundee. Pacheco continued working with Ali until 1977, when after recommending that Ali retire and Ali disregarding the advice, Pacheco left the association.

He then began working as a television boxing analyst, continuing that job for 25 years with the National Broadcasting Company, Showtime, and Univision. His fluency in Spanish enabled him to interview Hispanic boxers who otherwise would not have been interviewed on television.

In addition to his boxing interests, Pacheco is also an accomplished artist and has won awards for his paintings. He has written 14 books, including a biography and a cookbook.

PACQUIAO, EMMANUEL DAPIDRAN "MANNY," "PAC MAN". B. 17 December 1978, Kibawe, Bukidnon, **Philippines**. Manny Pacquiao is arguably the most outstanding fighter of the 21st century. He is also one of very few fighters who has campaigned in 11 weight classes from **light flyweight** to **light middleweight** and is the only fighter to win titles in eight different weight classes. As an **amateur** boxer, he claimed a record of 60–4.

He began **professional boxing** at the age of 16, with his first recorded **bout** on 25 January 1995 in Sablayan, Philippines. He weighed 106 pounds for that bout, which was held in the light flyweight class. After compiling a record of 23–1 with all but one bout occurring in the Philippines, he won the **World Boxing Council (WBC) flyweight** title on 4 December 1998 on an eighth round **knockout** of the Thai boxer Chatchai Sasakul in **Thailand**.

In his second defense of this title, not only did Pacquiao fail to make the weight for his bout with Medgoren Singsurat, he was stopped in the third round and lost the title. Pacquiao then put on a little weight and skipped over two weight classes, **super flyweight** and **bantamweight**, and began competing at the 122-pound class—**super bantamweight**. After winning something called the WBC International super bantamweight title—one of boxing's pseudo-titles—he came to the **United States** for the first time and won the more legitimate **International Boxing Federation (IBF) super bantamweight** championship on 23 June 2001 with a sixth-round knockout of South African Lehlo Ledwaba in **Las Vegas**.

Pacquiao defended that title successfully and then stopped former **featherweight** champion Marco Antonio Barrera in 11 rounds. On 8 May 2004, Pacquiao again moved up in weight and challenged Juan Manuel Márquez for the **World Boxing Association** and IBF featherweight titles but could only manage a **draw** with Márquez. The two fighters would meet three more times in their careers. On 19 May, Pacquiao lost a close but **unanimous decision** to Erik Morales for the **International Boxing Association** and WBC International **super featherweight** titles. Six months later, Pacquiao won the WBC International super featherweight—another pseudo-title—and defended that title five times, defeating Morales twice and Barrera once.

On 15 March 2008, Manny won the more legitimate **WBC super featherweight** title on a **split decision** over Juan Manuel Márquez—the second meeting between the two. Pacquiao immediately moved up to **lightweight** and won the **WBC lightweight title** over David Díaz with a ninth-round **technical knockout** on 28 June 2008. With the victory, Pacquiao became the first Asian fighter to win world titles in four weight classes.

In his next fight, Pacquiao fought another legendary fighter, **Óscar De La Hoya**, in a 12-round **welterweight** bout with no titles at stake. Pacquiao easily handled De La Hoya, with the bout stopped after eight rounds. After the bout, De La Hoya announced his retirement from the ring.

In 2009 on 2 May, Pacquiao took on another one of the era's best fighters, Englishman Ricky Hatton, who entered the **ring** with a record of 45–1. Pacquiao knocked out Hatton with one second remaining in the second round in a bout billed for the International Boxing Organization **light welterweight** title—the fifth weight class title for Pacquiao, albeit one of the minor organization's titles. In his next fight in 2009, Pacquiao won one of the major titles—the **World Boxing Organization (WBO) welterweight championship**—when he stopped Miguel Cotto in the 12th round of their fight on 14 November. This was Pacquiao's fifth major title and sixth overall. After one successful defense of this title, Pacquiao gained another world title. On 13

November 2010, he won a unanimous decision over Antonio Margarito for the **WBC light middleweight** title. He only weighed 144 pounds for the bout for the 154-pound weight title.

In his next three bouts, Pacquiao defended his WBO welterweight title and won a unanimous decision over Shane Mosley on 7 May 2011, won a **majority decision** over Juan Manuel Márquez on 12 November 2011, but lost his title on a close split decision to Timothy Bradley on 9 June 2012.

After the bout, in one of boxing's weird rulings, the WBO commissioned a panel of five **judges** to review the fight. They ruled that Pacquiao was the winner, but Bradley retained the championship.

Six months later, Pacquiao and Márquez fought their fourth bout, with Márquez knocking out Pacquiao with one second left in the sixth round in a **nontitle bout** for a special WBO belt—"Fighter of the Decade."

In addition to his boxing activities, Pacquiao has been elected to the Philippines House of Representatives, has appeared in more than a dozen films and television shows, and has released several albums of him singing.

Pacquiao is five foot six inches tall and has a 67-inch **reach**. He has fought at weights ranging from 106 to 147 pounds in weight classes from light flyweight to light middleweight. In 61 professional bouts, from 1995 to 2012, he won 54 (38 by knockout), lost five (three by knockout), had two draws, and fought a total of 371 rounds. He is a strong candidate to be inducted into the **International Boxing Hall of Fame** when he retires from active competition.

PALOMINO, CARLOS. B. 10 August 1949, San Luis Rio Colorado, Sonora, **Mexico.** Carlos Palomino is one of the few **professional boxing** champions who has a college degree. He was born in Mexico and as a young boy moved with his family to Los Angeles. While serving in the U.S. Army, he became interested in boxing and won the All-Army **welterweight** championship in 1971 and 1972. In 1972, he was also the National **Amateur Athletic Union light welterweight** champion. After being discharged from the army, he enrolled at Orange Coast College, a junior college in California, and later transferred to California State University, Long Beach, where he received a degree in recreational administration.

He began boxing as a professional on 14 September 1972 in Los Angeles and won 10 of 11 **bouts**, with a six-**round draw** the only mar on his record. He lost a **split decision** on 2 August 1974 to Andy Price and then did not lose again for five years.

He compiled a record of 19–1–3, with all bouts in California, and was matched with **World Boxing Council** welterweight champion Englishman John H. Stracey on 22 June 1976 in London, **England.** Palomino knocked

Stracey down twice in the 12th round of their scheduled 15-round bout before the bout was stopped, and Palomino became world welterweight champion.

He defended his title successfully seven times over the next two years, beating Armando Muñiz twice, Dave "Boy" Green, Everaldo Costa Azevedo, José Palacios, Ryu Sorimachi, and Mimoun Mohatar. On 14 January 1979, the undefeated (36–0–1) **Wilfredo Benítez** won a close 15-round split decision in his hometown of San Juan and took the welterweight championship from Palomino.

In Palomino's next bout, he fought another hall of famer, **lightweight** champion **Roberto Durán**, in a 10-round **nontitle bout**. Palomino was down in the sixth round and lost the one-sided bout by **unanimous decision**. Palomino retired after the 22 June 1979 bout. In retirement, he turned to acting and has since appeared in more than 30 films and television series. He was also named a commissioner on the California State Athletic **Commission** and served in that capacity for three years.

In 1980, Palomino's younger brother Paul was killed when the plane carrying the **United States** national amateur team, of which he was a member, crashed in **Poland**. Carlos felt especially guilty since he talked his brother out of becoming a professional and recommended that he first compete in the **Olympic Games**.

In 1997, at the age of 47, 18 years after his last bout, Palomino made a comeback of sorts. After the death of his father in 1997, Palomino went to a gym to work out. There he met **Héctor Camacho**, who was **training** for an upcoming bout with Roberto Durán. After **sparring** with Camacho for a few rounds, Palomino realized he still had some boxing ability left. He dedicated his comeback to the memory of his father and younger brother.

Palomino fought five fights in 1997 and 1998, winning his first four by **knockout**, including a win over former **light welterweight** champion René Arredondo. Palomino lost his last bout by **split decision** on 30 May 1998 to Wilfredo Rivera and hasn't fought since.

Palomino is five foot eight inches tall and has a 70-inch **reach**. He has fought at weights ranging from 145 to 152 pounds as a welterweight. In 38 professional bouts, from 1972 to 1998, he won 31 (19 by knockout), lost four (none by knockout), had three draws, and fought a total of 300 rounds. He was inducted into the **International Boxing Hall of Fame** in 2004.

PALOOKA. A palooka in boxing terminology is synonymous with "tomato can," "stiff," "stumblebum," "opponent," and just plain "bum." It is a derogatory term referring to a second-rate boxer. Ironically, the comic strip *Joe Palooka* was about a fictitious **heavyweight** boxing champion who was anything but a "palooka."

PANAMA. Although the small country of Panama has produced a substantial number of professional boxers, it does not have an extensive **amateur** program and only competed in **Olympic** boxing three times—1964, 1972, and 2012. Each of its four boxers was defeated in his first **bout**.

Professional boxing, however, is a different story, and Panama has had 27 world champions, include some of boxing's greatest competitors. Panama Al Brown, **Roberto Durán**, Ismael Laguna, and Eusebio Pedroza have all been inducted into the **International Boxing Hall of Fame**. Other Panamanian world champions include Pedro Alcázar, Celestino Caballero, Luis Concepción, Ricardo Córdoba, Victor Córdoba, Alfonso "Peppermint" Frazer, Julio César Green, Luis Ibarra, Guillermo Jones, Alfredo Layne, Alfonso López, Jorge Lujan, Ernesto Marcel, Mauricio Martínez, Vicente Mosquera, Anselmo Moreno, Carlos Murillo, Rafael Ortega, Rafael Pedroza, Enrique Pinder, Rigoberto Riasco, Santiago Samaniego, Roberto Vásquez, and Hilario Zapata.

PAPALEO, GUGLIELMO. *See* PEP, WILLIE "WILL O' THE WISP" (né GUGLIELMO PAPALEO).

PAPERWEIGHT. Paperweight was a name given to boxers of extremely low weights during the 19th and early 20th century. **Flyweight Jimmy Wilde** boxed in matches billed for the "108 lb. paperweight title," but the class never achieved much recognition and was never considered as an established weight division.
See also OTHER WEIGHT CLASSES.

PAPP, LASZLO "LACI". B. 25 March 1926, Budapest, **Hungary**. D. 16 October 2003, Budapest, Hungary. Had László Papp been a native of a noncommunist country, he undoubtedly would have been remembered by many more people. He was the first man to win three **Olympic Games** boxing **gold medals**, winning the **middleweight** class in 1948 and the **light middleweight** class in 1952 and 1956. He won his final **bout** in the 1956 Olympic tournament by defeating future professional world champion **José Torres**. Papp was finally allowed by the Hungarian government to become a professional boxer in 1957 at the age of 31, although he had to go to other countries to pursue his career as **professional boxing** was illegal in his native **Hungary**.

The five-foot-five-inch **southpaw** had his first professional fight on 18 May 1957 in Cologne, **Germany**. After winning his first seven bouts fighting in Germany, Austria, and **France**, he broke his hand early in a fight with Frenchman Germinal Ballarin in April 1959 and could only receive a **draw decision** in that bout. After a five-month layoff, he resumed boxing. He won four bouts in Austria and Yugoslavia but then was held to a 10-**round draw** by Italian Giancarlo Garbelli in Milan, **Italy**. In 1961 and 1962, Papp won six more bouts, including a decision over **Ralph "Tiger" Jones** in Vienna, Austria.

On 16 May 1962, Papp won the European middleweight championship by defeating the Dane Chris Christensen on a seventh-round **technical knockout** in Vienna. Over the next two years, Papp defended that title successfully six times at various European venues. He defeated Frenchman Hippolyte Annex, Englishman George Aldridge, German Peter Müller, Spaniard Luis Folledo, Dane Chris Christensen, and Irishman Mick Leahy. Papp also defeated Randy Sandy and Charley Cotton in **nontitle bouts** in Europe.

After the Leahy bout on 9 October 1964, Papp was offered a chance to fight for the world title, but the Hungarian government frowned on it and would no longer permit him an exit visa to leave the country, claiming that "boxing for financial gain was incompatible with socialist purposes."

Papp is one of the few world-class boxers to retire undefeated. The Papp László Sportarena in Budapest, an indoor ice hockey arena, is named for him.

Papp fought at weights ranging from 157 to 165 pounds as a middleweight. In 29 professional bouts, from 1957 to 1964, he won 27 (15 by **knockout**), lost none, had two draws, and fought a total of 225 rounds. He was inducted into the **International Boxing Hall of Fame** in 2001.

PARET, BERNARDO "BENNY," "KID". B. 14 March 1937, Santa Clara, **Cuba**. D. 3 April 1962, New York, New York. Benny "Kid" Paret made the fatal mistake of taunting **Emile Griffith** during the **weigh-in** for the **welterweight** championship **bout** in March 1962.

Paret was a competent if not outstanding boxer who began his **ring** career in his native Cuba, with his first recorded bout on 16 April 1954. After compiling a record of 21–3, with one of the three losses at the hands of future world welterweight champion Luis Manuel Rodríguez, Paret came to New York. There he fought some of the better welterweights and **middleweights** with mixed results. He defeated Argentinean Victor Zalazar twice but lost to **Gaspar Ortega** and drew with future middleweight and **light heavyweight** champion **José Torres**.

On 27 May 1960, he defeated Don Jordan on a 15-**round decision** in **Las Vegas** and became the world's welterweight champion. After losing a **nontitle bout** to Denny Moyer, Paret successfully defended his welterweight title with a 15-round **unanimous-decision** victory over Argentinean Luis Federico Thompson at **Madison Square Garden** on 10 December 1960.

After losing a nontitle bout to Ortega, Paret fought Emile Griffith in a title defense in Miami Beach, losing his title on a 13th-round **knockout** on 1 April 1961. Six months later, Paret regained the title on a **split decision** at Madison Square Garden on 30 September 1961.

Paret then attempted to move up to the middleweight ranks but was **knocked down** three times in the 10th round, the last time for the 10 count, by middleweight champion **Gene Fullmer** on 9 December 1961.

He then was scheduled to fight Griffith in a **rubber match** on 24 March 1962 at Madison Square Garden. During the prefight weigh-in, Paret taunted Griffith and called him a "maricón"—a Spanish derogatory term for a homosexual. This angered Griffith, who was ready to fight Paret right then and there (probably because the accusation was true, in part, as was later disclosed in Griffith's life).

In the fight, Paret knocked Griffith down in the sixth round, but Griffith had the better of the action throughout most of the fight. In the 12th round, Griffith caught Paret against the ropes and hit him 29 times in a row. Paret was caught in the ropes and unable to fall to the **canvas** and absorbed a frightful beating before **referee Ruby Goldstein** was able to step in and stop the bout.

Paret was unconscious and went into a coma by the time the fight was stopped. He remained in a coma at a hospital in New York before dying on 3 April 1962. The fight had been nationally **televised** and was the first **ring fatality** on national television. As has often been the case after a ring fatality, there was much public outrage that the sport of boxing was too brutal and should be outlawed, but as usual nothing came of it.

Paret was five foot seven inches tall and fought at weights ranging from 135 to 157 pounds as a welterweight and middleweight. In 50 professional bouts, from 1954 to 1962, Paret won 35 (10 by knockout), lost 12 (four by knockout), had three draws, and fought a total of 404 rounds.

PATTERSON, FLOYD. B. 4 January 1935, Waco, North Carolina. D. 11 May 2006, New Paltz, New York. Floyd Patterson would be at the top of most boxing historians' lists if they were asked to select the most mild-mannered, gentlemanly person to ever become world's **heavyweight** champion.

He was raised in Brooklyn, New York, and as a youth got in minor trouble and was sent to the Wiltwyck School for Boys in Esopus, New York, about eight miles south of Kingston near the Hudson River. He credits the two years he spent at the school with turning his life around. After returning home to Brooklyn, he began boxing at **Cus D'Amato's** Empire Sports Club at the Gramercy Gym in New York City. He was an exceptionally capable amateur boxer and, although underage, entered the New York **Golden Gloves** tournament as a **sub-novice welterweight** in 1950, winning two **bouts** before losing a **decision** in the third **round** of the tournament. Patterson won the 1951 **middleweight open** in both the New York Golden Gloves and Eastern Regionals tournaments but was defeated in the Intercity Golden Gloves. In 1952, as a **light heavyweight** he won all three of those tournaments. He also won the 1952 national **Amateur Athletic Union** middle-weight championship and the 1952 **Olympic Games** middleweight title. He claimed a record of 40–4 as an amateur boxer.

His first professional bout took place on 12 September 1952, a fourth-round **knockout** at **St. Nicholas Arena** in New York over Eddie Godbold. From 1952 to 1954, he won his first 13 bouts, eight by knockout, before losing a close eight-round decision to former light heavyweight champion **Joey Maxim** on 7 June 1954. Undeterred by the loss, he kept winning, and in 1956, after winning a 12-round **split decision** over Tommy "Hurricane" Jackson, the 21-year-old Patterson was matched with the 42-year-old light heavyweight champion **Archie Moore** for the world's heavyweight championship, made **vacant** by **Rocky Marciano's** retirement earlier that year.

Patterson knocked out Moore in the fifth round on 30 November 1956 and became the youngest heavyweight champion in boxing history—a feat later topped by **Mike Tyson** in 1986. Patterson's manager, Cus D'Amato did not want anything to do with the **International Boxing Club**, an organization later disclosed to have ties to organized crime, and consequently was very selective in Patterson's opponents as title challengers, with the result that both **Eddie Machen** and **Zora Folley**, the top two ranked heavyweights, were both bypassed.

For his first defense, Patterson won a rematch over Jackson, stopping him in 10 rounds on 29 July 1957. In his second title defense, a unique match was made. Patterson, a 1952 Olympic champion was pitted against **Pete Rademacher**, the 1956 Olympic **heavyweight** champion. What made this bout unique was that Rademacher, who was six and a half years older than Patterson, had never fought a professional bout. Although Patterson was **knocked down** in the second round, he got up and floored Rademacher six times, knocking him out in the sixth round of their bout on 22 August 1957 in Seattle, Washington, Rademacher's hometown.

Patterson's next defense was against another relatively unknown fighter, Roy Harris. Harris was a Texan (from the colorfully named town of Cut 'n' Shoot) who had compiled a record of 23–0 with only nine knockouts.

In the bout, which took place on 18 August 1958 in Los Angeles, California, Patterson easily won and stopped Harris after 12 rounds. Patterson then defended against the Englishman Brian London on 1 May 1959 in Indianapolis, Indiana. Patterson knocked out London in 11 rounds.

Patterson's next defense occurred less than two months after his defeat of London, a rarity in that era when heavyweight champions usually fought title bouts only once a year. On 26 June 1959 outdoors at Yankee Stadium, Patterson faced the European heavyweight champion, the Swede **Ingemar Johansson**, undefeated at 21–0. Johansson caught Patterson with a powerful right hand in the third round and knocked him down. Patterson got up and went down again a total of seven times in the round before being counted out at 2:03 of the third round.

For their rematch one year later (20 June 1960, at the Polo Grounds in New York), Patterson trained hard while Johansson enjoyed his celebrity and spent a minimum of effort in **training**. Patterson knocked out Johansson in the fifth round and became the first man to regain the heavyweight title.

They had one more rematch on 13 March 1961 in Miami Beach, Florida, and although Patterson was knocked down twice in the first round, he got up and knocked Johansson down in that round and eventually knocked him out in the sixth round. The two combatants eventually became lifelong friends and in the 1980s actually ran in marathon races together.

Patterson next defended against Tom McNeeley, an undefeated (23–0) boxer with no major victories to his credit. McNeeley was knocked down 11 times in the bout and lost on a fourth-round knockout.

Patterson then went against the wishes of his manager, Cus D'Amato, and scheduled his next title defense for 25 September 1962 in Chicago against the number one contender, Charles "Sonny" Liston, a former convict with mob connections. Liston knocked out Floyd at 2:06 of the first round and won the world's heavyweight title. Their rematch on 22 July 1963 in **Las Vegas** was almost identical to the first fight, as Liston caught Floyd early in the fight and knocked him out at 2:10 of the first round.

Floyd felt deep embarrassment and left the country, fighting twice in Sweden and once in **Puerto Rico** in 1964. He did finally meet Machen in Sweden and won a 12-round decision over him. In 1965, he defeated Canadian contender **George Chuvalo** and then on 22 November received a shot at **Muhammad Ali's** heavyweight title after Ali had twice defeated Liston to become the new champion. Patterson, who had injured his back prior to the Ali fight, was unable to put up a good showing throughout the fight and finally, after 12 rounds, **referee** Harry Krause stopped the bout to save Patterson from further punishment.

Patterson continued his boxing career and in 1966 knocked out British heavyweight champion Henry Cooper in four rounds in London, **England**. After fighting a close 10-round **draw** with contender **Jerry Quarry** and losing another close 12-round **majority decision** with him in 1967, Patterson fought yet another world heavyweight title fight. Jimmy Ellis, who had won the **World Boxing Association** title after Muhammad Ali was stripped of the title, defeated Patterson on a 15-round decision in Stockholm, Sweden, on 14 September 1968. After not boxing in 1969, Patterson resumed fighting in 1970, but his opponents were mostly of lower caliber. He did win a 10-round decision over Óscar Bonavena, a tough Argentinean.

Patterson's last bout was on 20 September 1972 with Ali—a **nontitle bout** since Ali had lost his title to **Joe Frazier** the previous year. The fight was stopped after the seventh round as Patterson's eye was cut and swollen shut. Although Patterson never officially announced his retirement, he never fought again. He settled in New Paltz, New York, and spent time working with young boxers. He legally adopted one of his students, Tracy Harris. Harris became known as Tracy Harris Patterson and won the New York **Golden Gloves** in 1984 and 1985 and later became **World Boxing Council super bantamweight** champion. Floyd was also a member of the **New York State Athletic Commission** and was its chairman from 1995 to 1998.

Patterson continued his friendship with former foe Ingemar Johansson, and the two would alternate annual visits between Johansson's Swedish home and Patterson's American one. The two former heavyweight champions died within three years of one another, both due to complications of Alzheimer's disease—Floyd in 2006 and Ingo in 2009.

Patterson was six feet tall and had a 71-inch **reach**. He fought at weights ranging from 163 to 200 pounds as a light heavyweight and heavyweight. In 64 professional bouts, from 1952 to 1972, he won 55 (40 by knockout), lost eight (five by knockout), had one draw, and fought a total of 419 rounds. He was inducted into the **International Boxing Hall of Fame** in 1991.

PAZ, VINNY. *See* PAZIENZA, VINCENZO EDWARD "VINNY," "THE PAZMANIAN DEVIL" (aka VINNY PAZ).

PAZIENZA, VINCENZO EDWARD "VINNY," "THE PAZMANIAN DEVIL" (aka VINNY PAZ). B. 16 December 1962, Cranston, Rhode Island. Vinny Pazienza overcame one of the worst injuries ever suffered by a boxer in his prime.

He began his **professional boxing** career on 26 May 1983 with a four-**round technical knockout** in **Atlantic City**. He won his first 14 **bouts**, 12 by **knockout**, before being stopped on cuts in the fifth round of a bout in **Italy**. After eight more victories, six by knockout, he fought Greg Haugen for the **International Boxing Federation lightweight** title in Providence, Rhode Island (10 miles north of Pazienza's hometown of Cranston), on 7 June 1987 and won a 15-round **unanimous decision**. In a rematch in Atlantic City eight months later, Haugen won a unanimous decision and regained the title.

In 1988, Pazienza challenged Roger Mayweather for Mayweather's **World Boxing Council light welterweight** title but lost a one-sided 12-round unanimous decision. Pazienza's next attempt at a world title occurred on 3 February 1990 when he faced **Héctor Camacho** for Camacho's **World Boxing Organization** light welterweight title. Again, Pazienza fell short, as he lost a unanimous decision.

In Vinny's next bout, he fought Haugen again, who by this time had lost his title, and defeated him on a 10-round decision in a **nontitle bout**. Four months later, Pazienza lost yet another attempt at a world title as Loreto Garza successfully defended his **World Boxing Association (WBA)** light welterweight championship when Pazienza, frustrated at the beating he was taking, threw Garza to the **canvas** and was **disqualified** in the 11th round.

On 1 October 1991, Pazienza finally won another title as he defeated Gilbert Delé, who was the WBA **light middleweight** champion. Pazienza stopped Delé with less than one minute to go in the 12th and final round.

This was Pazienza's last fight for nearly two years, as on 12 November 1991 he was in a horrific auto accident as a passenger in a car and, although he survived it, had two broken vertebrae in his neck and two other vertebrae damaged. He was told by doctors he would never box again and might not even be able to walk again.

He was placed in a metal halo that was screwed into his skull and had to wear that brace device for three months. One month after the accident, though, still wearing the brace, he was back in the gym working out. When the brace came off on 14 February, he was fitted with a hard plastic neck brace that he wore for a short time afterward before he discarded it.

While incapacitated, he vacated his newly won title. After receiving clearance from physicians, he returned to the **ring** on 15 December 1992, just 13 months after his accident, and won every round on all three **judges'** scorecards as he won a unanimous 10-round **decision**. After three more victories, including a 10th-round **technical knockout** of former **welterweight** champion Lloyd Honeyghan, Pazienza fought for a world title again.

The bout on 28 December 1993 was for one of the lesser organizations' titles—the International Boxing Organization (IBO) **super middleweight** championship—and Pazienza won it on an 11th-round knockout over Dan Sherry. After one more victory, Pazienza won a **unanimous decision** for the IBC super middleweight title over the legendary **Roberto Durán**, former multiple world champion who at 43 years of age and past his prime still was a dangerous opponent. Seven months later, Pazienza won a rematch with Durán also by 12-round unanimous decision.

On 24 June 1995, Pazienza was stopped in the sixth round after a third **knockdown** by the undefeated (28–0) **Roy Jones Jr.** in a bout for Jones's **International Boxing Federation** super middleweight title. In Pazienza's next bout, he stopped the previously unbeaten Dana Rosenblatt in four rounds and won the lightly regarded World Boxing Union super middleweight title. After a 12-round decision loss to Englishman Herol Graham in

London, Pazienza returned and won five consecutive bouts before losing a **split decision** to Rosenblatt for the IBO super middleweight title on 5 November 1999.

Pazienza was inactive for over a year and when he returned to the ring was stopped on cuts in eight rounds by Aaron Davis. After three more victories, Pazienza made one last bid for a world title, losing a unanimous decision to Eric Lucas on 1 March 2002 for the WBC super middleweight title. Vinny's last fight was on 27 March 2004, and after winning a 10-round decision, he retired from the ring. He has since dabbled in professional wrestling as a **referee**.

Pazienza is five foot seven inches tall and has a 70-inch **reach**. He fought at weights ranging from 135 to 171 pounds in weight classes from lightweight to super middleweight. In 60 professional bouts, from 1983 to 2004, he won 50 (30 by knockout), lost 10 (three by knockout), and fought a total of 460 rounds.

PEP, WILLIE "WILL O' THE WISP" (né GUGLIELMO PAPALEO). B. 19 September 1922, Middletown, Connecticut. D. 23 November 2006, Rocky Hill, Connecticut. The dictionary defines "will o' the wisp" as "a ghostly light seen by travellers at night, especially over bogs, swamps or marshes. It resembles a flickering lamp and is said to recede if approached, drawing travellers from the safe paths." The phrase "recede if approached" certainly describes Willie Pep's style. He was a consummate defensive fighter who reportedly once won a **round** on the **judges'** scorecards without throwing a punch (although the story has subsequently been deemed apocryphal).

He began as an **amateur** boxer in Connecticut and did well, claiming an amateur record of 62–3. One of those losses was to a boxer who outweighed him by about 20 pounds and later became world's **welterweight** and **middleweight** champion—**"Sugar Ray" Robinson**.

Pep's first **professional bout** was on 25 July 1940 in Hartford, Connecticut, and was won by Pep on a four-round **decision**. He continued fighting throughout New England and won 53 consecutive bouts. On 20 November 1942, he defeated Albert "Chalky" Wright on a 15-round decision at **Madison Square Garden** and won the **New York State Athletic Commission** world's **featherweight** championship. (At the time, the rival **National Boxing Association** recognized Jackie Wilson as their featherweight champion.)

Four months later, on 19 March 1943 at the Garden, Pep suffered his first professional loss, ending a winning streak that had reached 62 straight victories. Sammy Angott, then world's **lightweight** champion, defeated Pep on a close 10-round **unanimous decision** in a **nontitle bout**.

Pep's first title defense was on 8 June 1943 in Boston, Massachusetts, when he won a unanimous 15-round decision over Sal Bartolo. On 29 September 1944, Pep won a rematch with Wright in another title defense on a 15-round decision. Although Pep kept busy fighting nontitle bouts, he defended his title only about once a year. His 1945 title defense occurred on 19 February 1945, a 15-round unanimous decision over Phil Terranova.

On 13 December 1945, for only the second time in his professional career, Pep did not win when his 10-round bout with Jimmy McAllister in Baltimore, Maryland, was scored a draw. In Pep's 1946 title defense (7 June 1946), he knocked out Bartolo in 12 rounds.

Pep did not defend his title again for more than one year, but he had a good reason for this—he was recovering from injuries, including a broken back suffered in an airplane crash. On 5 January 1947, while returning from Miami, Florida, Pep was a passenger in a small plane that crashed in Millville, New Jersey. The copilot and two passengers were killed. Pep, who was one of 11 survivors, suffered a broken leg and broken back and spent five months in a body cast and back brace.

Pep returned to the **ring** on 17 June 1947, less than six months after his injuries. He won six straight bouts in June and July before knocking out Jock Leslie in 12 rounds on 22 August 1947 in Flint, Michigan, in defense of his featherweight title. Pep's next title defense was on 24 February 1948 against Humberto Sierra. In a bout held in the rain at the Orange Bowl in Miami, Florida **referee Jack Dempsey** stopped the bout after Sierra was knocked down in the 10th round.

Pep's next title defense occurred on 29 October 1948 at Madison Square Garden and marked the beginning of one of boxing's great series of bouts— Pep–Saddler. Going into the bout, Pep had the exceptional record of 134–1–1 while Joseph "Sandy" Saddler's record was 85–6–2, also an outstanding one. Saddler knocked Pep down twice in the third round and knocked him out in the fourth round and won the world's **featherweight** title.

Their subsequent rematch at the Garden on 11 February 1949 was voted the "Fight of the Year" by *Ring* **magazine** and was won by Pep on a 15-round unanimous decision. Pep then won three more title defenses—20 September 1949 (Eddie Campo, technical knockout, seven rounds); 16 January 1950 (Charley Riley, 5th round **knockout**); and 17 March 1950 (Ray Famechon, unanimous decision, 15 rounds).

On 8 September 1950, Pep fought Saddler for the third time and this time lost his title on an eighth-round retirement after he separated his shoulder. Their rematch one year later on 26 September 1951 was one of the dirtiest fights in ring history, and after nine tough rounds, Pep retired after suffering a deep cut over his eye, although he was ahead on the scorecards at that time.

Although Pep continuing boxing until 1966, he never again fought for a world championship. His next two losses were questionable, though. On 30 June 1952, he was stopped in six rounds by Tommy Collins, and on 26 February 1954 he was stopped in two rounds by Lulu Perez. In both of those fights, Pep was suspected of **taking a dive**, although nothing was ever proved.

On 30 March 1955, Pep lost a close **split decision** to Gil Cadilli for his seventh loss (three to Saddler). Pep defeated Cadilli in a rematch and by the end of 1957 had the remarkable record of 209–7–1. After losing a close split decision to **journeyman Tommy Tibbs**, Pep won his next 11 bouts. He then faced the world's featherweight champion Nigerian Hogan "Kid" Bassey in a nontitle bout. Bassey knocked Pep down twice in the ninth round before the bout was stopped and virtually ended Pep's career.

Pep did fight one more bout, in Caracas, **Venezuela**, on 26 January 1959 but was knocked down three times by journeyman Sonny Leon and lost a unanimous decision. He retired after that bout and worked as a referee and **trainer** of young boxers.

In 1965, Pep was working with some young boxers in Miami, Florida, and when one of his fighters got sick, the promoter asked the 43-year-old Willie if he could substitute for him. Pep did and found that he still had some boxing ability left. He had nine bouts that year against lower-class opposition and won them all. On 16 March 1966, Pep was scheduled to box an **exhibition** bout against Calvin Woodland in Richmond, Virginia. Just before the bout, he was told that it would not be an exhibition but a regular bout. Although out of shape, he lasted the full six rounds but lost the decision and never fought again. However, in retirement, he and Saddler boxed an occasional exhibition.

In retirement, he continued to work as a **referee** and worked bouts worldwide, including ones in **Australia**, Jamaica, **Canada**, the **Philippines**, and **Brazil**. He died at the age of 84 from complications of Alzheimer's disease while at a nursing home in Connecticut.

Pep was five foot five inches tall and had a 68-inch **reach**. He fought at weights ranging from 123 to 138 pounds, primarily as a featherweight. He had the remarkable total of 241 professional bouts from 1940 to 1966—many more than nearly all the fighters of his generation—and won 229 (65 by knockout), lost 11 (six by knockout), had one **draw**, and fought a total of 1,956 rounds. He was inducted as a member of the inaugural class of the **International Boxing Hall of Fame** in 1990.

PÉREZ, PASCUAL NICOLÁS "EL LEÓN MENDOCINO," "EL PEQUEÑO GIGANTE". B. 4 March 1926, Mendoza, **Argentina**. D. 22 January 1977. Pascual Pérez, at four foot 11 inches, was one of the smallest men ever to become a world champion. Although the lightest boxing weight class when he competed was the **flyweight** division, with a maximum weight limit of 112 pounds, Pérez fought most of his **bouts** weighing no more than 108 pounds.

As an **amateur** boxer, he won the 1948 **Olympic** flyweight **gold medal** and continued boxing as an amateur for three more years before becoming a **professional** boxer on 5 December 1952 with a four-**round technical knockout** of José Ciorino in Gerli, Buenos Aires. Pérez won his first 18 bouts by **knockout** and had a record of 23–0 when he met world flyweight champion Yoshio Shirai in a **nontitle bout** on 24 July 1954 in Buenos Aires. He held Shirai to a 10-round **draw** then won a unanimous 15-round **decision** over the **Japanese** Shirai in Tokyo, Japan, on 26 November to become the world's flyweight champion and the first Argentinean to win a world boxing championship.

In a rematch seven months later, Pérez stopped Shirai in five rounds in Tokyo to retain his title. From 1955 to 1958, he successfully defended his title six more times and won seven other bouts that were billed as nontitle, but since both boxers weighed in under the 112 pound limit the flyweight title was technically at stake. He suffered his first loss in a nontitle bout on a 10-round **unanimous decision** to Sadao Yaoita in Tokyo on 16 January 1959 but knocked out Yaoita in 13 rounds later that year in a world flyweight title bout.

In his next bout, on 16 April 1960 in Bangkok, **Thailand**, Pérez lost his title to the Thai boxer Pone Kingpetch on a 15-round **split decision**. Five months later, in neutral territory—Los Angeles, California—Kingpetch stopped Pérez in the eighth round and retained his title.

From 1961 to 1963, Pérez limited his boxing activity to his native Argentina and won 28 consecutive bouts, 19 of them by knockout or technical knockout. Pérez then traveled to the **Philippines**, where on 30 April 1963 he lost a 10-round split decision to the Filipino Leo Zulueta. Pérez had five more bouts in Latin America, losing three of them, including the final bout of his professional career on 15 March 1964, when he was stopped in six rounds by Eugenio Hurtado in **Panama**.

Pérez fought at weights ranging from 103 to 112 pounds as a flyweight. In 92 professional bouts, from 1952 to 1964, he won 84 (57 by knockout), lost seven (three by knockout), had one draw, and fought a total of 619 rounds. He was inducted into the **International Boxing Hall of Fame** in 1995.

PHILIPPINES. Boxing has always been a popular sport in the Philippines. In **amateur boxing**, the Philippines first competed in the 1932 **Olympic Games** and has entered 18 Olympic boxing tournaments—every one except 1980, when it boycotted the games. The country has yet to win an Olympic **gold medal** in boxing but has won two **silver** and three **bronze** medals. **Bantamweight** José Luis Villanueva won the first Olympic boxing medal in

1932, a bronze, and his son, Anthony, won a silver medal in 1964 in the **featherweight** class. **Light flyweights** Leopoldo Serrantes in 1988 and Roel Velasco in 1992 were bronze medalists. Velasco's brother, Mansueto, won the 1996 silver medal, also in the light flyweight class.

In **professional boxing**, the Philippines has produced 33 world champion boxers. The first was the **flyweight** Francisco Guilledo, who boxed as **Pancho Villa** and who won his championship in 1923. Gabriel "Flash" Elorde is another of the great Filipino world champions, and he was elected to the **International Boxing Hall of Fame** in 1993. His countryman, Villa, was elected to that hall in 1994. The most famous and best champion is **Manny Pacquiao**, who has won titles in eight different divisions—more than any other boxer in history. Other top Filipino world champions include Roberto Cruz, Ceferino Garcia, Rolando Navarrete, Donny Nietes, Dodie Boy Penalosa and his brother Gerry Penalosa, Erbito Salavarria, Ben Villaflor, Bernabe Villacampo, and Eleuterio Zapanta (Little Dado). In addition, one of boxing's best **referees**, Carlos Padilla Jr., is a native of the Philippines.

One of boxing's all time great **bouts** took place in the Philippines on 1 October 1975 in Quezon City, Metro Manila, when **Muhammad Ali** and **Joe Frazier** met for the third time. Ali stopped Frazier in the 14th **round** to retain his world's **heavyweight** title in a bout known as the "**Thrilla in Manila.**"

POINTS. See SCORING SYSTEMS.

POLAND. Boxing might not be the most popular sport in Poland, but Poland has had a strong tradition in the **amateur ring.** Polish boxers first competed in the 1924 **Olympic Games** and have entered 19 Olympic boxing tournaments. In those tournaments, Poland has had 105 competitors and has won 43 medals—sixth best of all nations. The country has won eight **gold medals**, nine **silver**, and 26 **bronze**. Only the **United States** with 34 has won more bronze Olympic boxing medals than Poland.

The eight gold medalists are Kazimierz Paździor, 1960 **lightweight**; Józef Grudzień, 1964 lightweight; Jan Szczepański, 1972 lightweight; Jerzy Kulej, 1964 and 1968 **light welterweight**; Zygmunt Chychła, 1952 **welterweight**; Marian Kasprzyk, 1964 welterweight; and Jerzy Rybicki, 1976 **light middleweight**.

Zbigniew Pietrzykowski was probably Poland's greatest amateur boxer. He won three Olympic boxing medals, light middleweight bronze in 1956, **light heavyweight** bronze in 1964, and light heavyweight silver in 1960, when he was defeated in the final by Cassius Clay (who would become the world's **heavyweight** champion as a professional and change his name to **Muhammad Ali**). Pietrzykowski later became a member of the Polish Parliament.

Eleven Polish boxers have each won more than one Olympic boxing medal. In addition to Pietrzykowski's three medals and Kulej's two medals, Aleksy Antkiewicz won the 1948 **featherweight** bronze medal and the 1952 lightweight silver medal. Artur Olech was the **flyweight** bronze medalist in 1964 and 1968. Marian Kasprzyk won a bronze medal in 1960 in the light welterweight class and returned four years later as a welterweight and won the gold medal. Leszek Błażyński won bronze medals as a flyweight in 1972 and 1976. Józef Grudzień won a silver medal in 1968 in the lightweight class to go along with his 1964 gold medal. Tadeusz Walasek competed in the 1956 welterweight class but did not medal; he returned as a **middleweight** and won a silver medal in 1960 and bronze medal in 1964. Janusz Gortat won bronze medals in 1972 and 1976 in the light heavyweight class. (Gortat's son, Marcin, is a professional basketball player in the National Basketball Association.) Kazimierz Szczerba was the 1976 bronze medalist as a light welterweight and 1980 bronze medalist as a welterweight. Jerzy Rybicki won the gold medal in 1976 as a light middleweight and the bronze medal as a middleweight in 1980. Brothers Krzysztof and Leszek Kosedowski were both featherweight bronze medalists—Leszek in 1976 and Krzysztof four years later.

Feliks Stamm was the most noteworthy coach in Polish boxing, and he was in charge of their Olympic team from 1936 to 1968, when Poland had their best Olympic boxing teams.

Since the fall of communism, Polish boxers have been allowed to box professionally, and several Polish boxing world champions have emerged. Among them are Tomasz Adamek, Dariusz Michalczewski, and Krzyzstof Włodarczyk. The 1988 Olympic bronze medalist Andrew (Andrzej) Gołota was one of the better professional **heavyweights** during the 1990s and faced champions **Riddick Bowe**, Lamon Brewster, **Lennox Lewis**, John Ruiz, **Mike Tyson**, and Tim Witherspoon during his career from 1992 to 2009.

In addition, there have been many notable Polish American boxers, among them world champions Bobby Czyz, **Stanley Ketchel** (Stanislaw Kiecal), Eddie "Babe" Risko (Henry Pylkowski), Teddy Yarosz, and **Tony Zale** (Antoni Zaleski).

PRELIMINARY BOUTS. Most boxing **cards** have several **bouts** scheduled. Bouts that take place prior to the **main event** are called preliminary bouts or prelims, are generally scheduled for four, six, or eight **rounds**, and feature boxers of lesser quality than those in main events. Professional boxers usually begin their careers boxing in preliminary bouts and as they gain in experience and fame move up to main events.

PROFESSIONAL BOXING. Professional boxing began in the **bareknuckle** era, when boxers would receive remuneration for their efforts by boxing fans or would challenge one another with the boxers' backers putting up the cash prize for the victors. Purses in modern-day professional boxing run the gamut from several dollars paid to boxers in **preliminary bouts** to multimillions that have been paid to some boxers in **world championship bouts**.

PUERTO RICO. Boxing is one of Puerto Rico's most popular sports, and there have been many boxers, both born on the island or born on the mainland, of Puerto Rican heritage who have excelled in the sport. Although the Commonwealth of Puerto Rico is part of the **United States**, its unique status has enabled it to have its own National Olympic Committee and send its own teams to the **Olympic Games**.

In **amateur boxing**, Puerto Rico first competed in the 1948 Olympic Games and has entered 15 Olympic boxing tournaments. The country has won six medals—one **silver** and five **bronze**. Luis Ortiz won the 1984 **lightweight** silver medal. Bronze medalists are Orlando Maldonado, 1976 **light flyweight**; Juan Venegas, 1948 **bantamweight**; Anibal Acevedo, 1992 **welterweight**; Daniel Santos, 1996 welterweight; and Aristides González, 1984 **middleweight**. Puerto Rican–born **José Torres** was the 1956 silver medalist in the **light middleweight** class while boxing for the United States team.

In recent years, Puerto Rican boxers have become, along with Mexican boxers and African American boxers, the largest ethnic groups in **professional boxing**. There have been more than 30 Puerto Rican world champions, among them **International Boxing Hall of Fame** members **Wilfred Benítez**, Sixto Escobar, **Wilfredo Gómez**, **Carlos Ortiz**, Edwin Rosario, and **José Torres**. Also in the hall of fame are **referee Joe Cortez** and nonchampions the Cocoa Kid (Herbert Hardwick) and Pedro Montañez. Other Puerto Rican world champions of note, some of whom will most likely be inducted into the hall once they are eligible, include **Héctor Camacho**, Miguel Ángel Cotto, Esteban de Jesús, Carlos de León, Alfredo Escalera, Daniel Jiménez, Juan LaPorte, Juan Manuel López, John John Molina, Eric Morel, Ossie Ocasio, Daniel Santos, Samuel Serrano, **Félix Trinidad**, Wilfredo Vázquez, and his son Wilfredo Jr.

Among the top Puerto Rican referees are Joe Cortez (born in New York but raised in Puerto Rico) and Waldemar Schmidt.

PUGILISTIC DEMENTIA. Pugilistic dementia (sometimes called dementia pugilistica) is a neurological condition brought on by repeated blows to the head such as occur to most **professional** boxers. Symptoms include slurred speech, memory loss, declining mental ability, and lack of coordination. It has occurred and continues to occur in many former boxers, and consequently medical authorities have suggested banning the sport, although to deaf ears for the most part.

It is a condition formerly known as punch-drunk and has often been used as a sterotypical portrait of former professional boxers in motion pictures.

PUNCH DRUNK. *See* PUGILISTIC DEMENTIA.

PUNCHSTAT. *See* COMPUBOX.

QUARRY, JERRY "IRISH," "THE BELLFLOWER BOMBER". B. 15 May 1945, Bakersfield, California. D. 3 January 1999, Templeton, California. Although the "era of the **white hope**," strictly speaking, occurred during the reign of **heavyweight** champion **Jack Johnson**, the phrase "white hope" has been used in describing many Caucasian boxers in the second half of the 20th century. **Jerry Quarry** was one such "white hope."

He began boxing at a very young age and won a junior championship at eight weighing just 45 pounds. He did a substantial amount of **amateur boxing** and claimed a record of 170–13 with 54 **knockouts**. In 1965, after winning the Western Regional **Golden Gloves** and National Golden Gloves titles, he became a professional boxer comanaged by his father, James Quarry, and Johnnie Flores, an established fight manager.

His first fight was on 7 May 1965 in Los Angeles and resulted in a four-**round decision** over Gene Hamilton in a heavyweight **bout**. He progressed rapidly and by November 1965 was featured in the **main event** at the Olympic Auditorium in Los Angeles. In 1966, he was fighting in the main event at **Madison Square Garden** in New York, where he fought a 10-**round draw** with Tony Alongi, a fighter with a record of 38–2–1. On 14 July 1966 in Los Angeles, Quarry was matched with **Eddie Machen**, a one-time number one ranked heavyweight. Although Machen was past his prime then and would retire less than one year later, he still defeated Quarry on a 10-round **unanimous decision**. After winning his next six bouts, Quarry met former heavyweight champion **Floyd Patterson** on 9 June 1967 in Los Angeles. The decision was a **majority draw**, with one **judge** voting for Quarry but the other two officials calling the bout even.

After **Muhammad Ali** refused to be inducted into the U.S. Army in 1967, the **World Boxing Association** stripped him of his title and arranged a heavyweight tournament among their top eight ranked boxers to determine a successor. Quarry defeated Patterson in the first round of the tournament on a 12-round **majority decision** and then stopped Thad Spencer in the 12th and final round in the semifinal of the tournament to set up a World Boxing

Association world heavyweight championship bout with Jimmy Ellis, Ali's one-time **sparring partner**. On 27 April 1968 in Oakland, California, Ellis won a 15-round majority decision over Quarry.

In March 1968, the rival **World Boxing Council** had **Joe Frazier** and Buster Mathis fight for their version of the heavyweight title, with Frazier winning on an 11th-round **technical knockout**. After successfully defending his version of the title three times, Frazier faced Quarry on 23 March 1969. In a bout selected as the "Fight of the Year" by *Ring* **magazine**, Frazier inflicted a bad cut to Quarry's eye, and the bout was stopped by **referee** Arthur Mercante after the seventh round. In 1970, as Ali was appealing his conviction of draft evasion, he was granted a boxing license. He chose to fight Quarry, who was still one of the top-rated contenders, for his first fight in nearly three and a half years. The eagerly anticipated fight, held in Atlanta, Georgia, drew a large crowd, but the fight lasted less than three rounds as Quarry was badly cut.

In 1972, Quarry fought a rematch with Ali in **Las Vegas** but again was stopped—this time in the seventh round. The following year Quarry scored one of the best victories of his career as he stopped the hard-hitting **Earnie Shavers** in the first round. This earned Quarry a rematch with Joe Frazier in 1974, but Frazier again stopped Quarry. On 24 March 1975, Quarry faced **Ken Norton** for the **vacant** North American Boxing Federation heavyweight title—a pseudo-title that Muhammad Ali held briefly after he was defeated by Joe Frazier. Norton stopped Quarry in five rounds.

Quarry retired following that bout and worked as a bodyguard for the music group Three Dog Night. Quarry should have stayed retired but instead came back in November 1977 with a ninth-round technical knockout over Lorenzo Zanon after losing the first eight rounds on all three officials' score-cards. Quarry retired after the bout.

In 1983, financial problems caused him to attempt a comeback, and although he won two bouts against **journeyman** fighters, he began to show signs of brain damage. He began working as a mobile home salesman and then a beer salesman. He also was involved with drug and alcohol abuse. In 1992, after seeing **George Foreman** come back successfully after a 10-year retirement, Quarry attempted to reenter the **ring** but was denied a license by the California State Athletic **Commission**. He managed to obtain one in Colorado and fought one more bout against a journeyman with a record of 3–4–1, but by then he had lost his boxing abilities and lost a six-round **unanimous decision**.

By 1995, Quarry was showing serious signs of **pugilistic dementia** and was being cared for by his brother, James, the only one of the four Quarry boys who did not become a professional boxer. Jerry Quarry was hospitalized for pneumonia in December 1998 and died a few days later from a heart attack. His caretaker brother, James Quarry, established the Jerry Quarry Foundation to help other disabled former boxers.

Quarry was six feet tall and had a 72-inch **reach**. He fought at weights ranging from 183 to 209 pounds as a heavyweight. In 66 hard-fought professional bouts, from 1965 to 1992, he won 53 (32 by knockout), lost nine (six by knockout), had four draws, and fought a total of 419 rounds.

QUICKEST KNOCKOUTS. On 23 September 1946, a **welterweight bout** between Al Couture and Ralph Walton in Lewiston, Maine, ended in a one-punch **knockout** in which the "official" time was recorded as 10 and a half seconds—a virtual impossibility since the **referee** had to use 10 seconds to count out the fallen boxer and the winning boxer had to rush across the **ring** and throw a knockout punch, but nonetheless that bout has been listed in boxing record books as the "quickest knockout," although boxing historians have recently changed the result to a more realistic 14-second knockout. (A footnote to that bout—Couture's son, Pete, later became one of the best professional bowlers and competed on the Professional Bowlers Tour.)

There have been more than 20 bouts, amateur and professional, that were stopped in 10 seconds or less. The quickest stoppage was one in Thailand on 23 July 2010 in a **flyweight** bout between Liempetch Sor Veerapol and Lookrak Kiatmungmee that was ended in just three seconds.

With referees stopping bouts much more quickly in recent years to prevent injuries in the ring, there have been several heavy punchers who have scored multiple knockouts or **technical knockouts** within 30 seconds or less. **Middleweight** Tyrone Brunson scored six in 2005 and 2006; **heavyweight** Shannon Briggs has scored five between 1997 and 2010; and Bobby Flores, a 330-plus pound heavyweight, had four in 2006 and 2007.

A **Golden Gloves** amateur bout in Minneapolis, Minnesota, on 4 November 1947 was stopped after only four seconds when Mike Collins knocked out Pat Brownson.

Southpaw Colombian featherweight Ever Beleño stopped Guillermo Salcedo in Sinceledo, Colombia, on 16 September 1994 in five seconds—the referee stopped the bout without counting. Beleño stopped 35 opponents in his 38 victories from 1989 to 2003 and twice challenged unsuccessfully for the world's featherweight championship.

Australian middleweight Paul Rees injured his opponent Charlie Hansen's eye with his first punch in a 19 June 1991 bout in Brisbane and the fight was stopped by referee Alan Simpson after only five seconds.

A **bareknuckle** bout in Leavenworth, Kansas, on 4 January 1868 reportedly only lasted seven seconds when Tom Dow defeated Ned Kiely.

Welterweight Teddy Barker scored a 10-second knockout over Bob Roberts on 2 September 1957 in Maesteg, **Wales**.

On 3 November 2000, in Ebbw Vale, Wales, Russell "Ducky" Rees knocked down Des Sowden four seconds after the opening bell, and the referee stopped the bout 10 seconds into the fight without completing his count over the fallen Sowden. Sowden had 11 professional bouts from 1998 to 2000, winning only one—and that by **disqualification** when his opponent hit him while he was down.

With today's modern technology, a few quick knockouts are available on YouTube. In one of them, on 15 June 2007 in St. Paul, Minnesota, **light heavyweight** Brandon Burke raced across the ring at the opening bell only to be met by a short right hand punch by his opponent, Phil Williams. Burke went straight down on his face, and referee Mark Nelson called a halt to the bout at 10 seconds.

Another one-punch knockout available on YouTube is heavyweight James Thunder's victory over Crawford Grimsley on 18 March 1997 in Flint, Michigan. The official time of the bout including, the 10-second count-out, was 13 seconds, although on the video it appears quicker. Thunder, a Samoan, born James Peau, was one of the better heavyweights during the 1990s and won several minor championships, including the OPBF, **World Boxing Council (WBC)** International, **International Boxing Federation (IBF)** Pan Pacific, Australian, **World Boxing Federation**, International Boxing Organization, and WBC Continental Americas.

Boxing's quickest knockouts in championship bouts are:

17 seconds—Daniel Jiménez over Harald Geier—3 September 1994, Wiener Neustadt, Austria, **World Boxing Organization (WBO) super bantamweight**

20 seconds—Gerald McClellan over Jay Bell—6 August 1993, Bayamon, **Puerto Rico**, WBC middleweight (McClellan's next two title defenses were also one-**round** knockouts)

24 seconds—**Bernard Hopkins** over Steve Frank—27 January 1996, Phoenix, Arizona, IBF middleweight

34 seconds—Pongsaklek Wonjongkam over Daisuke Naito—19 April 2002, Khon Kaen, **Thailand**, WBC flyweight

35 seconds—**Naseem Hamed** over Said Lawal, 16 March 1996, Glasgow, **Scotland**, WBO **featherweight**

R

RADEMACHER, THOMAS PETER "PETE". B. 20 November 1928, Tieton, Washington. If you examine the names of most fighters' first **professional** opponent, you would be hard-pressed to recognize any of them as competent fighters. Pete Rademacher is definitely the exception to that statement. In his first professional **bout**, he faced the world's **heavyweight** champion, **Floyd Patterson**—and actually knocked down Patterson during the fight.

Pete Rademacher had his first **amateur** bout as an eighth grader in Washington and then attended Castle Heights Military Academy in Lebanon, Tennessee, where he continued to box, winning a local military academy tournament there. In 1948, he enrolled at Washington State University, played on their football team, and continued amateur boxing. Following graduation with a Bachelor of Science degree in animal husbandry, he served in the U.S. Army at Fort Benning, Georgia.

His substantial amateur boxing career in the heavyweight division included quite a few major amateur championships. Among them were the Seattle **Golden Gloves** in 1949, 1951, 1952, 1953; National **Amateur Athletic Union (AAU)** in 1953; All-Army in 1956; All-Service in 1956; Olympic trials in 1956; and the **Olympic Games** in 1956. His Olympic Games victory was exceptional in that he won all three of his bouts by **knockout**—the first Olympic boxer to do so.

Following his discharge from the service, he challenged heavyweight champion Floyd Patterson to a title bout. **Cus D'Amato**, Patterson's manager, requested a guarantee of $250,000 for the bout to take place. Rademacher was able to raise the money from a Columbus, Georgia, organization called Youth Unlimited, and promoter Jack Hurley scheduled the bout for 22 August 1957 at Sicks Stadium in Seattle, Washington. The 28-year-old Rademacher, trained by George Chameres, scored a second-**round knockdown** over Patterson but then was unable to finish him. Patterson recovered and knocked Rademacher down once in the third round, four times in the fifth round, and twice more in the sixth round, with **referee** Tommy Loughran counting Rademacher out at 2:57 of that round.

Rademacher's next fight was nearly a year later when he faced top heavyweight contender **Zora Folley**, whom he had fought as an amateur, losing to Folley in the 1950 Seattle Golden Gloves and defeating Folley en route to winning the 1953 National AAU championship. On 25 July 1958, Folley knocked out Rademacher in four rounds in Los Angeles. Rademacher continued boxing professionally but against boxers of lesser ability than Patterson and Folley (who had a combined record of 72–3–2 at the time they fought Rademacher).

Rademacher won his next six bouts, four by knockout, but on 26 April 1960 in London, **England**, was stopped in seven rounds by Brian London, another top heavyweight. Rademacher then won his next seven bouts, including victories over **George Chuvalo**, **Lamar Clark**, and Willi Besmanoff, before losing three straight to the likes of Doug Jones, George Logan, and former world's **light heavyweight** champion **Archie Moore**.

Rademacher's final professional bout was a 10-round **unanimous decision** over former world's **middleweight** champion **Carl "Bobo" Olson** on 3 April 1962.

Rademacher became a quite successful businessman after retiring from boxing. He lived in Columbus, Georgia, for a while and in 1969 received a patent for a trapshooting target projector that was developed into a trap shooting range, which he then marketed. He then moved to Ohio and worked for a building contractor. He also occasionally promoted boxing and refereed and judged boxing in Ohio. He worked for the McNeil Corporation in Akron, eventually retiring as president. He then worked for the American Cancer Society as a golf director. He also developed a motorized unicycle that he has ridden in nearly 400 parades.

Rademacher is an anomaly in the boxing world—a man who did many things besides box, although he is remembered most for his historic failed bid for the world's heavyweight crown.

Rademacher is six foot one inch tall and has a 77-inch **reach**. He fought at weights ranging from 192 to 211 pounds as a heavyweight. In 23 professional bouts, from 1957 to 1962, he won 15 (eight by **knockout**), lost seven (six by knockout), had one **draw**, and fought a total of 155 rounds.

REACH. A boxer's reach is one of his significant physical measurements. It is the distance between the end of the fingertips of one hand and the end of the fingertips of the other when he has his arms outstretched sideways at a 90-degree angle. A boxer with a reach advantage over his opponent can more easily land **jabs**. The reach measurement can sometimes be misleading, as it includes the measurement from shoulder to shoulder, and the reach of a boxer with broad shoulders might not be a true barometer of his ability to keep his opponent at a distance.

REFEREE. The role of referee is essential to a boxing contest. The so-called third man in the **ring** originally did not appear with the boxers but called out commands from a position outside the ring. In modern times, referees must be licensed by a state athletic **commission** before they are permitted to work a **bout**.

Among the most popular and competent referees have been B. J. Angle, Zach Clayton (former Harlem Rens professional basketball player), Eugene Corri, Arthur Donovan, Harry Gibbs, **Ruby Goldstein**, Harry Kessler, Johnny LoBianco, Arthur Mercante Sr. and his son Arthur Jr., Ray Miller, Tony Perez, George Siler, and Richard Steele. In recent times, Kenny Bayless, Frank Cappuccino, Stanley Christodoulou, **Joe Cortez**, Jay Edson, Richard Greene, Mitch Halpern, Larry Hazzard, **Mills Lane**, Carlos Padilla, Davey Pearl, Steve "Triple S" Smoger, and Harold Valan have been among the most active referees in major bouts. Christodoulou, Cortez, Donovan, Goldstein, Hazzard, Lane, Mercante Sr., and Siler have all been inducted into the **International Boxing Hall of Fame**.

Quite a few former great boxers have been called upon to referee but have demonstrated various degrees of ability. One instance of lack of competence was the second **Sonny Liston–Muhammad Ali heavyweight** championship fight, when former heavyweight champion **Jersey Joe Walcott** as referee failed to realize that Liston had been down for a 10-count and only stopped the bout after writer **Nat Fleischer** at **ringside** intervened. Other world champions who refereed include Mushy Callahan, **Georges Carpentier**, **Jack Dempsey**, **Jim Jeffries**, Sonny Liston, Tommy Loughran, **Joe Louis**, **Willie Pep**, **Barney Ross**, **Jack Sharkey**, and **Benny Leonard** (who died in the ring while refereeing a bout in New York).

Other notable individuals who were selected for their neutrality and refereed bouts include boxing writer Nat Fleischer, legendary lawman William "Bat" Masterson, and promoter **George "Tex" Rickard**.

See also JUDGES; SCORING SYSTEMS.

REFEREE STOPS CONTEST. *See* TECHNICAL KNOCKOUT (TKO).

RELATIVES. Boxing has attracted many sets of brothers as well as fathers and sons and—in recent times—fathers and daughters. Among the brothers who became world champions were:

Arredondo—René (**light welterweight**), Ricardo (**super featherweight**)
Attell—Abe (**featherweight**), Monte (**bantamweight**)
Bredahl—Jimmi (super featherweight), Johnny (**super flyweight**, bantamweight)
Canizales—Gaby (bantamweight), Orlando (bantamweight)
Cruz—Carlos Teo (**lightweight**), Leonardo (**super bantamweight**)

Curry—Bruce (light welterweight), Donald (**welterweight**, **light middleweight**)

Dundee—Joe (welterweight), Vince (**middleweight**)

Galaxy—twins—Khaokor (bantamweight), Khaosai (super flyweight)

García—twins—Ramón (**light flyweight**), Raúl (**minimumweight**)

Hilton—Dave (**super middleweight**), Matthew (light middleweight)

Kameda—Daiki (**flyweight**), Koki (light flyweight, flyweight, bantamweight)

Klitschko—**Vitali** (**heavyweight**), **Wladimir** (heavyweight)

Márquez—Juan Manuel (featherweight, super featherweight, lightweight,
light welterweight), Rafael (bantamweight, super bantamweight)

Morales—Diego (super flyweight), Erik (super bantamweight, featherweight, super featherweight, light welterweight)

Norris—Orlin (**cruiserweight**), Terry (light middleweight)

Penalosa—Dodie Boy (light flyweight), Gerry (super flyweight, bantamweight)

Porpaoin—twins—Chana (minimumweight), Songkram (minimumweight)

Rocchigiani—Graciano (super middleweight, **light heavyweight**), Ralf
(cruiserweight)

Ruelas—Gabriel (super featherweight), Rafael (lightweight)

Sithbanprachan—Pichit (flyweight), Pichitnoi (light flyweight)

Sor Vorapin—Ratanachai (bantamweight), Ratanapol (minimumweight)

Spinks—**Leon** (heavyweight), **Michael** (light heavyweight, heavyweight)

Stecca—Loris (super bantamweight), Maurizio (featherweight)

Tiozzo—Christophe (super middleweight), Fabrice (light heavyweight,
cruiserweight)

Other champions whose brothers boxed but did not win championships include middleweight champion **Gene Fullmer** and brothers Don and Jay;
welterweight champion Fritzie Zivic and brothers Joe, Eddie, Pete, and Jack;
and middleweight champion Tommy Yarosz and brothers Tommy, Eddie,
and Victor.

Both brothers Mike and Tommy Gibbons were elected to the **International Boxing Hall of Fame**, although neither won a world championship.

Heavyweight champion Mike Weaver had triplet brothers, Floyd, Lloyd,
and Troy, who each boxed, although none of the three reached Mike's level
of success. On 31 January 1987 at Reseda, California, all four brothers appeared on the same boxing **card**. Floyd's record was 18–11–3 from 1985 to
2011, Lloyd's was 10–7 from 1985 to 2001, and Troy's was 20–9–2 from
1985 to 2011.

The 19th-century **bareknuckle** boxer known as **Bendigo** was one of a set of triplets, but there is no record of whether his brothers, Shadrach and Meshach, ever boxed.

Fathers and sons who both won championships include **Julio César Chávez** (super featherweight, lightweight, light welterweight) and his son Julio César Jr. (middleweight); Guty Espadas (flyweight) and son Guty Jr. (featherweight); **Floyd Patterson** (heavyweight) and his adopted son Tracy Harris Patterson (super bantamweight, super featherweight); Leon Spinks (heavyweight) and son Cory (welterweight, light middleweight); and Wilfredo Vázquez (bantamweight, super bantamweight, featherweight) and son Wilfredo Jr. (super bantamweight).

Roxell "Rocky" Mosley Sr. and his son Roxell "Rocky" Mosley Jr. both fought on the same boxing card on 23 September 1975 in Everett, Washington. Rocky Sr. was knocked out in two **rounds** while Rocky Jr. won his **bout** on a two-round **knockout**. Both Mosleys faced Mike Colbert at various times in their careers, and Colbert defeated both of them. **Héctor Camacho** and his son Héctor Jr. both were active boxers at the same time, and Héctor Jr. fought his first professional fight on 1 October 1996 in Fort Lauderdale, Florida, on the same card as his father.

Fathers and daughters who both boxed include both **Muhammad Ali** and his daughter Leila Ali, **Joe Frazier** and his daughter Jacqui Frazier-Lyde, **Archie Moore** and his daughter J'Marie Moore, **George Foreman** and his daughter Freeda George Foreman, and **Roberto Durán** and his daughter Irichelle Durán. On 8 June 2001, Leila Ali defeated Jacqui Frazier-Lyde on an eight-round **majority decision** in Verona, New York.

A few other relatives of boxers who enjoyed fame in other fields include Ernie Terrell's sister, Jean Terrell, who was the lead singer with the Supremes singing group; **Gene Tunney's** son, John, who became a U.S. senator; Frankie Campbell's brother, Dolph Camilli, a major league baseball player for 12 years from 1933 to 1945; **Jim Corbett's** brother Joe, who played major league baseball for four years from 1895 to 1904. **"Sugar Ray" Robinson's** son, Ronnie Robinson, became a roller derby star, one of the few black participants in that form of entertainment. The great-grandson of Young Corbett III (born Raffaelle Capobianca Giardano), Matt Giordano, has played defensive back in the National Football League for four teams from 2005 to 2012. **Ken Norton's** son, Ken Jr., was an All-Pro National Football League linebacker who played from 1988 to 2000 and won three Super Bowl rings.

REPUBLIC OF SOUTH AFRICA. *See* SOUTH AFRICA.

RICKARD, GEORGE LEWIS "TEX". B. 2 January 1870, Kansas City, Missouri. D. 6 January 1929, Miami Beach, Florida. Tex Rickard was one of the legendary characters of the early 20th century. He was raised in Texas, worked as a cowboy while in his teens, and drove cattle to Montana and Omaha. At the age of 23, he became a marshal in Henrietta, Texas. He traveled to Alaska in 1895 and took part in the gold rush, first as a prospector and then as a hotel and saloon owner. In 1899, he went to Nome, Alaska, in search of gold. After losing much of his holdings through gambling, he went to California. He spent a couple of years there and then headed for Nevada, where he opened another establishment.

To call attention to the town of Goldfield, Nevada, it was decided to stage a boxing match. Rickard arranged for **Joe Gans** to meet Battling Nelson for the world's **lightweight** championship on 3 September 1906 in a "**fight to a finish**" bout. Rickard put up $30,000 in gold to entice Nelson to go west to face Gans and promised Gans $10,000. The bout ended in the 42nd **round** when Nelson **fouled** Gans. Although everyone connected with the bout profited, Rickard was not interested in boxing promotion and did not promote any more bouts for four years, instead taking part in mining speculation during that time. In 1910, when former **heavyweight** champion **Jim Jeffries** was coming out of retirement to face **Jack Johnson** in an effort to restore the heavyweight championship to the white race, Rickard got involved with that promotion. Although many other promoters were vying for the bout, Rickard first met with Johnson in his hotel in Pittsburgh and later in New York's Harlem and impressed Johnson with his ready access to cash. When the sealed bids for the bout were opened, Rickard's bid of $101,000 far exceeded the others. He ensured being awarded the bout by advancing Johnson $20,000 in $1,000 bills on the spot.

The Johnson–Jeffries bout scheduled for 45 rounds took place on 4 July 1910 in Reno, Nevada, after the governor of California would not allow the bout to occur in his state. An arena was specially constructed for the fight. After a dispute between the two combatants as to who would **referee** the bout, it was decided that Rickard himself would act in that capacity, even though he had not previously worked as a referee. Although Jeffries was knocked out in the 15th round, the bout proved to be another financial success, as it drew a gate of $270,755, the largest boxing gate to that point in history, with 15,760 paying customers.

After the mixed-race bout won by the black man, rioting broke out in several cities, and Rickard was ostracized for promoting it. He vowed never again to promote a boxing match between a white and black boxer—one reason why **Harry Wills**, the great black boxer, never received a title fight opportunity.

Rickard then headed for South America, where he managed a cattle business in Paraguay. He lived there for six years, returning to the **United States** in 1916, where he got back into the boxing promotion business again.

This time he promoted a fight between the new heavyweight champion **Jess Willard** and Frank Moran, the challenger. The bout took place on 25 March 1916 at **Madison Square Garden** in New York. It was a 10-round **no-decision** fight that was a relatively dull affair but a financial success.

Jack "Doc" Kearns, the manager of heavyweight prospect **Jack Dempsey**, saw Rickard's promotional abilities and asked him to promote a fight between Dempsey and Willard. That bout on 4 July 1919 in Toledo, Ohio, saw Dempsey give Willard a savage beating and win the world's heavyweight title. That began a connection among Rickard, Kearns, and Dempsey, and Rickard staged some of boxing's biggest fights during the 1920s.

On 2 July 1921, Rickard promoted a bout between Dempsey and French war hero **Georges Carpentier** that drew 80,183 fans to a new wooden arena specially constructed for the bout. The total gate receipts were $1,789,238— the first boxing match to exceed one million dollars in gate revenue. Rickard's next major promotion was Dempsey against the Argentinean **Luis Ángel Firpo** on 14 September 1923 at the Polo Grounds in New York. The bout proved to be one of the most exciting in boxing history, although it lasted less than two rounds.

In 1925, Rickard helped to get a new Madison Square Garden constructed on 50th street and Eighth Avenue in New York. As one of the attractions at the Garden, a new ice hockey team was added to the National Hockey League (NHL) for the 1926 season. The team became known as Tex's Rangers, and the team has competed in the NHL since then as the New York Rangers.

Tex's next two promotions of Dempsey fights both occurred outside New York City, and both were two of that era's most written-about events. Dempsey lost his title to **Gene Tunney** outdoors in Philadelphia on 23 September 1926 at Sesquicentennial Stadium before 120,557 fans—the largest attendance for a boxing match to that point. One year later, the **Dempsey–Tunney** rematch, held in Chicago on 22 September 1927, drew 104,943 fans and was boxing's first two-million-dollar gate.

Rickard also helped **Nat Fleischer** found *Ring* magazine in 1922 and remained with the publication until his death following an appendectomy on 6 January 1929.

In 1990, Rickard was inducted as a member of the inaugural class of the **International Boxing Hall of Fame**.

RING. The ring is the roped-off elevated rectangular area in which boxing matches are contested. The dimensions vary and can range from 16 feet per side to 25 feet per side between the ropes, with an additional two to three feet outside the ropes. Three or, in recent years, four strands of ropes surround the ring. The surface of the ring platform is padded and covered with **canvas**.

The word *ring* stems from **bareknuckle** days when a circle was drawn on the ground to designate the area for the **bout**.

RING ANNOUNCERS. Although the **ring** announcer plays a relatively minor role in an evening of boxing, several have become memorable due to their unique voice, style, or trademark phrases.

One of the first announcers with a notable style was Harry Balogh, whose eloquence included the phrase "and may the better combatant emerge victorious." Johnny Addie (brother of *Washington Post* sportswriter Bob Addie) was a fixture at New York boxing matches during the 1950s and 1960s and announced boxing at **Madison Square Garden**, Yankee Stadium, and smaller **fight clubs** such as **St. Nicholas Arena**.

His West Coast counterpart was Jimmy Lennon, who did the announcing at Los Angeles matches at Olympic Auditorium among other venues. He was the uncle of the famous singing Lennon Sisters (regulars on the Lawrence Welk television show). His son, Jimmy Lennon Jr., continued the announcing tradition for California boxing and was inducted into the **International Boxing Hall of Fame** in 2013.

Perhaps the most well-known ring announcer since 1980 has been Michael Buffer. The good-looking Buffer has announced world championship **bouts** from all over the country. Buffer has established his own ring persona, and his phrase "Let's get ready to rumble" is one of the best-known in boxing history. He was inducted into the International Boxing Hall of Fame in 2012.

RING CARD GIRLS. *See* ROUND CARD GIRLS.

RING **MAGAZINE.** In 1922, newspaper writer **Nat Fleischer** founded *Ring* magazine along with promoter **Tex Rickard**. By 1929, Fleischer became sole owner of the publication. The magazine became the leading boxing magazine and was known as "the bible of boxing." In contrast to the most popular magazine that previously had covered boxing, *The Police Gazette*, which often featured risque "girlie pictures," Fleischer concentrated solely on boxing with a little bit of wrestling and had the following statement in each magazine: "*The Ring* is a magazine which a man may take home with him. He may leave it on his library table safe in the knowledge that it does not contain one line of matter either in the text or the advertisements which would be offensive. The publisher of the *Ring* guards this reputation of his magazine jealously. It is entertaining and it is clean."

In addition to Fleischer, sportswriter Dan Daniel became a regular contributor to the magazine, which in 1928 began giving out annual awards for the "Fighter of the Year." In each month's issue, the *Ring* also produced a top-10 ranking of boxers for each weight division, which became the standard for measuring a boxer's progress.

In 1942, Fleischer produced an all-time boxing record book that first appeared as *Nat Fleischer's All-Time Ring Record Book* and contained historical records of past fighters as well as those active in 1941. Through the years, this annual publication became the standard reference book for boxers, managers, and promoters. In 1953, he expanded the book with an encyclopedic section on **ring** history, and the title then became *Nat Fleischer's Ring Record Book and Boxing Encyclopedia*. In addition to the annual record book, the *Ring* also produced many of Fleischer's monographs and biographies of fighters.

Fleischer's son-in-law, Nat Loubet, was added to the staff after World War II, and after Fleischer became ill in the late 1960s, Loubet became the magazine's editor and, after Fleischer's death in 1972, its owner.

In 1977, the publication suffered a loss of prestige as it was found to have fabricated some results in its annual record book to enhance the records of certain fighters in the **United States Boxing Tournament**—a creation of promoter **Don King**. The discovery of this fact, along with alleged payoffs to enable some fighters to be included in the tournament, led to the tournament's demise. Owner Loubet decided to sell the publication, and a syndicate led by sports historian and memorabilia collector **Bert Randolph Sugar** purchased it.

One of Sugar's interests in acquiring the entity was its huge collection of memorabilia, which was displayed in its tiny office in New York City. Sugar's partners were former New York Knickerbocker basketball star Dave DeBusschere, sports public relations man Jim Bukata, and former collegiate basketball star Nick Kladis. Sugar became the editor and public spokesman for the organization.

As editor, Sugar changed the look of the publication, added several new features, and gave the periodical a more up-to-date look. He also continued with the annual record book and allowed the *Ring*'s managing editor, Herbert G. Goldman, to enhance the publication by correcting and expanding the records of some of the former champions included in the book. Sugar also encouraged Goldman and John Grasso to form an organization of boxing aficionados worldwide to work on improving boxing records through additional research. That organization is known as IBRO—the **International Boxing Research Organization**—and is still in existence today.

Under Sugar's leadership, while the quality of the magazine and its record book were substantially increased, it did not become the financial success its backers anticipated, and after a falling out with his partners, Sugar was replaced as editor by Randy Gordon, one of the publication's writers, and later by Nigel Collins, who returned as editor from 1997 to 2011.

By the late 1980s, the magazine was near bankruptcy and in 1989 nearly ceased publication. Fortunately, new ownership was found, and the enterprise was able to continue. Stanley Weston, who had worked for Fleischer at one time and who was a publisher of competing sports magazines, became editor in 1990. In 1993, the organization was sold to Kappa Publishing and relocated its offices to a suburb of Philadelphia.

In an era with multiple sanctioning organizations and champions, the *Ring* reestablished the concept of a single linear champion for each division and began naming lineal champions and awarding championship belts.

In August 2007, the magazine was again sold, this time to boxing champion **Óscar De La Hoya's** Golden Boy Productions. It continues to be the main print source for boxing information.

See also APPENDIX E and APPENDIX F.

RINGSIDE. The seats closest to the boxing **ring** are known as ringside seats and are generally the most expensive. Often the seats adjacent to the ring are reserved for the media and the boxing **judges**, with the "ringside" seats available for the general public extending back several rows from the ring.

ROBE. Boxers generally enter the **ring** wearing a robe. Some boxers' robes are extremely elaborate and feature their name on the back. Other boxers wear very plain robes, often not more than terrycloth.

ROBINSON, RAY "SUGAR RAY" (né WALKER SMITH JR.). B. 3 May 1921, Ailey, Georgia. D. 12 April 1989, Culver City, California. "Sugar Ray" Robinson was the original "Sugar Ray," whose style was described as "sweet as sugar." He is rated by many boxing historians as the greatest pound-for-pound boxer in history.

He began boxing as an **amateur** at the famed Salem-Crescent Athletic Club in Harlem, New York. In the 1938 New York **Golden Gloves**, he competed in the 118-pound junior class under his given name and after winning his first two **bouts** was defeated on a three-**round decision** by Pasquale Pesca on 16 February. Pesca went on to win that division in the finals but had a brief, unimpressive **professional** career. In 1939, Walker Smith entered the New York Golden Gloves as Ray Robinson and won the 126-pound **open** division, the Eastern Regionals 126-pound class, and the intercity 126-pound title. In 1940, he moved up to the 135-pound class and again won all three titles. His amateur record is sometimes listed as 85–0, but he lost at least two bouts as Walker Smith—one to Pesca and the other to future **welterweight** contender **Billy Graham**.

Robinson's first professional fight was on 4 October 1940 at **Madison Square Garden**. He won his first 40 fights from 1940 to 1942, with victories over **lightweight** champion Sammy Angott twice in **nontitle bouts**, future welterweight champion Marty Servo, former welterweight champion Fritzie Zivic twice, and future **middleweight** champion **Jake LaMotta**, before losing on 5 February 1943 to LaMotta on a 10-round decision in Detroit in a bout in which Robinson was outweighed by 16 pounds. Robinson then won his next 14 bouts before being held to a 10-round **draw** by José Basora on 14 May 1945. Included in those 14 victories were wins over LaMotta twice, former triple champion **Henry Armstrong**, and top contenders Izzy Jannazzo and California Jackie Wilson.

On 20 December 1946, Robinson (with a record of 73–1–1) finally got a shot at the world welterweight title, which was vacated by the retirement of Marty Servo. "Sugar Ray" won a unanimous 15-round decision over Tommy Bell at Madison Square Garden and was the new world's welterweight champion. On 24 June 1947, Robinson fought his first title defense against Jimmy Doyle in Cleveland, Ohio. Robinson **knocked out** Doyle in the eighth round, but although Doyle was saved by the bell, he never regained consciousness and was carried from the **ring** after the bell rang to start the ninth round. Doyle died the following day and became the first **fatality** in a world title bout.

Robinson was able to keep on fighting and less than two months later fought a benefit bout for Doyle's family. Robinson's next title defense was on 19 December 1947, a sixth-round **technical knockout** of Chuck Taylor. He than followed that with a 15-round **unanimous decision** victory over Bernard Docusen in his next title defense.

Robinson also kept busy with nontitle bouts and on 15 February 1949 was held to a 10-round draw with Henry Brimm, a relatively unknown **journeyman** who had a record of 23–9–2. Following that bout, Brimm fought 13 more bouts in his professional career and won just three of them.

Robinson's next welterweight title fight was a 15-round unanimous decision over future welterweight champion **Kid Gavilán** on 11 July 1949. By this time in his career, Robinson had developed into a middleweight, and most of his nontitle bouts were in the middleweight class. On 5 June 1950, he defeated Robert Villemain on a 15-round unanimous decision in Philadelphia in a bout that was recognized by the Pennsylvania State Athletic **Commission** for the world's middleweight title. Two months after that bout, Robinson trimmed down to the welterweight limit and successfully defended his title on a 15-round decision over Charlie Fusari. He then knocked out José Basora in one round in defense of his Pennsylvania middleweight title. Basora had held him to a draw in 1945. Robinson followed that bout with another middleweight title defense over **Carl "Bobo" Olson**, a man who would later become middleweight champion. Robinson then spent two months in Europe, where he won five bouts and discovered he enjoyed life abroad.

Returning to the **United States**, he fought LaMotta for the sixth time. This time it was for LaMotta's world middleweight title on 14 February 1951 in Chicago. "Sugar Ray" stopped LaMotta in the 13th round in a one-sided fight, later known as the St. Valentine's Day massacre, the first time in Jake's career that he was legitimately stopped. (He had lost in the fourth round in a 1947 bout that he later claimed to have thrown.)

Robinson returned to Europe in May 1952 accompanied by an entourage of about a dozen people, including his personal barber. While enjoying the good life there, he won six bouts. In his seventh bout in Europe, he lost his middleweight title to an Englishman, Randy Turpin, on a 15-round decision on 10 July in London, **England**. Turpin was not champion for long, however, as the two fought a return bout in New York in September, which Robinson won on a 10th-round technical knockout before 61,943 fans at the Polo Grounds.

Robinson then made two title defenses, winning a 15-round decision over Olson and knocking out former welterweight champion **Rocky Graziano** in three rounds.

Robinson's next bout was one of the most memorable in boxing history. He challenged the **light heavyweight** champion **Joey Maxim** for Maxim's title on an extremely hot and humid night in New York. The bout took place at Yankee Stadium before 47,983 fans on 25 June 1952. **Referee Ruby Goldstein** was overcome by the heat and retired after the 10th round and was replaced by Ray Miller. Robinson, well ahead on **points**, was felled by the heat and quit after the 13th round. Maxim, who retained his title, was never quite the same, and although he continued fighting until 1958, he won only four of his last 15 fights.

In December 1952, Robinson announced his retirement from the **ring** to pursue a career as a song-and-dance man. At that time, Robinson also owned a substantial amount of real estate in Harlem, including a nightclub, and was famed for his vehicle—a pink Cadillac.

He returned to the ring in 1955, and after six tune-up fights in which he won five (losing only to **Ralph "Tiger" Jones** on a 10-round decision), he challenged Carl "Bobo" Olson for the world's middleweight title. On 9 December 1955, he knocked out Olson in the second round and regained the middleweight title. In a rematch five months later, he again knocked out Olson, this time in four rounds.

On 2 January 1957, Robinson lost his title to **Gene Fullmer** at **Madison Square Garden** by a unanimous decision. Fullmer only held the title for four months, as Robinson knocked him out in five rounds in their rematch in May.

Robinson's next fight on 23 September 1957 earned the *Ring* **magazine** "Fight of the Year" designation, as he and welterweight champion **Carmen Basilio** went toe-to-toe for 15 rounds before Basilio was named the **split decision** winner. Prior to 1957, Robinson had only lost four of 145 fights, but in 1957 he lost twice, although both were memorable, hard-fought bouts.

In Robinson's next bout, on 25 March 1958, he rewon the middleweight title from Basilio on another split decision in 1958's "Fight of the Year." Ray then took 21 months off from the ring and did not fight again until December 1959—a nontitle bout that he won easily with a two-round knockout. During 1959, Robinson was stripped of his title by the **National Boxing Association (NBA)**, although he still was recognized as champion by the **New York State Athletic Commission** and the Massachusetts Athletic Commission.

His next title defense occurred on 22 January 1960 in Boston, Massachusetts, against a relatively unknown boxer, Massachusetts-born Paul Pender. Robinson again lost his title on a split decision. In a rematch in June 1960, Pender again was victorious by split decision.

Robinson made two more unsuccessful attempts at regaining the middleweight title. On 3 December 1960, he fought a 15-round **draw** with Fullmer for Gene's NBA middleweight title and in their rematch in March 1961 lost a 15-round unanimous decision.

Robinson continued fighting until 1965, fighting in Europe for part of 1962, 1963, and 1964. He had a record of 143–8–3 prior to his last match with Fullmer and ended his career with a record of 173–19–6. In his last 44 fights, from 1961 to 1965, his record was 30–11–3.

After he retired, he appeared in a few films but in his later years developed diabetes and then Alzheimer's disease.

Robinson was five foot 11 inches tall and had a 72-inch **reach**. He fought at weights ranging from 134 to 165 pounds, primarily as a welterweight and middleweight. In 200 professional bouts, from 1940 to 1965, he won 173 (108 by knockout), lost 19 (one by knockout), had six draws and two **no contests**, and fought a total of 1,403 rounds. He was inducted as a member of the inaugural class of the **International Boxing Hall of Fame** in 1990.

ROCKY. In 1975, actor Sylvester Stallone saw the **Chuck Wepner–Muhammad Ali heavyweight** championship match and became inspired to write a screenplay. At the time, Stallone was a struggling actor who had appeared in several films but had not had any major roles. He had then turned to writing screenplays, also with no success. Inspired by the Wepner–Ali fight, he wrote the screenplay for *Rocky* in about three and a half days of nonstop writing. He then attempted to sell the story to film producers Irwin Winkler and Robert Chartoff. They liked it and offered him $75,000 for it.

Stallone felt this was not enough and began negotiating the fee. The producers wanted to place a well-known actor in the role, and Stallone was convinced that he wanted to play the part and would not sell the script otherwise. Eventually, United Artists agreed to make the film for one million dollars and that Stallone could play the role. Stallone was to work for the union-minimum actor's fee and would receive a percentage of the profits.

The film tells the heartwarming story of Rocky Balboa, a Philadelphia-based heavyweight boxer who was an average fighter who never got a break. Apollo Creed, the heavyweight champion, decides to fight his next title defense in Philadelphia on 1 January 1976 in honor of the nation's bicentennial. After his original opponent is injured, Creed decides to select a local fighter as the opponent, and Balboa's nickname, "The Italian Stallion," has a ring to it and sounds marketable. Rocky trains for the fight with a former boxer and gymnasium owner, and Rocky's friend, Paulie, helps him train. The shy Rocky falls for Paulie's sister, Adrian, and that subplot is also advanced during the film. In the film's climax, Rocky fights Creed for the title and lasts the full 15 rounds in a thrilling fight, although he loses the decision. Creed's persona is similar to that of Muhammad Ali, the heavyweight champion at that time, and Balboa's is quite similar to that of Wepner.

John Avildsen directed the film, and Stallone helped cast it. After heavyweight boxer **Ken Norton**, who had previous acting experience, did not accept the role of Apollo Creed, Carl Weathers, a former professional football player turned actor, received the role. Burgess Meredith was cast as Rocky's **trainer**, Burt Young played Rocky's friend Paulie, and Talia Shire played Adrian. The original one million dollar budget forced the film to be shot quickly in just 28 days and caused Stallone to use several of his family members in minor roles, including his own dog, Butkus. The film was a huge box office success and grossed more than $225 million.

The film won the Academy Award as best film of 1976, Avildsen won one as best director, and the four leading players—Stallone, Meredith, Young, and Shire—each were also nominated for Academy Awards, although none of the four won one. The film inspired five sequels produced from 1979 to 2006 with many of the same actors, and although none of the sequels received the same critical acclaim, they all did well at the box office.

Wepner, unfortunately, never received public acknowledgment of his role in the creation of Rocky and never received any financial remuneration either. In 2003, Wepner sued Stallone over this fact, and the suit was settled out of court for an undisclosed sum.

Rocky appears on most lists of the top-10 sports films and made Stallone into a highly popular actor who went on to star in many other films.

ROMANIA. As was the case with most of the Iron Curtain countries prior to the fall of communism, Romania has a strong **amateur boxing** program. The country has competed in 17 **Olympic Games** boxing tournaments since 1936 (missing only 1948) and has won 25 medals. Surprisingly, though, it has only won one **gold medal**. It does have nine **silver medals** and 15 **bronze** medals, and the total of 25 medals places the country ninth among all nations in Olympic boxing competition. The one Olympic boxing gold medalist is Nicolae Linca, who won it in the 1956 **welterweight** competition.

Leonard Doroftei won two bronze medals—1992 **light welterweight** and 1996 welterweight. Marian Simion also won two medals—1996 welterweight bronze and 2000 **light middleweight** silver. Marian's brother, Dorel, won the bronze medal in 2000 as a welterweight. Ion Monea was another two-time Olympic boxing medalist—he won his first, a bronze, in 1960 as a **middleweight**. He lost in the 1964 middleweight quarterfinal round but returned in 1968 as a **light heavyweight** and won the silver medal. Brothers Calistrat Cutov (1968 bronze) and Simion Cutov (1976 silver) both won medals in the **lightweight** class.

In **professional boxing**, Lucian Bute, Adrian Diaconu, Leonard Doroftei, and Michael Loewe have all won world championships since Romania allowed its athletes to become professional boxers following the fall of communism. One of the few Romanians to box professionally in earlier years was the giant Gogea Mitu, whose height was reported at various times as from seven foot two to seven foot seven inches. He boxed in 1935 and 1936 and reportedly won eight of 11 **bouts**. Aurel Toma was another early Romanian professional boxer, and he began his career in 1931 in Romania, won the European Boxing Union **bantamweight** title, and then moved to the **United States** in 1937, where he fought most of his 74 fights, winning 48, losing 15, and having 11 draws.

ROPE-A-DOPE. Rope-a-dope was the name given by **Muhammad Ali** to a **ring** tactic he used in his **heavyweight** championship **bout** against **George Foreman** in Zaire on 30 October 1974. He leaned back against the ring ropes and allowed Foreman to throw punches at him while using his arms and **gloves** to protect himself. Foreman eventually became weary from throwing punches, and Ali was able to capitalize on Foreman's tiredness to knock him out and regain the heavyweight championship.

ROSENBLOOM, MAX EVERITT "SLAPSIE MAXIE". B. 1 November 1907, Leonard's Bridge, Connecticut. D. 6 March 1976, South Pasadena, California. Slapsie Maxie Rosenbloom was a world champion without a **knockout** punch. His slapping style of punching resulted in only 7 percent of his total **bouts** ending short of the distance—the lowest percentage of any major world champion boxer—but his defensive skills enabled him to win the vast majority of his fights. A colorful personage, after retiring from the ring he became nearly as well known as a character actor who appeared in more than 70 Hollywood films and television series.

He was raised on the Lower East Side of Manhattan in New York City and reportedly was spotted after a street fight by actor George Raft, who convinced Max to become a **professional** boxer. Rosenbloom's first recorded professional bout was on 8 October 1923 in New York City, and he won a six-**round decision**. After compiling a record of 25–3–5, he faced future **light heavyweight** champion Jimmy Slattery on 22 August 1925 but lost a six-round decision. On 30 August 1927, he faced Slattery in a light heavyweight championship bout but lost a 10-round decision. On 15 November 1929, Rosenbloom defeated future **heavyweight** champion **Jim Braddock** on a 10-round decision.

In 1930 on 25 June, Rosenbloom won the world's light heavyweight championship on a 15-round **split decision** in his sixth meeting with Slattery.

Over the next four years, Rosenbloom successfully defended the title six times. During these four years, Rosenbloom also fought 94 **nontitle bouts**, winning 66, losing 17, and drawing 10. He beat Abie Bain (22 October 1930, **technical knockout [TKO] round 11**); Slattery (5 August 1931, **unanimous decision** 15); Lou Scozza (14 July 1932, **majority decision** 15); Adolf Heuser (10 March 1933, unanimous decision 15); Bob Godwin (24 March 1933, TKO 4); **Mickey Walker** (3 November 1933, unanimous decision 15); and Joe Knight (5 February 1934, **majority draw** 15). On 16 November 1934, he lost his championship to Bob Olin on a 15-round unanimous decision.

He continued boxing until 1939, and after his bout with Al Ettore on 26 June, which Rosenbloom won on a third-round technical knockout, he retired. In retirement, he did a lot of movie and television work and for a time had a nightclub act with former world's heavyweight champion **Max Baer**.

Rosenbloom was five foot 10 inches tall and had a 71-inch **reach**. He fought at weights ranging from 151 to 198 pounds, primarily as a light heavyweight and heavyweight. In 298 professional bouts, from 1923 to 1939, he won 207 (19 by knockout), lost 39 (two by knockout), and had 26 draws, three **no contests**, and 23 no-decision bouts, in which he was awarded the **newspaper decision** in 15, lost three, and drew five. He fought a total of 2,765 rounds. He was inducted into the **International Boxing Hall of Fame** in 1993.

ROSOFSKY, BERYL DAVID. *See* ROSS, BARNEY (né BERYL DAVID ROSOFSKY).

ROSS, BARNEY (né BERYL DAVID ROSOFSKY). B. 23 December 1909, New York, New York. D. 17 January 1967, Chicago, Illinois. Not only was Barney Ross a multiple boxing champion, he was also a war hero decorated with a Silver Star for his work as a U.S. Marine at the Battle of Guadalcanal.

He was the son of a rabbi and was raised in Chicago after his immigrant parents moved there from New York. His father had taught him that Jews do not fight back—they are scholars, not fighters. But Beryl's feelings changed when he was 14 years old after his father was murdered during a robbery at the grocery that he owned. After his mother suffered a nervous breakdown, Barney and an older brother went to live with a cousin while the three youngest siblings were placed in an orphanage.

As a teen, Barney led a rough life, and one of his teenage pals was Jacob Rubenstein, later to become infamous as Jack Ruby, killer of Lee Harvey Oswald, the assassin of President John F. Kennedy.

Beryl, after changing his name to the American-sounding Barney Ross so as not to tarnish the memory of his father, began boxing in **amateur bouts** to earn money by, as was the custom in those days, pawning the medals he won for his boxing efforts. He became a quite successful amateur boxer and won the 1929 Chicago **Golden Gloves** and Intercity Golden Gloves **featherweight** titles.

He became a **professional** later that year and after compiling a record of 43–2–2 in his first four years of boxing met and defeated **Tony Canzoneri** on 23 June 1933 in Chicago on a **majority decision**. The 10-**round** bout was for both Canzoneri's world **lightweight** and **junior welterweight** titles. Ross also won a rematch three months later on a 15-round **unanimous decision** outdoors at the Polo Grounds in New York.

An active champion, Ross made five title defenses over the next 18 months, defeating Sammy Fuller, Pete Nebo, Kid Moro, and Bobby Pacho and fighting a **draw** with Frankie Klick. On 28 May 1934, Ross won his third title by defeating **Jimmy McLarnin** on a 15-round **split decision** outdoors at the **Madison Square Garden** Bowl in Long Island City, New York. Four months later, McLarnin recaptured the title in another close bout at the same venue, also by split decision.

Ross then concentrated his efforts on the junior welterweight title, which he still owned, and defended it successfully three times against Pacho, Klick, and Henry Woods but after the Woods bout vacated it. He then regained the **welterweight** title in a **rubber match** with McLarnin on 28 May 1935 by unanimous decision.

After nine victorious **nontitle bouts**, Ross defended the welterweight title successfully against Izzy Jannazzo on 27 November 1936. Ross won four nontitle bouts and then defended against Ceferino García on 23 September 1937 at the Polo Grounds as part of the **Carnival of Champions** multiple championship bouts **card**.

On 31 May 1938, Ross lost his welterweight title to **Henry Armstrong** on a 15-round unanimous decision. Although Ross took a beating, he stayed the distance, but then he retired from **ring** competition.

He was not through fighting, however, as in 1942 he enlisted in the U.S. Marine Corps at the age of 32. Many famous athletes and entertainers in the service at that time were used in noncombat positions, but Ross insisted on being employed in combat duty. He eventually wound up in Guadalcanal, where his bravery under fire earned him the Silver Star. He also contracted malaria and was wounded. The narcotics used to counter the pain of his wounds resulted in Ross becoming addicted to them, and after he was discharged from the service, he had yet another fight to overcome his drug addiction. His story was told in the 1957 film *Monkey on My Back*. After his recovery, he worked at promotional activities until his death from cancer in 1967.

Ross was five foot seven inches tall and had a 67-inch **reach**. He fought at weights ranging from 130 to 144 pounds, primarily as a lightweight and welterweight. In 81 professional bouts, from 1929 to 1938, he won 72 (22 by **knockout**), lost four (none by knockout), and had three draws and two no-decision bouts, in which he was awarded the **newspaper decision** in both. He fought a total of 622 rounds. He was inducted as a member of the inaugural class of the **International Boxing Hall of Fame** in 1990.

ROUND. A round is the interval of a boxing **bout**, usually three minutes long for **professional** bouts and either two or three minutes long for **amateur** bouts. A one-minute rest period between rounds is customary.

The word *round* is also used to designate cycles of a tournament. A tournament with 16 boxers will have four rounds. In the first round, there are eight bouts, with the losers eliminated from further competition. In the second round (or quarterfinal round), there will be four bouts, and so on.

ROUND CARD GIRLS. In recent years, boxing promoters have attempted to add interest to their **cards** by having scantily clad females walk around the **ring** between rounds of a **bout** holding a large card with the number of the upcoming round.

RUBBER MATCH. A rubber match in sports' terminology is a third match between two contestants in which each has won one of the previous two matches. The origin of the term is unknown, although one possibility attributes the phrase to the third and deciding hand in the card game of bridge.

RUMBLE IN THE JUNGLE. *See* ALI–FOREMAN.

RUSSIA. As a member of the **Union of Soviet Socialist Republics (USSR),** Russia did not permit **professional boxing**. It did, however, have an extensive **amateur boxing** program and furnished many of the boxers for international competition for the USSR. After the breakup of the Soviet Union, each of the former Soviet republics entered the **Olympic Games** as separate nations. Since 1996, Russia has competed in each Olympic boxing tournament. The results have been exceptional, with 26 medals being won—nine **gold,** five **silver,** and 12 **bronze.** Although only competing in five Olympic Games, Russia (as a separate country) is in eighth place among all nations in Olympic boxing.

Oleg Saitov has had the best performances since Russia became a separate nation and won three Olympic boxing medals in the **welterweight** class— gold in 1996 and 2000 and bronze in 2004. The three Russian boxers who each won two medals are Aleksey Tishchenko (gold medals in both 2004 **featherweight** and 2008 **lightweight**), Gaydarbek Gaydarbekov (2000 silver and 2004 gold as a **middleweight**), and Raimkul Malakhbekov (1996 bronze and 2000 silver in the **bantamweight** class).

Russia has only recently permitted boxers to become professional, but this has already produced 11 world champions. They are Yuri Arbachakov, Zaurbek Baysangurov, Sultan Ibragimov, Denis Inkin, Roman Karmazin, Dimitri Kirilov, Ahmed Kotiev, Oleg Maskaev, Dmitry Pirog, Alexander Povetkin (also a kick-boxing champion), and **Nikolai Valuev** (the seven-foot-tall **heavyweight** champion). **Kosta Tszyu** was born in Russia but moved to **Australia**.

RYAN, TOMMY (né JOSEPH YOUNGS). B. 31 March 1870, Redwood, New York. D. 3 August 1948, Van Nuys, California. Tommy Ryan boxed in an era when boxers often "claimed" titles and there was not always a clean transfer of a title from one boxer to another. At times, several different boxers claimed the same title. Once, Ryan laid claim to the **middleweight** title, though he faced all comers, and was not defeated prior to his retirement from the ring.

As a teenager, Tommy Ryan worked on railroad construction gangs in Michigan. The itinerant crews lived in camps and used boxing as their leisure-hour entertainment. Ryan became one of those who was handy with his fists, using the skin-tight **gloves** of the era.

His first recorded **professional bouts** occurred in 1887. He won most of his bouts and on 17 February 1891 defeated Danny Needham in Minneapolis in 76 **rounds** for the world's **welterweight** title. In December of that year, he knocked out Frank Howsom in 14 rounds in defense of that title.

On 26 July, Ryan **decisioned Mysterious Billy Smith** in 20 rounds in another title defense. Six months later, in January 1895, he ended the boxing career of another one of that era's best fighters—**Jack Dempsey, the Nonpareil**—stopping him in three rounds. Later that year, in a rematch with Smith, Ryan was ahead in the 18th round when the bout was stopped by police with Smith nearly knocked out.

On 2 March 1896, Ryan lost to **Charles "Kid" McCoy** by a **knockout** in the 15th round in a bout billed for the "world middleweight title." Ryan successfully defended his **welterweight** title in 1897 by stopping Tom Tracey in nine rounds. On 20 December 1897, Ryan knocked out Bill Heffernan in three rounds in Buffalo, New York, and then claimed the middleweight title. Three months later, Ryan found himself in San Francisco defending his middleweight claim by knocking out George Green in 18 rounds.

Ryan then returned east and in October 1898 won a 20-round decision over Jack Bonner in Brooklyn to enhance his title claim. From that point until 1905, he did not lose a bout billed for the middleweight title and was still regarded as middleweight champion when he retired.

From 1898 to 1904, he made successful title defenses against Johnny Gorman (23 November 1898, **technical knockout** [TKO] round 8); Dick O'Brien (23 December 1898, TKO 14); Charley Johnson (1 March 1899, knockout [KO] 8); Jack Moffat (31 August 1899, decision 20); Frank Craig (18 September 1899, TKO 10); Tommy West (4 March 1901, TKO 17); George Green (30 January 1902, KO 7); Johnny Gorman (24 June 1902, KO 3); and Kid Carter (15 September 1902, KO 6). On 27 January 1904, Ryan fought a six-round no-decision bout with **Philadelphia Jack O'Brien** that was ruled a **draw** by the newspapers covering the bout.

Ryan retired after his last bout in 1904 but came back in 1907 and fought two bouts, winning one by knockout and fighting a draw in the other. Four years later, he fought one more bout—a no decision with Denver Ed Martin in which Martin received the newspapers' verdict.

In retirement, Ryan appeared in vaudeville, often boxing **exhibitions** with **Bob Fitzsimmons**. He also had a gym in Syracuse, New York, managed a few boxers, and eventually retired to California.

Ryan was five foot seven inches tall and had a 73-inch **reach**. He fought at weights ranging from 137 to 160 pounds, primarily as a welterweight and middleweight. In 109 professional bouts, from 1887 to 1911, he won 85 (71 by knockout), lost four (one by knockout), and had 11 draws, two **no contests**, and seven no-decision bouts, in which he was awarded the **newspaper decision** in five, lost one, and drew one. He fought a total of 1,048 rounds. He was inducted into the **International Boxing Hall of Fame** in 1991.

S

SADDLER, JOSEPH "SANDY". B. 23 June 1926, Boston, Massachusetts. D. 18 September 2001. Sandy Saddler is best known for his four-**bout** series with **Willie Pep** from 1948 to 1951 in which they took turns holding the world's **featherweight** championship. Their 1949 bout was *Ring* magazine's "Fight of the Year."

Saddler was a tall, thin man whose fighting weight never exceeded 132 pounds. He began his **professional boxing** career in New England at the age of 17. He won an eight-**round decision** over Earl Roy in Hartford, Connecticut, on 7 March 1944. After being stopped in his second bout, Saddler won his next six, but only two were by **knockout**. His next two bouts, only one week apart, were a loss and a **draw** with Lou Alter. Saddler then began a winning streak that reached 37 before his next loss. In 1944, he had 22 bouts, and in 1945 had 24.

On 18 February 1946, he had his third loss, a 10-round decision to Bobby McQuillar, and later that year, on 23 July, Phil Terranova, former world's featherweight champion, defeated Saddler on a 10-round decision. Saddler then won his next 16 bouts, including a second-round knockout over future **lightweight** champion Joe Brown. One month later, Saddler fought a 10-round **draw** with another future lightweight champion, Jimmy Carter. After a 10-round decision loss to Humberto Sierra on 3 October 1947, Saddler went on another winning streak, this time for 14 bouts, including bouts in Caracas, **Venezuela**; Havana, **Cuba**; and Aruba. Louis "Chico" Rosa defeated Saddler in Hawaii, and then Saddler won two bouts in **Panama** before returning to the **United States**.

On 29 October 1948, he fought the first of his four bouts with Willie Pep and knocked him out in the fourth round to win the world's featherweight championship. At the time of the fight, Pep had lost only once in 136 bouts and had never been knocked out. After winning five **nontitle bouts**, Saddler faced Pep for the second time on 11 February 1949. This time Pep won a 15-round decision that was selected as the "Fight of the Year" by *Ring* magazine.

Saddler then won 12 straight bouts, nine by knockout, including victories over former **bantamweight** champion Harold Dade and future lightweight champion Paddy DeMarco. On 6 December 1949, Saddler defeated Orlando Zulueta for the world's **junior lightweight** title, one that in that era was not highly regarded. Saddler won his next 10 bouts, including a junior lightweight title defense against Lauro Salas, another fighter who would eventually become lightweight champion. He then faced Pep in their third bout on 8 September 1950. This time Saddler regained the **featherweight** championship, as Pep retired after seven rounds due to a separated shoulder.

Saddler's next loss occurred in a nontitle bout when undefeated (44–0–1) Del Flanagan outpointed him in 10 rounds on 6 December 1950. On 28 February, Saddler traveled to Havana, Cuba, to defend his junior lightweight title against Cuban Diego Sosa. In the second round of a rough fight, both fighters went down, with Saddler still punching Sosa as they fell. Saddler arose by the count of eight, but Sosa was not up by the count of 10, and the **referee** awarded the bout to Saddler, precipitating a riot by Sosa's supporters.

On 26 September 1951, one month after a loss to DeMarco in a nontitle bout, Pep and Saddler met for the fourth and final time, with Saddler's world featherweight title at stake. The bout, described by **ring** historians as one of the dirtiest in history, was won by Saddler after Pep retired after nine rounds. As a result of their actions, Pep's boxing license was revoked by the **New York State Athletic Commission** and Saddler's was suspended.

Saddler fought 23 more bouts in his ring career, winning 16, but only two of them were title defenses—a 25 February 1955 15-round **unanimous decision** over Teddy "Red Top" Davis and an 18 January 1956 ninth-round **technical knockout** of Gabriel "Flash" Elorde due to a cut. Saddler's last bout was a 10-round unanimous decision loss to Larry Boardman.

Saddler retired from boxing on 23 January 1957 due to a detached retina suffered when a taxicab in which Saddler was a passenger collided with another vehicle in July 1956. After he retired, he became a boxing **trainer**, with one of his students being **heavyweight** champion **George Foreman**. From time to time, Pep and Saddler would renact their ring wars by boxing brief **exhibitions** with one another.

Saddler was quite tall for his weight at five foot eight inches and had a 70-inch **reach**. He fought at weights ranging from 115 to 134 pounds, primarily as a featherweight. In 162 professional bouts, from 1944 to 1956, Saddler won 144 (103 by knockout), lost 16 (one by knockout), had two draws, and fought a total of 926 rounds. He was inducted as a member of the inaugural class of the **International Boxing Hall of Fame** in 1990.

SÁNCHEZ NARVÁEZ, SALVADOR "CHAVA". B. 26 January 1959, Santiago Tianguistenco, Edomex, **Mexico**. D. 12 August 1982, San Luis Potosi, Mexico. Salvador Sánchez was one of the few champions to die while still undefeated as a champion. He was one of the greatest Mexican **feather-weights** of all time and had made nine successful defenses of his title prior to his death.

His first **professional** fight (a three-**round knockout** of Al Gardeno in Vera Cruz, Mexico) was on 4 May 1975 at the age of 16 after having just a few **amateur** contests. Fighting exclusively in Mexico, he won his first 18 **bouts**, 17 by knockout, from 1975 to 1977. On 9 September 1977 in Mazlatán, Mexico, he fought Antonio Becerra for the **vacant** Mexican **bantamweight** championship. Sánchez lost a 12-round **split decision**. This was the only bout that Sánchez would lose as a professional boxer. Seven months later, on 15 April 1978, Sánchez fought a 10-round **majority draw** in Los Angeles with Juan Escobar in Sánchez's first fight outside of Mexico.

Sánchez then won his next 13 bouts and received the opportunity to box for the **World Boxing Council** world featherweight championship on 2 February 1980 in Phoenix, Arizona. He defeated Danny "Little Red" Lopez on a **technical knockout** in the 13th round and became champion. Over the next two and a half years, Sánchez successfully defended his title nine times. His opponents were Rubén Castillo (12 April 1980, **unanimous decision** round 15); Danny Lopez (21 June 1980, TKO 14); Pat Ford (13 September 1980, **majority decision** 15); Juan LaPorte (13 December 1980, unanimous decision 15); Roberto Castañon (22 March 1981, TKO 10); **super bantamweight** champion **Wilfredo Gómez** (21 August 1981, TKO 8); Pat Cowdell (12 December 1981, split decision 15); Jorge "Rocky" García (8 May 1982, unanimous decision 15); and **Azumah Nelson** (21 July 1982, TKO 15). Nelson, Gómez, and Ford were all undefeated when they met Sánchez; Castañon, LaPorte, and Castillo each only had one loss; and García and Cowdell had two losses each.

On 12 August 1982, Sánchez was killed in the early morning hours when he crashed his sports car while traveling on the federal highway from Santiago de Queretaro to San Luis Potosi in Mexico.

Sánchez was five foot seven inches tall and had a 67-inch **reach**. He fought at weights ranging from 118 to 129 pounds, primarily as a featherweight. In 46 professional bouts, from 1975 to 1982, he won 44 (32 by knockout), lost one (none by knockout), had one **draw**, and fought a total of 376 rounds. He was inducted into the **International Boxing Hall of Fame** in 1991.

SARDIÑAS MONTALVO, ELIGIO. See CHOCOLATE, KID "THE CUBAN BON BON" (né ELIGIO SARDIÑAS MONTALVO).

SAVATE. Savate is a French form of **kickboxing** and is the only form of kickboxing in which the contestants wear shoes. The French word *savate* means "old shoe." The sport originated in the early 19th century, possibly among sailors in Marseilles. It was included as a demonstration sport in the 1924 **Olympic Games** in Paris. It is more commonly referred to as La Boxe Française-Savate in **France**.

See also KICKBOXING; MIXED MARTIAL ARTS; MUAY THAI.

SAVON FABRE, FÉLIX "NIÑOTE". B. 22 September 1967, San Vicente, **Cuba**. Félix Savon is a boxer who is relatively unknown in the **United States** but who has compiled one of the most impressive boxing records of all time. As a Cuban boxer, he was not allowed to box **professionally**.

The six-foot-five-inch, 200-pound right-hander with an 82-inch reach is one of only three men to win three **Olympic** boxing **gold medals**, winning the **heavyweight** class in 1992, 1996, and 2000. Only the Cuban Olympic boycott in 1988 prevented him from winning four Olympic medals. He won the **International Boxing Association World Championships** an unprecedented six times, winning the heavyweight class in 1986, 1989, 1991, 1993, 1995, and 1997 and winning the **silver medal** in 1999 after the Cuban team withdrew from the competition in protest over a scoring **decision** in another **bout**.

Savon's 1997 gold medal was somewhat tainted, though, as he lost to **Uzbekistan's** Ruslan Chagaev in the final but Chagaev was later disqualified from the tournament and his medals stripped for having fought as a professional prior to the tournament. Although Chagaev was later reinstated as an **amateur**, when the bouts were declared **exhibitions** his medal was not restored. Savon was also a three-time Pan American Games winner in 1987, 1991, and 1995 and a four-time winner at the Central America and **Caribbean** Games, with victories in 1986, 1990, 1993, and 1998.

Included among his amateur victories are wins over Michael Bentt, Lamon Brewster, Shannon Briggs, and Sultan Ibragimov, all boxers who later won world professional heavyweight championships. Savon claims an amateur record 415–17, but as with nearly all boxers' amateur records, it is next to impossible to find complete documentation of it.

Savon announced his retirement from competition following the 2000 Olympic Games, in which he was the Cuban flagbearer, and has become a **trainer** for the Cuban national team. His nephew Erislandy Savon competed as a **super heavyweight** for Cuba at the 2012 Olympic Games but lost in his first bout.

SCHMELING, MAXIMILLIAN ADOLPH OTTO SIEGFRIED "MAX," "THE BLACK UHLAN OF THE RHINE". B. 28 September 1905, Klein Luckow, **Germany**. D. 2 February 2005, Wenzendorf, Germany. During the 1930s, Max Schmeling became synonymous with Nazi Germany, even though Schmeling himself was not a Nazi supporter. For much of his boxing career in the **United States**, he was a major villain, and his return **bout** with **heavyweight** champion **Joe Louis** in 1938 was one of the most symbolic good guy–bad guy fights in boxing history.

Schmeling began boxing as a **professional** in Düsseldorf, Germany, on 2 August 1924. Fighting exclusively in Germany, he built a record of 37–4–3 and gained the German **light heavyweight** and **heavyweight** and European light heavyweight championships. He came to the United States in November 1928 and, under the management of American Joe Jacobs, quickly established himself as one of the contenders for the **vacant** world's heavyweight title.

After winning three bouts against lower-quality opposition, he stopped Johnny Risko in nine **rounds** on 1 February 1929 at **Madison Square Garden** in a bout acclaimed by *Ring* **magazine** as the "Fight of the Year." After a 15-round **unanimous-decision** victory over the Basque fighter Paolino Uzcudun, Schmeling was matched with **Jack Sharkey** for the world's heavyweight championship, made vacant by champion **Gene Tunney's** retirement in 1928.

On 12 June 1930 at New York's Yankee Stadium, Schmeling became the world's heavyweight champion after a fourth-round blow that knocked him down and incapacitated him was ruled a low blow and **referee** Jim Crowley awarded him the bout on a **foul**. Although Sharkey demanded a rematch, Schmeling and his manager, Jacobs, refused to grant him one and instead made his first title defense against Young Stribling, a boxer from the state of Georgia known as the "King of the Canebrakes." Schmeling stopped Stribling in the 15th and final round of their bout and retained his title.

Although Schmeling did not want to fight a rematch with Sharkey, the **New York State Athletic Commission** threatened to prohibit him from boxing in New York again, and Schmeling and Jacobs relented and granted Sharkey the rematch.

In a closely contested bout, Sharkey won a **split decision** and the world's heavyweight title on 21 June 1932. Three months later, Schmeling defeated former **middleweight** champion **Mickey Walker**, then boxing as a heavyweight, on an eighth-round **technical knockout**.

In Germany at this time, the Nazi party had seized power. Schmeling began to be viewed as an extension of that regime and lost favor with North American boxing fans. In his next bout, he faced **Max Baer**, who while not a practicing Jew, had a Jewish father and wore a Star of David on his **ring** trunks. The bout was promoted by **Jack Dempsey**, who had recently retired from the ring and had embarked on a new, short-lived career as a boxing promoter. In a bout voted "Fight of the Year" by *Ring* magazine, Baer stopped Schmeling in the 10th round of their scheduled 15-round bout. After Schmeling lost a 10-round **decision** to Steve Hamas in his next bout, he returned to Europe.

In Europe, Schmeling fought a 12-round **draw** with Uzcudun in Barcelona, **Spain**. On 26 August 1936, Schmeling knocked out German Walter Neusel in the ninth round in Hamburg before the largest European crowd ever to see a fight, 102,000 spectators. Schmeling then stopped Hamas in nine rounds in Hamburg and won a 12-round decision over Uzcudun in Berlin.

Schmeling did not fight until nearly one year later, but when he did he scored one of boxing's biggest upsets. He returned to the **United States** and fought the undefeated (24–0) heavyweight contender **Joe Louis** at Yankee Stadium. He knocked Louis down in the fourth round and knocked him out in the 12th round for Louis's first defeat. Although Schmeling should then have been considered as the next challenger for **James J. Braddock's** heavyweight title, promoters were wary of allowing the German to fight for the championship. A fight with Braddock was signed for, but Braddock was injured in **training** and the bout was postponed and finally cancelled. Schmeling returned to Germany to bide his time. Louis received the title shot and easily defeated Braddock on 22 June 1937.

After three successful title defenses, Louis met Schmeling on 22 June 1938 at Yankee Stadium. In that fight, Louis, with the weight of the country on his shoulders and determined to avenge his only loss, tore into Schmeling from the opening bell and knocked Schmeling down twice before Schmeling was counted out at 2:04 of the first round.

In 1939, Schmeling had one fight in Germany and won the European and German heavyweight championship with a one-round **knockout** of Adolf Heuser in Stuttgart before World War II broke out. He was drafted into the German Army and served as a paratrooper.

After the war, needing money, Schmeling began a brief comeback in Germany at the age of 42. He fought five bouts in 1947 and 1948, winning three, losing two, and retiring after a 10-round decision loss to Richard Vogt on 31 October 1948.

In the 1950s, Schmeling began working for Coca-Cola in Germany. After a while, he owned his own bottling plant and was an executive for the company. He later became wealthy, started a friendship with Louis, and lived mainly in Berlin until the age of 99.

Schmeling was six foot one inch tall and had a 76-inch **reach**. He fought at weights ranging from 171 to 196 pounds as a heavyweight. In 70 professional bouts, from 1924 to 1948, he won 56 (40 by knockout), lost 10 (five by knockout), had four draws, and fought a total of 472 rounds. He was inducted into the **International Boxing Hall of Fame** in 1992.

SCORECARD. *See* JUDGES.

SCORING SYSTEMS. When **judges** score a **bout**, they are required to use the scoring system mandated by the jurisdiction that sanctions the bout. Various systems have been employed in boxing history. The simplest just awards each **round** to one of the contestants or calls the round even. Point systems used include the 10-point must system in which the winner of the round receives 10 points and the loser nine or less, with even rounds scored at 10 points each. A five-point must system has been employed for professional bouts, and a 20-point system has been used for amateur bouts.

SCOTLAND. Scotland is a country that is part of the United Kingdom, although its athletes compete internationally with those of **England**, **Wales**, and **Northern Ireland** as part of the **Great Britain** team. There have been seven boxers from Scotland who have won **Olympic** boxing medals—**lightweight** Richard McTaggart won the gold medal in 1956 and the **bronze** medal in 1960, George McKenzie was the 1920 **bantamweight** bronze medalist and his brother James, won the 1924 **flyweight silver medal**, and Alex Ireland, despite his name, was a Scot born in Edinburgh who won the 1920 **welterweight** silver medal. William Cuthbertson, 1920 flyweight bronze medal; John McCormack, 1956 **light middleweight** bronze; and Willie Fisher, 1960 light middleweight bronze, were the others. As with the other countries of the United Kingdom, boxing has been quite popular since the 19th century.

Professional world champions from Scotland include Benny Lynch and Ken Buchanan, who have both been elected to the **International Boxing Hall of Fame**. Other Scottish champions are Alex Arthur, Ricky Burns, Pat Clinton, Scott Harrison, Walter McGowan, Jackie Paterson, Murray Sutherland, Jim Watt, and Paul Weir.

SECONDS. *See* CORNERMAN.

SELBY, NORMAN. *See* McCOY, CHARLES "KID," "THE CORKSCREW KID" (né NORMAN SELBY).

SHARKEY, JACK "THE BOSTON GOB" (né JOSEPH PAUL ZU-KAUSKAS). B. 26 October 1902, Binghamton, New York. D. 17 August 1994, Beverley, Massachusetts. In 1920, Lithuanian American Joe Zukauskas joined the U.S. Navy and served two two-year stints. When his ship had liberty in Boston in 1924, he decided to earn some extra money by boxing a few **bouts**, as he had done some boxing while in the navy. He found a promoter who promised him a bout for $100 and then asked him his name. When he told him Joseph Paul Zukauskas, the promoter told him to go get himself a name. Zukauskas thought of the then **heavyweight** champion, **Jack Dempsey**, and former heavyweight challenger Tom Sharkey and said "Jack Sharkey." He returned on 29 January 1924 and stopped his opponent in the first **round**.

Over the next two years, he won 17 of 23 bouts, mostly in New England, and decided to go to New York, where most of the major boxing action took place. On 12 February 1926, he won the **main event** at **Madison Square Garden** by **decisioning** Eddie Huffman. Sharkey won his next five fights, including a decision over George Godfrey, and faced the great black fighter **Harry Wills** at Ebbets Field, the baseball park that was the home of the Brooklyn Dodgers. Wills was one of the greatest fighters of his era and had been avoided by heavyweight champion Jack Dempsey. Sharkey was well ahead of Wills when the **referee** stopped the bout in the 13th round of the scheduled 15-round bout claiming that Wills **fouled** Sharkey.

Sharkey began 1927 by stopping former world's **light heavyweight** champion Mike McTigue in 12 rounds at the Garden. Later that year at Yankee Stadium, he fought former heavyweight champion Jack Dempsey, who had just lost his title to **Gene Tunney**. The winner of the Dempsey–Sharkey bout would then face Tunney. Although Sharkey put up a good battle and staggered Dempsey in the first round, Dempsey was able to recover and knock out Sharkey in the seventh round. Sharkey's **corner** claimed it was a foul blow, but the referee did not agree.

Sharkey continued as one of the sport's top heavyweights and fought a **draw** with New Zealander Tom Heeney, knocked out former light heavyweight champion Jack Delaney in one round, handed KO Christner his first career loss after 16 bouts, defeated Young Stribling, and stopped light heavyweight champion Tommy Loughran and "Fainting" Phil Scott.

When Gene Tunney retired in 1928, the heavyweight title became **vacant**. The **New York State Athletic Commission** had Sharkey and **Max Schmeling** fight for the vacant title on 12 June 1930 at Yankee Stadium. In the fourth round, Schmeling was knocked down and claimed it was caused by a low blow. After some confusion, referee Jim Crowley (famed as one of football's Four Horsemen when he played college football at Notre Dame) awarded the bout and the championship to Schmeling on a foul.

Sharkey wanted a rematch but was unable to get one, as Schmeling avoided him, and did not fight for over a year. In his next bout, on 22 July 1931, Sharkey met former **middleweight** champion **Mickey Walker**, who was now fighting as a **heavyweight**. The 15-round bout was scored a draw. Three months later, Sharkey won a 10-round decision over **Primo Carnera**.

On 21 June 1932, Sharkey finally got his rematch with Schmeling for the heavyweight title. In Sharkey's words, as reported by Peter Heller in his book *In This Corner*, "Fifteen long rounds. I never hit him below the chin." Sharkey won a **split decision** and was now heavyweight champion of the world.

Sharkey kept his title for only one year and did not defend it until 29 June 1933. On that day, he fought the six-foot-six-inch, 260-pound Primo Carnera. Although big, Carnera was not a talented fighter. He was managed by New York mobsters who manipulated the results of many of his bouts. Carnera knocked out Sharkey in the sixth round in one of boxing's major upsets, and although Sharkey swore to his dying day that the fight was on the level, that fact still remains questionable in the minds of many boxing historians.

Sharkey lost decisions in his next two bouts that year to King Levinsky and Tommy Loughran and then did not fight for two years. In his next four bouts, against lesser-ranked opponents, he had mixed results, two wins, one loss, and one draw.

Sharkey's last professional bout was against the up-and-coming **Joe Louis**, making Sharkey the only man to fight both Dempsey and Louis. Joe easily knocked out Sharkey in the third round after knocking him down four times previously.

In retirement, Sharkey owned a bar and worked as a referee. He also was a noted fly fisherman and on occasion toured with baseball star Ted Williams making personal appearances promoting fly-fishing.

Sharkey was six feet tall and had a 72-inch **reach**. He fought at weights ranging from 181 to 207 pounds as a heavyweight. In 55 professional bouts, from 1924 to 1936, he won 37 (13 by **knockout**), lost 13 (four by knockout), had three draws, and had two no-decision bouts, in which he was awarded the **newspaper decision** in one and lost one. He fought a total of 460 rounds. He was inducted into the **International Boxing Hall of Fame** in 1994.

SHAVER, EARNIE DEE. *See* SHAVERS, EARNIE "THE ACORN," "THE BLACK DESTROYER" (né EARNIE DEE SHAVER).

SHAVERS, EARNIE "THE ACORN," "THE BLACK DESTROYER" (né EARNIE DEE SHAVER). B. 31 August 1945, Garland, Alabama. **Earnie Shavers** had one of the hardest punches in the history of boxing and appears on most boxing historians' lists of the 10 hardest hitters. He began boxing rather late in life, at age 22 in 1967, and had a relatively short but productive **amateur** career, with victories in 1969 in the **heavyweight** division of three **Golden Gloves** tournaments—Youngstown, Cleveland, and Ohio. He also won the National **Amateur Athletic Union** heavyweight championship that year.

He began boxing as a **professional** on 6 November 1969 with a second-**round knockout** of Silas Howell in Akron, Ohio. Shavers fought six more fights that year, winning five by knockout and losing a four-round **decision** to Stan Johnson. He won his next six by knockout in 1970 before being knocked out himself in five rounds by hard-hitting, undefeated Ron Stander. Shavers then won his next 33 **bouts**, 32 of them by knockout, with 13 first-round knockouts, including one of former heavyweight champion Jimmy Ellis.

In his next bout, Shavers was stopped in one round by **Jerry Quarry**. After winning another one-round knockout victory, Shavers went 10 rounds with Bob Stallings, a **journeyman** fighter with a record of 20–25. Stallings knocked Shavers down in the ninth round and won a close but unanimous 10-round decision. Three weeks later, Shavers fought a 10-round **draw** with Jimmy Young. This was the first time in Shavers's 51-bout career that he fought two consecutive fights without winning either.

He won his next three fights comfortably by knockout and on 13 September 1975 faced **Ron Lyle** in Lyle's hometown of Denver. Lyle and Shavers were two of the hardest-hitting heavyweights of all time and demonstrated this in their bout. Shavers knocked Lyle down in the second round, but Lyle came back to knock Shavers down and stop him in the sixth round.

After five more victories, four by knockout, Shavers was given the opportunity to fight **Muhammad Ali** for the world's heavyweight championship at **Madison Square Garden** on 29 September 1977. Shavers staggered Ali in the second round but could not finish him off. Both fighters remained on their feet for the entire 15 rounds, but in the last round, with both men fighting furiously, Ali staggered Shavers. The **unanimous decision** went in Ali's favor. After the fight, Ali said that Shavers was the hardest puncher he ever fought.

In his next fight, Shavers fought the other top heavyweight of the era, **Larry Holmes**, in a 12-round bout. Holmes dominated and won nearly every round as he gained a unanimous decision. Shavers's next five fights all ended in less than four rounds and included a first-round knockout of **Ken Norton**, former heavyweight champion. This gained Shavers another shot at Larry Holmes, who was now recognized by the **World Boxing Council** as heavyweight champion. On 28 September 1979 in **Las Vegas**, Shavers knocked Holmes down in the seventh round, but Holmes caught up with him and stopped him in the 11th round of their 15-round bout.

Shavers was stopped in two of his next three bouts by heavyweight contenders Bernardo Mercado and Randall "Tex" Cobb, and for the next three years, he fought much lower-caliber opponents, winning 12 of 15 bouts. He retired in 1983 but then fought three more fights against fighters with abysmal records—one in 1987 and two in 1995. In his last bout, he was knocked out in two rounds by a fighter with a record of 5–16–2.

In retirement, he became an ordained minister and lived in Phoenix for a while and then moved to **England**. He has worked as head of security in a bar in Liverpool and has done some **refereeing** of professional wrestling **exhibitions**.

Shavers is six feet tall and fought at weights ranging from 200 to 228 pounds as a heavyweight. In 90 professional bouts, from 1969 to 1995, he won 75 (69 by knockout), lost 14 (seven by knockout), had one **draw**, and fought a total of 370 rounds.

SHOMO, VINCENT O'NEAL "VINCE". B. 30 July 1940, New York, New York. Vince Shomo was one of the top **amateur** boxers in the **United States** during the 1950s. He attended DeWitt Clinton High School in the Bronx, New York, and then transferred to George Washington High School and played basketball at Washington.

He was the first boxer to win four New York **Golden Gloves** championships (1956 **featherweight sub-novice**; 1957, 1959, and 1960 **lightweight open**). He also won the 1957, 1959, and 1960 Eastern Regional Golden Gloves and the 1959 and 1960 Intercity Golden Gloves. In 1958, he entered the Golden Gloves in the **welterweight** division but lost a **decision** in the quarterfinal **round**. He was, however, selected as an alternate in the Intercity Golden Gloves that year and won his **bout**. He also won the 1957, 1958, and 1960 National **Amateur Athletic Union (AAU)** lightweight titles and 1959 Pan American Games **light welterweight** gold medal.

He was not as successful as a **professional** boxer, though. Boxing as a welterweight, Shomo fought his first professional bout on 10 October 1960 and won the six-round bout by decision. His boxing career then went up and down. He won his first five bouts. He only won two of his next five, with a **draw** among them. He then lost his next four bouts by decision. He won five in a row again, but then ended his career by losing four fights and having one draw. In his final fight, on 12 November 1968, he was stopped by Billy Backus, who later became a world welterweight champion.

In the mid-1960s, Shomo became an accountant and worked for Shell Oil Company and later in the 1980s was the comptroller for *Ring* **magazine**.

After retiring from the **ring**, he became licensed as an AAU official and often **refereed** Golden Glove bouts.

Shomo is five foot seven inches tall and fought at weights ranging from 141 to 153 pounds, primarily as a welterweight. In 24 professional bouts, from 1960 to 1968, he won 12, (three by **knockout**), lost 10 (three by knockout), had two draws, and fought a total of 171 rounds.

SILVER MEDAL. In international amateur boxing competition such as the **Olympic Games** and **World Championships**, the loser in the final tournament match is awarded a silver medal as the tournament runner-up.

SINCLAIR, FLOYD JOY. *See* MAYWEATHER, FLOYD JOY, JR., "PRETTY BOY," "MONEY" (né FLOYD JOY SINCLAIR).

SMITH, AMOS "MYSTERIOUS BILLY". B. 15 May 1871, Little River, Nova Scotia, **Canada**. D. 14 October 1937, Portland, Oregon. "Mysterious Billy" Smith was variously reported as being born in Nova Scotia; Eastport, Maine; or East Port, Missouri. What is agreed upon by most boxing historians is that he was one of the dirtiest fighters of all time. Included among his 90 recorded professional **bouts**, with 22 losses, are 11 bouts lost by **disqualification**. Five of his bouts were also recorded as "**no contest**," which meant in essence that the **referee** disqualified both fighters. He did win one of his bouts by disqualification as well. His bouts were also difficult to score, as evidenced by the fact that 26 of them were scored as draws. He is the only world champion to have more draws than victories.

Details of his early career are sketchy, but the first recorded bout listed for him took place in 1890 in New Brunswick, Canada. He then traveled to the West Coast and has bouts in Portland, Oregon, and San Francisco on his record. In 1893, he fought two bouts in Coney Island, Brooklyn, New York, and one in Chicago. In 1895, he fought a 20-**round draw** with **Tommy Ryan** in Coney Island for the world **welterweight** title.

During the latter part of that decade, Smith fought and defeated some of that era's top welterweights, such as **Joe Walcott**, Charlie McKeever, Matty Mathews, and Kid Lavigne. He claimed the world welterweight title after winning a 25-round **decision** over Matthews on 25 August 1898 in New York. On 15 January 1900, Smith fought Rube Ferns in a 25-round bout in Buffalo, New York, for Smith's welterweight title. Although Smith knocked Ferns down 15 times in the bout, he lost the bout by disqualification in the 21st round. Though Smith lost, he did not relinquish his claim to the title, and less than two weeks later defeated Frank McConnell in New York City by a **knockout** in the 22nd round in a bout billed as a welterweight title bout. After Matty Matthews knocked out Smith in the 19th round on 19 April 1900 in New York City, Smith no longer had a claim to the title. He continued boxing through 1903 with 16 bouts, of which he won only one, lost eight (three by knockout, four by disqualification, one by decision), drew six, and had one no contest. He made a brief, unsuccessful comeback with three bouts, one each in 1910, 1911, and 1915.

In retirement, he ran a saloon in Portland, Oregon, and his son boxed briefly as "Mysterious Billy" Smith Jr., winning only nine of 23 bouts during the 1920s.

Smith was five foot eight inches tall and fought at weights ranging from 139 to 156 pounds, primarily as a welterweight. In 90 professional bouts, from 1890 to 1915, Mysterious Billy Smith won 31 (22 by knockout), lost 22 (eight by knockout), had 26 draws, had five no contests, and fought six no-decision bouts in which he was awarded the **newspaper decision** in two, lost three, and drew one. He fought a total of 1,039 rounds. He was inducted into the **International Boxing Hall of Fame** in 2009.

SMITH, WALKER, JR. *See* ROBINSON, RAY "SUGAR RAY" (né WALKER SMITH JR.).

SOUTH AFRICA. In South Africa, cricket, rugby, and football (soccer) are the major sports. Boxing, though, has always been followed by quite a few avid fans, and South Africa has produced several world-class boxers.

In **amateur boxing**, South African boxers first competed in the 1920 **Olympic Games** and were in all nine games through 1960. In 1961, the country became known officially as the Republic of South Africa, and its three-letter Olympic abbreviation since then has been RSA. From 1964 to 1988, South Africa was not permitted to compete in the Olympics, but the nation was reinstated in 1992 and since then has entered each of the six Olympic boxing tournaments.

South Africans have won 19 Olympic boxing medals, including six gold medals, which places them in 13th place among all nations. Their gold medalists are Clarence "Sal" Walker, 1920 **bantamweight**; Willie Smith, 1924 bantamweight; Laurie Stevens, 1932 **lightweight**; Gerald Dreyer, 1948 lightweight; Dave Carstens, 1932 **light heavyweight**; and George Hunter, 1948 light heavyweight. South African Olympic boxing **silver** medalists are **featherweights** Charles Catterall, 1936, and Dennis Shepherd, 1948; **light middleweight** Theunis van Schalkwyk, 1952; and **heavyweight** Daan Bekker, 1960. From 1948 to 1960, South African heavyweights medalled in each of the four Olympics, with Bekker also winning a **bronze** in 1956 and John Arthur in 1948 and Dries Nieman in 1952 also winning bronze medals. Other South African Olympic bronze medalists are **flyweight** Willie Toweel, 1952; bantamweight Harry Isaacs, 1928; featherweights Len Leisching, 1952, and William Meyers, 1960; **light welterweight** Henry Loubscher, 1956; and **middleweight** Eddie Peirce, 1932.

Professional boxing in South Africa has always had a good following. World champions in the apartheid era include bantamweights Vic Toweel and Arnold Taylor, **super featherweight** Brian Mitchell, **cruiserweight** Piet Crous, and heavyweight Gerrie Coetzee. Peter Mathebula, who was recognized as the **World Boxing Association (WBA)** flyweight champion in 1980–1981, is the only black South African world champion in that era. Other top boxers from South Africa in the apartheid era who did not become world champions include Pierre Coetzer, Johnny DuPlooy, Pierre Fourie, Mike Holt, Kallie Knoetze, Willie Ludick, the seven-foot-two-inch Ewart Potgieter, George "Boer" Rodel, and the Toweel brothers—Alan, Jimmy, Fraser, and Willie—all brothers of bantamweight champion Vic. Not to be forgotten is the boxer with the most unpronounceable name (at least to English speakers), Nkosana Mgxaji, who compiled a creditable 89–9–3 record from 1969 to 1985, held the South African light welterweight title, and challenged Samuel Serrano for the WBA super featherweight title.

Since the end of apartheid in 1990, and coincidental with the rise of multiple boxing sanctioning organizations, there have been 18 South African world champion boxers, mostly black. Among them are Cassius Baloyi, Mbolelo Botile, Vuyani Bungu, Mzonke Fana, Isaac Hlatshwayo, Nkosinathi Joyi, Malcolm Klassen, Lehlohonolo Ledwaba, Thulani Malinga, Jeffrey Mathebula, Jacob Matlala, Moruti Mthalane, Welcome Ncita, Takalani Ndlovu, Simphiwe Nongqayi, Zolani Petelo, and Dingaan Thobela. The lone white South African world champion in that time was heavyweight Corrie Sanders.

Sportswriter Chris Greyvenstein has been South Africa's most noted boxing journalist and has been nominated for the **International Boxing Hall of Fame**, although not yet, as of 2012, been elected. South African **referee** Stanley Christodoulou was elected to the hall in 2004.

SOUTHPAWS. *See* LEFT-HANDED BOXERS.

SPAIN. In Spain, many other sports are more popular than boxing, but the country has produced several professional world champions and won four **Olympic** medals.

Spain first competed in Olympic boxing in 1924 but did not win an Olympic medal until 1972, when Enrique Rodríguez won the **bronze** medal as a **light flyweight**. Rafael Lozano, also a light flyweight, won bronze in 1996 and **silver** in 2000 in that class, and Faustino Reyes won the 1996 **featherweight** silver medal.

There have been 10 Spanish professional world champions—Gabriel Campillo, Pedro Carrasco, Javier Castillejo, José Manuel Durán, Perico Fernández, Cecilio Lastra, José López Bueno, Jorge Mata, Baltazar Sangchili, and Miguel Velásquez. Other notable Spanish nonchampion boxers include Luis Romero, Kid Tano, José Manuel Urtain, and Paolino Uzcudun.

SPARRING. When boxers practice their moves in the **ring** with an opponent, it is referred to as sparring. They usually wear extra protective equipment that they do not wear in actual competition, such as a leather headgear, and usually do not put all their power into their punches. The term is also used during a **bout** when both fighters are moving around looking for an opening to throw a punch.

SPARRING PARTNER. When a boxer is **training** for an upcoming match, he often hires other boxers to work with him in the **ring** in sparring sessions. These boxers are known as sparring partners and are usually of lesser ability.

Often the sparring partners are asked to mimic the style of the boxer's future opponent in order to best prepare him for the **bout**.

SPINKS, LEON "NEON LEON". B. 11 July 1953, St. Louis, Missouri. Leon Spinks was one of the most unlikely **heavyweight** champions. He had an excellent **amateur boxing** career, winning the National **Amateur Athletic Union light heavyweight** championship in 1974, 1975, and 1976 and the 1976 **Olympic Games** gold medal in the light heavyweight class.

His professional career began as a heavyweight on 15 January 1977 with a fifth-**round technical knockout** over Bob Smith in **Las Vegas**. Spinks won his next four fights by **knockout** before fighting a 10-round **draw** with heavyweight contender Scott LeDoux. After a 10-round **unanimous decision** over undefeated Italian heavyweight Alfio Righetti, Spinks was matched with **Muhammad Ali** for the world's heavyweight championship. They met in Las Vegas on 15 February 1978 after Spinks had only had seven professional fights. Ali took him lightly and spent much of the **bout** clowning and dancing. Spinks won a **split decision** in one of boxing's biggest upsets of all time.

Spinks and Ali signed for a rematch in September, and the **World Boxing Council (WBC)** then stripped Spinks of his title, requiring him to defend it against **Ken Norton** instead of Ali. The **World Boxing Association (WBA)** did not, and the Spinks–Ali rematch went on as scheduled in the Superdome in New Orleans, Louisiana, on 15 September. This time, Ali put forth a good effort and easily defeated Spinks by a unanimous decision to become the first man to regain the world's heavyweight title twice.

In Spinks's only fight in 1979, he was knocked down three times in the first round (an automatic stoppage) in his bout with **South African** Gerrie Coetzee in Monaco. He fought four more times in 1980, with three wins and a draw, and was matched with **Larry Holmes**, the WBC world heavyweight champion on 12 June 1981 in Detroit. This was Spinks's third heavyweight title fight in just 14 bouts. Holmes stopped him in the third round on a technical knockout.

Spinks continued his career but now boxed as a **cruiserweight**—a division with a 200-pound maximum weight as opposed to the unlimited weight heavyweight division. On 31 October 1982, he defeated Jesse Burnett on a 12-round unanimous decision and was awarded the North American Boxing Federation cruiserweight title—a relatively meaningless one.

After two more bouts as a cruiserweight, being stopped in six rounds by former world cruiserweight champion Carlos de León and stopping **journeyman** Lupe Guerra in four rounds, Spinks moved back to the heavyweight ranks. He won his next four bouts as a heavyweight, including an eight-round technical knockout over Kip Kane for another meaningless title—the WBC Continental Americas heavyweight title.

On 22 March 1986, in Reno, Nevada, Spinks fought his last significant fight, although he would continue to appear in the **ring** until 1995. His opponent in Reno was Dwight Muhammad Qawi, who had been the WBC world light heavyweight champion and who was now the WBA cruiserweight titleholder. The 15-round bout for the WBA world cruiserweight championship was won by Qawi in the sixth round on a **technical knockout**.

Spinks continued fighting, but his subsequent opponents were of a much lower caliber than he had previously fought. In his last 22 fights, from 1986 to 1995, he won only nine, lost 12, and drew one.

After retiring from the ring, he hit bottom and for a time was homeless. His life turned around somewhat, and he worked as a greeter at ex-football player Mike Ditka's restaurant in Chicago. He subsequently moved to Columbus, Nebraska, and has worked at McDonald's restaurants and at the local YMCA. He also does volunteer work with the homeless.

His brother, **Michael Spinks**, was also an Olympic champion in 1976 and as a professional defeated Larry Holmes in 1985 to win recognition as the **International Boxing Federation (IBF)** heavyweight champion. The Spinks brothers thus became the first pair of brothers to win the heavyweight championship—a feat matched two decades later by the **Klitschko** brothers. Leon's son Cory Spinks has also boxed and won the IBF **welterweight** title in 2003. Leon's other son, Leon Calvin, began his **professional boxing** career in 1990 but after winning his first two bouts was murdered. Leon Calvin's son, Leon Spinks III, began his professional boxing career in 2012 and as of 13 July 2013 had an undefeated record of six wins and one draw.

Spinks is six foot one inch tall and has a 76-inch **reach**. He fought at weights ranging from 190 to 225 pounds, primarily as a heavyweight. In 46 professional bouts, from 1977 to 1995, Leon Spinks won 26 (14 by knockout), lost 17 (nine by knockout), had three draws, and fought a total of 324 rounds.

SPINKS, MICHAEL "JINX". B. 13 July 1956, St. Louis, Missouri. Michael Spinks is the only man to have won the **Olympic** boxing gold medal as a **middleweight** and the world's **light heavyweight** and **heavyweight** titles as a **professional**. He is also one of the first pair of brothers (with brother **Leon Spinks**) to both win the world's professional heavyweight championship—a feat later matched by the **Klitschko** brothers.

As an **amateur** boxer, Spinks claimed a record of 93–7. He won the 1974 National **Golden Gloves light middleweight** title and the 1976 National Golden Gloves middleweight title. He was the **United States** entrant at the 1976 **Olympic Games** in the middleweight class. He had one of the easiest paths to the Olympic final **bout** of any boxer in history, competing in only one bout. He received a **bye** in his first **round**, won by a **walkover** in his second round bout when his Cameroonian opponent pulled out due to the African boycott, won his quarterfinal bout by **decision** over a Polish opponent, won his semifinal bout by a walkover when his **Romanian** opponent was injured, and then won the final bout when he outclassed his **Soviet** opponent and the **referee** stopped the contest in the third round.

After the Olympic Games, he became a professional boxer, with his first bout on 16 April 1977, a one-round **knockout**. He won his first 16 bouts, including wins over former light heavyweight champion Marvin Johnson and future **super middleweight** champion Murray Sutherland.

On 18 July 1981, Spinks defeated Eddie Mustafa Muhammad on a 15-round unanimous decision and won the **World Boxing Association (WBA)** light heavyweight title. In his sixth title defense, he decisioned the **World Boxing Council (WBC)** light heavyweight titleholder, Dwight Muhammad Qawi, and became WBC champion as well. Two fights later, Spinks won **International Boxing Federation (IBF)** recognition as light heavyweight champion when he defeated Eddie Davis. After two more defenses of the three titles, Spinks met heavyweight champion **Larry Holmes** for the IBF heavyweight title.

In a major upset, Spinks became the first light heavyweight champion to win the heavyweight title when he outpointed Holmes over 15 rounds on 21 September 1985. He again defeated him in a rematch on 19 April 1986, but only by a **split decision** this time. Spinks made one defense of his title against Steffan Tangstad and then was stripped of his IBF title for not fighting the IBF's choice of opponent, Tony Tucker, and opting to fight **Gerry Cooney** instead. Spinks stopped Cooney in five rounds in a **nontitle bout**.

Spinks then challenged the WBC and WBA heavyweight champion, **Mike Tyson**, and suffered his first and only loss in his **professional boxing** career as he was knocked out in just 91 seconds of the first round and then retired from the ring.

Spinks is six foot two inches tall and has a 76-inch **reach**. He fought at weights ranging from 166 to 212 pounds as a light heavyweight and heavyweight. In 32 professional bouts, from 1977 to 1988, he won 31 (21 by knockout), lost one by knockout, and fought a total of 226 rounds. He was inducted into the **International Boxing Hall of Fame** in 1994.

SPLIT DECISION. A split decision is one in which two of the three officials scoring the **bout** vote for one boxer while the other official votes for the other boxer as the bout's winner.

See also DRAW; MAJORITY DECISION; MAJORITY DRAW; TECHNICAL DECISION; UNANIMOUS DECISION.

ST. NICHOLAS ARENA. St. Nicholas Arena was located on 69 West 66th Street at Columbus Avenue in New York, New York, and was one of the **fight clubs** that featured regular weekly boxing shows. It was built in 1896 as an ice skating rink. Boxing was introduced there in 1906 as a private club. When the activity was legalized in 1911, boxing became a staple at the rink and by 1920 had supplanted it, resulting in the removal of the ice rink.

Regular boxing shows continued at the arena until 28 May 1962 and during the late 1940s and 1950s were **televised** weekly. During World War II, the arena was briefly renamed the Royal Windsor Arena. Although many top fighters began their careers at St. Nicks, there was only one world championship **bout** during the arena's existence—17 October 1938, Mike Belloise versus Joey Archibald for the world's **featherweight** title.

After the arena discontinued boxing shows, the American Broadcasting Company television network converted the facility to a television studio, which in 2012 was still being used for that purpose.

See also BLUE HORIZON; FELT FORUM; SUNNYSIDE GARDEN.

STEVENSON LAWRENCE, TEÓFILO. B. 29 March 1952, Puerto Padre, **Cuba**. D. 11 June 2012, Havana, Cuba. Teófilo Stevenson is one of just three men to win three **Olympic gold medals** in boxing. Had he been born in another country, he might have become one of the most popular and wealthy **heavyweight** champions in boxing history. Yet he never boxed as a **professional** due to his country's stringent stance against professional boxing.

He began boxing at the age of nine, and by the time he was 17, he was one of Cuba's best boxers. He was not yet the invincible warrior he would become and was defeated by Gabriel García in the Cuban national championships and by Duane Bobick in the 1971 Pan American Games. He did, however, win the **bronze medal** in the latter tournament. In a rematch with Bobick at the 1972 Olympic Games, Stevenson knocked Bobick down three times in the third **round** and won when the **referee** stopped the contest. In Stevenson's other three **bouts** in those games, the referee stopped the contest in two and Stevenson won the final bout on a **walkover** as his opponent had been injured in the semifinal bout and was not allowed to compete. Stevenson was the recipient of the **Val Barker Trophy** in 1972, the award given to the top boxer in the Olympic tournament.

The six-foot-five-inch, 220-pound Stevenson won the 1976 Olympic gold medal in a similar fashion, with a first-round **bye**, two clean **knockouts**, a bout stopped by the referee, and a retirement in the third round of his final bout. One of those knockouts was against the American entry, John Tate, who would later win the world's heavyweight title as a professional.

In 1980, the boycott by the **United States** and 62 other countries limited the opposition, but some of the world's best amateur boxers then were from Iron Curtain countries, who all participated. Stevenson knocked out a Nigerian in his first round bout, a Pole in his quarterfinal bout, and won **decisions** over a Hungarian and a **Russian** to win his third Olympic gold medal. Had Cuba not boycotted the Olympic Games in 1984 and 1988, Stevenson most likely would have added one or two more Olympic medals to his collection.

He also won two Pan American Games gold medals, in 1975 and 1979, and three **World Championship** gold medals, in 1974, 1978, and 1986. At the 1982 World Championships, Stevenson was defeated by future world professional heavyweight champion Francesco Damiani in a preliminary round and did not medal. Damiani won the **silver medal** in that tournament and would also win the Olympic silver medal in 1984.

In dual meet competition between the United States and **Cuba**, Stevenson won all six of his bouts from 1978 to 1984.

After winning his second Olympic gold medal, Stevenson was offered a reported five million dollars to become a professional boxer and fight the world champion **Muhammad Ali**. In a subsequent interview, he commented, "What is one million dollars compared to the love of eight million Cubans?" In response to the question, "Don't you wish you'd had the chance to fight Ali?" Stevenson replied, "You mean my brother?" Stevenson bore a strong physical resemblance to Ali, who visited Stevenson in Cuba in the mid-1990s and donated a substantial sum of money toward medical aid for the impoverished country.

Stevenson retired after the 1988 **Olympic Games**, which he was unable to enter due to Cuba's boycott. In his amateur career, he had a reported record of 302–22, which included victories over future professional **heavyweight** champions John Tate, Tony Tubbs, Michael Dokes, and Francesco Damiani.

STEWARD, EMANUEL "MANNY". B. 7 July 1944, Bottom Creek, West Virginia. D. 25 October 2012, Chicago, Illinois. Emanuel Steward was one of boxing's great **trainers**. The son of a West Virginia coal miner, at the age of 12 he moved with his mother to Detroit, Michigan, when his parents divorced. He took up boxing at the Brewster Recreation Center after receiving a pair of boxing **gloves** as a gift. He became an accomplished amateur boxer and won the 1963 National **Golden Gloves bantamweight** championship.

He became an electrical linesman to support his family and forsook a **professional boxing** career. In 1971, he brought his half-brother, James, to the nearby Kronk Gym in Detroit and became a part-time coach. He eventually gave up his day job and became a full-time boxing trainer.

His first two pupils, Hilmer Kenty and **Thomas Hearns**, became world champions in 1980. Over the next three decades, Steward worked with other champions such as Dennis Andries, **Julio César Chávez, Óscar De La Hoya**, John David Jackson, Hilmer Kenty, **Wladimir Klitschko, Lennox Lewis**, Mike McCallum, Milt McCrory, Michael Moorer, Jimmy Paul, and Duane Thomas. His fatherly style helped endear him to boxers, many of whom did not have fathers they respected. He often would take them to his home and gave them the love they lacked from their own families. He was much respected by his fellow trainers and received recognition from the Boxing Writers Association of America as the Manager of the Year in 1980 and 1989 and Trainer of the Year in 1993 and 1997.

He also worked for Home Box Office as a boxing analyst. He died from stomach cancer at the age of 68. He was inducted into the **International Boxing Hall of Fame** in 1996.

STILLMAN'S GYM. For most of its life, Stillman's Gym was located on 919 Eighth Avenue between 54th and 55th Streets, just two blocks north of **Madison Square Garden**. It was originally founded shortly after World War I by two philanthropists, Alpheus Geer and Hiram Mallinson, who established the Marshall Stillman Movement, an organization devoted to rehabilitating ex-convicts and juvenile delinquents. They opened a gymnasium in Harlem toward this end. In 1921, it was moved south to the Eighth Avenue location. Louis Ingber was hired to run it and eventually became its owner. Through the years, he became known as Lou Stillman and had his name legally changed.

He was a crusty character who sat on a high stool to oversee the activity and was continually insulting the fighters. As one article described him, "he was no sitcom character—crusty exterior with a heart of gold—he was all crust." He was said to have been either a former private detective or former policeman, and he always carried a loaded .38-caliber revolver with him.

Stillman's Gym was located in a three-story building with a two-story gymnasium on the second floor of the building. After climbing a steep flight of stairs to the gym, a visitor would be met by Stillman's manager and boxing instructor, Jack Curley, who would collect the 25 cent entry fee that enabled a spectator to climb another flight of stairs to sit in the gallery at one end of the gym to watch the boxers work out. There were two boxing **rings** on the floor, with only the best boxers allowed to use ring number one. A bell would ring every three minutes to mark the end of a **round**, and a second bell would ring one minute later for activity to resume.

The place was legendary for its lack of sanitation. The windows were always kept closed, and the air was heavy with cigar and cigarette smoke and perspiration and liniment. All of the best fighters trained there at one time or another since during that era most of the major fights took place at Madison Square Garden. All of the best **trainers** and managers would be there as well.

In 1959, the place was sold and Stillman retired. The gym was renamed the Eighth Avenue Gym but lasted only until 1962, when the building was demolished and replaced by an apartment house.

STONE. Stone is a British unit of weight measure equal to 14 pounds. British boxers' weights are usually given in stone and pounds.

STOPPAGE. *See* TECHNICAL KNOCKOUT (TKO).

STRAWWEIGHT. Strawweight is a boxing class with a maximum weight limit of 105 pounds. It is also referred to as minimumweight or mini flyweight. **Professional** sanctioning organizations first established this class in the late 1980s (**International Boxing Federation [IBF]**, June 1987; **World Boxing Council [WBC]**, October 1987; **World Boxing Association**, January 1988; **World Boxing Organization**, August 1989).

The IBF champion South **Korean** Kyung-Yun Lee was the first recognized champion in this division, and WBC champion Ricardo López of **Mexico** (champion from 1990 to 1999, 21 title defenses) was the most successful. Other of the best strawweights include José Antonio Aguirre, Iván Calderón, Roman González, Donnie Nietes, and Ratanapol Sor Vorapin.

SUB-NOVICE. In **Golden Gloves** boxing tournaments, the category subnovice is used for **amateur** boxers who have not previously competed in public competition. Boxers with previous experience compete in the **open** class.

SUGAR, HERBERT RANDOLPH "BERT". B. 7 June 1937, Washington, DC. D. 25 March 2012, Chappaqua, New York. Bert Sugar had a way with words. He also had a Damon Runyonesque charisma. He capitalized on both when he acquired *Ring* **magazine** in 1979 and became its editor. Although the magazine was not a financial success during his period of ownership, he became a staple in the boxing world during the next 30 years.

A graduate of the University of Maryland, he continued his education at the University of Michigan and earned a law degree in 1961. After passing the bar (he would later wisecrack "the only bar I ever passed"), he worked briefly in law but then moved into the advertising field. He became a collector of sports artifacts, mainly baseball, and eventually purchased *Boxing Illustrated* magazine in 1969 and edited it until 1973. Six years later, he, along with former professional basketball player Dave DeBusschere, Nick Kladis, and Jim Bukata, purchased *Ring* magazine from Nat Loubet, and Sugar became its editor. He proceeded to make the magazine more colorful and readible but unfortunately not more financially profitable. After four years at the magazine, he was ousted as its editor. In his inimitable style, he took over a table at his local watering hole, O'Reilly's Pub, and operated from there as a freelance writer for a short period of time, even changing his business card to read "corner table at O'Reilly's Pub." He eventually sued his former partners for breach of contract and settled out of court. As part of the settlement, he received ownership of *Boxing Illustrated*, which *Ring* had revived. He also edited a magazine called *Fight Game* into the 1990s.

He then had become well known in the boxing world for his gregarious personality, fund of boxing knowledge and trivia, always present fedora hat, and large cigar. He began appearing on television shows for his boxing knowledge and way with words. He also appeared in several films about boxing, including *Night and the City* and *Rocky Balboa*.

He was a prolific writer with more than 80 books to his credit, although quite a few were cowritten with other authors. In 1990, he won the **Nat Fleischer** Award for "Excellence in Boxing Journalism" from the Boxing Writers Association of America.

He was inducted into the **International Boxing Hall of Fame** in 2005. He died in his hometown of Chappaqua, New York, on 25 March 2012 of cardiac arrest, although he had previously contracted lung cancer.

SULLIVAN, JOHN LAWRENCE "JOHN L.," "BOSTON STRONG BOY". B. 15 October 1858, Roxbury, Massachusetts. D. 2 February 1918, Mattapan, Massachusetts. John L. Sullivan provides a bridge in **heavyweight** boxing history between the **bareknuckle** era (**London Prize Ring Rules**) and the gloved era (**Marquess of Queensberry Rules**).

Although John L. Sullivan was a competent baseball player who turned down an offer from the Cincinnati Red Stockings to play **professional** baseball, he preferred being a boxer who would enter a saloon and bellow, "I can lick any sonofabitch in the house." (That phrase, incidentally, was the title of his 1892 autobiography.)

His first recorded **bouts**, all in Boston, occured in 1879. By 1881, he was traveling across the country and had recorded bouts in New York, Philadelphia, and Chicago in addition to Boston. His first bout of significance occurred on 7 February 1882 when he and Paddy Ryan fought in Mississippi City, Mississippi, in a bareknuckle bout under London Prize Ring Rules for the "heavyweight championship of America"—a bout that Sullivan won in nine **rounds**. Throughout the next few years, he traveled in the eastern part of the **United States**, boxing **exhibitions** and issuing challenges, and was not defeated.

In November of 1887, he traveled to **England** and **Ireland**, issuing challenges and boxing exhibitions as he did in the United States. On 10 March 1888, he fought Charlie Mitchell in Chantilly, **France**, in 39 rounds in a bareknuckle affair. His last major bareknuckle fight and the last bareknuckle heavyweight championship bout took place in Richburg, Mississippi, on 8 July 1889. He and **Jake Kilrain** fought for 75 rounds, with Kilrain finally surrendering. As was not uncommon for the era, after the bout both participants and their seconds were arrested for an illegal prizefight and fined.

While Sullivan was champion, he drew a color line and refused to fight a black boxer. Sullivan's famous statement was "I will not fight a Negro. I never have and I never will." Consequently, **Peter Jackson**, a black boxer from **Australia** and one of the era's best boxers, was unable to fight Sullivan.

In 1890, John L. spent his time touring in a play, *Honest Hearts and Willing Hands*, which included some **sparring**. The following year he traveled to Hawaii and Australia for more exhibitions.

On 7 September 1892, he fought **Jim Corbett** in New Orleans, Louisiana, for the heavyweight championship of the world, using **gloves** and Marquess of Queensberry Rules. Corbett was a scientific boxer, whereas Sullivan was a brawler. The craftier Corbett won the title when he knocked out Sullivan in the 21st round.

Although Sullivan never fought a major bout again, he did box a few exhibitions over the next decade, including several with Kilrain in 1909 in Arizona. He owned bars, worked occasionally as a guest baseball umpire, and performed on the stage. In an ironic twist of fate, Sullivan, who had been a heavy drinker, gave up alcohol and became a speaker in favor of the temperance movement. The Great John L. remained a celebrity until his death from a heart attack in 1918.

Sullivan was five foot 10 inches tall and had a 74-inch **reach**. He fought at weights ranging from 190 to 229 pounds as a heavyweight. His boxing record is somewhat sketchy insofar as separating exhibition bouts from real bouts, and is also somewhat muddied by his boxing both bareknuckle and gloved contests, but his record for gloved contests as reported by Boxrec is 41 professional bouts, from 1879 to 1892, with 38 won (32 by knockout), one loss by knockout, one **draw**, and one **no contest**, and a total of 131 rounds fought. He was inducted as a member of the inaugural class of the **International Boxing Hall of Fame** in 1990.

SUNNYSIDE GARDEN. Sunnyside Garden (often misspelled Gardens) was one of New York City's neighborhood **fight clubs**. (Although the sign outside the building said "Sunnyside Garden Arena," no one ever referred to it by its full name—it was called just Sunnyside or Sunnyside Garden.) It was located in the Sunnyside section of the borough of Queens on Roosevelt Avenue between 44th and 45th Streets, underneath the Flushing line elevated subway's Bliss Street station. Its capacity was only about 2,400, but it was often filled, especially for New York **Golden Gloves bouts**.

It was originally built in 1926 as a private indoor tennis facility for millionaire Jay Gould, but after World War II it was no longer used for tennis and boxing became its main attraction, although at times **professional** wrestling and even roller derby matches were held there. It managed to survive until 24 June 1977 and was the last small fight club in New York. Although it never held a world championship bout, many top-notch fighters and world champions had their start there, including Vito Antuofermo, Óscar Bonavena, **Gerry Cooney**, Alfredo Escalera, Mustafa Hamsho, **Ralph "Tiger" Jones**, **José Torres**, Rodrigo Valdéz, and Eddie Mustafa Muhammad (then known as Eddie Gregory) , and as amateurs, **Floyd Patterson** and **Emile Griffith**. **Light heavyweight** champion Harold Johnson fought the last bout of his career there. Local **heavyweight** Irish Bobby Cassidy fought there 21 times—more than any other top boxer.

It was demolished in December 1977 and is now the site of a hamburger franchise.

See also BLUE HORIZON; FELT FORUM; ST. NICHOLAS ARENA.

SUPER BANTAMWEIGHT. Super bantamweight (sometimes called junior featherweight) is a boxing weight class in which the contestants cannot exceed 122 pounds. The **World Boxing Council** was the first sanctioning organization to recognize this class, and their first champion in this division was the **Panamanian** Rigoberto Riasco, who defeated the Kenyan-born **Japanese** fighter Waruinge Nakayama on a ninth-**round technical knockout** in Panama on 3 April 1976.

Among the best super bantamweights have been Marco Antonio Barrera, Celestino Caballero, Jeff Fenech, **Wilfredo Gómez**, Joan Guzmán, Kennedy McKinney, Steve Molitor, Erik Morales, **Manny Pacquiao**, Tracy Harris Patterson (**Floyd Patterson's** adopted son), Ismail Vásquez, and Daniel Zaragoza.

SUPER FEATHERWEIGHT. Super featherweight (more commonly known throughout boxing history as junior lightweight) is a boxing weight class in which the contestants cannot exceed 130 pounds. The class was first recognized (as junior lightweight) when Italian American Johnny Dundee defeated George "KO" Chaney on a fifth-**round disqualification** on 18 November 1921. The class was active through 1935, when champion **Barney Ross** vacated it in pursuit of heavier weight classes.

It was resurrected in 1959 when the **National Boxing Association** (forerunner of the present-day **World Boxing Association**) recognized Rhode Islander Harold Gomes as the division's champion following his win over Texan Paul Jorgensen on a 15-round **unanimous decision**.

Among the best super featherweights have been **Alexis Argüello**, **Julio César Chávez**, **Kid Chocolate**, Johnny Dundee, Gabriel "Flash" Elorde, Hiroshi Kobayashi, Rocky Lockridge, **Floyd Mayweather Jr.**, Brian Mitchell, John John Molina, **Azumah Nelson**, Barney Ross, and Samuel Serrano.

SUPER FLYWEIGHT. Super flyweight (sometimes called junior bantamweight) is a boxing weight class in which the contestants cannot exceed 115 pounds. The **World Boxing Council** was the first sanctioning organization to recognize this class, and their first champion in this division was the **Venezuelan** Rafael Orono, who defeated the **Korean** Seung-Hoon Lee on 2 February 1980 in Caracas, Venezuela, on a 15-**round split decision** to win the title.

Among the best super flyweights have been Vic Darchinyan, Khaosai Galaxy, Mark Johnson, Cristian Mijares, Alexander Muñoz, Luis Alberto Pérez, Ellyas Pical, Gilberto Roman, Danny Romero, Johnny Tapia, Masumori Tokuyama, and Jiro Watanabe.

SUPER HEAVYWEIGHT. Super heavyweight is the name given to the unlimited weight division in **amateur boxing**. Until 1984, the unlimited division in amateur boxing (over 175 pounds) was referred to as the **heavyweight** division, but in that year a new category for boxers between 175 and 201 pounds was added. That division was called heavyweight, and the former unlimited division, now over 201 pounds, was renamed the super heavyweight class. **Professional boxing** does not use that terminology, but its weight class between 175 and 200 is called the **cruiserweight** division.

See also KLITSCHKO, VOLODOMYR VOLODOMYROVICH "WLADIMIR," "DR. STEELHAMMER"; LEWIS, LENNOX CLAUDIUS "THE LION".

SUPER LIGHTWEIGHT. *See* LIGHT WELTERWEIGHT.

SUPER MIDDLEWEIGHT. Super middleweight (sometimes called junior light heavyweight) is a boxing weight class in which the contestants cannot exceed 168 pounds. The **International Boxing Federation** was the first sanctioning organization to recognize this class, and their first champion in this division was the Scotsman Murray Sutherland, who defeated Philadelphian Ernie Singletary by **unanimous decision** in **Atlantic City**, New Jersey, on 28 March 1984. Among the best super middleweights have been Nigel Benn, Markus Beyer, **Joe Calzaghe**, **Roy Jones Jr.**, Mikkel Kessler, Anthony Mundine, Sven Ottke, Chong-Pal Park, Graciano Rocchigiani, and Andre Ward.

SUPER WEIGHT CLASSES. With the rise to power of the **World Boxing Council (WBC)**, **World Boxing Association (WBA)**, and other boxing sanctioning organizations, they discovered that by adding additional boxing weight classes they could make more money since they charged sanctioning fees for world championship bouts. By creating additional weight classes with weight limits in between the existing ones, they could double their profits. Initially, the WBA referred to them as "junior" classes, but the WBC called them "super" weight classes, although in recent years both WBC and WBA use the "super" prefix while the **International Boxing Federation** and **World Boxing Organization** use the "junior" one. Thus a boxer competing in the division between the 112-pound **flyweight** and 118-pound **bantamweight** at the division limit of 115 pounds was either a "**junior bantamweight**" or a "**super flyweight**." To add to the confusion in terminology, some classes (especially in **amateur boxing**) are called "light" classes, such as "**light welterweight**" or "**light middleweight**."

SUPER WELTERWEIGHT. *See* LIGHT MIDDLEWEIGHT.

T

TAKE A DIVE. Throughout boxing history, there have been many instances in which a fighter deliberately allows himself to be **knocked down** and counted out. This action is known as "taking a dive." It is usually done when he is paid to do so by gamblers who have bet on his opponent, but there have been instances when the fighter simply knew he was outclassed and did not want to suffer a physical beating. It is also sometimes referred to as "throwing a fight."

TECHNICAL DECISION. A technical decision occurs in some boxing jurisdictions when a **bout** is stopped short of the distance due to an accidental cut. If the bout goes more than three **rounds**, the **judges'** scorecards are consulted, and the boxer leading on **points** at that time is awarded the victory by technical decision.

TECHNICAL KNOCKOUT (TKO). A technical **knockout** occurs when the **bout** is stopped prior to the scheduled distance when a fighter is not **knocked down** and counted out. It can be stopped by a boxer refusing to continue, by the **referee** deciding that a boxer is not defending himself or has taken too much punishment, by the **ring** physician deciding that a boxer should not continue for fear of severe damage, or by the boxer's **seconds** who feel that their man is taking too much of a beating. It is also referred to as a stoppage. In **amateur boxing**, the result is recorded as RSC (referee stops contest).

TELEVISED BOXING. When commercial television first began in the late 1940s, one of the most popular shows was boxing. It was easy to televise since all the action took place in a relatively small area. Boxing matches then were plentiful, as many arenas had weekly boxing **cards**. The first owners of television sets were often bars, and boxing was a big attraction for bar patrons.

Television, however, proved to be the downfall of the small boxing club, as fans stayed home to watch boxing on television and live attendance dwindled. By the 1960s, many of the small boxing clubs closed, although boxing could be seen on network television two or three times each week.

In the 1960s, the death of **Benny "Kid" Paret** at the hands of **Emile Griffith** on live television almost brought an end to televised boxing. But as the decade moved on, it was quickly forgotten and the story of **Muhammad Ali** made for good television. Unlike some of the previous **heavyweight** champions, Ali kept busy and fought several heavyweight championship **bouts** each year. Network television covered them, and it brought a resurgence to televised boxing.

The American Broadcasting Company (ABC) television network, with **Howard Cosell** as announcer, began broadcasting boxing on a regular basis, and the **United States'** success at the 1976 Olympic boxing tournament helped increase the networks' interest in covering live boxing.

During the 1980s, though, the televised death of Deuk-Koo Kim in his bout against **Ray Mancini**, coupled with the rise of cable television, quickly ended the networks' interest in the sport. Boxing became a staple of cable television on Home Box Office, Showtime, Entertainment and Sports Programming Network, and the USA networks and virtually disappeared from the noncable networks such as Columbia Broadcasting System, National Broadcasting Company, and ABC.

By the 21st century, the concept of pay-per-view, where home television viewers must pay to watch an individual event, has caused boxing to virtually disappear from cable television and has helped cause a decline in interest in the sport.

THAILAND. Boxing in Thailand is quite a popular sport, both the traditional style that is practiced worldwide and the Thai variant of **Muay Thai** (a form of kickboxing) being among of the country's favorite sporting events. In **amateur boxing**, Thai boxers first competed in the 1956 **Olympic Games** and have entered 14 Olympic boxing tournaments. Thai boxers have won 14 Olympic medals, winning medals in nearly every class from **light flyweight** to **middleweight**. Wijan Ponlid in 2000 and Somjit Jongjohor in 2008 were **flyweight** gold medalists, Somluck Kamsing (one of the few four-time Olympic boxers) was a 1996 **featherweight** gold medalist, and Manus Boomjunong was the 2004 **light welterweight** champion. He also won a **silver medal** in 2008.

It is common in Thailand for professional boxers to discard their given names in favor of **ring** names, and few Thai boxers are known by their real names. The first **professional** world champion from Thailand was Pone Kingpetch, who was flyweight champion from 1960 to 1962, rewon the title in 1963, held it for nine months, regained it again in 1964, and held it for one more year. In 1966, Chartchai Chionoi became Thailand's second world champion, also in the flyweight division. He held the **World Boxing Council** title until 1969, rewon it in March 1970, lost it in December 1970, won the **World Boxing Association** title in 1973, and finally lost it in 1974.

Other Thai boxing champions include Venice Borkhorsor, Sot Chitalada, the Galaxy twins Khaosai and Kaokor, Muangchai Kittikasem, Saensak Muangsurin, Netrnoi Sor Vorasingh, and Pongsaklek Wonjongkam.

Khaosai Galaxy was inducted into the **International Boxing Hall of Fame** in 1999.

THOMPSON, WILLIAM ABEDNEGO. See BENDIGO (né WILLIAM ABEDNEGO THOMPSON).

THRILLA IN MANILA. See ALI–FRAZIER TRILOGY.

THROW A FIGHT. See TAKE A DIVE.

THROW IN THE TOWEL. In earlier days in **professional boxing**, if a boxer's seconds thought that he was being badly beaten, they would throw a towel into the **ring** as a sign of surrender. In modern-day boxing, only the **referee** or ring doctor can stop the **bout**, and if a towel is thrown into the ring by the **corner**, the referee will disregard it, although he should seriously consider the state of the boxer and generally does stop the match.

This expression, originating in the boxing ring, has made its way into the language, and the phrase "throw in the towel" is often used to mean surrender or resign.

TIBBS, TOMMY. B. 23 July 1934, Lancaster, Ohio. D. 15 May 1975, Roxbury, Massachusetts. Tommy Tibbs is a name probably unknown to most sports fans and is a fighter remembered by only the most ardent boxing fans, yet from 1949 to 1972 he was one of boxing's most active fighters who never failed to compete, even though he was on the short end of more than half his boxing **bouts**.

He began his **professional boxing** career on 13 May 1949 with a four-**round decision** victory over Joe Brian in Columbus, Ohio. After winning his second bout, he began a stretch of 17 bouts in 1950 and 1951 in which he won only two, lost 13, and drew two, fighting mostly in Ohio and West Virginia. Undaunted, Tibbs continued boxing in the **featherweight** class and would win a few and lose a few, almost always by decision.

In 1952, he moved to New England and fought in that area for most of the rest of his career. On 21 April 1952, he lost a six-round decision to Harold Gomes, who was undefeated at that time and would later win the **junior**

lightweight championship. Tibbs was a very active fighter, often fighting weekly during this time. By 1953, he had progressed to 10-round **main events**, winning as often as he lost. On 28 January 1954, he ended Gomes's undefeated streak at 22 when he won a 10-round decision over Gomes. He fought Gomes twice more that year and won both times by **knockout** or **technical knockout**.

Tibbs fought three bouts with former lightweight champion Lauro Salas in 1956 and 1957, winning one, losing one, and drawing one. Possibly the biggest win in Tibbs's career was a 10-round **split-decision** victory on 14 January 1958 over former featherweight champion **Willie Pep**, a man considered by boxing historians **Bert Randolph Sugar** and **Teddy Atlas** to be the third best pound-for-pound fighter of all time.

Tibbs was quite inconsistent, though, and following the Pep win he lost seven consecutive bouts and nine of 11, usually by decision. At this point in his career, he was a quite popular selection as an opponent for many promoters, and over the next 10 years he fought in **Mexico, Canada**, Hawaii, the **Philippines, Cuba, England**, Jamaica, **Puerto Rico, Italy, France, South Africa**, and **Australia** as well as **Madison Square Garden** and never failed to give the fans their money's worth even though he lost as many bouts as he won.

He never fought for a major championship, although on 29 June 1959 he fought and defeated Tommy Garrow in a 12-round bout billed for the New England **lightweight** title. He defended it once successfully before losing it in 1963. He ended his career with an 11-bout losing streak, retiring in 1967 but returned to the **ring** for a final bout in 1972.

As was the case with many boxers, he came to a tragic end when, after a dispute, he was shot to death outside a bar in Roxbury, Massachusetts, in 1975.

Tibbs was five foot four inches tall and fought at weights ranging from 120 to 138 pounds, primarily as a featherweight and lightweight. In 142 professional bouts, from 1949 to 1972, he won 60 (14 by knockout), lost 78 (eight by knockout), had four draws, and fought a total of 1,150 rounds.

TIGER, DICK (né RICHARD IHETU). B. 14 August 1929, Amaigbo, Nigeria. D. 14 December 1971, Aba, Nigeria. Dick Tiger began his **professional boxing** career in Nigeria on 1 January 1952. During his early career in Africa, he fought fighters with names like Easy Dynamite, Lion Ring, Koko Kid, Blackie Power, Mighty Joe, and Super Human Power. After compiling a record of 14–3, with all three defeats coming at the hands of Tommy West, Tiger traveled to Liverpool, **England**, in December 1955. Tiger then lost his next four **bouts** in Liverpool but then turned his career around and won 15 of his next 18 bouts, earning him a shot at the British Empire **middleweight**

title on 27 March 1958. On that date in Liverpool, he knocked out Pat McAteer in the ninth **round** to win the first of many titles in his boxing career.

After splitting two bouts with former New York **Golden Gloves welter-weight** champion Randy Sandy in England, Tiger came to the **United States** in June 1959. For the rest of his boxing career, which lasted until 1970, Tiger fought nearly all of his bouts in the United States. In the rest of 1959, Tiger fared well against several of the top middleweights and drew and lost to Rory Calhoun, split two bouts with future middleweight champion **Joey Giardel-lo**, and defeated Gene Armstrong twice and Holly Mims and Victor Zalazar once each in his first 10 months in the United States.

On 22 June 1960, he traveled to Edmonton, Alberta, **Canada**, and lost his British Empire title via a 15-round **split decision** to Wilfie Greaves. Five months later, he stopped Greaves in nine rounds and regained his title. After six more winning fights against top middleweights, Tiger was matched with **Gene Fullmer** for the **World Boxing Association** world middleweight title at Candlestick Park in San Francisco on 23 October 1962. Tiger won a **unanimous decision** and the world middleweight title and was named "Fighter of the Year" by *Ring* **magazine**. Tiger's next two fights were also with Fullmer—a 15-round **draw** in **Las Vegas** in February 1963 and a seven-round **technical knockout** over Fullmer in August 1963 in the first world championship bout ever held in Nigeria.

Returning to the United States in December, Tiger lost his title to Joey Giardello by **decision** in 15 rounds in **Atlantic City**, New Jersey. It took Tiger two years to gain a rematch with Giardello, but when he did, on 21 October 1965 in **Madison Square Garden**, Tiger comfortably won a 15-round unanimous decision and regained the world middleweight title. Less than a year later, on 25 April 1966 also at the Garden, Tiger was defeated by former welterweight champion **Emile Griffith** on a unanimous 15-round decision.

Tiger then moved up in weight and challenged **light heavyweight** cham-pion **José Torres**. Although he only weighed 167 pounds, eight pounds under the light heavyweight limit, Tiger easily outpointed Torres on 16 De-cember 1966 at Madison Square Garden and added the world's light heavy-weight championship to his list of boxing titles. He successfully defended it twice before being knocked out by **Bob Foster** on 24 May 1968 in Madison Square Garden.

Tiger's next fight on 25 October 1968 against Frankie DePaula was named the *Ring* magazine "Fight of the Year" even though it was only a 10-round **nontitle bout**. Tiger was knocked down twice in the second round and got up to knock DePaula down twice in the third round. Both fighters remained on their feet for the rest of the fight, which Tiger won on a unanimous decision. Tiger fought three more fights in his career—all 10-round nontitle main events at Madison Square Garden—defeating former middleweight champion **Nino Benvenuti** and Andy Kendall and losing to Emile Griffith, all three bouts by unanimous decision.

After retiring from the ring, Tiger gave his efforts to support Biafra in its fight for independence from Nigeria. He then worked briefly as a guard at the Metropolitan Museum of Art in New York but then returned to Nigeria, where he died of liver cancer at the age of 42 in 1972.

Tiger was five foot eight inches tall and had a 71-inch **reach**. He fought at weights ranging from 158 to 168 pounds as a middleweight and light heavyweight. In 82 professional bouts, from 1952 to 1970, he won 60 (27 by **knockout**), lost 19 (two by knockout), and fought a total of 677 rounds. He was inducted into the **International Boxing Hall of Fame** in 1991.

TILELLI, CARMINE ORLANDO. *See* GIARDELLO, JOEY (né CARMINE ORLANDO TILELLI).

TONEY, JAMES NATHANIEL "LIGHTS OUT". B. 24 August 1968, Grand Rapids, Michigan. James Toney is one of the few boxers to be successful as a **middleweight, light heavyweight**, and **heavyweight**. In his 25-year **professional boxing** career, he has fought at weights ranging from 157 to 257 pounds.

A graduate of Huron High School in Ann Arbor, Michigan, he had college scholarship offers to play football but injured an ankle and did not pursue them. He had a good career as an **amateur** boxer, with a reported record of 33–2 with 32 **knockouts** and various local amateur championships in 1983, 1984, 1987, and 1988.

His first **bout** as a professional boxer was on 26 October 1988 in Mount Clemens, Michigan, where as a 160-pound middleweight he stopped Stephen Lee in two **rounds**. Toney won his first 19 bouts, 14 by knockout, and in his 20th victory won the **International Boxing Council** middleweight title—not one of the more prestigious titles.

In his 21st bout, Toney was held to a 10-round **majority decision** by Sanderline Williams, a competent but not exceptional boxer with a 24–11 record at the time. In a rematch three months later, Toney won a **unanimous decision** over Williams. After three more victories, Toney, weighing only 157 pounds, fought Michael "Second To" Nunn for the **International Boxing Federation (IBF)** middleweight championship—one of the four that are most widely recognized by the boxing world. The 12-round bout took place on 10 May 1991 in Davenport, Iowa—not one of the major boxing towns—and was won by Toney on an 11th-round **technical knockout**.

Toney successfully defended that title against Reggie Johnson in **Las Vegas** and Francesco d'Aquila in Monte Carlo, Monaco, then fought a 12-round **draw** with **World Boxing Association (WBA)** middleweight champion Mike McCallum on 13 December 1991. Toney's success in 1991 earned his recognition by *Ring* **magazine** as "Fighter of the Year." In a rematch with McCallum on 29 August 1992, Toney was the victor by a majority decision.

Toney then moved up in weight and won the IBF **super middleweight** title by stopping Iran Barkley in nine rounds on 13 February 1992. After seven nontitle victories and three super middleweight title defenses, the undefeated Toney (44–0–2) faced the undefeated **Roy Jones Jr.** (26–0) on 18 November 1994. Jones dominated the fight, and Toney's undefeated streak came to an end, along with his reign as super middleweight champion.

Toney then moved up in weight and began fighting in the light heavyweight division, with his first fight in that class a 12-round majority decision loss to Montell Griffin for the IBF Inter-Continental light heavyweight title, one of boxing's useless titles, created solely to make the bout appear to be a "championship" bout. After two victories as a light heavyweight, Toney won the World Boxing Union (WBU) (another sanctioning organization with little credibility) light heavyweight title by stopping Freddie Delgado in five rounds. After one defense of that title, Toney moved up in weight again and fought at 189 pounds for the WBU Continental **cruiserweight** title. In his next fight, Toney had ballooned up to 200 pounds for a **nontitle bout**. He then dropped back to the light heavyweight limit up 175 and made three successful title defenses.

On 22 February 1997, Toney fought McCallum for the third time, this time for the WBU cruiserweight title. Toney ended McCallum's boxing career with a 12-round unanimous decision. Three months later, Toney fought Drake Thadzi for the International Boxing Organization (IBO) light heavyweight title. Although Toney lost a majority decision to Thadzi, he was over the light heavyweight limit and would not have won the title had he won the fight.

On 14 June 1997, Toney won the IBO cruiserweight title by defeating Steve Little by unanimous decision. He then fought a series of nontitle bouts and on 26 April 2003 won the IBF cruiserweight title with a unanimous-decision victory over the previously undefeated (31–0) Vassily Jirov. On 4 October 2003, Toney, now weighing 217 pounds, stopped former heavyweight champion **Evander Holyfield** in nine rounds in a nontitle bout scheduled for 12 rounds. This earned him recognition by *Ring* magazine again as "Fighter of the Year."

On 23 September 2004, Toney, now up to 227 pounds, won the **International Boxing Association (IBA)** heavyweight championship with a 12-round unanimous decision over previously undefeated (22–0) Rydell Booker. Toney now became the first man to win titles in each of the five weight classes from middleweight to heavyweight, although some of the titles were from lesser sanctioning organizations. In his next bout, Toney won the more prestigious WBA world heavyweight championship with a 12-round unanimous decision over John Ruiz. But after the bout, it was discovered that Toney tested positive for a banned substance (the anabolic steroid stanozol), and the result of the fight was changed to "**no contest**" and Toney stripped of his title.

Toney then defeated Dominic Guinn in an IBA heavyweight title defense and fought a **draw** with Hasim Rahman for Rahman's **World Boxing Council** heavyweight championship. Toney lost his next two fights with Samuel Peter by **split decision** and unanimous decision. On 24 May 2007, Toney won a 10-round **decision** over Danny Batchelder and again tested positive for a banned substance. He was banned from boxing for one year but managed to have the ban reduced to six months after claiming that he was set up and his water bottle tampered with.

His next bout was a rematch with Rahman, which was stopped in the third round due to a severe cut suffered by Rahman. The cut was ruled to have been caused by an accidental clash of heads and the bout was ruled no contest. After winning two more bouts, Toney, weighing 257 pounds, easily defeated Damon Reed on 24 February 2011.

Less than nine months later, after probably setting a record for the greatest weight loss between bouts, Toney weighed only 199 pounds for a **cruiserweight** bout with Denis Lebedev in Moscow, **Russia**, which Toney lost on a unanimous decision. In Toney's next bout on 7 April 2012, he was back to 248 pounds and stopped Bobby Gunn in five rounds. As of 2012, Toney, now 44 years old, still has not announced his retirement.

In 2010, Toney attempted to compete in **mixed martial arts** but lost his only bout in August by a first-round submission. In 2001, Toney had one of the leading roles in the film biography *Ali*, playing the part of **Joe Frazier**.

Toney is five foot 10 inches tall and has a 72-inch **reach**. He has fought at weights ranging from 157 to 257 pounds in weight classes ranging from middleweight to heavyweight. In 86 professional bouts, from 1988 to 2012, he won 74 (45 by knockout), lost seven (none by knockout), had three draws and two no contests, and fought a total of 646 rounds.

TORRES, JOSÉ "CHEGÜI". B. 3 May 1936, Ponce, **Puerto Rico**. D. 19 January 2009, Ponce, Puerto Rico. José Torres was an accomplished person on many levels. He was an Olympic **silver medalist**, New York **Golden Gloves** champion, **professional** world champion, author, commissioner of the **New York State Athletic Commission**, community leader, president of the **World Boxing Organization**, and national anthem singer.

He began boxing while in the U.S. Army and represented the **United States** in the 1956 **Olympic Games**. After winning his first three **bouts** in the **light middleweight** division, he met two-time Olympic champion **László Papp** in the final. Papp prevailed by **decision** and became the first boxer to win three Olympic gold medals—a feat duplicated only twice since by **Cubans Teófilo Stevenson** and **Félix Savon**. After the Olympic Games, Torres returned to the army and boxed two more years as an **amateur**, winning the 1958 New York Golden Gloves as a representative of the Empire Sporting Club, the Eastern Regionals Golden Gloves, and the Intercity Golden Gloves tournaments in the **middleweight** division. He also won the National **Amateur Athletic Union** tournament in 1958.

He fought his first professional bout on 24 May 1958, with a one-**round knockout** of Gene Hamilton at the Eastern Parkway Arena in Brooklyn, New York. After winning his first 13 bouts (11 by knockout), mostly in the New York City area, he traveled to Puerto Rico, where he fought a 10-round **draw** with future **welterweight** champion **Benny "Kid" Paret**. Torres won his next 11 bouts (eight by knockout) and returned to San Juan, Puerto Rico, with a record of 24–0–1 to fight Obdulio Nuñez for the Puerto Rican middleweight championship on 27 July 1962. He knocked out Nuñez in the seventh round of their scheduled 12-round bout.

After winning one more bout, Torres suffered his first loss and the only loss of his career in which he did not finish the fight. Hard-hitting Cuban Florentino Fernández knocked Torres down twice before stopping Torres in the fifth round of their 25 May 1963 bout in San Juan. Torres won his next eight bouts, including a one-round knockout of former middleweight champion **Carl "Bobo" Olson**.

On 30 March 1965, Torres, managed by **Cus D'Amato**, stopped Willie Pastrano after nine rounds and became the world's **light heavyweight** champion. Torres made three successful defenses before losing his championship by unanimous decision to **Dick Tiger** on 16 December 1966 at **Madison Square Garden**. Six months later, Torres failed in an attempt to regain the title on a **split decision** also at the Garden.

Torres fought just twice more after that—the first was a six-round **technical knockout** victory over **Australian** Bob Dunlop in Melbourne in 1968. In his last fight, Torres was knocked down in both the first and second rounds before getting up and scoring a two-round knockout of Charlie Green at Madison Square Garden on 14 July 1969.

After retiring from the **ring**, Torres led a busy life. He authored books on **Muhammad Ali** and **Mike Tyson** and wrote columns in English for the *Village Voice* as well as in Spanish for *El Diario La Prensa*, both New York City newspapers. He became a leader of the Puerto Rican community in New York. From 1984 to 1988, he was the commissioner of boxing for the New York State Athletic Commission. In 1986, he sang the national anthem before a **lightweight** championship bout in **Atlantic City**. From 1990 to 1995, he was the president of the World Boxing Organization. In 2007, he moved back from New York to his hometown of Ponce, Puerto Rico, to concentrate on writing, but he died two years later of a heart attack.

Torres was five foot 10 inches tall and had a 74-inch **reach**. He fought at weights ranging from 158 to 182 pounds as a middleweight and light heavyweight. In 45 professional bouts, from 1958 to 1969, he won 41 (29 by knockout), lost three (one by knockout), had one **draw**, and fought a total of 300 rounds. He was inducted into the **International Boxing Hall of Fame** in 1997.

TOUGHMAN COMPETITION. Toughman contests were originated by boxing promoter Art Dore in Bay City, Michigan, in 1979. They were open to men who had not won more than five fights previously in public competition. Three one-minute **rounds**, with one-minute rest periods, are fought wearing 16-ounce **gloves** and headgear. The name has been trademarked, and competitions have been fought in several states, usually in a tournament format. Several men who competed in toughman contests later became professional boxers in ordinary boxing competition, such as Grady Brewer, **Eric "Butterbean" Esch**, and Tommy Morrison.

TRAINER. A trainer is one of the most important assistants that a boxer has. Not only does he supervise a boxer's preparations for upcoming matches, he also works as an instructor, teaching skills and tactics necessary for the boxer to be successful. A good trainer also serves as a boxer's confidant and at times will be used as a cheerleader to help a boxer's mental preparations for a bout. Some trainers specialize in handling cuts and other injuries that a boxer might incur during a fight and are called **cutmen**. A few trainers also serve as a boxer's manager and schedule bouts and negotiate contracts with boxing promoters.

Some of the sport's best trainers include **Ray Arcel, Teddy Atlas**, Tony Ayala Sr., **George Benton**, Whitey Bimstein, Jack Blackburn, Chuck Bodak, Drew "Bundini" Brown, **Gil Clancy, Cus D'Amato, Angelo Dundee**, Lou Duva, Eddie Futch, Richie Giachetti, Charlie Goldman, Panama Lewis, Floyd Mayweather Sr., Buddy McGirt, **Dr. Ferdie Pacheco**, Goody Petronelli, Freddie Roach, Kevin Rooney, **Emanuel Steward**, and Victor Vallee.

Trainers elected to the **International Boxing Hall of Fame** are Bimstein, Clancy, Duva, Futch, Goldman, Roach, and Steward.

TRAINING. In most sports, the methods of training used in the early 20th century have changed dramatically during the past 100 years. All sorts of sophisticated gym equipment have been developed, and modern athletes undergo quite different training routines than their counterparts of a century ago.

Not so in boxing. A 21st-century boxer generally does the same type of training regiment that his predecessors did 100 years ago. They have traditionally done roadwork (jogging several miles daily—usually in the early morning hours). They have also used a light punching bag or speed bag to practice throwing punches rapidly and a heavy bag to practice power punches. They will jump rope rapidly to improve footwork, shadow box (practice throwing punches at an invisible opponent), and have **sparring** sessions with a real opponent. Since most boxers (with the exception of heavyweights) must weigh-in at a specified weight limit for each **bout**, they watch their diets carefully. Boxers normally train daily regardless of whether or not they have a future fight scheduled. Most boxers employ a **trainer** to help them work out and advise them on boxing technique.

See also STILLMAN'S GYM.

TRINIDAD GARCÍA, FÉLIX JUAN, JR., "TITO". B. 10 January 1973, Fajardo, **Puerto Rico**. Félix Trinidad Jr. is the son of a professional boxer. Félix Trinidad Sr. was a competent boxer who fought mostly in Puerto Rico from 1975 to 1981 and won the Puerto Rico **featherweight** title. In his only fight on the mainland, in Houston, Texas, he fought Salvador Sánchez, who six months after they fought became the world's featherweight champion.

Félix Jr. began **professional boxing** in 1990 at the age of 17. His first **bout** was on 10 March, and he **knocked out** Ángel Romero in two **rounds** at Miramar, Puerto Rico. After winning his first 15 fights in Puerto Rico and Miami, Florida, he traveled to Paris, **France**, where he stopped Alberto de las Mercedes Cortes in three rounds, although Trinidad himself was **knocked down** in the second round. After winning three more bouts by knockout, Trinidad (with a record of 19–0 and 16 knockouts) faced Maurice Blocker for the **International Boxing Federation (IBF) welterweight** title. Trinidad knocked out Blocker in two rounds on 19 June 1993 in San Diego and became the new IBF world welterweight champion.

Trinidad defended his title 14 times from 1993 to 1999, including victories over former three-division champion **Héctor Camacho** (29 January 1994, **unanimous decision**); previously undefeated (56–0) Luis Ramón Campas (17 September 1994, **technical knockout** [TKO] round 4); previously undefeated (32–0) Oba Carr (10 December 1994, TKO 8); and former four-division champion **Pernell Whitaker** (20 February 1999, unanimous decision).

On 18 September 1999, Trinidad met **World Boxing Council (WBC)** welterweight champion **Óscar De La Hoya** in **Las Vegas** and gained that title also by winning a 12-round unanimous decision. In his next fight, Trinidad moved up in weight class and won the **World Boxing Association (WBA) light middleweight** championship with a 12-round unanimous decision over David Reid. After two defenses of that title, Trinidad fought William Joppy for the WBA **middleweight** championship. He stopped Joppy in five rounds to win his third world championship title.

On 21 September 2001, Trinidad fought **Bernard Hopkins**, then holder of the WBC and IBF middleweight crowns. Hopkins stopped Trinidad in the 12th round of their fight at **Madison Square Garden**. Trinidad has fought sparingly since then.

He won one bout in 2002, another in 2004, and was defeated by Ronald "Winky" Wright in 2005. He then announced his retirement, but three years later fought **Roy Jones Jr.**, losing a 12-round decision to Jones.

In 2009, Trinidad became involved with professional wrestling in the capacity of **referee**.

Trinidad is five foot 11 inches tall and has a 72-inch **reach**. He fought at weights ranging from 138 to 170 pounds, primarily as a welterweight and middleweight. In 45 professional bouts, from 1990 to 2008, he won 42 (35 by knockout), lost three (one by knockout), and fought a total of 238 rounds.

TSZYU, KONSTANTIN BORISOVICH "KOSTYA," "THUNDER FROM DOWN UNDER". B. 19 September 1969, Serov, **Russia, Union of Soviet Socialist Republics**. Kostya Tszyu is of mixed **Korean**–Russian parentage and started boxing at the age of nine in Russia. He compiled an outstanding record reported to be 259–11 as an **amateur** boxer for the Soviet Union. He won the 1986 Junior European **featherweight** championship, won a **silver medal** at the 1987 Junior World Championships as a **lightweight**, competed in the 1988 **Olympic Games** but lost his third **bout** in the lightweight class, won the 1989 and 1991 European Championships, and won the Goodwill Games in 1990 and the 1991 **World Championships**.

He immigrated to **Australia** following the collapse of the Soviet Union in 1992 and had his first **professional** bout there in Melbourne on 1 March 1992, a first-**round technical knockout** of Darrell Hiles in the **light welterweight** class. He won his next five bouts in Australia, four by **knockout**, and was brought to the **United States**. He won his first bout there on 30 January 1993 on a second-round technical knockout and then returned to Australia, where he won three more, including a 10-round **unanimous decision** over former lightweight champion **Livingstone Bramble**. After three more victories, one in the United States and two in Australia, he stopped Jake Rodríguez in six rounds in **Las Vegas** on 28 January 1995 and won the **International Boxing Federation (IBF)** light welterweight title.

He successfully defended that title four times in Australia, including a 12-round unanimous decision over former light welterweight champion Roger Mayweather. He returned to the United States for a title defense against Leonardo Mas in Las Vegas, which was ruled a **no contest** after Tszyu knocked out Mas in the first round but Mas's **cornermen** complained that the knockout blow was thrown after referee **Joe Cortez** gave the command to break. The Nevada Athletic **Commission** was unsure and declared the bout no contest. Four months later, Tszyu lost his title to Vince Phillips in **Atlantic City** via a 10-round technical knockout.

Tszyu then won four bouts by knockout and on 21 August 1999 in Miami, Florida, regained the light welterweight title by stopping Miguel Ángel González in 10 rounds. In his next bout, Tszyu successfully defended against Ahmed Santos in Connecticut with an eighth-round technical knockout. On 29 July 2000 in Phoenix, defended against the legendary **Julio César Chávez**, who entered the **ring** with a record of 103–4–2 but was 38 years old and had lost two of his previous five bouts. Tszyu stopped Chávez in the sixth round.

Tszyu, the holder of the **World Boxing Council (WBC)** version of the light welterweight title, then challenged the **World Boxing Association (WBA)** light welterweight champion, Sharmba Mitchell. Kostya added that belt to his collection by stopping Mitchell in seven rounds on 3 February 2001 in Las Vegas. After a successful defense of both titles against Oksay Urkal, Tszyu then challenged the IBF light welterweight champion, the undefeated (27–0) Zab Judah. After stopping Judah in two rounds, Tszyu then held three of the four widely recognized light welterweight championships. He fought one bout in 2002 and one in 2003, defending all three titles. He won a rematch with Mitchell in 2004, although by this time both the WBC and WBA had stripped Tszyu of their titles, and the bout was solely for the IBF belt.

Tszyu's last fight took place in Manchester, **England**, on 4 June 2005 against the undefeated (38–0) Englishman Ricky Hatton. Tszyu retired in his corner after the 11th round of the scheduled 12-round bout and lost his championship.

Although he has not officially announced his retirement from the ring, Tszyu has not fought since then. He has worked as a **trainer** for several fighters. One of them is Alexander Povetkin, the WBA world **heavyweight** champion.

Tszyu is five foot seven inches tall and has a 67-inch **reach**. He fought at weights ranging from 136 to 141 pounds as a light welterweight. In 34 professional bouts, from 1992 to 2005, Tszyu won 31 (25 by knockout), lost two (both by knockout), had one **no contest** bout, and fought a total of 202 rounds. He was inducted into the **International Boxing Hall of Fame** in 2011.

TUNNEY, JAMES JOSEPH "GENE," "THE FIGHTING MARINE".

B. 25 May 1897, New York, New York. D. 7 November 1978, Greenwich, Connecticut. Gene Tunney is best known for his two memorable **bouts** with **Jack Dempsey** for the world's **heavyweight** championship. Tunney is also the only heavyweight champion whose son became a **United States** senator.

Gene Tunney was raised in the Greenwich Village section of New York City and began boxing at the Greenwich Village Athletic Club. His first **professional** fight was on 3 July 1915. After winning 11 of his first 12 bouts (with a **draw** the only mar on his record), he enlisted in the U.S. Marines on 2 May 1918. He continued boxing while in the service and won the American Expeditionary Forces **light heavyweight** championship in 1919. After his discharge, he resumed his **professional boxing** career and was often billed as "The Fighting Marine."

Tunney built his undefeated record to 40–0–1 and on 23 May 1922 fought **Harry Greb** in a bout billed for the "American light heavyweight" title. In a close fight, Greb outpointed Tunney in 15 rounds at **Madison Square Garden**. This was Tunney's only loss as a professional boxer. Over the next three years, Tunney and Greb would meet four more times in the **ring**, with Tunney winning twice in 1923, the two fighting a draw in 1924, and a "no decision" bout in 1925 in which Tunney received the **newspaper decision**.

One of Tunney's other major victories was a 15th-**round technical knockout** over former world's light heavyweight champion **Georges Carpentier** in a one-sided fight on 24 July 1924. Tunney also scored wins over contenders Tommy Gibbons and Johnny Risko.

On 23 September 1926, one of the largest crowds ever to see a boxing match in person, 120,557, saw Tunney win the world's heavyweight championship on a 10-round **unanimous decision** over Jack Dempsey at Sesquicentennial Stadium in Philadelphia, Pennsylvania. Their rematch, one year later at Soldier Field in Chicago, drew nearly as many fans (104,943) and was also won by Tunney on a 10-round unanimous decision. In the seventh round of that contest, Tunney was knocked down by Dempsey, who forgot the relatively new rule that a boxer who scores a **knockdown** must retreat to a neutral **corner**. He stood over Tunney for several seconds before **referee** Dave Barry sent Dempsey to a neutral corner and then began the count. Tunney got up at the count of nine, although he was actually on the floor for 14 seconds. The gate for the bout was $2,658,660—the first two-million-dollar gate in ring history. For his share, Tunney received $990,000, although he asked for a check for one million dollars and wrote a check for the difference.

Tunney was married in 1928 to a Connecticut socialite, Mary "Polly" Lauder, a relative of industrialist Andrew Carnegie. Tunney promised his wife he would retire after just one more title defense, which he made on 26

July 1928—an 11th-round technical knockout of New Zealander Tom Heeney. Tunney was one of the few champions who retired as undefeated champion and who did not attempt a comeback in the ring.

In retirement, Tunney became involved with several businesses and also owned real estate. He was on the board of directors of several companies and died a very wealthy man. His son, John V. Tunney, a Yale University graduate, was a member of the House of Representatives from 1965 to 1971 and a United States Senator from 1971 to 1977, representing the state of California.

Tunney was six feet tall and had a 76-inch **reach**. He fought at weights ranging from 165 to 192 pounds as a light heavyweight and heavyweight. In 86 professional bouts, from 1915 to 1928, Gene Tunney won 65 (48 by **knockout**), lost one (none by knockout), and had one draw, one **no contest**, and 18 no-decision bouts, in which he was awarded the **newspaper decision** in 15 and drew three. He fought a total of 599 rounds. He was inducted as a member of the inaugural class of the **International Boxing Hall of Fame** in 1990.

TYSON, MICHAEL GERARD "MIKE," "IRON MIKE" (aka MALIK ABDUL-AZIZ). B. 30 June 1966, Brooklyn, New York. When Mike Tyson first began boxing professionally, it appeared that he was going to be the next **Jack Dempsey**, **Joe Louis**, **Rocky Marciano**, and **Muhammad Ali** combined into one invincible fighter. After his first five years, in which he won 37 fights, 33 by **knockout**, these predictions seemed to be true. But then he self-destructed, and the next 15 years saw one negative incident followed by another and his career became one which he summed up in a 2005 interview by saying, "My whole life has been a waste—I've been a failure."

Tyson had a troubled youth and wound up in a reform school in Johnstown, New York. While there, he began boxing, and counselor Bobby Stewart introduced him to **trainer Cus D'Amato**, who ran a gymnasium in Catskill, New York. Cus saw potential in Tyson, and after Mike's mother passed away, Cus adopted Tyson and removed him from the school. Cus, helped by Kevin Rooney and briefly by **Teddy Atlas**, taught Tyson the peek-a-boo style that was used successfully by former **heavyweight** champion **Floyd Patterson**, in which the boxer's **gloves** are held high to protect the face. As an **amateur** boxer, Tyson's record was claimed to be 48–6, although other totals have also been published. He did win the 1984 National **Golden Gloves** heavyweight division and was twice beaten by Henry Tillman in **Olympic** trials.

Cus introduced Tyson to his friends Bill Cayton and **Jim Jacobs**, and they became Tyson's managers as Tyson became a **professional** boxer. His first professional **bout** was on 6 March 1985 in Albany, New York, and Tyson easily scored a first-**round** knockout. D'Amato died on 4 November 1985 and would not see the results of his work with Tyson.

Tyson won his first 19 bouts by knockout before winning 10-round **decisions** over James "Quick" Tillis and Mitch "Blood" Green in May 1986. After six more knockout victories, including one in just 30 seconds over **Joe Frazier's** overmatched son, Marvis Frazier, Tyson was matched with **World Boxing Council (WBC)** heavyweight champion Trevor Berbick on 22 November 1986 in **Las Vegas**. Tyson became the youngest world's heavyweight champion in boxing history at the age of 20 years, four months, and 22 days as he easily won the bout, which was stopped in the second round after Berbick was knocked down twice.

In Tyson's next fight, he won **World Boxing Association (WBA)** recognition as champion when he decisioned James "Bonecrusher" Smith in 12 rounds on 7 March 1987. After a sixth round stoppage of Pinklon Thomas, Tyson won universal recognition as heavyweight champion by decisioning Tony Tucker on 1 August 1987. Over the next two years, Tyson made six successful defenses of his titles, with victories over Tyrell Biggs (16 October 1987, **technical knockout** [TKO] round 7); **Larry Holmes** (22 January 1988, TKO 4); Tony Tubbs (21 March 1988, TKO 2); **Michael Spinks** (27 June 1988, knockout [KO] 1); Frank Bruno (25 February 1989, TKO 5); and Carl Williams (21 July 1989, TKO 1).

Tyson's life changed significantly in 1988 when manager Jim Jacobs died. Jacobs's partner Bill Cayton sold Tyson's managerial contract, and promoter **Don King** began to be the major managerial figure in Tyson's life, although he could not be manager of record as it would be a conflict of interest with his role as promoter. **Trainer** Kevin Rooney was let go by Tyson's new management team, and that would play a significant part in Tyson's future.

On 11 February 1990, Tyson returned to Tokyo, **Japan**, where he had previously defeated Tony Tubbs in March 1988. Tyson was matched with James "Buster" Douglas. In one of the biggest upsets in boxing history, Douglas, a 42–1 underdog, controlled the fight from round one, but was knocked down in the eighth round. He got up from the **knockdown** as the round ended and came back strong in the ninth and 10th rounds. He knocked Tyson down in the 10th round (the first knockdown of Tyson's career), and when Tyson did not appear able to defend himself, **referee** Octavio Meyrán stopped the fight.

Tyson won his next four bouts, and then disaster struck. In July 1991, Tyson was arrested for an alleged rape that occurred when he invited a girl to his hotel room in Indianapolis on 19 July 1991. In February 1992, he was convicted of the charge and sentenced to six years in prison in March 1992.

He was released in March 1995 after serving three years of the sentence. While in prison, he converted to Islam and adopted the name Malik Abdul-Aziz, although unlike some other notable boxers he retained the name Mike Tyson for future boxing matches.

After Tyson was released, he knocked out Peter McNeeley, a relatively unknown boxer whose main claim to fame was that his father, Tom McNeeley, fought Floyd Patterson for the world's heavyweight championship in 1961. Tyson easily stopped McNeeley in the first round. After one more tune-up fight, a three-round knockout of Buster Mathis Jr., Tyson challenged Frank Bruno for the WBC heavyweight title on 16 March 1996 and after stopping Bruno in three rounds regained the title. Tyson won the WBA title on 7 September 1996 by stopping Bruce Seldon in the first round.

Tyson was then stopped in the 11th round by **Evander Holyfield** on 9 November 1996 and never again regained recognition as heavyweight champion, even though he fought for nine more years. On 28 June 1997, Tyson was involved in one of the most bizarre heavyweight title fights. He and Holyfield engaged in a rematch. Early in the fight, the two fighters' heads clashed and Tyson suffered a bad cut over his right eye. In the third round, as the fighters were fighting in close, Tyson suddenly bit a chunk off Holyfield's right ear. Referee **Mills Lane** stopped the fight and deducted two points from the scorecards for Tyson, although Mike claimed the injured ear was caused by a punch. Later in the round, Tyson bit Holyfield's left ear, and after the referee discovered that, he awarded the fight to Holyfield by **disqualification**.

Tyson's last major fight was on 8 June 2002 when he challenged **Lennox Lewis** for the heavyweight title. During a prefight press conference in January 2002 to announce the signing for the match, Tyson and Lewis got into an altercation and both got knocked down. While down, Tyson reportedly bit Lewis on the leg. In the actual fight in June, Lennox won on an eighth-round knockout.

To add to Tyson's legacy of strangeness, in 2003 he had a tattoo etched onto his face. Tyson had three more bouts after the Lennox one and retired after a loss to Kevin McBride on 11 June 2005.

Tyson is five foot 10 inches tall and has a 71-inch **reach**. He fought at weights ranging from 212 to 239 pounds as a heavyweight. In 58 professional bouts, from 1985 to 2005, he won 50 (44 by knockout), lost six (five by knockout), had two **no-contest** bouts, and fought a total of 217 rounds. He was inducted into the **International Boxing Hall of Fame** in 2011.

U

UKRAINE. The Ukraine was one of the former Soviet Socialist Republics, and as such the county's athletes competed for the **Union of Soviet Socialist Republics** until 1992. It has since competed as an independent nation and sent boxing teams to the **Olympic Games** in each of the five tournaments from 1996 to 2012, winning medals in four of the five years. In those five tournaments, the Ukraine has won a total of 14 medals—four **gold**, three **silver**, and seven **bronze**. The gold medalists were Vasyl Lomachenko, who won two gold medals, 2008 **featherweight** and 2012 **lightweight**; Oleksandr Usik, 2012 **heavyweight**; and **Volodomyr Klitschko**, 1996 **super heavyweight**.

Klitschko and his brother, **Vitali**, both have won the heavyweight championship as professional boxers, and Vyacheslav Senchenko, Wladimir Sidorenko (2000 Olympic **flyweight** bronze medalist), Andreas Kotelnik (2000 Olympic lightweight silver medalist), Sergei Dzinziruk, and Yuriy Nuzhenko have also won professional world titles.

UNANIMOUS DECISION. A unanimous decision is one in which all three officials scoring the **bout** agree on the winner.

See also DRAW; MAJORITY DECISION; MAJORITY DRAW; SPLIT DECISION; TECHNICAL DECISION.

UNATTACHED. In **amateur boxing**, fighters usually are affiliated with an athletic club. Those boxers who do not have such affiliations are said to be boxing unattached.

UNDERCARD. Most boxing **cards** have one or two feature **bouts** called **main events**. The cards are supplemented by several other **preliminary bouts** that are collectively referred to as the undercard.

UNION OF SOVIET SOCIALIST REPUBLICS (USSR). Professional **boxing** was not permitted in the Soviet Union, but it excelled in **amateur boxing**. It first competed in the 1952 **Olympic Games** and entered nine

Olympic boxing tournaments—each one from 1952 to 1988 except for 1984, when it boycotted the games. After the breakup of the Soviet Union, a team competing as the "Unified team," consisting of boxers from former Soviet republics, entered the 1992 Olympic Games. Since 1996, **Russia** has competed in each Olympic boxing tournament, and many of the former Soviet Union republics, such as Armenia, Estonia, **Kazakhstan**, Latvia, Lithuania, Moldova, Turkmenistan, and **Uzbekistan**, have each entered Olympic Games boxing teams.

In the nine Olympic boxing tournaments that the Soviet Union entered, it won 51 Olympic boxing medals—14 **gold**, 19 **silver**, and 18 **bronze**. This places it fourth among all nations. If the two medals won by the Unified Team in 1992 and the 26 medals that Russia has won from 1996 to 2012 are added to the Soviet Union's total, the resulting 79 medals places them second behind the **United States'** total of 111 in the all-time Olympic boxing medal count.

Boris Lagutin has been the Soviet Union's best boxer. Competing in the **light middleweight** class, he won a bronze medal in 1960 and gold medals in 1964 and 1968. He is one of only nine boxers to win three Olympic medals, and one of only 16 to win two or more gold medals.

Alexei Kiselov (silver medalist in both 1964 **light heavyweight** and 1968 **middleweight**), Viktor Savchenko (1976 light middleweight bronze, 1980 middleweight silver), and Viktor Rybakov (bronze medalist in both 1976 **bantamweight** and 1980 **featherweight**) each won two medals.

UNITED KINGDOM. *See* GREAT BRITAIN.

UNITED STATES. Boxing in the United States has been a popular sport since the 19th century, although in recent years interest has markedly decreased. During the first half of the 20th century, boxing was one of the country's most popular sports along with baseball.

In **amateur boxing**, the **Amateur Athletic Union** first conducted annual amateur boxing tournaments in 1888. United States boxers first competed in the 1904 **Olympic Games** and have entered every Olympic boxing tournament since then with the exception of 1908 and 1980. The United States has won more Olympic boxing **gold medals**, 50, more **silver medals**, 23, and more **bronze** medals, 38, than any other country. The total of 111 is more than 40 greater than the second place country, **Great Britain**.

Since amateur boxers in the United States tend to become **professional** as soon as they achieve success in the amateur ranks, there have been only four U.S. Olympic boxers to win multiple medals, and they all did so in 1904 in St. Louis, which was the first games that had a boxing competition. It was held over two days with only 18 entrants in the seven weight classes. Oliver

Kirk, at 115 pounds, entered both the **bantamweight** and **featherweight** classes and needed to win only one **bout** in each of the divisions (which he did) to become the first, and only, Olympic boxer to win two gold medals in one Olympic boxing tournament. In that same tournament, Charles Mayer won the **middleweight** gold medal by winning just one bout and was the runner-up in the **heavyweight** class by losing his only bout in that division. George Finnegan won the **flyweight** class in his only bout and lost to Kirk in the bantamweight division. Harry Spanier, the **lightweight** winner, was **welterweight** runner-up.

Many U.S. Olympic boxers have done quite well as professional boxers, especially in the heavyweight ranks, where **Riddick Bowe**, Cassius Clay **(Muhammad Ali)**, **George Foreman**, **Joe Frazier**, **Evander Holyfield**, Ray Mercer, **Floyd Patterson**, **Leon Spinks**, and John Tate have all won world's heavyweight titles.

Professional boxing in the United States has been popular since the 19th century. The preponderance of world championship bouts during the first half of the 20th century were held in the United States, and more than half of the sport's recognized world champions were Americans.

During the first half of the 20th century, boxing matches for the world's heavyweight championship were among the most highly anticipated sports events, and the popularity of such champions as **Jack Dempsey**, **Joe Louis**, and **Rocky Marciano** exceeded those of nearly all other sports figures. The sport continued its popularity during the early years of television in the 1940s and 1950s, and with the rise of champions such as Muhammad Ali, Joe Frazier, George Foreman, **Larry Holmes**, and **Mike Tyson**, continued into the 1980s. But with the increase in championship sanctioning organizations, the increased number of weight classifications, and the corresponding rise of multiple championship claimants, fan interest and newspaper coverage of boxing in the United States has declined substantially during the past 30 years.

UNITED STATES AMATEUR BOXING FEDERATION. *See* AMATEUR ATHLETIC UNION (AAU).

UNITED STATES CHAMPIONSHIP TOURNAMENT. The **United States** Championship Tournament was a creation of promoter **Don King**. After having promoted several of **Muhammad Ali's** fights, Ali changed promoters and signed with King's rival, **Bob Arum**. King then decided to create a tournament to capitalize on the patriotism resulting from the bicentennial celebration and the U.S. success at the 1976 Olympic Games boxing competition. King's tournament would feature solely U.S.-born **professional** boxers since at that time many of the world titles were held by foreign boxers and this tournament would restore interest to boxing in the United States. Plans were for competition to be held in the six major weight classes, with eight boxers selected for each weight class. Venues were also selected to promote patriotism, with an aircraft carrier and the U.S. Naval Academy being chosen to host fights.

King got Roone Arledge, head of the American Broadcasting Company (ABC) television network sports department, to agree to televise the fights and *Ring* **magazine** to provide rankings of the boxers in order to select the best ones in each division. New York State boxing **commissioner** James Farley was named chairman of the tournament committee.

With the financial backing of ABC, purses for the fighters were to be distributed as follows: **heavyweights**—$15,000 for quarterfinalist losers, $30,000 for semifinalist losers, $45,000 for finalist losers, and $135,000 for the champion. In the **light heavyweight** and **middleweight** division, purses were $10,000, $15,000, $19,500, and $45,500. Purses for the other weights were $7,500, $10,000, $12,000, and $28,000.

The following fighters were initially selected:

- Heavyweight—Johnny Boudreaux, Dino Dennis, **Larry Holmes**, Leroy Jones, Scott LeDoux, Tom Prater. Alternates Kevin Isaacs and Jeff Merritt.
- Light heavyweight—Tom Bethea, Bobby Cassidy, Donald "Biff" Cline, Ray Elson, Tony Greene, Len Hutchins, Vonzell Johnson, Richie Kates, Willie Taylor.
- Middleweight—Johnny Baldwin, Tony Chiaverini, Mike Colbert, Roy Edmonds, Ike Fluellen, David Love, Willie Monroe, Bobby Watts.
- **Welterweight**—Randy Shields, Harold Weston, others not named.
- **Lightweight**—Edwin Viruet, others not named.
- **Featherweight**—not named.

The first round of **bouts** was on Sunday 16 January 1977 aboard the USS *Lexington* aircraft carrier in Pensacola, Florida—all quarterfinal bouts scheduled for eight **rounds**.

- Heavyweight—Larry Holmes defeated Tom Prater by **unanimous decision**.
- Light heavyweight—Bobby Cassidy defeated Willie Taylor by **split decision**.
- Middleweight—Mike Colbert defeated Jackie Smith, scoring not announced.
- Welterweight—Randy Shields defeated Juan Cantres by split decision.
- Lightweight—John Sullivan defeated Paddy Dolan, scoring not announced.

- Featherweight—Walter Seeley defeated Hilbert Stevenson by unanimous decision.

The second round of bouts was on Sunday 13 February 1977 at the Halsey Field House, Annapolis, Maryland, and all were scheduled eight-round bouts in the quarterfinal round.

- Heavyweight—Johnny Boudreaux defeated Scott LeDoux by unanimous decision.
- Light heavyweight—Ray Elson defeated Donald "Biff" Cline by **technical knockout** (TKO) at 1:48 of the fourth round.
- Middleweight—Casey Gacic defeated Leo Saenz by unanimous decision.
- Welterweight—Johnny Gant defeated Anthony House by TKO at 1:43 of the second round.
- Lightweight—Edwin Viruet defeated Tommy Rose by TKO at 2:49 of the fourth round.
- Featherweight—Richard Rozelle defeated Davey Vásquez by unanimous decision.

The third round of bouts was on Sunday 6 March 1977 at the Marion Correctional Facility, Marion, Ohio (where King had previously been incarcerated). All bouts were scheduled eight-round bouts in the quarterfinal round.

- Heavyweight—Stan Ward defeated Kevin Isaac by unanimous decision.
- Middleweight—Rocky Mosely Jr. defeated Johnny Baldwin by TKO in the fourth round.
- Welterweight—**Wilfred Benítez** defeated Melvin Dennis by unanimous decision.
- Lightweight—Ruby Ortiz defeated Vinnie DeBarros by unanimous decision.
- Featherweight—Ruben Castillo defeated Kenny Weldon by unanimous decision.

The fourth round of bouts was on Sunday 27 March 1977 at Randolph AFB, San Antonio, Texas. All bouts were scheduled eight-round bouts in the quarterfinal round.

- Heavyweight—Leroy Jones defeated John "Dino" Denis by unanimous decision.
- Light heavyweight—Vonzell Johnson defeated Tony Greene by TKO in the third round.

- Middleweight—Bobby "Boogaloo" Watts defeated David Love by TKO at 1:41 of the first round.
- Welterweight—Floyd Mayweather Sr. defeated Miguel Barreto by decision.
- Lightweight—Greg Coverson defeated Jerry Kornele by decision.
- Featherweight—James Martinez defeated Warren Matthews by split decision.

The first semifinal round of bouts was on Saturday 2 April 1977 at the Convention Center, San Antonio, Texas. Bouts were scheduled for 10 rounds.

- Lightweight—Ruby Ortiz defeated John Sullivan by unanimous decision.
- Featherweight—Ruben Castillo defeated Walter Seeley by unanimous decision.

The second semifinal round was originally scheduled for Sunday 10 April 1977 at the Fontainebleau Hotel, Miami Beach, Florida, but was held on Saturday 16 April 1977.

- Middleweight—Mike Colbert defeated Rocky Mosely Jr. by split decision.
- Featherweight—Richard Rozelle defeated James Martinez by unanimous decision.

The tournament was then abruptly canceled.

In April, rumors surfaced that payoffs were made to ensure that certain boxers were included in the tournament. *Ring* magazine's ratings were also accused of inaccuracy, and one fighter originally included, Ike Fluellan, who had not fought for one year previously, had been credited with fictitious victories and included. A federal grand jury in Baltimore was convened to investigate the legitimacy of the tournament. ABC's reaction was to cancel the 16 April telecast. Don King's reaction was to suspend his assistants, Al Braverman and Paddy Flood, although they were later reinstated.

It was disclosed that King's contract with ABC called for him to receive only "production costs," but had the tournament reached its scheduled conclusion King would have had a controlling interest in all the tournament winners. It was also disclosed that King paid *Ring* $30,000 for their part in the event.

ABC staffer Alex Wallau and independent boxing newsletter editor Malcolm "Flash" Gordon were the first two individuals who found problems with the boxers' records and selection for the tournament. As the tournament went on, more and more problems surfaced, resulting in the cancellation of the tournament.

Although investigations were made and many allegations of improprieties surfaced, no criminal charges were ever made.

UPPERCUT. An uppercut is a type of boxing punch that is thrown underhand.

See also BOLO PUNCH; COUNTERPUNCH; CROSS; HAYMAKER; HOOK; JAB.

USA BOXING. *See* AMATEUR ATHLETIC UNION (AAU).

UZBEKISTAN. Uzbekistan was one of the former Soviet Socialist Republics, and as such their athletes competed for the **Union of Soviet Socialist Republics** until 1992. The country has since competed as an independent nation and sent boxing teams to the **Olympic Games** in each of the five tournaments from 1996 to 2012, winning medals in four of the five years. The nation has had quite a bit of success, winning seven medals—one **gold** and six **bronze**. **Light welterweight** Mukhammad Kadyr Abdulayev won the 2000 gold medal in addition to being his country's flagbearer during the opening ceremony. The six bronze medalists are **light middleweight** Karim Tulyaganov in 1996, **light heavyweight** Sergey Mikhaylov in 2000, **super heavyweight** Rustam Saidov in 2000, light heavyweight Utkirbek Khaydarov in 2004, **bantamweight** Bakhodirdzhon Sultanov in 2004, and **middleweight** Abbos Atayev in 2012.

In **professional boxing**, Saidov has won recognition as the world's **heavyweight** champion by the **World Boxing Association**, and Artur Grigorian, who competed in the 1992 Olympic Games as a member of the Unified Team, has won the **World Boxing Organization lightweight** championship.

V

VACANT. Boxing sanctioning organizations will declare a championship vacant when the champion retires, abandons the title claim to move to another weight class, does not fight the man the organization designates as the next challenger, or commits some other infraction that causes them to not recognize his championship claim any longer. When a title is declared vacant, the sanctioning organization usually selects the top two boxers in that weight class to fight for the vacant title. On occasion, the organization awards a boxer the championship by acclamation.

See also NORTON, KENNETH HOWARD SR.

VAL BARKER TROPHY. The Val Barker Trophy is presented to the boxer in the **Olympic** boxing tournament who "exemplifies style during competition." In general, it has been awarded to the tournament's outstanding boxer regardless of weight class. **Bronze medalist** American **flyweight** Louis Lauria in 1936 and Kenyan **featherweight** Philip Waruinge in 1968 and **silver medalist** American **light middleweight Roy Jones Jr.** in 1988 were the only Val Barker Trophy winners to not win the Olympic gold medal.

See also APPENDIX B for a list of recipients.

VALERO, EDWIN "EL INCA," "DINAMITA". B. 3 December 1981, Bolero Alto, Mérida, **Venezuela**. D. 19 April 2010, Valencia, Carabobo, Venezuela. The story of Edwin Valero is a tragic one. A left-hander, he began boxing at the age of 12 and reportedly had an **amateur** record of 86–6, with 45 **knockouts**. On 5 February 2001, prior to beginning a **professional boxing** career, he was injured severely in a motorcycle accident and suffered a fractured skull. He was cleared by a doctor in Venezuela to resume boxing, and on 27 July 2002 he began boxing professionally with a one-round knockout of Eduardo Hernández in Caracas. After winning his first 12 fights, all by first-round knockouts (or **technical knockouts**), including three in California, he attempted to fight in New York State in January 2004 but was denied a license for failing an MRI examination.

This ban was recognized by other state athletic **commissions**, and Valero was unable to box in the **United States** until 2009. In the meantime, he fought throughout the world—in **Argentina**, **Panama**, Venezuela, **Japan**, and **France**—and won his first 18 **bouts** all by first-round knockouts or technical knockouts, an all-time record for a professional boxer. The streak lasted until 25 March 2006 when Genaro Trazancos lasted until the second round of their bout in Japan.

In his next bout, on 25 August 2006, Valero met Panamanian Vicente Mosquera for the **World Boxing Association super featherweight** title in Panama City. Although knocked down in the third round, Valero went on to stop Mosquera in the 10th round and win the championship. After four successful title defenses Valero moved up to the **lightweight** division and won the **World Boxing Council** lightweight title on 4 April 2009 by knocking down Antonio Pitalua three times in the second round of their bout in Austin, Texas. Valero made two successful defenses of that title before tragedy struck his life.

In March 2010, Valero's wife was hospitalized with cracked ribs and a punctured lung. Later that month, he was admitted to a substance abuse clinic for alcohol and drug dependency and anger management problems. On 18 April, he was arrested after his wife was found murdered. He confessed to the murder and the following day was found hanging in his cell. It was officially stated that he committed suicide, although Venezuelan President Hugo Chávez publicly stated that he thought Valero had been murdered.

Valero was five foot six inches tall and had a 69-inch **reach**. He fought at weights ranging from 126 to 135 pounds as a super featherweight and lightweight. In 27 professional bouts, from 2002 to 2010, he won all 27 by knockout—a unique feat in boxing history—and fought a total of only 67 rounds.

VALUEV, NIKOLAI SERGEYEVICH "THE RUSSIAN GIANT," "THE BEAST FROM THE EAST". B. 21 August 1973, Leningrad, **Russia**, **Union of Soviet Socialist Republics**. Nikolai Valuev, at seven feet tall (2.13 meters), is by far the tallest man to win a world's boxing championship. There have been other men who have boxed professionally who were in excess of seven feet tall, such as **South African** Ewart Potgieter (seven foot two inches, with a record of 11–2–1 from 1954 to 1957); **Romanian** Gogea Mitu (variously reported as seven foot four inches to seven foot seven inches, 2–1–1 from 1935 to 1936); Carl Chancellor (seven foot one inch, with weights ranging from 296 to 440 pounds; 4–6–2 from 1988 to 1998); and Marcellus Brown (seven feet tall, 26–17–1 from 1989 to 2008).

Valuev began boxing professionally on 15 October 1993 when he knocked out John Morton in two **rounds** in Berlin, **Germany**. He fought sporadically after that, with two wins in 1994 and one in 1995 in Russia.

In October 1996, he began boxing in earnest with two **bouts** in London and then went to **Australia** in 1997, where he won two more. On 31 May 1997, he boxed in the **United States** for the first time, winning a two-round **knockout** over Terrell Nelson at Trump Taj Mahal in **Atlantic City**, New Jersey. He had five more bouts that year all over the world—in **Japan**, Russia, **Germany**, and Australia. He won three more in 1998 in Russia and on 22 January 1999 won the Russian **heavyweight** championship by stopping Alexei Osokin in six rounds. On 6 June 2000, Valuev won a 12-round **unanimous decision** over Yuriy Yuristratov in St. Petersburg, Russia, and became the Pan Asian Boxing Association (PABA) world's heavyweight champion. The PABA, however, is one of a multitude of boxing associations whose titles do not carry much weight among boxing fans.

In 2001, Valuev returned to the Trump Taj Mahal and successfully defended his PABA title with a **technical knockout** of George Linberger in just 1:20 of the first round. Valuev then won the **World Boxing Association (WBA)** Inter-Continental heavyweight title (another one with limited recognition) with a sixth-round technical knockout on 24 July 2004 in Frankfurt, Germany, against Richard Bango, who was undefeated prior to that match.

On 17 December 2005, Valuev made boxing history when he won a 12-round **majority decision** over John Ruiz in Berlin, Germany, to win the WBA world's heavyweight championship—one of the four major boxing sanctioning organizations—and he became the tallest and heaviest man to win a major world's heavyweight championship. After successfully defending that title three times, Valuev lost the championship on a 12-round majority decision to Ruslan Chagaev on 14 April 2007 in Baden-Wurttemberg, Germany. Valuev regained it on 30 August 2008 by again winning a decision over John Ruiz. He defended it by majority decision against former world's heavyweight champion **Evander Holyfield** on 20 December 2008 in Zurich, Switzerland, but then lost it by majority decision to David Haye on 7 November 2009 in Nuremberg, Germany, and retired three days after that bout.

After retiring from boxing, he has written an autobiography, was elected to public office, and was named general manager of the Russian national bandy (a variation of ice hockey) team.

Valuev has an 85-inch **reach**. He fought at weights ranging from 310 to 348 pounds as a heavyweight. In 53 professional bouts, from 1993 to 2009, he won 50 (34 by knockout), lost two (none by knockout), had one **no contest**, and fought a total of 276 rounds.

VENEZUELA. Although boxing is not one of the major sports in Venezuela, the country nevertheless has produced both **Olympic amateur** champions as well as **professional** champions. Baseball, by far, and football (soccer), basketball, rugby, tennis, cycling, and golf all exceed boxing in popularity there. The **World Boxing Association** has a strong influence on the sport in Venezuela and during the 1990s maintained its office in Caracas.

In **amateur boxing**, Venezuelan boxers first competed in the 1952 **Olympic Games** and have entered 15 Olympic boxing tournaments—every one from 1952 to 2012 except 1964. Their best year was 1968, when Francisco Rodríguez became the first winner in the new **light flyweight** class. Rodríguez returned in 1972 but was knocked out in his first **bout** in one of that year's major upsets. Venezuelans won four other Olympic boxing medals—Pedro José Gamarro, 1976 **welterweight silver**; Bernardo José Piñango, 1980 **bantamweight** silver; Omar Catari, 1984 **featherweight bronze**; and José Marcelino Bolivar, 1984 light flyweight bronze.

In **professional boxing**, Venezuela has done quite well, with 32 boxers gaining world championships. They include Miguel Acosta, Noel Arambulet, José Bonilla, Antonio Cermeño, Israel Contreras, Crisanto España, Ernesto España, Antonio Esparragoza, Luis Estaba, Leo Gamez, Alimi Goitia, Antonio Gómez, Betulio González, David Griman, Aquiles Guzmán, Carlos Hernández, Jorge Linares, Félix Machado, Alfredo Marcano, Eidy Moya, Alexander Muñoz, Fulgencio Obelmejias, Rafael Orono, Yober Ortega, Lorenzo Parra, Bernardo Piñango, Eloy Rojas, Jesús "Kiki" Rojas, Vicente Rondón, José Sanabria, Gilberto Serrano, and **Edwin Valero**.

A world's **heavyweight** championship bout was contested at the Poliedro in Caracas, Venezuela, on 26 March 1974 when **George Foreman** defended his title by stopping **Ken Norton** in the second round.

VILLA, PANCHO (né FRANCISCO VILLARUEL GUILLEDO). B. 1 August 1901, Ilog, Negros Occidental, **Philippines**. D. 14 July 1925, San Francisco, California. Pancho Villa was the **ring** name of one of the greatest Asian boxers in history, although he remains relatively unknown to modern boxing fans. He began boxing **professionally** as a **flyweight** in Manila, Philippines, in 1919. He was discovered by American boxing promoter Frank Churchill, who was promoting boxing in the Philippines, which at that time was a territory of the **United States**. Guilledo was given the ring name of Pancho Villa after the Mexican guerrilla leader of that era. From 1919 to 1922, Villa fought 56 **bouts** exclusively in the Philippines and is credited with winning 51 of them.

In 1922, Villa and Churchill, as his manager, came to the United States and on 7 June, Villa was matched with Abe Goldstein in a 12-**round** no-decision bout. He acquitted himself well, although the **newspaper decision** went to Goldstein. One month later, Villa was matched with Olympic champion **Frankie Genaro** in another 12-round no-decision contest and again lost a newspaper decision. On 14 September, Villa met Johnny Buff for the American flyweight championship and won by an 11th-round **knockout**. He retained that title until 1 March 1923, when Genaro defeated him on a 15-round **decision**. On 18 June 1923, world flyweight champion **Jimmy Wilde**, a Welshman, came to the United States to defend his world title, which he had held since 1916. In an upset, Wilde was knocked out by Villa, who then became the world champion. Over the next two years, Villa continued fighting as a flyweight and **bantamweight** in the United States and was undefeated, although most of his bouts were nontitle ones.

On 4 July 1925, Villa was matched with **Jimmy McLarnin** in Oakland, California. The morning of the bout, Villa had an infected tooth extracted. Villa fought that night with a face still swollen from the infection and lost a 10-round decision to McLarnin. The infection worsened, and on 13 July it had spread to Villa's throat in a condition known as Ludwig's angina. He was operated on but died the next day still holding the title of world flyweight champion.

Villa was five foot one inch tall and fought at weights ranging from 102 to 116 pounds as a flyweight. Of the 107 recorded bouts in his career, he won 80 (23 by knockout), lost five (none by knockout), and had three draws and two **no-contest** bouts. He also boxed 17 no-decision bouts, of which he won the newspaper decisions in 12, lost four, and had one draw. He fought a total of 860 rounds. His fighting weight never exceeded 116 pounds and might have been as low as 102 pounds in one of his early bouts. In 1994, he was inducted into the **International Boxing Hall of Fame**.

W

WALCOTT, JERSEY JOE (né ARNOLD RAYMOND CREAM). B. 31 January 1914, Merchantville, New Jersey. **D.** 25 February 1994, Camden, New Jersey. Jersey Joe Walcott was a **professional** boxer for 17 years before he got a chance to fight for the world's **heavyweight** title. When he did, he lost a 15-**round decision** that even his opponent felt was an injustice.

Walcott began boxing professionally in 1930, with his first recorded professional **bout** on 9 September in Vineland, New Jersey. He adopted the name of a boxer from the West Indies he admired, **Joe Walcott**, who had been the world's **welterweight** champion in the early 20th century.

Jersey Joe's early record is rather sketchy, and he might have fought prior to 1930. He also has no recorded bouts in 1932 or 1934 but apparently was ill in 1934 with typhoid fever.

During the 1930s, he compiled a known record of 25–7–2, with victories over Elmer "Violent" Ray, Willie Reddish (later a well-known **trainer**), and former **Golden Gloves** champion Lorenzo Pack and losses to Tiger Jack Fox and Al Ettore, among his more notable opponents.

In February 1940, Walcott was knocked out in six rounds by Abe Simon. Walcott then was virtually out of boxing and fought only a couple of times during the war years. In 1945, a Camden businessman, Felix Bocchicchio, met Walcott and helped to turn his boxing career around.

Walcott fought nine times in 1945 and won all but one. In 1946, he beat top contender Jimmy Bivins and Lee Oma but was defeated by future **light heavyweight** champion **Joey Maxim** and Elmer Ray. In 1947, Walcott avenged those defeats by twice beating Maxim and once defeating Ray.

He then got the chance of his lifetime and was matched with heavyweight champion **Joe Louis** for the world's heavyweight title. The bout took place at **Madison Square Garden** on 5 December 1947 and went the full 15 rounds.

Walcott knocked Louis down in the first and fourth rounds and to most observers appeared to have won the bout. The officials thought otherwise, and although **referee Ruby Goldstein** voted for Walcott by a score of 7–6–2, both **judges** saw it for Louis, who retained his title. Louis himself thought that he had lost the fight.

On 25 June 1948, the two fought a rematch, and this time Louis left no doubts, as he knocked out Walcott in the 11th round of their fight at Yankee Stadium. Louis retired after the bout. One year later, on 22 June 1949, Walcott fought **Ezzard Charles** for the **vacant National Boxing Association** heavyweight title. Walcott again went home disappointed, as Charles won a unanimous 15-round decision.

He continued boxing and won five of his next six bouts, stopping future light heavyweight champion Harold Johnson in three rounds but losing a 10-round decision to contender Rex Layne.

Walcott received another title shot at Charles on 7 March 1951 and for the fourth time lost a heavyweight championship bout, again on a 15-round **unanimous decision**. Surprisingly, Charles granted Walcott a rematch, and on 18 July 1951 Walcott prevailed, knocking out Charles in the seventh round and winning the world's heavyweight championship at the age of 37, the oldest man to do so to that point in history.

In 1952, the two fought again (their fourth heavyweight title fight against each other—the most bouts between two fighters for the heavyweight title). Walcott retained his title on a 15-round unanimous decision in a bout refereed by former basketball and Negro League baseball star Zach Clayton—the first heavyweight title bout with a black referee.

Three months later, on 23 September 1952, Walcott lost his title to **Rocky Marciano** on a 13th-round **knockout**. Walcott had knocked Rocky down for the first time in his career in the first round and was ahead on points when Marciano ended the bout. Walcott's final bout, at the age of 39, occurred on 15 May 1953 when he was knocked out in the first round by Marciano.

In retirement, Walcott had a role in the film *The Harder They Fall*. He also worked as a referee, working the second Liston–Ali heavyweight fight, among others, and had a brief career as a professional wrestler. During the 1970s, he was elected sheriff of Camden County in New Jersey and later became chairman of the New Jersey State Athletic **Commission**.

Walcott was six feet tall and had a 74-inch **reach**. He fought at weights ranging from 158 to 201 pounds, primarily as a heavyweight. He died at the age of 80 from complications of diabetes. In 71 professional bouts, from 1930 to 1953, he won 51 (32 by knockout), lost 18 (six by knockout), had two draws, and fought a total of 475 rounds. He was inducted as a member of the inaugural class of the **International Boxing Hall of Fame** in 1990.

WALCOTT, JOE "BARBADOS JOE," "BARBADOS DEMON". B. 13 March 1873, Demerara, British Guiana. D. 1 October 1935, Massillon, Ohio. Boxing has had two great fighters who were called Joe Walcott. One of the two was born with that name, while the other, born Arnold Raymond Cream, admired the original and was known as **Jersey Joe Walcott**.

The original Joe Walcott, sometimes referred to as Barbados Joe Walcott, was born in British Guiana, a South American country known as Guyana since its independence in 1966. He spent much of his youth, however, on the **Caribbean** island of Barbados. He worked as a cabin boy on ships and eventually landed in Boston, Massachusetts. There he held various odd jobs, one of which was in a local gymnasium as a **sparring partner**. He began a **professional boxing** career in 1890, with his first recorded **bout** occurring on 28 February 1890 in South Boston. Although only a shade taller than five foot one inch, he boxed as a **welterweight** throughout much of his career.

By 1894, boxing primarily in New England, he had won 29 of 33 fights with two **draws**. On 19 April 1894, he defeated Tom Tracey in Boston and won a bout billed for the "world 140-pound championship." After winning nine of 10 bouts, with one **no contest** included, he defended that title against **"Mysterious Billy" Smith** on 1 March 1895 in a bout that resulted in a 15-round draw. Over the next two years, Walcott fought 16 bouts, winning 12, losing two, and fighting two draws. The two losses were to George "Kid" Lavigne and Tommy West.

On 29 October 1897 in San Francisco, California, Walcott fought a rematch with Lavigne for the world's **lightweight** title but was stopped in the 12th round. The following year, on 6 December 1898, Walcott again fought Smith, this time for the world's welterweight title, but lost a 20-round decision in their bout in New York City.

In 1900, Walcott scored a seventh-round **technical knockout** over Joe Choynski, a boxer who had fought some of the era's best **heavyweights** and who weighed 163 pounds for the bout with Walcott. Walcott also scored two victories over Smith in 1900 in **nontitle bouts**.

Walcott won recognition as world's welterweight champion on 18 December 1901 when he defeated James "Rube" Ferns in Fort Erie, Ontario, **Canada**, on a fifth-round technical knockout. He then successfully defended that title against Tommy West, Billy Woods, Young Peter Jackson, and Mose LaFontise. On 29 April 1904 in San Francisco, Walcott lost his title to the Dixie Kid on a 20-round **disqualification**. Walcott was easily winning the bout when **referee** James Sullivan stopped it in the final round for an alleged kidney blow and awarded the fight to the Kid. It was later disclosed that the referee had bet on the Dixie Kid, and Walcott was allowed to retain his title.

Walcott then fought a 15-round draw with the great **Sam Langford** in his next title defense and then fought a 20-round nontitle bout with another black great from that era, **Joe Gans**. After the Gans bout, it was reported that Walcott accidentally shot himself in the hand and he did not fight for the next 16 months.

In 1906, he made two more successful title defenses—an eighth-round **knockout** of Jack Dougherty and a 20-round draw with Billy Rhodes. The Rhodes bout was an interesting example of boxing in the early 20th century.

It was fought on a sandbar off of an island in the Missouri River near Kansas City, Missouri, to avoid the state boxing bans of that time. Presumably, the bout's location was not within the jurisdiction of either of the surrounding states.

Walcott lost the title in his subsequent bout—a 15-round decision to Bill "Honey" Mellody in Chelsea, Massachusetts, on 16 October 1906. In a rematch one month later, Mellody stopped Walcott in 12 rounds. Walcott continued boxing until 2 November 1911 but had a poor record in his final years, winning only seven, losing 13, and drawing seven in his final 27 bouts.

In retirement, he worked as a fireman and a porter on a freighter, and when he was unable to find employment elsewhere, New York City mayor Jimmy Walker interceded and got Walcott a job as a custodian at **Madison Square Garden**.

Walcott died after being hit by a car in Massillon, Ohio.

Walcott had a 65-inch **reach** and fought at weights ranging from 133 to 148 pounds, primarily as a welterweight. In 166 professional bouts, from 1890 to 1911, he won 95 (61 by **knockout**), lost 25 (nine by knockout), and had 24 draws, three **no contests**, and 19 no-decision bouts, in which he won the **newspaper decision** in nine, lost seven, and drew three. He fought a total of 1,332 rounds. He was inducted into the **International Boxing Hall of Fame** in 1991.

WALES. Wales is a country that is part of the United Kingdom, although its athletes compete internationally with those of **England, Scotland**, and **Northern Ireland** as part of the **Great Britain** team. Welsh **Olympic** boxing champions were Fred Evans, 2012 **welterweight silver medalist**, and Ralph Evans (no relation), 1972 **light flyweight bronze** medalist. As with the other countries of the United Kingdom, boxing has been quite popular since the 19th century.

Professional world champions from Wales include three of boxing's all-time great champions—**Jimmy Wilde**, Freddie Welsh, and **Joe Calzaghe**. Both Wilde and Welsh have been elected to the **International Boxing Hall of Fame**, and Calzaghe most likely will be also once he is eligible. Other Welsh champions are Nathan Cleverly, Barry Jones, Percy Jones, Enzo Maccarinelli, Gavin Rees, Robbie Regan, Steve Robinson, and Howard Winstone. **Jem Driscoll** was an all-time great, although not a champion, and is a member of the International Boxing Hall of Fame.

WALKER, EDWARD PATRICK "MICKEY," "THE TOY BULL-DOG". B. 13 July 1901 or 1903, Elizabeth, New Jersey. D. 28 April 1981, Freehold, New Jersey. Mickey Walker was a **welterweight** champion who ended his career boxing and defeating **heavyweights**. Only five foot seven inches tall, he was tough and scrappy and earned himself the nickname "The Toy Bulldog" for his voraciousness.

He had very few **amateur bouts**, if any, and his first recorded **professional** bout took place on 10 February 1919 in his native Elizabeth, New Jersey. He began fighting during the "no decision" era but was credited with the **newspaper decision** in most of his early bouts. On 18 July 1921, he went 12 **rounds** with welterweight champion **Jack Britton** but lost a newspaper decision. Later that year, Walker stopped top contender Dave Shade in eight rounds but lost a 12-round newspaper decision in a rematch. Through 1921, Walker had fought 47 bouts and had a record of 18–2 with 27 no-decision bouts in which he had a record of 20–6–1. In 1922, after winning his first six bouts (five via newspaper decision), he hit a bad spell and won only one of seven bouts—five losses and one **no contest**—but after just one victory in his next bout somehow earned a shot at Britton's world welterweight title. Walker made the most of this opportunity and defeated Britton by a 15-round **unanimous decision** on 1 November 1922 at **Madison Square Garden** and became world's welterweight champion.

After several **nontitle** victories, Walker defended his championship on 22 March 1923 in Newark, New Jersey, and won a 12-round newspaper decision over Pete Latzo. In Walker's next title defense, on 8 October 1923 in Newark, New Jersey, he and challenger Jimmy Jones boxed nine rounds, but both were disqualified in the ninth round by **referee** Danny Sullivan for "not trying," although Walker claimed he had hurt his hands. The bout was ruled "no contest," and both fighters were suspended for a year by the New Jersey State Athletic **Commission**.

Walker defended his welterweight title twice more on 24 June 1924 (Lew Tendler, 10-round **decision**) and on 1 October 1924 (Bobby Barrett, sixth-round **knockout**) before moving up in weight class and challenging heavier fighters. Although Walker weighed just slightly over the welterweight limit of 147 pounds, he fought **light heavyweight** champion Mike McTigue on 7 January 1925 for the light heavyweight title. Walker went 12 rounds with McTigue in a no-decision bout and, although awarded the newspaper decision, did not gain the title. In Walker's next bout, he fought **middleweight** champion **Harry Greb** for Greb's middleweight title on 2 July 1925 but was outpointed by Greb over 15 rounds in a bout chosen as "Fight of the Year" by *Ring* magazine.

Walker then returned to the welterweight ranks and defended his title twice more against Dave Shade (21 September 1925, 15-round **split decision**) and William "Sailor" Friedman (25 November 1925, 12-round no decision).

On 20 May 1926, Walker lost his welterweight title to Latzo on a 10-round unanimous decision in Scranton, Pennsylvania. Walker then moved up in weight class and boxed as a middleweight. On 3 December 1926, Walker won a disputed 10-round decision over Theodore "Tiger" Flowers in Chicago and became the world middleweight champion. Referee Benny Yanger, the sole arbiter, scored the bout for Walker, even though most other observers thought that Flowers had dominated.

Walker made his first title defense on 30 June 1927 in London, **England**, and knocked out Scot Tommy Milligan in 10 rounds. In nontitle bouts later in 1927, Walker defeated two former light heavyweight champions—knocking out Mike McTigue in one round and winning a 10-round decision over Paul Berlenbach. In 1928, Walker successfully defended his middleweight title with a 10-round newspaper decision over Jock Malone and a 10-round split decision victory over Ace Hudkins.

On 28 March 1929, Walker again challenged for the world's light heavyweight title. This time he went 10 rounds with champion Tommy Loughran in Chicago but lost a split decision. In October, Walker again defeated Hudkins in defense of his middleweight title.

Although Walker still weighed only a few pounds over the 160-pound middleweight limit, he began fighting light heavyweights and heavyweights almost exclusively and, although outweighed by more than 25 pounds in several of his bouts, defeated heavyweight contenders Johnny Risko, Meyer "KO" Christner, Ed "Bearcat" Wright, Kingfish Levinsky, and Paulino Uzcudun and fought a 15-round **draw** with future heavyweight champion **Jack Sharkey**. Walker took a beating from former heavyweight champion **Max Schmeling** in a bout that was stopped in the eighth round on 26 September 1932.

Walker made yet another attempt at the light heavyweight championship on 3 November 1933 but lost a 15-round decision to **Maxie Rosenbloom**. Walker defeated Rosenbloom the following year, although Rosenbloom's title was not a stake in that bout.

Walker retired after a 2 December 1935 bout in which he was stopped by Erich Seelig. In retirement, Walker owned a popular bar near **Madison Square Garden** and in later life became an accomplished painter as well as an avid golfer.

Walker had a 67-inch **reach** and fought at weights ranging from 139 to 179 pounds in weight classes from welterweight to heavyweight. In 164 professional bouts, from 1919 to 1935, he won 94 (60 by **knockout**), lost 19 (six by knockout), and had four draws, two **no contests**, and 45 no-decision bouts, in which he received the newspaper decision in 37, lost seven, and drew one. He fought a total of 1,251 rounds. He was inducted as a member of the inaugural class of the **International Boxing Hall of Fame** in 1990.

WALKOVER. A walkover occurs in **amateur boxing** when a boxer's opponent does not show up to box at the scheduled time. This can be due to failure to make the weight, illness or injury, or political action (a country refusing to allow their fighter to meet a representative from another country for political reasons).

WALLACE, COLEY. B. 5 April 1927, Jacksonville, Florida. D. 30 January 2005, New York, New York. Coley Wallace bore a striking facial resemblance to **Joe Louis**, so much so that he portrayed Louis in the 1953 Hollywood film biography of Louis, *The Joe Louis Story*.

The best portion of Wallace's boxing career was as an **amateur** boxer. Boxing for the Salem-Crescent Athletic Club in Harlem, New York, Wallace won the 1948 New York **Golden Gloves open** division **heavyweight** championship. He was invited to compete in the subsequent Tournament of Champions and won that title by defeating Bob Baker of Pittsburgh. In the following New York–Chicago Intercity competition, Wallace again won, this time by defeating Clarence Henry of the Chicago team.

In his first-**round bout** in the Tournament of Champions, Wallace was matched against Rocco "Socko" Marchegiano of the Lowell, Massachusetts, team in a bout held in the afternoon on Monday 1 March 1948 at Ridgewood Grove, Brooklyn. Wallace, a more polished boxer, won a close **decision** over the wild-swinging, unpolished Marchegiano. This turned out to be the only loss in Marchegiano's career as he soon afterward changed his name to **Rocky Marciano** and won all 49 of his **professional** bouts as well as the world's heavyweight championship. In 1949, Wallace again won the Golden Gloves tournament, but this time he lost to Baker in the Tournament of Champions semifinal round.

Wallace became a professional fighter in 1950, winning his first bout on 15 March 1950 with a second-round **knockout** of Willie Brown. Wallace won his first 12 bouts before being knocked out in the second round by Elkins Brothers at **Madison Square Garden** on 15 June 1951. After five more victories in 1951 and 1952, Wallace was again knocked out on 19 September 1952, this time by Jimmy Bivins, one of the best heavyweights of that era but one who never fully received due recognition for his abilities. Wallace also faced former heavyweight champion **Ezzard Charles** and former amateur opponent Bob Baker in losing efforts.

Wallace was managed by Frank "Blinky" Palermo, an organized crime figure who was later convicted of conspiracy and extortion, and as such Wallace's professional boxing career proved to be far from successful even though he retired in 1957 with a winning record.

He supplemented his boxing income by working as a bouncer at the famous Harlem Savoy Ballroom during the 1950s and later worked occasionally as an actor. Among the films he appeared in was the rarely seen 1957 film *Carib Gold*, in which he costarred with Ethel Waters. He also reprised his role as Joe Louis in the 1979 television biography of Rocky Marciano and in the award-winning 1980 film *Raging Bull*. After retiring from the **ring**, Wallace worked as a liquor salesman, a rather strange occupation for a man who was once a teetotaler.

Wallace was six foot two inches tall and had a 78-inch **reach**. He fought at weights ranging from 196 to 211 pounds as a heavyweight. In 28 professional bouts, from 1950 to 1956, he won 21 (16 by knockout), lost seven (four by knockout), and fought a total of 161 rounds.

WEIGH-IN. At a specified interval prior to a **bout** (usually 12–36 hours), both boxers are required to be weighed in the presence of representatives of the boxing **commission**. Boxers must not exceed the maximum weight agreed upon for the bout. In championship bouts, boxers must not exceed the weight limit for the class.

WELTERWEIGHT. Welterweight is a boxing weight class in which the contestants cannot exceed 147 pounds. One of the eight traditional weight classes, its first champion was Paddy Duffy, who defeated William McMillan on 30 October 1888. Welterweight is one of the more popular weight classes, and its champions have included some of the best boxers in **ring** history regardless of weight.

Some of the best professional welterweights have included **Henry Armstrong**, **Carmen Basilio**, **Jack Britton**, Charley Burley, **Óscar De La Hoya**, **Kid Gavilán**, **Emile Griffith**, **Thomas Hearns**, **"Sugar Ray" Leonard**, Ted "Kid" Lewis, **Jimmy McLarnin**, **José Nápoles**, **"Sugar Ray" Robinson**, **Barney Ross**, **Félix Trinidad**, **Mickey Walker**, and **Pernell Whitaker**. Robinson is generally regarded as the best champion in this division.

See also GRAHAM, WILLIAM WALTER, JR., "BILLY"; ORTEGA, GASPAR "EL INDIO"; PALOMINO, CARLOS; PARET, BERNARDO "BENNY," "KID"; SHOMO, VINCENT O'NEAL "VINCE"; SMITH, AMOS "MYSTERIOUS BILLY"; WALCOTT, JOE "BARBADOS JOE," "BARBADOS DEMON".

WEPNER, CHARLES "CHUCK," "THE BAYONNE BLEEDER". B. 26 February 1939, New York, New York. Had Chuck Wepner not fought **Muhammad Ali** in Cleveland, Ohio, on 24 March 1975 for the **heavyweight** championship, he would have been just another game heavyweight contender who won some and lost some, such as the likes of Jack O'Halloran, Pedro Agosto, and James J. Woody. But on that day, Wepner (nicknamed the "Bayonne Bleeder" due to his propensity to cut easily) proved he had the heart of a champion if not the skills of one. When he entered the **ring** with a record of 30–9–2—including a streak from 1969 to 1971 in which he lost six of 10 fights, being stopped in four of the six—Wepner knocked Ali down in the ninth **round** of their title fight, but was thoroughly outclassed in most of the other rounds. He did, however last until 2:41 of the 15th and final round.

The fact that Ali gave Wepner, basically a **journeyman** fighter, a chance at the **heavyweight** title, and Wepner rose to the occasion and did battle with Ali for 15 rounds, inspired Sylvester Stallone to write a screenplay he entitled *Rocky*. Stallone later was able to produce the film, which won an Academy Award.

After becoming interested in boxing while serving in the U.S. Marines from 1956 to 1959, Wepner joined the Bayonne (New Jersey) Police Athletic League and won the 1964 New York **Golden Gloves** heavyweight **sub-novice** championship as a representative of the club. He became a **professional** boxer with his first **bout** on 5 August 1964 in Bayonne. After his first eight bouts, he had only won four with two losses and two **draws**. From 1966 to 1969, his fortunes improved, and he won 14 of 15 bouts, but the quality of his opposition was mostly journeymen boxers. From 1969 to 1971, he had the slump referred to earlier where he lost six of 10 bouts. One of those losses was to former heavyweight champion **Sonny Liston**, in which Wepner was stopped in the ninth round and cut so badly that he later needed 120 stitches in his face.

After the losing streak, Wepner then won eight straight bouts, including a **decision** over former heavyweight champion Ernie Terrell. Ali, who had just won the title from **George Foreman** in a difficult bout, was looking for a relatively easy opponent for his first title defense. Promoter **Don King** came up with the idea of a white opponent for Ali, and Wepner's winning streak provided Ali with a credible opponent for a title defense. King's promotional phrase for the fight was "Give the white guy a break."

After his 15 rounds of fame, Wepner returned to being a journeyman boxer and after winning only five of his last nine bouts retired after a 26 September 1978 loss to Scott Frank.

In 1976, Wepner met professional wrestler Andre the Giant and lost when Andre threw him out of the ring.

Wepner ran into hard times during the 1980s and served time for cocaine possession but later turned his life around and became a salesman for a wine and liquor distributor.

He was never acknowledged by Stallone and never received any remuneration nor even a bit part in one of the *Rocky* films, and in 2003 he filed a suit against Stallone that was eventually settled in 2006. A 2011 ESPN documentary about Wepner titled *The Real Rocky* provides an excellent summary of Wepner's story.

Wepner is six foot five inches tall and fought at weights ranging from 202 to 225 pounds as a heavyweight. In 51 professional bouts, from 1964 to 1978, he won 35 (17 by **knockout**), lost 14 (nine by knockout), had two draws, and fought a total of 360 rounds.

WHITAKER, PERNELL "SWEET PEA". B. 2 January 1964, Norfolk, Virginia. Pernell Whitaker was a top **amateur** boxer who won **professional** world championships in four different weight classes. As a youth, Pernell was known as "Pete" to his friends. At one of his early **bouts** as an amateur boxer, his friends called him "Sweet Pete." A **ringside** reporter misunderstood the name and described him as "Sweet Pea." The name stuck, and he became "Sweet Pea" for the rest of his **ring** career.

As an amateur boxer, he was one of the best in the world and claimed a record of 201 victories and only 13 defeats. He won the 1982 National **Amateur Athletic Union lightweight** championship and was a **silver medalist** at the 1982 **World Championships**, losing to **Cuban** Ángel Herrera in the finals. In 1983 at the Pan American Games, he won the lightweight **gold medal** by defeating Herrera in the finals. In the **Olympic Games** in 1984, Cuba did not participate, so Whitaker had an easier path to the championship.

He became a professional boxer on 23 November 1984 on a **card** at **Madison Square Garden** with five other former Olympians. Although his first opponent, Farrain Comeaux, had an undefeated record of 9–0, Whitaker handled him easily and scored a second-**round technical knockout**.

After Whitaker won his first 15 bouts, he lost a controversial **split decision** to José Luis Ramírez, a veteran of over 100 fights, for the **World Boxing Council (WBC)** world's lightweight championship in **France** on 12 March 1988. The following year, Whitaker again fought for a lightweight title—this time against Greg Haugen, a fighter with a record and experience level more similar to Whitaker's. At the time of the bout on 18 February 1989, Haugen had been fighting professionally for about six years and had won 23 of 24 bouts. Whitaker had been fighting professionally for about four years and had won 16 of 17 bouts. Whitaker won a 12-round **decision** in the bout in Hampton, Virginia, and became the **International Boxing Federation (IBF)** world's lightweight champion.

After one successful title defense against Louie Lomeli, Whitaker defeated Ramírez in a rematch in Norfolk, Virginia, and added the **vacant** WBC lightweight title to his collection. He then successfully defended against Freddie Pendleton and **Azumah Nelson**. On 11 August 1990, Whitaker knocked out Juan Nazario in the first round and gained **World Boxing Association (WBA)** title recognition. After three successful defenses of the three lightweight titles, Whitaker abandoned them to move up in weight class. On 17 July 1992, Whitaker won a unanimous 12-round decision over Rafael Pineda and became IBF **light welterweight** champion. He did not remain at that weight long, and eight months later he defeated James "Buddy" McGirt for the WBC **welterweight** title.

Whitaker's first defense of the welterweight crown was against legendary champion **Julio César Chávez**. At that time, Chávez had won all 87 of his prior bouts and had had no losses or draws. His was bidding for his fourth different weight class championship as he already had won the **super featherweight** and **lightweight** titles and was the current light welterweight champion. Whitaker appeared to most observers to have won the bout, but it was scored a **majority draw** as one **judge** voted for Chávez while the other two judges saw the bout even.

Whitaker made two successful defenses of the welterweight title before moving up to his fourth weight division—**light middleweight**. On 4 March 1995, Whitaker defeated Julio César Vásquez to win the WBA light middleweight title and became one of the few boxers in **ring** history to win championships in four different weight classes. He never defended that title, though, and returned to the welterweight division, where he won five consecutive bouts in defense of that title.

On 12 April 1997, Whitaker fought another one of that era's legendary fighters—**Óscar De La Hoya**. De La Hoya had also been an Olympic champion and won three professional world championships and was bidding for his fourth. In a relatively close but **unanimous decision**, De La Hoya won, although he was knocked down briefly in the ninth round. Whitaker's next fight six months later was ruled a **no contest** after he won a decision but tested positive for cocaine. Whitaker did not fight in 1998, but in February 1999 he challenged **Félix Trinidad** for the IBF welterweight title. In this fight, Whitaker was soundly beaten and was down in the second round.

Whitaker only fought once more after the Trinidad bout—two years later—and lost when he broke his clavicle while throwing a punch in round two. He lasted one more round, and the bout was stopped by the ring physician at 27 seconds of the fourth round.

In retirement, Whitaker has turned to **training** and has worked with Dorin Spivey, Calvin Brock, and Zab Judah.

Whitaker is five foot six inches tall and has a 69-inch **reach**. He fought at weights ranging from 134 to 155 pounds, primarily as a lightweight and welterweight. In 46 professional bouts, from 1984 to 2001, he won 40 (17 by **knockout**), lost four (one by knockout), had one draw and one no contest, and fought a total of 379 rounds. He was inducted into the **International Boxing Hall of Fame** in 2008.

WHITE HOPE. After the black fighter **Jack Johnson** won the world's **heavyweight** championship and deported himself in a manner that antagonized many white people, the sporting public began to search for a Caucasian boxer who could dethrone Johnson. These boxers were referred to as "white hopes" in the vernacular of that era. Among the boxers considered as "white hopes" were Bill Brennan, Dan "Porky" Flynn, "Fireman" Jim Flynn, Fred Fulton, Al Kaufman, Luther McCarty, Frank Moran, Carl Morris, Arthur Pelkey, George "Boer" Rodel, Ed "Gunboat" Smith, and **Jess Willard**. Retired undefeated heavyweight champion **Jim Jeffries** came out of retirement in an attempt to defeat Johnson but failed. Kaufman, Flynn, and Moran also failed in heavyweight title **bouts** against Johnson.

On 5 April 1915, Jess Willard succeeded by knocking out Johnson in the 26th **round** of their scheduled 45-round bout in Havana, **Cuba**, and the era of the white hope ended.

The phrase came into use again in the 1970s and 1980s when the heavyweight title had been controlled by black fighters for nearly 20 years and most heavyweight contenders were also black. White contenders such as **Jerry Quarry**, **Gerry Cooney**, and Randall "Tex" Cobb were often referred to as "white hopes" by promoters looking to capitalize on the race of those contenders, although racial animosity among the participants just did not exist then.

WILDE, WILLIAM JAMES "JIMMY," "THE MIGHTY ATOM". B. 15 May 1892, Pentwyn Deintyr, **Wales**. D. 10 March 1969, Whitchurch, **England**. For a little guy (five foot two inches, 94 pounds) Jimmy Wilde had one of the most devastating **knockout** punches and was rated by **Bert Randolph Sugar** as the 13th greatest puncher in boxing history, regardless of weight, as well as the best **flyweight** of all time.

Wilde began working as a coal miner at the age of 12 and also fought in **boxing booths**. His earliest recorded **professional bout** was on 1 January 1911 in Pontypridd, Wales, although it is likely that he fought prior to that date. In his third professional bout, on 20 January 1911, Wilde fought a six-**round draw** with Dai Jones in Pontypridd. This would be Wilde's last bout that he did not win until 25 January 1915—a span of time in which he won 89 consecutive bouts.

Although there were no formal weight classes at extremely light weights when Wilde began boxing, he did win a bout on 20 July 1912 in Cardiff, Wales, that was billed for the "British 94 lb. title" by stopping Kid Morris in five rounds. Wilde's 16 November 1912 victory over Jim Ransford in the second round at Tonypandy, Wales, was billed for the "flyweight championship of England." His 1 January 1913 18-round **technical knockout** over Billy Padden in Glasgow, **Scotland**, was for the "English 98 lb. championship," and three weeks later on 18 January 1913, Wilde defeated Tommy Hughes in seven rounds for the English 100-pound title in Tonypandy. On 6 December 1913 Wilde, weighing only 96 pounds, defeated Young George Dando in 10 rounds at Merthyr Tydfil, Wales, for the "English and Welsh 108 lbs. **paperweight**" title. On 30 March 1914, Wilde stopped Frenchman Eugene Husson in six rounds at the **National Sporting Club (NSC)** in London in a bout billed for the European Boxing Union flyweight title (and also for the world gnatweight title). Wilde weighed only 94 pounds for this bout, while Husson was just 87.5 pounds.

On 25 January 1915, Wilde suffered the first defeat of his professional career when he was stopped in the 17th round by the 20-pounds heavier Tancy Lee for the British Empire flyweight title, European Boxing Union flyweight title, and International Boxing Union (IBU) flyweight title. Wilde won the British Empire and IBU titles the following year when he stopped Joe Symonds in 12 rounds at the NSC on 14 February 1916. Later that year, Wilde defeated Tancy Lee and was also credited with the IBU title.

In 1916, he joined the army and worked as a physical education instructor.

On 18 December 1916, Wilde received world recognition as flyweight champion when he defeated the Italian American Giuseppe Di Melfi, who boxed as the Young Zulu Kid, in an 11th-round technical knockout.

In 1918, Wilde suffered only the second loss of his professional career when in a **bantamweight** tournament, after winning two three-round bouts in two days, he was **decisioned** by Memphis Pal Moore in the three-round tournament championship bout on 12 December at Royal Albert Hall in London. He defeated Moore by 20-round decision on 17 July 1919, also in London.

In 1919, Wilde traveled to the **United States**, where most states still did not allow decisions in boxing contests, and he fought several no-decision bouts there. He spent most of 1919 and 1920 in the United States and **Canada**. In 1921, he returned to London for a bout with **Pete Herman**, the former world's bantamweight champion. Wilde weighed in at 110 pounds, his heaviest ever, against Herman's 119 pounds and was stopped in the 17th round of their scheduled 20-round bout.

Wilde retired after that bout but came back two and a half years later. His last fight was on 18 June 1923 outdoors at the Polo Grounds in New York against the Filipino **Pancho Villa**. Villa knocked out Wilde in the seventh round, and Wilde retired from the **ring** permanently shortly afterward.

In retirement, he lived comfortably, as he had saved much of his ring earnings, but later lost much of them in failed enterprises, such as a Welsh cinema chain and a cafe. He was president of the British National Union of Boxers and wrote a book published in 1923—part autobiography and part instruction manual, *The Art of Boxing*.

Wilde had a 66-inch **reach** and fought at weights ranging from 94 to 110 pounds as a flyweight. In 152 recorded professional bouts, from 1911 to 1923, he won 134 (100 by knockout), lost four (three by knockout), and had two draws, seven **no contests**, and five no-decision bouts, in which he was awarded the **newspaper decision** in four and lost one. He fought a total of 1,132 rounds. He was inducted as a member of the inaugural class of the **International Boxing Hall of Fame** in 1990.

WILLARD, JESS "THE POTTAWATOMIE GIANT". B. 29 December 1881, Pottawatomie County, Kansas. D. 15 December 1968, Los Angeles, California. Jess Willard was one of the largest men to become **heavyweight** champion. He was slightly more than six foot six inches tall, had an 83-inch **reach**, and weighed about 240 pounds. Raised on a ranch in Kansas, he worked as a cowboy and, after he married, moved to Oklahoma working as a mule salesman and wagon driver. When his business ventures were not successful, he decided to take advantage of his size and try his luck as a prizefighter.

His first recorded professional **bout** was on 15 February 1911 at the age of 29 in Sapulpa, Oklahoma. His awkwardness and lack of **ring** generalship resulted in his being **disqualified** in the fourth **round** for throwing his opponent to the mat. He did better in his next six matches, winning four by **knockout** and two by **decision**. After being stopped in the fifth round of his next contest, he then traveled to Illinois and Indiana, winning three more by knockout.

He ended his travels in New York City, where he fought two of the better "**white hopes**" of the era, Arthur Pelkey and Luther McCarty. The bouts were no-decision ones, and Willard received the **newspaper decision** over Pelkey, and the McCarty bout was ruled a **draw**. (Ironically, less than one year later, on 24 May 1913, Pelkey killed McCarty in the ring in a bout in Calgary, Alberta, **Canada**.)

After two more bouts in New York, one in Buffalo and one in New York City, in which Willard knocked out a sailor (Sailor White) and a soldier (Soldier Kearns), Willard headed for the West Coast, stopping along the way in Indiana, where he won two more bouts by knockout.

Willard lost a 20-round decision to another of the white hopes, Ed "Gunboat" Smith, in Colma, California, on 20 May 1913. Three bouts later, he fought Jack "Bull" Young in Vernon, California, on 22 August 1913. Willard knocked him out in the 11th round, and Young died the following day due to a brain hemorrhage suffered in the bout. Willard then traveled back cross-country, stopping in Milwaukee, Wisconsin, where he lost a **newspaper decision** to George "Boer" Rodel. After a two-round knockout in Indiana, Willard faced a man who was about his size, the six-foot-four-inch, 234-pound Carl Morris, in **Madison Square Garden**. Although the bout was officially no decision, Willard won a one-sided newspaper decision.

Over the next 16 months, Willard fought five bouts, winning four by knockout and, in a fight that Willard took on short notice acting as a substitute, losing a newspaper decision to Tom McMahon, a fighter who was about 60 pounds lighter.

Willard's big day in boxing history occurred on 5 April 1915 when **Jack Johnson**, the heavyweight champion, met him in Havana, **Cuba**, for a scheduled 45-round bout. Johnson was ahead throughout most of the fight but lost when he was counted out in the 26th round. Johnson later claimed he threw the fight, but most boxing experts do not believe that story. As a result, Willard was the new world's heavyweight champion.

Willard successfully defended the title only once, on 25 March 1916 against Frank Moran at Madison Square Garden in **Tex Rickard's** first promotion there. The bout, according to New York State law at the time, was limited to 10 rounds and would be a no-decision bout with the title only changing hands if Moran scored a knockout. He did not, and the bout went into the record books simply as a no decision, although Willard won the decision in the eyes of the sportswriters.

For the next three years, Willard did not fight. He did remain in the public eye and appeared in Buffalo Bill's Wild West Show and in movie serials as a cowboy. He also appeared on the vaudeville stage. Although not particularly fond of this, he preferred it to boxing.

He finally returned to the **ring** on 4 July 1919 in Toledo, Ohio, against **Jack Dempsey** and suffered one of the worst beatings a boxer ever did in the ring. Dempsey knocked him down seven times in the first round, although Willard stayed on his feet after that until the fight was stopped in the third round. After the fight, Willard was diagnosed with a broken jaw, broken cheekbone, and broken ribs and he had also lost some teeth.

Willard retired after the Dempsey bout, but four years later he was talked into a brief comeback. He stopped Floyd Johnson in 11 rounds on 12 May 1923 at Yankee Stadium and was knocked out by **Luis Ángel Firpo** in eight rounds on 12 July 1923.

In retirement, he was a successful businessman both in real estate and supermarkets, and occasionally he would **referee** professional wrestling matches.

Willard fought at weights ranging from 214 to 259 pounds as a heavyweight. In 35 professional bouts, from 1911 to 1923, he won 23 (20 by knockout), lost five (three by knockout), had one draw, and fought six no-decision bouts, in which he was awarded the newspaper decision in three, lost two, and drew one. He fought a total of 268 rounds. He was inducted into the **International Boxing Hall of Fame** in 2003.

WILLIAMS, CLEVELAND T. "BIG CAT". B. 6 June 1933, Griffin, Georgia. D. 3 September 1999, Houston, Texas. Cleveland Williams was one of the hardest-punching **heavyweights** during the 1950s and 1960s but never got a chance at the heavyweight title until he was past his prime. A big man at six foot three inches tall with an 80-inch **reach**, he began his **professional boxing** career on 11 December 1951 with a three-**round knockout** in Tampa, Florida. He won his first 27 **bouts**, with 23 knockouts, fighting mostly in the southern **United States**, before he lost a four-round **decision** to Sylvester Jones on the **undercard** of the **Rocky Marciano**–Roland LaStarza heavyweight title fight at the Polo Grounds on 24 September 1953, a bout in which Williams was **knocked down** twice.

After winning four more bouts by knockout, including a return bout with Jones in which he knocked out Jones in seven rounds, Williams was a last-minute substitute as an opponent for the tough Bob Satterfield on 22 June 1954 in Miami Beach, Florida. Satterfield gave Williams his second loss and first by knockout as he knocked him out in the third round.

Williams was inactive for the next two years as he was drafted into the U.S. Army. After his discharge, he continued his winning ways with 12 consecutive victories, eight by knockout, but none against the top contenders. On 15 April 1959, he met **Sonny Liston** and was stopped in three rounds by the powerful future heavyweight champion. Following that bout, Williams won an easy three-round knockout and then did not fight for five months. On 1 October 1959, Williams faced a young heavyweight with a record of 18–1 named Curley Lee. Williams knocked Lee down twice in the fifth round and then knocked him out in the 10th. Lee was badly hurt and suffered brain damage that ended his promising career. Williams then fought a rematch with Liston but this time did not last two rounds. He rebounded from that loss and won eight straight, including a seventh-round stoppage of future heavyweight champion Ernie Terrell. Williams then fought a **draw** with top contender **Eddie Machen** and followed that bout with three more victories before losing a **split decision** in a rematch with Terrell. Williams then won five straight bouts before his life changed in 1964.

On 29 November 1964, Williams was driving at night in his hometown of Houston. He was pulled over by a highway patrolman who accused Williams of speeding. Reportedly, Williams resisted arrest, and the patrolman pulled his gun out and shot Williams in the stomach. Since this occurred during the segregation era in the South, the true story will never be known. Over the next seven months, Williams underwent four operations; his hip was broken, his colon was damaged, and his kidney had to be removed. Miraculously, he recovered, and his weight, which had gone down to 145 pounds from his normal 220, eventually returned.

On 8 February 1966, he returned to the **ring** and won a one-round knockout. After three more victories, **Muhammad Ali** gave Williams a shot at the world's heavyweight championship. The two fought on 14 November 1966 at the Houston Astrodome, and with Ali at his prime and Williams far from it, Williams was stopped in the third round.

Williams did not fight in 1967 but returned in 1968. He continued boxing until 1972, but in the 20 bouts he fought over those five years, he won only 13 and was knocked out or stopped in four of them. His last fight was on 28 October 1972 in Denver, and he won a 10-round decision over **journeyman** Roberto Davila.

As a result of his abdominal injuries, he began undergoing dialysis weekly in the early 1990s. On 3 September 1999, while crossing a street in Houston, he was hit by a hit-and-run driver and died.

Williams fought at weights ranging from 190 to 236 pounds as a heavyweight. In 92 professional bouts, from 1951 to 1972, he won 78 (58 by knockout), lost 13 (eight by knockout), had one draw, and fought a total of 478 rounds.

WILLIAMS, IKE. B. 2 August 1923, Brunswick, Georgia. D. 5 September 1994, Los Angeles, California. Ike Williams was one of the best fighters in boxing history (selected by boxing historian **Bert Randolph Sugar** as number 47 in his book *The 100 Greatest Boxers of All Time*), yet his career could possibly have been greater had he not had the misfortune of being managed by Frank "Blinky" Palermo, one of the underworld's leaders in the 1950s.

Williams was born in Georgia but was raised in Trenton, New Jersey. He attended Trenton Central High School and began boxing as a teenager. In 1938, he won the Trenton **Golden Gloves featherweight** championship. He had his first **professional bout** on 15 March 1940 in New Brunswick, New Jersey, at the age of 16. After his first 16 bouts, his record was 10–4–2, but he then won his next 34 consecutive bouts. On 25 January 1944 in Philadelphia, Williams fought Bob Montgomery, who had recently lost his **lightweight** championship to Beau Jack. Montgomery knocked out Williams with only 11 seconds remaining in the 12th and final **round** of their **nontitle bout**.

Following that bout, Williams fought 19 more fights in 1944, winning all but one—a **split decision** loss to Willie Joyce. Included in his 18 victories were two split-decision wins over former lightweight champion Sammy Angott.

Williams's 11 bouts in 1945 included three more with Joyce. Williams won the first but lost the next two. He also was stopped by Angott in nine rounds after he tore a stomach muscle. The highlight of the year for Williams occurred on 18 April when he traveled to **Mexico** and stopped Mexican lightweight Juan Zurita and won the world's lightweight title. The Mexican fans began rioting, and Williams had his newly won world championship belt stolen from him at gunpoint.

Although Williams kept busy by fighting over-the-weight nontitle bouts, he was not able to arrange a defense of his title. Williams became upset with his manager, Connie McCarthy, and attempted to go out on his own without a manager. The managers' organization, the Boxing Guild, then blackballed Williams and threatened to do the same to any promoter who hired Williams for a fight. Williams then attempted to organize some of the top boxers, but they did not want to become organized for fear of repercussions. He was then approached by Frank "Blinky" Palermo, who offered to manage Williams and promised to get him fights. Williams's first title defense was against Enrique Bolaños in Los Angeles on 30 April 1946. Williams stopped him in eight rounds.

Williams's next defense came on 4 September 1946. He traveled to Cardiff, **Wales**, and knocked out the Welsh challenger Ronnie James in the ninth round after knocking him down six times in the fight. On 4 August 1947, Williams fought a rematch with Bob Montgomery, who at this time was recognized as lightweight champion by the **New York State Athletic Commission**. Williams had recognition from the **National Boxing Association** as lightweight champion. Williams stopped him in six rounds and achieved universal recognition as lightweight champion.

After he defeated future **welterweight** champion **Kid Gavilán** in a nontitle bout, he defended his lightweight title against Bolaños again on 25 May 1948, winning a split-decision 15-round bout in Los Angeles. In Williams's next title defense on 12 July 1948 he stopped former lightweight champion Beau Jack in six rounds. Williams's first fight in 1949 was a 10-round **unanimous-decision** win over future welterweight champion Johnny Bratton. He followed that with two more nontitle fights with Kid Gavilán, losing both in close bouts. On 21 July 1949, Williams fought Bolaños for the third time in a lightweight championship bout and defeated him for the third time—this time by a fourth-round **technical knockout**.

Although Williams kept busy fighting nontitle bouts, his next lightweight title defense did not take place until 25 May 1951, when he lost his championship to Jimmy Carter via a 14th-round technical knockout after being knocked down three times.

In 1951, the **United States** Senate appointed a special commission to investigate organized crime in the country, and Williams was one of the individuals who was called upon to testify. During the investigation, it was disclosed that Palermo never paid Williams for several of his bouts and owed him more than $60,000 for two of the fights. He claimed that he never threw a fight but that at times he carried his opponent so that the gambling interests might be satisfied.

He continued boxing but lost to several of the top fighters of the era, including Gil Turner, who stopped him in 10 rounds; Chuck Davey, who stopped him in five (although Williams later admitted he threw the fight); and future welterweight and **middleweight** champion **Carmine Basilio**, who won a 10-round unanimous decision.

Williams's last two fights were with Beau Jack in 1955—the first was scored a **draw**, and Jack retired in the eighth round of the second fight. Both fighters retired from the **ring** after that fight.

After retiring, Williams's generosity in giving money to his friends and his penchant for gambling caught up with him, and he lost two apartment houses that he had owned. He eventually worked as a day laborer. During the 1970s, **Muhammad Ali** attempted to help him by offering work at his **training** camp, but it did not work out. A decade later, promoter **Don King** and boxer **Mike Tyson** helped Williams relocate to Los Angeles.

Williams was five foot nine inches tall and had a 68-inch **reach**. He fought at weights ranging from 128 to 155 pounds, primarily as a lightweight and welterweight. In 157 professional bouts, from 1940 to 1955, he won 127 (61 by **knockout**), lost 24 (six by knockout), had four draws, and fought two no-decision bouts, in which he received the **newspaper decision** in one and drew one. He fought a total of 1,159 rounds. He was inducted as a member of the inaugural class of the **International Boxing Hall of Fame** in 1990.

WILLS, HARRY "THE BLACK PANTHER". B. 15 May 1889, New Orleans, Louisiana. D. 21 December 1958, New York, New York. Had **Jack Johnson** not led the life he did, Harry Wills might have been the world's **heavyweight** champion. Wills was the top challenger for **Jack Dempsey's** heavyweight title during the 1920s, but due to race riots that occurred following Johnson's winning the heavyweight title and his arrogant behavior while champion that alienated many white fans, promoter **Tex Rickard** refused to make an interracial match for the heavyweight title once the Caucasian **Jess Willard** won it.

Wills began boxing as a professional in 1911 in New Orleans but had limited opportunities against white fighters. He found himself boxing other good black boxers such as **Sam Langford**, Sam McVey, **Joe Jeannette**, Battling Jim Johnson, Jeff Clark, George "Kid" Cotton, Kid Norfolk, and

John Lester Johnson quite often. In his 107 recorded fights, he had 23 with Langford, of which 15 were no-decision **bouts**. Six of the eight bouts that either ended in a **knockout** or **decision** were won by Wills.

On 7 September 1915, Wills defeated Sam McVey on a 12-**round** decision in Boston and claimed the "colored heavyweight title." He lost it to Langford a few months later when Langford knocked him out in the 19th round of their scheduled 20-round bout in New Orleans on 11 February 1916.

Although Wills and Langford met on at least seven occasions in 1916 and 1917 with the title at stake, they were all "no decision" bouts, and the title did not change hands as they went the scheduled distance each time.

In December 1917, Wills traveled to **Panama** and for the next seven months met his usual foes, Langford, Clark, and McVey. He knocked out Langford twice, beat McVey twice, once by knockout, and knocked out Clark. As a result of his defeats of Langford, Wills again claimed the colored title when they returned to the states in the summer of 1918.

In bouts against white fighters, Wills defeated Willie Meehan in four rounds in 1914, and Meehan later defeated Jack Dempsey twice in four rounders. Wills also knocked out Fred Fulton in three rounds in 1920 and broke three of Fulton's ribs in the process. In 1921, Wills knocked out Edward "Gunboat" Smith in one round. In 1924, Wills won a 12-round **newspaper decision** over **Luis Ángel Firpo**. The closest Wills came to a heavyweight title bout occurred on 12 October 1926 when he fought future heavyweight champion **Jack Sharkey** but lost on a **disqualification** in the 13th round of their 15-round bout. Wills was disqualified for an illegal back-hand blow but had been losing the fight by a large margin.

In Wills's next fight, he was knocked out in four rounds by the Basque boxer Paolino Uzcudun on 13 July 1927. Wills continued fighting until 1932 and had his last bout on 19 October 1932, a one-round knockout of a relatively unknown fighter.

In retirement, Wills invested his money wisely and owned real estate in Harlem. Upon his death from diabetes in 1958, he left an estate of over $100,000.

Wills was six foot two inches tall and had a 76-inch **reach**. He fought at weights ranging from 203 to 225 pounds as a heavyweight. In 107 professional bouts, from 1911 to 1932, he won 67 (54 by knockout), lost nine (five by knockout), had three draws and five **no contests**, and fought 23 no-decision bouts, in which he was awarded the newspaper decision in 19, lost one, and drew three. He fought a total of 706 rounds. He was inducted into the **International Boxing Hall of Fame** in 1992.

WOMEN IN BOXING. For most of the 19th and 20th centuries, women did not compete in the boxing **ring**. With the rise of the women's equality movement, several began boxing in the 1970s. By the 21st century, there are quite a few women boxers, and in the 2012 **Olympic Games** women's boxing was included for the first time. Many boxing fans still do not look kindly on seeing women competing in the ring, and women's boxing still does not have the fan appeal that women's basketball or women's tennis has.

One of the first female boxers to achieve fame was Cathy "Cat" Davis, who fought during the 1970s and even appeared on the cover of *Ring* magazine. During the 1980s, there was not much activity with women's boxing, but it resurfaced in the 1990s and fighters such as Christy Martin as well as the daughters of **heavyweight** champions **Joe Frazier** (Jacqui Frazier-Lyde) and **Muhammad Ali** (Leila Ali) became well known. **Golden Gloves** boxing tournaments also began being held for women.

In 2012, a women's division was added for the Olympic Games, and 36 competitors took part in three weight divisions. Gold medals were won by Nicola Adams of **Great Britain (flyweight)**, Katie Taylor of **Ireland (light welterweight)**, and Claressa Shields of the **United States (light heavyweight)**.

The 2004 Academy Award–winning film *Million Dollar Baby* was about the relationship between a female professional boxer and her **trainer**.

There have been a few women who were involved in the boxing business. Several were boxing promoters—Jackie Kallen, **Aileen Eaton**, and boxer **Sean O'Grady's** mother, Jean O'Grady. "KO" Becky O'Neill, a four-foot-seven-inch former vaudevillian was the manager of **bantamweight** champion Jeff Chandler. Carol B. Polis became the first female boxing **judge** in 1973. Eva Shain was the first female to judge a heavyweight title fight when she worked the **Muhammad Ali–Earnie Shavers** championship **bout** in 1977. Eugenia Williams and Barbara Perez (wife of **referee** Tony Perez) have also served as boxing judges. In 2008, Melvina Lathan was appointed chairperson of the **New York State Athletic Commission**. She is the first African American female to hold that post and had been licensed as a boxing judge in New York State since 1991.

WORLD BOXING ASSOCIATION (WBA). The World Boxing Association is a boxing sanctioning organization that began in 1921 in the **United States** as the National Boxing Association (NBA). In 1962, the NBA was renamed and has since become predominantly a Latin American organization with offices in **Panama** or **Venezuela** (1990–2007). Its championships are rated on a par by boxing fans with those of the **World Boxing Council**.

WORLD BOXING COUNCIL (WBC). The World Boxing Council is a boxing sanctioning organization that was formed in 1963 in **Mexico** City. Since 1975, the WBC president has been José Sulaimán, a controversial figure who has been accused of corruption and who has worked closely with the controversial promoter **Don King**. Nonetheless, the WBC's championships, along with those of the competing **World Boxing Association**, carry the most weight among boxing fans, and many of boxing's greatest fighters in the latter half of the 20th century have won WBC championships.

WORLD BOXING FEDERATION (WBF). The World Boxing Federation is a boxing sanctioning organization that was formed in 1988 in Bristol, Tennessee, and since 2009 has been based in the country of Luxembourg. It is one of many such organizations whose championships do not carry much weight among boxing fans.

WORLD BOXING ORGANIZATION (WBO). The World Boxing Organization is one of the four major boxing sanctioning organizations. It was created in 1988 after several members of the **World Boxing Association** left that organization due to a rules dispute. It is based in San Juan, **Puerto Rico**, and is the least prestigious of the four major sanctioning bodies.

WORLD CHAMPIONS. The ultimate goal of all professional boxers is to be recognized as world champion. As boxing traditionally has been one of the most loosely organized sports, the title "world champion" in each division began with a **bout** promoted for the world championship. There has never been any organized world championship tournament, but rather the individual champions would defend their titles at their discretion, although usually at least once annually. For most of the 20th century, there was usually only one boxer in each weight class who was world champion. Occasionally, when a champion retired or outgrew his weight class, more than one bout would be promoted as a "world championship" match and more than one boxer would be so recognized, but usually the two so-called world champions would meet in the **ring** and the title status would be clarified.

During the latter half of the 20th century, as various sanctioning organizations gained power, each one would recognize their own champions and most weight divisions had four or more different world champions. This remains the case in the 21st century, and consequently only the most diehard boxing fans can name the current world champions.

WORLD CHAMPIONSHIPS. A biannual men's **amateur boxing** tournament promoted by the **International Boxing Association (AIBA)** is known as the World Championships. It was first held in 1974 in Havana, **Cuba**, and the first four World Championships were held quadrennially from 1974 to 1986. The fifth World Championships occurred in 1989, and since then, beginning in 1991, the event has been held in alternate years. The 2013 AIBA World Championships are scheduled for 4–13 October in Almaty, **Kazakhstan**.

Cuban boxers have dominated the World Championships. In the 16 tournaments that have been held from 1974 to 2011, Cuba has won 65 **gold medals**, 28 **silver medals**, and 23 **bronze medals**—116 in total. **Russia** and the Soviet Union combined have won a total of 99 medals, with 35 gold medals, 29 silver medals, and 35 bronze medals.

A similar amateur **women's** event began in 2001 in Scranton, Pennsylvania. Subsequent women's world championships have been held in 2002, 2005, 2006, and biannually since then. The 2014 women's world championships are scheduled to take place in **Canada**. In the seven events from 2001 to 2012, Russian women have won the most medals—48 (18 gold, 8 silver, and 22 bronze). China is second with 31 medals (11 gold, 8 silver, and 12 bronze).

WRIGHT, ARCHIBALD LEE. *See* MOORE, ARCHIE "THE OLD MONGOOSE" (né ARCHIBALD LEE WRIGHT).

Y

YOUNGS, JOSEPH. *See* RYAN, TOMMY (né JOSEPH YOUNGS).

Z

ZALE, TONY "THE MAN OF STEEL" (né ANTON FLORIAN ZALE-SKI). B. 29 May 1913, Gary, Indiana. D. 20 March 1997, Portage, Indiana. The names Tony Zale and **Rocky Graziano** will forever be linked in boxing history. In less than two years, from 1946 to 1948, they fought three of boxing's greatest fights. Although each of the two boxers fought memorable **bouts** with other opponents, the Zale–Graziano battles are the ones that fight fans remember the most.

Tony Zale did well as an **amateur** and represented Chicago in the 1934 Chicago–New York Intercity **Golden Gloves** bouts but lost a decision to future **light heavyweight** champion Melio Bettina. Zale had worked at the steel mills in his hometown of Gary, Indiana, and gained the nickname "Man of Steel" for his ability to take a punch as well as his former employment.

Shortly after the Golden Gloves ended in 1934, Zale became a professional boxer and had his first bout on 11 June 1934 in Chicago. Over the next two months, he won his first nine bouts before losing consecutive six-**round decisions** on 13 and 15 August. On 5 November 1934, Zale had a record of 15–3 but then lost six of his next eight bouts.

Zale's record was relatively unimpressive over the next four years, but in 1939 and 1940 he won 11 consecutive bouts, nine by **knockout**, and earned a shot at the **middleweight** title. On 19 July 1940, Zale stopped Al Hostak in the 13th round in Hostak's hometown of Seattle, Washington, and won the **National Boxing Association (NBA)** middleweight title. Zale made two successful defenses of that title in 1941, stopping Steve Mamakos in 14 rounds and demolishing Hostak in a rematch that saw Hostak down eight times in the second round.

Between those two title defenses, Zale took part in one of boxing's more unusual events. The Pabst Brewing Company sponsored a boxing card with free admission on 16 August 1941 in Milwaukee, Wisconsin, at a time when the national convention of the Fraternal Order of Eagles was taking place. The main event of the six-bout card was won by Zale on a ninth-round knockout of Billy Pryor and was refereed by former heavyweight champion Jack Dempsey. A record 135,132 fans attended the matches at the Juneau Park outdoor arena.

Zale then won a 15-round **unanimous decision** over Georgie Abrams at **Madison Square Garden** in a bout recognized by both the NBA and **New York State Athletic Commission** for the middleweight title. Zale then lost a 12-round decision to **Billy Conn**, former light heavyweight champion who had nearly won the world's **heavyweight** title from **Joe Louis** the preceding year.

Zale went into the U.S. Navy, and his title was "frozen for the duration" in the vernacular of the day. He resumed boxing in January 1946 after his discharge. Later that year, Zale engaged in the first of his three battles with Rocky Graziano.

On 27 September 1946 at Yankee Stadium, Zale knocked out Graziano in a middleweight championship bout in which Graziano was knocked down in the first round and Zale in the second round. The bout was named "Fight of the Year" by *Ring* **magazine**.

After Zale won five **nontitle bouts** in 1947, he again met Graziano in a middleweight title fight—this time in Chicago on 16 July 1947. Graziano was knocked down in the third round but in the sixth round caught Zale with a multitude of punches before the bout was stopped, with Graziano being the new world's middleweight champion. This bout was also named *Ring*'s "Fight of the Year."

Zale took six months off then won three bouts by knockout in early 1948 before meeting Graziano for the third time. The **rubber match** was held outdoors in Newark, New Jersey, on 10 June 1948. Zale rewon the title by knocking Graziano down in the first and third rounds before knocking him out in third round.

Three months later, on 21 September 1948 in Jersey City, New Jersey, Zale fought the last bout of his career. European middleweight champion Frenchman **Marcel Cerdan**, with a record of 108–3, stopped Zale at the end of the 11th round and won the world's middleweight championship. This fight also was named "Fight of the Year." Zale retired following the loss.

In retirement, Zale worked for the Chicago Department of Parks and for Catholic Youth Organizations as a youth mentor. He died at the age of 83 from the effects of Parkinson's disease and Alzheimer's disease at a nursing home in Indiana.

Zale was five foot seven inches tall and had a 69-inch **reach**. He fought at weights ranging from 154 to 164 pounds as a middleweight. In 87 professional bouts, from 1934 to 1948, he won 67 (45 by knockout), lost 18 (five by knockout), had two draws, and fought a total of 501 rounds. He was inducted into the **International Boxing Hall of Fame** in 1991.

ZALESKI, ANTON FLORIAN. *See* ZALE, TONY "THE MAN OF STEEL" (né ANTON FLORIAN ZALESKI).

ZÁRATE SERNA, CARLOS "CAÑAS". B. 23 May 1951, Tepito, Distrito Federal, **Mexico**. Carlos Zárate had one of the most powerful punches for a man his size. While only 118 pounds, 90 percent of his **bouts** ended with him winning by **knockout**, an extraordinary percentage, better than nearly every **professional** boxer regardless of weight class.

He began boxing professionally on 2 February 1970 after winning the Mexican **Golden Gloves** title and claimed an **amateur boxing** record of 33–3 with 30 knockouts. He won his first 23 professional bouts by knockout, with all but two of those knockouts coming in the first three **rounds**. On 8 May 1976, with an undefeated record of 39–0, he challenged Rodolfo Martínez for the **World Boxing Council (WBC) bantamweight** championship at the Forum in Inglewood, California. Zárate stopped Martínez in the ninth round and became champion.

Zárate made three successful title defenses. The **World Boxing Association** bantamweight champion at that time was Alfredo Zamora, another Mexican who was also undefeated. A match between the two champions for the undisputed bantamweight championship was eagerly awaited by boxing fans, but the two sanctioning organizations demanded too much money. The California Boxing **Commission** eventually sanctioned the bout as a 10-round **nontitle bout**. On 23 April 1977, the match took place, and the 45–0 Zárate established his superiority with a fourth-round **stoppage** of the 29–0 Zamora.

After five more successful title defenses, Zárate attempted to move up in weight class and challenged **Wilfredo Gómez** for the WBC **super bantamweight** (122 pound) title on 28 October 1978 in Gómez's homeland of **Puerto Rico**. Entering the bout, Gómez had a record of 21–0–1 (with 21 knockouts), and Zárate was 52–0 with 51 knockouts. Gómez knocked Zárate down twice in the fourth round and once in the fifth before the bout was stopped.

Zárate then made one more successful defense of his bantamweight championship before losing the title to Lupe Pintor in an extremely close **split decision** on 3 June 1979 in **Las Vegas**. After the bout, Zárate retired from the **ring** with a career record of 54–2.

As with many boxers, Zárate did not remain retired and attempted a comeback in 1986. After winning 12 straight bouts (10 by knockout), Zárate challenged the undefeated WBC super bantamweight champion, Jeff Fenech, in Fenech's hometown of Sydney, **Australia**, on 16 October 1987. The bout ended unsatisfactorily, as Fenech suffered a cut from an accidental collision of heads and the bout was stopped after only four rounds. The WBC rules for that situation required the **judges'** scorecards up to that time to be used to determine a winner, and Fenech was ahead on points on all three scorecards and was named the winner by **technical decision**.

After Fenech abandoned his title to compete in the **featherweight** division, Zárate and Daniel Zaragoza fought for the **vacant** WBC super bantamweight title on 29 February 1988 at the Great Western Forum in Inglewood, California. Zaragoza stopped Zárate in the 10th round, and this time Zárate retired permanently from the ring.

Zárate is five foot eight inches tall and has a 67-inch **reach**. He fought at weights ranging from 113 to 127 pounds, primarily as a bantamweight and super bantamweight. In 70 professional bouts, from 1970 to 1988, he won 66 (63 by knockout), lost four (two by knockout), and fought a total of 298 rounds. He was inducted into the **International Boxing Hall of Fame** in 1994.

His son, Carlos Zárate Jr., became a boxer and, although not nearly as competent as his father, compiled a record of 17–1 with 12 knockouts as a **lightweight** from 2009 to 2012. His nephew Joel Luna Zárate also boxed from 1988 to 2000 and won 34 of 40 bouts in the **super flyweight** class.

ZUKAUSKAS, JOSEPH PAUL. *See* SHARKEY, JACK "THE BOSTON GOB" (né JOSEPH PAUL ZUKAUSKAS).

Appendix A

International Boxing Hall of Fame Inductees

Modern Boxers

Year	Inducted	Year	Inducted
1990	Muhammad Ali	2009	Lennox Lewis
1998	Sammy Angott	1991	Sonny Liston
2003	Fred Apostoli	2003	Nicolino Locche
1992	Alexis Argüello	2005	Duilio Loi
1990	Henry Armstrong	2010	Danny Lopez
1990	Carmine Basilio	2007	Ricardo Lopez
1996	Wilfred Benítez	1990	Joe Louis
1992	Nino Benvenuti	1990	Rocky Marciano
1994	Jack "Kid" Berg	2010	Lloyd Marshall
1999	Jimmy Bivins	1994	Joey Maxim
1996	Joe Brown	2003	Mike McCallum
2000	Ken Buchanan	2005	Barry McGuigan
1992	Charley Burley	2009	Brian Mitchell
2009	Orlando Canizales	1995	Bob Montgomery
1998	Miguel Canto	1990	Carlos Mónzon
2006	Michael Carbajal	1990	Archie Moore
2000	Jimmy Carter	1990	José Napoles
2001	Marcel Cerdan	2004	Azumah Nelson
1998	Antonio Cervantes	2005	Terry Norris
2005	Bobby Chacon	1992	Ken Norton
2000	Jeff Chandler	1991	Ruben Olivares
2010	Jung-Koo Chang	2000	Carl "Bobo" Olson
1990	Ezzard Charles	1991	Carlos Ortiz
2011	Julio César Chávez	1996	Manuel Ortiz
2012	Cocoa Kid	2004	Carlos Palomino
2003	Curtis Cokes	2001	László Papp
1990	Billy Conn	2001	Willie Pastrano
2002	Pipino Cuevas	1991	Floyd Patterson

2007	Roberto Durán	1999	Eusebio Pedroza
1993	Flash Elorde	1990	Willie Pep
2002	Jeff Fenech	1995	Pascual Pérez
2003	George Foreman	2008	Eddie Perkins
1990	Bob Foster	1996	Aaron Pryor
1990	Joe Frazier	2004	Dwight Muhammad Qawi
1991	Gene Fullmer	2001	Sugar Ramos
1999	Khaosai Galaxy	1990	Ray Robinson
2002	Victor Galindez	1997	Luis Rodriguez
2013	Arturo Gatti	2006	Edwin Rosario
1990	Kid Gavilán	1998	Matthew Saad Muhammad
1993	Joey Giardello	1990	Sandy Saddler
1995	Wilfredo Gómez	1999	Vicente Saldivar
2006	Humberto González	1991	Salvador Sánchez
1992	Billy Graham	1992	Max Schmeling
1991	Rocky Graziano	1994	Michael Spinks
1990	Emile Griffith	1991	Dick Tiger
1993	Marvelous Marvin Hagler	1997	José Torres
1995	Fighting Harada	2011	Kostya Tszyu
2012	Thomas Hearns	2001	Randy Turpin
2013	Virgil Hill	2011	Mike Tyson
2008	Larry Holmes	1990	Jersey Joe Walcott
1991	Beau Jack	2008	Pernell Whitaker
1999	Lew Jenkins	2008	Holman Williams
1992	Éder Jofre	1990	Ike Williams
2002	Ingemar Johansson	1997	Chalky Wright
1993	Harold Johnson	2013	Myung-Woo Yuh
2012	Mark Johnson	1991	Tony Zale
2001	Ismael Laguna	2004	Daniel Zaragoza
1990	Jake LaMotta	1994	Carlos Zárate
1997	Ray Leonard	1993	Fritzie Zivic

Oldtimers

Year	Inducted	Year	Inducted
1992	Lou Ambers	1990	Sam Langford
2004	Baby Arizmendi	1998	George "Kid" Lavigne
1990	Abe Attell	1990	Benny Leonard

1995	Max Baer	2000	Battling Levinsky
2000	Jimmy Barry	2008	Harry Lewis
2002	Benny Bass	1994	John Henry Lewis
2003	Battling Battalino	1992	Ted "Kid" Lewis
2001	Paul Berlenbach	1991	Tommy Loughran
2001	James J. Braddock	1998	Benny Lynch
1990	Jack Britton	2005	Joe Lynch
2006	Lou Brouillard	2005	Sammy Mandell
2012	Newsboy Brown	1995	Jack McAuliffe
1992	Panama Al Brown	1992	Kid McCoy
1996	Tommy Burns	1991	Packey McFarland
1990	Tony Canzoneri	1990	Terry McGovern
1991	Georges Carpentier	1991	Jimmy McLarnin
1991	Kid Chocolate	1999	Sam McVey
1998	Joe Choynski	1997	Freddie Miller
1990	James J. Corbett	2010	Billy Miske
2010	Young Corbett II	2002	Charley Mitchell
2004	Young Corbett III	2007	Pedro Montanez
1999	Johnny Coulon	2002	Owen Moran
2005	Eugene Criqui	2011	Memphis Pal Moore
1993	Les Darcy	1992	Battling Nelson
1996	Jack Delaney	1997	Kid Norfolk
1992	Jack "Nonpareil" Dempsey	1994	Philadelphia Jack O'Brien
1990	Jack Dempsey	2001	Billy Papke
1995	Jack Dillon	2000	Billy Petrolle
2002	Dixie Kid	2013	Wesley Ramey
1990	George Dixon	2004	Willie Ritchie
1990	Jem Driscoll	1993	Maxie Rosenbloom
1991	Johnny Dundee	1990	Barney Ross
2002	Sixto Escobar	2011	Jack Root
2004	Jackie Fields	1991	Tommy Ryan
1990	Bob Fitzsimmons	2011	Dave Shade
1993	Tiger Flowers	1994	Jack Sharkey
1990	Joe Gans	2003	Tom Sharkey
1998	Frankie Genaro	2006	Jimmy Slattery
1992	Mike Gibbons	2009	Mysterious Billy Smith
1993	Tommy Gibbons	2013	Jeff Smith

Year		Year	
2007	George Godfrey	2009	Billy Soose
1990	Harry Greb	1999	Freddie Steele
1991	Young Griffo	1996	Young Stribling
2002	Harry Harris	2005	Charles "Bud" Taylor
2008	Len Harvey	1999	Lew Tendler
1997	Pete Herman	2005	Marcel Thil
2012	Leo Houck	1990	Gene Tunney
1990	Peter Jackson	1994	Pancho Villa
1997	Joe Jeannette	1991	Barbados Joe Walcott
1990	James J. Jeffries	1990	Mickey Walker
1990	Jack Johnson	1997	Freddie Welsh
2009	Gorilla Jones	1990	Jimmy Wilde
2010	Rocky Kansas	2003	Jess Willard
2003	Louis "Kid" Kaplan	1996	Kid Williams
1990	Stanley Ketchel	1992	Harry Wills
1995	Johnny Kilbane	2000	Ad Wolgast
2012	Jake Kilrain	2001	Midget Wolgast
2008	Frank Klaus	2006	Teddy Yarosz
1996	Fidel LaBarba		

Pioneers

Year	Inducted	Year	Inducted
2001	Barney Aaron	1992	John Jackson
2007	Young Barney Aaron	1995	Tom Johnson
2003	Caleb Baldwin	2010	Paddington Tom Jones
1992	Jem Belcher	1992	Tom King
1994	Ben Brain	1992	Nat Langham
1990	Jack Broughton	1990	Jem Mace
1992	James Burke	1990	Daniel Mendoza
2006	Jem Carney	1997	Tom Molineaux
2000	Arthur Chambers	1996	John Morrissey
2013	Joe Coburn	1993	Henry Pearce
1991	Tom Cribb	2005	Jack Randall
2007	Dick Curtis	2005	Bill Richmond
2008	Dan Donnelly	1997	Dutch Sam
1998	Prof. Mike Donovan	2002	Young Dutch Sam
2008	Paddy Duffy	1990	Tom Sayers

2004	Billy Edwards	1992	Tom Spring
1992	James Figg	1990	John L. Sullivan
2003	Joe Goss	1991	William "Bendigo" Thompson
2011	John Gully	1995	Jem Ward
2002	John C. Heenan	2012	James Wharton (Young Molineaux)
2009	Tom Hyer		

Nonparticipants

Year	Inducted	Year	Inducted
1992	Thomas S. Andrews	2009	Abe J. Greene
1991	Ray Arcel	2010	Larry Hazzard
1999	Bob Arum	2013	Arturo "Cuyo" Hernández
2006	Jarvis Astaire	2009	Akihiko Honda
1999	Giuseppe Ballarati	1997	Joe Humphreys
2001	George Benton	2000	Sam Ichinose
2011	Nacho Beristain	1993	Jimmy Jacobs
2011	A.F. Bettinson	1990	Mike Jacobs
2006	Whitey Bimstein	1999	James J. Johnston
1992	Jack Blackburn	1990	Jack Kearns
1998	William A. Brady	1997	Don King
2004	Umberto Branchini	2013	Mills Lane
1993	Teddy Brenner	2000	Tito Lectoure
2007	Amilcar Brusa	2013	Jimmy Lennon Jr.
2012	Michael Buffer	1992	A. J. Liebling
2005	William D. Cayton	1990	Lord Lonsdale
1990	John Graham Chambers	1992	Harry Markson
2001	Don Chargin	1990	Marquess of Queensberry
2004	Stanley Christodoulou	2012	Hugh McIntosh
1993	Gil Clancy	1995	Arthur Mercante
1991	James W. Coffroth	2000	Dan Morgan
2002	Irving Cohen	1996	William Muldoon
2007	Cuco Conde	1995	Gilbert Odd
2011	Joe Cortez	1999	Dan O'Rourke
1995	Cus D'Amato	2008	Mogens Palle
2000	Jeff Dickson	1996	Dan Parker
1993	Arthur Donovan	1991	George Parnassus

1999	Mickey Duff	2004	J. Russell Peltz
1992	Angelo Dundee	1990	Tex Rickard
1994	Chris Dundee	2012	Freddie Roach
1993	Don Dunphy	1999	Irving Rudd
2003	Dan Duva	2006	Rodolfo Sabatini
1998	Lou Duva	2005	Lope Sarreal
2002	Aileen Eaton	2010	Wilfried Sauerland
1991	Pierce Egan	1995	George Siler
2010	Shelly Finkel	2002	Sam Silverman
1990	Nat Fleischer	1995	Jack Solomons
1997	Richard K. Fox	1996	Emanuel Steward
2003	Dewey Fragetta	2007	Jose Sulaiman
2005	Don Fraser	1994	Sam Taub
1994	Eddie Futch	1998	Herman Taylor
2009	Billy Gibson	2010	Bruce Trampler
1992	Charley Goldman	2012	Rip Valenti
1994	Ruby Goldstein	2004	Lou Viscusi
2009	Bob Goodman	1992	James J. Walker
1999	Murray Goodman	2008	Frank Warren
2008	Bill Gore	2003	Al Weill

Observers

Year	Inducted	Year	Inducted
2008	Dave Anderson	2005	Jersey Jones
2012	Al Bernstein	2005	Hank Kaplan
2001	Lester Bromberg	2012	Michael Katz
2002	Jimmy Cannon	2008	Joe Koizumi
2011	Harry Carpenter	2009	Hugh McIlvanney
2013	Ted Carroll	2009	Larry Merchant
2001	Ralph Citro	2005	Harry Mullan
2010	Howard Cosell	2004	Barney Nagler
2007	Tad Dorgan	2007	LeRoy Neiman
2003	Jack Fiske	2002	Damon Runyon
2009	Paul Gallico	2003	Budd Schulberg
2001	Bill Gallo	2010	Ed Schuler
2002	Reggie Gutteridge	2011	Sylvester Stallone
2013	Colin Hart	2005	Bert Sugar

2004   W. C. Heinz   2006   Stanley Weston

Appendix B

Olympic Games Boxing Champions

Light Flyweight (108 pounds)

1904–1964	not contested	1992	Rogelio Marcelo, CUB
1968	Francisco Rodríguez, VEN	1996	Daniel Petrov, BUL
1972	György Gedó, HUN	2000	Brahim Asloum, FRA
1976	Jorge Hernández, CUB	2004	Yan Bartelemí, CUB
1980	Shamil Sabarov, URS	2008	Zou Shiming, CHN
1984	Paul Gonzalez, USA	2012	Zou Shiming, CHN
1988	*Ivailo Khristov, BUL		

Flyweight (112 pounds)

1904	George Finnegan, USA	1968	Ricardo Delgado, MEX
1908	not contested	1972	Georgi Kostadinov, BUL
1912	no Olympic boxing	1976	Leo Randolph, USA
1920	Frankie Genaro, USA	1980	Petar Lesov, BUL
1924	Fidel LaBarba, USA	1984	Steve McCrory, USA
1928	Antal Kocsis, HUN	1988	Kim Kwang-Sun, KOR
1932	István Énekes, HUN	1992	Choi Chol-Su, PRK
1936	Willy Kaiser, GER	1996	Maikro Romero, CUB
1948	Pascual Pérez, ARG	2000	Wijan Ponlid, THA
1952	Nate Brooks, USA	2004	Yuriokis Gamboa, CUB
1956	Terence Spinks, GBR	2008	Somjit Jongjohor, THA
1960	Gyula Török, HUN	2012	Robeisy Ramírez, CUB
1964	Fernando Atzori, ITA		

Bantamweight (119 pounds)

1904	Oliver Kirk, USA	1968	Valerian Sokolov, URS
1908	Henry Thomas, GBR	1972	Orlando Martínez, CUB
1912	no Olympic boxing	1976	Gu Yong-Ju, PRK
1920	Clarence Walker, RSA	1980	Juan Hernández Pérez, CUB

1924	William Smith, RSA	1984	Maurizio Stecca, ITA
1928	Vittorio Tamagnini, ITA	1988	Kennedy McKinney, USA
1932	Horace Gwynne, CAN	1992	Joel Casamayor, CUB
1936	Ulderico Sergo, ITA	1996	István Kovács, HUN
1948	Tibor Csík, HUN	2000	Guillermo Rigondeaux, CUB
1952	Pentti Hämäläinen, FIN	2004	Guillermo Rigondeaux, CUB
1956	Wolfgang Behrendt, GER	2008	Enkhbatyn Badar-Uugan, MGL
1960	Oleg Grigoryev, URS	2012	Luke Campbell, GBR
1964	Takao Sakurai, JPN		

Featherweight (126 pounds)

1904	Oliver Kirk, USA	1968	Antonio Roldán, MEX
1908	Richard Gunn, GBR	1972	Boris Kuznetsov, URS
1912	no Olympic boxing	1976	Angel Herrera, CUB
1920	Paul Fritsch, FRA	1980	Rudi Fink, GDR
1924	Jackie Fields, USA	1984	Meldrick Taylor, USA
1928	Bep van Klaveren, NED	1988	Giovanni Parisi, ITA
1932	Carmelo Robledo, ARG	1992	Andreas Tews, GER
1936	Oscar Casanovas, ARG	1996	Somluck Kamsing, THA
1948	Ernesto Formenti, ITA	2000	Bekzat Sattarkhanov, KAZ
1952	Ján Zachara, TCH	2004	Aleksei Tishchenko, URS
1956	Vladimir Safronov, URS	2008	Vasyl Lomachenko, UKR
1960	Francesco Musso, ITA	2012	not contested
1964	Stanislav Stepashkin, URS		

Lightweight (132 pounds)

1904	Harry Spanjer, USA	1968	Ronnie Harris, USA
1908	Frederick Grace, GBR	1972	Jan Szczepański, POL
1912	no Olympic boxing	1976	Howard Davis, USA
1920	Samuel Mosberg, USA	1980	Angel Herrera, CUB
1924	Hans Jacob Nielsen, DEN	1984	Pernell Whitaker, USA
1928	Carlo Orlandi, ITA	1988	Andreas Zülow, GDR
1932	Lawrence Stevens, RSA	1992	Oscar de la Hoya, USA
1936	Imre Harangi, HUN	1996	Hocine Soltani, ALG
1948	Gerald Dreyer, RSA	2000	Mario Kindelán, CUB
1952	Aureliano Bolognesi, ITA	2004	Mario Kindelán, CUB
1956	Dick McTaggart, GBR	2008	Aleksei Tishchenko, RUS

1960	Kazmierz Pazdzior, POL	2012	Vasyl Lomachenko, UKR
1964	Józef Grudzień, POL		

Light Welterweight (140 pounds)

1904–1948	not contested	1984	Jerry Page, USA
1952	Charles Adkins, USA	1988	Vyacheslav Yanovskiy, URS
1956	Vladimir Yengibaryan, URS	1992	Héctor Vinent, CUB
1960	Bohumil Němeček, TCH	1996	Héctor Vinent, CUB
1964	Jerzy Kulej, POL	2000	Mahammat. Abdoolayev, UZB
1968	Jerzy Kulej, POL	2004	Manus Boonjumnong, THA
1972	Ray Seales, USA	2008	Félix Díaz, DOM
1976	Ray Leonard, USA	2012	Roniel Iglesias, CUB
1980	Patrizio Oliva, ITA		

Welterweight (147 pounds)

1904	Albert Young, USA	1968	Manfred Wolke, GDR
1908	not contested	1972	Emilio Correa, CUB
1912	no Olympic boxing	1976	Jochen Bachfeld, GDR
1920	Bert Schneider, CAN	1980	Andrés Aldama, CUB
1924	Jean Delarge, BEL	1984	Mark Breland, USA
1928	Ted Morgan, NZL	1988	Robert Wangila, KEN
1932	Edward Flynn, USA	1992	Michael Carruth, IRL
1936	Sten Suvio, FIN	1996	Oleg Saitov, RUS
1948	Július Torma, TCH	2000	Oleg Saitov, RUS
1952	Zygmunt Chychła, POL	2004	Bakhtiyar Artayev, KAZ
1956	Nicolae Linca, ROU	2008	Bakhyt Sarsekbayev, KAZ
1960	Giovanni Benvenuti, ITA	2012	Serik Sapiyev, KAZ
1964	Marian Kasprzyk, POL		

Light Middleweight (154 pounds)

1904–1948	not contested	1980	Armando Martínez, CUB
1952	László Papp, HUN	1984	Frank Tate, USA
1956	László Papp, HUN	1988	Park Si-Hun, KOR
1960	Wilbert McClure, USA	1992	Juan Carlos Lemus, CUB
1964	Boris Lagutin, URS	1996	David Reid, USA

1968	Boris Lagutin, URS	2000	Yermakhan Ibraimov, KAZ
1972	Dieter Kottysch, FRG	2004–2012	not contested
1976	Jerzy Rybicki, POL		

Middleweight (165 pounds)

1904	Charles Mayer, USA	1968	Chris Finnegan, GBR
1908	John Douglas, GBR	1972	Vyacheslav Lemeshev, URS
1912	no Olympic boxing	1976	Michael Spinks, USA
1920	Harry Mallin, GBR	1980	Jose Gomez, CUB
1924	Harry Mallin, GBR	1984	Shin Joon-Sup, KOR
1928	Piero Toscani, ITA	1988	Henry Maske, GDR
1932	Carmen Barth, USA	1992	Ariel Hernández, CUB
1936	Jean Despeaux, FRA	1996	Ariel Hernández, CUB
1948	László Papp, HUN	2000	Jorge Gutiérrez, CUB
1952	Floyd Patterson, USA	2004	Gaydarbek Gaydarbekov, RUS
1956	Gennadiy Shatkov, URS	2008	James DeGale, GBR
1960	Eddie Crook, USA	2012	Ryoto Murata, JPN
1964	Valeri Popenchenko, URS		

Light Heavyweight (178 pounds)

1904	not contested	1968	Danas Pozniakas, URS
1908	not contested	1972	Mate Parlov, YUG
1912	no Olympic boxing	1976	Leon Spinks, USA
1920	Eddie Eagan, USA	1980	Slobodan Kačar, YUG
1924	Harry Mitchell, GBR	1984	Anton Josipović, YUG
1928	Victor Avendaño, ARG	1988	Andrew Maynard, USA
1932	David Carstens, RSA	1992	Torsten May, GER
1936	Roger Michelot, FRA	1996	Vassiliy Jirov, KAZ
1948	George Hunter, RSA	2000	Aleksandr Lebziak, RUS
1952	Norvel Lee, USA	2004	André Ward, USA
1956	James Boyd, USA	2008	Zhang Xiaoping, CHN
1960	Cassius Clay, USA	2012	Egor Mekhontcev, RUS
1964	Cosimo Pinto, ITA		

Heavyweight (unlimited until 1980, 201 pounds afterward)

1904	Samuel Berger, USA	1968	George Foreman, USA

1908	Albert Oldman, GBR	1972	Téofilo Stevenson, CUB
1912	no Olympic boxing	1976	Téofilo Stevenson, CUB
1920	Ronald Rawson, GBR	1980	Téofilo Stevenson, CUB
1924	Otto von Porat, NOR	1984	Henry Tillman, USA
1928	Arturo Rodriguez, ARG	1988	Ray Mercer, USA
1932	Santiago Lovell, ARG	1992	Félix Savón, CUB
1936	Herbert Runge, GER	1996	Félix Savón, CUB
1948	Rafael Iglesias, ARG	2000	Félix Savón, CUB
1952	Ed Sanders, USA	2004	Odlanier Solis, CUB
1956	Peter Rademacher, USA	2008	Rakhim Chakhkiev, RUS
1960	Franco De Piccoli, ITA	2012	Oleksandr Usyk, UKR
1964	Joe Frazier, USA		

Super Heavyweight (unlimited pounds)

1904–1980	not contested	2000	Audley Harrison, GBR
1984	Tyrell Biggs, USA	2004	Aleksandr Povetkin, RUS
1988	Lennox Lewis, CAN	2008	Roberto Cammarelle, ITA
1992	Roberto Balado, CUB	2012	Anthony Joshua, GBR
1996	Wladimir Klitschko, UKR		

Women's Champions

2012	Flyweight (112 pounds), Nicola Adams, GBR
2012	Lightweight (132 pounds), Katie Taylor, IRL
2012	Middleweight (165 pounds), Claressa Shields, USA

* Name originally Ismail Mustafov Huseinov, later changed to Ivailo Marinov Khristov.

Val Barker Trophy Winners

1936   Louis Laurie, USA, FLY

1948   George Hunter, RSA, LHV

1952   Norvel Lee, USA, HVY

1956   Dick McTaggart, GBR, LIT

1960   Giovanni Benvenuti, ITA, WEL

1964   Valeri Popenchenko, URS, MID

1968   Philip Waruinge, KEN, FEA

1972   Téofilo Stevenson, CUB, HVY

1976   Howard Davis, USA, LIT

1980   Patrizio Oliva, ITA, LWE

1984   Paul Gonzales, USA, LFL

1988   Roy Jones Jr., USA, LMD

1992   Roberto Balado, CUB, SHV

1996   Vassiliy Jirov, KAZ, LHV

2000   Oleg Saitov, RUS, WEL

2004   Bakhtiyar Artayev, KAZ, WEL

2008   Vasyl Lomachenko, UKR, FEA

2012   Serik Sapiyev, KAZ, WEL

Medals by Country	Gold	Silver	Bronze	Total
United States	50	23	38	111
Cuba	34	19	14	67
Great Britain	17	12	24	53
Soviet Union	14	19	18	51
Italy	15	15	17	47
Poland	8	9	26	43
Germany	5	12	11	28
Russia	9	5	12	26
Romania	1	9	15	25
Argentina	7	7	10	24
Hungary	10	2	8	20
Korea	3	7	10	20
South Africa	6	4	9	19
France	4	7	8	19
Bulgaria	4	5	9	18
Kazakhstan	6	5	6	17

Canada	3	7	7	17
Ireland	2	5	9	16
Thailand	4	4	6	14
Ukraine	4	3	7	14
Finland	2	1	11	14
East Germany	5	2	6	13
Mexico	2	3	7	12
Denmark	1	5	6	12
Yugoslavia	3	2	6	11
Sweden	0	5	6	11
China	3	2	3	8
North Korea	2	3	3	8
Kenya	1	1	5	7
Uzbekistan	1	0	6	7
Czechoslovakia	3	1	2	6
Mongolia	1	2	3	6
Netherlands	1	1	4	6
Algeria	1	0	5	6
West Germany	1	0	5	6
Nigeria	0	3	3	6
Puerto Rico	0	1	5	6
Azerbaijan	0	0	6	6
Japan	2	0	3	5
Norway	1	2	2	5
Venezuela	1	2	2	5
Philippines	0	2	3	5
Turkey	0	2	3	5
Belgium	1	1	2	4
Uganda	0	3	1	4
Spain	0	2	2	4
Australia	0	1	3	4
Brazil	0	1	3	4
New Zealand	1	1	1	3
Ghana	0	1	2	3
Chile	0	1	2	3
Egypt	0	1	2	3

Colombia	0	0	3	3
Morocco	0	0	3	3
Dominican Republic	1	0	1	2
Belarus	0	2	0	2
Unified Team	0	1	1	2
Cameroon	0	1	1	2
India	0	0	2	2
Moldova	0	0	2	2
Tunisia	0	0	2	2
Czech Republic	0	1	0	1
Tonga	0	1	0	1
Estonia	0	1	0	1
Australasia	0	1	0	1
Bermuda	0	0	1	1
Uruguay	0	0	1	1
United Arab Republic	0	0	1	1
Niger	0	0	1	1
Tajikistan	0	0	1	1
Pakistan	0	0	1	1
Lithuania	0	0	1	1
Armenia	0	0	1	1
Mauritius	0	0	1	1
Syria	0	0	1	1
Zambia	0	0	1	1
Georgia	0	0	1	1
Guyana	0	0	1	1

Appendix C

Nicknames and Ring Names

Many boxers during the 19th century and first half of the 20th century adopted ring names, often to hide their occupation from family and, in an era of ethnic prejudice, just as often to change their nationality to a more acceptable one. They often were given sobriquets such as "The Manassa Mauler" by promoters and sportswriters to add to their gate appeal.

In recent years, while most boxers use their given names in the ring, they have adopted the use of nicknames to enhance their marketability. The following lists are far from all-inclusive but do include most of the more popular or successful boxers as well as some of the more colorful ring names and nicknames. Note that minor variations occur in the spelling of several boxers' given names, especially those of foreign origin. The ones listed below are those most commonly seen.

BOXERS

Ring Name	Given Name
Abe the Newsboy	Abraham Hollandersky
Bones Adams	Clarence Richard Adams
Kid Akeem	Akeem Anifowoshe
Pedro Alcazar	Guillermo González
Muhammad Ali	Cassius Marcellus Clay Jr.*
Terry Allen	Edward Albert Govier
Lou Ambers	Luigi Giuseppe d'Ambrosio
Sammy Angott	Samuel Engotti
Tony Anthony	Ernest Anthony
Baby Arizmendi	Alberto Arizmendi
Gene "Ace" Armstrong	Genorace Armstrong
Henry Armstrong	Henry Jackson Jr.
Kid Azteca	Luis Villanueva Paramo
Buddy Baer	Jacob Henry Baer
Yama Bahama	William Horatio Butler Jr.

Snowy Baker	Reginald Leslie Baker
Sonny Banks	Lucien Banks
Nick Barone	Carmine Barone
Sam Baroudi	Sam Crandall
Soldier Bartfield	Jakob Bartfeldt
Sal Bartolo	Salvatore Interbartolo
Carmen Basilio	Carmine Basilio
Hogan "Kid" Bassey	Ogun Asuguo Bassey
Battling Battalino	Christopher Battaglia
Fahsan 3K Battery	Narongrit Pirang
Frenchy Belanger	Albert Belanger
Bendigo	William Abednego Thompson
Nino Benvenuti	Giovanni Benvenuti
Jack "Kid" Berg	Judah Bergman
Jack Bernstein	John Dodick
Black Bill (1920–1931)	Eladio Valdés
Black Bill (1897–1916)	Claude Brooks
Johnny Bizzarro	John Lorio
Jack Blackburn	Charles Henry Blackburn
Lou Bogash	Luigi Boccasio
Venice Borkhorsor	Prawet Ponchiengkwang
Joe Bowker	Thomas Mahon
Battling Bozo	James Curtis Hambright
James J. Braddock	James Walter Braddock
KO Bill Brennan	Wilhelm Schenck
Jack Britton	William J. Breslin
Kid Broad	William M. Thomas
Buster Brown	Sebastian M. Catanzaro
Knockout Brown	Valentine Braunheim
Newsboy Brown	David Montrose
Panama Al Brown	Alfonso Teófilo Brown
Johnny Buff	John Lesky
Young Gene Buffalo	Eugene Coker
St. Mary's County Bully	Charles McElderry
Tommy Burns	Noah Brusso
Butterbean	Eric Scott Esch
Chic Calderwood	Charles Calderwood

Rory Calhoun	Herman Calhoun
Mushy Callahan	Vincent Morris Scheer
Frankie Campbell	Francisco Camilli
Yori Boy Campas	Luis Ramón Campas
Eddie Campi	Edward De Campus
Gaby Canizales	Jose Canizales
Chango Carmona	Eudibiel Guillen Chapin
Kid Carter	Edward Blaswick
Rocky Castellani	Attilio Castellani
Chucho Castillo	Jesús Castillo Aguillera
Chartchai Chionoi	Naris Chionoi
George Chip	George Chipulonis
Kid Chocolate (1910–1988)	Eligio Sardiñas Montalvo
Kid Chocolate (1983–)	Peter Quillin
KO Christner	Meyer Wilson Christner
George Chuvalo	Jure Čuvalo
Elky Clark	William Clark
Jeff Clark	Winlock Jefferson Clarke
Biff Cline	Donald Cline
Frankie Conley	Francesco Conte
Young Corbett II	William J. Rothwell
Young Corbett III	Raffaele Capabianca Giordano
Lulu Costantino	Carlo Joseph Costantino
Leach Cross	Louis Charles Wallach
Pipino Cuevas	José Isidro Cuevas González
Little Dado	Eleuterio Zapanta
Speedy Dado	Diosdado Posadas
Les Darcy	James Leslie Darcy
Al "Bummy" Davis	Albert Abraham Davidoff
Teddy "Red Top" Davis	Murray Cain
Indian Benny Deathpaine	Bennetto Payne
Jack Delaney	Ovila Chapdelaine
Al Delmont	Alberto Delmonte
Tony DeMarco	Leo Liotta
Jack Dempsey (1895–1983)	William Harrison Dempsey
Jack Dempsey (1862–1895)	John Edward Kelly
Doug DeWitt	Douglas Anthony Ittaglio

Jack Dillon	Ernest Cutler Price
Gus Dorazio	Justine Vincolota
Leonard Dorin	Leonard Dorin Doroftei
Joe Dundee	Samuel Lazzaro
Johnny Dundee	Giuseppe Carrora
Vince Dundee	Vincent Lazzaro
Bunty Doran	Edward Doran
Flash Elorde	Gabriel Elorde
Young Erne	George A. Nieb
Guty Espadas	Gustavo Hernán Espadas Cruz
Guty Espadas Jr.	Gustavo Espinosa Espadas
Rocky Estafire	Mustafa Hamsho
Rube Ferns	James Ferns
Chris Eubank	Christopher Livingstone Eubanks
Young Firpo	Guido Bardelli
Fitzie Fitzpatrick	Hilton J. Fitzpatrick
Tiger Flowers	Theodore Flowers
"Fireman" Jim Flynn	Andrew Chiariglione
Jackie Fields	Jacob Finkelstein
"Tiger" Jack Fox	John Linwood Fox
Sailor Friedman	William Friedman
Khaokor Galaxy	Nirote Saenkham
Khaosai Galaxy	Sura Saenkham
Tony Galento	Domenico Antonio Galento
Italian Joe Gans	Antonio Camberlengo
Joe Gans	Joseph Gant
Rocky Garcia	Jorge García
Pappy Gault	William Henry Gault Jr.
Kid Gavilán	Gerardo González
Frankie Genaro	Frank DiGennaro
Joey Giardello	Carmine Orlando Tilelli
Mike Glover	Michael J. Cavanaugh
George Godfrey	Feab Smith Williams
Jimmy Goodrich	James Edward Moran
Bushy Graham	Angelo Geraci
Bunny Grant	George Leslie Grant
Kid Graves	Perry Ivan Graves

Rocky Graziano	Thomas Rocco Barbella
Harry Greb	Edward Henry Greb
Corn Griffin	John Charles Griffin
Philly Griffin	Phillip DeLuca
Tuffy Griffiths	Gerald Ambrose Griffiths
Young Griffo	Albert Griffiths
Joe Grim	Saverio Giannone
Marvelous Marvin Hagler	Marvin Nathaniel Hagler*
Iron Hague	William Hague
Henry Hank	Joseph Harrison
Fighting Harada	Masahiko Harada
Kid Herman	Herman Landfield
Pete "Kid" Herman	Peter Gulotta
Herbie Hide	Herbert Okechukwu Maduagwu
Him	Horst Geisler
Big Boy Hogue	Willard Joseph Hogue
Chief Crazy Horse	Frankie Martin
Ace Hudkins	Asa Hudkins
Guts Ishimatsu	Yuji Suzuki
Beau Jack	Sidney Walker
Young Beau Jack	Elwood Thornton
Dynamite Jackson	Ernest Bendy
Melody Jackson	Henry Jackson
Young Peter Jackson	Sim Thompkins
Johnny Jadick	John J. Jadich
Izzy Jannazzo	Anthony Jannazzo
Joe Jeannette	Jeremiah Jeannette
Ben Jeby	Morris Jebaltowski
Harry Jeffra	Ignacius Pasquale Guiffi
Lew Jenkins	Verlin E. Jenkins
Frankie Jerome	Frank Doherty
Tom Johnson	Thomas Jackling
Young Jack Johnson	John Lee Storey
Gorilla Jones	William Jones
Tiger Jones	Ralph Jones
Rocky Kalingo	Ramón Pérez Kalingo
Rocky Kansas	Rocco Tozzo

Hugo Kelly	Ugo Micheli
Stanley Ketchel	Stanislaw Kiecal
Alabama Kid	Clarence Oland Reeves
Cocoa Kid	Herbert Lewis Hardwick
Danny Kid	Florencio Solente
Dixie Kid	Aaron Lister Brown
Georgia Kid	James Bussey
Young Zulu Kid	Giuseppe DiMelfi
Jake Kilrain	John J. Killion
Buddy King	Frank King
Pone Kingpetch	Mana Sridokbuab
Klondike	John W. Haynes
Royal Kobayashi	Kazuo Kobayashi
Solly Krieger	Danny Auerbach
George LaBlanche	George Blais
Jake LaMotta	Giacobbe LaMotta
Tippy Larkin	Antonio Pilleteri
Kitione Lave	Lavernai Kitione Takitau
Curley Lee	Lee Chapman
Casper Leon	Gaspare Leoni
Sonny Leon	Victor Adams
Benny Leonard	Benjamin Leiner
Sugar Ray Leonard	Ray Charles Leonard
Battling Levinsky	Barney Lebrowitz
King Levinsky	Harris Krakow
Harry Lewis	Henry Besterman
Ted "Kid" Lewis	Gershon Mendeloff
Sonny Liston	Charles L. Liston
Rocky Lockridge	Rick Lockridge
Brian London	Brian Sidney Harper
Yaqui Lopez	Alvaro Lopez
Joe Louis	Joseph Louis Barrow
Louisiana	Joseph Biderberg
Fred "Dummy" Mahan	Federico Mesa
Ray Mancini	Ray Mancino
Sammy Mandell	Salvador Mandala
Rocky Marciano	Rocco Francis Marchegiano

Dado Marino	Salvador Marino
Eddie "Cannonball" Martin	Eduardo Vittorio Martino
Silent Martin	Thomas F. Martin
Young Martin	Martin Marco Voto
Tami Mauriello	Stefano Mauriello
Joey Maxim	Giuseppe Antonio Berardinelli
Floyd Mayweather Jr.	Floyd Joy Sinclair
Jock McAvoy	Joseph Patrick Bamford
Al McCoy	Alexander Rudolph
Charles "Kid" McCoy	Norman Selby
Elbows McFadden	George McFadden
Packey McFarland	Patrick McFarland
Buddy McGirt	James Walter McGirt
Eddie McGoorty	Eddie Van Dusart
Phil McGraw	Mitchell Karmanos
Barry McGuigan	Finbarr Patrick McGuigan
Kid McPartland	William Lawrence McPartland
Willie Meehan	Eugene Walcott
Honey Mellody	William J. Mellody
Midget Mexico	Bricio Garcia
Pinky Mitchell	Myron Herbert Mitchell
Gunner Moir	James Moir
Young Molineaux	James Wharton
Rinty Monaghan	John Joseph Monaghan
Monk the Newsboy	Harry Kronski
Small Montana	Benjamin Gan
Young Montreal	Maurice Billingkoff
Archie Moore	Archibald Lee Wright
Memphis Pal Moore	Thomas Wilson Moore
Philadelphia Pal Moore	Paul Walter Von Franzke
Tod Morgan	Albert Morgan Pilkington
Rocky Mosley Sr.	Roxell Mosley Sr.
Rocky Mosley Jr.	Roxell Mosley Jr.
Irish Bob Murphy	Edwin Lee Conarty
Torpedo Billy Murphy	Thomas William Murphy
Eddie Mustafa Muhammad	Edward Dean Gregory*
Waruinge Nakayama	Philip Waruinge

Sugar Boy Nando	Fernando Mueller
Battling Nelson	Oscar Mattheus Nelson
Johnny Nelson	Ivanson Ranny Nelson
George Nichols	Philip John Nicolosi
Kid Norfolk	William Ward
Philadelphia Jack O'Brien	Joseph Francis Hagen
Packy O'Gatty	Pasquale Agati
Elisha Obed	Everett Ferguson
Fully Obel	Fulgencio Obelmejias
Bobo Olson	Carl Olson
Lee Oma	Frank Czjewski
Con Orem	John Condle Orem
Young Otto	Arthur Susskind
Pedlar Palmer	Thomas Palmer
Little Pancho	Eulogio Tingson
Benny "Kid" Paret	Bernardo Paret
Routier Parra	Alejandro Romero Castillo
Tommy Paul	Gaetano Alfonso Papa
Vinny Paz	Vincenzo Edward Pazienza
Arthur Pelkey	Andrew Arthur Peltier
Willie Pep	Guglielmo Papaleo
Lulu Perez	Luis Pérez
Young Perez	Victor Perez
Big Boy Peterson	Clayton Peterson
Lupe Pintor	José Guadalupe Pintor Guzmán
Dwight Muhammad Qawi	Dwight Braxton*
Sugar Ramos	Ultiminio Ramos Zaqueira
Rip Randall	Garland Jerome Randall
Sheik Rangel	Richard Rangel
Sonny Ray	Rogers J. Moten
Eddie "Babe" Risko	Henry Pelkowski
Willie Ritchie	Gerhardt A. Steffen
Rocky Rivero	Juan Carlos Rivero
Mexican Joe Rivers	José Ybarra
Sugar Ray Robinson	Walker Smith Jr.
Spike Robson	Frank Robson
George "Boer" Rodel	Lodewikus van Vuuren

Sugar Baby Rojas	Bebis José Rojas
Jack Root	Janos Ruthaly
Kentucky Rosebud	Walter Edgerton
Charley Phil Rosenberg	Charles Green
Barney Ross	Beryl David Rosofsky
Tony Ross	Antonio Rossilano
Mike Rossman	Michael Albert DePiano
Gustave Roth	Gustave Scillie
Tommy Ryan	Joseph Youngs
Matthew Saad Muhammad	Maxwell Antonio Loach
Sandy Saddler	Joseph Saddler
Dutch Sam	Samuel Elias
Dave Sands	David Ritchie
Randy Sandy	Randolph Sandy
Baltasar Sangchili	Baltasar Belenguer Hervás
Clever Sencio	Inocencio Moldes
Marty Servo	Mario Severino
Jack Sharkey	Joseph Paul Zukauskas
Little Jackie Sharkey	Giovanni Cervati
Earnie Shavers	Earnie Dee Shaver
Battling Shaw	Jose Perez Flores
Battling Siki	Amadou M'Barick Fall, aka Louis Phal
Kimbo Slice	Kevin Ferguson
Tiger Smalls	Priest George Young Smalls
Gunboat Smith	Edward J. Smyth
Jeff Smith	Jerome Jeffords
Jewey Smith	Joseph Smith
Mysterious Billy Smith	Amos Smith
Jimmy Soo	James Joseph Bark
Saman Sorjaturong	Saman Sriprated
Netrnoi Sor Vorasingh	Net Ladnork
Cory Spinks	Cory A. Calvin
Digger Stanley	George Stanley
Freddie Steele	Frederick Earl Burgett
Popper Stopper	James Richard Paul
Young Stribling	William Lawrence Stribling Jr.
Felix Sturm	Adnan Ćatić

Chick Suggs	Edward Murray Suggs
Leopard Tamakuma	Yukito Tamakuma
Kid Tano	Cayetano Ojeda Herrera
Bud Taylor	Charles Taylor
Young Jack Thompson	Cecil Lewis Thompson
Jimmy Thunder	James Peau
Dick Tiger	Richard Ihetu
Battling Torres	José Raymundo Torres Anzaldua
Kid Tunero	Evelio Celestino Mustelier
Gene Tunney	James Joseph Tunney
King Tut	Henry Tuttle
Niño Valdés	Geraldo Ramos Ponciano Valdéz
Chico Vejar	Francis Vejar
Pancho Villa	Francisco Guilledo
Jersey Joe Walcott (1914–1994)	Arnold Raymond Cream
Mickey Walker	Edward Patrick Walker
Nunc Wallace	Edwin Wallace
Spider Webb	Ellsworth Webb
Freddie Welsh	Frederick Hall Thomas
Whitey Wenzel	Otto Wenzel
Sonny Boy West	Alfred West
Barney Williams	Barney Lebrowitz
Ike Williams	Isiah Williams
Kid Williams	John Gutenko
California Jackie Wilson	George Dudley Wilson
Johnny Wilson	Giovanni Panica
Unknown Winston	Edward Robert Winston Jr.
Midget Wolgast	Joseph Robert Loscalzo
Bearcat Wright	Ed Wright
Chalky Wright	Albert Garfield Wright
Winky Wright	Ronald Lamont Wright
Benny Yanger	Frank Angone
Tony Zale	Anton Florian Zaleski
Charley Zivic	Charley Affif
Fritzie Zivic	Ferdinand Henry John Zivcich
Zulu Kid	Joseph Dimelfi

Ring Name	Nickname
Barney Aaron	Star of the East
Virgil Akins	Honey Bear
Muhammad Ali	The Greatest
Lou Ambers	Herkimer Hurricane
Sammy Angott	The Clutch
Art Aragon	Golden Boy
Alexis Argüello	El Flaco Explosivo (explosive thin man)
Henry Armstrong	Homicide Hank
Abe Attell	The Little Hebrew
Max Baer	Livermore Larruper
Carlos Manuel Baldomir	El Tata
Iran Barkley	The Blade
Jimmy Barry	Little Tiger
Carmen Basilio	Upstate Onion Farmer
Benny Bass	Little Fish
Wilfred Benítez	El Radar
George Benton	The Professor
Jack "Kid" Berg	Whitechapel Whirlwind
Paul Berlenbach	Astoria Assassin
Jack Blackburn	Chappie
Craig Bodzianowski	Gator
Riddick Bowe	Big Daddy, Sugar Man
James J. Braddock	Cinderella Man
Jack Britton	Boxing Marvel
Jack Broughton	Father of Boxing
Henry Brown	Toothpick
Joe Brown	Old Bones
James Burke	Deaf
Tommy Burns	Little Giant of Hanover
Butterbean	King of the Four Rounders
Joe Calzaghe	Pride of Wales, Italian Dragon
Héctor Camacho	Macho Man
Héctor Camacho Jr.	Machito
Miguel Canto	El Maestro
Michael Carbajal	Manitas de Piedra

Primo Carnera	Ambling Alp
Georges Carpentier	The Orchid Man
Rubin Carter	Hurricane
Joel Casamayor	El Cepillo (The Brush)
Marcel Cerdan	Casablanca Clouter
Antonio Cervantes	Kid Pambelé
Jeff Chandler	Joltin' Jeff
Ezzard Charles	Cincinnati Cobra
Julio César Chávez Sr.	El César del Boxeo
Kid Chocolate (1910–1988)	Cuban Bon Bon
Cassius Clay	Louisville Lip
Randall Cobb	Tex
Gerrie Coetzee	Bionic Hand
Billy Conn	Pittsburgh Kid
Gerry Cooney	Gentleman Gerry
Jim Corbett	Gentleman Jim
Johnny Coulon	Cherry Picker from Logan Square
Leach Cross	Fighting Dentist
Floyd Cummings	Jumbo
Donald Curry	The Cobra
Les Darcy	Maitland Wonder
Al Davis	Bummy
Teddy Davis	Red-Top
Óscar De La Hoya	Golden Boy
Jack Delaney	Bright Eyes
Jack Dempsey (1895–1983)	Manassa Mauler
Jack Dempsey (1862–1895)	The Nonpareil
Jack Dillon	Hoosier Bearcat
George Dixon	Little Chocolate
Michael Dokes	Dynamite
Mike Donovan	Professor
James Douglas	Buster
Jim Driscoll	Peerless Jim
Johnny Dundee	Scotch Wop
Roberto Durán	Manos de Piedra (Hands of Stone)
Yvon Durelle	Fighting Fisherman
Sixto Escobar	El Gallito (The Rooster)

Jeff Fenech	Marrickville Mauler
Dick Finnegan	Honeyboy
Luis Ángel Firpo	Wild Bull of the Pampas
Bob Fitzsimmons	Ruby Robert, The Freckled Wonder
Frank Fletcher	The Animal
Tiger Flowers	Georgia Deacon
George Foreman	Big George
Billy Fox	Blackjack
Alfonso Frazer	Peppermint
Joe Frazier	Smokin' Joe
Gene Fullmer	Cyclone
Khaosai Galaxy	Thai Tyson
Tony Galento	Two Ton
Victor Galíndez	El Leopardo de Morón
Joe Gans	Old Master
Arturo Gatti	Thunder
Kid Gavilán	Cuban Hawk
Michael Gibbons (1983–)	Godfather, Fighting Pride of Birmingham, Al
Mike Gibbons (1887–1956)	St. Paul Phantom
George Godfrey (1897–1947)	Feab S. Williams
Ruby Goldstein	Jewel of the Ghetto
Wilfredo Gómez	Bazooka
Humberto González	Chiquita
Rocky Graziano	The Rock
Harry Greb	Pittsburgh Windmill
Mitch Green	Blood
Horace Gwynne	Lefty
Naseem Hamed	Prince, Naz
Harry Harris	Human Hairpin, Human Scissors
Joe Harris	Gypsy Joe
Garnet Hart	Sugar
Marvin Hart	Fightin' Kentuckian, Louisville Plumber
Stanley Hayward	Kitten
Tommy Hearns	Hitman, Motor City Cobra
Virgil Hill	Quicksilver
Larry Holmes	Easton Assassin

Evander Holyfield	Real Deal
Bernard Hopkins	The Executioner
Ace Hudkins	The Nebraska Wildcat
John Jackson	Gentleman John
Peter Jackson	Black Prince, Peter the Great
Tommy Jackson	Hurricane
Jim Jeffries	Boilermaker
Lew Jenkins	Sweetwater Swatter
Éder Jofre	Galinho de Ouro (Golden Rooster)
Ingemar Johansson	Hammer of Thor, Ingo
George Johnson	Scrap Iron
Jack Johnson	Galveston Giant, Li'l Arthur
Tom Johnson (1964–)	Boom Boom
Stanley Ketchel	Michigan Assassin
Tom King	Fighting Sailor
Vitaly Klitschko	Dr. Ironfist
Wladimir Klitschko	Dr. Steelhammer
Ismael Laguna	El Tigre Colonense
Donny Lalonde	Golden Boy
Jake LaMotta	Bronx Bull
Sam Langford	Boston Tar Baby
George "Kid" Lavigne	Saginaw Kid
Scott LeDoux	Fighting Frenchman
William Lee	Caveman
Benny Leonard	Ghetto Wizard
Ray Leonard	Sugar Ray
Julian Letterlough	Mr. KO
Lennox Lewis	The Lion
Ted Lewis	Kid
Rafael Limón	Bazooka
Danny Lopez	Little Red
Ernie Lopez	Indian Red
Miguel Lora	Happy
Tommy Loughran	Phantom of Philly
Joe Louis	Brown Bomber
Raúl Macías	Ratón
Ray Mancini	Boom Boom

Sammy Mandell	Rockford Sheik
Rocky Marciano	Brockton Blockbuster
Everett Martin	Big Foot
Floyd Mayweather Jr.	Pretty Boy, Money
Roger Mayweather	Black Mamba
Jack McAuliffe	Napoleon of the Ring
Charles "Kid" McCoy	Corkscrew Kid
George McFadden	Elbows
Terry McGovern	Terrible Terry
Barry McGuigan	Clones Cyclone
Victor McLaglen	Sharkey
Jimmy McLarnin	Baby-Faced Assassin
Alan Minter	Boom Boom
Willie Monroe	The Worm
Bob Montgomery	Bobcat
Carlos Monzón	Escopeta (Shotgun)
Archie Moore	Old Mongoose
Owen Moran	The Fearless
Tommy Morrison	The Duke
Shane Mosley	Sugar
John Mugabi	The Beast
Eddie Mustafa Muhammad	Flame
Nkosana Mxgaji	Happy Boy
José Napoles	Mantequilla (Butter)
Azumah Nelson	Professor
Battling Nelson	Durable Dane
Michael Nunn	Second To
Sean O'Grady	Bubble-Gum kid
Rubén Olivares	El Púas
Carl "Bobo" Olson	Hawaiian Swede
Gaspar Ortega	El Indio (Indian)
Manny Pacquiao	Pac Man
Billy Papke	Illinois Thunderbolt
László Papp	Laci
Vinny Pazienza	Pazmanian Devil
Eusebio Pedroza	Alacrán (Scorpion)
Willie Pep	Will o' the Wisp

Gregorio Peralta	Goyo
Pascual Pérez	El Pequeño Gigante (Little Giant)
Billy Petrolle	Fargo Express
Emile Pladner	Spider
Aaron Pryor	Hawk
Jerry Quarry	Irish, Bellflower Bomber
Garland Randall	Rip
Ray Robinson	Sugar Ray
Luis Manuel Rodríguez	El Feo
Jose Roman	King
Edwin Rosario	El Chapo
Maxie Rosenbloom	Slapsie Maxie
Mike Rossman	Kosher Butcher, Jewish Bomber
Donovan Ruddock	Razor
Matthew Saad Muhammad	Miracle Matthew
Lauro Salas	Lion of Monterrey
Vicente Saldivar	Zurdo de Oro (Golden Leftie)
Salvador Sánchez	Chava
Félix Savon	Niñote
Max Schmeling	Black Uhlan of the Rhine
Gustav Scholz	Bubi
John Scully	Iceman
Ray Seales	Sugar Ray
Jack Sharkey	Boston Gob
Earnie Shavers	Black Destroyer
Hardy Smallwood	Bazooka
Charley Smith	Tombstone
James Smith	Bonecrusher
Jeff Smith	Globetrotter
Wallace Smith	Bud
Renaldo Snipes	Mister
Leon Spinks	Neon Leon
Michael Spinks	Jinx
Ron Stander	Council Bluffs Butcher
Freddie Steele	Tacoma Assassin
Willie Stevenson	Pineapple
Bruce Strauss	The Mouse

Young Stribling	King of the Canebrakes
Jack Sullivan	Twin
Mike Sullivan	Twin
Tony Thornton	The Punching Postman
James Tillis	Quick
James Toney	Lights Out
José Torres	Chegüi
Félix Trinidad	Tito
Tony Tucker	TNT
Gene Tunney	Fighting Marine
Randy Turpin	Leamington Larruper
Kosta Tszyu	Thunder from Down Under
Mike Tyson	Iron Mike
Paulino Uzcudun	Basque Woodchopper
Mickey Walker	Toy Bulldog
Joe Walcott (1873–1935)	Barbados Demon
Bobby Watts	Boogaloo
Billy Wells	Bombardier
Freddie Welsh	Welsh Wizard
Chuck Wepner	Bayonne Bleeder
Pernell Whitaker	Sweet Pea
Jimmy Wilde	Mighty Atom
Jess Willard	Pottawatomie Giant
Carl Williams	The Truth
Harry Wills	Black Panther
Ad Wolgast	Michigan Wildcat
Tony Zale	Man of Steel
Carlos Zárate	Cañas
Fritzie Zivic	Croat Comet

* legally changed name

NONBOXERS (TRAINERS, PROMOTERS, WRITERS, ETC.)

Nickname	Given Name
Al Albert	Alan Aufrichtig
Marv Albert	Marvin Philip Aufrichtig

Steve Albert	Stephen Aufrichtig
Nacho Beristáin	Ignacio Beristáin
A. F. "Peggy" Bettinson	Arthur Frederick Bettinson
Whitey Bimstein	Morris Bimstein
Jack Blackburn	Charles Henry Blackburn
Chuck Bodak	Vasil Bodak
Dr. Joyce Brothers	Joyce Diane Bauer
Bundini	Drew Brown
Frank Cappuccino	Frank Capcino
Frankie Carbo	Paolo Giovanni Carbo
Cuco Conde	Carlos Conde
Pepe Correa	Jose Correa
Howard Cosell	Howard William Cohen
Jack Curley	Jacques Armand Schuel
Joey Curtis	George Curtis
Cus D'Amato	Constantine D'Amato
Dan Daniel	Daniel Margowitz
Tad Dorgan	Thomas Aloysius Dorgan
Mickey Duff	Monek Prager
Angelo Dundee	Angelo Mirena
Chris Dundee	Cristofo Mirena
Yank Durham	Yancey Durham
Cal Eaton	Alvah M. Eaton
Win Elliot	Irwin Elliot Shalek
Jack Fiske	Jacob Quincy Finkelstein
Jack Fugazy	Humbert J. Fugazy
Pincho Gutierrez	Luis Gutierrez
W. C. Heinz	Wilfred Charles Heinz
Sarge Johnson	Thomas Johnson
Jersey Jones	Willis Jones
Jack "Doc" Kearns	John Leo McKernan
Tito Lectuore	Juan Carlos Lectuore
Butch Lewis	Ronald Everett Lewis
Panama Lewis	Carlos Lewis
A. J. Liebling	Abbott Joseph Liebling
Lord Lonsdale	Hugh Cecil Lowther
Ace Marotta	Adolph Marotta

Marquess of Queensberry	John Sholto Douglas
Bat Masterson	William Barclay Masterson
Rock Newman	Eugene Roderick Newman
Blinky Palermo	Frank Palermo
Goody Petronelli	Guerino Petronelli
Tex Rickard	George Lewis Rickard
Damon Runyon	Alfred Damon Runyan
Sylvester Stallone	Michael Sylvester Gardenzio Stallone
Lou Stillman	Louis Ingber
Bert Sugar	Herbert Randolph Sugar
Rip Valenti	Anthony Valenti
Mickey Vann	Micheal Van Norman
Al Weill	Armand Weill

BAREKNUCKLE FIGHTERS

Many of the fighters in the bareknuckle era had colorful sobriquets often reflecting their occupation.

Given Name	Nickname
James Ambrose	Yankee Sullivan
Jem Belcher	The Napoleon of the Ring
Benjamin Brain	Big Ben
Harry Broome	The Unknown
Jack Broughton	The Father of Boxing
James Burke	The Deaf 'Un
Tom Cannon	The Great Gun of Windsor
Ben Caunt	The Torkard Giant
Peter Corcoran	The Irish Champion
Peter Crawley	Young Rump Steak
Tom Cribb	The Black Diamond
William Darts	The Dyer
Bob Gregson	The Lancashire Giant
John Gully	The Potter
John C. Heenan	The Benicia Boy
Tom Hickman	The Gasman
William Hooper	The Tinman

Josh Hudson	The John Bull Fighter
Richard Humphries	The Gentleman Fighter
Sam Hurst	The Staleybridge Infant
Jacob Hyer	Father of the American Ring
George Ingleston	The Brewer
John Jackson	Gentleman
Tom Jones	Paddington Tom
Tom Juchau	The Pavior
Tom King	The Fighting Sailor
Tom Lyons	The Waterman
Jem Mace	The Gypsy
George McChester	Country McCluskey
Mike McCoole	The Deck Hand Champion
George Meggs	The Collier
Daniel Mendoza	The Jewish Champion
George Millsom	The Baker
Tom Molineaux	The Virginia Slave
John Morrissey	Old Smoke
Bill Neate	The Bristol Bull
Ned O'Baldwin	The Irish Giant
Thomas Owen	The Fighting Oilman
Tom Paddock	The Redditch Needlepointer
Henry Pearce	The Game Chicken
William Perry	The Tipton Slasher
Bill Richmond	The Black Terror
Paddy Ryan	The Trojan Giant
Tom Sayers	The Brighton Boy
Harry Sellers	The West Countryman
Jack Slack	The Norfolk Butcher
John Smith	Buckhorse
Tom Spring	The Light Tapper
William Stevens	The Nailer
George Stevenson	The Coachman
John L. Sullivan	The Boston Strong Boy
George Taylor	The Barber
William Thompson	Bendigo
Bob Travers	The Black Wonder

| Jem Ward | The Black Diamond |
| William Wood | The Coachman |

Appendix D

Weight Classes

Weight limits have varied throughout history. The limits listed are as of 2012.

PROFESSIONAL

Pounds	Class
105	Strawweight (Mini Flyweight) (Minimumweight)
108	Junior Flyweight (Light Flyweight)
112	Flyweight
115	Junior Bantamweight (Super Flyweight)
118	Bantamweight
122	Junior Featherweight (Super Bantamweight)
126	Featherweight
130	Junior Lightweight (Super Featherweight)
135	Lightweight
140	Junior Welterweight (Super Lightweight) (Light Welterweight)
147	Welterweight
154	Junior Middleweight (Super Welterweight) (Light Middleweight)
160	Middleweight
168	Junior Light Heavyweight (Super Middleweight)
175	Light Heavyweight
200	Cruiserweight (Junior Heavyweight)
Over 200	Heavyweight

AMATEUR

Kilograms (Pounds)	Class
46–49 (101.4–108.0)	Light Flyweight
49–52 (108.0–114.6)	Flyweight
52–56 (114.6–123.5)	Bantamweight
56–60 (123.5–132.3)	Lightweight
60–64 (132.3–141.1)	Light Welterweight
64–69 (141.1–152.1)	Welterweight
69–75 (152.1–165.3)	Middleweight
75–81 (165.3–178.6)	Light Heavyweight
81–91 (178.6–200.6)	Heavyweight
Over 91 (over 200.6)	Super Heavyweight

Appendix E

Ring *Magazine Fighter of the Year*

The Ring magazine, founded in 1922 by Nat Fleischer, is boxing's most respected publication. In 1928, Fleischer began a series of annual awards. Although the magazine's ownership has changed hands several times since Fleisher's death in 1973, the publication has continued to issue annual awards for boxing excellence during the year.

1928	Gene Tunney
1929	Tommy Loughran
1930	Max Schmeling
1931	Tommy Loughran
1932	Jack Sharkey
1933	no award
1934	Tony Canzoneri and Barney Ross
1935	Barney Ross
1936	Joe Louis
1937	Henry Armstrong
1938	Joe Louis
1939	Joe Louis
1940	Billy Conn
1941	Joe Louis
1942	Sugar Ray Robinson
1943	Fred Apostoli
1944	Beau Jack
1945	Willie Pep
1946	Tony Zale
1947	Gus Lesnevich
1948	Ike Williams
1949	Ezzard Charles
1950	Ezzard Charles
1951	Sugar Ray Robinson

1952	Rocky Marciano
1953	Bobo Olson
1954	Rocky Marciano
1955	Rocky Marciano
1956	Floyd Patterson
1957	Carmen Basilio
1958	Ingemar Johansson
1959	Ingemar Johansson
1960	Floyd Patterson
1961	Joe Brown
1962	Dick Tiger
1963	Cassius Clay
1964	Emile Griffith
1965	Dick Tiger
1966	no award
1967	Joe Frazier
1968	Nino Benvenuti
1969	Jose Napoles
1970	Joe Frazier
1971	Joe Frazier
1972	Muhammad Ali and Carlos Monzon
1973	George Foreman
1974	Muhammad Ali
1975	Muhammad Ali
1976	George Foreman
1977	Carlos Zarate
1978	Muhammad Ali
1979	Sugar Ray Leonard
1980	Thomas Hearns
1981	Sugar Ray Leonard and Salvador Sanchez
1982	Larry Holmes
1983	Marvin Hagler
1984	Thomas Hearns
1985	Marvin Hagler and Donald Curry
1986	Mike Tyson
1987	Evander Holyfield
1988	Mike Tyson

1989	Pernell Whitaker
1990	Julio César Chávez
1991	James Toney
1992	Riddick Bowe
1993	Michael Carbajal
1994	Roy Jones Jr.
1995	Oscar De La Hoya
1996	Evander Holyfield
1997	Evander Holyfield
1998	Floyd Mayweather Jr.
1999	Paulie Ayala
2000	Felix Trinidad
2001	Bernard Hopkins
2002	Vernon Forrest
2003	James Toney
2004	Glen Johnson
2005	Ricky Hatton
2006	Manny Pacquiao
2007	Floyd Mayweather Jr.
2008	Manny Pacquiao
2009	Manny Pacquiao
2010	Sergio Martinez
2011	Andre Ward
2012	Juan Manuel Márquez

Appendix F

Ring *Magazine Fight of the Year*

Ring magazine, founded in 1922 by Nat Fleischer, is boxing's most respected publication. Although the magazine's ownership has changed hands several times since Fleisher's death in 1973, the publication has continued to issue annual awards for boxing excellence during the year.

23 May 1922	Harry Greb Unan. Dec. 15 Gene Tunney
14 Sep 1923	Jack Dempsey KO 2 Luis Ángel Firpo
24 Jul 1924	Gene Tunney TKO 15 Georges Carpentier
2 Jul 1925	Harry Greb Unan. Dec. 15 Mickey Walker
23 Sep 1926	Gene Tunney Unan. Dec. 10 Jack Dempsey
22 Sep 1927	Gene Tunney Unan. Dec. 10 Jack Dempsey
6 Jan 1928	Tommy Loughran Unan. Dec. 15 Leo Lomski
1 Feb 1929	Max Schmeling TKO 9 Johnny Risko
7 Aug 1930	Jack "Kid" Berg Split Dec. 10 Kid Chocolate
3 Jul 1931	Max Schmeling TKO 15 Young Stribling
4 Nov 1932	Tony Canzoneri Unan. Dec. 15 Billy Petrolle
8 Jun 1933	Max Baer TKO 10 Max Schmeling
28 May 1934	Barney Ross Split Dec. 15 Jimmy McLarnin
24 Sep 1935	Joe Louis KO 4 Max Baer
19 Jun 1936	Max Schmeling KO 12 Joe Louis
30 Aug 1937	Joe Louis Unan. Dec. 15 Tommy Farr
17 Aug 1938	Henry Armstrong Split Dec. 15 Lou Ambers
20 Sep 1939	Joe Louis KO 11 Bob Pastor
1 Mar 1940	Ceferino Garcia Draw 10 Henry Armstrong
18 Jun 1941	Joe Louis KO 13 Billy Conn
20 Nov 1942	Willie Pep Unan. Dec. 15 Chalky Wright
21 May 1943	Beau Jack Unan. Dec. 15 Bob Montgomery
3 Mar 1944	Bob Montgomery Split Dec. 15 Beau Jack
29 Jun 1945	Rocky Graziano KO 10 Freddie Cochrane
27 Sep 1946	Tony Zale KO 6 Rocky Graziano

16 Jul 1947	Rocky Graziano TKO 6 Tony Zale
21 Sep 1948	Marcel Cerdan TKO 12 Tony Zale
11 Feb 1949	Willie Pep Unan. Dec. 15 Sandy Saddler
13 Sep 1950	Jake LaMotta KO 15 Laurent Dauthuille
18 Jul 1951	Jersey Joe Walcott KO 7 Ezzard Charles
23 Sep 1952	Rocky Marciano KO 13 Jersey Joe Walcott
24 Sep 1953	Rocky Marciano TKO 11 Roland LaStarza
17 Sep 1954	Rocky Marciano KO 8 Ezzard Charles
30 Nov 1955	Carmen Basilio TKO 12 Tony DeMarco
12 Sep 1956	Carmen Basilio TKO 9 Johnny Saxton
23 Sep 1957	Carmen Basilio Split Dec. 15 Sugar Ray Robinson
25 Mar 1958	Sugar Ray Robinson Split Dec. 15 Carmen Basilio
28 Aug 1959	Gene Fullmer TKO 14 Carmen Basilio
20 Jun 1960	Floyd Patterson KO 5 Ingemar Johansson
18 Apr 1961	Joe Brown Ref. Dec. 15 Dave Charnley
30 Jan 1962	Joey Giardello Maj. Dec. 10 Henry Hank
13 Mar 1963	Cassius Clay Unan. Dec. 10 Doug Jones
25 Feb 1964	Cassius Clay TKO 7 Sonny Liston
1 Feb 1965	Floyd Patterson Unan. Dec. 12 George Chuvalo
15 Aug 1966	Jose Torres Unan. Dec. 15 Eddie Cotton
17 Apr 1967	Nino Benvenuti Unan. Dec. 15 Emile Griffith
25 Oct 1968	Dick Tiger Unan. Dec. 10 Frank DePaula
23 Jun 1969	Joe Frazier TKO 7 Jerry Quarry
7 Nov 1970	Carlos Monzon TKO 12 Nino Benvenuti
8 Mar 1971	Joe Frazier Unan. Dec. 15 Muhammad Ali
26 Sep 1972	Bob Foster KO 14 Chris Finnegan
22 Jan 1973	George Foreman KO 2 Joe Frazier
30 Oct 1974	Muhammad Ali KO 8 George Foreman
1 Oct 1975	Muhammad Ali TKO 14 Joe Frazier
24 Jan 1976	George Foreman KO 5 Ron Lyle
17 Mar 1977	Jimmy Young Unan. Dec. 12 George Foreman
15 Feb 1978	Leon Spinks Split Dec. Muhammad Ali
17 Jun 1979	Danny Lopez KO 15 Mike Ayala
13 Jul 1980	Matthew Saad Muhammad TKO 14 Yaqui Lopez
16 Sep 1981	Sugar Ray Leonard TKO 14 Thomas Hearns
11 Dec 1982	Bobby Chacon Unan. Dec. 15 Rafael Limon
15 May 1983	Bobby Chacon Unan. Dec. 15 Cornelius Boza-Edwards

3 Nov 1984	Jose Luis Ramirez TKO 4 Edwin Rosario
15 Apr 1985	Marvelous Marvin Hagler TKO 3 Thomas Hearns
23 Jun 1986	Steve Cruz Unan. Dec. 15 Barry McGuigan
6 Apr 1987	Sugar Ray Leonard Split Dec. 12 Marvelous Marvin Hagler
23 July 1988	Tony Lopez Unan. Dec. 12 Rocky Lockridge
24 Feb 1989	Roberto Duran Split Dec. 12 Iran Barkley
17 Mar 1990	Julio César Chávez TKO 12 Meldrick Taylor
15 Jun 1991	Robert Quiroga Unan. Dec. 12 Akeem Anifowoshe
13 Nov 1992	Riddick Bowe Unan. Dec. 12 Evander Holyfield
13 Mar 1993	Michael Carbajal KO 7 Humberto Gonzalez
10 Dec 1994	Jorge Fernando Castro TKO 9 John David Jackson
15 Jul 1995	Saman Sorjaturong TKO 7 Humberto Gonzalez
9 Nov 1996	Evander Holyfield TKO 11 Mike Tyson
4 Oct 1997	Arturo Gatti TKO 5 Gabriel Ruelas
22 Aug 1998	Ivan Robinson Split Dec. 10 Arturo Gatti
26 Jun 1999	Paulie Ayala Unan. Dec. 12 Johnny Tapia
19 Feb 2000	Erik Morales Split Dec. 12 Marco Antonio Barrera
13 Jul 2001	Micky Ward Unan. Dec. 10 Emanuel Augustus
18 May 2002	Micky Ward Maj. Dec. 10 Arturo Gatti
7 Jun 2003	Arturo Gatti Unan. Dec. 10 Micky Ward
27 Nov 2004	Marco Antonio Barrera Maj. Dec. 12 Erik Morales
7 May 2005	Diego Corrales TKO 10 Jose Luis Castillo
18 Mar 2006	Somsak Sithchatchawal TKO 10 Mahyar Monshipour
4 Aug 2007	Israel Vasquez TKO 6 Rafael Marquez
1 Mar 2008	Israel Vasquez Split Dec. 12 Rafael Marquez
28 Feb 2009	Juan Manuel Marquez TKO 9 Juan Diaz
28 Aug 2010	Giovani Segura KO 8 Ivan Calderon
16 Apr 2011	Victor Ortiz Unan. Dec. 12 Andre Berto
8 Dec 2012	Juan Manuel Márquez KO 6 Manny Pacquiao

Appendix G

Professional Boxing Heavyweight Champions

BAREKNUCKLE ERA

1719–1730   James Figg

1730–1734   Tom Pipes

1734–1736   George Taylor

1736–1750   Jack Broughton

1750–1760   Jack Slack

1760–1761   William Stevens

1761–1762   George Meggs

1762–1765   George Millsom

1765–1766   Tom Juchau

1766–1769   William Darts

1769–1769   Tom Lyons

1769–1771   William Darts

1771–1776   Peter Corcoran

1776–1779   Harry Sellers

1779–1779   Jack "Duggan" Fearns

1779–1787   none

1787–1791   Tom Johnson

1791–1794   Ben Brain

1794–1795   Daniel Mendoza

1795–1796   John Jackson

1796–1797   Thomas Owen

1797–1800   Jack Bartholomew

1800–1805   Jem Belcher

1805–1807   Hen Pearce

1807–1808   John Gully

1808–1822   Tom Cribb

1810–1815   Tom Molineaux (American)

1823–1824   Tom Spring

1824–1825   Tom Cannon

1825–1827   Jem Ward

1827–1827   Peter Crawley

1827–1832   Jem Ward

1833–1839   James "Deaf" Burke

1839–1840   William "Bendigo" Thompson

1840–1841   Ben Caunt

1841–1851   Tom Hyer (American)

1841–1841   Nick Ward

1841–1845   Ben Caunt

1845–1850   William "Bendigo" Thompson

1850–1851   William Perry

1851–1856   Harry Broome

1853–1859   John Morrissey (American)

1856–1858   Tom Paddock

1858–1860   Tom Sayers

1860–1861   Sam Hurst

1860–1863   John C. Heenan (American)

1861–1862   Jem Mace

1862–1863   Tom King

1863–1865   Joe Coburn (American)

1865–1870   Jimmy Elliott (American)

1866–1871   Jem Mace

1866–1873   Mike McCoole (American)

1869–1870   Tom Allen (American)

1873–1876   Tom Allen (American)

1876–1880   Joe Goss (American)

1880–1882   Paddy Ryan (American)

1882–1889   John L. Sullivan (American)

MARQUESS OF QUEENSBERRY RULES ERA

1889–1892   John L. Sullivan

1892–1897   Jim Corbett

1897–1899   Bob Fitzsimmons

1899–1905   Jim Jeffries

1905–1906	Marvin Hart
1906–1908	Tommy Burns
1908–1915	Jack Johnson
1915–1919	Jess Willard
1919–1926	Jack Dempsey
1927–1928	Gene Tunney
1928–1930	vacant
1930–1932	Max Schmeling
1932–1933	Jack Sharkey
1933–1934	Primo Carnera
1934–1935	Max Baer
1935–1937	James J. Braddock
1937–1949	Joe Louis
1949–1951	Ezzard Charles
1950–1951	Lee Savold*
1951–1952	Jersey Joe Walcott
1952–1956	Rocky Marciano
1956	vacant
1956–1959	Floyd Patterson
1959–1960	Ingemar Johansson
1960–1962	Floyd Patterson
1962–1964	Sonny Liston
1964–1969	Cassius Clay (Muhammad Ali)
1965–1967	Ernie Terrell*
1968–1970	Joe Frazier*
1968–1970	Jimmy Ellis*
1970–1973	Joe Frazier
1973–1974	George Foreman
1974–1978	Muhammad Ali
1978	Leon Spinks*
1978	Ken Norton*
1978–1983	Larry Holmes*
1978–1979	Muhammad Ali*
1979–1980	John Tate*
1980–1982	Mike Weaver*
1982–1983	Michael Dokes*
1983–1984	Gerrie Coetzee*

1983–1985	Larry Holmes*
1984	Tim Witherspoon*
1984–1986	Pinklon Thomas*
1984–1985	Greg Page*
1985–1986	Tony Tubbs*
1985–1987	Michael Spinks*
1986	Tim Witherspoon*
1986	Trevor Berbick*
1986–1987	Mike Tyson*
1986–1987	James Smith*
1987	Tony Tucker*
1987–1989	Mike Tyson
1989–1991	Francesco Damiani*
1989–1990	Mike Tyson*
1990	James "Buster" Douglas*
1990–1992	Evander Holyfield*
1991	Ray Mercer*
1992–1993	Michael Moorer*
1992–1993	Riddick Bowe*
1992–1994	Lennox Lewis*
1993	Tommy Morrison*
1993–1994	Michael Bentt*
1993–1994	Evander Holyfield*
1994–1995	Herbie Hide*
1994	Michael Moorer*
1994–1995	Oliver McCall*
1994–1995	George Foreman*
1995–1996	Riddick Bowe*
1995–1996	Bruce Seldon*
1995–1996	Frank Bruno*
1996	Mike Tyson*
1996–1997	Michael Moorer*
1996–1997	Henry Akinwande*
1996–1999	Evander Holyfield*
1997–1901	Lennox Lewis*
1997–1999	Herbie Hide*
1999–2000	Vitali Klitschko*

2000	Chris Byrd*
2000–2001	Evander Holyfield*
2000–2003	Wladimir Klitschko*
2001–2003	John Ruiz*
2001	Hasim Rahman*
2001–2004	Lennox Lewis*
2002–2006	Chris Byrd*
2003–2004	Roy Jones Jr.*
2003	Corrie Sanders*
2004–2005	John Ruiz*
2004–2006	Lamon Brewster*
2004–2005	Vitali Klitschko*
2005–2006	Hasim Rahman*
2005–2007	Nikolai Valuev*
2006	Siarhei Liakhovich*
2006–2012	Wladimir Klitschko*
2006–2008	Oleg Maskaev*
2006–2007	Shannon Briggs*
2007–2008	Ruslan Chagaev*
2007–2008	Sultan Ibragimov*
2008	Samuel Peter*
2008–2009	Nikolai Valuev*
2008–2012	Vitali Klitschko*
2009–2011	David Haye*
2011–2012	Alexander Povetkin*

* Title not recognized by all governing organizations.

Appendix H

Broughton's Rules

After severely beating George Stevenson in a fight to the extent that Stevenson died a few days afterward, the remorseful prizefighter Jack Broughton drew up a set of boxing rules to prevent a reoccurrence. The rules were used by Broughton to regulate bouts in his boxing academy. These rules governed the London Prize Ring until superseded by the London Prize Ring Rules of 1838.

I. That a square of a yard be chalked in the middle of the stage, and on every fresh set-to after a fall, or being parted form the rails, each Second is to bring his Man to the side of the square, and place him opposite to the other, and till they are fairly set-to at the Lines, it shall not be lawful for one to strike at the other.

II. That, in order to prevent any Disputes, the time a Man lies after a fall, if the Second does not bring his Man to the side of the square, within the space of half a minute, he shall be deemed a beaten Man.

III. That in every main Battle, no person whatever shall be upon the Stage, except the Principals and their Seconds, the same rule to be observed in bye-battles, except that in the latter, Mr. Broughton is allowed to be upon the Stage to keep decorum, and to assist Gentlemen in getting to their places, provided always he does not interfere in the Battle; and whoever pretends to infringe these Rules to be turned immediately out of the house. Every body is to quit the Stage as soon as the Champions are stripped, before the set-to.

IV. That no Champion be deemed beaten, unless he fails coming up to the line in the limited time, or that his own Second declares him beaten. No Second is to be allowed to ask his man's Adversary any questions, or advise him to give out.

V. That in bye-battles, the winning man to have two-thirds of the Money given, which shall be publicly divided upon the Stage, notwithstanding any private agreements to the contrary.

VI. That to prevent Disputes, in every main Battle the Principals shall, on coming on the Stage, choose from among the gentlemen present two Umpires, who shall absolutely decide all Disputes that may arise about the Battle; and if the two Umpires cannot agree, the said Umpires to choose a third, who is to determine it.

VII. That no person is to hit his Adversary when he is down, or seize him by the ham, the breeches, or any part below the waist: a man on his knees to be reckoned down.

As agreed by several Gentlemen at Broughton's Amphitheatre, Tottenham Court Road, August 16, 1743.

Appendix I

Revised London Prize Ring Rules

The rules of 1853 (which were somewhat different to the rules of 1838) are as follows:

1. That the ring shall be made on turf, and shall be four-and-twenty feet square, formed of eight stakes and ropes, the latter extending in double lines, the uppermost line being four feet from the ground, and the lower two feet from the ground. That in the centre of the ring a mark be formed, to be termed a scratch; and that at two opposite corners, as may be selected, spaces be enclosed by other marks sufficiently large for the reception of the seconds and bottle-holders, to be entitled "the corners."

2. That each man shall be attended to the ring by a second and a bottle-holder, the former provided with a sponge and the latter with a bottle of water. That the combatants, on shaking hands, shall retire until the seconds of each have tossed for choice of position, which adjusted, the winner shall choose his corner according to the state of the wind or sun, and conduct his man thereto, the loser taking the opposite corner.

3. That each man shall be provided with a handkerchief of a colour suitable to his own fancy, and that the seconds proceed to entwine these handkerchiefs at the upper end of one of the center stakes. That these handkerchiefs shall be called "the colours;" and that the winner of the battle at its conclusion shall be entitled to their possession, as the trophy of victory.

4. That two umpires shall be chosen by the seconds or backers to watch the progress of the battle, and take exception to any breach of the rules hereafter stated. That a referee shall be chosen by the umpires, unless otherwise agreed on, to whom all disputes shall be referred; and that the decision of this referee, whatever it may be, shall be final and strictly binding on all parties, whether as to the matter in dispute or the issue of the battle. That the umpires shall be provided with a watch, for the purpose of calling time; and that they mutually agree upon which this duty shall devolve, the call of that umpire only to be attended to, and no other person whatever to interfere in calling time. That the referee shall withhold all opinion till appealed to by the umpires, and that the umpires strictly abide by his decision without dispute.

5. That on the men being stripped, it shall be the duty of the seconds to examine their drawers, and if any objection arise as to insertion of improper substances therein, they shall appeal to their umpires, who, with the concurrence of the referee, shall direct what alterations shall be made.

6. That in future no spikes be used in fighting boots except those authorized by the Pugilistic Benevolent Association, which shall not exceed three-eights of an inch from the sole of the boot, and shall not be less than one-eight of an inch broad at the point; and, it shall be in the power of the referee to alter, or file in any way he pleases, spikes which shall not accord with the above dimensions, even to filing them away altogether.

7. That both men being ready, each man shall be conducted to that side of the scratch next his corner previously chosen; and the seconds on the one side and the men on the other, having shaken hands, the former shall immediately return to their corners, and there remain within the prescribed marks till the round be finished, on no pretence whatever approaching their principals during the round, under penalty of 5s. for each offence, at the option of the referee. The penalty, which will be strictly enforced, to go to the funds of the Association. The principal to be responsible for every fine inflicted on his second.

8. That at the conclusion of the round, when one or both of the men shall be down, the seconds and bottle-holders shall step forward and carry or conduct their principal to his corner, there affording him the necessary assistance, and no person whatever be permitted to interfere with this duty.

9. That at the expiration of thirty seconds (unless otherwise agreed upon) the umpire appointed shall cry "Time," upon which each man shall rise from the knee of his bottle-holder and walk to his own side of the scratch unaided, the seconds and the bottle-holders remaining at their corner; and that either man failing so to be at the scratch within eight seconds, shall be deemed to have lost the battle.

10. That on no consideration whatever shall any person be permitted to enter the ring during the battle, nor till it shall have been concluded; and that in the event of such unfair practice, or the ropes and stakes being disturbed or removed, it shall be in the power of the referee to award the victory to that man who in his honest opinion shall have the best of the contest.

11. That the seconds and bottle-holders shall not interfere, advise, or direct the adversary of their principal, and shall refrain from all offensive and irritating expressions, in all respects conducting themselves with order and decorum, and confine themselves to the diligent and careful discharge of their duties to their principals.

12. That in picking up their men, should the seconds or bottle-holders wilfully injure the antagonist of their principal, the latter shall be deemed to have forfeited the battle on the decision of the referee.

13. That it shall be "a fair stand-up fight," and if either man shall wilfully throw himself down without receiving a blow, whether blows shall have previously been exchanged or not, he shall be deemed to have lost the battle; but that this rule shall not apply to a man who in a close slips down from the grasp of his opponent to avoid punishment, or from obvious accident or weakness.

14. That butting with the head shall be deemed foul, and the party resorting to this practice shall be deemed to have lost the battle.

15. That a blow struck when a man is thrown or down, shall be deemed foul. That a man with one knee and one hand on the ground, or with both knees on the ground, shall be deemed down; and a blow given in either of those positions shall be considered foul, providing always, that when in such position, the man so down shall not himself strike or attempt to strike.

16. That a blow struck below the waistband shall be deemed foul, and that, in a close, seizing an antagonist below the waist, by the thigh, or otherwise, shall be deemed foul.

17. That all attempts to inflict injury by gouging, or tearing the flesh with the fingers or nails, and biting, shall be deemed foul.

18. That kicking, or deliberately falling on an antagonist, with the knees or otherwise when down, shall be deemed a foul.

19. That all bets shall be paid as the battle-money, after a fight, is awarded.

20. That no person, on any pretence whatever, shall be permitted to approach nearer the ring than ten feet, with the exception of the umpires and referee, and the persons appointed to take charge of the water or other refreshment for the combatants, who shall take their seats close to the corners selected by the seconds.

21. That due notice shall be given by the stakeholder of the day and place where the battle-money is to be given up, and that he be exonerated from all responsibility upon obeying the direction of the referee; and that all parties be strictly bound by these rules; and that in future all articles of agreement for a contest be entered into with a strict and willing adherence to the letter and spirit of these rules.

22. That in the event of magisterial or other interference, or in case of darkness coming on, the referee shall have the power to name the time and place for the next meeting, if possible, on the same day, or as soon after as may be.

23. That should the fight not be decided on the day, all bets, instead of being drawn, shall be put together and divided, unless the fight shall be resumed the same week, between Sunday and Sunday, in which case the bets shall stand and be decided by the event. That where the day named in the articles for a fight to come off is altered to another day in the same week, the bets shall stand. The battle-money shall remain in the hands of the stakeholder until fairly won or lost by a fight, unless a draw be mutually agreed upon.

24. That any pugilist voluntarily quitting the ring previous to the deliberate judgment of the referee being obtained, shall be deemed to have lost the fight.

25. That on an objection being made by the seconds or umpire, the men shall retire to their corners, and there remain until the decision of the appointed authorities shall be obtained; that if pronounced "foul," the battle shall be at an end, but if "fair," "time" shall be called by the party appointed, and the man absent from the scratch in eight seconds after shall be deemed to have lost the fight. The decision in all cases to be given promptly and irrevocably, for which purpose the umpires and the referee should be invariably close together.

26. That if in a rally at the ropes a man steps outside the ring, to avoid his antagonist or escape punishment, he shall forfeit the battle.

27. That the use of hard substances, such as stones, or sticks, or of resin, in the hand during the battle shall be deemed foul, and that on the requisition of the seconds, of either man, the accused shall open his hands for the examination of the referee.

28. That where a man shall have his antagonist across the ropes in such a position as to be helpless, and to endanger his life by strangulation or apoplexy, it shall be in the power of the referee to direct the seconds to take their man away, and thus conclude the round, and that the man or his seconds refusing to obey the direction of the referee, shall be deemed the loser.

29. That all stage fights be as nearly as possible in conformity with the foregoing rules.

Appendix J

Marquess of Queensberry Rules

1. To be a fair stand-up boxing match in a 24-foot ring, or as near that size as practicable.
2. No wrestling or hugging (clinching) allowed.
3. The rounds to be of three minutes duration, and one minute's time between rounds.
4. If either man falls through weakness or otherwise, he must get up unassisted, 10 seconds to be allowed him to do so, the other man meanwhile to return to his corner, and when the fallen man is on his legs the round is to be resumed and continued until the three minutes have expired. If one man fails to come to the scratch in the 10 seconds allowed, it shall be in the power of the referee to give his award in favour of the other man.
5. A man hanging on the ropes in a helpless state, with his toes off the ground, shall be considered down.
6. No seconds or any other person to be allowed in the ring during the rounds.
7. Should the contest be stopped by any unavoidable interference, the referee to name the time and place as soon as possible for finishing the contest; so that the match must be won and lost, unless the backers of both men agree to draw the stakes.
8. The gloves to be fair-sized boxing gloves of the best quality and new.
9. Should a glove burst, or come off, it must be replaced to the referee's satisfaction.
10. A man on one knee is considered down and if struck is entitled to the stakes.
11. That no shoes or boots with spikes or sprigs be allowed.
12. The contest in all other respects to be governed by revised London Prize Ring Rules.

Appendix K

They Go Through Plenty

Paul Gallico, as sports editor of the *New York Daily News*, was responsible for creating the New York Golden Gloves tournament in 1927. He later became a world-renowned author of such works as *The Snow Goose* and *The Poseidon Adventure*. The following column appeared in the *New York Daily News* on 18 February 1930, the day before the Golden Gloves finals at Madison Square Garden. It gives a good illustration of the sacrifices that an individual must make in order to become an amateur boxing champion.

How brightly the fires of ambition burn in the Golden Glovers who will perform in Madison Square Garden tomorrow evening can only be appreciated by one who has followed them in their travels from the time they appear before the doctor as candidates to that proud moment when they scramble through the ropes of the most famous ring in the country. The things they put up with, the obstacles they overcome and the energy they expend would be enough to overcome anyone but a potential champion. And that probably is what has made the Golden Gloves such a blue ribbon event. None but the worthy reach Madison Square. Everybody knows they have to be good to get there.

When the last bout in the Garden is over there will have been exactly 800 fights during the holding of the Golden Gloves for this year. Now, when you figure that out that's a lot of arguments. And through it all they kept on winning, winning and winning. They went to the doggondest places in the Metropolitan area. I know. I went around with them. And I marveled at their endurance and their patience. You know, a tournament like this isn't all peaches and cream. All the auditoriums in the city aren't like Madison Square Garden. Nor are all of them as centrally located.

Picture a typical Golden Glover in the sub-novice[1] class. From 9 to 5 he works at his job, whatever it is. Most of them are tough ones, requiring hard work. When they're through they're pretty tired. Well, a long ride home on car.[2] or subway, no dinner, because it won't do to fight on a full stomach, business of tossing paraphernalia into a bag, picking up the handlers and then off to the wars. Now comes another long ride on subway or train or car. The tiny auditoriums where the eliminations are held are scattered over the vast city and the boys have to get there as best they can. Mostly there's a walk after the subway ride. And sometimes it is raining.

They get there around seven o'clock, undress themselves, get themselves weighed in and drawn and then begins a long, tedious wait stretched out in stuffy dressing rooms until their turn comes to go on. This, too, is decided by lot. Some of the boys must wait two or three hours before they go on. There is no help for it in a tournament of the magnitude of the Golden Gloves. Perhaps due to the particular stage in which the tournament finds itself, the boy must fight twice that night. Then he goes on early and comes back and waits and waits and waits.

At last he fights. He wins, of course, because he is going into the Garden tomorrow night, and only winners show there. But it has been a tough fight. His body is bruised and battered; his chin is sore; possibly he has received a bloody nose or a cut on his face. Back to the dressing room where the News doctor renders first aid if necessary. Then for a quick shower, and sometimes the shower facilities are not all they should be, because the small amateur and social clubs which hold these eliminations are far from being millionaires. Well it is pretty late now. Probably after eleven o'clock. And our sub-novice friend has to ride clear across Brooklyn to get home. Possibly a couple of changes of cars or trains. I suggested that probably it is raining. He drags himself home about one in the morning, victorious, it is true, but sore and dog-tired.

But no staying in bed late the next morning to rest up. No sir! Jobs must be protected. Up at seven again and taking a right hand punch at the time clock at nine. Life and the grind goes on, doesn't it? Five o'clock again, and into the gym to limber up. Weight must be kept just right and muscles kept in shape. He should do road work, too, but probably doesn't for which you can hardly blame him. And he should eat the right kind of food but doesn't because (1) he doesn't know what the right kind of food is, and (2) he hasn't got the money.

Two or three nights later, he must do it all over again, this time going some place else to fight. Three, four, five, six times, sometimes before he even reaches the Garden. That's the kind of tournament it is and that is why a Golden Glover is like no other amateur boxer. He's got stuff in him. He heals quickly from everything—cuts, fatigue, beatings, overwork. He has no time to be sick or let his troubles get the better of him. No matter what knocks him down he gets up. And that is why he is making the Garden tomorrow and why we are taking him to Chicago.[3]

NOTES

1. The sub-novice class was for boxers who hadn't boxed in previous years.
2. A streetcar or trolley car.

3. The winners at Madison Square Garden competed against a team from Chicago in the Intercity Golden Gloves.

Appendix L

Boxing Movies

This list includes films in which boxing and boxers play a major part in the story. Quite a few real-life boxers have bit parts in many of these films. There have also been many boxers who appeared in nonboxing films—often in small parts as a mobster, tough guy, or bodyguard. Those films are not included here.

Year	Title	Star or Subject	Type
1894	Corbett and Courtney Before the Kinetograph	Jim Corbett	Silent documentary
1897	The Corbett–Fitzsimmons Fight	Jim Corbett	Silent documentary
1919	Broken Blossoms	Lillian Gish	Silent drama
1919	The Egg Crate Wallop	Charles Ray	Silent comedy
1920	A Son of David	Ronald Colman	Silent drama
1921	The Croxley Master	Dick Webb	Silent drama
1924	Dynamite Dan	Kenneth MacDonald	Silent drama
1924	The Great White Way	Tom Lewis	Silent comedy
1926	Battling Butler	Buster Keaton	Silent comedy
1927	The Ring	Carl Brisson	Silent drama
1929	Speakeasy	Paul Page	Drama
1930	Hold Everything	Joe E. Brown	Musical comedy
1931	The Champ	Wallace Beery	Drama
1932	The Big Timer	Ben Lyon	Drama
1932	They Never Come Back	Regis Toomey	Drama
1932	Winner Take All	James Cagney	Drama
1933	The Bermondsey Kid	Esmond Knight	Drama
1933	The Big Chance	John Darrow	Drama
1933	The Prizefighter and the Lady	Max Baer	Drama
1934	Palooka	Stuart Erwin	Comedy
1936	Cain and Mabel	Clark Gable	Comedy
1936	Conflict	John Wayne	Drama

1936	*Excuse My Glove*	Len Harvey	Comedy
1936	*The Milky Way*	Harold Lloyd	Comedy
1937	*Fifty-Shilling Boxer*	Bruce Seton	Comedy
1937	*Flying Fists*	Bruce Bennett	Drama
1937	*Kid Galahad*	Edward G. Robinson	Drama
1937	*When's Your Birthday*	Joe E. Brown	Comedy
1938	*The Crowd Roars*	Robert Taylor	Drama
1938	*Hollywood Stadium Mystery*	Neil Hamilton	Drama
1938	*Spirit of Youth*	Joe Louis	Bio: Joe Louis
1939	*Golden Boy*	William Holden	Drama
1939	*There Ain't No Justice*	Jimmy Hanley	Drama
1939	*They Made Me a Criminal*	John Garfield	Drama
1940	*City for Conquest*	James Cagney	Drama
1940	*The Notorious Elinor Lee*	Robert Earl Jones	Drama
1941	*Bowery Blitzkrieg*	Huntz Hall	Comedy
1941	*Here Comes Mr. Jordan*	Robert Montgomery	Drama
1941	*The Miracle Kid*	Tom Neal	Drama
1942	*Gentleman Jim*	Errol Flynn	Bio: Jim Corbett
1943	*Kid Dynamite*	Leo Gorcey	Comedy
1943	*The Man from Down Under*	Charles Laughton	Drama
1944	*The Contender*	Buster Crabbe	Drama
1945	*The Great John L.*	Greg McClure	Bio: John L. Sullivan
1946	*Gentleman Joe Palooka*	Joe Kirkwood Jr.	Comedy
1946	*Joe Palooka, Champ*	Joe Kirkwood Jr.	Comedy
1946	*The Kid from Brooklyn*	Danny Kaye	Comedy
1947	*Body and Soul*	John Garfield	Drama
1947	*Joe Palooka in The Knockout*	Joe Kirkwood Jr.	Comedy
1947	*Killer McCoy*	Mickey Rooney	Drama
1948	*Joe Palooka in Fighting Mad*	Joe Kirkwood Jr.	Comedy
1948	*Joe Palooka in Winner Take All*	Joe Kirkwood Jr.	Comedy
1948	*Whiplash*	Dane Clark	Drama
1949	*Champion*	Kirk Douglas	Drama
1949	*Diez Segundos*	Ricardo Duggan	Drama
1949	*Duke of Chicago*	Tom Brown	Drama
1949	*Fighting Fools*	Leo Gorcey	Comedy

1949	*Joe Palooka in The Big Fight*	Joe Kirkwood Jr.	Comedy
1949	*Joe Palooka in The Counterpunch*	Joe Kirkwood Jr.	Comedy
1949	*No Way Back*	Terence de Marney	Drama
1949	*The Set-Up*	Robert Ryan	Drama
1950	*The Golden Gloves Story*	James Dunn	Drama
1950	*Joe Palooka in Humphrey Takes a Chance*	Joe Kirkwood Jr.	Comedy
1950	*Joe Palooka Meets Humphrey*	Joe Kirkwood Jr.	Comedy
1950	*Joe Palooka in The Squared Circle*	Joe Kirkwood Jr.	Comedy
1950	*Night and the City*	Richard Widmark	Drama
1950	*Right Cross*	Dick Powell	Drama
1951	*Joe Palooka in Triple Cross*	Joe Kirkwood Jr.	Comedy
1952	*The Fighter*	Richard Conte	Drama
1952	*Kid Monk Baroni*	Leonard Nimoy	Drama
1952	*The Quiet Man*	John Wayne	Drama
1952	*The Ring*	Lalo Rios	Drama
1953	*The Joe Louis Story*	Coley Wallace	Bio - Joe Louis
1953	*Off Limits*	Bob Hope	Comedy
1953	*The Square Ring*	Jack Warner	Drama
1954	*On the Waterfront*	Marlon Brando	Drama
1955	*Killer's Kiss*	Frank Silvera	Drama
1956	*The Harder They Fall*	Humphrey Bogart	Drama
1956	*The Leather Saint*	Paul Douglas	Drama
1956	*Somebody Up There Likes Me*	Paul Newman	Bio: Rocky Graziano
1956	*The Square Jungle*	Tony Curtis	Drama
1956	*World in My Corner*	Audie Murphy	Drama
1957	*Monkey on My Back*	Cameron Mitchell	Bio: Barney Ross
1960	*Rocco and His Brothers*	Alain Delon	Drama
1962	*Kid Galahad*	Elvis Presley	Musical
1962	*Requiem for a Heavyweight*	Anthony Quinn	Drama
1964	*Belarmino*	Belarmino Fragoso	Documentary
1968	*Legendary Champions*	Jack Dempsey	Documentary
1970	*A.K.A. Cassius Clay*	Muhammad Ali	Documentary
1970	*The Great White Hope*	James Earl Jones	Bio: Jack Johnson

1970	*Jack Johnson*	Jack Johnson	Documentary
1970	*The Super Fight*	Muhammad Ali	Documentary
1971	*Below the Belt*	John Tull	Comedy
1972	*Fat City*	Stacy Keach	Drama
1972	*Hammer*	Fred Williamson	Drama
1973	*The All-American Boy*	Jon Voight	Drama
1975	*Hard Times*	Charles Bronson	Drama
1975	*Let's Do It Again*	Sidney Poitier	Comedy
1975	*Mandingo*	James Mason	Drama
1976	*Rocky*	Sylvester Stallone	Drama
1977	*The Greatest*	Muhammad Ali	Bio: Muhammad Ali
1978	*Every Which Way But Loose*	Clint Eastwood	Comedy
1978	*Matilda*	Elliott Gould	Comedy
1978	*Ring of Passion*	Bernie Casey	Bio: Louis–Schmeling
1979	*The Champ*	Jon Voight	Drama
1979	*Flesh & Blood*	Tom Berenger	Drama
1979	*The Hitter*	Ron O'Neal	Drama
1979	*The Main Event*	Ryan O'Neal	Comedy
1979	*Marciano*	Tony Lo Bianco	Bio: Rocky Marciano
1979	*Penitentiary*	Leon Isaac Kennedy	Drama
1979	*The Prize Fighter*	Tim Conway	Comedy
1979	*Rocky II*	Sylvester Stallone	Drama
1980	*Raging Bull*	Robert De Niro	Bio: Jake LaMotta
1982	*Bomber*	Bud Spencer	Comedy
1982	*Honeyboy*	Erik Estrada	Drama
1982	*Penitentiary II*	Leon Isaac Kennedy	Drama
1982	*Rocky III*	Sylvester Stallone	Drama
1983	*Dempsey*	Treat Williams	Bio: Jack Dempsey
1983	*The Fighter*	Gregory Harrison	Drama
1983	*The Last Fight*	Ruben Blades	Drama
1983	*Tough Enough*	Dennis Quaid	Drama
1984	*Terrible Joe Moran*	James Cagney	Drama
1985	*Doin' Time*	Jeff Altman	Comedy
1985	*Heart of a Champion: The Ray Mancini Story*	Robert Blake	Bio: Ray Mancini
1985	*Rocky IV*	Sylvester Stallone	Drama

1986	*Busted Up*	Paul Coufos	Drama
1986	*Split Decisions*	Gene Hackman	Drama
1986	*Streets of Gold*	Klaus Maria Brandauer	Drama
1987	*Broken Noses*	Andy Minsker	Documentary
1987	*Heart*	Brad Davis	Comedy
1987	*Penitentiary III*	Leon Isaac Kennedy	Drama
1987	*Teen Wolf Too*	Jason Bateman	Comedy
1988	*Aryan*	Mohanlal	Drama
1988	*Homeboy*	Mickey Rourke	Drama
1988	*Spike of Bensonhurst*	Sasha Mitchell	Comedy
1989	*Champions Forever: World Heavyweight Champs*	Muhammad Ali	Documentary
1989	*Dotsuitarunen*	Hidekazu Akai	Drama
1989	*Fist Fighter*	Jorge Rivero	Drama
1989	*Thunderground*	Michael Copeman	Drama
1989	*Triumph of the Spirit*	Willem Dafoe	Drama
1990	*Crossing the Line*	Kenny Ireland	Drama
1990	*Rocky V*	Sylvester Stallone	Drama
1991	*Blonde Fist*	Margi Clarke	Drama
1991	*Rose Against the Odds*	Paul Williams	Bio: Lionel Rose
1992	*Far and Away*	Tom Cruise	Drama
1992	*Gladiator*	James Marshall	Drama
1992	*Night and the City*	Robert De Niro	Drama
1992	*The Power of One*	Stephen Dorff	Drama
1993	*Diggstown*	Bruce Dern	Drama
1993	*Fallen Champ: The Untold Story of Mike Tyson*	Mike Tyson	Documentary
1993	*Percy and Thunder*	James Earl Jones	Drama
1994	*In This Corner*	Gene Lythgow	Drama
1995	*Sonny Liston: The Mysterious Life and Death of a Champion*	Sonny Liston	Documentary
1995	*Tokyo Fist*	Kaori Fujii	Drama
1995	*Tyson*	Michael Jai White	Bio: Mike Tyson
1996	*The Great White Hype*	Samuel L. Jackson	Comedy
1996	*Kids Return*	Ken Kaneko	Drama
1996	*Lucky Punch*	Karl Makinen	Drama

1996	*The Mouse*	John Savage	Comedy
1996	*Muhammad Ali: The Whole Story*	Muhammad Ali	Documentary
1996	*Real Money*	Jimmy Flint	Drama
1996	*When We Were Kings*	Muhammad Ali	Documentary
1997	*The Boxer*	Daniel Day-Lewis	Drama
1997	*Champions Forever: The Latin Legends*	Kid Gavilán	Documentary
1997	*Don King: Only in America*	Ving Rhames	Bio: Don King
1997	*The Kid*	Jeff Saumier	Drama
1997	*Twenty Four Seven*	Bob Hoskins	Drama
1998	*Legionnaire*	Jean-Claude Van Damme	Drama
1998	*Like It Is*	Steve Bell	Drama
1998	*Snake Eyes*	Nicholas Cage	Drama
1998	*Sugar Ray Robinson: The Bright Lights and Dark Shadows of a Champion*	Ray Robinson	Documentary
1999	*Fight Club*	Brad Pitt	Drama
1999	*The Hurricane*	Denzel Washington	Bio: Rubin Carter
1999	*On the Ropes*	Martin Goldman	Documentary
1999	*Play It to the Bone*	Woody Harrelson	Comedy
1999	*Rocky Marciano*	Jon Favreau	Bio: Rocky Marciano
1999	*Shadow Boxers*	Michael Bentt	Documentary
1999	*Southpaw*	Francis Barrett	Documentary
2000	*Ali: An American Hero*	David Ramsey	Bio: Muhammad Ali
2000	*Billy Elliot*	Jamie Bell	Drama
2000	*Body and Soul*	Ray Mancini	Drama
2000	*A Fighter's Blues*	Andy Lau	Drama
2000	*Girlfight*	Michelle Rodriguez	Drama
2000	*King of the World*	Terrence Ramsey	Bio: Muhammad Ali
2000	*Knockout*	Sophia Adella Luke	Drama
2000	*The Opponent*	Erika Eleniak	Drama
2000	*Price of Glory*	Jimmy Smits	Drama
2000	*Shiner*	Michael Caine	Drama
2000	*Straight Right*	Brent Smith	Drama
2001	*Ali*	Will Smith	Bio: Muhammad Ali
2001	*Carman: The Champion*	Carman	Drama

2001	*Honeybee*	Senait Ashenafi	Drama
2001	*Ladies and the Champ*	Olympia Dukakis	Comedy
2001	*Made*	Vince Vaughn	Comedy
2002	*Champion*	Oh-seong Yu	Drama
2002	*I Spy*	Eddie Murphy	Comedy
2002	*Joe and Max*	Leonard Roberts	Bio: Louis–Schmeling
2002	*Undisputed*	Wesley Snipes	Drama
2003	*More Than Famous*	Carlos Hernandez	Documentary
2003	*N.B.T.*	Rick Lindland	Drama
2003	*Southside*	Brian Austin Green	Drama
2003	*Undefeated*	John Leguizamo	Drama
2004	*Against the Ropes*	Meg Ryan	Bio: Jackie Kallen
2004	*Bashing*	Jason "Wee Man" Acuna	Drama
2004	*Beautiful Boxer*	Asanee Suwan	Drama
2004	*Before the Fall*	Max Riemelt	Drama
2004	*Black Cloud*	Eddie Spears	Drama
2004	*The Calcium Kid*	Mark Heap	Comedy
2004	*Casablanca Driver*	Maurice Barthelemy	Comedy
2004	*The Collector*	Kim Bodnia	Comedy
2004	*Fight Night*	John B. Nelson Jr.	Drama
2004	*Fighting Tommy Riley*	Eddie Jones	Drama
2004	*Million Dollar Baby*	Hilary Swank	Drama
2004	*Unforgivable Blackness: The Rise and Fall of Jack Johnson*	Jack Johnson	Documentary
2005	*Blood of a Champion*	Bokeem Woodbine	Drama
2005	*Cinderella Man*	Russell Crowe	Bio: Jim Braddock
2005	*Crying Fist*	Min-sik Choi	Drama
2005	*One More Round*	Tony Amendola	Comedy
2005	*Ring of Fire: The Emile Griffith Story*	Emile Griffith	Documentary
2005	*Short Fuse*	Frank Acosta	Drama
2006	*Annapolis*	James Franco	Drama
2006	*The Black Dahlia*	Josh Hartnett	Drama
2006	*Blue Blood*	James Boyle	Documentary

2006	*Pacquiao: The Movie*	Jericho Rosales	Bio: Manny Pacquiao
2006	*Revoloution [sic]*	Bret Carr	Drama
2006	*Rocky Balboa*	Sylvester Stallone	Drama
2006	*They're Just My Friends*	Malik Yoba	Drama
2006	*Undisputed II: Last Man Standing*	Michael Jai White	Drama
2007	*Apne*	Dharmendra	Drama
2007	*The Hammer*	Adam Carolla	Comedy
2007	*Magic Man*	Paul Malignaggi	Documentary
2007	*Orthodox Stance*	Dmitriy Salita	Documentary
2007	*Poor Boy's Game*	Rossif Sutherland	Drama
2007	*Resurrecting the Champ*	Samuel L. Jackson	Drama
2007	*Strength and Honor*	Michael Madsen	Drama
2007	*Triumph and Tragedy: The Ray Mancini Story*	Ray Mancini	Documentary
2008	*Assault in the Ring*	Eric Drath	Documentary
2008	*Joe Louis: America's Hero Betrayed*	Joe Louis	Documentary
2008	*Nurse. Fighter. Boy*	Clark Johnson	Drama
2008	*Phantom Punch*	Ving Rhames	Bio: Sonny Liston
2008	*Rigged*	Rebecca Neuenswander	Drama
2008	*Two Fists, One Heart*	Daniel Amalm	Drama
2008	*Tyson*	Mike Tyson	Documentary
2008	*Victoire Terminus, Kinshasa*	Jeanette Mukendi	Documentary
2009	*The Boxer*	Josh Dallas	Drama
2009	*Facing Ali*	George Foreman	Documentary
2009	*From Mexico with Love*	Kuno Becker	Drama
2009	*The Kid: Chamaco*	Martin Sheen	Drama
2009	*Sons of Cuba*	Yosvani Bonachea	Documentary
2010	*Featherweight*	Holly Anderson	Drama
2010	*The Fighter*	Mark Wahlberg	Bio: Micky Ward
2010	*Lahore*	Farooq Shaikh	Drama
2010	*Love Ranch*	Joe Pesci	Comedy
2010	*Max Schmeling*	Henry Maske	Bio: Max Schmeling
2010	*Risen*	Stuart Brennan	Bio: Howard Winstone

2011	*Klitschko*	Vladimir Klitschko	Documentary
2011	*Knockout*	Steve Austin	Drama
2011	*Knuckle*	James Quinn McDonagh	Documentary
2011	*New City Fighter*	Jimmy Andrews	Drama
2011	*On the Ropes*	Mark Noyce	Comedy
2011	*Real Steel*	Hugh Jackman	Drama
2012	*China Heavyweight*	Qi Moxiang	Documentary

Appendix M

The Nonpareil's Grave

Boxing's most famous poem (at least until Muhammad Ali came along) was written in 1899 by M. J. MacMahon of Portland, Oregon, the lawyer of middleweight Jack Dempsey, the Nonpareil. Dempsey was buried in an unmarked grave, and MacMahon wrote the poem, originally published anonymously, to call attention to that fact and attempt to raise funds to erect a proper monument.

The Nonpareil's Grave

I

Far out in the wilds of Oregon,
On a lonely mountain side,
Where Columbia's mighty waters,
Roll down to the ocean tide;
Where the giant fir and cedar
Are imaged in the wave,
O'ergrown with firs and lichens,
I found Jack Dempsey's grave.

II

I found no marble monolith,
No broken shaft, or stone,
Recording sixty victories,
This vanquished victor won;
No rose, no shamrock could I find,
No mortal here to tell
Where sleeps in this forsaken spot
Immortal Nonpareil.

III

A winding wooden canyon road
That mortals seldom tread,
Leads up this lonely mountain,
To the desert of the dead.
And the Western sun was sinking
In Pacific's golden wave,
And those solemn pines kept watching
Over poor Jack Dempsey's grave

IV

Forgotten by ten thousand throats,
That thundered his acclaim,
Forgotten by his friends and foes,

Who cheered his very name,
Oblivion wraps his faded form,
But ages hence shall save
The memory of that Irish lad
That fills poor Dempsey's grave

V

Oh Fame, why sleeps thy favored son
In wilds, in woods, in weeds,
And shall he ever thus sleep on,
Interred his valiant deeds?
'Tis strange New York should thus forget
Its "bravest of the brave"
And in the fields of Oregon,
Unmarked, leave Dempsey's grave.

Bibliography

INTRODUCTION

Although the popularity of boxing has declined somewhat in the last 50 years, there is no shortage of books on the sport, especially in the English language. With the rise of Internet self-publishing companies, there have been quite a few that have appeared in the 21st century that might not have otherwise been published in earlier times.

In the first half of the 20th century, various annual record books were issued containing the records of some of the major boxers of the era. Thomas S. Andrews produced one from 1903 to 1938, *The Police Gazette's Record Book* (edited by Sam Austin) appeared sporadically from 1896 to 1930, Everlast produced one from 1923 to 1938, Post from 1934 to 1938, and the *Boxing News Record* from 1937 to 1939. They were superseded by Nat Fleischer's *Ring Record Book,* which first appeared in 1942.

For nearly 50 years, the *Ring Record Book and Boxing Encyclopedia* was considered the bible of boxing and was the standard reference for sports writers as well as individuals in the boxing business, such as managers and promoters. Since its demise, there has not been an adequate annual book to replace it, but several websites (notably Boxrec) have been created to fill the gap. Former *Ring Record Book* editor Herbert G. Goldman, in 2012, produced a four-volume set that includes the records of more than 2,500 boxers throughout ring history as well as an extensive encyclopedic section.

Both Goldman's book and the *Ring Record Books* are very useful to the researcher although much of the information contained in them can also be found at the Boxrec website. The earlier record books are interesting from a historical perspective but provide little useful record information that can't be found in more modern sources.

Boxing history has been approached in several manners. Some books provide an overall general history while others concentrate on a particular weight class, ethnic group, era, or fight. Bert Randolph Sugar's *100 Years of Boxing* and his *100 Greatest Fighters of All Time* present good overviews of the sport in Sugar's inimitable writing style.

For bareknuckle boxing history, Pierce Egan's 19th-century writing in *Boxiana: Sketches of Ancient and Modern Pugilism* (which is available in reprints) gives a good flavor of what the sport was like in its early years. The "white hope" era is thoroughly chronicled in Graeme Kent's *The Great White Hopes* and in Geoffrey C. Ward's *Unforgivable Blackness: The Rise and Fall of Jack Johnson.* This is the companion book to the Ken Burns's film on Johnson of the same title.

Kevin Mitchell's *Jacobs Beach: The Mob, the Fights, the Fifties* and Barney Nagler's *James Norris and the Decline of Boxing* both provide excellent insights into boxing in the early television era.

Another way of looking at boxing history has been presented by Arcadia Press. They have a series of books detailing the history of boxing in a specific United States city. Their books are written by local historians and, to date, include Baltimore, Boston, Chicago, Cincinnati, Detroit, Philadelphia, and San Francisco.

Quite a few books have been written solely on one memorable fight. Among the best in this category are Norman Mailer's *The Fight* on the Muhammad Ali–George Foreman fight in Zaire, Jeremy Schaap's *Cinderella Man* on the James J. Braddock–Max Baer bout, and Alan Lloyd's *The Great Prize Fight* on the John C. Heenan–Tom Sayers bareknuckle bout of 1860.

As with all sports, many boxing books are biographies, although there are not nearly as many autobiographies written in the first person with an established author as coauthor as there are for other sports, such as baseball or football. Biographies exist for many former champions of the past, and like many other sports, there are also quite a few biographies of nonchampions, including a number of boxers that most fans have never even heard mention of. Among the best are Rocky Graziano's (with Rowland Barber) *Somebody Up There Likes Me*, Jake LaMotta's *Raging Bull*, and Gerald Astor's biography of Joe Louis, *". . . And a Credit to His Race": The Hard Life and Times of Joseph Louis Barrow, a.k.a. Joe Louis*. Muhammad Ali has had more books written about him than any other boxer. Thomas Hauser's *Muhammad Ali: His Life and Times* is among the best.

Instructional books are available, although not nearly as many as will be found for other individual sports such as tennis, golf, or bowling. Most boxers learn the sport from trainers in gymnasiums and gain experience as amateur boxers in tournaments such as the Golden Gloves.

Boxing has appealed to some of the world's best writers, such as Ernest Hemingway, and there have been collections of essays on boxing as well as some excellent fiction by well-known authors. A. J. Liebling's *The Sweet Science* is one of the best. *The Fireside Book of Boxing* is an excellent anthology that includes many short pieces written by the best authors, among them Ernest Hemingway, Paul Gallico, O. Henry, Victor Hugo, George Bernard Shaw, and the classical writers Homer, Plato, and Virgil.

Novelty books on boxing include George Plimpton's humorous account of his ring appearance with Archie Moore in *Shadow Box* and Bert Sugar and Teddy Atlas's *The Ultimate Book of Boxing Lists*, which enumerates their choices for the top 10 in categories such as Most Fragile Chins, Flattest Noses, and various ethnic groups.

Boxing websites of interest include the outstanding aforementioned Boxrec, the Cyber Boxing Zone, and that of the International Boxing Research Organization (IBRO). Several contemporary boxers also maintain their own sites with varying levels of thoroughness.

The International Boxing Hall of Fame, located in Canastota, New York, has a huge library that may be consulted by the researcher by appointment. The listing below provides a comprehensive selection of boxing resources.

I. REFERENCE

A. Encyclopedias

Goldman, Herbert G. *Boxing: A Worldwide Record of Bouts and Boxers*. 4 vols. Jefferson, NC: McFarland, 2012.

Golesworthy, Maurice. *The Encyclopedia of Boxing*. London: Robert Hale, 1971.

Odd, Gilbert. *Encyclopedia of Boxing*. New York: Crescent, 1983.

The Ring Record Book and Boxing Encyclopedia. New York: Ring Bookshop, 1941–1972. (From 1941 to 1972, Nat Fleischer edited an annual boxing record book that appeared under various titles. He gradually added historical information in addition to boxers' records, and by 1953 the book was known as *The Ring Record Book and Boxing Encyclopedia*. Upon his death in 1972, Nat Loubet became editor from 1973 to 1979. Bert Randolph Sugar was editor from 1980 to 1983, and Herbert G. Goldman edited the 1984 and 1985 editions. None was produced in 1986, and the last in the series appeared with a 1986–1987 title.)

B. Annuals

Andrews, Thomas S. *World's Annual Sporting Records 1938*. Milwaukee: Evening Wisconsin, 1904–1938.

Austin, Sam C. *Police Gazette Sporting Annual*. New York: Richard K. Fox, 1896–1918, 1930.

Blair, George D. *Minnesota Boxing Record Book*. St. Paul, MN: self-published, 1984–1994.

Blewett, Bert. *King Korn Record Book*. Johannesburg, South Africa, 1981–1990.

Boxing News. *Boxing News Annual and Record Book*. London: Ring, 1945–1985.

Citro, Ralph. *Computer Boxing Update*. Blackwood, NJ: self-published, 1984–1993.

Editors of *The Ring*. *The Ring Boxing Almanac and Book of Facts*. Fort Washington, PA: London, 1996–2011.

Everlast Boxing Record. New York: Everlast Sports, 1923–1938.

Foley, Tom J. *The Old Timer Sporting Records Compilation*. 1908.

Gibbons, Les. *The Small Glove News Record Book.* Leumeah, New Zealand: Small Glove News, 1977–1979, 1981, 1983.

Gordon, Malcolm "Flash." *Flash Gordon's 1986 East Coast Boxing Yearbook.* Sunnyside, NY: self-published, 1986.

Hugman, Barry. *British Boxing Yearbook.* Feltham, UK: Newnes, 1985–2010.

Innes, Nelse. *Ring Record and Fistic Facts.* Boston: Nelse Innes, 1893–1899.

Jones, Robert E. *Bob Jones's N.Z. Boxing Yearbook.* Wellington, New Zealand: Robert Jones Holdings, 1972–1973.

MacDonald, Robert. *The Tartan Boxing Annual 1984.* Wick, Caithness, UK: R.W.M. Productions, 1984.

Miley, Bill. *Mid-American Boxing News Record Book.* Davison, MI: self-published, 1986–1987.

Noble, Reg. *Boxing Illustrated Record Book.* Montreal: Fax, 1979–1980.

Romano, John J. *Post Boxing Record Book and Sports Annual.* New York: John J. Romano, 1934–1938.

Solomons, Jack. *Jack Solomons International Boxing Annual.* London: Playfair, 1948–1953.

Vaccare, Peter. *The Ringside Boxing Record of 1940.* New York: Ringside, 1940.

———. *Ringside Boxing Record Quarterly 1961.* New York: RBRQ, 1962.

Wignall, Trevor. *Sporting Record Boxing Annual 1949.* London: Country and Sporting Publications, 1949.

Winn, George. *Boxing News Record.* New York: George Winn, 1937–1939.

C. Official Reports

Amateur Athletic Union of the United States. *Official AAU Boxing Handbook 1973–76.* Indianapolis: Amateur Athletic Union of the United States, 1973.

Organizing Committee Third World Boxing Cup. *Official Report.* Rome, 1983.

D. Miscellaneous Reference Books

1. Amateur

Grasso, John, ed. *The Olympic Games Boxing Record Book.* Guilford, NY: International Boxing Research Organization, 1984.

Official NCAA Guide: Boxing. New York: National Collegiate Athletic Bureau, 1943–1956.

Wallechinsky, David, and Jaime Loucky. *The Complete Book of the Olympics, 2012 Edition*. London: Aurum, 2012.

2. Professional

Andrews, Thomas S. *Ring Battles of Centuries*. 1914.
———. *Ring Battles of Centuries and Sporting Almanac*. Rev. ed. Milwaukee, WI: T. S. Andrews, 1925.
Morrison, Ian. *Boxing: The Records*. Enfield, UK: Guinness, 1986.
———. *Guinness Boxing Who's Who*. Enfield, UK: Guinness, 1991.
Roberts, James B., and Alexander G. Skutt. *The Boxing Register*. Ithaca, NY: McBooks, 2002.

II. HISTORY

A. General

Arnold, Peter. *The Pictorial History of Boxing*. New York: Gallery, 1988.
Batchelor, Denzil. *Big Fight*. London: Phoenix House, 1954.
Bell, Leslie. *Inside the Fight Game*. London: Rockliff, 1952.
———. *Men Behind the Gloves*. London: C&J Temple, 1950.
Bodia, Kasia. *Boxing: A Cultural History*. London: Reaktion, 2009.
Brooke-Ball, Peter, Derek O'Dell, and O. F. Snelling. *The Boxing Album: An Illustrated History; The Complete Story of Boxing from the Pugilists of the Classic Amphitheatre to the Heroes of Today*. Wigston, Leicester, UK: Anness, 2012.
Buchanan-Taylor, W., and James Butler. *What Do You Know about Boxing?* London: Heath Cranton, 1947.
Burroughs, Chuck. *Come Out Fighting: True Fight Tales for Fight Fans*. Albert City, IA: Appeal, 1977.
Butler, James, and Frank Butler. *The Fight Game*. Kingswood, UK: World's Work, 1954.
Carpenter, Harry. *Boxing: An Illustrated History*. New York: Crescent, 1982.
Durant, John, and Edward Rice. *Come Out Fighting*. New York: Duell, Sloan and Pierce, 1946.
Edmundson, Joseph. *Great Moments in Boxing*. London: Carousel, 1974.
Fleischer, Nat, and Sam Andre. *A Pictorial History of Boxing*. New York: Bonanza, 1959.
Garber, Angus G., III. *Boxing Legends*. New York: Gallery, 1988.
Greyvenstein, Chris. *Gloves and Glory*. South Africa: Limosin Brandy, n.d.
———. *This Brutal Glory*. Cape Town, South Africa: Buren, 1969.

Johnston, Alexander. *Ten and Out!* New York: Ives Washburn, 1947.

Kent, Graeme. *Boxing's Strangest Fights.* London: Robson, 2000.

Mills, Freddie. *Battling for a Title: A Kaleidoscope of Boxing.* London: Stanley Paul, 1954.

Odd, Gilbert E. *Debatable Decisions.* London: Nicholson & Watson, 1953.

————. *Ring Battles of the Century.* London: Nicholson & Watson, 1949.

————. *Was the Referee Right?* London: Nicholson & Watson, 1952.

Prospero, Angelo, Jr. *Great Fights and Fighters.* Rochester, NY: self-published, 1986.

Sanford, Harry, and Max Steeber. *The Square Jungle.* London: Panther, 1960.

Strong, L. A. G. *Shake Hands and Come Out Fighting.* London: Chapman & Hall, 1953.

Sugar, Bert Randolph. *100 Years of Boxing.* New York: Routledge, 1982.

Weston, Stanley, and Steve Farhood. *The Ring: Boxing in the 20th Century.* New York: BDD, 1993.

Wilson, Peter. *Ringside Seat.* London: Rich and Cowan, 1949.

B. Specific Eras

1. Bareknuckle Era

a. General   Brier, Warren J. *The Frightful Punishment.* Missoula: University of Montana Press, 1969.

Edwards, Billy. *Legendary Boxers of the Golden Age.* 1984. Reprint, Secaucus, NJ: Chartwell, 1990.

Egan, Pierce. *Boxiana: Sketches of Ancient and Modern Pugilism.* London: G. Smeeton, 1812. Reprint, Leicester, UK: Vance Harvey, 1971.

Ford, John. *Prizefighting: The Age of Regency Boximania.* Newton Abbot, UK: Davis and Charles, 1971.

Golding, Louis. *The Bare-Knuckle Breed.* London: Hutchinson, 1952.

Gorn, Elliott J. *The Manly Art: Bare-Knuckle Prize Fighting in America.* Ithaca, N.Y.: Cornell, 1986.

Lynch, Bohun. *The Prize Ring.* London: Country Life, 1925.

Mee, Bob. *Bare Fists: The History of Bare-Knuckle Prize-Fighting.* New York: Overlook, 2002.

Reid, J. C. *Bucks and Bruisers: Pierce Egan and Regency England.* London: Routledge and Kegan Paul, 1971.

Smith, Kevin. *Black Genesis: The History of the Black Prizefighter, 1760–1870.* Bloomington, IN: iUniverse, 2003.

b. Biography   i. John Gully

Darwin, Bernard. *John Gully and His Times*. London: Harper and Brothers, 1935.

ii. Daniel Mendoza

Ribalow, Harold U. *Fighter from Whitechapel*. New York: Farrar, Straus and Cudahy, 1962.

iii. Tom Molineaux

Fraser, George MacDonald. *Black Ajax*. New York: Avalon, 1999. (Fictionalized account of Molineaux's life.)

iv. John L. Sullivan

Chidsey, Donald Barr. *John the Great: The Times and Life of a Remarkable American, John L. Sullivan*. Garden City, NY: Doubleday, Doran, 1942.

Fleischer, Nat. *John L. Sullivan: Champion of Champions*. New York: G.P. Putnam's Sons, 1951.

Isenberg, Michael T. *John L. Sullivan and His America*. Urbana: University of Illinois Press, 1988.

Sullivan, John L. *I Can Lick Any Sonofabitch in the House!* Carson City, NV: Proteus, 1892. Reprint, London: Proteus, 1979.

2. White Hope Era

Fredrick, Oswald. *White Hope: The Story of the Jack Johnson Era*. London: Pendulum, 1947.

Kent, Graeme. *The Great White Hopes*. Thrupp, Stroud, Gloucestershire, UK: Sutton, 2005.

Lardner, John. *White Hopes and Other Tigers*. Philadelphia: J.B. Lippincott, 1951.

3. 1950s

Mitchell, Kevin. *Jacobs Beach: The Mob, the Fights, the Fifties*. New York: Pegasus, 2010.

Nagler, Barney. *James Norris and the Decline of Boxing*. Indianapolis: Bobbs-Merrill, 1964.

Rondinone, Troy. *Friday Night Fighter: Gaspar "Indio" Ortega and the Golden Age of Television Boxing*. Champaign: University of Illinois Press, 2013.

4. 1980s

Kimball, George. *Four Kings: Leonard, Hagler, Hearns, Duran, and the Last Great Era of Boxing*. Ithaca, NY: McBooks, 2008.

C. Weight Classes

1. Heavyweights

Cooper, Henry. *The Great Heavyweights*. London: Hamlyn, 1978.
Durant, John. *The Heavyweight Champions*. New York: Hastings House, 1960.
Fleischer, Nat. *The Heavyweight Championship: An Informal History of Heavyweight Boxing from 1719 to the Present Day*. New York: G.P. Putnam's Sons, 1961.
Leigh-Lye, Terry. *A Century of Great Boxing Drama*. London: Mayflower, 1971.
————. *In This Corner*. London: Mayflower, 1963.
McCallum, John D. *The World Heavyweight Boxing Championship: A History*. Radnor, PA: Chilton, 1974.
Odd, Gilbert. *Kings of the Ring: 100 Years of World Heavyweight Boxing*. Feltham, UK: Newnes, 1985.
Ryan, Pat. *The Heavyweight Championship*. Mankato, MN: Creative Education, 1993. (Youth.)
Weston, Stanley. *The Heavyweight Champions*. New York: Ace, 1970.

2. Light Heavyweights

Mills, Freddie. *Forward the Light-Heavies*. London: Stanley Paul, 1956.

3. Middleweights

De Cristofaro, S. *Boxing's Greatest Middleweights*. Rochester, NY: self-published, 1982.

4. Lightweights

Suster, Gerald. *Lightning Strikes: The Lives and Times of Boxing's Lightweight Heroes*. London: Robson, 1994.

E. Single Bout

1. Ali–Foreman

Mailer, Norman. *The Fight*. Boston: Little, Brown, 1975.

2. Ali–Frazier I

Fisher, Art, and Neal Marshall. *Garden of Innocents*. New York: E.P. Dutton, 1972.

3. Ali–Frazier III

Kram, Mark. *Ghosts of Manila: The Fateful Blood Feud between Muhammad Ali and Joe Frazier*. New York: Perennial, 2001.

4. Braddock–Baer

Schaap, Jeremy. *Cinderella Man: James J. Braddock, Max Baer, and the Greatest Upset in Boxing History*. Boston: Houghton Mifflin, 2006.

5. Dempsey–Carpentier

Waltzer, Jim. *The Battle of the Century: Dempsey, Carpentier, and the Birth of Modern Promotion*. Santa Barbara, CA: Praeger, 2011.

6. Dempsey–Gibbons

Kelly, Jason. *Shelby's Folly: Jack Dempsey, Doc Kearns, and the Shakedown of a Montana Boomtown*. Lincoln: University of Nebraska Press, 2010.

7. Dempsey–Tunney

Heimer, Mel. *The Long Count*. New York: Atheneum, 1969.

8. Heenan–Sayers

Lloyd, Alan. *The Great Prize Fight*. New York: Coward, McCann & Geoghegan, 1977.

9. Johnson–Burns

Wells, Jeff. *Boxing Day: The Fight That Changed the World*. New York: HarperCollins, 1999.

10. Johnson–Jeffries

Frederick, Steven. *The Last Great Prize-Fight: Johnson vs. Jeffries, Reno July 4, 1910, a Tex Rickard Promotion.* San Francisco: Create Space, 2010.

11. Louis–Schmeling

Margolick, David. *Beyond Glory: Joe Louis vs. Max Schmeling, and a World on the Brink.* New York: Alfred A. Knopf, 2005.
Myler, Patrick. *Ring of Hate: Joe Louis vs. Max Schmeling; The Fight of the Century.* New York: Arcade, 2005.

12. Sullivan–Corbett

Luckman, George E., and John A. Peterson. *John L. Sullivan, Heavyweight Champion of the World; James J. Corbett, Challenger of the Title Holder and Their Great Fight New Orleans 1892.* Lawndale, CA: Luckman-Peterson, c. 1985. (Reprint of an original undated pamphlet, no author given.)

13. Tyson–Douglas

Layden, Joe. *The Last Great Fight: The Extraordinary Tale of Two Men and How One Fight Changed Their Lives Forever.* New York: St. Martin's Griffin, 2008.

14. Collection of Individual Bouts

Farnol, Jeffery. *Famous Prize Fights: Or Epics of "The Fancy."* Boston: Little, Brown, 1928.
Pacheco, Ferdie, with Jim Moskovitz. *The 12 Greatest Rounds of Boxing.* Toronto: Sport Media, 2003.

F. Ethnic Groups

1. Black Boxers

Ashe, Arthur. *A Hard Road to Glory—Boxing: The African-American Athlete in Boxing.* New York: Amistad, 1993.

Aycock, Colleen. *The First Black Boxing Champions: Essays on Fighters of the 1800s to the 1920s*. Jefferson, NC: McFarland, 2011.
Fleischer, Nat. *Black Dynamite: The Story of the Negro in Boxing*. 5 vols. New York: Ring, 1938.

2. Irish and Irish American Boxers

Anderson, Roger. *The Fighting Irish*. Edinburgh, UK: Mainstream, 2005.

3. Jewish Boxers

Blady, Ken. *The Jewish Boxers Hall of Fame*. New York: Shapolsky, 1988.
Bodner, Alan. *When Boxing Was a Jewish Sport*. Westport, CT: Praeger, 1997.
Goldman, Arthur. *Stars of David*. Johannesburg, South Africa: South African Maccabi Counsel, n.d.
Joseph, Daniel. *Dandy: A Jewish Boxer's Journey from Russian Immigrant to Boxing Champion*. Self-published, 2011.

G. Specific Geographic Area

1. Australia

Mitchell, Ray. *Great Australian Fights*. London: Horwitz, 1965.

2. Canada

Greig, Murray. *Goin' the Distance*. Toronto: Macmillan, 1996.

3. Cuba

Duncan, John. *In the Red Corner*. London: Yellow Jersey, 2001.

4. Great Britain

Batchelor, Denzil. *British Boxing*. London: Collins, 1948.
Harding, John. *Lonsdale's Belt: The Story of Boxing's Greatest Prize*. London: Robson, 1996.
Hilton, Trevor. *British Boxers: First Series*. London: Beverley, 1956.

5. Philippines

Gonzalez, Joaquin Jay, III, and Angelo Michael F. Merino. *From Pancho to Pacquiao: Philippine Boxing In and Out of the Ring*. Minneapolis: Mill City, 2012.

6. South Africa

Greyvenstein, Chris. *The Fighters*. Cape Town, South Africa: CTP, 1981.

7. United States

a. Baltimore, Maryland Schaif, Thomas. *Baltimore's Boxing Legacy, 1893–2003*. Charleston, SC: Arcadia, 2003.

b. Boston, Massachusetts Smith, Kevin. *Boston's Boxing Heritage: Prizefighting from 1882 to 1955*. Mount Pleasant, SC: Arcadia, 2002.

c. Chicago, Illinois Johnston, J. J., Sean Curtin, and David Mamet. *Chicago Boxing*. Charleston, SC: Arcadia, 2005.

Johnston, J. J., and Sean Curtin. *Chicago Amateur Boxing*. Charleston, SC: Arcadia, 2006.

d. Cincinnati, Ohio Grace, Kevin, Joshua Grace, and Buddy LaRosa. *Cincinnati Boxing*. Charleston, SC: Arcadia, 2006.

e. Cleveland, Ohio Fitch, Jerry. *Cleveland's Greatest Fighters of All Time*. Self-published, 1980.

f. Delaware County, Pennsylvania Hasson, Chuck. *The Delaware County Boxing Record and Capsule History*. Self-published, 1986.

g. Detroit, Michigan Lindell, Lindy. *Metro Detroit Boxing*. Charleston, SC: Arcadia, 2001.

h. Los Angeles, California Callis, Tracy, and Charles Johnston. *Boxing in the Los Angeles Area: 1880–2005*. Bloomington, IN: Trafford, 2009.

i. Montana Bell, Frank. *Gladiators of the Glittering Gulches*. Helena, MT: Western Horizons, 1985.

j. New Mexico Cozzone, Chris, and Jim Boggio. *Boxing in New Mexico: A History, 1868–1940*. Jefferson, NC: McFarland, 2013.

k. New York, New York Corpas, Jose. *New York City's Greatest Boxers*. Charleston, SC: Arcadia, 2006.

l. Philadelphia, Pennsylvania Callis, Tracy, Chuck Hasson, and Mike DeLisa. *Philadelphia's Boxing Heritage, 1876–1976*. Charleston, SC: Arcadia, 2002.

m. San Francisco, California Lang, Arne K. *The Nelson–Wolgast Fight and the San Francisco Boxing Scene, 1910–1914*. Jefferson, NC: McFarland, 2012.

Somrack, F. Daniel. *Boxing in San Francisco*. Charleston, SC: Arcadia, 2005.

H. Amateur Boxing

50 Years of the International Amateur Boxing Association. Berlin: Druckhaus Mitte, 1996.

Farrell, Bill. *Cradle of Champions: 80 Years of New York Daily News Golden Gloves*. Champaign, IL: Sports Publishing, 2007.

Grasso, John. *Complete Roster of All Competitors in the New York Golden Gloves, Tournament of Champions (Eastern Regionals), and New York–Chicago Intercity Golden Gloves*. Unpublished, 1979.

———. *The New York Golden Gloves, 1927–1978*. Unpublished, 1979.

———. *The New York Golden Gloves Complete Records of All Finalists*. Unpublished, 1979.

Plummer, William. *Buttercups and Strong Boys: A Sojourn at the Golden Gloves*. New York: Penguin, 1990.

I. Death in the Ring

Broadbent, Rick. *The Big If: The Life and Death of Johnny Owen*. London: Macmillan, 2006.

Mitchell, Ray. *Fight for Your Life*. London: Scripts, 1967.

III. BIOGRAPHY

In addition to conventional biographies, this section includes books that are a series of reminiscences by a fighter and not strictly a complete biography, or in the case of *Ali Rap*, a collection of sayings by Muhammad Ali. Some, such as *Henry Cooper's Book of Boxing*, combine personal reminiscence with boxing instruction.

A. Collections

Burrill, Bob. *Who's Who in Boxing*. New Rochelle, NY: Arlington House, 1974.

Carpenter, Harry. *Masters of Boxing*. New York: A.S. Barnes, 1964.

Encinosa, Enrique G., and Hank Kaplan. *Boxing—This Is It*. Palm Springs, CA: ETC, 1985.

Heller, Peter. *In This Corner: Forty World Champions Tell Their Stories.* New York: Simon & Schuster, 1973.

Helliwell, Arthur. *The Private Lives of Famous Fighters.* London: Cedric Day, 1949.

Pep, Willie, with Robert Sacchi. *Willie Pep Remembers . . . Friday's Heroes.* New York: Frederick Fell, 1973.

Porter, David L. *Biographical Dictionary of American Sports.* 4 vols. New York: Greenwood, 1989.

Scurti, Richard. *Boxing's Greatest Interviews!!: Boxing's Biggest Stars Speak! Ray Leonard to Oscar De La Hoya to Sylvester Stallone!* Bloomington, IN: iUniverse, 2008.

Sugar, Bert Randolph. *The 100 Greatest Boxers of All Time.* New York: Bonanza, 1984.

B. Single Individual

1. Boxers

a. Abe the Newsboy (Abraham Hollandersky)   Hollandersky, Abe. *The Life Story of Abe the Newsboy.* Los Angeles: self-published, 1953.

b. Muhammad Ali (Cassius Clay)   Ali, Muhammad, with Hana Yasmeen Ali. *The Soul of a Butterfly: Reflections on Life's Journey.* New York: Simon & Schuster, 2004.

Ali, Muhammad, with Richard Durham. *The Greatest: My Own Story.* New York: Random House, 1975.

Atyeo, Don, and Felix Dennis. *The Holy Warrior: Muhammad Ali.* London: Bunch, 1975.

Bingham, Howard, and Max Wallace. *Muhammad Ali's Greatest Fight: Cassius Clay vs. the United State of America.* New York: M. Evans, 2000.

Bortstein, Larry. *Ali.* New York: Scholastic, 1976. (Youth.)

Denenberg, Barry. *The Story of Muhammad Ali: Heavyweight Champion of the World.* New York: Dell, 1990. (Youth.)

Early, Gerald, ed. *The Muhammad Ali Reader.* New York: William Morrow, 1998.

Edwards, Audrey, with Gary Wohl. *Muhammad Ali: The People's Champ.* Boston: Little, Brown, 1977.

Garrett, Leslie. *The Story of Muhammad Ali.* New York: Scholastic, 2002. (Youth.)

Hauser, Thomas. *Muhammad Ali: His Life and Times.* New York: Simon & Schuster, 1991.

Kaletsky, Richard. *Ali and Me: Through the Ropes.* Bethany, CT: Adrienne, 1982.

Kindred, Dave. *Sound and Fury: Two Powerful Lives, One Fateful Friendship*. New York: Simon & Schuster, 2006.

King, David. *I Am King: A Photographic Biography of Muhammad Ali*. Harmondsworth, UK: Penguin, 1975.

Lardner, Rex. *Ali*. New York: Grosset & Dunlap, 1975.

Lipsyte, Robert. *Free to Be Muhammad Ali*. New York: Bantam, 1978.

Lois, George. *Ali Rap: Muhammad Ali, the First Heavyweight Champion of Rap*. Cologne, Germany: Taschen, 2006.

Milverstedt, F. M. *In This Corner: Muhammad Ali*. Milwaukee: Raintree, 1976. (Youth.)

Odd, Gilbert. *Ali, the Fighting Prophet*. London: Pelham, 1975.

Oliver, Ann, and Paul Simpson, eds. *The Rough Guide to Muhammad Ali: The Man, the Fights, the Mouth*. London: Penguin, 2004.

Olsen, James T. *Muhammad Ali: I Am the Greatest*. Mankato, MN: Creative Education, 1974. (Youth.)

Pacheco, Ferdie. *Muhammad Ali: A View from the Corner*. New York: Carol, 1992.

Remnick, David. *King of the World*. New York: Random House, 1998.

Ricella, Christopher. *Muhammad Ali*. Los Angeles: Melrose Square, 1991.

Rummel, Jack. *Muhammad Ali*. New York: Chelsea House, 1988.

Schulberg, Budd. *Loser and Still Champion: Muhammad Ali*. Garden City: Doubleday, 1972.

Sheed, Wilfrid. *Muhammad Ali: A Portrait in Words and Photographs*. New York: New American, 1975.

Torres, Jose. *Sting Like a Bee: The Muhammad Ali Story*. New York: Abelard-Schuman, 1971.

Wilson, Beth P. *Muhammad Ali*. New York: G.P. Putnam's Sons, 1974. (Youth.)

   c. Alex Argüello   Giudice, Christian. *Beloved Warrior: The Rise and Fall of Alexis Arguello*. Dulles, VA: Potomac, 2012.

   d. Henry Armstrong   Armstrong, Henry. *Gloves, Glory and God: An Autobiography*. Westwood, NJ: Fleming H. Revell, 1946.

   e. Max Baer   Fleischer, Nat. *Max Baer: The Glamour Boy of the Ring*. New York: Ring, 1970.

   f. Reginald "Snowy" Baker   Growden, Greg. *The Snowy Baker Story*. Milsons Point, Australia, 2003.

   g. Carmen Basilio   Youmans, Gary. *The Onion Picker: Carmen Basilio and Boxing in the 1950s*. Syracuse, NY: Campbell Road Press North, 2007.

   h. Nigel Benn   Benn, Nigel. *Dark Destroyer*. London: Blake, 1999.

   i. Riddick Bowe   Vick, Christian. *The Triumph and Tragedy of Riddick Bowe*. Tamarac, FL: Llumina, 2011.

   j. Frank Bruno   Bruno, Frank, with Norman Giller. *Frank Bruno from Zero to Hero*. London: Andre Deutsch, 1997.

k. Ken Buchanan   Buchanan, Ken. *The Tartan Legend: The Autobiography.* London: Headline, 2000.

l. Charley Burley   Rosenfeld, Allen S. *Charley Burley: The Life and Hard Times of an Uncrowned Champion.* Bloomington, IN: Authorhouse, 2003.

m. Tommy Burns   Pollack, Adam J. *In the Ring with Tommy Burns.* Iowa City, IA: WIN by KO, 2011.

n. Joe Calzaghe   Calzaghe, Joe. *No Ordinary Joe: The Autobiography of the Greatest British Boxer of All Time.* London: Random House UK, 2007.

o. Primo Carnera   Page, Joseph S. *Primo Carnera: The Life and Career of the Heavyweight Boxing Champion.* Jefferson, NC: McFarland, 2010.

p. Georges Carpentier   Carpentier, Georges. *Carpentier by Himself.* London: Hutchinson, 1955.

q. Rubin "Hurricane" Carter   Chaiton, Sam, and Terry Swinton. *Lazarus and the Hurricane: The Freeing of Rubin "Hurricane" Carter.* New York: St. Martin's Griffin, 1999.

r. George Chuvalo   Brignall, Richard. *Fearless: The Story of George Chuvalo, Canada's Greatest Boxer.* Toronto: Lorimer, 2010.

s. Gerrie Coetzee   Wilson, Marshall. *Gerrie.* Johannesburg, South Africa: Macmillan, 1979.

t. Billy Conn   O'Toole, Andrew. *Sweet William: The Life of Billy Conn.* Champaign: University of Illinois Press, 2010.

u. John Conteh   Conteh, John. *I, Conteh.* London: Harrap, 1982.

v. Henry Cooper   Cooper, Henry. *Henry Cooper: An Autobiography.* London: Cassell, 1974.

———. *Henry Cooper's Book of Boxing.* Feltham, UK: Hamlyn, 1982.

Wilson, Peter. *King Henry: The Fighting Life of Henry Cooper.* London: Daily Mirror, 1971.

w. Jim Corbett   Fleischer, Nat. *Gentleman Jim: The Story of James J. Corbett.* New York: Ring, 1942.

x. Billy Costello   Hauser, Thomas. *The Black Lights: Inside the World of Professional Boxing.* New York: McGraw-Hill, 1986.

y. Leach Cross   Schutte, William. *Fighting Dentist: The Boxing Career of Dr. Leach Cross.* Fullerton, CA: self-published, 1977.

z. Tony DeMarco   DeMarco, Tony. *Nardo: Memoirs of a Boxing Champion.* Ottawa: Legas, 2011.

aa. Jack Dempsey   Dempsey, Jack, as told to Bob Considine and Bill Slocum. *Dempsey: By the Man Himself.* New York: Avon, 1960.

Dempsey, Jack, with Barbara Piattelli Dempsey. *Dempsey.* New York: Harper & Row, 1977.

Dempsey, Jack, with Myron M. Stearns. *Round by Round.* New York: Whittlesey House, 1940.

Diamond, Wilfrid. *Blood, Sweat, and Jack Dempsey.* Kingswood, UK: World's Work, 1953.

Fleischer, Nat. *Jack Dempsey: The Idol of Fistiana.* New York: Bantam, 1949.

———. *Jack Dempsey.* New Rochelle, NY: Arlington House, 1972.

Hay, Jack. *A Pair of Jacks: Jack Dempsey & Son.* Los Alamitos, CA: Hwong, 1982.

Kahn, Roger. *A Flame of Pure Fire.* New York: Harcourt, Brace, 1999.

Roberts, Randy. *Jack Dempsey: The Manassa Mauler.* Baton Rouge: Louisiana State University Press, 1979.

ab **Terry Downes**   Downes, Terry. *My Bleeding Business.* London: Stanley Paul, 1964.

ac. **Jack Duggan**   Duggan, Jack. *Fighting for Glory.* Oakville, ON: Humanity, 1981.

ad. **Roberto Duran**   Giudice, Christian. *Hands of Stone: The Life and Legend of Roberto Duran.* Preston, UK: Milo, 2009.

ae. **Yvon Durelle**   Fraser, Raymond. *The Fighting Fisherman.* Halifax, NS: Formac, 1981.

af. **Eddie Eagan**   Eagan, Eddie. *Fighting for Fun.* New York: Macmillan, 1932.

ag. **Bob Fitzsimmons**   Odd, Gilbert. *The Fighting Blacksmith: A Biography of Bob Fitzsimmons.* London: Pelham, 1976.

ah. **Del Flanagan**   Blair, George D. *Del Flanagan: The Last of Minnesota's Great Fighters.* St. Paul, MN: self-published, n.d.

ai. **Glen Flanagan**   Blair, George D. *Glen Flanagan: St. Paul's Fighting Irishman.* St. Paul, MN: self-published, n.d.

aj. **George Foreman**   Foreman, George, and Joel Engel. *By George: The Autobiography of George Foreman.* New York: Villard, 1995.

Foreman, George, with Ken Abraham. *God in My Corner: A Spiritual Memoir.* Nashville: Thomas Nelson, 2007.

ak. **Joe Frazier**   Frazier, Joe, with Phil Berger. *Smokin' Joe: The Autobiography of a Heavyweight Champion of the World, Smokin' Joe Frazier.* New York: Macmillan, 1996.

al. **Joe Gans**   Gildea, William. *The Longest Fight: In the Ring with Joe Gans, Boxing's First African American Champion.* New York: Farrar, Straus and Giroux, 2012.

am. **Joey Giambra**   Giambra, Joey, and Fred Villani. *The Uncrowned Champion.* Las Vegas: Joey One, 1979.

an. **Rocky Graziano**   Graziano, Rocky, with Rowland Barber. *Somebody Up There Likes Me.* New York: Simon & Schuster, 1955.

Graziano, Rocky, with Ralph Corsel. *Somebody Down Here Likes Me Too.* New York: Stein and Day, 1981.

ao. Harry Greb   Fair, James R. *Give Him to the Angels: The Story of Harry Greb*. New York: Smith and Durrell, 1946.

Paxton, Bill. *The Fearless Harry Greb: Biography of a Tragic Hero of Boxing*. Jefferson, NC: McFarland, 2009.

ap. Emile Griffith   Ross, Ron. *Nine, Ten and Out!: The Two Worlds of Emile Griffith*. New York: DiBella, 2008.

aq. Marvin Hart   Pollack, Adam J. *In the Ring with Marvin Hart*. Iowa City, IA: WIN by KO, 2010.

ar. Thomas Hearns   Hughes, Brian, and Damian Hughes. *Hit Man: The Thomas Hearns Story*. Wrea Green, UK: Milo, 2009.

as. Larry Holmes   Holmes, Larry, and Phil Berger. *Larry Holmes: Against the Odds*. New York: St. Martin's, 1998.

at. Peter Jackson   Langley, Tom. *Life of Peter Jackson: Champion of Australia*. Leicester, UK: Vance Harvey, 1974.

au. James J. Jeffries   Nicholson, Kelly Richard. *A Man among Men: The Life and Ring Battles of Jim Jeffries, Heavyweight Champion of the World*. Draper, UT: Homeward Bound, 2002.

av. Ingemar Johansson   Johansson, Ingemar. *Seconds Out of the Ring*. London: Stanley Paul, 1960.

aw. Jack Johnson   Farr, Finis. *Black Champion*. Greenwich, CT: Fawcett, 1969.

Fradella, Sal. *Jack Johnson*. Boston: Brandon, 1990.

Johnson, Jack. *Jack Johnson: In the Ring and Out*. London: Proteus, 1927. Reprint, London: Proteus, 1977.

———. *Jack Johnson Is a Dandy: An Autobiography with Pictures*. New York: Chelsea House, 1969.

Ward, Geoffrey C. *Unforgivable Blackness: The Rise and Fall of Jack Johnson*. New York: Vintage, 2006.

ax. Stanley Ketchel   Mora, Manuel A. *Stanley Ketchel: A Life of Triumph and Prophecy*. Bloomington, IN: Authorhouse, 2010.

ay. Jake LaMotta   La Motta, Jake, with Joseph Carter and Peter Savage. *Raging Bull: My Story*. Englewood Cliffs, NJ: Prentice-Hall, 1970.

az. Sam Langford   Moyle, Clay. *Sam Langford: Boxing's Greatest Uncrowned Champion*. Seattle: Bennett & Hastings, 2008.

ba. Benny Leonard   Fleischer, Nat. *Leonard the Magnificent*. Norwalk, CT: O'Brien, 1947.

bb. Ray Leonard   Goldstein, Alan. *A Fistful of Sugar*. New York: Coward, McCann & Geoghagen, 1981.

Leonard, Sugar Ray, with Michael Arkush. *The Big Fight: My Life In and Out of the Ring*. New York: Viking, 2011.

bc. Lennox Lewis   Lewis, Lennox, and Melissa Mathison. *Lennox*. London: Trafalgar Square, 2002.

bd. Charles "Sonny" Liston Steen, Rob. *Sonny Liston: His Life, Strife and the Phantom Punch*. London: JR Books, 2008.

Tosches, Nick. *The Devil and Sonny Liston*. New York: Little, Brown, 2000.

be. Joe Louis Astor, Gerald. *". . . And a Credit to His Race": The Hard Life and Times of Joseph Louis Barrow, a.k.a. Joe Louis*. New York: E.P. Dutton, 1974.

Barrow, Joe Louis, Jr., with Barbara Munder. *Joe Louis: 50 Years an American Hero*. Boston: G.K. Hall, 1990.

Diamond, Wilfrid. *How Great Was Joe Louis?* New York: Paebar, 1950.

Edmonds, Anthony O. *Joe Louis*. Grand Rapids, MI: William B. Eerdmans, 1973.

Louis, Joe, with Edna Rust and Art Rust Jr. *Joe Louis: My Life*. New York: Berkley, 1981.

Mead, Chris. *Champion: Joe Louis, Black Hero in White America*. New York: Charles Scribner's Sons, 1985.

Van Every, Edward. *Joe Louis: Man and Super Fighter*. New York: Frederick A. Stokes, 1936.

bf. Benny Lynch Burrowes, John. *Benny: The Life and Times of a Fighting Legend*. Edinburgh, UK: Mainstream Sport, 2002.

bg. Ray Mancini Kriegel, Mark. *The Good Son: The Life of Ray "Boom Boom" Mancini*. New York: Simon & Schuster, 2012.

bh. Rocky Marciano Cameron, John. *Redemption: The Life & Death of Rocky Marciano*. Vol. 1. N.p.: CreateSpace, 2012.

Sullivan, Russell. *Rocky Marciano: The Rock of His Times*. Urbana: University of Illinois Press, 2005.

bi. Jack McAuliffe Fleischer, Nat. *Jack McAuliffe: The Napoleon of the Prize Ring*. New York: Ring, 1944.

bj. Kid McCoy Cantwell, Robert. *The Real McCoy: The Life and Times of Norman Selby*. Princeton, NJ: Auerbach, 1971.

bk. Terry McGovern Fleischer, Nat. *Terrible Terry, the Brooklyn Terror: The Fistic Career of Terry McGovern*. New York: Ring, 1943.

bl. Jimmy McLarnin Gallimore, Andrew. *Babyface Goes to Hollywood: Fighters, Mobsters and Film Stars; The Jimmy McLarnin Story*. Dublin: O'Brien, 2009.

bm. Freddie Mills Bell, Leslie. *Focus on Freddie Mills*. London: Cobham House, 1949.

Mills, Freddie. *Twenty Years*. London: Nicholson & Watson, 1950.

bn. Billy Miske Moyle, Clay. *Billy Miske: The St. Paul Thunderbolt*. Iowa City, IA: WIN by KO, 2011.

bo. Archie Moore Fitzgerald, Mike. *Ageless Warrior: The Life of Boxing Legend Archie Moore*. Champaign, IL: Sports Publishing, 2004.

bp. Con O'Kelly Ulyatt, Michael E. *The Fighting O'Kellys*. Beverley, UK: Hutton, 1991.

bq. Manny Pacquiao Poole, Gary Andrew. *Pac-Man: Behind the Scenes with Manny Pacquiao—the Greatest Pound-for-Pound Fighter in the World*. Cambridge, MA: DaCapo, 2010.

br. Jackie Paterson Morrison, John. *Triumph to Tragedy*. Glasgow, UK: Mac Ghille Mhuire, 2000.

bs. Floyd Patterson Newcombe, Jack. *Floyd Patterson: Heavyweight King*. New York: Bartholomew House, 1961.

Patterson, Floyd, with Milton Gross. *Victory over Myself*. London: Pelham, 1962.

Stratton, W. K. *Floyd Patterson: The Fighting Life of Boxing's Invisible Champion*. New York: Houghton Mifflin Harcourt, 2012.

bt. Aaron Pryor Terrill, Marshall. *Flight of the Hawk: The Aaron Pryor Story*. Sun Lakes, AZ: Book World / Blue Star, 1998.

bu. Jerry Quarry Springer, Steve, and Blake Chavez. *Hard Luck: The Triumph and Tragedy of "Irish" Jerry Quarry*. Guilford, CT: Lyons, 2011.

bv. Ray Robinson Haygood, Wil. *Sweet Thunder: The Life and Times of Sugar Ray Robinson*. Chicago: Chicago Review, 2011.

Robinson, Sugar Ray, with Dave Anderson. *Sugar Ray*. New York: New American, 1970.

bw. Charlie Rose Rose, Charlie. *Life's a Knock-Out*. London: Hutchinson, 1953.

bx. Barney Ross Century, Douglas. *Barney Ross: The Life of a Jewish Fighter*. New York: Schocken, 2009.

Ross, Barney. *No Man Stands Alone*. Philadelphia: Lippincott, 1957.

by. Fraser Scott Scott, Fraser. *Weigh-In: The Selling of a Middleweight*. New York: Thomas Y. Crowell, 1974.

bz. Earnie Shavers Shavers, Earnie. *Welcome to the Big Time: Earnie Shavers*. Champaign, IL: Sports Publishing, 2002.

ca. Billy Soose Rubin, Rusty, and Tom Donelson. *Billy Soose: The Champion Time Forgot*. Bloomington, IN: Authorhouse, 2005.

cb. Leon Spinks Spinks, Betty. *Leon Spinks and Me*. Bloomington, IN: Authorhouse, 2008.

cc. Young Stribling Jones, Jimmy. *King of the Canebrakes*. Macon, GA: Southern, 1969.

cd. Dick Tiger Makinde, Adeyinka. *Dick Tiger: The Life and Times of a Boxing Immortal*. Tarentum, PA: Word Association, 2005.

ce. Gene Tunney Jarrett, John. *Gene Tunney: The Golden Guy Who Licked Jack Dempsey Twice*. London: Robson, 2003.

cf. Randy Turpin Birtley, Jack. *The Tragedy of Randolph Turpin*. London: New English Library, 1975.

cg. Mike Tyson Berger, Phil. *Blood Season: Tyson and the World of Boxing*. New York: William Morrow, 1989.

Heller, Peter. *Bad Intentions: The Mike Tyson Story.* New York: Penguin, 1989.

Hennessey, John. *Mike Tyson.* New York: Gallery, 1990.

Torres, Jose. *Fire & Fear: The Inside Story of Mike Tyson.* New York: Warner, 1989.

    ch. Jersey Joe Walcott   Curl, James. *Jersey Joe Walcott: A Boxing Biography.* Jefferson, NC: McFarland, 2012.

    ci. Mickey Walker   Walker, Mickey. *The Will to Conquer.* Hollywood, CA: House-Warven, 1953.

    cj. Micky Ward   Halloran, Bob. *Irish Thunder: The Hard Life and Times of Micky Ward.* Guilford, CT: Lyons, 2008.

    ck. Bruce Woodcock   Bell, Leslie. *Focus on Bruce Woodcock.* London: Cobham House, 1949.

Woodcock, Bruce. *Two Fists and a Fortune.* London: Hutchinson, 1951.

    cl. Jimmy Young   Dolan, Edward F., Jr., and Richard B. Lyttle. *Jimmy Young, Heavyweight Challenger.* Garden City, NY: Doubleday, 1979. (Youth.)

2. Trainers and Managers

    a. Ray Arcel   Dewey, Donald. *Ray Arcel: A Boxing Biography.* Jefferson, NC: McFarland, 2012.

    b. Teddy Atlas   Atlas, Teddy, and Peter Alson. *Atlas: From the Streets to the Ring, a Son's Struggle to Become a Man.* New York: HarperCollins, 2006.

    c. Angelo Dundee   Dundee, Angelo, with Bert Randolph Sugar. *My View from the Corner: A Life in Boxing.* New York: McGraw-Hill, 2008.

    d. Jack "Doc" Kearns   Kearns, Jack (Doc), as told to Oscar Fraley. *The Million Dollar Gate.* New York: Macmillan, 1966.

    e. Eddie Shapiro   Shapiro, Eddie. *Peddlers of Flesh.* New York: Vantage, 1959.

    f. Benny Singh   Singh, Benny. *My Champions Were Dark.* Durban, South Africa: Pennant, 1963.

3. Referees

    a. Collection   Fitzgerald, Mike, and Patrick Morley. *Third Man in the Ring: 33 of Boxing's Best Referees and Their Stories.* Dulles, VA: Potomac, 2013.

    b. Harry Gibbs   Gibbs, Harry, with John Morris. *Box On: The Autobiography of Harry Gibbs.* London: Pelham, 1981.

    c. Ruby Goldstein   Goldstein, Ruby, as told to Frank Graham. *Third Man in the Ring.* New York: Funk & Wagnalls, 1959.

d. Eugene Henderson   Henderson, Eugene. *Box On: The Autobiography of Eugene Henderson.* London: Stanley Paul, 1957.

e. Harry Kessler   Kessler, Harry, as told to Alma Kessler and Robert A. Suhosky. *The Millionaire Referee.* St. Louis: Harkess, 1982.

f. Arthur Mercante   Mercante, Arthur, with Phil Guarnieri. *Inside the Ropes.* Ithaca, NY: McBooks, 2006.

4. Others: Promoters, Writers, Ring Physicians, etc.

a. Vince Bagnato   Bagnato, Vince. *Half-a-Buck Nobody and Me.* Erin, ON: Boston Mills, 1984.

b. Al Bernstein   Bernstein, Al. *Al Bernstein: 30 Years, 30 Undeniable Truths about Boxing, Sports, and TV.* New York: Diversion, 2012.

c. Tom Fisher   Fisher, Tom, with Gilbert M. Allnutt. *Boxing Was My Sport.* London: Croydon Ex Boxers' Association, 1976.

d. Reg Gutteridge   Gutteridge, Reg. *Reg Gutteridge: King of Commentary.* London: Blake, 1998.

e. Mike Jacobs   Daniel, Daniel M. *The Mike Jacobs Story.* New York: Ring, 1950.

f. Don King   Newfield, Jack. *Only in America: The Life and Crimes of Don King.* New York: William Morrow, 1995.

g. Ferdie Pacheco   Pacheco, Ferdie. *Blood in My Coffee: The Life of the Fight Doctor.* Champaign, IL: Sports Publishing, 2005.
———. *Fight Doctor.* New York: Simon & Schuster, 1977.

h. Tex Rickard   Aycock, Colleen, and Mark Scott. *Tex Rickard: Boxing's Greatest Promoter.* Jefferson, NC: McFarland, 2012.

i. George Bernard Shaw   Green, Benny. *Shaw's Champions: G.B.S. and Prizefighting from Cashel Byron to Gene Tunney.* London: Elm Tree, 1978.

j. Jack Solomons   Solomons, Jack. *Jack Solomons Tells All.* London: Rich & Cowan, 1951.

k. Sylvester Stallone   Stallone, Sylvester. *The Official Rocky Scrapbook.* New York: Grosset & Dunlap, 1977.

IV. INSTRUCTIONAL

A. Rules and Officiating

Clark, Norman. *The Boxing Referee.* London: Methuen, 1926.

Rodriguez, Robert G. *Regulation of Boxing: A History and Comparative Analysis of Policies among American States*. Jefferson, NC: McFarland, 2009.

B. Boxing

Clarke, Richard E. *Amateur Boxing*. London: Thorsons, 1949.

Elmer, William. *Boxing*. New York: American, 1902.

Gotay, Al. *Boxing Basics: The Techniques and Knowledge Needed to Excel in the Sport of Boxing*. Denver: Outskirts, 2008.

Haislet, Edwin L. *Boxing*. New York: A.S. Barnes, 1940.

Halbert, Christy. *The Ultimate Boxer: Understanding the Sport and Skills of Boxing*. Brentwood, TN: Impact Seminars, 2003.

Harvey, Len. *Modern Boxing*. London: Blackie & Son, 1937.

Lachica, Alan, and Doug Werner. *Boxing's Ten Commandments: Essential Training for the Sweet Science*. San Diego, CA: Tracks, 2007.

LaFond, Eddie, and Julie Menendez. *Better Boxing: An Illustrated Guide*. New York, Ronald, 1959.

Schroeder, Charles Roy. *Boxing Skills*. St. Louis: Regmar, 1973.

Sullivan, George. *Better Boxing for Boys*. New York: Dodd, Mead, 1966.

Trotter, J. C. *Boxing*. London: George Routledge and Sons, 1902.

Wilde, Jimmy. *The Art of Boxing*. London: W. Foulsham, 1923.

C. Training

Fleischer, Nat. *Training for Boxers*. New York: Ring, 1970.

Hatmaker, Mark. *Boxer's Book of Conditioning and Drilling*. Chula Vista, CA: Tracks, 2011.

Roca, Hector, and Bruce Silverglade. *The Gleason's Gym Total Body Boxing Workout for Women: A 4-Week Head-to-Toe Makeover*. New York: Simon & Schuster, 2006.

Todd, Gary. *Workouts from Boxing's Greatest Champs: Get in Shape with Muhammad Ali, Fernando Vargas, Roy Jones, Jr., and Other Legends*. Berkeley, CA: Ulysses, 2004.

VI. OTHER BOOKS

A. Anthology

Batchelor, Denzil, ed. *Best Boxing Stories*. London: Faber and Faber, 1953.

Heinz, W.C., ed. *The Fireside Book of Boxing*. New York: Simon & Schuster, 1961.

Oates, Joyce Carol, and Daniel Halpern. *Reading the Fights*. New York: Prentice-Hall, 1988.

Shepherd, T. B., ed. *The Noble Art*. London: Hollis and Carter, 1950.

Silverman, Jeff, ed. *The Greatest Boxing Stories Ever Told: Thirty-six Incredible Tales from the Ring*. Guilford, CT: Lyons, 2002.

B. Bibliography

Hartley, R.A. *History & Bibliography of Boxing Books*. Alton, UK: Nimrod, 1989.

C. Essays

Collins, Nigel. *Boxing Babylon: Behind the Shadowy World of the Prize Ring*. New York: Citadel, 1990.

Hauser, Thomas. *And the New . . . : An Inside Look at Another Year in Boxing*. Fayetteville: University of Arkansas Press, 2012.

Kimball, George, and John Schulian. *At the Fights: American Writers on Boxing*. New York: Library of America, 2011.

Liebling, A. J. *The Sweet Science*. New York: Viking, 1956.

Lotierzo, Frank, and Tom Donelson. *Viewing Boxing from Ringside*. San Jose, CA: Writers Club, 2002.

McIlvanney, Hugh. *McIlvanney on Boxing: An Anthology*. New York: Beaufort, 1982.

Oates, Joyce Carol. *On Boxing*. Hopewell, NJ: Ecco, 1995.

Rendall, Jonathan. *This Bloody Mary Is the Last Thing I Own: A Journey to the End of Boxing*. Hopewell, NJ: Ecco, 1997.

Rotella, Carlo. *Cut Time: An Education at the Fights*. New York: Houghton Mifflin, 2003.

Schulberg, Budd. *Sparring with Hemingway: And Other Legends of the Fight Game*. Chicago: Ivan R. Dee, 1995.

Schulian, John. *Writers' Fighters & Other Sweet Scientists*. Fairway, KS: Andrews & McMeel, 1983.

Sugar, Bert Randolph. *Bert Sugar on Boxing: The Best of the Sport's Most Notable Writer*. Guilford, CT: Lyons, 2003.

Warner, Fred, and James Barbour, eds. *A Neutral Corner: Boxing Essays by A.J. Liebling*. New York: Simon & Schuster, 1990.

D. Fiction

1. Novels

Gardner, Leonard. *Fat City*. New York: Farrar, Straus and Giroux, 1969.
Harkins, Philip. *Knockout*. New York: Grosset & Dunlap, 1950.
Lipsyte, Robert. *The Chief.* New York: HarperCollins, 1983.
———. *The Contender.* New York: HarperCollins, 1967.
Merrill, Walter Anthony. *K.O.* N.p.: Keystone, 1933.
Mihailovic, Dragoslav. *When Pumpkins Blossomed*. New York: Harcourt Brace Jovanovich, 1971.
Schulberg, Budd. *The Harder They Fall*. New York: Random House, 1947.
Wallace, Francis. *Kid Galahad*. New York: Bantam, 1962.

2. Short Stories

Greenberg, Martin H. *In the Ring: A Treasury of Boxing Stories*. New York: Crown, 1987.
Staudohar, Paul D., ed. *Boxing's Best Short Stories*. Chicago: Chicago Review, 1999.
VanLoan, Charles E. *Inside the Ropes*. Boston: Small, Maynard, 1913.
Wallace, Edgar. *Fighting Snub Reilly and Other Stories*. Cleveland: World, 1934.

3. Novelizations of Screenplays

Grant, James Edward. *The Great John L.* Cleveland: World, 1945.
Merwin, Sam, Jr. *Body and Soul*. Chicago: Century, 1947.
Parent, Gail, and Andrew Smith. *The Main Event*. New York: Bantam, 1979.
Serling, Rod. *Requiem for a Heavyweight*. London: Transworld, 1962.

4. Plays

Sackler, Howard. *The Great White Hope*. New York: Dial, 1968.

E. Women in Boxing

Bell, Leslie. *Bella of Blackfriars*. London: Odhams, 1961.
Odd, Gilbert E. *The Woman in the Corner*. London: Pelham, 1978.

Snowden Picket, Lynn. *Looking for a Fight: A Memoir*. New York: Random House, 2000.

F. Humor

Plimpton, George. *Shadow Box*. New York: G.P. Putnam's Sons, 1977.

G. Photographic Essay

Bennett, George, and Pete Hamill. *Fighters*. Garden City, NY: Doubleday, 1978.
Keifel, Holger. *BOX: The Face of Boxing*. San Francisco: Chronicle, 2010.
Schatz, Howard, and Beverly J. Ornstein. *At the Fights: Inside the World of Professional Boxing*. New York: Sports Illustrated, 2012.

H. Quiz Books

Mitchell, Ray. *Ray Mitchell's Boxing Quiz, Book 1*. London: Horwitz, 1966.
Nash, Bruce, and Julian E. Compton. *The World Championship Boxing Quiz Book*. New York: Drake, 1976.
Sugar, Bert R., and John Grasso. *505 Boxing Questions Your Friends Can't Answer*. New York: Walker, 1982.

I. Boxing Films

Romano, Frederick V. *The Boxing Filmography: American Features, 1920–2003*. Jefferson, NC: McFarland, 2004.
Streible, Dan. *Fight Pictures: A History of Boxing and Early Cinema*. Berkeley: University of California Press, 2008.

J. Miscellaneous

Avis, F. C. *Boxing Reference Dictionary*. New York: Philosophical Library, 1958.
Grasso, John, ed. *First Annual Journal*. Guilford, NY: International Boxing Research Organization, 1983.
———. *Second Annual Journal*. Guilford, NY: International Boxing Research Organization, 1984.
———. *Third Annual Journal*. Guilford, NY: International Boxing Research Organization, 1985.

Sugar, Bert Randolph, and Teddy Atlas. *The Ultimate Book of Boxing Lists*. Philadelphia: Running Press, 2010.
Williams, Joe. *TV Boxing Book*. New York: D. Van Nostrand, 1954.
Willoughby, David P. *The Super Athletes*. New York: A.S. Barnes, 1970.

K. Foreign Language

1. French

Arroyo, Eduardo. *Panama Al Brown 1902–1951*. Paris: Grasset et Fasquel, 1982.
Bouttier, Jean-Claude, avec la collaboration de Christian Montaignac. *Quinze Rounds de Ma Vie*. Paris: Calmann-Levy, 1972.
Cangioni, Pierre. *La Fabuleuse Histoire de la Boxe*. Paris: Editions O.D.I.L., 1977.
Colombini, Robert. *Histoires de . . . Boxe*. Paris: Calmann-Lévy, 1968.
Denis, Georges. *Annuaire du Ring Edition 1957–58*. Paris: Editions Arcadiennes, 1958.
Loiseau, Jean-Claude. *Marcel Cerdan*. Paris: Flammarion, 1989.
Severin, Kurt. *Cassius Clay: Toujours Le Plus Grand?* Verviers, Belgium: Marabout, 1971.

2. German

Grothe, Sebastian. *Wer Kommt Nach Henry Maske?* Saarbrücken, Germany: VDM Verlag, 2011.
Kluge, Volker. *Max Schmeling: Eine Biographie in 15 Runden*, Berlin: Aufbau, 2004.
Sturm, Felix and Stefan Becker. *Fitness-Boxen mit Felix Sturm: Mein Power-Programm für Kraft und Ausdauer*. Südwest Verlag, 2009.

3. Italian

Ballarati, Giuseppe. *Campioni del Passato, Volume 1*. Rome: Giuseppe Ballarati, 1983.
———. *La "Bibbia" del Pugilato edizione*. Rome: Giuseppe Ballarati, 1962–1994.
Benvenuti, Nino. *Il Mondo in Pugno*. Milan: Sperling & Kupfer, 2001.
Degrasse, Roberto. *Tiberio Mitri, Il Pugile, La Favola, Il Dramma*. Villorba, Italy: Edizioni Anordest, 2010.

Giuliano, Orlando. *Rocky Marciano L'Invincible*. Arezzo, Italy: Limina, 2011.

Toffolo, Davide *Carnera—La Montagna Che Cammina N.E.* Bologna, Italy: Coconino, 2012.

Torti, Roberto. *Il Pugno Invisibile—Essere Giovanni Parisi*. Torino, Italy: ADD Editore, 2010.

4. Norwegian

Gjennom Ringen. Lund, Norway: Lund Historical Society, 2006.

5. Polish

Gryzewski, Kazimerz. *Pamietnik Feliksa Stamma*. Warsaw: Sport i Turysty-ka, 1973.

Olszewski, Lucjan. *Bokserzy* walczą o tytuły *(1924–1978)*. Krakow, Poland: Polish Boxing Federation, 1979.

Osmólski, Piotr. *Leksykon boksu*. Warsaw: Sport i Turystyka, 1989.

Skotnicki, Jan, and Slawomir Rojek. *Zawadowcy Historia Championatu Wszechwag: I Poczet Mistrzow Swiata 1719–1993*. Lodz, Poland: Wydawnictwo Kask., 1997.

Slowinski, Przemyslaw. *Urodzony, by walczyc. Historia Stanleya Ketchela, najlepszego polskiego piesciarza wszech czasów*. Chorzów, Poland: Videograf II, 2007.

6. Russian

Belenkii, A. *Boks. Bolshie chempiony*. Moscow: AST, 2008.

7. Spanish

De La Hoya, Oscar, and Steve Springer. *Un Sueno Americano: Mi Historia*. New York: Rayo, 2008.

Encinosa, Enrique. *Azucar y Chocolate: Historia del Boxeo Cubano*. Miami: Ediciones Universal, 2004.

Garmabella, José Ramon. *Grandes Leyendas del Boxeo*. Barcelona: Grijalbo, 2010.

Pomares, Maria. *Guia Pugilistica 1984*. Buenos Aires, 1984.

Ramos, Alberto Salcedo. *El Oro y La Obscuridad: La Vida Gloriosa y Tragica de Kid Pambele*. Madrid, Spain: Debate, 2003.

Rodriguez Feu, Francisco. *Los Grandes Campeones del Mundo de los Pesos Pesados*. Barcelona: Ediciones el cobre, 2004.

Tapia, Johnny. *Mi Vida Loca: The Crazy Life of Johnny Tapia*. Chicago: Bonus, 2009.

Valero, Roberto. *El Boxeo Mexicano en Records*. Mexico City: self-published, 1985, 1986.

VI. PERIODICALS

Boxing Digest. New York, 1998–2010, monthly.

Boxing Illustrated. New York, 1958–1995, monthly.

Boxing Monthly. London, monthly.

Boxing News. London, 1909–2012, weekly.

KO Magazine. Blue Bell, PA, 1980–2007, monthly 1980–2000, bimonthly 2001–2003, quarterly 2004, and three times a year 2005–present.

Official Boxing Record. Hollywood, CA, 1976–1990, monthly.

Ring, Blue Bell, PA, 1922–2012, monthly.

Small Glove News. New Zealand, ca. 1975–1985, monthly.

South African Boxing World. Johannesburg, 1976–2005, monthly.

VII. WEBSITES OF INTEREST

Comprehensive list of ring deaths, compiled by historian Miguel Velazquez: http://ejmas.com/jcs/velazquez/Muerte2011_pdf_Sep_2011.pdf.

Extensive website of Olympic Games information: http://www.sports-reference.com/Olympics.

Excellent comprehensive boxing encyclopedia: http://www.cyberboxingzone.com.

Complete details of virtually every professional fight (the source used for boxers' records contained in this historical dictionary): http://boxrec.com.

International Boxing Hall of Fame: http://www.ibhof.com/pages/about/inductees/inducteeindex.html.

International Boxing Research Organization: http://www.ibroresearch.com.

Some boxers or fans of boxers have their own websites. One of the better ones is http://www.harrygreb.com.

About the Author

John Grasso was born in New York City and raised in Whitestone, New York. Educated as an accountant, he spent most of his working life in data processing. He moved to Guilford in central New York State in 1980, has written on boxing, basketball, football, and tennis, and has traveled extensively, visiting more than 40 countries and attending eight Olympic Games with his wife, Dorothy, and two children, Steven and Laurel.

A sports historian, he has been the treasurer of the International Society of Olympic Historians (ISOH) since 2004 and is a member of the Association for Professional Basketball Research (APBR), the North American Society for Sport History (NASSH), and the Professional Football Researchers Association (PFRA), and was the founder of the International Boxing Research Organization (IBRO) in 1982. He is on the board of electors of the International Boxing Hall of Fame and helps to elect new members.

His published boxing work includes *505 Boxing Questions Your Friends Can't Answer* with Bert R. Sugar, *The 100 Greatest Boxers of All Time* with Bert R. Sugar, *The Olympic Games Boxing Record Book*, and the *1984 Ring Record Book and Boxing Encyclopedia* (Olympic editor). He has also contributed boxing essays to the *Biographical Dictionary of American Sports* and the *American National Biography* as well as *Ring* magazine and *Boxing Illustrated*. He is also the author of the unpublished history *The New York Golden Gloves, 1927–1978*.

His eclectic interest in all sports resulted in his being the author of the *Historical Dictionary of Basketball*, *Historical Dictionary of Tennis*, and *Historical Dictionary of Football*.

He is currently a consulting editor for Scarecrow Press, responsible for acquiring new sports titles and working with their authors to help produce the final product.